Financial A
for HR Ma

Financial Analysis for HR Managers

Tools for Linking HR Strategy to Business Strategy

Steven Director

Vice President, Publisher: Tim Moore
Associate Publisher and Director of Marketing: Amy Neidlinger
Executive Editor: Jeanne Glasser Levine
Editorial Assistant: Pamela Boland
Operations Specialist: Jodi Kemper
Marketing Manager: Megan Graue
Cover Designer: Alan Clements
Managing Editor: Kristy Hart
Project Editor: Betsy Harris
Copy Editor: Apostrophe Editing Services
Proofreader: Language Logistics, LLC
Indexer: Lisa Stumpf
Compositor: Nonie Ratcliff
Manufacturing Buyer: Dan Uhrig

FT Press offers excellent discounts on this book when ordered in quantity for bulk purchases
or special sales. For more information, please contact U.S. Corporate and Government Sales,
1-800-382-3419, corpsales@pearsontechgroup.com. For sales outside the U.S., please contact
International Sales at international@pearsoned.com.

Pearson Education LTD.
Pearson Education Australia PTY, Limited.
Pearson Education Singapore, Pte. Ltd.
Pearson Education Asia, Ltd.
Pearson Education Canada, Ltd.
Pearson Educación de Mexico, S.A. de C.V.
Pearson Education—Japan
Pearson Education Malaysia, Pte. Ltd.

Library of Congress Cataloging-in-Publication Data
Director, Steven M.
  Financial analysis for HR managers : tools for linking HR strategy to business stategy / Steven
Director.
    p. cm.
  ISBN 978-0-13-299674-7 (hardcover : alk. paper)
  1. Personnel management. 2. Strategic planning. 3. Business enterprises--Finance. 4.
Human capital. I.
Title.
  HF5549.D5266 2013
  658.15024'6583--dc23
                            2012041385

To Elissa, Syril, Rustin, Mara, Torin,
Judah, and Hazel.

Contents

Acknowledgments

I would like to express my gratitude to my colleagues and my students at Rutgers. Over the years, they have taught me far more than I ever learned in graduate school. Particularly valuable were the insights I gained from the experienced and very bright professionals who participated in the Rutgers Executive Masters in HR Leadership program and in the executive education programs offered by the Rutgers Center for Management Development. Among many other things, these individuals taught me the importance of communicating core concepts with a minimum of academic jargon and mathematical notation. To the extent that I failed to do that in this book, the fault is my own. My students also often asked me to recommend a book on corporate finance that would be appropriate for HR managers. The difficulty I had in identifying books that would provide what they were looking for prompted me to begin thinking about doing this volume. It was my colleague and friend Dr. Paula Caligiuri who encouraged me to move beyond just thinking about it and actually submit a book proposal to FT Press. I am therefore particularly grateful to Paula for making this book happen.

The ideas expressed in this volume are largely a synthesis of the writings and contributions others have made to the finance and human resource strategy literatures. My dependence on their work cannot be overstated. Unfortunately, the list is far too large to acknowledge them all. I have, however, tried to cite many of these individuals in the following chapters. Finally, I would like to express my greatest gratitude to my parents. Though neither had a degree in finance, or anything else, their exceptional level of business acumen (and hard work) provided our family with the resources that enabled my siblings and me to attend college and graduate school.

About the Author

Steven Director is a professor in the Rutgers University School of Management and Labor Relations. He has held a number of leadership positions at Rutgers, including serving as Associate Dean, as Chair of the Human Resource Management Department, and as Director of the PhD program in Industrial Relations and Human Resources. Prior to joining Rutgers he was an Employment Policy Fellow at the Brookings Institution and on the faculty of Michigan State University. He received his Ph.D. and MBA degrees from the Northwestern University Kellogg School of Management.

Dr. Director teaches courses in Labor Economics, Statistics, and Finance. His most frequent and preferred teaching assignment is a course in Financial Analysis for Human Resource Managers. In addition to his on-campus teaching, Dr. Director has taught Finance for HR to senior executives in the U.S., Europe, and Asia. Recognized for his ability to effectively communicate financial concepts to non-financial audiences, Dr. Director has also developed and delivered customized finance training for scientists, engineers, and physicians. His publications have appeared in numerous journals and edited volumes.

His research interests include the financial aspects of HR, compensation and benefits policy, and the interaction between national and corporate employment policy. In January, 2003 he developed and partnered with the Society of Human Resource Management to produce the monthly Leading Indicator of National Employment (LINE) Report. Dr. Director continues to serve as economic advisor to this project and SHRM has now published over 100 consecutive monthly LINE reports. This data series is followed closely by financial analysts and business economists.

1

Business Strategy, Financial Strategy, and HR Strategy

What makes one company more successful than another? Is it because it has nicer office buildings, newer research labs, or better manufacturing equipment? If it is the differences in people that create differences in corporate value, then the HR function (though not necessarily the HR department) is critical to a corporation's success. Clearly line managers have an important role in hiring, developing, and motivating the people that can make an organization successful. Perhaps surprisingly it is the role of human resource managers in this process that is less clear. Should human resource managers have primarily an administrative role focusing on the processing of transactions and compliance with regulations? Should human resource managers be business partners charged with developing and maintaining a workforce with the specific capabilities required to execute their firm's business strategy? Or should human resource managers be true strategic partners participating along with top management, and their counterparts from other functional areas, in the actual development and monitoring of a firm's business strategy? In many organizations HR departments play only one or two of these three roles. It is a premise of this book that many firms fail to achieve their maximum success because they do not utilize their HR departments optimally. It must be acknowledged, however, that line managers may be underutilizing their HR departments because they are not confident that HR can perform at higher levels.

Is HR Weakest in the Most Critical Areas?

A study conducted by the Corporate Leadership Council (CLC)[1] found that in the opinion of the 16,000 line managers who were surveyed, fewer than one in five HR business partners were highly effective in their strategy roles. That's a statement that the HR profession should find troubling. The good news is that there's lots of room for improvement, and we know how to generate those improvements. The CLC study also estimated the relationship between HR staff competencies and degree of success as a strategic partner. Their findings are summarized in Exhibit 1-1. Each vertical bar represents an estimate of the maximum impact on strategic role effectiveness of a particular HR capability. The maximum impact was calculated by comparing the strategic role performance of individuals rated high and individuals rated low on each capability. Of far greater importance than expertise in any HR specialization was overall business acumen. What are the implications of that statement for the way you select and train HR professionals? Does it mean you don't need individuals with specialized training or experience in HR? No, but it suggests that while specialized HR skills are necessary, they are not sufficient.

HR professionals need both HR knowledge and a high degree of business acumen. Most individuals in the field today have strong HR skills. There is, however, a wide range in the level of business acumen they possess. That creates substantial competitive advantages for corporations whose HR staffs possess both sets of skills. For individuals who have both sets of skills, it also creates great opportunities for them to advance within their HR careers. The specific mix of skills required depends, of course, on the individual's job duties and position in the corporate hierarchy. In general, the higher the individual is (or hopes to be) in the corporate hierarchy, the greater the need for strong business acumen to complement their HR knowledge.

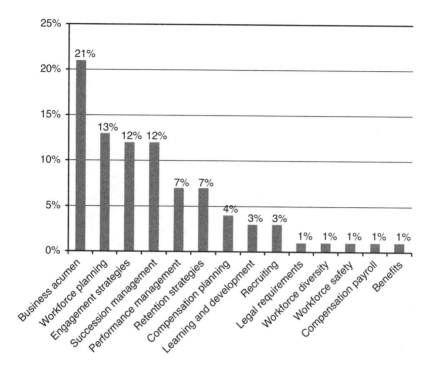

Exhibit 1-1 Impact of HR competencies on strategic role effectiveness

Source: Graph created using data from Corporate Leadership Council, "Building Next-Generation HR-Line Partnerships," Corporate Executive Board, 2008, p. 32.

What is business acumen, anyway? At the most fundamental level, it is an understanding of how your company makes money and how your decisions and behaviors can impact the company's financial performance. The business acumen needed by HR managers includes an understanding of their firm's business strategy, the key drivers of their firm's success, and the interrelationships among the different components of the organization. This understanding is necessary to develop and execute an effective HR strategy. There is no business department, function, or activity whose success is not dependent upon the firm's HR strategy. An organization's HR strategy determines who is employed in each functional area, how much will be invested to enhance their skills and capabilities, and what behaviors will be encouraged or discouraged through the compensation system. A firm's HR strategy must be tailored to support its business strategy. To produce this alignment, HR managers need the ability to analyze which choices will add value to the firm and which will weaken it. Do most individuals in the HR profession have that ability? In a survey conducted by Mercer Consulting,[2] HR leaders were asked to assess the skills of their staffs. They rated their staffs weakest on the following skill sets:

- Financial skills
- Business strategy skills
- Organizational assessment
- Cross-functional expertise
- Cost analysis and management

They felt their staffs were strongest at the following:

- Interpersonal skills
- Recordkeeping/data maintenance
- Team skills
- Functional HR expertise
- Customer service

The skill sets where these HR staffs were strong are important, but they are not the skill sets that drive corporate success or the career success of individual HR managers. No company is going to become an industry leader because of the interpersonal skills or recordkeeping abilities of its HR staff. It is rather striking that the areas in which these HR staffs were weakest are exactly the skill sets that are most likely to contribute to a corporation's success, and exactly the skills that individual HR managers need to progress in their careers.

You Don't Need to Be a Quant to Make Good Business Decisions

In most cases HR managers need only a modest level of quantitative skills. There is certainly no need to be the kind of individual the Wall Street firms refer to as a *quant*. Analyzing business decisions generally requires no more than a tolerance for basic arithmetic and a comfort with the creation and use of spreadsheets. Actually, in many cases more important than the ability to crunch the numbers is the ability to think analytically and creatively about the business challenges a firm faces. Some HR managers are limited in their ability to do this simply because they do not understand all the jargon used in their company's financial statements or in the models their firm uses to evaluate business alternatives. Without that understanding it's impossible to know, for example, whether a proposal made by a colleague is brilliant or nonsense.

Fortunately, gaining an understanding of basic financial jargon and concepts is not difficult to do. You don't need a degree in finance to use financial tools to make better decisions. The goal of this book is to help HR professionals deepen their understanding of business economics and finance. Hopefully an increased understanding of these issues can enable them to make better decisions about resource allocations within the HR function. The bigger potential benefit, however, is that an increased understanding of these issues can enable them to more effectively tailor an HR strategy to the firm's business strategy. If this can be done they can significantly improve their firm's competitiveness and add value to the firm's shareholders. At the same time they can enhance their own prospects for career advancement. Too many HR professionals underestimate the role HR can and should play in strategic decisions. They should not be deterred simply because these decisions involve financial models or analyses.

Which HR Decisions Are Important?

In many organizations, human resource costs (recruitment, selection, compensation, training, and workforce administration) are the largest component of the firm's operating expenses. In some service organizations these items constitute 70% to 80% of the firm's total costs. Properly managing those costs is therefore critical to the success of any corporation. Other things equal, a 10% reduction in a firm's HR costs can produce a huge increase in its bottom line profit. Still, of greater importance than managing workforce costs is creating workforce value. Firms do not become industry leaders because they have the lowest turnover rate, the smallest health insurance premiums, or the lowest cost per hire. Firms succeed because they create value for their customers. Firms succeed because they have a workforce that skillfully executes a value-creating business strategy. A firm's objective must be to maximize the return on the investment (ROI) it makes in its workforce. The relationship between the ROI and HR costs can be summarized as: HR ROI = Workforce value / HR costs. Yes, other things equal, reducing HR costs in the denominator of this ratio produces an increase in ROI. Of course, increasing HR costs in the denominator of this ratio could also improve ROI. That would be the case when these additional HR expenditures result in even larger increases in workforce value.

Reducing inefficiencies in HR processes and increasing workforce value are both important. Increases in workforce value, however, are most likely to explain a firm's level of success. Consider these two firms. Company A's management and workforce are by far the most talented and engaged in the industry. Company B's management and workforce are about average for the industry, but its cost per hire is much less than average. Which HR department is doing the better job? In which firm will more value be created for shareholders? The amount a firm can save by reducing inefficiencies in HR processes is usually insignificant compared to the amount it can gain by building a more talented and engaged work force. Of course if you can do both, you should. Several books have been written that focus on using financial tools to improve the efficiency of resource allocation within the HR department. This book discusses those issues but focuses on the financial understanding needed to align HR strategy with business strategy and create shareholder value.

What This Book Attempts to Do

When should financial analyses precede HR decisions? The answer to that question is always. That doesn't mean that in all cases you need to develop spreadsheet models and utilize their built-in financial functions. That may be necessary when decisions involve many factors or substantial amounts of money. However, even in situations in which no formal modeling is warranted, you need to consider the potential financial implications of your recommendations and actions. To do that requires an understanding of and appreciation for the importance of the following:

- Basic financial concepts such as the difference between profit and cash flow
- Difference between the market value and the book value of a company
- Cost of capital
- Time value of money
- Return on investment
- Risk reward trade-offs
- Risk management tools such as diversification and real options

Most of these concepts are just as relevant for your personal decision making as for your decisions at work. HR managers also need to understand the strengths and weaknesses of the various financial performance measures used to assess how well a company is doing and as a basis for allocating incentive pay.

This book provides you with an intuitive understanding of each of these topics. Algebraic notation and equations are avoided, and these concepts are illustrated using spreadsheet examples. Not all HR managers are comfortable with algebraic notation, and in any case spreadsheets are the format in which they are most likely to encounter these concepts on the job. Where appropriate the keystrokes for utilizing Microsoft Excel's built-in financial functions are provided and discussed. This book does not attempt to include an introduction to the HR strategy or to corporate compensation policies. There are excellent volumes devoted to these topics.[3] What it does attempt to do is provide HR managers with an understanding of the financial jargon and methods often central to strategy development and compensation policy.

Chapter 2 ("The Income Statement: Do We Care About More Than the Bottom Line?"), Chapter 3 ("The Balance Sheet: If Your People Are Your Most Important Asset, Where Do They Show Up on the Balance Sheet?"), and Chapter 4 ("Cash Flows: Timing Is Everything") use data from the annual reports of Home Depot, Inc., to review the interpretation of corporate income statements, balance sheets, and cash flow statements. If you are familiar with the interpretation of basic financial statements and the differences between profit and cash flow, you may want to skip over these chapters. Chapter 5 ("Financial Statements as a Window into Business Strategy") provides a case study on using financial statements to gain insights into a firm's business strategy. Chapter 6 ("Stocks, Bonds, and the Weighted Average Cost of Capital") and Chapter 7 ("Capital Budgeting and Discounted Cash Flow Analysis") discuss the concepts of cost of capital and time value of money. Chapter 8 ("Financial Analysis of Human Resource Initiatives") uses these concepts to look at resource allocation within the HR function. Chapter 9 ("Financial Analysis of Corporation's Strategic Initiatives") begins with the premise that if HR managers are going to be true strategic partners they must understand the financial models used to develop and evaluate corporate strategy. These techniques are discussed in spreadsheet illustrations. Chapter 10 ("Equity-Based Compensation: Stock and Stock Options") looks at equity pay and the implications of paying in stock versus paying in stock by stock options. Pensions are of enormous financial significance to the U.S. economy and to most large corporations, and they are the subject of Chapter 11 ("Financial Aspects of Pension and Retirement Programs"). The chapter includes a discussion of the way pension accounting choices can affect the company's bottom line profit. Chapter 12 ("Creating Value and Rewarding Value Creation") attempts to pull all these concepts together to look at the conditions under which shareholder value is created and at the strengths and weaknesses of alternative measures of value creation. These topics are discussed within the context of incentive pay and the choice of performance metrics that encourage the development and execution of strategies that create long-term value for the firm and its stakeholders.

2

The Income Statement: Do We Care About More Than the Bottom Line?

Suppose you resign from your corporate HR position and use your life savings, say $1,000,000, to start your own headhunting firm. One year later, what are the financial questions that you will be asking? Perhaps number one on your list will be, "Did your firm make a profit?" In addition to profitability you will want to know about the financial condition of your business, that is, "Will your firm have the financial strength to ride out difficult economic conditions should you encounter them?" Or on the flipside, "Will your firm have the financial strength to take advantage of any attractive expansion opportunities?" A third question you will no doubt ask is, "What rate of return are you earning on your $1,000,000 investment?" Could you have earned a comparable or better return from an alternative investment, perhaps one that was less much risky than starting up a small business? Your accountant may point out to you that you should be closely monitoring your firm's cash flow from operations. What's the difference between cash flow and profit? Why is cash flow even important as long as you make a profit large enough to give you a good return on your investment? The questions you would want answered as the owner of a small privately held business are the same ones that the CEOs, CFOs, and other executives of large corporations worry about. How close can the standard financial statements come to providing useful answers to these questions?

It has become a cliché to say that trying to manage a business based on its financial statements is like trying to drive a car by looking in the rear view mirror. That criticism is a bit too simplistic. A driver cannot plan his route forward without knowing where he is now and how much gas he has in the car. Financial statements tell you where you are now and what resources you can draw upon to move forward. Furthermore, a key component of strategic planning is almost always a forecast of what future financial statements would look like under different business scenarios. In addition to these internal uses, financial statements are a primary mechanism through which external constituencies (for example, stockholders, bondholders, financial analysts, banks, partners, suppliers, customers, competitors, and prospective employees) form opinions about a firm. It's hard to overstate the importance of financial statements. That doesn't mean that the standard financial statements (the balance sheet, the income statement, the statement of cash flows, and statement of retained earnings) don't have significant weaknesses and limitations. However, understanding those limitations makes them more, not less, useful. Financial metrics are also more valuable when combined with nonfinancial measures such as customer satisfaction, product quality, product innovation, process efficiency, and the ability to attract and retain highly talented employees.

The following sections discuss the interpretation and analysis of the basic financial statements using as examples data from the Securities Exchange Commission (SEC) filings by the nation's largest home improvement retailer Home Depot, Inc., and its major competitor Lowe's Companies, Inc. This chapter looks at income statements. The income statements show profit as the amount by which revenues exceed expenses. The next two chapters focus on the balance sheet and cash flow statement. A balance sheet provides an indication of a company's financial strength by comparing the amount the company owns (assets) to the amount it owes (liabilities). Annual cash flow statements provide a comparison of the amount of cash coming in during the year and the amount paid out during that period. A key objective of these chapters is to help the reader understand how net cash flow differs from net profit.

Income Statements

Income statements are sometimes referred to as an Earnings Statement, Statement of Operations, Profit and Loss Statement, or P&L Statement. No matter how complex the corporation may be, the logic of an income statement can be nothing more than Revenues minus Expenses = Profits. Exhibit 2-1 presents Home Depot's income statement for the 2011 fiscal year. Perhaps the first thing you notice is that Home Depot's top-line sales revenue grew by a modest 3.5%, whereas its bottom line net income grew by a substantial 16.3%. How can profits grow so much faster than sales? Before getting into that analysis, review the definition of each of the components shown on an income statement.

Amounts in Millions For 12-Month Period Ending	January 30, 2012 FY 2011	January 30, 2011 FY 2010	% Change
NET SALES	$ 70,395	$ 67,997	3.5%
Cost of Sales	46,133	44,693	3.2%
GROSS PROFIT	24,262	23,304	4.1%
Selling, General, and Administrative Expenses	16,028	15,849	1.1%
EBITDA	8,234	7,455	10.4%
Depreciation and Amortization	1,573	1,616	-2.7%
EBIT	6,661	5,839	14.1%
Interest and Other Expense (Net)	593	566	4.8%
EARNINGS BEFORE INCOME TAX	6,068	5,273	15.1%
Provision for Income Tax	2,185	1,935	12.9%
NET EARNINGS	$ 3,883	$ 3,338	16.3%

Exhibit 2-1 The Home Depot, Inc., and subsidiaries consolidated statement of earnings

Source: Form 10-K filed with U.S. Securities Exchange Commission on 3/22/2012, page 30.

Sales Revenue

When analysts speak about a company's top-line growth, they are referring to growth in the dollar value of sales, which is the top line of the income statement. The top line of Home Depot's fiscal year (fy) 2011 income statement shows sales of just under $70.4 billion, up 3.5% from fy2010. As is typically done, the top line in the Home Depot income statement is labeled Net Sales, indicating that this number is net of (that is, after subtracting out) any discounts off of list price, sales returns, or other deductions from the original sale price. Sales taxes are also not included in this number. You must remember that Home Depot, like all major corporations, uses the accrual method of accounting. That means they assign (accrue) revenues and expenses to particular time periods using the following logic. Revenues for a specific time period, say fy2011, are the revenues earned during that year regardless of whether Home Depot has collected the cash from those sales. Any amounts that remain uncollected at the end of the year show up as Accounts Receivable on the balance sheet (see Exhibit 3-1).

Cost of Goods Sold

The first category of expenses subtracted out on an income statement is the cost of the merchandise sold during that period. The cost of the merchandise sold by Home Depot in fy2011 was $46.1 billion. Remember that is what it cost Home Depot to purchase this merchandise from its suppliers, not the price Home Depot charged its customers when this merchandise was resold. The accrual accounting method requires that the expenses subtracted out on the fy2011 income statement be those expenses, and only those expenses, that were necessary to generate Home Depot's fy2011 revenues. The amount of merchandise Home Depot purchases from its suppliers in a given year can be either more or less than the amount it actually sells in that year. The amount subtracted on its income statement will always be the cost of the merchandise sold that year. For example, if in a given year Home Depot purchased merchandise costing $50 billion but sold merchandise only costing $45 billion, a $45 billion cost of goods expense would be subtracted on its income statement. Inventory levels shown on its balance sheet would increase by $5 billion. In a year when year Home Depot purchased merchandise costing $50 billion and, by drawing down on previous inventory, sold merchandise costing $53 billion, the $53 billion cost of goods sold would be subtracted on its income statement. Inventory levels shown on its balance sheet would decrease by $3 billion.

SG&A

Ignore, just for the moment, the subtotals shown in bold type in the income statement (Gross Profit, EBIT, EBITDA, and Pretax Profit). The next major category of expenses subtracted out is Selling, General, and Administrative Expense (SG&A). Home Depot's

SG&A expense in fy2011 was $16.0 billion. This category is sometimes referred to as Operating Expenses because it is a catch-all category that includes almost all the costs of operating a business. The only things it does not include are the costs shown elsewhere on the income statement (merchandise costs, depreciation, interest, and income taxes). It will come as no surprise to HR managers that for most corporations the largest component of operating expenses is compensation costs (wages and benefits). That is just one of the compelling reasons why HR managers need to understand financial statements and why CEOs, CFOs, and others need to appreciate the role HR plays to determine a firm's financial success (or lack thereof). In addition to compensation costs, SG&A includes expenses for the following:

- Advertising
- Office supplies
- Rent
- Insurance
- Utilities
- Bad debt write-offs
- Payroll taxes
- Shipping costs
- Travel and entertainment
- And much more

Under the accrual accounting method, all operating expenses for the year are included in SG&A even if the company has not paid all those bills by the end of the fiscal year. As discussed in the next chapter, any operating expenses not paid by the end of fy2011 were recorded on the company's balance sheet as an accounts payable liability. It's not a consideration for a retailer like Home Depot, but in some industries, for example pharmaceuticals, research and development is so important that operating expenses on their income statements are disaggregated on to two lines: one labeled R&D and the other labeled SG&A. Pfizer, Inc., for example, in its fy2011 income statement shows $9.1 billion spent on R&D and another $19.5 billion for other SG&A expenses.[1]

Depreciation and Amortization

Suppose Home Depot builds a new store at a cost of $60 million and that store generates $20 million in revenues during its first year of operation. When trying to determine whether that new store was profitable in its first year, would it make sense to subtract from its first year revenues its first year operating expenses and the full $60 million construction cost? Of course not. Both common sense and Generally Accepted Accounting Principles (GAAP) require that when estimating this store's profit you treat the $60 million construction cost as if it had been spread over the useful life of that store. The accounting term for that process is *depreciation*. There are various ways to calculate depreciation expense, but the simplest to illustrate is called *straight line depreciation*. If Home Depot were using straight line depreciation to allocate this $60 million construction cost over a 30-year life of the building, it would on its income statement subtract a $2 million ($60 million / 30) depreciation expense in each of those 30 years. In the first year $60 million would have been paid to construct the building but only a $2 million expense would be included on the income statement. In the second and later years, no cash would be been paid out for this construction, but a $2 million expense would be included on the income statement. This method of calculating profits can produce large differences between the profit a company reports in a given a year and its actual net cash flow in that year. The implications of that statement for business planning are extremely important and are examined in detail in later chapters.

In fy2011 Home Depot's income statement included a depreciation expense charge of almost $1.6 billion. That $1.6 billion was not, however, paid out in fy2011. It was just an accounting recognition of a portion of the cash Home Depot paid out in earlier years to purchase buildings and other long-term assets. Firms depreciate not just their buildings, but almost all long-term assets. Long-term assets are assets that have a useful life of greater than one year. These might include furniture and fixtures, trucks, forklifts, lab equipment, computers, and almost any other type of fixed asset that is required for the firm's operation. The most significant exception is real estate. Firms depreciate the cost of buildings and other improvements on the land but not the cost of the land itself. The assumption is that land does not have a finite useful life and does not decrease in value with usage.

How can you determine the appropriate useful life over which to spread the cost of each type of depreciable asset? You could argue, quite reasonably, that a firm should make the most realistic forecast possible of how long each of its long-term assets will be used and then allocate their cost over that that life span. For tax purposes, however, firms typically use the minimum asset life span permitted under the federal income tax code. The shorter the life span assumed, the larger the annual depreciation expense will be. Larger annual depreciation deductions reduce the company's taxable income and therefore the taxes that must be paid. An exception might be a firm that is not profitable now but expects to be profitable in the future. In that situation a firm might prefer smaller deductions now and larger reductions in the future. When firms use a different asset life estimate for financial reporting than for tax purposes, this is disclosed in a footnote to its financial statements.

The term *deprecation* refers to allocating the cost of a long-term tangible asset over an estimate of its useful life. Until recently, the term *amortization* referred to an analogous process used to allocate the cost of an intangible asset, for example, a purchased patent or brand name over an estimate of its useful life. The logic behind this approach was not always clear. Does a brand name have a finite useful life? Is it always true that over time a brand name decreases rather than increases in value? To sidestep these difficulties, accountants have generally stopped assigning arbitrary economic lives to intangible assets. Intangible assets are now carried on a company's books at their initial value until there is evidence that their value has declined. If and when such declines in value of an intangible asset do occur, the company shows a charge on their income statement labeled amortization expense.

Interest Expense

Almost all corporations have both interest bearing debt such as bank borrowing and bonds and noninterest bearing debt such as accounts payable. This line on the income statement shows the cost for this period of the interest bearing debt. Interest is shown on a separate line and is not lumped into the broad category of operating expenses because it is not a cost of operating the business. It is a cost of financing the business. This distinction is important when you begin analyzing the income statement to assess the success of the firm's business model. The label used on the Home Depot income statement is Interest and Other Expenses (Net). Other expenses that can be included are loan application and processing fees, points charged by lenders, and legal and other fees associated with obtaining loans. In fy2011 Home Depot's interest expense of $606 million was offset by $13 million of interest and investment income producing a net interest expense of $593 million. In a foot note to its income statement, Home Depot states that the interest expense shown for 2012 is net of capitalized interest of $3 million. Capitalized interest is interest that instead of being expensed on the current period's income statement is treated as part of the asset's cost reported on the balance sheet. It then becomes part of the asset's depreciation expense reported on future income statements.

Income Taxes

Income tax expense is the total amount the corporation must pay in federal and state income taxes. It does not include other nonincome taxes such as the employer share of unemployment and social security taxes. These nonincome taxes are included in operating expenses. Home Depot's income tax expense in fy2011 was just more than $2 billion. Its combined effective income tax rate decreased to 36.0% for fy2011 (2,185 / 6,068) from 36.7% in fy2010 (1,935 / 5,273).

Net Income

When managers talk about being "bottom line focused" they mean focused on net income, which is the bottom line of the income statement. Net income (which is the same as net earnings or net profit) is what's left when you take top-line sales revenue and then net out (subtract out) all the categories of expenses shown on the income statement. Companies whose stock is publicly traded are required to report Earnings Per Share (EPS). EPS is exactly what it sounds like: Net Income divided by the number of stock shares outstanding. Stock options and certain other financial instruments give their owners the right to obtain additional stock shares from the company. When such share distributions occur, the denominator in the EPS ratio, the number of shares outstanding, increases and the earnings per share is reduced (if the same profit figure is used in the numerator). To alert shareholders to this possibility, publicly traded companies are also required to report Diluted Earnings Per Shares. In the diluted EPS measure, the denominator is the number of shares currently outstanding plus the number that could potentially be issued through stock options and other securities that could be converted into stock. A big difference between a company's basic EPS and diluted EPS may make investors nervous because of the risk that their ownership percentage will decline at some point in the future. Expressed on a per share basis, Home Depot's net income converts to a basic EPS of $2.49 and diluted EPS of $2.47.

Profit Can Be Measured at Various Levels

The income statements in Exhibit 2-1 show five measures of profit:

- Gross Profit
- EBITDA
- EBIT (Earnings Before Income Taxes)
- Net Income

Which profit measure is most important? That depends on which business question you want to answer at the moment. Each of these measures provides important information for managers and investors.

Gross Profit

Gross profit is sales revenue minus only the first category of expenses, the cost of goods sold. Gross profit, often referred to as gross margin, is just the mark-up a company receives over its cost of purchasing or producing the items sold. If Home Depot buys a hammer for $5.00 from its supplier and then sells it at retail for $8.00, the gross profit or gross margin on that item is $3.00. To be successful a company's gross profit must be large enough to cover all other costs of operating and financing the business and still leave a sufficient bottom line profit.

EBIT

EBIT is an acronym for Earnings Before Interest and Taxes are subtracted out. Its calculation is exactly that: sales revenue minus all expenses other than interest and taxes. What critical business question does knowing that quantity answer? Why exclude interest expense that is a real and sometimes large expense? Another name for EBIT is operating profit. Interest expense is not subtracted out in this calculation because it is a not a cost of operating the business. It is a cost of financing the business. Suppose Home Depot and Lowe's had the same sales revenue, the same cost of goods sold, and the same operating expenses, but that Home Depot had more debt and therefore more interest expense than Lowe's. In this hypothetical situation, both companies would have equally successful business operations and exactly the same pretax operating profit (EBIT). However, because of financing differences Home Depot would have a smaller bottom line net income. If the question you are interested in at the moment is, "Which business model is more successful?" comparing the two firms on EBIT would be the best choice. If the question you are interested in at the moment is, "Which firm generated the greatest profit for its shareholders?" comparing the two firms on net income would be the best choice. Remember that net income is always the result of two things: the profitability of the firm's business operations (which is measured by EBIT) and the way those operations were financed, that is, how much was borrowed at what interest rate.

EBITDA

EBITDA is an acronym for Earnings Before Interest, Taxes, Depreciation and Amortization are subtracted out. Though sometimes referred to as a profit measure, it is probably more correct to view EBITDA as one form of cash flow measure. Remember that depreciation and amortization expenses do not represent cash outflows during the period in which they appear on the income statement. They are accounting reallocations of cash that was actually paid out at the time specific tangible or intangible assets were originally acquired. In fy2011, Home Depot's depreciation and amortization expense was $1.573 billion, so its EBITDA was $1.573 greater than its EBIT. EBITDA is a widely used performance metric in many industries including telecom. One telecom firm that eventually got into financial trouble was boasting each quarter about how rapidly its EBITDA was growing. Its EBITDA, the revenues it received from subscribers minus only the current cost of providing telecom services to those subscribers, was actually a positive and growing number. However, the monthly cost to provide telephone service after the fiber, electronics, and other network components are in place is relatively small. EBITDA would have been a good estimate of the positive cash flow its business would generate each quarter *if* there were no additional expenditures for building out its network. As a profit measure, however, EBITDA can be misleading. For this telecom firm viewing EBITDA as a profit measure was the equivalent of saying, "Yes, we are profitable if we don't subtract out the biggest costs our industry incurs, the costs of fiber, electronics, and network construction." The networks are a long-term asset, and the costs to create them show up on an income statement only as depreciation expense.

Net Income

Net income is the profit reaming after all expenses have been subtracted. It is determined by the level of success achieved by the firm's business operations, the amount borrowed to finance those operations, the average interest rate paid on that debt, and the company's tax bracket. These bottom line profits can be retained by the corporation to support future business operations or distributed to shareholders as dividends.

Seeing the Big Picture

Understanding the definition and calculation of the various income statement components is only the first step to use this information to make better business decisions. One way to begin an analysis of the business implications of this information is to calculate a common size income statement. This is easily done by expressing each row in the income statement as a percentage of top-line revenues. By expressing each item as a percentage of a common size (100%), you can easily make comparisons between a company's income statements from different years or between the income statements of different companies for the same year. Exhibit 2-2 provides an example of common size income statements for Home Depot and its largest competitor Lowe's Companies, Inc. Several factors are immediately obvious. Both firms charge almost exactly the same mark-up on the merchandise they sell. Gross margins at Home Depot are 34.5%, and gross margins at Lowe's are 34.6%. This is not surprising given the similarities in their product lines and competitive pressures to match the prices others offer. The similar gross margins are an important insight into the business strategies of these two firms. The relationship of gross margins to business strategy is discussed in the next chapter.

Amounts in Millions of $ For 12-Month Period Ending	Home Depot Jan 30, 2012 FY 2011	% of Sales	Lowe's Feb 3, 2012 FY 2011	% of Sales
NET SALES	$70,395	100%	$50,208	100%
Cost of Sales	46,133	65.5%	32,858	65.4%
GROSS PROFIT	24,262	34.5%	17,350	34.6%
Selling, General, and Administrative Expenses	16,028	22.8%	12,593	25.1%
EBITDA	8,234	11.7%	4,757	9.5%
Depreciation and Amortization	1,573	2.2%	1,480	2.9%
EBIT	6,661	9.5%	3,277	6.5%
Interest and Other Expense (Net)	593	0.8%	371	0.7%
EARNINGS BEFORE INCOME TAX	6,068	8.6%	2,906	5.8%
Provision for Income Tax	2,185	3.1%	1,067	2.1%
NET EARNINGS	$3,883	5.5%	$1,839	3.7%

Exhibit 2-2 Common size income statements for Home Depot and Lowe's

Source: Lowe's calculations based Form 10-K filed with U.S. Securities Exchange Commission on 3/20/2012, page 32. Home Depot calculations based Form 10-K filed with U.S. Securities Exchange Commission on 3/22/12, page 30.

Operating Efficiency

There is a bigger difference between the two firms in terms of operating efficiency. SG&A at Lowe's is equal to 25.1% of sales revenue, whereas at Home Depot it is only 22.8%. If Lowes's had generated the same $50.2 billion of sales with an SG&A percentage equal to Home Depot's, its operating profit (EBIT) would have been $1.15 billion larger! ([25.1% – 22.8%] x $50.2 billion). This data raises the question, "Why are operating expenses greater at Lowe's?" Is it because it is less efficient, or is it because it is intentionally spending more on marketing or more to provide a different customer experience?

Store Growth

Depreciation expense at Home Depot was larger in dollar terms but smaller as a percentage of sales (refer to Exhibit 2-2). This percentage difference is largely the result of the difference in the rate of store expansion. Between the end of 2007 and the end of 2011, the number of Lowe's stores increased by almost 14%, from 1,534 to 1,745. During that same period the number of Home Depot stores increased by less than 1%, from 2,234 to 2,252.

Operating Profit Margin

Because as a percentage of sales revenue, both SG&A and depreciation expense are larger at Lowe's than at Home Depot, it is not surprising that Lowe's operating profit margin (EBIT/sales revenue) is much smaller. For every $100 of sales revenue, Home Depot in 2011 earned an operating profit of $9.50. For every $100 of sales revenue, Lowe's earned an operating profit of only $6.50. Even if Home Depot and Lowe's had the same sales revenue, Home Depot's operating profit would have been 46% greater!

Profit per Store

Another way to see this difference is to calculate EBIT per store. At Home Depot this was $2.96 million ($6.66 billion / 2,252 stores).

At Lowe's, it was only $1.88 million ($3.28 billion / 1,745 stores). By strategically closing down underperforming stores, Home Depot has optimized its capital allocation and concentrated on its core business activities. The introduction of new warehousing and transportation systems has also helped to reduce its supply chain costs.

Year-Over-Year Change

Between 2010 and 2011, Home Depot's bottom line net income grew by 16.3%, even though its top-line revenues grew by only 3.5%. It can do this because during 2011 as a percentage of sales, its gross margins were up and its SG&A and depreciation expenses were down.

Financing Costs

EBIT provides the most direct measure of the success of Home Depot's business model. Bottom line net income is always the result of two things: the success of the company's business model and how that business was financed, that is, how much was borrowed at what interest rate. Home Depot and Lowe's were not dramatically different in terms of interest expense. At Home Depot it was equal to 0.8% of sales and at Lowe's 0.7% of sales.

The Bottom Line

After subtracting from Home Depot's operating profit of $6.7 billion, an interest expense of $593 million, and almost $2.2 billion in income taxes, you see that Home Depot's 2011 bottom line net income (which it label Net Earnings) was almost $3.9 billion. The 5.5% net profit margin means that for every $100 in sales revenue that comes in, $5.50 remains after all expenses are subtracted. Does that level of profitability constitute a strong business performance? Is that enough profit to provide the company's shareholders with an attractive return on their investment? Alternative techniques for answering those questions are examined in later chapters.

3

The Balance Sheet: If Your People Are Your Most Important Asset, Where Do They Show Up on the Balance Sheet?

If you want to calculate your personal net worth, you subtract from the value of everything you own the value of everything you owe. No matter how complex a corporation may be, its balance sheet is nothing more than that, a list of everything the company owns (assets) minus the list of everything the company owes (liabilities). Although you could describe the difference between these two quantities as a corporation's net worth, the standard accounting terminology for the excess of assets over liabilities is *owners' equity* or *shareholders' equity*. A corporation with assets of $5 billion and liabilities of $3 billion would calculate its shareholders' equity as $2 billion (5 − 3 = 2). Just as you might assess your personal financial health by comparing the value of what you own to the value of what you owe, you can assess the financial condition of a corporation by comparing the value of its assets to the value of its liabilities. When you assess a corporation's financial condition, you seek to determine whether it has the financial strength to ride out difficult economic times should it encounter them. On the flipside, you are also interested in whether it has the financial strength to take advantage of any attractive growth opportunities. Balance sheets are sometimes described as a snapshot in that they show what the company owned and what it owed on a specific date, the last day of the reporting period. The balance sheet excerpts in Exhibits 3-1 and 3-2 show Home Depot's assets and liabilities as of January 30, 2012, which was the last day of its 2011 fiscal year. By contrast, an income statement does not refer to a specific date but to an interval of time. Home Depot's 2011 income statement (refer to

Exhibit 2-1) reports the company's revenues and expenses over the 12-month period ending on January 30, 2012.

Assets on the Balance Sheet

The balance sheet balances because of simple arithmetic. Assets are usually listed on the left side (or top) of the balance sheet, and liabilities and shareholders' equity on the right side (or bottom). Because shareholders' equity is calculated by subtracting liabilities from assets (in the previous example 5 − 3 = 2), assets on the left side always equal the sum of liabilities and shareholders' equity on the right side (5 = 3 + 2). The assets listed in Exhibit 3-1 are divided into two groups: Current Assets and Long-Term Assets. Current assets are assets that the company expects to convert into cash, sell, or consume within 1 year of the balance sheet date.[1] Current assets are presented in the order of liquidity, that is, the speed with which they can be converted to cash. The typical sequence is cash, temporary investments, accounts receivable, inventory, supplies, and prepaid expenses. Then long-term assets are shown at their original purchase price minus accumulated depreciation. A few of these items may warrant some additional explanation.

Accounts Receivable

The income statement shows that Home Depot's sales in fy2011 were $70.395 billion (refer back to Exhibit 2-1). Some of those sales were credit sales, and not all that money was collected by the end of the year. The amount remaining uncollected was added to the accounts receivables balance in the current assets section of Home Depot's balance sheet in Exhibit 3-1. Receivables increased by $160 million between January 30, 2011 and January 30, 2012. That tells you that the amount Home Depot collected from sales in fy2011 was $70.235 billion ($70.395 billion in sales minus the $160 million that was uncollected as of January 30, 2012).

THE HOME DEPOT, INC., AND SUBSIDIARIES
CONSOLIDATED BALANCE SHEETS

Amounts in Millions

		Jan 30, 2012 FY 2011	Jan 30, 2011 FY 2010
ASSETS			
Current Assets:			
Cash and Cash Equivalents		1,987	545
Receivables, Net		1,245	1,085
Merchandise Inventories		10,325	10,625
Other Current Assets		963	1,224
	Total Current Assets	**14,520**	**13,479**
Long-Term Assets			
Property and Equipment, at Cost			
Land		8,480	8,497
Buildings		17,737	17,606
Furniture, Fixtures, and Equipment		10,040	9,687
Leasehold Improvements		1,372	1,373
Construction in Progress		758	654
Capital Leases		588	568
	Gross Property and Equipment	**38,975**	**38,385**
Less Accumulated Depreciation and Amortization		14,257	13,325
	Net Property and Equipment	**24,448**	**25,060**
Notes Receivable		135	139
Goodwill		1,120	1,187
Other Assets		295	260
	Total Assets	**$40,518**	**$40,125**

Exhibit 3-1 Assets section of Home Depot's balance sheet
Source: Form 10-K filed with U.S. Securities Exchange Commission on 3/22/2012, page 31.

Accounts Receivable Turnover Ratio

Dividing annual sales revenue from the top line of the income statement by the accounts receivable balance yields a measure known as an accounts receivable turnover ratio ($70.395 billion / $1.25 billion = 56.5). Dividing this ratio into 52 weeks gives the average sales collection period in weeks (52 / 56.5 = 0.92 weeks). Home Depot's average collection period of less than 1 week is obviously much shorter than the collection period you might observe in other types of businesses. Remember this is an average with many sales paid for at the time of purchase, whereas others are credit sales that may take much longer than 1 week to collect. Tracking the average collection period from year to year should provide an early indication if a firm is beginning to have difficulty collecting from its customers.

Inventories

To be conservative, inventories are shown on a company's balance sheet at the company's cost of acquiring that merchandise or the current market value of that merchandise, whichever is smaller. Determining a company's cost of acquiring (purchasing or manufacturing) the merchandise in inventory is not always straightforward. Home Depot uses the first-in, first-out (FIFO) method of calculating its inventory costs. For example, suppose it buys 5,000 hammers at $7.00 each and later another 3,000 identical hammers at $8.00 each. It then sells 6,000 of these hammers at $10.00 each. All the hammers are identical, so it makes no difference whether when stocking the shelves the warehouse employee grabs a box from the first shipment or from the second shipment. The question is just whether the first hammers sold will be treated for accounting purposes as having been purchased at the $7.00 price or the $8.00 price. Because Home Depot uses the FIFO method, for purposes of the income statement they would treat the first 5,000 sold (the first out of inventory) as having the first cost of $7.00 each. The next 1,000 that were sold would be treated as having a cost of $8.00 each. The 2,000 that were not sold would be included in the inventory section of the balance sheet at $8.00 each.

If Home Depot had instead opted to use the last-in, first-out (LIFO) method of inventory accounting, it would have treated the first 3,000 sold (the first out) as having a cost of $8.00 each (the last cost) and the next 3,000 as having a cost of $7.00 each. The 2,000 remaining in inventory would be valued at $7.00 each. The important point here is that in both cases the business reality is exactly the same. In both scenarios 8,000 hammers were purchased at an average price of $7.38 each, and 6,000 were sold at $10.00 each. Nevertheless, opting to use the FIFO instead of the LIFO accounting method would make the *reported* profits higher and the *reported* inventory values lower. With the FIFO method the cost of goods sold subtracted out on the income statement would be $43,000 (5,000 at $7 plus 1,000 at $8). With the LIFO accounting choice, the cost of goods sold subtracted out on the income statement would be $45,000 (3,000 at $8 and 3,000 at $7). Obviously, subtracting a smaller cost of goods sold on the income statement increases *reported* profits. Remember that *true* profits, at least at the pretax level, are unaffected by this accounting choice. Why would a company elect the LIFO accounting option which, during periods of rising prices, lowers reported profits? They might select LIFO precisely because lower taxable profits mean lower tax payments. The choice between LIFO and FIFO is more significant during periods of rapid inflation. If in this example the price per hammer had been the same in both the first and second purchases, the choice of FIFO versus LIFO would have no effect. With today's computerized inventory control systems, it is often possible to at all times know the exact cost of the items currently in inventory. That makes it possible to avoid both LIFO and FIFO and use an average cost method for inventory costing. Home Depot, however, like most companies chooses to stay with one of the more traditional methods of inventory costing.

Inventory Turnover Ratio

Dividing the Cost of Goods Sold expense from Home Depot's income statement by the value of inventories shown on its balance sheet yields a measure known as an inventory turnover ratio ($46.133 billion / $10.325 billion = 4.47). Dividing this ratio into 52 weeks gives the average inventory holding period in weeks (52 / 4.47 = 11.6 weeks). Home Depot turns its inventory over 4.47 times a year compared to only 3.93 times a year at Lowe's. This is another area where Home Depot's performance is stronger. A key goal of modern supply chain management techniques and Just-in-Time (JiT) inventory practices is reducing the amount of capital tied up in inventory. Of course, if inventories become too lean, there is a risk of losing sales because some products may not be available for immediate delivery.

Property, Plant, and Equipment

The long-term assets section of the balance sheet lists the firm's property, plant, and equipment at the original purchase price and then subtracts the accumulated depreciation to determine the net (or book) value of these assets. Suppose Home Depot were to buy for $50,000 a delivery truck that has an estimated useful life of 5 years. Allocating this cost over 5 years using straight-line depreciation would result in a $10,000 ($50,000 / 5) depreciation expense subtracted on the income statement in each of those years. Regardless of its market value, at the end 1 year, this truck would be shown on the company's balance sheet as having a value of $40,000 (original purchase price of $50,000 minus accumulated depreciation of $10,000). At the end of year 2, this truck would be shown on the company's balance sheet as having a value of $30,000 (original purchase price of $50,000 minus accumulated depreciation of 2 times $10,000). At the end of year 5, even if this truck were in good condition and fully operable, it would be shown on the company's balance sheet as having a value of zero (original purchase price of $50,000 minus the accumulated depreciation of 5 times $10,000). You never depreciate more than 100% of an asset's original cost. So even if this truck remained in use in year 6 and beyond, there would be no additional depreciation expense for this truck on the company's income statement.

Home Depot's balance sheet (refer to Exhibit 3-1) shows that the total originally paid for its property, plant, and equipment was $38.975 billion. This quantity is sometimes referred to a gross property plant and equipment. Subtracting the accumulated depreciation, the amount that has already been expensed on the current and previous income statements, yields the $24.448 billion net (or book value) of these long-term assets. Home Depot lists seven categories of property and equipment. Most of the labels are straightforward. Leasehold improvements are just alterations it made to property Home Depot leases from others. Capital leases are a long-term lease that are so similar to purchasing an asset that for accounting purposes they are reported as if the asset had been purchased. For example, a lease would be treated as a purchase if the lease covers 75% or more of the asset's useful life or if the present value[2] of the lease payments is greater than 90% of the asset's market value.

Goodwill

Also shown in the assets section of Home Depot's balance sheet are long-term notes receivable and goodwill. Whenever *goodwill* appears on a balance sheet, it indicates that there has been an acquisition and that the price paid was greater than the fair market value of net assets acquired. Paying a price greater than the value of the assets acquired does not necessarily mean you have paid a price greater than the value of the on-going firm containing those assets. For example, during fy2006 Home Depot made a number of acquisitions at a total cost of $4.5 billion. The cash and other identifiable assets acquired through those acquisitions, minus the liabilities assumed along with those acquisitions, had an estimated fair market value of $1.5 billion. When Home Depot consolidated these acquisitions into its balance sheet, it recorded these assets and liabilities with a net value of $1.5 billion and an additional "plug number" of $3 billion labeled goodwill. The sum of the $1.5 billion in net assets and the $3 billion in goodwill, therefore, balanced the $4.5 billion that was paid to acquire these firms.

The term goodwill sounds like you are paying for the good feelings customers and others may have about a firm being acquired. That, however, is not the case, and many firms are abandoning the goodwill label and replacing it with more precise language like "excess of purchase price over fair value of assets acquired." There are many reasons why a firm might be worth more than the fair market value of its net assets. One reason that should be obvious to HR managers is the value of a firm's workforce. What is required in dollars and time to recruit, select, and develop one top executive (or one executive secretary, or one engineer, or one sales rep, or one highly competent employee in any position)? Given the magnitude of those HR costs, a successful corporation with all its employees in place is obviously worth far more than it would be with same net assets but none of those employees in place. Examples of other factors that may add value beyond the sum of a corporation's net assets are market position, brand recognition, customer loyalty, first-mover advantage, and strategic fit with the acquiring firm.

Companies no longer amortize (write down the value of) goodwill over a specified number of years. Instead goodwill remains as an asset on the balance sheet until the company has evidence that its value has decreased. Home Depot's 2011 balance sheet (refer to Exhibit 3-1) shows goodwill valued at more than $1.1 billion. When there is evidence that the value of goodwill has declined, a goodwill impairment charge is subtracted on the income statement, and the value of the goodwill asset shown on the balance sheet is reduced. (The value of goodwill is usually written down when there is a significant decrease in the present value of expected future cash flows from the acquired asset. The logic behind and techniques for calculating the present value of future cash flows is discussed in Chapter 7, "Capital Budgeting and Discounted Cash Flow Analysis.")

Liabilities on the Balance Sheet

The section of the Home Depot balance sheet reproduced in Exhibit 3-2 shows total liabilities as of January 30, 2012 of $22.62 billion. Of this amount $9.38 billion are current liabilities that must be paid within the upcoming 12 months. The balance of $13.24 billion consists of long-term liabilities that will not come due within the next 12 months. If a firm has a 20-year mortgage, 1 year of it is shown as a current liability, and the other 19 years as a long-term liability. The current liabilities section of Home Depot's balance sheet shows $30 million as the near-term installments associated with long-term debt. Most of the labels in the liabilities section of this balance sheet are straightforward, with the possible exceptions of deferred revenue and deferred income taxes. *Deferred revenue* is money received for goods or services that have not yet been delivered. Under the accrual accounting methodology, these funds are included in cash on the assets side of the balance sheet, and a corresponding liability is recorded until delivery is made, at which time it is converted into revenue on the income statement. *Deferred income tax* entries indicate that there has been a difference between the accounting treatment and the tax treatment of some item of income or expense. A deferred income tax entry may appear on either the asset side or the liabilities side of the balance sheet. A deferred tax asset indicates this difference will result in a future tax savings. A deferred tax liability indicates that this difference will result in an increase in the firm's future tax obligations. For example, income already earned and recognized for accounting but not tax purposes creates a tax liability. You must pay taxes on that income in a future year.

THE HOME DEPOT, INC., AND SUBSIDIARIES
CONSOLIDATED BALANCE SHEETS, continued.
LIABILITIES AND STOCKHOLDERS' EQUITY

Amounts in Millions

	Jan 30, 2012	Jan 30, 2011
Current Liabilities:		
Accounts Payable	4,856	4,717
Accrued Salaries and Related Expenses	1,372	1,290
Sales Taxes Payable	391	368
Deferred Revenue	1,147	1,177
Income Taxes Payable	23	13
Current Installments of Long-Term Debt	30	1,042
Other Accrued Expenses	1,557	1,515
Long-term Liabilities:		
Long-Term Debt, Excluding Current Installments	10,758	8,707
Other Long-Term Liabilities	2,146	2,135
Deferred Income Taxes	340	272
Total Liabilities	$ 22,620	$ 21,236
Components of Stockholders' Equity		
Common Stock, Par Value $0.05 x 1.722 Billion Shares Issued	87	86
Additional Paid-In Capital	6,966	6,556
Retained Earnings	17,246	14,995
Accumulated Other Comprehensive Income	293	445
Treasury Stock at Cost	(6,694)	(3,193)
Total Stockholders Equity	$ 17,898	$ 18,889
Total Liabilities Plus Stockholder's Equity	$ 40,518	$ 40,125

Exhibit 3-2 Liabilities and equity section of Home Depot balance sheet

Source: Form 10-K filed with U.S. Securities Exchange Commission on 3/22/2012, page 31.

Stockholders' Equity on the Balance Sheet

As of June 30, 2012, Home Depot had assets totaling $40.518 billion and liabilities totaling $22.620 billion. Subtracting from the sum of everything Home Depot owned the sum of everything Home Depot owed, yields a shareholders' equity of $17.898 billion (40.518 – 22.620). That is the amount that would be left if all assets were sold at their book value and all liabilities were paid off at their book value. Paying off all liabilities at their book value is certainly possible if you have the cash to do that. Selling all assets at their book value is extremely unlikely. Assets, particularly long-term assets, may have a market value quite different from their book value. For example, a building constructed 20 years ago for $300,000 and depreciated straight line over 30 years will have a book value of $100,000 ($300,000 original purchase price minus 20 years of depreciation at $10,000 per year). The cost to replace that building in today's market could easily be $400,000 or more. In that example, the current market value is more than four times the book value. The book value of shareholders equity is therefore seldom the price you would pay to acquire a corporation. The assets on the balance sheet may have a book value that is quite different from the market value, and the balance sheet value does not include intangibles like brand value or the talent of the company's management and workforce.

The Capital Invested Component of Stockholders Equity

Current stockholders' equity is what the stockholders originally invested in the business plus any profits that were earned and retained in the business. The Home Depot balance sheet shows the components of its shareholders' equity. As of January 30, 2012, 1.722 billion shares of Home Depot stock had been issued. The individuals purchasing those shares paid Home Depot $7.053 billion. On the balance sheet this $7.053 billion is disaggregated into $87 million, which reflects the $0.05 par value of each share issued and $6,966 billion in additional paid-in capital. That disaggregation adds very little useful information for most readers of a balance sheet. The $0.05 a share par value is an arbitrary number chosen by the lawyers and accountants who structured the stock offering. When these shares were issued, they were not sold for 5 cents each but for as much as the market would pay. Dividing $7.053 billion by 1.722 billion shares tells you that the average price paid when the company originally sold these shares was $4.10 per share. This number, of course, has little relationship, if any, to what those shares sell for in today's market. On January 30, 2012, Home Depot stock was selling for just under $45 a share. Fluctuations in the current market price of its stock price generally have no impact on Home Depot's income statement or on the value of shareholder's equity shown on its balance sheet. The current market price is what individuals external to Home Depot agree to when buying and selling stock to each other. Current stock prices impact a company's financial statements only in years when the company chooses to issue new shares or buy back shares that are currently outstanding.

The Retained Earning Component of Stockholders Equity

There are only two possibilities for what a company can do with its net profits. It can distribute them to shareholders as dividends or retain them within the corporation to support its future operations. The stockholders equity section of Home Depot's January 30, 2012 balance sheet shows that out of the profits the company earned in the years since its incorporation $17.246 billion was retained to grow the business. The balance of its net profits was distributed as dividends.

Other Comprehensive Income

The Home Depot balance sheet also shows $293 million of Accumulated Other Comprehensive Income. Other comprehensive income includes changes in the value of certain assets or liabilities before these changes are recognized on the income statement. These assets are not usually assets like buildings or land, but instead are securities, derivative contracts, pension liabilities, and foreign operation assets. An example would be unrealized gains or losses on securities or derivatives held by Home Depot. These changes will eventually be recognized on the income statement when the security is sold or the derivative position is closed. In the meantime the security is shown at its increased value in the assets section of the balance sheet. This increases the value of total assets and therefore the value of stockholders equity. The other comprehensive income category shows the source of this increase in stockholder equity.

Treasury Stock

The last entry on the Home Depot balance sheet is labeled Treasury stock. These are shares of the company's own stock that Home Depot has purchased in the external market. Why would a company buy shares of its own stock? Sometimes these shares are acquired for re-issuance through stock-based employee compensation plans. Buying back shares in the open market prevents the dilution that would occur if the company issued new stock to support these compensation needs. Companies may also buy back stock because they feel that their stock is undervalued in the open market. During 2011, Home Depot announced plans to buy back $3.5 billion of its outstanding shares. This was in addition to substantial share repurchases in earlier years. As of January 30, 2012 Home Depot had spent $6.696 billion to repurchase its own stock. The amount paid to purchase these shares is subtracted from stockholders' equity. Owning shares of its own stock cannot make a company more valuable. It can, however, make each outstanding share more valuable because the company's value is divided among a smaller number of shares outstanding.

Which Numbers on a Balance Sheet Can You Believe?

Assuming a complete absence of fraud and that all entries were prepared in a manner consistent with generally accepted accounting principles (GAAP), can you have equal confidence in all the numbers in a balance sheet? The answer is usually "no." The cash amounts shown should be exact. The liabilities listed should also be precise because the firm and its creditors have written contracts specifying exactly how much is owed. You need to be a bit more cautious, however, when looking at the noncash current assets. The accounts receivable number shown is net of an allowance for accounts that may never be collected. Such bad debt allowances are based on historical experience, but as always history is no guarantee of what the future will bring. For example, a significant percentage of Home Depot's customers are professional contractors. It's certainly possible that the percentage of contractors paying their debts in a timely manner might decline during a prolonged housing recession. Inventory is shown on a balance sheet at the lower of its cost or its current market value. However, firms may vary considerably in the speed and aggressiveness with which inventory is written down in response to a decline in its market value.

Book Value Versus Market Value of Long-Term Assets

You need to be most cautious when basing decisions on the balance sheet valuations of long-term assets. The book value of long-term assets, the original purchase price minus accumulated depreciation, can be a millions of dollars above or below the market value of those assets. A building constructed 15 years ago for $3 million and now shown on a firm's balance sheet at a depreciated value of $1.5 million could easily have a replacement cost of $5 million. It's also possible for market values to be well below book values. Both U.S. and International Financial Reporting Standards (IFRS) do require that assets be written down when their economic value to a firm declines. That doesn't mean you don't need to be cautious. Consider the case of a steel mill[3] that was operating with outdated technology at a time when there was excess capacity in the global steel industry. As is standard for an on-going concern, this steel mill was shown on the parent company's balance sheet at its original construction cost minus accumulated depreciation. When the parent company decided to discontinue operations at this location, there were no buyers willing to purchase this mill for even one-half of its book value.

If the Asset Value Is Imprecise, so Is the Equity Value

Remember that equity is just assets minus liabilities. If in a firm with $3 million in liabilities, the book value of assets is $8 million, the book value of equity will be $5 million. If the book value of assets overstates (understates) its market value by $2 million, the balance sheet value of the equity would also be overstated (understated) by $2 million. It's important to keep those caveats in mind when using financial performance measures such as return on assets (net income / assets) and return on equity (net income / equity). You usually focus on changes in the numerator of those ratios, but those ratios are equally affected by the validity of the numbers in the denominator.

What Can a Balance Sheet Tell You About a Company's Financial Condition?

To assess your personal financial condition, you might begin by calculating your net worth. To do that you would subtract from the sum of everything you own, the sum of everything you owe. If the amount you owe is large compared to your net worth, you probably have cause for concern. In that situation, you would certainly find it more difficult to obtain a mortgage or a car loan. You can apply exactly the same logic to a corporate balance sheet. You can subtract from the sum of everything Home Depot owns (assets of $40.518 billion) the sum of everything Home Depot owes (liabilities of $22.620 billion) to obtain Home Depot's net worth (shareholder's equity of $17.898 billion). Dividing total liabilities by the shareholders equity ($22.620 billion / $17.898) reveals that Home Depot's debt to equity ratio is 1.26. Home Depot uses $1.26 in borrowed money for every $1.00 of shareholders' equity. The debt-to-equity ratio is a measure of financial leverage. A firm is said to be more highly leveraged if it increases the percentage of its assets that are financed through borrowing. Home Depot's debt equity ratio of 1.26 in January 2012 is up from 1.11 in January 2010. An increasing debt equity ratio can signal a problem with a firm's business operations. However, in this case it appears that Home Depot's leverage was increasing not because of operating problems but because of an intentional shift in its financial strategy. During 2011, the company borrowed $2 billion through the sale of 10-year and 30-year bonds.[4] Those funds were used to pay off $1 billion of bonds originally issued in 2006 that matured in 2011. The balance was used by Home Depot to buy back shares of its own stock. Home Depot was intentionally increasing its debt/equity ratio based on the expectation that borrowing long term at low rates would enable the company to generate even larger increases in shareholder value.

Any debt-to-equity ratio more than 1.0 indicates that the company is relying more heavily on borrowed money than on the owner's money. For small or struggling firms, a ratio above 1.0 can lead to serious problems. But for large, well-established firms, like Home Depot, a debt equity ratio of 1.26 is not a large amount of leverage. By comparison, the ratio of liabilities to equity on IBM's January 2012 balance sheet was 4.75.[5] Like Home Depot, IBM was taking advantage of historically low interest rates to borrow funds and use them to repurchase its own shares.

Use Caution When Using Published Financial Ratios

To properly interpret the level of any financial ratio, you must compare it to the level of that ratio in that firm in earlier years and to the value of that ratio in other firms with a similar product/industrial mix. For companies whose stock is publicly traded, numerous financial ratios can be obtained at no cost from MSN Money, Yahoo Finance, Google Finance, and many other Internet sites. For instance, the MSN money site provides six ratios related to financial condition, six related to profit margins, six related to return on investment, six related to operational efficiency, and six related to stock price. There are no accounting standards that specify how these financial ratios should be defined. Managers, investors, or financial analysts may calculate a ratio in the manner they believe is most relevant for their purposes. When utilizing financial ratios calculated by others, it is therefore critical that you know the definitions that were used. For example, the Home Depot leverage ratio calculated in the previous section was 1.26. The measure used was debt to equity. The MSN Money site reports a different leverage ratio for Home Depot of 2.3. The measure used was assets to equity. These are just two different ways to say exactly the same thing. If Home Depot has $1.26 in debt for $1.00 of equity, it has $2.26 in assets for every $1.00 of equity ($1.00 of equity + $1.26 of debt = $2.26 in total assets). MSN Money divided the $2.26 in total assets by the $1.00 of equity to get a ratio of 2.26, which it rounded to 2.3. It is also common to see published debt/equity ratios calculated with long-term debt, not total liabilities, in the numerator. Unfortunately, it's not always easy as it should be to find a clear statement of the definitions used to calculate published ratios. You may sometimes need to go back to the original financial statements and replicate the calculations to be sure a published ratio is what you think it is.

Ratio of Current Assets to Current Liabilities

A ratio called the Current Ratio is often used to assess the short-run implications of a company's debt. It is usually defined as current assets divided by current liabilities. Dividing Home Depot's current assets of $14.520 billion by its current liabilities of $9.376 billion yields a current ratio of 1.54. A ratio of 1.54 suggests that during the upcoming year Home Depot will have $1.54 in current assets to pay off for every $1.00 of current liabilities. A current ratio close to or below 1.0 can be a flag that a company may have difficulty raising the cash to cover its short-term debts. A variation that provides an even more stringent test of a firm's capability to make the payments on its short-term obligations is the acid test ratio. It is defined the same way as the current ratio but excludes from the current assets measure in the numerator the value of less liquid items such as inventories and prepaid expenses. There is no guarantee that all the merchandise in inventory will be sold, and prepaid expenses (for example, rent or insurance paid for in advance) are not assets that can be converted into cash. Calculating this ratio using Home Depot's January 2012 balance sheet ([$14.520 billion in current assets − $10.325 billion in inventory] / $9.376 billion of liabilities) yields a value of 0.45, that is, only $0.45 in liquid assets available to cover each $1.00 of short term debt. That would be cause for serious concern if you believed Home Depot would be unable to convert most of its $10 billion of inventory into cash. Because there is no reason to believe that, the acid test in this case is not a particularly useful measure. It might however be a critically important tool if you were evaluating the balance sheet of, say, a cell phone manufacturer that had a large inventory of phones that consumers were rejecting in favor of the latest-and-greatest release from one of its competitors.

Financial Leverage Can Increase the Shareholders' Return on Investment

The previous section discussed using a debt equity ratio to assess the amount of financial leverage reflected on a firm's balance sheet. Why do almost all firms have debt on their balance sheet? It's not because they couldn't raise all the money needed by selling stock.

It's because they believe that by borrowing a portion of the amount needed they can provide their shareholders with a greater rate of return on their investment. Exhibit 3-3 illustrates how this can be achieved. A common measure of the rate of return earned by the shareholders is Return on Equity (ROE), calculated by dividing Net Income from the bottom line of the income statement by Shareholders Equity from the balance sheet. The top panel illustrates the effect of leverage under the assumption that management can earn an operating profit of 10% on every dollar of assets they have to work with. If this company's $500 million in assets had been paid for with funds raised through the sale of stock, its EBIT would be $50 million and its net income $35 million. That $35 million divided by the shareholders' investment of $500 million would have been a return on equity of 7%. Now suppose only $100 million of that $500 million in assets had been financed through the sale of stock and that the balance, $400 million, was money borrowed from a bank or by selling bonds. If the average interest rate on the debt was 5%, the firm must pay 20 million in interest, reducing its net income to $21 million. However, because the shareholders had invested only $100 million, that $21 million net income represents a 21% return on the equity. In this case the use of substantial financial leverage tripled the shareholders' rate of return on their investment. Would you rather earn a 7% return or a 21% return on the funds in your 401K? You would jump at the chance to earn 21% unless you thought that investment was too risky. Does using financial leverage make a firm more risky?

Financial Leverage Can Reduce the Shareholders' Return on Investment

To see how financial leverage can reduce the return to shareholders, refer to the bottom panel of Exhibit 3-3. Suppose the business described in this exhibit were a Home Depot retail outlet, and Lowe's had just opened a new store one block away, and that the new Lowe's store reduces Home Depot's profit by cutting into its market share. This Home Depot outlet is still profitable but now earns an operating profit equal to 2% of assets utilized instead of the previous 10%. Referring to the bottom panel of Exhibit 3-3, you can see if this firm had no debt, its net income would be $7 million and its return on equity would be 1.4%. On the other hand, if this firm had $400 million in debt, its net income, actually a net loss, would be –$10 million. Under this scenario, the effect of financial leverage was to reduce the return on equity from +1.4% to –10%. So when is leverage helpful, and when is it harmful? Simply, it is helpful when you can earn more on a borrowed dollar than it costs you to borrow it. Exhibit 3-3 shows the average interest rate was 5%. When the firm earned 10% on each dollar of assets, the use of leverage was highly beneficial. When the firm earned only 2% on each dollar of assets, the use of leverage was detrimental. The more highly leveraged a firm is, the larger these positive and negative effects can be. Leverage can magnify a good year into a great year. It can also transform a mediocre year into a disastrous year. Highly leveraged firms are generally considered to be riskier because the effect of leverage is to take whatever volatility there is in business operations and magnify that into even greater swings in bottom-line profit and return on equity.

Assumption 1: Management can earn an operating profit of 10% on every dollar.

	No Leverage	Highly Leveraged
Equity	$500	$100
Debt	$0	$400
Total Assets	$500	$500
EBIT @ 10 % of Assets	$50	$50
- Interest @ 5% of Debt	$0	-$20
Profit Before Tax	$50	$30
Tax @ 30%	-$15	-$9
Net Income	$35	$21
Return on Equity (NI/Equity)	7.0%	21.0%

Assumption 2: Management can earn an operating proit of 2% on every dollar.

	No Leverage	Highly Leveraged
Equity	$500	$100
Debt	$0	$400
Total Assets	$500	$500
EBIT @ 2% of Assets	$10	$10
- Interest @ 5% of Debt	$0	-$20
Profit Before Tax	$10	-$10
Tax @ 30%	-$3	$0
Net Income	$7	-$10
Return on Equity (NI/Equity)	1.4%	-10.0%

Exhibit 3-3 Impact of leverage on return on equity

An Alternative Calculation of Return on Equity

The return on equity measure used in the previous example was calculated by dividing net income by the book value, that is, the balance sheet value, of shareholders equity. It is certainly possible that the stock market value of shareholders equity could be above or below the value of shareholders equity shown on the balance sheet. The stock market value of shareholders equity, the company's market capitalization, is the dollar value of all shares currently outstanding. It is calculated by multiplying the number of shares outstanding by the current price per share. For example, if there are 10 million shares of XYZ Company's stock outstanding and XYZ stock is trading at $50 per share, the market capitalization of XYZ is $500 million. Some analysts prefer to calculate return on equity as net income divided by market value of equity, instead of as net income divided by the balance sheet value of equity. Using the market value of equity avoids needing to rely on accounting statements that may not reflect the true replacement cost of a firm's assets and may completely omit the value of workforce quality and other intangible assets. Of course, using the market value of equity has a different set of problems. This number can be highly volatile and influenced by stock market conditions and other external factors unrelated to the firm's performance.

4

Cash Flows: Timing Is Everything

What's the difference between operating profit and cash flow from operations? When measuring profits you make a series of timing adjustments. For example, you define top-line revenues as total sales during the period even if you have not yet collected all the cash from those sales. You subtract from that number only the cost of the merchandise sold during that period, even if you paid your suppliers for that merchandise and other merchandise that is still in inventory. Similarly you don't subtract from the current period's revenues the full amount paid to purchase long-term assets. You allocate, or depreciate, those costs over an estimate of the economic life of that asset. Those timing assumptions are all quite reasonable if your goal is to estimate the amount of profit earned during a particular time period. When calculating cash flow from operations, you make none of those timing adjustments. When calculating cash flow you attempt to answer the question, "How much cash did your business operations actually bring in during the period and how much cash did your business operations actually pay out during that period?" The net of those two numbers determines whether your cash flow for the period was positive or negative.

The example in Exhibit 4-1 illustrates how different profit and cash flow can be during the same period. This firm had a profit of $15 million in 2012, but its cash flow was a negative $6 million. The company's cash flow from the operations was calculated as follows:

15	Net income
+ 6	Depreciation
–4	Increase in Accounts Receivable
–8	Increase in inventory
–15	Increase in long-term assets
–6	Cash flow from operations

Income Statement and Excerpt from Balance Sheet
All Figures in Millions of $

Income Statement for Year 2012

Revenue	100
Cost of Goods Sold	60
Operating Expenses	12
Depreciation	6
Interest	2
Tax	5
Net Income	15

Balance Sheet at the End of 2012		Balance Sheet at the End of 2011	
Cash	4	Cash	10
Accounts Receivable	8	Accounts Receivable	4
Inventory	20	Inventory	12
Long-Term Assets, Gross	65	Long-Term Assets, Gross	50
Accumulated Depreciation	31	Accumulated Depreciation	25
Long-Term Assets, Net	29	Long-Term Assets, Net	25
Total Assets	61	Total Assets	51
Short-Term Liabilities	15	Short-Term Liabilities	15
Long-Term Liabilities	25	Long-Term Liabilities	25
Equity	21	Equity	11
Total Liabilities Plus Equity	61	Total Liabilities Plus Equity	51

Exhibit 4-1 Information needed to calculate cash flow from operations

Calculating operating cash flows involves two steps. The first is to determine what the income statement tells you about cash flows. The second is to review the assets and liabilities shown on the balance sheet to determine whether there were any changes during the year in these items that had cash flow implications. When you assess the cash flow impact of a particular transaction, you are doing nothing more than saying, "If all this company's cash were kept in a single account, would that account balance go up or down because of this transaction?"

Cash Flow Information from the Income Statement

The company (refer to Exhibit 4-1) earned a net profit of $15 million. That's a cash inflow. But one of the items subtracted on the income statement was depreciation. As you know, depreciation is not a real cash outflow. It's just an accounting recognition in the current period of a portion of the cash that was spent at the time the long-term assets were acquired. The cash generated in 2012 was therefore more than $15 million profit. When you add back the $6 million in depreciation expense, you see that the cash generated was $21 million. The company's current business operations during 2011 brought in $21 million more than was paid out. You could stop there if there were no changes over the year in the balance sheet. But there usually are, so look at that next.

Cash Flow Information from the Balance Sheet

What changes occurred in this company's balance sheet between the end of 2011 and the end of 2012? Did those changes add to or reduce the company's cash on hand? An increase in an asset category required cash to purchase those additional assets, so subtract from the cash generated the amount of any asset increase. A reduction in an asset category would mean assets were sold, so you would add the cash received from selling those assets. An increase in any category of liabilities would mean additional funds were borrowed, so add the amount of cash obtained through any additional borrowing. A reduction in any category of liabilities would mean debts were being paid off. In that case, you would subtract the amount of cash used to pay off those debts.

In this example, inventories increased by $8 million, and long-term assets increased by $15 million. The cash used to acquire those additional assets was subtracted in the preceding calculation. Accounts Receivable also increased over the year. Accounts Receivable, that is, uncollected funds, increased by $4 million, so the company has

$4 million less in the bank than if accounts receivables had remained at the 2011 level. In this example liabilities were unchanged between the end of 2011 and the end of 2012.

The logic of the Home Depot cash flow statement shown in Exhibit 4-2 is exactly the same as the approach used in the simplified previous example. Home Depot starts with the $3.9 billion in net income from the bottom line of its 2011 income statement and then adds back the two noncash items, depreciation, and stock-based compensation expense, which had been subtracted on that income statement. Chapter 10, "Equity-Based Compensation: Stock and Stock Options," discusses the expensing of stock-based compensation. The key point for this discussion is that granting employees stock options or other forms of equity does not require a cash outlay at the time of the grant. Home Depot then goes through each of the categories of assets and liabilities that appear on its balance sheet. If an asset category increases, the cash required to increase those assets is subtracted. If an asset category decreases, the proceeds from those asset reductions are added. If a liability category increases, the funds obtained through that borrowing are added. If a liability category decreases, funds used to pay down that debt are subtracted. During the 12-month period that ended January 29, 2012, Home Depot's business operations produced a net cash inflow of $6.651 billion. Of that amount the company spent $1.129 billion to build new stores and acquire other long-term business assets. That still left a net inflow of $5.522 billion.

What can a company do with that much cash? There are only a few possibilities. The cash could be retained within the company to expand current business operations or to acquire new businesses. Funds not retained in the business can be returned to the shareholders as dividends or used to repurchase the company shares in the open market. Home Depot during 2011 did all three of those things.

It paid dividends of $1.632 billion and repurchased a $3.47 billion of its own stock. After a stock repurchase, each of the remaining shareholders will own a larger percentage of the company. These remaining shareholders will have benefited if at the time of the repurchase the stock was undervalued in the external market. The remaining shareholders will have incurred an economic loss if at the time of the repurchase the shares were overvalued in the external market.

CASH FLOWS FOR YEAR ENDING JANUARY 30, 2012
Amounts in Millions

		Net Earnings	$3,883
Add Back	Depreciation and Amortization		1,682
Add Back	Stock-Based Compensation Expense		215

Changes in Operating Assets:

Subtract	Increase in Receivables, Net	(170)
Add	Decrease in Merchandise Inventories	256
Add	Decrease in Other Current Assets	159

Changes in Operating Liabilities:

Add	Increase in Accounts Payable and Accrued Expenses		422
Subtract	Decrease in Deferred Revenue		(29)
Add	Increase in Income Taxes Payable		14
Add	Increase in Deferred Income Taxes		170
Subtract	Decrease in Other Long-Term Liabilities		(2)
Add	Other		51
	Net Cash Provided by Operating Activities		**$6,651**

CASH FLOWS FROM INVESTING ACTIVITIES:

Subtract	Purchase of Property and Equipment	(1,221)	
Add	Proceeds from Sales of Property and Equipment	56	
Subtract	Payments for Business Acquired	(65)	
Add	Proceeds from Sale Business, Net	101	
	Net Cash Used in Investing Activities		**(1,129)**

CASH FLOWS FROM FINANCING ACTIVITIES:

Add	Proceeds from Long-Term Borrowings	1,994	
Subtract	Repayments of Long-Term Debt	(1,028)	
Subtract	Repurchases of Common Stock	(3,470)	
Add	Proceeds from Sales of Common Stock	306	
Subtract	Cash Dividends Paid to Stockholders	(1,632)	
Subtract	Net Cash Used in Other Financing Activities	(218)	
	Net Cash Used in Financing		**(4,048)**

INCREASE IN CASH AND CASH EQUIVALENTS   **$1,474**

Effect of Exchange Rate Changes on Cash and Cash Equivalents	(32)
Cash and Cash Equivalents at Beginning of Year	**$545**
Cash and Cash Equivalents at End of Year	**$1,987**

Exhibit 4-2 Cash flow statement for Home Depot
Source: Form 10-K filed with U.S. Securities Exchange Commission on 3/22/2012, page 32.

At the same time that Home Depot was distributing cash by repurchasing shares, it was raising cash by selling bonds. Home Depot paid off $1.028 billion in bonds originally issued in 2006 that matured in 2011. This cash outflow was more than offset by borrowing $1.994 billion through the sale of new 10-year and 30-year bonds. Of course, buying back shares at the same time you're taking on additional debt makes the company more highly leveraged. As explained in Chapter 2

("The Income Statement: Do We Care About More Than the Bottom
Line?") increasing leverage creates additional opportunities and also
additional risk.

   The combined effect of all these activities was to increase Home
Depot's cash on hand by $1.474 billion, from $545 million at the start
of the year to $1.987 billion at the end of the year.

5

Financial Statements as a Window into Business Strategy

When looking at financial statements, the challenge for most people is to not fail to see the forest for the trees. Can a corporation's balance sheet and income statement provide clues not only about its financial performance, but also about its business and financial strategy? Try an exercise to see how far you can get. The income statements and balance sheets in Exhibits 5-1 and 5-2 describe real companies that you're probably familiar with. For the moment, however, the names are withheld to see how much you can learn about each of them just by looking at the numbers in their financial statements. Suppose as an experienced HR executive, you have been asked to recommend which company's management team deserves a bigger performance bonus. Chapter 12, "Creating Value and Rewarding Value Creation," discusses in more detail the selection and construction of bonus drivers, but for the purpose of this exercise, you will use only some simple financial ratios.

	Company A		Company B	
Total Revenue	10,877	100.0%	446,950	100.0%
Cost of Revenue, Total	6,592	60.6%	335,127	75.0%
Gross Profit	**4,285**	**39.4%**	**111,823**	**25.0%**
Selling /General /Administrative Expense	3,036	27.9%	85,265	19.1%
EBIT	**1,249**	**11.5%**	**26,558**	**5.9%**
Interest Expense	130	1.2%	2,160	0.5%
Income Tax--Total	436	4.0%	7,944	1.8%
Income After Tax	**683**	**6.3%**	**16,454**	**3.7%**
Minority Interest	0	0.0%	-688	-0.2%
Total Extraordinary Items	0	0.0%	-67	0.0%
Net Income	**683**	**6.3%**	**15,669**	**3.5%**

Exhibit 5-1 Income statements for companies A and B

Assets	Company A		Company B	
Cash and Short-Term Investments	1,877	22%	6,003	3%
Total Receivables, Net	2,033	24%	5,937	3%
Total Inventory	1,148	14%	40,714	21%
Prepaid Expenses	282	3%	1,685	1%
Other Current Assets, Total	220	3%	636	0%
Total Current Assets	**5,560**	**65%**	**54,975**	**28%**
		0%		0%
Property/Plant/Equipment, Total--Net	2,469	29%	112,324	58%
Goodwill, Net	175	2%	20,651	11%
Other Long-Term Assets, Total	287	3%	5,456	3%
Total Assets	**8,491**	**100%**	**193,406**	**100%**
Liabilities				
Accounts Payable	917	11%	36,608	19%
Accrued Expenses	388	5%	18,154	9%
Notes Payable/Short-Term Debt	0	0%	4,047	2%
Current Port. of LT Debt/Capital Leases	506	6%	2,301	1%
Other Current Liabilities, Total	764	9%	1,190	1%
Total Current Liabilities	**2,575**	**30%**	**62,300**	**32%**
Long-Term Liabilities	3,960	47%	59,791	31%
Total Liabilities	**6,535**	**77%**	**122,091**	**63%**
Equity	**1,956**	**23%**	**71,315**	**37%**
Total Liabilities & Shareholders' Equity	**8,491**	**100%**	**193,406**	**100%**

Exhibit 5-2 Balance sheets for companies A and B

Common Size Financial Statements

It's immediately obvious that Company B has much larger sales revenue and profits. You can assume, however, that the size difference between these two organizations is reflected in the base salaries of the two management teams. The challenge is to recommend which team should get the larger performance bonus, perhaps as a percentage of its base salary. To control for the size difference between the two firms, you can calculate common size income statements and balance sheets (refer to Exhibits 5-1 and 5-2). The common size income statements simply express all entries as a percentage of top-line sales revenue. The common size balance sheets simply express each asset category as a percentage of total assets and each component of liabilities and shareholders' equity as a percentage of the total liabilities and shareholders' equity.

Profit Margin

You might start your analysis by comparing the two firms on net profit margin. On this measure Company A looks stronger. For every $100 in sales revenue, Company A ended up with $6.30 of bottom line net income. Company B generated only $3.50 of bottom line net income from every $100 in sales revenue. If you recommend that bonuses be distributed in proportion to the net profit margin, Company A managers will receive bonuses almost twice as large as those received by the team at Company B.

Net profit margin = Net income / sales revenue

Company A looks much stronger

Company A: 683 / 10,877	**= 6.3%**
Company B: 15,699 / 446,950	= 3.5%

Return on Assets

In addition to looking at profit as a percentage of sales revenue, you could calculate profit as a percentage of the assets used to generate that profit. Maximizing the profit they can earn given the bundle of assets they have to work with is a key economic goal of any management team. If you recommend that bonuses be distributed in proportion to return on assets, the teams in both companies would receive similar bonuses. There is no significant difference between the two companies on this measure.

Return on assets = Net income / total assets

No significant difference between companies A and B

Company A: 683 / 8,491	**= 8.0 %**
Company B: 15,699 / 193,406	**= 8.1 %**

Asset Turnover

Clearly, it is going to make a big difference which bonus driver you choose. The question you may be asking yourself is, "How could two companies be so different on net profit margin and so similar on return on assets?" To answer that question you probably need to calculate one more ratio. The ratio defined as sales revenue divided by total assets is sometimes referred to as *asset turnover*. This is the first measure on which Company B's performance is the stronger one. Company B generated $2.31 in sales revenue for every $1 of assets it had to work with. Company A generated only a $1.28 in sales revenue for every $1 of assets. If bonuses are distributed based on asset turnover, the Company B team would receive bonuses almost twice as large as those received by its counterparts in Company A.

Asset turnover = Sales revenue / total assets

Company B looks much stronger

Company A: 10,877 / 8,491   = 1.28

Company B: 446,950 / 193,406   **= 2.31**

Connecting the Dots

So what are you going to recommend? On the first measure, Company A looks better. On the second measure, there is no real difference between the two firms. On the third measure, Company B looks better. To make sense of this information, you need to ask what business scenario explains this constellation of data points. Perhaps it can help to recognize that Return on Assets = Profit Margin × Asset Turnover, as shown in Exhibit 5-3. When you multiply the fractions on the right side of this equation, the two sales terms cancel, and you are left with NI over assets, which is ROA (return on assets). This equation is simply saying that ROA, the net income a company earns on each dollar of assets, is equal to the profit it makes on every dollar of sales revenue, times the number of sales dollars it can generate with each dollar of assets. You can now see that Company A and Company B achieved almost exactly the same ROA through two different business strategies. The Company A data suggests a high-margin, low-volume business strategy. The Company B data is consistent with a low-margin, high-volume business strategy. Company B made much less profit on each dollar of sales but offset that by generating more sales per dollar of assets.

Return on Assets	=	Profit Margin	x	Asset Turnover
Net Income / Assets	=	Net Income / Sales	x	Sales / Assets
Company A 8.0%	=	6.3%	x	1.28
Company B 8.1%	=	3.5%	x	2.31

Exhibit 5-3 The determinants of ROA

Return on Equity

You have now figured out how these two firms could be so different in profit per dollar of sales while so close in profit per dollar of assets. Company A offset its lower margins with higher volumes. There is, however, an additional performance measure that you should consider: profit per dollar of shareholders equity. This measure shows how much profit is earned for every dollar shareholder investment.

Return on equity = Net income / equity

Company A looks much stronger

Company A: 683 /1,956	= **34.9%**
Company B: 15,699 /71,315	= 22.0%

If performance is judged on this measure of ROE, Company A looks much stronger. This raises a new question. How can two companies be so similar on ROA yet so different when it comes to return on equity (ROE)? The equation in Exhibit 5-4 provides the answer.

Return on Equity	=	Profit Margin	x	Asset Turnover	x	Financial Leverage
Net Income / Equity	=	Net Income / Sales	x	Sales / Assets	x	Assets / Equity
Company A 34.9%	=	6.3%	x	1.28	x	4.34
Company B 22.0%	=	3.5%	x	2.31	x	2.71

Exhibit 5-4 The determinants of ROE

The first two terms on the right side of this equation are exactly the ones you used to calculate the ROA. The additional term on the right side is a measure of financial leverage, calculated as the ratio of assets to equity. Company A's assets to equity ratio of 4.34 suggests that for every $1.00 of equity, the company borrowed an additional $3.34. Company B's assets to equity ratio of $2.71 suggests that for every $1.00 of equity that company borrowed $1.71. When you multiply the fractions on the right side of this equation, the two sales terms cancel, the two assets terms cancel, and you are left with net income over equity, which is ROE. This equation is simply saying that ROE, the net income a company earns on each dollar of equity, is equal to the profit it makes on every dollar of assets multiplied by the amount of assets it has per dollar shareholder investment. As explained in Chapter 3 ("The Balance Sheet: If Your People Are Your Most Important Asset, Where Do They Show Up on the Balance Sheet?"), whenever you see a company whose ROE is different from its ROA, that difference is the result of financial leverage. When the ROE is greater than the ROA, the financial leverage was beneficial, that is, the company earned more on the borrowed money than it cost to borrow it. When the ROE is less than the ROA, the financial leverage turned out to be detrimental, that is, the company earned less on the borrowed money than it cost to borrow it. The larger the amount of financial leverage (that is, borrowing), the larger these beneficial or harmful effects can be.

Differential Impact of Financial Leverage

The impact of financial leverage was beneficial at both of these firms. Company B's ROE of 22% was well above its ROA of 8.1%. There was even a larger difference between Company A's ROE of 34.9% and its ROA of 8.0%. Company A had the bigger benefit from financial leverage because it engaged in more borrowing. That can be confirmed by referring to Company A's higher assets to equity ratio in Exhibit 5-4. The first two terms on the right side of the equation are the components ROA. The third term on the right side of this equation is the leverage multiplier. The larger it is, the more borrowing there has been, and the larger the impact of financial leverage will be. You've now figured out how the two companies could have similar ROAs but such different ROEs. The explanation is that Company A was much more highly leveraged.

It is interesting to note that in percentage terms Company A has both borrowed more from others and has more owed to them. The accounts receivable number shown on Company A's balance sheet (2,033) is equal to 19% of the top-line sales number on its income statement (10,877). The comparable percentage for Company B is only 1%. It appears that Company A makes much greater use of credit sales.

The Big Picture

By reviewing their financial statements, and without relying on any external information, you got clues about the business strategies and the financial strategies of these two firms. Company A appeared to have a high-margin, low-volume business strategy. Company B appeared to employ a low-margin, high-volume strategy. Company A's financial strategy appeared to depend upon a far greater amount of financial leverage. The data in Exhibits 5-1 and 5-2 is real and was excerpted from the March 2012 10-K filings of two well-known retailers. The figures are in millions of U.S. dollars. That information is probably enough for you to identify Company B with 2011 sales revenues of just under $447 billion as Wal-Mart Stores, Inc. Company A is Nordstrom, Inc. Now that you know who these two companies are, you can see that your speculations based on their financial statements were accurate. Wal-Mart's low-margin, high-volume strategy is widely understood and has been hugely successful. During 2011 Nordstrom matched Wal-Mart's ROA through a quite different high-margin, low-volume strategy. Nordstrom is willing to compromise some market share to focus on the subset of consumers who are willing to pay a premium price for its differentiated merchandise and its higher level of customer service. If the objective were to reward operating managers in proportion to the success of their 2011 business operations, managers at both the firms should probably receive similar bonuses. Both firms achieved the same ROA but through different business strategies.

Even though their operating performances as measured by ROA were similar, Nordstrom (Company A) had a greater ROE; that is, it earned more profit per dollar shareholder investment. Nordstrom's larger ROE was the result of its financial strategy, not the result of a stronger operating performance. Financial strategy decisions are typically made at corporate headquarters, and ROE is therefore usually not an appropriate measure to gauge the performance of divisional or operating managers. The difference between a firm's ROE and its ROA could be an important factor when evaluating the performance of the CFO or the CEO. Remember, however, that although greater financial leverage may boost a firm's ROE, it also makes the firm riskier. You must carefully assess whether the increase in the ROE is large enough to justify taking on that additional risk. In the previous example, you saw that Nordstrom was both more highly leveraged (it borrowed more) and had much more owed to them (that is, much higher receivables on its balance sheet). The explanation is that Nordstrom is one of the few U.S. retailers that still own its credit card receivables. Nordstrom's wholly owned federal savings bank, Nordstrom FSB, provides a private label credit card, two Nordstrom VISA credit cards, and a debit card. Nordstrom's financial statements reflect the combination of retail businesses that are typically only moderately leveraged and banking operations that are typically more highly leveraged.

The Link Between HR Strategy and Business Strategy

Becker, Huselid, and Beatty in their excellent book, *The Differentiated Workforce*[1] explain how the HR strategies at Wal-Mart and Nordstrom are aligned with the business strategies that you uncovered through a review of their financial statements. At both firms HR strategy is focused on attracting, developing, and retaining exceptionally talented individuals to occupy those key positions that are most critical to maintaining the firm's strategic capabilities. They explain that at Nordstrom these individuals are the personal shoppers that shape the customer experience, and that at Wal-Mart they are the distribution and logistics specialists that enable the firm's operating processes to work so efficiently.

Remember this was only an exercise used to demonstrate how you can extract clues about both business strategy and financial strategy from a review of a firm's income statement and balance sheet. A more detailed discussion of selecting bonus drivers is contained in Chapter 12. However, one key take away from the previous example should be that a firm's ROA is always a function of its profit margin and asset turnover. When a firm selects a business strategy, it makes a statement about the combination of profit margin and asset turnover that it believes can maximize its ROA. HR strategy including employee selection and employee compensation should be tailored to support the firm's business strategy. Those business strategies can differ between firms and even between different divisions of the same firm. For example, Tiffany and Company has one division that manufactures and sells finished jewelry and another division that imports and distributes loose diamonds. Both divisions have the same economic goal, to maximize ROA, the profit earned on the assets invested in that division. The strategies it utilizes to pursue this goal are, however, polar opposites. The finished jewelry division pursues a high-margin strategy. This division's products are differentiated from the competition not only by the quality of the materials and workmanship, but also by the Tiffany and Company brand. This division believes its brand is its single-most important asset[2] and targets a market niche that pays a premium for its differentiated product.

Branding is much less important in the loose diamond division because a loose diamond of a given size and quality has the same value whether distributed by Tiffany or any other firm. Product differentiation is not practical in this market. This division pursues a low-margin strategy. Its approach is to employ competitive, not premium, pricing and to seek the largest share possible of the diamond importation and distribution business. If Tiffany is going to be successful in this market, it will be because of the scale and efficiency of its operations. If you are the SVP of HR at Tiffany's, you don't want to evaluate the financial statements of these two divisions without an understanding of these differences in business strategies. It would be foolish to deny bonuses to managers in the loose diamond division because they did not achieve profit margins comparable to those earned in the finished jewelry division, or to criticize the managers in the finished jewelry division because they did not match the market share of the loose diamond division.

6

Stocks, Bonds, and the Weighted Average Cost of Capital

Why Is the Cost of Capital Important to HR Managers?

No business strategy and no HR strategy can create value for the firm unless it generates a return on investment greater than the firm's cost of capital. For that reason it is critical to understand what determines a firm's cost of capital and the implications of the cost of capital for all strategic and operating decisions made by the firm. The basic concept is a simple one. For example, suppose you want to open a restaurant where you can show off your skills as a chef and make enough money to support your family. To get this business started, you need $500,000, all of which you borrow from your brother-in-law at 8%. Your cost of capital is 8%, and each year you must pay your brother-in-law $40,000 in interest. Unless the operating profit from your restaurant is greater than $40,000 per year, you may show off your culinary skills, but you won't be generating any economic value for yourself and your family. In this example, 8% is the minimum return you must earn on the $500,000 invested in this restaurant if your business is to be successful. A firm's cost of capital is the minimum rate of return it must it must generate through its business operations to cover the cost of raising the money used to acquire the assets invested in those operations.

Where Does the Money Come From?

The example in the previous paragraph is an unrealistic one in that 100% of the funds came from borrowing. Most corporations are financed through a combination of equity and debt. Equity financing refers to funds raised through the sale of stock. This can be common stock or preferred stock. Each share of common stock represents an ownership interest in the corporation. Owners of common stock typically have the right to vote for members of the Board of Directors and on other corporate issues. Common stockholders have the right to receive dividends in proportion to their ownership interest. For example, if you own 3% of the outstanding stock and management chooses to declare a dividend, you are entitled to 3% of the dividends distributed. If the company is liquidated, common shareholders also have a right to receive a percentage of the proceeds. However, common shareholders have the lowest priority claim. They receive a percentage of whatever, if anything, is left after the claims of creditors, bondholders, and preferred stockholders have been paid.

Preferred stock is a type of stock that may have no voting rights but pays a fixed dividend amount. Corporations cannot pay any dividends to common stockholders until this obligation to preferred stockholders has been satisfied. For example, GM's offered its series B preferred shares with a fixed dividend of $2.38 per year. GM cannot pay any dividends to its common stockholders unless it first pays $2.38 per share to the preferred stockholders. After it does that, the dividend to common stockholders could be less than $2.38 a share or much larger than that. Preferred stock may be *cumulative* or *noncumulative*. Cumulative preferred requires that if a company fails to pay a dividend at the stated rate, it must make it up at a later time. The GM series B preferred shares are cumulative. That means if these preferred shareholders received no dividend in 2013, they must be paid $4.76 per share (2 x $2.38) in 2014, or no dividends can be paid to common shareholders in 2014.

Debt financing, that is, borrowing, can take the form of loans from a bank or other institution, or the sale of bonds or commercial paper. Bonds and commercial paper are just IOUs that the corporation provides to lenders. Bonds and commercial paper are debt instruments and do not represent any ownership interest in the company. Commercial paper is usually short term and unsecured, that is, not backed by specific assets. Bonds may be secured or unsecured and can have terms as long as 20 or 30 years. If you buy a $10,000 bond from IBM, IBM gives you a bond certificate (an IOU) stating that it will repay the $10,000 you have loaned it on the bonds maturity date. That bond certificate will also state the annual interest rate that IBM will pay you on your $10,000 between the date of purchase and the maturity date. Bond pricing and bond yields are discussed in more detail in Chapter 7, "Capital Budgeting and Discounted Cash Flow Analysis."

Calculating the WACC

Firms often refer to their weighted average cost of capital (WACC). This is just the weighted average of the cost of raising equity capital from the firm's shareholders and the cost of borrowing from the firm's creditors. Consider the hypothetical firm described in Exhibit 6-1 with $50 million of assets. Equity capital, that is, proceeds from the sale of stock, was used to purchase assets costing $30 million (60% of the total). Borrowed funds were used to purchase the remaining $20 million of assets (40% of the total). If the cost of raising equity capital is 11% and the average cost of borrowings is 6%, the firm's weighted average cost of capital is 9% [(.60x 11%) + (.40x6%) = 9%]. This firm's business operations must produce a return of at least 9% to cover the cost of the assets utilized. That 9% is sometimes described as the *hurdle rate* that must be exceeded by all its strategic and operating investments.

	Cost of Capital	Proportion of Total Assets
Equity	11%	0.6
Debt	6%	0.4
Weighted Average	9% = (.6 x 11%) + (.4 x 6%)	

Exhibit 6-1 Weighted average cost of capital

The Cost of Debt

Of course, to do the calculation (refer to Exhibit 6-1) you must start with an estimate of the cost of debt and the cost of equity. As you will see, the cost of debt is the easier number to determine. The cost of debt is just the average after-tax interest rate that the firm pays. Because interest, like other business expenses, reduces a firm's taxable income, its after-tax cost is less than its pretax cost. If a firm were in a 25% tax bracket, every $100 in interest expense would reduce the firm's taxable income by $100 and therefore its tax obligation by $25. The net after-tax cost of the interest payment would be $75 ($100 interest payment minus $25 tax reduction). This relationship can be expressed as

After tax cost of debt = (Average interest rate) × (1 – tax rate).

If a firm's pretax interest rate were 8% and its tax rate were 25%, its after-tax interest rate would be 6% (8% × (1 – .25) = 6%).

The Cost of Equity

The *cost of equity* is the minimum rate of return that will entice investors to purchase shares of stock in this firm. Of course, stockholders are not promised any specific rate of return. Their stock purchase decision is based on the return they expect to receive. Their actual returns may turn out to be much more or much less than was expected. The riskier a firm is perceived to be, the higher the expected return will need to be to attract equity investors. The capital asset pricing model, often abbreviated as CAPM, is by far the most frequently used method for estimating the expected return that will be required. Recent survey data indicates an overwhelming majority of all organizations and more than 90% publicly traded companies utilize the CAPM when estimating their cost of equity.[1] The underlying logic of the CAPM is just that investors won't pursue a risky investment unless they expect to earn more than they could on a less risky investment. Exhibit 6-2 is an illustration of using CAPM to estimate the expected return on a company's stock.

Expected Return on This Stock = Return on a Risk-Free Investment + Premium for Accepting Risk Associated with This Stock
= Return on a Risk-Free Investment + Beta x (Market Rate of Return - Risk-Free Rate of Return)
11%   =   5%   + 1.5 x (9% - 5%)

Exhibit 6-2 Using CAPM to estimate the cost of equity

The yield on government bonds is usually assumed to be your best proxy for the return on a risk-free investment. Just less than one-half of all firms report using the yield on the 10-year U.S. government bonds as their estimate of the risk-free rate.[2] Others use the yield on either shorter or longer treasury bonds. The illustration in Exhibit 6-2 assumes that during a particular time period government bonds were yielding 5% and the average return on equities in the U.S. stock market was 9%. In other words, the U.S. stock market was providing a risk premium of 4 percentage points above government bonds. Because there are billions of dollars invested in the U.S. stock market, it is clear that an additional 4% added to their expected return was enough to entice many investors to put money in the risky stock market rather than leave it in safer government bonds.

Is Your Company of Above Average or Below Average Risk?

The capital asset pricing model assumes that if a company's stock is perceived to be of above average risk, it will attract investors only if they believe they can earn an above-average return. Similarly, a company whose stock is perceived to be of below average risk will attract investors even though it is expected to provide a below average return. The company's stock (refer to Exhibit 6-2) was assumed to be one and one-half times as risky as the market on average, so investors would require a risk premium of 1.5 times the market risk premium of 4 percentage points. A risk premium of 6 percentage points (1.5 × 4%) above the risk-free rate of 5% suggests investors would purchase this company's stock only if they expected to earn an 11% return on their investment.

The term *beta* (the second letter of the Greek alphabet) in this illustration is a measure of how risky a firm is relative to the overall stock market. It is a measure of a stock's price volatility in relation to the rest of the market. In other words, does the stock's price tend to fluctuate more or less than the average for all other stocks? When a stock's volatility equals that of an average share in the market, beta equals 1.0. *Volatility*, uncertainty about what the stock price will be in the future, is treated as an indication of risk. Stocks of above average volatility and therefore above average risk have a beta greater than 1.0, and stocks of below average volatility and risk have a beta of less than 1.0. Beta is usually estimated by comparing the volatility in a stock's price during some sample period to the volatility in a broad market index such as the S&P 500 index. For example, you could record on a sample of 100 days the value of a company's stock price and the level of the S&P 500 index. You could then plot those 100 paired observations in a graph similar to the one in Exhibit 6-3 and use regression analysis (or a ruler) to find the straight line that best summarized the historical relationship between this company's stock price and the S&P 500 index. The slope of that line is the beta.

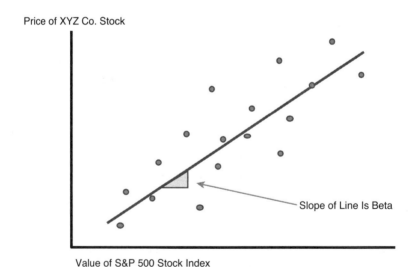

Exhibit 6-3 Estimating beta by plotting a company's stock price versus the overall market

Stated differently, a change in the company stock price equals beta times the change in the market index. If the beta were 1.2, that would mean that every time the S&P index moves by 1%, this company stock tends to move by 1.2%. If the S&P went up by 10%, the stock would on average rise by 12%. If the S&P fell 5%, the stock would on average fall 6%. Similarly, the price of a stock with a beta of 0.8 would on average rise by 8% when the S&P index climbs by 10% and fall by 4% when the S&P index declines by 5%.

Remember that the betas reflect the average responses during a sample time period. There is no guarantee that these historical patterns will persist into the future. Estimates of the betas for the stocks of publicly traded companies are readily available at no cost from a large variety of Internet financial data services.

Capital Costs in 2012

To review, a company's cost of capital is the weighted average of its cost of borrowing and its cost of raising money through the sale of stock. The cost of debt is the average after-tax interest rate it pays on the amount borrowed. The cost of equity is the minimum rate of return that will entice investors to purchase shares of stock in this firm. If the company is perceived to be of above average risk, that is, it has a beta greater than 1.0, investors will purchase the stock only if they expect to earn a return that is sufficiently above average for the market. If the company is perceived to be of below average risk, that is, it has a beta less than 1.0, investors will expect to earn a return that is below average of the market. Estimates of the average cost of capital for a sample of industries are shown in Exhibit 6-4. If you review these you can notice that in each industry the cost of equity is substantially above the after-tax cost of debt. Equity investors require a higher return because they expose themselves to considerably more risk. There is no promise about what will happen to the market price of the shares they purchase or what level of, if any, dividends they will receive. On the other hand, bond purchasers and others who loan funds to the firm receive a contractual promise that their principal will be returned along with a specified amount of interest. Their risk is not zero; the firm could default on these promises, but it is substantially less than the risk absorbed by equity investors.

Industry Name	Cost of Equity	After-Tax Cost of Debt	Weighted Average Cost of Capital
Semiconductor Equip	12.70%	3.28%	11.46%
Advertising	14.09%	5.24%	11.42%
Furn/Home Furnishings	12.81%	3.48%	10.98%
Retail (Hardlines)	12.57%	3.75%	10.84%
Metal Fabricating	11.48%	2.84%	10.32%
Auto Parts	12.13%	3.54%	10.27%
Retail (Softlines)	10.55%	2.54%	10.13%
Heavy Truck & Equip	12.76%	3.07%	9.82%
Chemical (Diversified)	11.02%	2.64%	9.48%
Computers/Peripherals	9.71%	4.30%	9.21%
Electrical Equipment	9.89%	3.21%	9.14%
Steel	12.03%	2.66%	9.06%
Apparel	9.71%	3.67%	8.77%
Petroleum (Producing)	9.97%	3.88%	8.76%
Human Resources	9.34%	2.89%	8.73%
Healthcare Information	8.95%	3.01%	8.60%
Engineering & Const	9.26%	2.85%	8.57%
IT Services	8.25%	3.13%	7.96%
Retail Automotive	10.13%	2.21%	7.95%
Computer Software	8.17%	3.83%	7.87%
E-Commerce	8.08%	3.83%	7.83%
Biotechnology	8.09%	5.72%	7.81%
Telecom. Equipment	8.00%	3.79%	7.52%
Electronics	8.31%	3.92%	7.51%
Homebuilding	10.62%	3.67%	7.14%
Bank	6.52%	2.83%	4.27%

Exhibit 6-4 2012 Average cost of capital in a sample of industries

Source: January 2012 estimates by Dr. Aswath Damodaran, Stern School of Business, New York University. Downloaded May 23, 2012 from http://pages.stern.nyu.edu/~adamodar/New_Home_Page/datafile/wacc.htm.

Impact of WACC on Value Creation

Value is created only when the assets employed in the firm's operations generate a return greater than the firm's cost of capital. Greater value is created when the return on the assets employed increases and/or the cost of capital falls. Increasing the return on the assets employed is the primary challenge facing operating managers. However, before addressing that topic, look at how important a reduction in the firm's cost of capital can be. The data in Exhibit 6-5 describe one division of a large company. During 2012, this division had pre-tax operating profits of $700,000 and after-tax operating profits of $462,000. The economic value created by this division during 2012 was $22,000. In other words, its business operations earned $462,000, which was $22,000 more than the $440,000 (10% × $4,400,000) it costs the parent corporation to keep $4,400,000 in assets tied up in this division.

Economic profit = (After-tax operating profit) – (WACC × capital employed)

$22,000 = ($462,000) – (10% × $4,400,000)

	Year 2012	200% Growth	No Growth, but WACC Reduced by 1 Point
Revenue	$5,000,000	$15,000,000	$5,000,000
Cost of Goods Sold	3,000,000	9,000,000	3,000,000
Operating Expense	1,000,000	3,000,000	1,000,000
Depreciation	300,000	900,000	300,000
EBIT	$700,000	$2,100,000	$700,000
EBIT -33% Tax	462,000	1,386,000	462,000
WACC	10.0%	10.0%	9.0%
Capital Employed	4,400,000	13,200,000	4,400,000
Economic Profit	$22,000	$66,000	$66,000

Exhibit 6-5 Relationship between economic profit and WACC

Now look at two different scenarios for 2013. The first one is described in the middle column of Exhibit 6-5 labeled 200% growth. This scenario assumes the firm triples in size. Revenues, expenses, profits, and assets are all three times what they were in 2012. Not surprisingly, that generates an economic profit of $66,000, three times the level of the previous year. Of course, few managers can ever achieve 200% growth in a single year. Is there an alternative way to triple the size of this division's economic profit? Consider the scenario in the third column of this exhibit. This scenario assumes no growth, that is, revenues, expenses, profits, and assets all unchanged from 2012. However, in this scenario the firm's weighted average cost of capital declines by one percentage point from 10% to 9%. A decline of that magnitude would increase economic profit by exactly as much is tripling the size of the firm with no change in its cost of capital. That occurs because the firm is saving 1% of the $4,400,000 in assets tied up in this division. In this example, the impact of reducing the cost of capital was large because the amount of assets tied up in this division was large. In other situations the impact may not be as dramatic, but you must understand that changes in the cost of capital can be just as significant as changes in operating performance. Of course, it's not either–or. Firms must simultaneously strive to maximize their operating performance and minimize their cost of capital.

Reducing the Weighted Average Cost of Capital

How can a firm reduce its cost of capital? Refer to the WACC calculation in Exhibit 6-1. This firm raised 60% of its capital from equity investors and 40% of its capital through borrowing. Using the calculation shown in this exhibit, you can determine its weighted average cost of capital was 9%. Could this firm lower its weighted average cost of capital by using less of the expensive money (equity, which costs 11%) and more of the cheap money (debt that costs 6%)? If this firm reduced its equity proportion to 20% and raised its debt proportion to 80%, would its WACC fall to 7%? Probably not, even though $[.20 \times 11\%] + [.80 \times 6\%] = 7\%$. That result could be obtained only if the cost of debt and the cost of equity remained unchanged. If the company were to become more highly leveraged, relying more heavily on debt financing, it would be perceived as a riskier firm. As a result, its cost of equity and its cost of borrowing would probably both rise. Changing the amount of leverage might reduce or might increase this firm's weighted average cost of capital.[3] Choosing the optimal debt and equity proportions requires judgments about how equity investors, lenders, and bond rating agencies respond to the firm's capital structure. In practice, a firm's capital structure is often driven more by the need for external funds than by attempts to reach an optimal balance between debt and equity. Highly profitable firms with limited investment opportunities tend to pay down their debt. Firms whose investment opportunities exceed their internally generated funds tend to increase their debt.

Decisions Based on WACC

Capital budgeting is the term often used to describe the planning process through which firms determine whether investments are worth pursuing. Such investments might include purchasing new machinery or replacement machinery, offering training programs, allocating R&D funds, undertaking advertising campaigns, introducing new products, engaging in mergers and acquisitions, and countless others. The weighted average cost of capital is critical to all these decisions and all long-term investments a firm makes. The WACC serves as the hurdle rate that must be surpassed before any of these projects can be approved. If a project does not offer a rate of return greater than the firm's WACC, undertaking it will destroy rather than create shareholder value. In many cases these investments are evaluated using the firmwide WACC. However, an even higher hurdle rate may be used if the project's risk level is greater than the risk level for the firm as a whole. HR managers need to understand this concept to allocate resources within the HR function and to design HR systems that encourage managers in all functional areas to develop and execute strategies that create shareholder value. The types of techniques and models typically used to make these decisions are discussed in the next chapter.

7

Capital Budgeting and Discounted Cash Flow Analysis

Discounted cash flow analysis is probably the most important financial tool that you will encounter. Fortunately, present values are easy to understand and easy to calculate. If you had the opportunity to choose between receiving $1,000 a year from today or receiving $1,000 today, which would you prefer? Clearly you would prefer to receive the cash today. If you received the money today, you could invest it and earn a return during the upcoming year. If you could invest at 5%, at the end of the year you would have $1,050 (your original $1,000 plus $50 in interest). So if 5% is the correct interest rate, a choice between $1,000 a year from now and $1,000 today is equivalent to a choice between $1,000 a year from now and $1,050 a year from now. Obviously, $1,050 is the better outcome. A dollar received today is always worth more than a dollar received in the future. The sooner you receive the money, the sooner you can invest it and begin receiving a return or borrow less and avoid paying out interest.

Calculating Present Values

You'll no doubt hear financial analysts referring to the present value of future cash flows. The present value of any future amount is just the amount you would have to invest today to grow to that future amount in the assumed time period at the assumed interest rate. So at 5% interest, $1,000 is the present value of $1,150 to be received

2 years from now. This relationship can be summarized by the equation in Exhibit 7-1. In this equation, the interest rate is expressed in decimal form (5% = .05), and t is the number of years the funds remain invested.

Present Value x (1 + Interest Rate)^t = Future Value at End of Year t

$1,000 x 1.05 x 1.05	= $1,150	= Future Value at End of 2 Years
$1,000 x 1.05^2	= $1,150	= Future Value at End of 2 Years

Exhibit 7-1 Relationship between present value and future value

This equation is nothing more than a sixth-grade compound interest formula. Fortunately, that's all you need to calculate present values and perform discounted cash flow analyses. You will usually find it more convenient to work with that equation if you rearrange the terms. When you divide both sides of that equation by (1 + Interest rate)^t you get

Present value = Future Value / (1 + Interest rate)^t

Using that expression, it is straightforward to calculate the present value of any future amount.

Discounted Cash Flow Analysis (DCF)

Present values are sometimes referred to as *discounted cash flows* (*DCFs*), and the interest rate is sometimes referred to as the *discount rate*. Financial models that utilize present value calculations are therefore often referred to DCF analyses. Capital budgeting is the process corporations use to determine whether long-term investments are worth pursuing. This typically involves calculating the DCF valuation of each potential project. Discounted cash flow analyses are essential tools for assessing almost all corporate expenditures. Examples could range from deciding which copy machine to purchase, to assessing the costs and benefits of an employee training program, to evaluating merger and acquisition (M&A) opportunities. It is, of course just as important to consider the time value of money when making personal financial decisions such as buying a house, saving for a child's education, or choosing whether to buy or lease a new car. DCF techniques are also used to value financial instruments such as stocks, bonds, and employee stock options. The basic concepts are illustrated next, and specific applications are discussed in later chapters.

Reading a Present Value Table

Present value tables are tools that were created to reduce the amount of arithmetic involved in DCF calculations. They are seldom still used for that purpose because financial calculators and spreadsheets are now much better alternatives. However, before moving on to spreadsheets, the present value table in Exhibit 7-2 illustrates some basic time value of money concepts. Interpreting the numbers in the present value table is straightforward. If you think of the column headings as annual interest rates, you can think of the row headings as years. If the column headings were monthly interest rates, the row headings would represent months. Determining what interest rate to use is extremely important and is a topic discussed in detail later in this chapter in the section, "Selecting the Appropriate Discount Rate." For the moment, assume the relevant annual interest rate is 10%. The table tells you that the present value of $1.00 received 1 year from now is .909 dollars, or just under 91 cents. That figure was calculated by dividing $1.00 by 1.10. If you put $.91 into an account earning 10%, at the end of 1 year your account balance would be $1.00. The table shows that the present value of $1 received 2 years from now is .826 dollars, or just under 83 cents ($1.00 / 1.10^2). The present value of $1 received 3 years from now is .751 dollars, or just more than 75 cents ($1.00 / 1.10^3). All other entries in the table were calculated in the same way.

Present Value of $1 Discounted at Discount Rate *i*, for *n* Years

Discount Rate (i)

n	1%	2%	3%	4%	5%	6%	7%	8%	9%	10%	11%	12%
1	0.990	0.980	0.971	0.962	0.952	0.943	0.935	0.926	0.917	0.909	0.901	0.893
2	0.980	0.961	0.943	0.925	0.907	0.890	0.873	0.857	0.842	0.826	0.812	0.797
3	0.971	0.942	0.915	0.889	0.864	0.840	0.816	0.794	0.772	0.751	0.731	0.712
4	0.961	0.924	0.888	0.855	0.823	0.792	0.763	0.735	0.708	0.683	0.659	0.636
5	0.951	0.906	0.863	0.822	0.784	0.747	0.713	0.681	0.650	0.621	0.593	0.567
6	0.942	0.888	0.837	0.790	0.746	0.705	0.666	0.630	0.596	0.564	0.535	0.507
7	0.933	0.871	0.813	0.760	0.711	0.665	0.623	0.583	0.547	0.513	0.482	0.452
8	0.923	0.853	0.789	0.731	0.677	0.627	0.582	0.540	0.502	0.467	0.434	0.404
9	0.914	0.837	0.766	0.703	0.645	0.592	0.544	0.500	0.460	0.424	0.391	0.361
10	0.905	0.820	0.744	0.676	0.614	0.558	0.508	0.463	0.422	0.386	0.352	0.322
11	0.896	0.804	0.722	0.650	0.585	0.527	0.475	0.429	0.388	0.350	0.317	0.287
12	0.887	0.788	0.701	0.625	0.557	0.497	0.444	0.397	0.356	0.319	0.286	0.257
13	0.879	0.773	0.681	0.601	0.530	0.469	0.415	0.368	0.326	0.290	0.258	0.229
14	0.870	0.758	0.661	0.577	0.505	0.442	0.388	0.340	0.299	0.263	0.232	0.205
15	0.861	0.743	0.642	0.555	0.481	0.417	0.362	0.315	0.275	0.239	0.209	0.183
16	0.853	0.728	0.623	0.534	0.458	0.394	0.339	0.292	0.252	0.218	0.188	0.163
17	0.844	0.714	0.605	0.513	0.436	0.371	0.317	0.270	0.231	0.198	0.170	0.146
18	0.836	0.700	0.587	0.494	0.416	0.350	0.296	0.250	0.212	0.180	0.153	0.130
19	0.828	0.686	0.570	0.475	0.396	0.331	0.277	0.232	0.194	0.164	0.138	0.116
20	0.820	0.673	0.554	0.456	0.377	0.312	0.258	0.215	0.178	0.149	0.124	0.104
25	0.780	0.610	0.478	0.375	0.295	0.233	0.184	0.146	0.116	0.092	0.074	0.059
30	0.742	0.552	0.412	0.308	0.231	0.174	0.131	0.099	0.075	0.057	0.044	0.033

Exhibit 7-2 Present value table

Basic Time Value of Money Concepts

So how can you use this present value table? If the table tells you the present value of $1 received in the future, you can calculate the present value of any number of dollars. Suppose you want to buy your daughter a $1,000 computer when she graduates from high school 1 year from now. How much would you need to put in a bank account tomorrow morning at 10% to have that $1,000 ready when she graduates? You would need to deposit $909 ($1000 × .909), which is the present value of $1,000 received or paid 1 year from now. How much would you need to invest today if she were not going to graduate for 10 years? The present value of $1,000 in 10 years is only $386 ($1000 × .386). You would need to invest much less today because 10 years of compound interest, instead of just 1, would be added before you make your withdrawal. Other things equal, the present value will always be less when the time period is longer. Other things equal, the present value will always be larger when the interest rate is smaller. Suppose you will need $1,000 in 10 years but the annual return on your investment will be only 2%. You would need to invest $820 ($1000 × .820) instead of $386. That makes sense. If your investment will be growing more slowly, you need to start with an amount closer to your eventual target. When you start modeling corporate operating and strategic investments, it will be important to remember that, other things equal, a longer time period always reduces the present value of a future amount, and a lower interest rate always increases the present value of a future amount.

Do the Future Benefits Justify the Upfront Costs?

Now assume that your time value of money is 10%, for example, your money is currently in an account earning 10% per year. The most you should pay for a $1,000 benefit to be received 1 year from now is $909. If you had to pay more than that, you would be better off leaving the money in the account where it was earning 10%. In that account any amount greater than $909 would grow to more than $1,000 by the end of the year. Similarly, if your firm's weighted average cost of capital were 10%, $909,000 is the most it should pay for a benefit of $1,000,000 to be received 1 year from now. If that same $1,000,000 benefit would not be received for 10 years, the most your firm should pay is $386,000.

Calculating the Present Value of a Series of Cash Flows

The same approach you have used to calculate the present value of a single payment can be used to calculate the present value series of cash flows. Suppose you have just learned that you won $1,000,000 in the New Jersey State lottery. You rush to the lottery commission office to pick up your $1 million check. They say, "Sorry, that's not how it is done." They explain that they will pay you $50,000 per year for the next 20 years and that $50,000 × 20 is $1,000,000. What lump sum amount would you be willing to accept today instead of receiving $50,000 per year for the next 20 years? This calculation is shown in Exhibit 7-3. The first two columns show the year and the amount to be received at the end of each year. The third column shows the 10% present value discount factors obtained from Exhibit 7-2. The right column is the product of the cash flow in each year and the present value discount factor for that year. For example, $45,455 is how much you would have to invest today to grow to $50,000 at the end of 1 year. If your time value of money is 10%, you would be indifferent between receiving $45,455 today or $50,000 1 year from now. This table also illustrates how dramatic the impact of compound growth rates can be. You would be indifferent between receiving the final $50,000 payment or only $7,432 today. That's true because if you put $7,432 in an account earning 10%, it would after 20 years grow to exactly $50,000. The present value of the series of twenty $50,000 payments, the sum of the numbers in the right column, is $425,678. If your time value of money is 10%, you would be indifferent between receiving $425,678 today or $1 million spread out in $50,000 payments over the next 20 years. For the moment you are ignoring taxes and risk. Those factors are discussed in later chapters.

Year	Cash Flow	PVDF@10%	PV
1	$ 50,000	0.909	$ 45,455
2	$ 50,000	0.826	$ 41,322
3	$ 50,000	0.751	$ 37,566
4	$ 50,000	0.683	$ 34,151
5	$ 50,000	0.621	$ 31,046
6	$ 50,000	0.564	$ 28,224
7	$ 50,000	0.513	$ 25,658
8	$ 50,000	0.467	$ 23,325
9	$ 50,000	0.424	$ 21,205
10	$ 50,000	0.386	$ 19,277
11	$ 50,000	0.350	$ 17,525
12	$ 50,000	0.319	$ 15,932
13	$ 50,000	0.290	$ 14,483
14	$ 50,000	0.263	$ 13,167
15	$ 50,000	0.239	$ 11,970
16	$ 50,000	0.218	$ 10,881
17	$ 50,000	0.198	$ 9,892
18	$ 50,000	0.180	$ 8,993
19	$ 50,000	0.164	$ 8,175
20	$ 50,000	0.149	$ 7,432
			$ 425,678 Total PV

Exhibit 7-3 Calculating the present value of a series of payments

Using DCF on the Job

In case you don't get to use this analysis in exactly that context, look at some work-related examples. Your colleague has calculated that if your firm were to purchase a more energy-efficient heating and cooling (HVAC) system for its corporate headquarters, it could reduce its energy bills by $50,000 per year for the next 20 years. He has also determined that a system with the appropriate energy efficiency rating and the necessary heating and cooling capacity would cost $600,000. He's proud of the memo he has written to the boss recommending that the firm spend the $600,000 to achieve $1,000,000 in energy savings. If your firm's weighted average cost of capital is 10%, would the investment he is recommending be a cost-effective one? No, if energy cost reductions are the only reason for putting in the new system, the most your firm should spend for the new system is $425,678. A basic premise of DCF analysis is that the economic value of any asset is the present value of the cash flows you receive as a result of owning that asset. That's true whether the asset is an HVAC system, a piece of investment real estate, a share of stock, a bond, or even a company that you plan to acquire.

HR Applications

Here are some HR illustrations using the same numbers. Today is your 65th birthday, and you are about to retire. Under the terms of your company's defined-benefit pension plan, you have a choice of receiving a $50,000 per year pension payment for the rest of your life or a one-time upfront lump sum payment of $450,000. If you assume that you will live for 20 years after you retire and that your time value of money is 10%, which alternative would you choose? Under those assumptions you would be better off taking the $450,000 upfront. Exhibit 7-3 showed that if you put $425,678 into an account earning 10% and then withdrew $50,000 at the end of each year, you would exactly empty that account at the end of the 20th year. That's true because the $425,678 is the sum of the $45,455 that you would have to put in to grow to the first $50,000 withdrawal, the $41,322 needed to cover the second $50,000, and the amount needed to cover each of the other 18 withdrawals. If $425,678 is how much you have to deposit inured to draw out $50,000 per year, with a $450,000 deposit you could withdraw more than $50,000 in each of the next 20 years. That example could just as easily have been worded, "What's the most you should spend on a training program that will increase workforce productivity by $50,000 per year in each of the next 20 years?" or "What's the most you should spend on a HRIS program that will in each of the next 20 years eliminate the need for one data-entry position costing $50,000?" Of course, you may argue quite reasonably that you've never seen a software package with a useful life of 20 years. If the software package has a 3-year useful life, you just add up the first three rows ($45,455 + $41,322 + $37,556 = $124,343). These are generic models that can be easily customized to fit almost any business investment you are considering. If appropriate, a different cash flow could be entered for each year, and the number of years could be adjusted to reflect the length of the benefit stream you expect.

How Important Is It to Consider the Time Value of Money?

You need to consider the time value of money whenever you are comparing, adding, subtracting, or performing any calculations on cash flows that occur during different time periods. A mile is not equal to a kilometer, so you would not add one distance expressed in miles to another distance expressed in kilometers. The result would be meaningless. Before doing any calculations on those two numbers, you would need to express them both in the same unit of measurement, that is, both in miles or both in kilometers. Just as a mile is always bigger than a kilometer, a dollar received today is always worth more than a dollar received in the future. So before performing any calculations involving cash flows from different time periods, you need to express them in the common metric of present value.

Individuals sometimes assume that time value of money adjustments are only of real-world importance when the time horizons are long. For example, constructing a new manufacturing facility or starting an R&D project that might produce cash flows over a 20- or 30-year time frame. Now look at the example described in Exhibit 7-4 that involves a much shorter time horizon. In a past labor negotiation, the Chrysler Corporation offered the 70,000 members of its UAW collective-bargaining unit immediate lump sum bonuses averaging $2,120 each. How much more would it have cost Chrysler to increase its lump sum offer to $2,250, but spread the payments out over the 3-year life of the labor contract? Assume that at the time Chrysler's WACC was 10% and that under the second option the $750 payments would be made at the end of each contract year. Because Option A involves only an immediate payment, there is no present value adjustment required. To calculate the present value of the series of payments under Option B, multiply each payment by the appropriate discount factor from the 10% column of the present value table in Exhibit 7-2. You see that Chrysler, given its 10% cost of raising money, would be indifferent between paying each worker $1,865 up front, or $750 at the end of each of the next 3 years. Now that both options have been expressed in present value terms, you can compare them. Option B costs $256 less per worker. Because at the time Chrysler had 70,000 active employees, *increasing* its offer to $2,250 would have *saved* Chrysler almost $17.8 million! If you had ignored the time value of money, you would have mistakenly concluded that $2,250 over the term of the contract was more expensive than $2,120 upfront. This example demonstrates that even over relatively short time horizons ignoring the time value of money can lead to seriously flawed decisions.

Still need to convince yourself how real that $17.8 million savings is? Suppose Chrysler were to immediately deposit into a bank account earning 10% the amount needed to fund Option A and the amount needed to fund Option B. To fund Option A would require depositing 70,000 × $2,120. To fund Option B would require depositing 70,000 × $1,865. Do the math. That's a $17.8 million difference. Less is needed to fund Option B because the initial deposit would grow by 10% before the first $750 payments are made. The remainder would grow by another 10% in year 2 before the second payment is made, and the balance would grow by 10% in the third year before the last payment is made. The effect would be exactly the same as in that hypothetical, but a more likely scenario would be that instead of pre-funding these payments and investing the funds at 10%, the firm would simply not need to raise the money immediately, avoiding the 10% cost of capital on those amounts.

Option A: $2,120 Immediate Lump Sum Payment

Year	Payment	Discount Factor @10%	Present Value
0	$2,120		$2,120

Option B: $2,250 Spread Over Three Years

Year	Payment	Discount Factor @10%	Present Value	
0				
1	$750	0.909	$682	
2	$750	0.826	$620	
3	$750	0.751	$563	
Total	$2,250		$1,865	Total

Option B costs $256 less per worker.
$256 x 70,000 covered employees is a savings of $17,780,000.

Exhibit 7-4 Using present value to compare alternative compensation schemes

Using Spreadsheets to Calculate Present Values

Although present value tables may be useful for illustrating how DCF models work, they are no longer the most efficient way to calculate them. The analysis in Exhibit 7-3 could be accomplished easily using the time value of money functions built into Microsoft Excel and most other spreadsheet programs. Exhibit 7-5 shows an Excel spreadsheet that does this. The cash flows are typed into any range of cells you prefer, and then in any cell you type the Excel formula to calculate the net present value of those cash flows. The general syntax of the Excel net present value formula is

**=NPV(Interest rate, Range of cells
where the cash flows are located)**

In Exhibit 7-5 the formula in cell E4 is =NPV(.10,B2:B21). The result returned is the same $425,678 that you calculated in Exhibit 7-3. An alternative formula that would produce exactly the same result is =NPV(E3,B2:B21). In this second formula the interest rate is replaced with a cell address showing where the interest rate is located. The advantage of this second approach is that you can more easily plug in different discount rates to determine their impact on the present value. For example in this case, lowering the interest rate from 10% to 5% increases the present value to $623,111. If this firm could raise money only at 10%, it should pay no more than $425,678 for this stream of benefits. If this firm could raise money at a cost of 5%, it could pay up anything to $623,111 for the same stream of benefits. Obviously, a business deal is more attractive if the funds used to finance it can be raised at a lower cost.

	A	B	C	D	E
1	Year	Cash Flow			
2	1	$ 50,000			
3	2	$ 50,000		Discount Rate	10%
4	3	$ 50,000		Present Value	$425,678
5	4	$ 50,000			
6	5	$ 50,000			
7	6	$ 50,000			
8	7	$ 50,000			
9	8	$ 50,000			
10	9	$ 50,000			
11	10	$ 50,000			
12	11	$ 50,000			
13	12	$ 50,000			
14	13	$ 50,000			
15	14	$ 50,000			
16	15	$ 50,000			
17	16	$ 50,000			
18	17	$ 50,000			
19	18	$ 50,000			
20	19	$ 50,000			
21	20	$ 50,000			

Exhibit 7-5 Using an Excel spreadsheet to replicate analysis in Exhibit 7-3

In the earlier lottery example, you assumed the $50,000 payment was received at the end of each year. If those amounts were received at the start of each year, you could adjust the spreadsheet, as shown in Exhibit 7-6. Note the difference is that only 19 cash flows are listed in Column A. Because the first $50,000 would be received at the beginning of the first year, there is no time value of money adjustment required for that amount. The second payment would be received at the end of year 1 (the start of year 2), the third payment at the end of year 2, and so forth. The 20th payment would be received at the end of the 19th year. The present value of the 20 payments ($468,246) is therefore the initial $50,000 plus the $418,246 present value of the 19 future cash flows.

	A	B	C	D	E
1	Year	Cash Flow			
2	1	$ 50,000			
3	2	$ 50,000		Discount Rate	10%
4	3	$ 50,000		Present Value of Future Cash Flows	$418,246
5	4	$ 50,000			
6	5	$ 50,000		Initial Upfront Payment	$50,000
7	6	$ 50,000			
8	7	$ 50,000		Total	$468,246
9	8	$ 50,000			
10	9	$ 50,000			
11	10	$ 50,000			
12	11	$ 50,000			
13	12	$ 50,000			
14	13	$ 50,000			
15	14	$ 50,000			
16	15	$ 50,000			
17	16	$ 50,000			
18	17	$ 50,000			
19	18	$ 50,000			
20	19	$ 50,000			

Exhibit 7-6 Present value when cash flows occur at beginning of each period

Example of Using Excel's NPV Function to Analyze a Buy Versus Lease Decision

Now look at a buy versus lease analysis using Excel's built-in NPV function. You have decided that you need a new BMW 328i. The dealer says he agrees with you and explains that he has two ways that he can help you get that car. He will be glad to sell you the car for $35,200, or he will be equally happy to lease it to you. The 4-year lease would require an immediate $5,000 down payment, and then payments of $5,400 at the end of each year. Assume all funds will be taken out of an account earning 8% per year. The first step is to write down the pattern of cash flows associated with each alternative, as shown in Exhibit 7-7. The negative numbers represent cash you will have to pay out, and the one positive number, $18,300, is what you estimate you will receive if you sell the car at the end of year 4. The formula typed into cell B9 is =B2+NPV(0.08, B3:B6). The formula typed into cell C9 is =C2+NPV(0.08, C3:C6). In both cases the initial payment occurs at the present and is therefore not included in the range of cells specified in the NPV function. Excel assumes that the first entry in an NPV range is one period out, that the second is two periods out, and so forth. Had the $35,200 purchase price or the $5000 down payment been included within the NPV range, Excel would have treated them as occurring one year from now. The results in Exhibit 7-7 indicate that with this particular set of assumptions, buying the car would be approximately $1,000 cheaper than leasing it. Suppose however that you were taking the funds out of an account earning 15% or that you were borrowing the money from your brother-in-law who was charging you 15%. To make this change you would simply alter the NPV formulas to =B2+NPV(0.15, B3:B6) and =C2+NPV(0.15, C3:C6). At this higher cost of capital, the buy option becomes the more expensive one. Does that make intuitive sense? The buy option requires you to commit a much larger amount up front. The greater your cost of capital is, the greater the cost of tying that much cash up right away.

	A	B	C
1	Year	Buy	Lease
2	0	-$35,200	-$5,000
3	1	0	-$5,400
4	2	0	-$5,400
5	3	0	-$5,400
6	4	$18,300	-$5,400
7			
8			
9	NPV @ 8%	-$21,749	-$22,885
10			
11	NPV @ 15%	-$24,737	-$20,417

Exhibit 7-7 Lease or buy a BMW 328i

Determining the Relevant Cash Flows

An important aspect of the previous example is that it assumed the same end points under both alternatives, that is, that you did not own the car at the end of the 4 years. You sold it after 4 years under the buy option or turned it in after 4 years under the lease option. Had you not modeled equivalent end points, you would not be evaluating just the difference between buying and leasing. You would have also included the difference between owning and not owning the car at the end of year 4. If the objective is to isolate the cost differences between buying and leasing, you must model the same end point under both alternatives.

Another key assumption in the previous example was the choice of the 4-year time horizon. How could you model the cash flows if you were not sure whether you would keep this new car for 4, 6, or even 10 years? The approach shown in Exhibit 7-8 accommodates that scenario by assuming that you will own the car after 4 years under both options. Under the buy option you do not sell it and therefore receive no cash at the end of year 4. Under the lease option you purchase the car at the end of the lease for (you can assume) $19,000 and therefore pay out $24,400 ($19,000 plus the final lease payment of $5,400). Because under both alternatives you own the car at the end of year 4, how long you keep it after that is irrelevant to the original buy versus lease choice.

	A	B	C
1	Year	Buy	Lease
2	0	-$35,200	-$5,000
3	1	0	-$5,400
4	2	0	-$5,400
5	3	0	-$5,400
6	4	$0	-$24,400
7			
8			
9	NPV @ 8%	-$35,200	-$36,851

Exhibit 7-8 Lease/buy analysis when the time frame is unclear

Should maintenance costs be included in the model when analyzing the buy-versus-lease decision? Yes, if maintenance costs would be different under the buy and lease options. No, if maintenance costs would be the same under both the buy and lease options. When constructing DCF analyses you can determine whether a particular cash flow needs to be considered using what is sometimes referred to as the with-without rule. The only relevant cash flows are those that differ with a particular choice versus without that choice. For example, suppose you must pay for gasoline whether you buy the car or lease a car. The cost of the gas is real. It's just not relevant to the choice between buying or leasing the car.

Selecting the Appropriate Discount Rate

The interest rate in present value calculations is often referred to as the discount rate. The appropriate discount rate is the one that reflects the decision-maker's opportunity cost of capital, in other words how much the decision-maker could have benefited from the use of this money had it not been committed to this project. If the cash is already on hand, the appropriate discount rate is the rate of return you could have earned on alternative investments. If cash must be raised to undertake this project, the appropriate discount rate is the rate that must be paid to obtain those funds. The logic is the same whether the decision-maker is a for-profit corporation, a nonprofit organization, or you or your family. If you're going to make the payments on a car lease by taking the funds out of your bank account, the appropriate discount rate is the amount you would have earned had the money remained in that account. If you are going to make those payments by borrowing the money from your brother-in-law, the appropriate discount rate is the interest rate he charges you on that loan.

As discussed in Chapter 6, "Stocks, Bonds, and the Weighted Average Cost of Capital," most corporations are financed through a combination of debt and equity. The weighted average of the cost of debt and the cost of equity is the firm's cost of capital (WACC). The WACC is the interest rate that firms typically use when conducting discounted cash flow analyses. An important exception would be situations in which the investment being considered is of greater risk than the activities usually undertaken by that corporation. In such cases a risk-adjusted interest rate, one higher than the company's WACC, would be more appropriate. Incorporating risk considerations into DCF analyses is discussed in Chapter 9, "Financial Analysis of a Corporation's Strategic Initiatives."

Money Has Time Value Because of Interest Rates, Not Because of Inflation

A dollar received in the future is always worth less than a dollar received today. That would be true even if you lived in a zero inflation world. Money has time value because if you receive it sooner, you can either invest it and earn interest or borrow less and avoid paying interest. If you lived in a zero inflation world, interest rates would be lower, but they would still exist. You would still need to make time value of money adjustments. Nominal interest rates, those that exist in the marketplace, are themselves affected by inflationary expectations. For example, a banker who requires a 2% real return and expects inflation to average 7% might offer you a mortgage at 9%. If the banker had expected inflation to average only 4%, she could have offered you a 6% mortgage. When performing DCF analyses you can use either real, that is, inflation-adjusted, interest rates or nominal interest rates, but you need to be consistent. If you project cash flows that do not include anticipated future price changes, you need to discount those using real interest rates. If you project nominal cash flows, you need to discount those using nominal interest rates. This second approach is usually the easier one for managers to understand and work with. Project the dollar amounts you think you will actually receive or have to pay in future years, and discount those using the firm's nominal weighted average cost of capital.

Using NPV to Evaluate an Investment or Project

Consider the example shown in Exhibit 7-9. This project involves a $100,000 upfront cost and then produces the benefits shown in years 1 through 5. The formula in cell B9 is =+B2+NPV(A11,B3:B7). Remember that because the –$100,000 shown in cell B2 is an immediate expenditure, it is not included within the range of cells specified within the NPV function. Excel assumes the first entry in that range is 1 year into the future. If this firm's weighted average cost of capital is 12%, this project would have an NPV of $17,513. In other words, the net benefit to shareholders from this project is $17,513. The present value of the benefits in years 1 to 5 is $117,513, which is $17,513 more than the $100,000 initial cost. An investment is attractive when its NPV is greater than zero because that indicates that the present value of future benefits is greater than the upfront costs.

	A	B
1	**Year**	**Cash Flow**
2	0	-$100,000
3	1	$20,000
4	2	$30,000
5	3	$35,000
6	4	$40,000
7	5	$44,775
8		
9	**NPV**	**$17,513**
10		
11		12% = Interest Rate

Exhibit 7-9 Find the interest rate that makes the NPV = 0

IRR as an Alternative to Net Present Value

To make investment decisions using NPV analyses, you must start with an assumption about the appropriate discount rate. The internal rate of return (IRR) approach reverses that sequence. Instead of starting with an estimate of the appropriate discount rate, this approach calculates the largest rate that could be used and still have the investment be an attractive one. At any cost of capital less than the IRR the project is worth pursuing; that is, the present value of the future benefits is greater than the upfront cost. At any cost of capital greater than that, the project is not worth pursuing; that is, the present value of the future benefit is less than the costs. Suppose you returned to the spreadsheet in Exhibit 7-9 and change the value in cell A11 to 14%. Discounting the benefits at this higher rate, the NPV would fall to $11,190. If you continued to incrementally increase the interest rate in cell A11, you would see that as you discount the future benefits at higher and higher rates, the NPV continues to decline. As shown in Exhibit 7-10, at an interest rate of 18%, the NPV reaches zero, and at any interest rate larger than 18%, the NPV is negative. The interest rate that makes the NPV equal the zero is defined as the IRR (see Exhibit 7-11).

Discount Rate	Present Value
8%	$31,897
10%	$24,394
12%	$17,513
14%	$11,190
16%	$5,369
IRR 18%	$0
20%	-$4,961
22%	-$9,553

Exhibit 7-10 Present value of cash flows shown in Exhibit 7-9, calculated at different discount rates

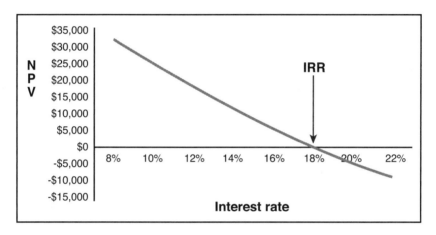

Exhibit 7-11 IRR is the interest rate that makes NPV = 0.

Using Excel's Built-In IRR Functions

Exhibit 7-10 used a trial-and-error process to find the IRR. You can always begin by plugging a discount rate into the NPV formula and observing whether the resulting NPV is a positive number. If it is, you could keep trying larger and larger discount rates until the NPV dropped to zero. If the initial NPV estimate were a negative number, you could plug in successively smaller discount rates until the NPV rose to zero. A more efficient approach would be to use Excel's built-in IRR function. The spreadsheet in Exhibit 7-12 contains the same cash flows shown in Exhibit 7-9. The general syntax of the Excel formula for calculating an internal rate of return is

=IRR(range of cells where the cash flows are located)

The formula in cell B9 of the spreadsheet in Exhibit 7-12 is =IRR(B2:B7). Note that when working with the IRR function, the time zero cash flow is included in the range. The result calculated in cell B9 is exactly the same 18% you found by trial and error in Exhibit 7-10.

	A	B
1	**Year**	**Cash Flow**
2	0	-$100,000
3	1	$20,000
4	2	$30,000
5	3	$35,000
6	4	$40,000
7	5	$44,775
8		
9	**IRR**	18%

Exhibit 7-12 Using Excel's built-in IRR function

IRR analyses are popular with CFOs and line executives for at least two reasons. In many cases, they enable you to avoid having to make estimates of the appropriate discount rate. For example, there might be a disagreement within the finance department about whether the NPV of a particular project should be calculated using a discount rate of 10%, 12%, or 14%. If you know the project has an IRR of 18%, you won't need to worry about resolving that disagreement. The project would add economic value to the firm at any of those rates and at any discount rate up to 18%. A second way IRR analyses are often used is to rank alternative investments. Giving up a project with an IRR of 20% would make economic sense if that were necessary to undertake a project with an IRR of 30%.

Two Different Ways to Answer the Same Question

To summarize you have considered two alternative decision rules. To utilize the NPV decision rule, you must begin with an estimate of cash flows and an estimate of the appropriate discount rate. Using the IRR decision rule, on the other hand, does not require you to begin with an estimate of the appropriate discount rate. Instead, this approach calculates the largest discount rate that could be applied to these cash flows and still have their present value be large enough to offset the project's upfront costs. These two rules can be summarized as follows:

> **NPV decision criteria: Invest if NPV > zero**
>
> **IRR decision criteria: Invest if IRR > WACC**

The following example illustrates the use of these techniques to analyze financial securities such as bonds. Subsequent chapters utilize these two decision rules to evaluate HR initiatives and corporate operating and strategic investments.

Example of Using NPV to Price the Bonds in Your 401(k)

Suppose today is June 30, 2013, and your broker phones to suggest a bond she believes you should purchase for your 401(k). The bond that was originally issued in 2003 has a $1,000 par value, a coupon rate of 6%, and a maturity date of July 1, 2018. If you purchase the bond, the par value is the amount you will receive when the bond matures. The coupon rate is the percentage of par value the bond issuer promises to pay you annually as interest. The coupon rate was established based on market conditions existing at the time the bond was issued and is locked in for the life of the bond. The individual who purchased this bond in 2003 is now eager to sell it to you. How much would you pay for a $1,000 par value bond with a 6% coupon that will mature in another 5 years? That, of course, depends on what bonds of comparable riskiness and maturity are yielding in today's market. Assume that in the current market 5-year bonds of comparable risk are yielding 8%.

Because the economic value of any asset is the present value of the cash flows you would get out of owning it, you can use the Excel NPV function to calculate an appropriate market price for this bond. The first step is to lay out cash flows you will receive if you purchase this bond, which are shown in Exhibit 7-13. Assume the interest is paid on the last day of each year. Each year you would receive $60 interest (6% coupon × $1,000 par value). At the end of the fifth year when the bond matures, you would receive the final $60 interest payment plus the $1,000 par value. The Excel formula in cell A12 is =NPV(A10,B4:B8). This bond would sell in the current market for $920, a substantial discount from its $1,000 par value. The bond would sell at a discount because for the next 5 years it will pay only the 6% coupon rate, not the 8% available on comparable bonds. If you were to purchase this bond for $920 today, receive $60 interest in each of the next 5 years, and then $1,000 when the bond matures, you would end up with exactly the same 8% yield to maturity as someone who purchased a newly issued $1,000 bond at par, received $80 interest the next 5 years, and then $1,000 when that bond matured.

	A	B	C	D
1	\$1,000 Bond with 6% Coupon Maturing in Five Years:			
2				
3	Year	Cash Flow		
4	1	$60		
5	2	$60		
6	3	$60		
7	4	$60		
8	5	$1,060		
9				
10	8%	= Market Yield on Bonds of Same Maturity and Risk		
11				
12	$920	= Bond Value		

Exhibit 7-13 Using NPV to calculate the value of a bond

Bond prices always move in the opposite direction from interest rates. If you were to enter 5% in cell A10 of the spreadsheet in Exhibit 7-13, you would see that the bond value becomes $1,043. The bond would sell at a premium to its par value because in that scenario the locked-in 6% coupon rate was greater than the 5% available on comparable bonds. If you pay $1,043 to purchase the bond, you will receive only the $1,000 par value when it matures. That $43 loss will exactly offset the above market interest you earned, and you will net the same 5% yield to maturity available on comparable bonds.

Example of Using IRR to Decide Which Bonds to Purchase

Suppose the investment manager for your firm's defined-benefit pension plan is choosing between two bonds of comparable maturity and riskiness. Both bonds have a $1,000 par value and an 8-year maturity. Bond A is selling at par with a 9% coupon. Bond B has only an 8% coupon but can be purchased for $879. Which bonds offers the higher yield to maturity? To determine this begin by typing the cash flows associated with each bond into the spreadsheet in Exhibit 7-14. You can then use Excel's built-in internal rate of return function to calculate the yield on each bond. The formula in cell B15 is =IRR(B5:B13). The formula cell in C15 is =IRR(C5:C13). You see that the yield on Bond A is 9%. That's no surprise because it is selling par and has a 9% coupon. Bond B had only a 7% coupon, but because you can purchase it at a deep discount, it actually offers a higher yield. Bond B with a 9.2% yield would be the better buy.

	A	B	C
1	Bond A is selling at par with a 9% coupon.		
2	Bond B with a coupon rate of 7% is selling at $879.		
3			
4	Year	Bond A	Bond B
5	0	-1000	-879
6	1	90	70
7	2	90	70
8	3	90	70
9	4	90	70
10	5	90	70
11	6	90	70
12	7	90	70
13	8	1090	1070
14			
15	IRR	9.00%	9.20%

Exhibit 7-14 Using IRR to calculate the yield on a bond

Caution About the IRR Reinvestment Rate Assumption

The IRR criterion is extremely useful and widely used. Nevertheless, it has some potential weaknesses that you should understand. When comparing two projects, the one with the higher NPV will usually also have the higher IRR. There are however some situations in which that is not the case. The spreadsheet in Exhibit 7-15 calculates the IRR and NPV of Projects A and B. Project A has a higher IRR, but Project B has a higher NPV. That occurred because the IRR formula assumes the interim cash flows are reinvested at the same rate of return as the project that generated them. That assumption is too optimistic in situations in which the interim cash flows are reinvested at something closer to the firm's weighted average cost of capital. In this example, Project A had larger cash flows in the early years and was therefore more affected by the high reinvestment rate assumption.

	A	B	C	D
1		A		B
2	0	-$20,000		-$20,000
3	1	$15,000		$0
4	2	$10,000		$5,000
5	3	$5,000		$10,000
6	4	$5,000		$35,000
7				
8	IRR	36%		30%
9				
10	NPV @ 10%	$9,072		$15,551
11				
12	MIRR	21%		27%

Exhibit 7-15 IRR and NPV do not always provide the same ranking.

Which project should you select when the NPV and IRR imply different rankings? You should base your choice on the NPV measures because there is no risk that they will be distorted by an unrealistically high unrealistic reinvestment rate assumption.[1] An alternative would be to re-evaluate the projects using Excel's MIRR function. The Excel formula for calculating this modified internal rate of return measure is

=MIRR(range, initial financing right, reinvestment rate)

This function enables you to specify the rate that will be earned by reinvesting the cash flows that are received prior to the project's end. In Exhibit 7-15, the entries in cells B12 and D12 were =MIRR(B2:B6,10%,10%) and =MIRR(D2:D6,10%,10%). Project A had the larger IRR, but after entering a more realistic reinvestment rate assumption into the MIRR function, it is clear that Project B would be the better choice. As a practical matter, the capital budgeting spreadsheets illustrated in Chapter 9 include both NPV and IRR measures. This practice requires only a few extra keystrokes and will highlight any instances in which the NPV and IRR criterion might lead to different choices.

Why Decisions Should Not Be Based on Payback Periods

The *payback period* is usually defined as the original investment divided by the annual benefit. For example, if a new energy-efficient furnace costs $4,000 and then reduces fuel bills $800 per year, it would "pay for itself" in 5 years. The usual assumption is that the shorter the payback period, the more attractive the investment. Because they are easy to understand and easy to calculate, payback periods are often used in capital budgeting. Unfortunately, relying on payback periods can lead to a serious misallocation of resources. One problem with simple payback formulas is that they do not take into account the time value of money. This limitation can, of course, be overcome by calculating the number of periods it takes for the present value of future cash flows to just equal the initial investment. A more serious weakness in payback measures, even if based on discounted cash flows, is that they completely ignore the magnitude and duration of all benefits that occur after the payback period. Consider the two alternative projects described in Exhibit 7-16. Using the payback decision rule, you would prefer Project A because costs are recovered in 5 years instead of 7. In this case, that would be a bad choice. The NPV of Project B is $4.6 million, twice what this firm would earn on Project A. If you're still not convinced of the limitations of payback models, consider that the option with the shortest payback period is always to do nothing at all. You might want to use payback periods as a tie-breaker if two projects are close in terms of projected NPV. That would be the equivalent of adopting a bird-in-hand philosophy assuming that the option with the shorter payback involves less risk. You should avoid, however, using payback periods instead of an NPV- or IRR-based decision model.

	(Cash Flows in Millions of Dollars)	
Year	Project A Cash Flows	Project B Cash Flows
0	-10	-10
1	2	1
2	2	1
3	2	1
4	2	1
5	2	2
6	2	2
7	2	2
8	2	5
9	2	7
10	2	7
Payback Period	5 Years	7 Years
NPV @10%	$2.3	$4.6

Exhibit 7-16 Payback periods can lead to the wrong decision.

8

Financial Analysis of Human Resource Initiatives

Obviously, making good HR decisions does not always require developing spreadsheets and utilizing their built-in financial functions. However, it does always require thinking logically and carefully about the financial implications of your recommendations and actions. It is neither possible, nor desirable, for this chapter to provide plug-in templates for all the kinds of decisions your HR department will make. Instead, this chapter has three goals. The first is to highlight situations in which financial analyses can improve HR decision making. The second is to provide examples of how you can apply the simple financial tools discussed in the previous chapter in these situations. The third is to convince you that even if you have had no formal training in finance you can use these tools and concepts to develop useful financial models tailored to the specific HR issues your firm faces.

These tools and models can also do more than just improve your own decision making. They can be extremely valuable for packaging and communicating your "bright idea" to others. The ability to support your recommendations or resource requests with the kinds of analyses and metrics that management is used to seeing can dramatically increase the probability that you will get the approvals you are seeking. If every $1,000 that the HR department spends doesn't produce a greater return on investment (ROI) than that amount could have earned in some other functional area, then those funds should be shifted out of the HR budget. This chapter provides a number of examples of how to think through HR issues from a ROI perspective. Later chapters make use of many of these same financial tools to analyze other HR topics such as pensions, stock options, and incentive pay.

Decisions Involving Cash Flow That Occur at Different Points in Time

Almost all the decisions that an HR department makes involve cash flow that occurs at different points in time. You spend money now, and if things go well, you reap the benefits months or years later. Few, if any, of the expenditures your HR department makes for recruitment, selection, training, and compensation can be properly analyzed without being sensitive to, if not to actually calculating, the net present value of the associated cash flows. Remember the discussion in Chapter 7, "Capital Budgeting and Discounted Cash Flow Analysis," of Chrysler's choice between offering its employees either one immediate payment or a series of three future payments? In that example, you saw that without calculating the present value of each alternative, it was impossible to know which one would cost Chrysler more.

Decision About Overtime Usage

For an example of how you should incorporate present value considerations into your HR decision making, look at the question of whether to ask employees to work overtime. Having employees work overtime usually means paying them time and one-half. That's a 50% increase in wage costs. Why would you ever do that instead of hiring additional workers who would receive the base wage but not the overtime premium? The answer is obvious. Bringing on new workers would require to you incur additional recruitment, selection, and training cost and quite possibly additional health insurance and other employee benefits costs. You would pay the overtime premiums when its cost is less than the cost of hiring the additional workers. To make that determination you need to first express the cost of both alternatives in present value terms.

Exhibit 8-1 contains a spreadsheet that illustrates an analysis of this type. Assume that one of your manufacturing units has 2,000 employees working 40 hours per week. Your firm has just signed a large contract that will mean for the next 3 years the output of this unit will need to be expanded by 10%. You quickly realize that you could expand output in one of two ways.

1. You could keep hours per week constant and expand the workforce by 10%. That would mean hiring 200 new employees. In addition to their wages, each new employee would receive a benefits package costing $8,850 per year.

2. You could hire no new employees but have the current employees increase their workweek by 10%. That would mean each worker would work 44 hours instead of 40, with the last 4 being paid at time and one-half. If the current average hourly wage in this unit is $18.50, the overtime premium would be $9.25 per hour.

	A	B	C	D	E	F	G	H	
1	**Cost to Use Overtime**								
2	400,000	Hours of Overtime							
3	$ 9.25	Overtime Premium							
4									
5	$ 3,700,000	Premium Cost of Overtime in Year 1							
6	$ 3,700,000	Premium Cost of Overtime in Year 2							
7	$ 3,700,000	Premium Cost of Overtime in Year 3							
8									
9	**$9,201,352**	Present Value of Overtime Costs							
10									
11									
12	**Cost to Hire Additional Workers**								
13	200	Additional Workers Needed							
14	$10,000	Recruitment, Selection, Processing, & Training Cost per Worker							
15	$2,000,000	Total Recruitment, Selection, Processing, & Training Costs							
16									
17	$ 1,770,000	Extra Benefits Costs in Year 1							
18	$ 1,770,000	Extra Benefits Costs in Year 2							
19	$ 1,770,000	Extra Benefits Costs in Year 3							
20	**$4,401,728**	Present Value of Extra Benefits							
21									
22	$ 1,800	End of Year 3 Termination Costs per Worker							
23	80	Number of Employees Terminated (40%)							
24	$ 108,189	Present Value of Total Termination Costs							
25									
26	$ (901,578)	Savings on Recruitment, Selection, Processing, & Training Costs (60%)							
27									
28									
29	**$5,608,340**	Total Cost of Hiring Additional Workers							

Exhibit 8-1 Using present values to make decisions about overtime usage

Begin by costing out the overtime option. Because the overtime costs will be spread over 3 years, you cannot simply sum them. You must first express them as present values. Cell A2 in this spreadsheet shows the number of overtime hours that would be needed per year ((10% of 40) × 50 weeks × 2000 workers). Multiplying this number by the overtime premium in cell A3 produces the annual overtime costs shown in cells A5, A6, and A7. If you thought wage rates would rise in the second and third years, it would be easy to increase the amounts in cells A6 and A7 by the appropriate percentages. Because the firm's WACC is 10%, the formula in cell A9 is =NPV(0.1,A5:A7). You see that the present value of the 3 years of overtime premiums is $9,201,352. Note that following the with-without logic described in the previous chapter, you must consider only the premium costs of the overtime, not the base wage costs. The base wage will be paid whether the additional work is done by new employees who would receive no overtime premium or by current employees who would receive an overtime premium. It is therefore not relevant to the choice between using overtime or hiring new employees.

Now cost out the hiring alternative. If you assume that recruitment, selection, processing, and training costs would average $10,000 per new hire, the cost for 200 hires would be $2,000,000, and this amount is shown in cell A15. If 200 new employees were hired, the firm's benefits costs would rise by $1,777,000 per year (200 × $8,840). These amounts are shown in cells A17, A18, and A19. If you project benefits costs to rise in years 2 and 3, you could easily multiply the amounts in these cells by the appropriate percentages. Entering the formula =NPV(0.1,A17:A19) into cell A20 reveals that the present value of the 3 years of benefits costs is $4,401,728.

This spreadsheet model also assumes that at the end of the 3-year spike in demand it will be necessary to terminate some of the recently hired workers. If 80 employees must be terminated at an average termination cost (processing, unemployment insurance, and so on) of $1,800, the total would be $144,000. However, because that amount would be spent 3 years from now, you enter the present value of that amount ($108,189) into cell A24. The formula in cell A24 is =+(A22*A23)/(1.1^3). The present value adjustment was accomplished by dividing by $(1+i)^t$, in this case (1.10^3).

The final assumption incorporated into this spreadsheet was that the remaining 120 of the recent hires would be moved into vacancies elsewhere in the firm. That would avoid having to spend an additional $10,000 to fill each of those vacancies, saving the firm $1,200,000. The present value of that amount, $901,578, was entered into cell A26. The formula in cell A26 is =(-120*10000)/(1.1^3)

You can now sum the values in cells A15, A20, A24, and A26 to find that the total cost of the additional hires option is $5,608,340. With this set of assumptions, hiring 200 additional employees for 3 years would cost the firm almost $3.6 million less than having all current employees work an extra 4 hours per week at time and one-half. Of course, had the additional work effort been needed for only a short period of time, the overtime option would have been the cheaper alternative. It would not be difficult to do a sensitivity analysis to determine the minimum period of increased labor demand required before the hiring option becomes the more cost-effective one. This example was not intended as a one-size-fits-all template but rather as an illustration of how HR decisions involving cash flow over a period of time could be modeled. Certainly you could improve this model by changing the assumptions or incorporating additional factors that would make it more appropriate for use in your organization. The important thing is that you understand that this and all other choices between alternatives involving cash flow at different time periods should not be made without first adjusting for the time value of money. In each case you must draw upon your knowledge of HR to identify the factors and cash flows that need to be considered. After you have done that, it is relatively easy to build a spreadsheet and let Excel do the present value calculations.

Using NPV and IRR to Guide HR Budget Allocations

Before looking at examples to calculate the NPV of specific HR initiatives, consider the use of NPV and IRR as budget allocation tools. Suppose you are the training manager for a large firm with a division in each of the four states, as shown in Exhibit 8-2. That figure also shows your estimates of the cost to train the workers in each state and the net present value and internal rate of return that you believe the training would produce. The total cost to train the workers in all four divisions would be $8,500,000. How would you allocate a $4 million training budget across these four divisions? The answer is that you shouldn't need to. You have already generated data that show that increasing the training budget to $8,500,000 would be in the best interest of the firm and its shareholders. A firm should undertake every investment that has a positive NPV. The NPV is an estimate of how much value will be created and how much shareholder wealth will be increased, as a result of that project. If your firm can raise the funds necessary to train all four groups at its 10% cost of capital, it should do so. HR managers need to make that kind of reasoned and documented argument to the CFO or others who make the budgetary decisions. Value creation consistent with the firm's business strategy, not fixed operating budgets, should determine which projects to undertake. Nevertheless, the planning requirements in large organizations do often constrain investments, at least in the short term, to the amount available in a fixed budget. So assume that in spite of your well-reasoned and well-documented arguments your training budget remains fixed at $4 million. What's the most you can do for the shareholders within this constraint? More specifically, what's the maximum NPV you can generate with this $4 million budget?

Division	Cost	NPV @10%	IRR
Ohio	$4,000,000	$210,000	12.5%
Michigan	$2,000,000	$150,000	13.3%
Wisconsin	$1,500,000	$170,000	15.8%
Indiana	$1,000,000	$120,000	16.8%

How would you allocate your $4 million training budget?

Exhibit 8-2 Four divisions whose employees could benefit from training

Before making that determination you must answer one additional question. Is it practical to train just some of the workers in a division, or will the training be useful only if everyone in that division is trained? Suppose your answer was that it would be useful to train some individuals even if it is not possible to train everyone in that division. In that situation you would maximize the return on your $4 million budget by ranking the divisions in terms of IRR. Allocate your budget first to the division offering the highest IRR and then work down the list until your budget is exhausted. In this example that would mean training the Indiana division, the Wisconsin division, and 75% of the Michigan division. The combined cost of training the Indiana and Wisconsin divisions would be $2.5 million. That would leave you with $1.5 million in unallocated funds. That $1.5 million would be enough to train only 75% of the Michigan division ($1.5 million available / $2 million cost). When partial investments are practical, you can fully utilize your budget. You can maximize the NPV generated by the total budget by allocating that budget over the projects that offer the highest rate of return.

If it were not practical to train just a portion of the employees in a division, you would maximize the return on your budget by comparing all clusters of investments that are possible within your budget constraint and then selecting the cluster that produces the largest NPV. This approach is illustrated in Exhibit 8-3. After reviewing the cost estimates in Exhibit 8-2, you can realize there are four possible ways to allocate your $4 million budget. You could train just the Ohio division, the Michigan and Wisconsin divisions, the Wisconsin and Indiana divisions, or the Michigan and Indiana divisions. Of these four possibilities providing the training to the Michigan and Wisconsin divisions produces the largest total NPV and would be the most effective use of your training dollars. Note that the Indiana division, which was the highest priority allocation when partial investments were practical, would not be among the divisions trained if partial investments were inappropriate.

If it is not practical to train just part of a division:		
Divisions Trained	**Cost**	**NPV**
Ohio	$4,000,000	$210,000
Michigan & Wisconsin	$3,500,000	$320,000
Wisconsin & Indiana	$2,500,000	$290,000
Michigan & Indiana	$3,000,000	$270,000

Exhibit 8-3 Budget allocation if partial investments are not practical

To review, when partial investments are not practical, it may not be impossible to fully utilize the funds in your budget. You can, however, maximize the achievable return on your budget by selecting the bundle of affordable investment opportunities with the highest NPV. The goal is the same as in the case when partial investments were practical. The difference is in the way you should go about identifying the projects to achieve that goal. In the first case you would rank projects by IRR and then allocate your budget over those offering the highest rates of return. In the second case in which partial invest-ments were not practical, you should select the bundle of projects that offer the highest NPV.

Allocating Budgets When There Are a Larger Number of Alternatives

In the previous example there were only four bundles of projects that could have been undertaken within the $4 million budget. That made it relatively easy to do the calculations (refer to Exhibit 8-3) and identify the bundle that would produce the largest total NPV. Sup-pose however that you must allocate your budget not just across four divisions but across the 15 potential projects. The logic is exactly the same, but the number of different bundles of projects to be consid-ered is extremely large. Fortunately, Excel has a built-in function that simplifies tasks such as this. Exhibit 8-4 shows the estimated NPV and cost of these 15 projects. Column F will be set to 1 for each project you choose to fund out of this budget, and to 0 for each project you choose not to fund. Only three cells have formulas entered into them:

C20: =SUMPRODUCT(C4:C18,F4:F18)

C21: =SUM(F4:F18)

C22: =SUMPRODUCT(E4:E18,F4:F181)

The total NPV is calculated in cell C20, which multiplies each project's NPV by 1 if the project is funded and by 0 if it is not. These products are then summed. Obviously, NPVs multiplied by zero add nothing to the total. The total cost is calculated in C22 using the same approach. Each project's cost is multiplied by 1 if the project is funded and by 0 if it is not. Costs multiplied by zero add nothing to the total. You can now use Excel's Solver function to select the proj-ects to pursue.

The Solver function can be accessed by clicking the Data tab at the top of an Excel spreadsheet. (If Solver is not visible on the right side of the Data menu, you must enable this add-in. The Excel Help function describes the steps for doing that.) When the Solver window opens, you can enter the parameters shown in Exhibit 8-5. These parameters instruct Excel to find the bundle of projects that will maximize the total NPV shown in cell C20. Excel will do this by comparing all possible combinations of ones and zeros in the range F4 to F18. The values in F4 to F18 are restricted to one or zero by the constraint defining this range as binary. The other constraint simply says the total cost in C22 must be less than or equal to the $60 million budget shown in cell C23.

	A	B	C	D	E	F
1			Estimated NPV		Current Cost	Fund ?
2		Project	in Millions of $		in Millions of $	Yes = 1, No = 0
3						
4		1	57.28		4.19	0
5		2	11.85		6.80	0
6		3	709.64		28.06	0
7		4	983.55		64.90	0
8		5	419.77		17.64	0
9		6	876.98		7.88	0
10		7	112.89		2.52	0
11		8	53.28		3.47	0
12		9	31.98		1.78	0
13		10	84.47		6.91	0
14		11	260.43		18.01	0
15		12	102.52		3.16	0
16		13	587.82		11.10	0
17		14	74.59		6.40	0
18		15	135.12		3.78	0
19						
20		Total NPV	0.00			
21		Projects Funded	0			
22		Total Spent	0.00			
23		Budget	60.00			

Exhibit 8-4 How would you allocate a $60 million budget across these 15 projects?

Exhibit 8-5 Setting parameters in Excel's Solver function

As soon as you click the Solve button, the spreadsheet is adjusted, as shown in Exhibit 8-6. Pursuing the seven projects identified by 1s in column F produces the largest total NPV achievable within this budget. This is calculation is, of course, only as good as your estimates of the NPVs and the costs. Chapter 9, "Financial Analysis of a Corporation's Strategic Initiatives," illustrates techniques for incorporating risk and uncertainty into estimates of this type.

	A	B	C	D	E	F
1			Estimated NPV		Current Cost	Fund ?
2		Project	in Millions of $		in Millions of $	= 1, No = 0
3						
4		1	57.28		4.19	0
5		2	11.85		6.80	0
6		3	709.64		28.06	1
7		4	983.55		64.90	0
8		5	419.77		17.64	0
9		6	876.98		7.88	1
10		7	112.89		2.52	1
11		8	53.28		3.47	1
12		9	31.98		1.78	0
13		10	84.47		6.91	0
14		11	260.43		18.01	0
15		12	102.52		3.16	1
16		13	587.82		11.10	1
17		14	74.59		6.40	0
18		15	135.12		3.78	1
19						
20		Total NPV	2578.25			
21	Projects Funded		7			
22		Total Spent	59.96			
23		Budget	60.00			

Exhibit 8-6   Optimal allocation of $60 million budget across these 15 projects

Are Models Such as the Previous One Really Useful for HR Managers?

There are potentially three benefits HR managers can gain from understanding models such as the previous one. First, they provide a framework for thinking about the choices managers must make. It is almost always the case that the number of plausible projects is larger than what can be accomplished within the available budget. Whenever this is true, some procedure will be used to determine which projects to fund. The objective of that procedure should be to select the bundle of projects that maximizes the total NPV that can be achieved within this budget. Even in a situation in which no numerical estimates of the potential benefits are produced, that principle should guide decision making. Second, on some occasions it will be useful to prepare a spreadsheet such as the one in Exhibit 8-6, even if the numbers plugged into it are only rough estimates. Suppose the numbers in column C of Exhibit 8-6 were your best estimates of the net benefit from each project. Without the spreadsheet, identifying the subset of projects that would maximize the return on your budget would require a trial-and-error process that could take hours to complete. Finally, HR managers must understand models of this type if they are going to be successful in their role as strategic partners. HR managers often encounter models of this type while working with colleagues in finance, R&D, manufacturing, or marketing.

Calculating NPV of Specific HR Initiatives

HR initiatives can, of course, take many forms. Examples could include enhancing the firm's selection procedures, in-person or online training programs, job redesign, employee wellness programs, efforts to increase employee engagement, updating the HRIS system, changing the compensation mix, and countless other activities. Though quite diverse in their substance and perhaps significance, all these should be considered from an ROI perspective. Because it is not feasible in this chapter to provide dozens of templates each focused on a different HR activity, the discussion focuses on four examples chosen to illustrate a range of analytical issues. These four examples (purchasing HRIS software, cost-benefit analysis of a training program, a turnover reduction effort, and building a daycare center for the children of your employees) will hopefully contribute to your understanding of and comfort with approaches that you can then adapt to fit the specific HR initiatives that your firm is considering.

Mutually Exclusive Alternatives: Which HRIS Software to Purchase?

Your firm is considering a major investment in human resource information system (HRIS) software. After months of research you have narrowed the choice to the two alternatives described in Exhibit 8-7. The first is a basic HRIS package that would cost $1 million to purchase and install. You estimate that having that package would reduce your data entry and data processing costs by $250,000 per year for the next 10 years. The other alternative is a high-end HRIS package that would cost $3 million to purchase and install. This software, you estimate, would reduce your data entry and data processing costs by $650,000 per year for the next 10 years. You have estimated the IRR and NPV for both alternatives. The formulas in cells C16 and E16 are =IRR(C3:C13) and =IRR(E3:E13). The formulas in cells C18 and E18 are =C3+NPV(0.1,C4:C13) and =E3+NPV(0.1,E4:E13).

	A	B	C	D	E
1			Basic		High-End
2	Year		HRIS		HRIS
3	0		-$1,000,000		-$3,000,000
4	1		$250,000		$650,000
5	2		$250,000		$650,000
6	3		$250,000		$650,000
7	4		$250,000		$650,000
8	5		$250,000		$650,000
9	6		$250,000		$650,000
10	7		$250,000		$650,000
11	8		$250,000		$650,000
12	9		$250,000		$650,000
13	10		$250,000		$650,000
14					
15					
16	IRR		21%		17%
17					
18	NPV @10%		$536,142		$993,969

Exhibit 8-7 Use NPV, not IRR, to rank mutually exclusive alternatives.

Which software package will you recommend to your boss? The IRRs tell you the basic package can provide your company with a higher rate of return on the company's investment. On the other hand, the high-end package will produce a larger NPV. You should recommend the high-end system. It will provide your firm with a much larger net benefit. Yes, it costs more, but the NPV calculation has already taken into consideration the 10% cost of raising those additional amounts. When alternatives are mutually exclusive (if you purchase one, you won't purchase the other), you should rank them using NPV, not IRR. It's true that if you could buy and use three of the basic systems, your total NPV would be even greater. Of course, that is not practical in this case.

Sunk Costs Are Irrelevant

Suppose the HRIS software your firm has purchased must be customized to fit your firm's HR practices. Actually, in some cases you may need to modify your HR practices so that they can be accommodated using this software. Those are both time-consuming and expensive activities. At the time the project was approved, you estimated that process would cost $1 million and take 1 year. You were willing to make that investment because you believed that when implemented the new HRIS system would produce benefits with a present value of $1.5 million. In other words, you thought this HRIS project would have an NPV of $500,000. Things didn't turn out exactly as planned. It's now been 2 years. You have already spent $2 million, and the system is still not ready to go live.

When you ask the team leader what happened, he responds, "Well, we've learned a lot. With another $500,000 and another year, we can get the system up and running." Should you fire the team leader and dump the project? Whether you should fire the team leader depends on whether you think the delays were his fault. Now focus on the second question: Should you dump the project? Assuming the latest forecast is an accurate one, 1 year from now you will have spent a total of $2.5 million for a project that provides benefits with a present value of $1.5 million. You will wish you had never started this project, but at this point you should continue it. The only cash flows relevant in making that decision are the additional $500,000 you must put in to complete the project and the $1.5 million benefit you will receive after it is completed. The $2 million that has already been spent is a sunk cost. That amount will be unchanged by what you decide today, so it should not influence what you decide today. Even if the sunk costs were $100 million (or any other number), you would continue the project if you thought spending $500,000 now would produce $1.5 million in benefits. At any given point in the life of a project, the only two things that should influence a continuation decision are the costs to complete the project and the present value of the cash flow that will be obtained if the project is completed.

Cost-Benefit Analysis of a Training Program

If training is successful it produces increases in employee performance in the months or years following the training program. To judge the ROI from training, you must determine whether the present value of the future performance increases is greater than the upfront training costs. It is easy to do this in a spreadsheet after the costs and benefits have been estimated. Obtaining useful estimates of the training costs is usually straightforward. You can begin by preparing a laundry list of cost components and attempting to put a dollar value on each of them. Exhibit 8-8 contains a checklist of potential training cost components. In your situation some of these may be insignificant, and there may be others not shown on this list that you will want to include.

Program development costs:

  Out-of-pocket costs for materials and supplies

  Number of hours spent on program development x average hourly compensation of program developers

  Number of hours spent consulting with program developers x average hourly compensation of managers involved in program design

  Payments to outside consultants or vendors

Program planning costs:

  Out-of-pocket costs for materials and supplies

  Number of hours spent recruiting and selecting trainees x average hourly compensation of individuals performing this task

  Number of hours spent on scheduling trainers, facilities, and trainees x average hourly compensation of individuals performing this task

  Payments to outside consultants or vendors

Program delivery costs:

  Out-of-pocket costs for materials and supplies

  Cost of facilities used

  Length of training in hours x average hourly compensation of trainees x number of trainees

  Total hours of participation by all trainers x average hourly compensation of trainers

  Costs to replace trainees or trainers while they are participating in training

  Payments to outside consultants or vendors

Program evaluation costs:

  Number of hours spent on post-program evaluation x average hourly compensation of individuals performing this task

---

Exhibit 8-8 Examples of possible training program costs

Determining Program Impacts Using Pre-Post Changes

Estimating the cost of training is almost always easier than estimating the benefits from training. Conceptually, the benefit is the dollar value of the increased employee performance that results from the training. Measuring that requires you to determine how much performance has changed as a result of the training, and to place a dollar value on that performance change. In some cases direct measures of performance are available. Examples of directly measurable outputs might be the revenues generated by a group of sales reps or the number of manufacturing defects attributable to worker error. In both of these cases, it would be easy to determine how much performance changed between the pre- and post-training periods. It would also be relatively straightforward to calculate the profits resulting from the increased sales or reduction in manufacturing costs due to a lower defect rate. However, even in situations such as these, you must be extremely cautious about the assumption that the pre-post change was caused by the training. Is it possible that pre-post-changes were fully or partially the result of other factors? For example, could the higher sales during the post-training period be because external business conditions improved? Could the lower defect rate be because business conditions weakened allowing workers to operate at a less frantic pace? Or could the lower defect rate be because workers were more experienced in the post-period than during the pre-period? Only if you are comfortable ruling out alternative causes of the pre-post change, can you be confident using that pre-post change as a measure of the training effect.

Determining Program Impacts Using Comparison Groups

If you are not confident that most of the observed pre-post change was caused by the training, things become more complex. One option might be to compare the performance change of the trainees to the performance change in a group of similar employees who did not receive the training. If the trainees improved more than the nontrainees, this might be a reasonable measure of the training's effect.

Even when a comparison group is available, the data needs to be interpreted cautiously. Suppose you send a group of managers to a week-long executive education program at a prestigious university. You observe that their performance ratings after participating in this program are substantially higher than they were in the past. That's encouraging, but before reaching any conclusions, you decide to review the change in performance ratings during the same period for a group of managers who did not attend this program. You find that the average performance rating increase among the attendees was much larger than the average performance rating increase among the nonattendees. Is that solid evidence that the program was effective? Maybe. What determined why some managers attended the program and others did not? For example, if you selected your highest potential managers to attend this program, even if the training program had no effect, those high-potential individuals would have probably performed better than the nonattendees in the year after the training. Those differences in individual ability might be misinterpreted as program effects.

You should always ask yourself what caused some individuals to end up in the treated group and others to end up in the comparison group. The answer to that question may suggest there would be post-program differences between the participants and the nonparticipants even if the program itself had no effect. HR managers seldom achieve laboratory-like conditions for isolating the effect of training programs or other initiatives. However, you need to carefully think about the program impact numbers you enter into your NPV models. Hopefully, you can rule out alternative explanations and be relatively confident that the observed changes came about because of the program being evaluated. Unless that can be done, there is a danger that the financial analyses based on these numbers will be misleading.

...But What If Everybody Gets the Training?

Identifying a comparable group of nontrainees can be difficult in situations in which management wants everyone to be trained.

However, if all employees do not receive the training at the same time, it may be possible to utilize the individuals who are trained in later periods as the comparison group for the individuals trained in earlier periods. In the following diagram, the Os represent observations about employee performance, and the Xs represent training or some other HR program.

	Time 1	Time 2	Time 3	Time 4
Group 1	O X	O		
Group 2	O	O X	O	
Group 3	O	O	O X	O

You could between Time 1 and Time 2 use the experience of Groups 2 and 3 as the comparison for the trainees in Group 1. Between Time 2 and Time 3, you could use the experience of Group 3 as the comparison for the trainees in Group 2. If it is not possible to construct a reasonable comparison group, managers will be forced to rely upon their judgment about what percentage the pre-post performance change was the result of the training.

Measuring the Dollar Value of Program Impacts

Determining what portion of the change in employee performance was the result of a training program or other HR initiative is only one of two challenges you will face. The second is putting a dollar value on the change that occurred as a result of this training. In cases like the manufacturing worker or sales rep examples previously discussed, calculating these values is relatively straightforward. At other times, such as sending managers for advanced training in strategic planning, quantifying and valuing the results is extremely difficult. What can you do when the dollar value of the performance change is not directly measurable? Some HR scholars[1] have proposed statistical techniques for estimating the value of a high performer compared to an average performer. If an organization can measure, in financial terms, output at the workgroup level and has performance data on individual employees, regression analysis can be used to estimate the dollar value of a one standard deviation increase in performance. If the dollar value of a one standard deviation increase in performance was, say, $30,000 per year, then a training program that increased performance ratings on average by 0.5 standard deviations could be assumed to produce a benefit of $15,000 per worker per year. Of course, in addition to the possible imprecision in the estimate of the dollar value of one standard deviation of performance, this approach offers no assistance in answering the previous question: "By how much (or how many standard deviations) did the training increase performance?" That question still must be answered by looking at pre-post changes in performance ratings or comparisons to a group of nontrainees.

Using Breakeven Levels as a Planning Tool

In situations in which the dollar value of performance increases is not directly measurable, and where the data required to generate statistical estimates are not available, managers may find that the most practical approach is to work with breakeven levels. Suppose your best estimate is that a proposed training program will increase productivity by 10% to 30%. You realize that's a large range but unfortunately do not have any sound basis to make a more precise forecast. One option would be to calculate the minimum increase in productivity necessary for the program to cover its own costs, that is, a breakeven level. If the breakeven level were 5%, you could approve the program, believing an impact of at least that size was likely. Had the breakeven level been 40%, you might have rejected the program because you felt a benefit of that magnitude was unrealistically optimistic. Making a judgment about whether a breakeven level can be reached is often much easier than making a point estimate of what a program's effect will be.

Exhibit 8-9 provides an example of applying a breakeven approach within the context of an NPV analysis. Assume one of your high-potential managers approaches you and says she would like to enroll in an executive MBA program at a local university. The degree can be completed in 1 year. She will do the course work during evenings and weekends but wants the company to pay the $75,000 tuition costs. Would this be a cost-effective investment for your firm?

	A	B	C	D	E
1	Year	Cash Flow	Cash Flow	Cash Flow	Cash Flow
2	1	-$75,000	-$75,000	-$75,000	-$75,000
3	2	$10,000	$20,000	$30,000	$40,000
4	3	$10,000	$20,000	$30,000	$40,000
5	4	$10,000	$20,000	$30,000	$40,000
6	5	$10,000	$20,000	$30,000	$40,000
7	6	$10,000	$20,000	$30,000	$40,000
8					
9	NPV	-$33,720	$742	$35,203	$69,665

Exhibit 8-9 Estimating breakeven level benefits of a training program

Your experience has been that employees stay with your firm for on average 6 years after completing their MBA. For that reason, you decide to model the benefits over a 6-year time horizon. Columns B, C, D, and E calculate the NPV at a 10% discount rate under four different assumptions. The assumptions are that completion of her MBA would increase this employee's value to your firm by 10, 20, 30, or 40 thousand dollars per year. This simple analysis reveals that paying these tuition expenses will not be cost-effective unless as a result of obtaining her degree the employee's value to your firm increases by at least $20,000 per year. If you think that's a realistic expectation, there is a solid basis for approving this employee's request.

Training That Doesn't Increase Productivity Could Still Be a Good Investment

When interpreting a specific NPV or IRR result, you must not lose sight of the broader context. Suppose that paying for this individual's MBA did not have a large impact on her productivity at your firm but did signal to her that she was a highly appreciated and highly valued member of the organization. That signal might be important in her decision to stay with your firm rather than jump to a competitor. In that scenario the training served not to increase productivity but as a way to retain highly valued talent. If the MBA increased her productivity by only $10,000 per year, the NPV would be negative (refer to Column B of Exhibit 8-9). You must decide whether you are willing to pay $33,720 to increase your chances of retaining this employee. Note that the cost of this retention device would be the NPV of this training, not the full $75,000. There may be times when you know you will undertake a project even if its NPV is negative. That does not necessarily mean calculating the NPV is unimportant. A supermarket may sell string beans at a loss to make money on steak. It does, however, need to calculate how much it loses on the string beans to ensure it can more than make up that amount on the steak.

Benefit/Cost Analysis of a Turnover Reduction Program

Costing turnover presents methodological problems of a different type. If you knew that employee turnover was costing your firm $600,000 per year, it would be simple to determine the maximum you should spend per year to reduce turnover costs by 25% (.25 × $600,000 = $150,000). You could easily justify spending $100,000 per year to increase wages, restructure your benefits package, or undertake any other HR program you thought would reduce turnover by 25%. Obviously, before making such judgments you need an estimate of your current turnover costs. Think of turnover costs as the sum of the following five components:

- Separation costs
- Replacement costs
- Training costs
- Change in compensation costs
- Change in performance

The process for calculating separation, replacement, and training costs is relatively straightforward. You sum all the out-of-pocket costs for each activity plus the cost of the staff time devoted to each activity. Exhibit 8-10 provides a list of potential turnover cost components. The Society for Human Resource Management (SHRM) also provides a useful and free web-based tool designed by Wayne Cascio and John Boudreau[2] for calculating separation, replacement, and training costs.

Examples of separation costs:

> Time spent conducting exit interviews and processing exit interview data
> Time spent on administrative functions related to separation
> Separation pay
> Unemployment insurance taxes
> Lost productivity during the period the position remains vacant

Examples of replacement costs:

> Time spent preparing job descriptions and gaining approvals
> Costs of advertising the open positions
> Fees paid to search firms
> Time spent reviewing applications and identifying finalists
> Tme spent traveling to and conducting on-campus interviews
> Expenses for travel to conduct on-campus and other off-site interviews
> Travel costs for applicants invited for on-site interviews
> Time spent conducting on-site interviews
> Preemployment testing of applicants
> Medical exams and background screening for applicants
> Time spent in meetings to identify preferred applicants
> Time spent negotiating the terms of employment offers
> Travel and moving expenses for new hires
> Time spent on administrative functions related to hiring (HRIS, payroll, benefits, and so on)

Training and orientation costs:

> Time spent on orientation and on-boarding activities
> Formal training program costs as described in Figure 8-7
> Informal training costs
> > Extra supervisor time devoted to new hires
> > Reduced productivity before new hire is fully up to speed

(The cost of time spent is the hours devoted by each group x average hourly wage for that group. Groups that should be included are the HR staff, non-HR staff, leaving employees, and new hires who devote compensated time to each activity.)

Exhibit 8-10 Examples of turnover cost components

The Composition of Turnover Can Be More Important Than the Level of Turnover

The change in performance between departing employees and their replacements is a factor that can be of far greater strategic significance than the types of costs listed in Exhibit 8-10. If departing employees are below average performers, replacing them with individuals who will perform at an average or above-average level can contribute dramatically to a firm's competitiveness. You would actually want to increase turnover when the value of the increased productivity is larger than the increases in separation, replacement, and training costs. Conversely, if employees with above-average talent are disproportionately represented among those choosing to leave, the cost of turnover to your firm will be far greater than on the kinds of activities listed in Exhibit 8-10. In some positions productivity differences resulting from turnover will impact only a firm's operating costs. Turnover in other positions, those that are critical to the successful implementation the firm's business strategy, can be a primary determinant of a firm's success or failure. Changing the composition of turnover (who leaves) can be more important than reducing the level of turnover (how many leave).

Comparing the Leavers and Their Replacements

If the difference in performance between employees who leave and their replacements is a critical factor, can the financial impact of this difference be measured? The SHRM website previously referenced includes a module designed by Casio and Boudreau that generates an estimate of the dollar value of the change in performance between employees who leave and their replacements. Cascio and Boudreau assume, "The difference in pay between leavers and their replacements is an indicator, although an imperfect one, of the uncompensated performance differential due to firm-specific human capital."[3] The idea is that employees who have firm-specific human capital, that is, knowledge or skill that is valuable only to their current employer, will not need to be fully compensated for the value of these skills. The employee does not have the bargaining leverage to demand full compensation for these skills because they could not be sold to other employers. That implies that when employees have firm-specific skills, employers are getting some value they don't need to pay for.

Casico and Boudreau assume that the amount of firm-specific skill and therefore the amount of uncompensated performance is positively correlated with wages. In other words, if the replacement earns more than the leaver, the firm is gaining more of this uncompensated value. If the replacement is paid less than the leaver, they assume the amount of uncompensated value declines. The module they designed for SHRM assumes turnover costs go down when you pay the replacement more and go up when you pay the replacement less. For example, if an employee paid $65,000 leaves and is replaced by an individual paid $75,000, their model assumes turnover costs are $10,000 less than if the replacement had been paid $65,000. Their model assumes that a more highly paid replacement will have more (uncompensated) firm-specific skills. That may not be the case. In many organizations, replacement employees, regardless of wage level, will have limited or no firm-specific skills at the time they are hired.

Managers in many organizations would argue that paying replacements more has the opposite effect—it increases turnover costs. That argument would certainly be valid when replacements are paid more—not because they have more skills, but just because salary rates in the external job market have risen.

If you do not feel the replacement assumptions made by the Cascio-Boudreau model are appropriate for your organization, you can calculate turnover costs by adding to the sum of the separation, replacement, and training costs the actual change in salaries between the leavers and the replacements, and your own estimate of the dollar value of any increase or decrease in performance. In some situations firms can directly measure performance difference between the leavers and their replacements. In others, you may need to rely upon a judgment made by an appropriate supervisor. For example, suppose a group of employees earning on average $50,000 per year leave and are replaced by individuals earning on average $60,000. If the supervisor estimates that the replacements are 10% more productive than the employees who left, you could add to the sum of the separation, replacement, and training costs the salary increase of $10,000 per employee minus the productivity increase of $5,000 per employee (10% × $50,000). If the supervisor estimated that the replacements were 10% less productive than employees who left, you could add to the sum of the separation, replacement, and training costs the salary increase of $10,000 per employee plus the productivity decrease of $5,000 per employee.

Net Present Value of an Investment Involving Facilities and Equipment

This example differs from the previous ones in that it involves investments in facilities and equipment. To analyze such investments properly, you need to consider depreciation expense and taxes and the differences between profit and cash flow. Suppose your firm is considering constructing a daycare facility for the children of your employees. You have carefully estimated that the new facility would have the following benefits and costs.

Initial cost	$500,000
Annual benefits	$165,000
Annual operating costs exclusive of depreciation	$85,000
Expected life	8 years
Salvage value after taxes	$100,000
Annual depreciation	$50,000
Tax rate	30%

Your only remaining task is to draft a memo to your boss explaining what your estimates imply about the economic feasibility of the proposed childcare center. If your firm's weighted average cost of capital is 11%, what is the expected net present value of this project?

As in all DCF analyses, you must begin by laying out the pattern of cash flow associated with this project. You know the initial cash outflow will be the $500,000 you estimated it will cost to build this facility. Exhibit 8-11 contains a spreadsheet that calculates the annual cash inflow for years 1 to 8. Cell B2 contains your estimate of the annual benefits. Factors you considered when deriving that estimate might have included decreased absenteeism because fewer employees will miss work because their childcare arrangements are disrupted; increased work effort if employees are less likely to arrive late or leave early because of childcare responsibilities; and perhaps increased productivity or lower required salaries if this childcare facility makes it easier for you to attract highly qualified employees. From your estimate of the annual benefit, subtract annual operating expenses and the depreciation expense. In this example the depreciation expense was calculated on a straight-line basis over 10 years ($500,000/10 years = $50,000 per year). If your estimates are correct, your firm's pretax profit will increase by $30,000 per year and its after-tax profit by $21,000 per year.

	A	B	C	D	E	F
1						
2	Benefits	165,000		Year		Cash Flow
3	- Operating Expenses	85,000		0		-$500,000
4	- Depreciation	50,000		1		$71,000
5	Pretax Income	30,000		2		$71,000
6	- Tax @ 30%	9,000		3		$71,000
7	Net Income	21,000		4		$71,000
8	+ Depreciation	50,000		5		$71,000
9	Cash Flow	$ 71,000		6		$71,000
10				7		$71,000
11				8		$171,000
12						
13				NPV		-$91,233

Exhibit 8-11 NPV of proposed childcare center

   DCF analyses, however, must be based on changes in cash flows, not on changes in profit. To properly analyze this investment, you must first determine how much cash is paid out in each year and how much cash will come in for each year. To convert your profit estimate in cell B7 to a cash flow estimate, add back the $50,000 depreciation expense. As you know the annual depreciation expense is not an additional cash outflow. It is an accounting reallocation of the $500,000 that was paid out initially. You may be wondering why you should subtract out the depreciation expense on row 4 if you are going to add it back on row 8. If you don't subtract out the depreciation expense on row 4, you have overestimated the pretax income and therefore the amount of tax due. Taxes are a real cash outflow, so it is important to accurately estimate the tax payments.

   Column F in this spreadsheet shows the pattern of cash flow associated with this project. Year zero is the $500,000 initial expenditure to construct the facility. The $71,000 annual cash flow you just calculated is shown in years 1 through 7. The year 8 cash flow is the sum of the final $71,000 annual cash flow net plus the $100,000 salvage value. In the interest of brevity, this example assumed the annual cash flow was the same in each of the 8 years. This is probably unrealistic, and you could easily expand this spreadsheet to model different benefits, costs, and therefore cash flow for each of the 8 year. The net present value of the nine cash flow amounts is calculated in cell F13 with the formula =F3+NPV(11%,F4:F11). If this project is evaluated on a standalone economic basis, it would not be good idea. It would produce no net economic benefit and would consume $91,233 of shareholder wealth. Of course, there might be other reasons, not reflected in your estimate of the annual benefits, for undertaking this project. If that is the case, you have demonstrated that it will cost your firm $91,233 (not $500,000) to pursue those other benefits.

What Is Your Firm's HR Budget?

What does your firm spend per year to attract, develop, compensate, and retain its human resources? That seems like a simple question, but it's surprising how many firms cannot answer it. If you don't know the size of your total HR budget, how can you be sure you have allocated it optimally? If firm level aggregations are difficult, you might begin by thinking about the total HR budget for divisions or departments. The annual human resource cost for a firm or unit is far more than just the budget of the HR department. The total cost can be thought of as having the following four components: recruitment and selection, training and development, compensation, and administration. Typically, compensation costs and perhaps also some of the recruitment, selection, and training costs appear in the budgets of the operating units not in the budget the HR department. The HR department budget often consists primarily of administrative costs but may not include all administrative costs. Payroll processing costs, for example, are often not included in the budget of the HR department. Because HR costs are distributed across a range of budgets it is difficult to identify and sum them. More important, it makes it difficult to manage them from an HR systems perspective.

The complexities of managing total HR costs from a systems perspective is probably easiest to illustrate at the job level. Assume your firm's IT department is recruiting to fill an applications engineer position. In your firm the average tenure in these positions is 7 years. The components of the total cost to fill this position for 7 years are calculated in the spreadsheet shown in Exhibit 8-12. If the cost of the individual's starting salary and benefits is $100,000 and increases by 5% per year, the present value of the compensation cost discounted at a 10% cost of capital over 7 years is $555,870 (cell B11). The total cost is shown in cell A19. If your firm spends $633,000 to fill this position, is the allocation shown in Exhibit 8-12 the optimal one? Could performance have been improved or costs reduced by spending more on one component and less on another? Perhaps the $100,000 initial compensation was required because you needed an individual familiar with a particular software application. Could you have hired an individual without this specialized knowledge for $80,000 and then brought her up to speed through a carefully designed training program? At that lower compensation level, the present value of the compensation cost over the 7 years would be would be $444,696 (cell D11). You could have spent anything up to $111,000 on the training and still saved money.

	A	B	C	D	E
1		Compensation		Compensation	
2	year	Scenario 1		Scenario 2	
3	1	$100,000		$80,000	
4	2	$105,000		$84,000	
5	3	$110,250		$88,200	
6	4	$115,763		$92,610	
7	5	$121,551		$97,241	
8	6	$127,628		$102,103	
9	7	$134,010		$107,208	
10					
11	NPV at 10%	$555,870		$444,696	
12					
13					
14	$30,000	Recruitment and Selection Costs			
15	$10,000	Initial Training			
16	$32,000	Present Value of Other Development Costs			
17	$555,870	Present Value of Compensation Costs			
18	$5,000	Present Value of Administrative Costs			
19	$632,870	Total Cost to Fill Position for Seven Years			

Exhibit 8-12 Cost of filling applications engineer position for 7 years

Is Your HR Budget Allocation Optimal?

Should a firm spend more on training to save money on compensation, or spend more on compensation to save money on training? Such make-or-buy choices are not the only possible trade-offs. As illustrated in Exhibit 8-13, there are trade-offs possible among all the HR budget components. Here are some examples. Should a firm spend more on selection to save money on training, or spend more on training to save money on selection? Spending $10,000 more on selection might enable a firm to identify individuals who can complete the training more quickly and therefore more cheaply. That would be a good idea if the reduction in training cost were greater than $10,000. On the other hand, spending $10,000 less on selection might be a good idea even if it meant the incoming employees were slightly less well-qualified. That trade-off would make sense if the reduction in new-hire quality could be more than offset by a $5,000 increase in training expenditures. Should a firm spend more on compensation to save money on recruitment and selection, or spend more on recruitment and selection to save money on compensation? Offering higher wages might attract more and better applicants and therefore reduce recruitment and selection costs. If so, that would be a good trade-off if the present value the extra wages were less than the savings in recruitment and selection. They are not highlighted in Exhibit 8-13, but there might also be trade-offs between administrative cost and these other factors. Spending more on any component of the HR budget could potentially save you money on the others. Those savings may or may not be large enough to justify the extra costs. Who in your organization analyzes questions like whether HR should shift money from A to B or from B to A?

For every position in your organization, there is a total cost to fill that position and a current allocation of that total cost across recruitment and selection, training and development, and compensation. Is that allocation optimal? How was that allocation determined? Too often it is the unplanned result of disjointed decisions by individuals responsible for unrelated budgets. Do the individuals setting compensation levels think about whether paying more could produce an even larger decrease in other HR costs? Do the individuals responsible for the recruitment, selection, training, and development of budgets think about questions such as whether increasing another unit's expenditures by $10,000 would enable them to cut their own budget by more than $10,000? In many organizations questions like those fall through the cracks. It is possible to model these kinds of trade-offs formally, but in many organizations simply requiring managers to think about the allocation of the total HR budget (not the budget of the HR department) can produce major benefits. Those benefits can include substantial cost-savings or perhaps much more important, an increase in the quality of the workforce that can be achieved at a given budget level.

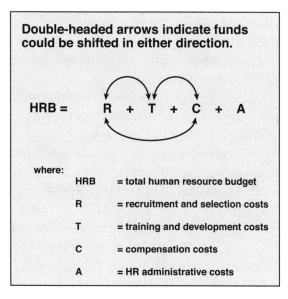

Exhibit 8-13 Trade-offs among HR budget components

Maximizing the ROI on Your Analysis Efforts

A consideration of the potential financial costs and benefits is essential in all HR decision making. Not all decisions, however, require the development of spreadsheets or other quantitative models. You won't want to spend a lot of time developing such models unless the issues you deal with are of financial or strategic significance. The criterion for assessing financial significance is clear; the dollar value of the potential costs and benefits is large. In making that determination you must consider which projects will have widespread impact. The individual case you analyze may not involve large budgets, but if it will set a precedent for companywide practice, its importance may be substantial. Projects of strategic significance (those that constitute a critical link in the firm's value creation process) certainly warrant careful analysis. In these cases, however, successful execution may be more important than cost minimization. Spending additional funds to reduce the risk that the activity will not be completed properly and on time is often the appropriate course of action.

You won't want to spend a lot of time on the analysis of projects that are not of financial or strategic significance. However, don't overestimate the amount of time the analysis will require. The most time-consuming component of the types of analyses described in this chapter is the data collection. If you are fortunate enough to have an HRIS system that can generate the specific data needed, the amount of time required to analyze that data is often not large. When hard data is not available, models of the type described in this chapter may still be useful based on your own or your colleagues' best estimates. Any time you decide to go ahead with a specific HR initiative, you are at least implicitly saying you believe the NPV from the activity will be positive. Any time you decide not to go ahead, you are saying you believe the NPV from that project will be negative. Plugging your own best estimates about potential costs and benefits into a spreadsheet can help you determine whether your gut feeling about whether to proceed with the project is consistent with your best estimates about the specifics. Constructing those spreadsheets is usually not a difficult or time-consuming activity.

When constructed, these models can also be useful for thinking through alternative possibilities. Before plugging in the numbers, it's not always intuitively obvious how large the impact would be if one of the input variables turns is above or below what you anticipate. "What-if" models of this type are often a valuable planning tool. The bottom line is that the benefits from such models can be large, and the costs of creating them are usually low.

9

Financial Analysis of a Corporation's Strategic Initiatives

Successful HR strategies are those that align with and support the firm's business strategy. Successful business strategies are those that create shareholder value. To align a firm's HR strategy with its business strategy, HR professionals must have at least a basic understanding of the financial models firms use to develop, describe, and evaluate strategic initiatives. That understanding is as important as, or maybe more important than, the ability to use financial models to evaluate operational decisions within the HR function. Recent survey data indicate that approximately 80% of all firms and more than 90% of large firms use discounted cash flow techniques to evaluate strategic investments.[1]

This chapter has two goals. The first is to demonstrate to HR professionals that they can easily understand enough about these models to be valuable contributors to cross-functional teams using these approaches. The second is to clarify that even when formal modeling is not used, the logic of these models provides an essential framework for thinking about business strategy and the creation of shareholder value. This chapter provides illustrations of models for

- Estimating the NPV of a strategic initiative
- Estimating multiple NPVs using scenario analysis
- Estimating an expected NPV based on judgments about the likelihood of each scenario
- Estimating the NPV when an strategic initiative involves real options

- Estimating the distribution of possible outcomes around an expected NPV
- Calculating the DCF value of a potential acquisition

Estimating the NPV of a Strategic Initiative Such as a New Product Introduction

The logic behind the financial analysis of a strategic investment is, of course, no different than the logic behind the analysis of any other investment. Strategic investment decisions do usually differ in that a larger number of inputs will need to be considered, the amount of risk exposure will be greater, and the consequences of success or failure will be much larger. As an initial example of a strategic investment, consider the introduction of a new product line. Assume your firm is considering producing and marketing a new version of windows. These are energy-efficient, duel casement, out-swing windows for use in new home construction. Exhibit 9-1 is spreadsheet of the type that might be used for modeling this decision. The overall logic of this spreadsheet is to forecast revenues by year, subtract all costs to determine projected profits, and then convert the profit estimates to cash flows. After that is done, it's straightforward to calculate the NPV and IRR of the proposed product introduction.

Capital Expenditures and Revenue Forecasts

Rows 2 and 3 of this spreadsheet show the initial capital and planning expenditures that must be made before this new manufacturing facility can be put into operation. Rows 5 through 12 are used to generate a sales forecast. You can begin in cell B5 with government or industry data on the number of new homes currently constructed each year. That number is then increased annually by the estimated growth rates you enter in Row 6. Multiplying the number of homes constructed each year times the Row 7 estimate of the percentage of homes using this type of window times the Row 8 estimate of average number of these windows per house produces an estimate of the industry sales volume in units. Multiplying the industry sales volume by your anticipated market share provides the Row 11 estimate of the number of windows you expect to sell each year. Multiplying the number of windows you expect to sell times the anticipated sales price per window generates the sales revenue projections on Row 12.

	YEAR	2013	2014	2015	2016	2017	2018	2019	2020	2021	2022	2023	2024	2025
2	Capital Expenditures	$30,000	$70,000	$50,000	$100,000						$100,000			
3	Planning and Startup Costs	$11,677	$50,000	$50,000	$60,000									
5	New Homes Constructed	2,000,000	2,060,000	2,121,800	2,185,454	2,251,018	2,318,548	2,388,105	2,459,748	2,533,540	2,609,546	2,687,833	2,768,468	2,851,522
6	% Growth		3%	3%	3%	3%	3%	3%	3%	3%	3%	3%	3%	3%
7	% Using Thermal Dual Casement Windows				18%	18%	18%	18%	18%	18%	18%	18%	18%	18%
8	Average Number per House				8	8	8	8	8	8	8	8	8	8
9	Market Share				10%	18%	26%	30%	35%	40%	40%	40%	40%	40%
10	Sales Price / Unit				$87	$88	$89	$90	$91	$91	$91	$92	$93	$94	$95
11	Sales Volume in Units				9,441	17,504	26,042	30,950	37,191	44,011	45,093	46,446	47,839	49,274
12	Sales Revenue				$821,381	$1,538,069	$2,311,188	$2,774,225	$3,367,031	$4,024,295	$4,164,437	$4,332,263	$4,506,854	$4,688,480
14	Raw Material per Unit				$26	$27	$27	$28	$28	$29	$29	$30	$30	$31
15	Utilities per Unit				$4	$4	$4	$4	$4	$4	$4	$4	$4	$4
16	Packaging per Unit				$8	$8	$8	$8	$8	$8	$8	$8	$8	$8
17	Sales & Distribution per Unit				$24	$24	$24	$24	$24	$24	$24	$24	$24	$24
18	Total Variable Cost per Unit				$62	$63	$63	$64	$64	$65	$65	$66	$66	$67
19	Total Variable Costs				$585,352	$1,094,345	$1,641,954	$1,968,144	$2,385,576	$2,847,796	$2,943,679	$3,059,188	$3,179,538	$3,304,946
20	Contribution per Unit				$25	$25	$26	$26	$26	$27	$27	$27	$28	$28
21	Total contribution to Profit				$236,029	$443,724	$669,233	$806,082	$981,455	$1,176,499	$1,220,758	$1,273,076	$1,327,315	$1,383,534
23	Depreciation (P,P,& E /10)				$25,000	$25,000	$25,000	$25,000	$25,000	$25,000	$35,000	$35,000	$35,000	$35,000
24	Personnel				$400,000	$408,000	$416,160	$424,483	$432,973	$441,632	$450,465	$459,474	$468,664	$478,037
25	Maintenance & Repairs				$6,000	$6,000	$6,000	$6,000	$6,000	$6,000	$6,000	$6,000	$6,000	$6,000
26	Consumables				$3,000	$3,000	$3,000	$3,000	$3,000	$3,000	$3,000	$3,000	$3,000	$3,000
27	Other Costs or Savings				$0	$0	$0	$0	$0	$0	$0	$0	$0	$0
28	Corporate Overhead (4% of Sales)				$32,855	$61,523	$92,448	$110,969	$134,681	$160,972	$166,577	$173,291	$180,274	$187,539
29	Total Fixed Costs	$0	$0	$0	$441,855	$478,523	$517,608	$544,452	$576,654	$611,604	$626,042	$641,765	$657,938	$674,576
31	Operating Profit Before Tax (EBI	$0	$0	$0	-$205,826	-$34,799	$151,626	$261,629	$404,801	$564,895	$594,716	$631,311	$669,377	$708,958
32	Taxes on Income	$0	$0	$0	$0	$0	$45,488	$78,489	$121,440	$169,468	$178,415	$189,393	$200,813	$212,687
33	Operating Profit After Tax	$0	$0	$0	-$205,826	-$34,799	$106,138	$183,141	$283,361	$395,426	$416,301	$441,918	$468,564	$496,271
34	+ Depreciation				$25,000	$25,000	$25,000	$25,000	$25,000	$25,000	$35,000	$35,000	$35,000	$35,000
35	Working Cap. (Inv.+AR-AP@35%of sales)				$287,483	$538,324	$808,916	$970,979	$1,178,461	$1,408,503	$1,457,553	$1,516,292	$1,577,399	$1,640,968
36	- Increase in Working Capital				$287,483	$250,841	$270,592	$162,063	$207,482	$230,042	$49,050	$58,739	$61,107	$63,569
37	- Increase in Property, Plant, & Equipment	$41,677	$120,000	$100,000	$150,000	$0	$0	$0	$0	$0	$100,000	$0	$0	$0
38	+Cash out of WC & P, P, & Equip.													$1,700,968
40	Cash Flow	($41,677)	($120,000)	($100,000)	($618,310)	($260,639)	($139,453)	$46,077	$100,879	$190,384	$302,251	$418,178	$442,457	$2,168,669
41	WACC	11%												
42	NPV	$244,049												
43	IRR	14.3%												

Exhibit 9-1 Estimating NPV and IRR of a strategic initiative

Variable Costs and Breakeven Levels

Variable costs are costs that vary with the level of output. In this example, the variable costs are raw materials, utilities, packaging, and sales and distribution costs. Fixed costs are costs that do not vary with the level of output. In this example the fixed costs are property, plant, and equipment (P, P, & E), personnel costs, maintenance and repairs, consumables, and corporate overhead charges. Row 20 shows the contribution to profit per unit. This is calculated as price per unit minus the variable cost per unit. For example, in the year 2016, the sales price of each window (shown on Row 10) is $87, and the total variable cost per window is $62 (shown on Row 18). There-fore, the contribution to profit per window is $25 ($87 – $62). In other words, each window sold covers its own variable cost and provides $25 toward covering the division's fixed costs. What's the value in knowing the contribution to profit? You can use that number to calculate the breakeven sales level. If you divide the year 2016 total fixed costs of $441,855 (shown on row 29) by the $25 per window contribution to profit, you see that you must sell 17,674 windows just to cover your fixed costs. This division will be profitable only if sales exceed that number.

Converting Profits Back to Cash Flows

As explained in the previous chapter, your investment decision must be based on the present value of the cash flow in each year, not on the present value of the profits. That is the only way you can answer the question, "Does it make sense to inject cash into this project during the early years to draw out cash in the later years?" The annual profit estimates are not measurements of how much cash will be paid out or received in a given year. To derive the cash flow estimates on Row 40 from the profit estimates on Row 33, you must do three things. Exhibit 9-2 illustrates this process using the data for the year 2019. First, you add back on Row 34 whatever deprecia-tion expense was subtracted out on Row 23. As you know, the annual depreciation expenses are not additional cash outflows but just reallo-cations for accounting and tax purposes of cash used in earlier periods to purchase long-term assets such as plant and equipment. Second, in any year when you do utilize cash to purchase long-term assets, those amounts are subtracted on Row 37. The third and final step is to sub-tract on Row 36 the cash used to increase working capital. *Working capital* is the net amount of cash the firm has tied up in inventories and accounts receivable. Remember that when calculating profit you did not subtract the cost of additions to inventory but only the cost of the windows actually sold in each year. If additional cash were used to build up inventories beyond what was sold that year, we now have to subtract that from the cash on hand. On Row 40, you see that the firm must inject substantial amounts of cash into this venture in the years

2013 to 2018. The cash flows are then projected to become positive in 2019 to 2025. This model, in cell N38, assumes that at the end of year 2025, the firm will cash out the working capital and the property, plant, and equipment invested in this project for $1,700,968. Even if the firm does not actually liquidate these assets, this would be a reasonable way to model the fact that at the end of 2025 this firm will own assets worth $1,700,968.

(Example Using Data for Year 2019)		Shown in Cell
Operating Profit After Tax	$183,141	H33
+ Depreciation	$25,000	H34
- Increase in Property, Plant, & Equipment	$0	H37
- Increase in Working Capital	-$162,063	H36
Cash Flow from Operations	$46,077	H40

Exhibit 9-2 Converting profits to cash flows

Should You Introduce This New Product Line?

This project requires your firm to inject substantial amounts of cash into this venture in the years 2013–2018 to receive the positive cash flow projected for years 2019 to 2025. If you express all those outflows and inflows in present value terms and then sum them, will this project produce a net gain or a net loss for the shareholders? That is the question answered by the NPV formula in cell B42. That formula is = B40+NPV(B41,C40:N40). If the firm's weighted average cost of capital is 11% and the cash flow turns out as projected, shareholder value increases by 244,049. An alternative way to evaluate this project would be to calculate its internal rate of return. The formula in cell B43 is =IRR(B40:N40). Remember that the IRR decision rule is that you would proceed with the project only if the IRR is greater than the cost of capital. In this case, the 14% IRR is greater than the firm's 11% cost of capital, so the project is an attractive one. The NPV in cell B42 was calculated using an 11% discount rate. If the IRR had not been larger than 11%, this NPV would have been negative.

How Useful Are Models of This Type?

A common reaction to models of the type shown in Exhibit 9-1 is that their real-world usefulness is limited by the large number of input assumptions required. It's true that models of this type are vulnerable to the GIGO (garbage in, garbage out) problem. If your input assumptions are all garbage, the model's output will be garbage. But think carefully before concluding that is a reason to reject this type of model. There is no assumption that is any more important because you typed it into a spreadsheet than if you made the decision without using a spreadsheet. If whether this initiative is a good idea depends on production costs in year 5, or market share year 2, or interest rates in year 8, you cannot escape that risk reality. Your only choice is to make strategic decisions with or without thinking through the underlying assumptions. Every time you decide to go ahead with a project, you assume that those factors will play out in a way that permits the project's success. Spreadsheet modeling does not increase the number of assumptions required; it make those assumptions explicit.

There are, of course, a number of potential benefits from the use of models such as the one in Exhibit 9-1. First, they provide guidance as to how you should proceed given your own best estimates of the input factors. Few people, even if they were extremely confident in their estimates of all the input factors shown in Exhibit 9-1, could determine without using a spreadsheet or similar model whether the project would produce a gain or a loss. A second major benefit of making all input assumptions explicit is that they can then be reviewed by your colleagues. If a colleague believes one of your assumptions is too high or too low, it is easy to plug in their estimates instead of yours to determine whether that difference would change the go/no-go policy implications for this project. A third potential benefit from models of this type is the ability to determine which input assumptions are particularly critical and which are of more limited importance. Suppose, for example, you adjust each of the input assumptions up and down by 10%. You might find, for example, that small differences in market share have a much larger impact than small differences in raw materials cost, or you might find the reverse. Identifying which input variables are most critical can help you determine which factors must be studied most carefully during the planning process, and perhaps which factors must be managed most carefully after the project has been implemented.

Models of this type might also assist you in redesigning a strategic initiative. Suppose based on your best assumptions the new initiative you are considering would have a negative NPV. Spreadsheet models of this type may enable you to determine what changes must be made for the project to become an attractive one. How much larger would the selling price need to be? How much lower would the costs need to be? How much larger would our market share need to be? Using spreadsheets it would be easy to answer these and similar questions. You could then determine which, if any, of these changes would be achievable with a project redesign.

Estimating Multiple NPVs Using Scenario Analysis

A natural extension of the previous approach would be to estimate multiple NPVs using scenario analysis. In the previous example, the product was an energy-efficient window used in new home construction. The firm might want to re-estimate the spreadsheet in Exhibit 9-1 under multiple scenarios about how quickly the demand for new homes will grow or how high energy costs will be. Each of these re-estimations would, of course, yield a different potential NPV for this product introduction. The benefit of scenario analysis is that management can now see a range of possible outcomes before making a decision on this project. The limitation of this approach is that it does explicitly incorporate any information about the likelihood of the various scenarios. When judgments can be made about the relative likelihood of alternatives scenarios, it is possible to utilize this information to calculate an expected NPV. An example of that approach is provided in the next section.

Estimating an Expected NPV Based on Judgments About the Likelihood of Each Scenario

Before illustrating the estimation of expected NPVs, it may be useful to review the concept of expected values. Suppose you are playing a casino game that requires you to make a $50 bet. If you win, you get back $100. If you lose, you get back nothing. The casino has designed the game so that on each play you have a 30% chance of winning and a 70% chance of losing. What would your average outcome be if you played that game 1,000 times? With that many plays, you can be relatively confident that you would win approximately 300 times and lose approximately 700 times. You could calculate your average outcome by adding up your winnings (300 × +$100) and your losses (700 x –$50) and dividing by 1,000. You average outcome would be a loss of $5.00 per game. You could do exactly the same calculation more quickly by adding the probability of a win times the amount of a win, plus the probability of a loss times the amount of a loss. In this example that would be (.30 ×$100) + (.70 x –$50) = –$5. Note that if you play this game only once there is no chance that you will lose $5. You will either lose $50 or win $100. The –$5 is an estimate of what the average outcome will be if you play this game many times. Looking at it this way, you can see that expected values are just weighted averages. Each potential outcome is weighted by the probability that it will occur.

You can use this same logic to calculate the expected net present value when there are multiple scenarios describing potential business outcomes. The example in Exhibit 9-3 assumes your firm is considering the introduction of a new cell phone model. Introducing this new phone would have an upfront cost of $100 million. If consumers prefer your phone to the competition, you will in years 1 to 5 receive the positive cash flow shown on Row 2. If consumers prefer the competition over your phone, your firm will experience the negative cash flow shown on Row 3. You could, of course, calculate the NPV for the success scenario and the NPV for the failure scenario. However, if you can make a business judgment about the probabilities of these two scenarios, you can calculate the expected net present value from this product introduction. Your marketing department tells you predicting consumer preferences is difficult and that the new cell phone would have only a 50% probability of success. Using that information you can calculate the expected cash flow shown on Row 5 of the spreadsheet. Each one is calculated by multiplying the probability of success times the cash flow if the product is successful and adding that to the probability of failure times the cash flow if the product is not successful. For example, the year 1 expected cash flow is (.50 × $60) + (.50 × –$40), which is $10. Had you assumed the year 1 probability of success was 70%, the expected cash flow would have been (.70 × $60) + (.30 × –$40), which is $30. Because Row 5 now shows the expected cash flow series, the NPV of this row is the expected NPV of this risky new product introduction. The formula in cell C6 is =C5+NPV(0.12,D5:H5). You would not proceed with the project because the expected outcome is a loss of $40 million. Note that if you introduce this new phone, there is no chance that the expected NPV will result. The project will either be successful or not successful. The expected NPV is an estimate of the average result you would obtain if you made business decisions like this many times. You can improve your organization's long-run probability of success if you invest only in projects where the expected NPV is positive.

	A	B	C	D	E	F	G	H
1	U.S. Launch of New Cell Phone Model		0	1	2	3	4	5
2		Success (50% Probability)	-$100	$60	$70	$80	$75	$50
3		Failure (50% Probability)	-$100	-$40	-$30	-$20	-$40	-$40
4								
5		Expected	-$100	$10	$20	$30	$18	$5
6		NPV@12%	-$40					

Exhibit 9-3 Calculating the expected NPV when there are multiple scenarios (all dollar amounts in millions)

The NPV When There Are Real Options Like the Ability to Abandon or Expand the Project

The analysis contained Exhibit 9-3 suggests the introduction of the new cell phone would have a negative NPV of $40 million. Obviously, you would not undertake the project if you thought it would reduce shareholder value by $40 million. Perhaps, however, your analysis did not go far enough. If this new product launch goes badly in years 1 and 2, you may be able to withdraw the product and cut your losses. If you believe that is a realistic option, you must adjust the cash flow projections for the failure scenario. Row 2 in Exhibit 9-4 differs from row 2 in Exhibit 9-3 in that the negative cash flow for years 3, 4, and 5 have been replaced with zeros. The assumption is that after the product is withdrawn there will be no more positive or negative cash flows. Changing this scenario changes the expected cash flow series and the expected NPV. The expected NPV from the U.S. launch is now –$9 million, instead of –$40 million. The option to abandon this project if it goes badly was worth $31 million. Of course, you would still not undertake a project with an expected NPV of $–9 million.

	A	B	Formula Bar C	D	E	F	G	H	I	J
1	U.S. Launch if Have Option to Abandon		0	1	2	3	4	5		
2		Success (50% Probability)	-$100	$60	$70	$80	$75	$50		
3		Failure (50% Probability)	-$100	-$40	-$30	$0	$0	$0		
4										
5		Expected	-$100	$10	$20	$40	$38	$25		
6		NPV@12%	-$9							
7										
8	Global Expansion if U.S. Launch is Successfu		0	1	2	3	4	5	6	7
9		Success (80% Probability)	$0	$0	-$500	$250	$300	$300	$250	$225
10		Failure (20% Probability)	$0	$0	-$500	-$200	-$200	$100	$0	$0
11										
12		Expected	$0	$0	-$500	$160	$200	$260	$200	$180
13		NPV@12%	$173							
14										
15										
16	NPV with Options to Abandon and Expand									
17	U.S. NPV of -$9 Plus (.50 x Global NPV of $1		$78							

Exhibit 9-4 Calculating the expected NPV when there are options to abandon or expand (all dollar amounts in millions)

There may, however, be an additional option that you should consider. You know that if this project goes badly you can abandon it and cut your losses. But what if the project is a success? Can you expand it and magnify your gains? Suppose that if the U.S. launch of this new phone is successful in years 1 and 2, you will in year 3 introduce it in Europe and Asia. This global expansion option is modeled in Rows 9 and 10 of the spreadsheet in Exhibit 9-4. Because the global expansion will not occur unless the U.S. launch has already proven successful, you might assign a higher success probability to the global launch. The example in Exhibit 9-3 assumes the global launch will have an 80% probability of success. The NPV of the expected cash flow from the global launch is $173 million.

You can now calculate the expected NPV of this new product introduction incorporating both the option to abandon the project if it goes badly and the option to expand it if it goes well. To do this, add the expected NPV of the U.S. launch to one-half of the expected NPV from the global launch. You are including only one-half of the expected NPV from the global launch because it will happen only if the U.S. launch has already been successful and there is only a 50% probability that the U.S. launch will succeed (–9 + .5x173 = 78). Options such as the ability to abandon or expand a project are often referred to as real options to differentiate them from financial options of the type that will be discussed in the next chapter. In this example, had the new product introduction been evaluated without consideration of these real options, the project would have been rejected because its expected NPV was negative. Only when the value of the real options was recognized did it become clear that the expected NPV of the proposal was positive and quite large.

Estimating the Distribution of Possible Outcomes Around an Expected NPV

The previous examples illustrate approaches corporations can use to estimate the expected net present value of a strategic initiative. If possible strategic planners would, of course, like to know more than just the expected NPV from a project under consideration. They would also like to know the distribution of possible NPVs around that expectation. Suppose for example, the most likely NPV from Project A were $10 million and you were confident the actual NPV would fall between $7 million and $13 million. Contrast that with Project B that also has an expected NPV of $10 million, but where the range of possible outcomes is between –$5 million and + $25 million. Even though both projects have the same expected NPV, Project B is a much higher risk. Firms that could not tolerate the possibility of a $5 million loss would need to rule out Project B entirely. Having estimates of the distribution potential investment outcomes can be extremely helpful to those contemplating high-risk business strategies.

All firms making risky investments must consider both the most likely outcome and the range of possible outcomes. Some firms find it useful to develop formal models to estimate those items. The pharmaceutical industry is one that makes large, high-risk invest-ments. Large pharmaceutical companies spend $4 to $8 billion per year per firm on research and development. Ninety-five percent of the projects they initiate end up at a dead end; that is, they do not result in an FDA approvable drug. Because the stakes are so high and the risks are so large, that industry has devoted substantial effort to developing models for assessing the risk associated with strategic investments. Hopefully reviewing the pharmaceutical industry exam-ple shown in Exhibit 9-5 demonstrates just how generic these models are and that they can be utilized by firms in most industries.

The spreadsheet reproduced in Exhibits 9-5a and 9-5b describes a strategic choice faced by large pharmaceutical firm. The choice is whether to in-license, that is, license the rights to, a new drug for treating type II diabetes. Rows 1 through 25 of this spreadsheet are shown in Exhibit 9-5a. The approach used to generate the revenue forecasts is similar to the approach used in Exhibit 9-1, so there is probably no need to review each of the steps. It starts with the estimate that 24.5 million people in the United States had type II diabetes in the year 2010. The assumptions shown are then used to calculate the revenue that year. The formula in cell E20 is =+E3*E6*E8*E10*E12*E14*E16*E18. The same approach was used to estimate revenue in each of the other years. The second half of this spreadsheet is shown in Exhibit 9-5b. Rows 27 to 42 contain estimates of the variable and fixed costs to manufacture and sell this drug. The deal costs are shown on Row 44. To in-license this drug would require an upfront payment of $100 million in 2010 and then additional milestone payments in the years 2013 to 2020. With this information you can calculate the after-tax profit shown on row 50. Then using the same logic described earlier, you convert the profit estimates to cash flow estimates. The cash flow is shown on Row 56. The NPV of the proposed deal is shown in cell B58 where the formula is =+B56+NPV(B57,C56:L56). The IRR for this project is shown in cell B59 where the formula is =IRR(B56:L56). The NPV is positive ($188.6 million), and the IRR is greater than the weighted average cost of capital. Both measures suggest this is a project worth pursuing.

Type II Diabetes - U.S. Opportunity	Project: In-license of new oral antihyperglycemic agent										
	2010	2011	2012	2013	2014	2015	2016	2017	2018	2019	2020
Disease Prevalence (thousands)	24,500	25,235	25,992	26,772	27,575	28,402	29,254	30,132	31,036	31,967	32,926
% growth		3%	3%	3%	3%	3%	3%	3%	3%	3%	3%
Diagnosis Rate	60%	60%	61%	62%	63%	64%	65%	65%	65%	65%	65%
% Treated with Drug	70%	70%	71%	72%	73%	74%	75%	75%	75%	75%	75%
% treated with Drug Class	20%	20%	20%	22%	23%	24%	26%	28%	30%	30%	30%
Market share	0%	0%	0%	1%	3%	6%	10%	13%	15%	16%	16%
Price per Day	$4.00	$4.12	$4.24	$4.37	$4.50	$4.64	$4.78	$4.92	$5.07	$5.22	$5.38
Average days of Therapy	300	315	330	345	360	360	360	360	360	360	360
Persistence Rate	42%	43%	44%	45%	46%	47%	48%	49%	50%	50%	50%
Gross Sales Revenue (thousands)	0	0	0	$17,841	$65,237	$151,975	$306,030	$464,004	$620,985	$702,724	$745,519
% growth					266%	133%	101%	52%	34%	13%	6%
Gross to Net Discounts	12%	12%	12%	12%	12%	12%	12%	12%	12%	12%	12%
Net Sales revenue (thousands)				$15,700	$57,409	$133,738	$269,307	$408,324	$546,467	$618,397	$656,057

Exhibit 9-5a Monte Carlo simulation of a strategic initiative

Type II Diabetes - U.S. Opportunity	Project: In-license of new oral antihyperglycemic agent										
	2010	2011	2012	2013	2014	2015	2016	2017	2018	2019	2020
Net Sales revenue (thousands)				$15,700	$57,409	$133,738	$269,307	$408,324	$546,467	$618,397	$656,057
Cost of Sales				$2,355	$8,611	$20,061	$40,396	$61,249	$81,970	$92,760	$98,409
Gross Margin				$13,345	$48,798	$113,677	$228,911	$347,075	$464,497	$525,637	$557,648
% of sales				85%	85%	85%	85%	85%	85%	85%	85%
Distribution				$51	$186	$432	$868	$1,312	$1,751	$1,803	$1,858
Advertising/Promotion			$15,000	$35,000	$35,000	$35,000	$35,000	$39,362	$52,522	$54,100	$55,575
Salesa Force				$50,000	$50,000	$50,000	$50,000	$50,000	$52,000	$52,522	$54,100
Medical Education				$2,500	$2,500	$2,529	$5,000	$5,000	$5,000	$5,000	$5,000
Depreciation		$1,500	$1,500	$1,500	$1,500	$1,500	$1,500	$1,500	$1,500	$1,500	$1,500
Product Contribution			($16,500)	($75,706)	($40,388)	$24,216	$136,543	$249,901	$351,724	$410,712	$439,615
Marketing				$1,000	$1,000	$1,000	$1,730	$3,000	$3,000	$3,000	$3,000
G&A				$500	$500	$865	$1,000	$1,000	$1,000	$1,000	$1,000
R&D Development	$45,000	$30,000									
Licensing/Royalties (thousands)	$100,000			$25,000	$25,000	$25,000	$25,000	$26,241	$35,014	$36,066	$37,150
Pre-Tax Earnings	($145,000)	($30,000)	($16,500)	($102,206)	($66,868)	($2,649)	$108,813	$219,660	$312,710	$370,646	$398,465
Taxes @ 30%	-$43,500	-$9,000	-$4,950	-$30,662	-$20,067	-$795	$32,644	$65,898	$93,813	$111,194	$119,540
After-tax Earnings (thousands)	($101,500)	($21,000)	($11,550)	($71,544)	($46,822)	($1,854)	$76,169	$153,762	$218,897	$259,452	$278,926
add back Depreciation		$1,500	$1,500	$1,500	$1,500	$1,500	$1,500	$1,500	$1,500	$1,500	$1,500
subtract increase in Working Capital				$1,531	$4,045	$7,397	$13,075	$13,314	$13,159	$1,578	$1,625
subtract Capital Expenditures	$15,000										
After-tax cashflow (thousands)	($116,500)	($19,500)	($10,050)	($71,575)	($49,367)	($7,751)	$64,594	$141,948	$207,238	$259,374	$278,801

WACC	10%
NPV	$188,632
IRR	19.7%

Exhibit 9-5b Monte Carlo simulation of a strategic initiative (second half)

Using the Spreadsheet to Structure the Deal

Before expanding this model to include a Monte Carlo simulation, look at how it could be used to help negotiate the proposed drug in-licensing. Suppose you are on the team deciding whether to in-license this drug. The firm you are negotiating with feels the terms you have offered, and shown on Row 44, are not sufficiently generous. How attractive would this deal be for your firm if you increased your offer by $10 million? The answer depends heavily on how you structure the payments. Reducing the initial year 2010 payment by $50 million and increasing the year 2020 payments by $60 million would increase your total payments by $10 million. What impact would those changes have on the NPV of this deal? Exhibit 9-5c reveals that entering this altered payment series into Row 44 of the spreadsheet would increase your NPV from $188,632,000 to $207,439,000. Offering to pay an additional $10 million but restructuring the payment sequence would increase your firm's net benefit by almost $19 million. How is that possible? It is a consequence of the time value of money. In this hypothetical you moved a $50 million payment from 2010 to 2020. If the firm's weighted average cost of capital is 10% each year that the firm does not have to come up with this $50 million, the firm saves $5 million ($50 million × 10%). Those savings more than offset the present value of the extra $10 million added in year 2020.

Type II Diabetes - U.S. Opportunity			Project: In-license of new oral antihyperglycemic agent								
	2010	2011	2012	2013	2014	2015	2016	2017	2018	2019	2020
Net Sales revenue (thousands)				$15,700	$57,409	$133,738	$269,307	$408,324	$546,467	$618,397	$656,057
Cost of Sales				$2,355	$8,611	$20,061	$40,396	$61,249	$81,970	$92,760	$98,409
Gross Margin				$13,345	$48,798	$113,677	$228,911	$347,075	$464,497	$525,637	$557,648
% of sales				85%	85%	85%	85%	85%	85%	85%	85%
Distribution				$51	$186	$432	$868	$1,312	$1,751	$1,803	$1,858
Advertising/Promotion			$15,000	$35,000	$35,000	$35,000	$35,000	$39,362	$52,522	$54,100	$55,575
Salesa Force				$50,000	$50,000	$50,000	$50,000	$50,000	$52,000	$52,522	$54,100
Medical Education				$2,500	$2,500	$2,529	$5,000	$5,000	$5,000	$5,000	$5,000
Depreciation		$1,500	$1,500	$1,500	$1,500	$1,500	$1,500	$1,500	$1,500	$1,500	$1,500
Product Contribution				($16,500)	($75,706)	($40,388)	$24,216	$136,543	$249,901	$361,724	$410,712	$439,615
Marketing				$1,000	$1,000	$1,000	$1,730	$3,000	$3,000	$3,000	$3,000
G&A				$500	$500	$865	$1,000	$1,000	$1,000	$1,000	$1,000
R&D Development	$45,000	$30,000									
Licensing/Royalties (thousands)	$50,000			$25,000	$25,000	$25,000	$25,000	$26,241	$35,014	$36,066	$97,150
Pre-Tax Earnings	($95,000)	($30,000)	($16,500)	($102,206)	($66,888)	($2,649)	$108,813	$219,660	$312,710	$370,646	$338,465
Taxes @ 30%	-$28,500	-$9,000	-$4,950	-$30,662	-$20,067	-$795	$32,644	$65,898	$93,813	$111,194	$101,540
After-tax Earnings (thousands)	($66,500)	($21,000)	($11,550)	($71,544)	($46,822)	($1,854)	$76,169	$153,762	$218,897	$259,452	$236,926
add back Depreciation		$1,500	$1,500	$1,500	$1,500	$1,500	$1,500	$1,500	$1,500	$1,500	$1,500
subtract increase in Working Capital				$1,531	$4,045	$7,397	$13,075	$13,314	$13,159	$1,578	$1,625
subtract Capital Expenditures	$15,000										
After-tax cashflow (thousands)	($81,500)	($19,500)	($10,050)	($71,575)	($49,367)	($7,751)	$64,594	$141,948	$207,238	$259,374	$236,801
WACC	10%										
NPV	$207,439										
IRR	22.4%										

Exhibit 9-5c Impact on NPV of restructuring licensing and royalty payments

Using Monte Carlo Simulations to Model Risk and Uncertainty

If your estimate for each of the input variables is correct, the proposed drug in-licensing deal will produce a large net benefit for your firm. Of course, there's almost no chance that all your estimates are correct. It has been said that whenever you make a cash flow forecast, you know you are wrong. You just don't know by how much or in which direction. Monte Carlo simulation is a technique that can be used to model the uncertainty in your forecasts and to assess the implications of this uncertainty. When Monte Carlo simulations are applied to spreadsheets such as the one in Exhibit 9-5, you have the option to enter into each input cell not just your best estimate but also information about the possible distribution around that estimate. For example, in cell F14 of this spreadsheet, the year 2014 price per dose for this drug is shown as $4.50. Assume that number was the best estimate that your marketing team could provide. However, when pressed they acknowledged that it was only an estimate and that the actual price might be above or below that. If further questioning revealed that they believed the price could be $3.50, $4.50, or $5.50, you could then ask them for their judgments about how likely it was that each of these prices would occur. Suppose their judgment is that there is a 30% chance the price will be $3.50, a 50% chance the price will be $4.50, and a 20% chance the price will be $5.50. How can their judgments about the likelihood of each of the different prices be incorporated into a spreadsheet? Before discussing software for doing that, review what you are trying to achieve.

Suppose you take 10 scraps of paper. On three of them you write $3.50. On five you write $4.50, and on two you write $5.50. You then put all 10 pieces of paper into your desk drawer. You could now recalculate the spreadsheet in Exhibit 9-5 with one difference. When you get to cell F14, you reach into your desk drawer and without looking randomly pull out one of the pieces of paper. Whatever price is on that piece of paper is the number you plug into cell F14. If you did that once, the resulting NPV would be meaningless. However, suppose you repeated that exercise 1,000 times and recorded the 1,000 NPVs that resulted. You could now plot those 1,000 NPVs on a graph and observe both the range of possible NPVs and the frequency with which each NPV occurred. That is in essence what a Monte Carlo simulation does. You could replicate that process in the cells with the price for each of the other years. Actually, you could apply a similar process in any or all of the almost 200 input cells in Exhibit 9-5. Assume you identified 50 key input cells where you thought it was important to consider not just information about the most likely value but also information about the range of possible values. If you were doing this manually, you would need to make a random draw from each of 50 different distributions, plug in those values, and then calculate the first NPV. Make a second draw from each of those 50 distributions, calculate the second NPV, and so on. To repeat that process 1,000 times would be tedious and slow. Fortunately, there is software available that can perform equivalent analyses quickly and simply.

Several companies sell Monte Carlo simulation software that works as an Excel add-in. When this software runs, you have the option to enter into any spreadsheet cell either a specific value or information about the distribution of possible values. The distribution information can be entered in a variety of formats. You could, as in the previous example, enter three prices and estimates of the probability that each of those prices will occur. You could specify a normal distribution by providing the mean and standard deviation. You could specify a distribution that is skewed left or skewed right, or truncated at a particular minimum and/or maximum value. Because these software packages provide a graphical image of the distribution you have specified, using them does not require a mathematics background. When you start the simulation, the software evaluates the spreadsheet 1,000 times (or whatever number of times you specify). Each time, for any cells in which you have specified a distribution, it makes a random draw from that distribution. It then plots the 1,000 NPVs in a graph similar to the one shown in Exhibit 9-6.

Interpreting the Output from a Monte Carlo Simulation

You use a simulation like this when you are concerned about the uncertainty of key assumptions. You don't know whether when you implement this project each of those factors will turn out to be close to what you assumed, or perhaps more favorable or less favorable for the success of the project. Most of the time most of the factors will have values close to their expectation. However, it is possible that all or most of the factors could turn out to be much less favorable than anticipated causing the project to have a much lower than expected NPV. On the other hand, all or most the factors could turn out to be much more favorable than anticipated causing the project to have a much higher than expected NPV. Monte Carlo simulation gives you a way to estimate the magnitude and likelihood of these extreme outcomes. It attempts to answer the questions, "What would the distribution of NPVs be if you undertook projects like this one many times? What would be the average outcome? How much could you lose if things go badly, and what is the likelihood of that? How much could you make if things go well, and what is likelihood of that?"

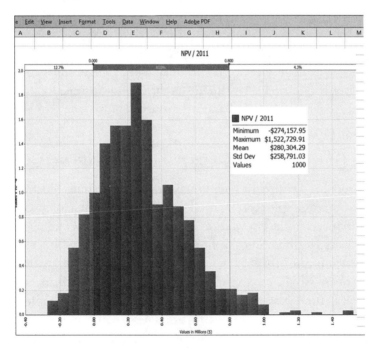

Exhibit 9-6 Output from Monte Carlo simulation showing range of possible NPVs

Exhibit 9-6 is a plot of the NPV value in cell B58 from each of 1,000 independent recalculations on the spreadsheet shown in Exhibit 9-5. In each recalculation when Excel reached a cell where a distribution rather than a single value had been entered, the Monte Carlo add-in made a random draw from that distribution, and the resulting value was used in the spreadsheet calculation. It is exactly analogous to your reaching into your desk drawer and randomly picking one of those 10 scraps of paper to determine which price to plug in to the spreadsheet. In this example, you see that the mean NPV from those 1,000 recalculations of the spreadsheet was $280,304,000. This suggests that if your company made business investments like this many times, you would have an average net benefit of approximately $280 million. In that sense, this project is an attractive one. However, the simulation results also revealed a wide distribution around that average. The largest NPV that occurred during those 1,000 trials was $1,522,730. The smallest NPV was a loss of $274,158. The percentages on the top row of the graph show that the NPV was below zero; that is, the company lost money in 12.7% of those 1,000 trials. A large company that makes many such investments might approve projects such as this because on average they would produce a net gain. A small company making only one such investment might choose to reject it to avoid exposing itself to a 12.7% chance of losing money.

Using DCF to Analyze Mergers and Acquisitions

Discounted cash flow techniques similar to the ones illustrated in the previous examples can be used to estimate the value of a potential acquisition. As in the previous examples, the most challenging part of the process is estimating the future cash flow. Even with a detailed knowledge of the firm to be acquired, its business strategy, its markets, its cost structure, and its competitors, it is difficult to estimate future cash flow. Nevertheless, most buyers use both discounted cash flow models and comparables to estimate the maximum purchase price they should offer. The use of comparables involves comparing the target company to similar companies whose stock is publicly traded or have been acquired recently. If a comparable company's P/E ratio (stock price divided by earnings per share) was, say, 14, that would imply that its market cap (the value of its outstanding stock) is 14 times its net income. You might then conclude that the appropriate price to pay for the target company is an amount equal to 14 times the target company's net income. In addition to price to net income, other comparable measures that might be used include a price to EBIT, price to EBITDA, price to sales, price to book value of assets, and price to book value of equity. The two major challenges in using the comparables approach are, of course, identifying companies that are sufficiently similar to the acquisition target and deciding which comparables measure to use. Because using different measures can produce widely varying estimates of the value of a target company, a common approach is to value the target company using multiple comparables measures and discounted cash flow analysis.

An example of using discounted cash flow analysis to evaluate a potential acquisition is shown in Exhibit 9-7. The spreadsheet reproduced in this exhibit assumes that an analysis is being done in the year 2012 for an acquisition that would take place at the beginning of 2013. Rows 6 through 13 contain the forecasts of sales, expenses, and profits for the years 2013 to 2020. Following exactly the same process and logic that was discussed in the earlier capital budgeting examples, you must convert the profit estimates to cash flow estimates. On Row 14, the depreciation expense is added back because it does not represent a cash outflow in that year. On Row 15 and Row 16, any cash used to expand property plant and equipment and to increase the firm's working capital are subtracted. The resulting cash flow is shown on Row 17.

Dividing Cash Flows into an Initial Time Horizon and a Terminal Value

Theoretically, the value of a company is the present value of all future cash flow. However, when estimating the value of a potential takeover target, a common approach is to estimate the present value of cash flow over an initial time horizon of 5 to 15 years and then add to that an estimate of what the company will be worth at the end of that initial time horizon. That estimate of what the company will be worth at the end of the initial time horizon is referred to as the terminal value. The assumption is that during this initial time horizon the company driven by its new owners will be undergoing change and that a specific forecast of the cash flow for each year is warranted, but that by the end of this time horizon the company will have reached a steady-state and that cash flow will begin to grow at a constant rate. Selecting the right time horizon is difficult and is just one of the practical problems faced when trying to apply DCF models. Recent survey data indicates that almost one-half of all firms (46%) discount an explicit cash flow forecast for the first 5 years and then add to that an estimate of the terminal value. Just more than one-third (34%) reported using a 10-year explicit forecast period, and only 4% incorporated a specific forecast for 20 years of more.[2] The spreadsheet in Exhibit 9-7 treats the years 2013 to 2019 as the initial time horizon and the year 2020 as the estimate of the steady-state condition. The present value of the cash flow in 2013 to 2019 is calculated in cell J20. The formula in that cell is =NPV(D32,B17:H17). D32 is a reference to the cell where the weighted average cost of capital is located.

	A	B	C	D	E	F	G	H	I	J
1	**Discounted Cash Flow Analysis of Firm Value**									
2	($ in Millions Except per Share)									
3										
4		2013	2014	2015	2016	2017	2018	2019	2020	
5										
6	Sales Revenue	2,888	3,032	3,184	3,343	3,510	3,686	3,870	4,064	
7	- Cost of Goods Sold	1,502	1,577	1,656	1,738	1,825	1,917	2,013	2,113	
8	Gross Pofit	1,386	1,456	1,528	1,605	1,685	1,769	1,858	1,951	
9	- Operating Expenses	481	505	531	557	585	614	645	677	
10	- Depreciation	232	253	276	300	327	341	330	330	
11	EBIT	673	697	722	748	773	814	883	943	
12	Tax at 35%	236	244	253	262	271	285	309	330	
13	Earnings After Tax	437	453	469	486	502	529	574	613	
14	+ Depreciation	232	253	276	300	327	341	330	330	
15	- Increase in P, P, & E	234	239	243	248	253	258	264	269	
16	- Increase in Working Capital	144	151	159	167	175	184	193	203	
17	Free Cash Flow	$ 291	$ 316	$ 343	$ 371	$ 401	$ 428	$ 447	$ 472	
18										
19										
20					Present Value of Cash Flows 2013 to 2019 =					$ 1,639
21					Terminal Value at End of 2019 Using Perpetual Growth model =			$ 5,897		
22					PV of Terminal Value =					$ 2,667
23										
24					Value of Operations =					$ 4,306
25					Add Value of Excess Marketable Securities			$ 1,100		
26					Value of Firm =					$ 5,406
27					Subtract Value of Liabilities			$ 851		
28					Value of Equity =					$ 4,555
29					Number of Shares Outstanding = 175 million					
30					Value per Share =					$ 26.03
31	Assumptions:									
32			Weighted average cost of capital is		12%					
33	Beginning in 2020 annnual growth in FCF will be				4%					
34	* Perpetual growth terminal value calculated as [FCF in 2020 / WACC - g]									

Exhibit 9-7 Using DCF analyses to evaluate mergers and acquisitions (M&A)

Which Cost of Capital Should Be Used?

Firms do not typically use their own WACC when valuing a potential acquisition. To more accurately reflect the risk level associated with the target company, it is common to use the target company's cost of capital or the cost of capital for a group of companies comparable to the target company.

Present Value of a No-Growth Perpetuity

The terminal value at the end of 2019 is calculated in cell I20. The terminal value is estimated as what the finance literature sometimes referred to as a perpetuity. A *perpetuity* is a perpetual or never-ending annuity. If you assume a no-growth perpetuity, that is, that the cash flow this firm was generating in 2020 would continue unchanged for the indefinite future, the present of that series value could be calculated using this formula:

**Present value of a fixed perpetuity =
annual cash flow / discount rate**

You may feel it is counterintuitive to put a finite value on an infinite series of payments, but perhaps the following example will make this seem more reasonable. How much would you pay for the right to receive $10,000 per year forever? Suppose you put $100,000 in a bank account paying 10% and instructed that bank to send you your interest at the end of each year and roll over the principal to the next year. For a single $100,000 payment, you could receive $10,000 per year forever. That is assuming the bank continued to exist and to follow your instructions, and that 10% continued to be the correct interest rate. Applying the perpetuity formula you see that at a discount rate of 10% the present value of a cash flow $10,000 per year forever is $10,000/.10 or $100,000.

Present Value of a Growth Perpetuity

In this example is it unrealistic to assume that cash flow would remain indefinitely at the year 2020 level. If you can estimate the rate at which these cash flows grow, you can calculate the present value of a growth perpetuity using this formula:

Present value of a growth perpetuity = annual cash flow / (discount rate – growth rate)

Subtracting the growth rate from the discount rate makes the denominator of this fraction smaller, and therefore the present value is larger. The larger the assumed growth rate, the greater the present value of this cash flow series. The formula in cell I20 of this spreadsheet is =+I17/(D32-D33). That formula divides the 2020 cash flows of $472 million by the 12% weighted average cost of capital minus the 4% growth rate. The result is an estimate that at the end of 2019 this firm's value will be $5.897 billion. Because that is the value at the end of 2019, you need to convert it to today's present value by dividing by $(1+i)^t$. The formula in cell J22 is =I21/(1+D32)^7. The Excel symbol for exponentiation, raising a number to a power, is ^. A recent survey of corporate financial professionals revealed that the perpetuity growth model is the approach most frequently used to estimate the terminal or continuing value of a project or other strategic investment.[3] The present value of this firm's business operations is therefore estimated in cell J24 to be $4.306 billion. That is the sum of present value of the cash flows during the initial time horizon (cell J20) and the present value of the terminal value (cell J22). If this firm has cash or marketable securities in an amount greater than what is needed to support the firm's business operations, this excess cash represents additional real value to the acquirer. When this amount is added to the value of the firm's operations, you see that the value of the firm is $5.406 billion. Firm value minus liabilities is the value of the equity in this firm. Dividing the $4.555 billion equity value by the number of shares of stock outstanding yields a price per share of $26.03. Acquisitions are, of course, a negotiation process, and $26.03 per share is the maximum that one would pay. The initial offer would almost certainly be much below that.

Stand-Alone Value Plus Synergies Minus Deal Costs Equals Acquisition Value

The previous example considered only the stand-alone value of the potential acquisition. Anticipated synergies between the purchasing company and the acquired company are often a primary motivation for undertaking an acquisition. Synergies may increase revenues and/or decrease costs. The acquired company's sales may increase because its products are now marketed through the distribution networks of the purchasing company or because they benefit from association with the purchasing company's brand. The sales of the purchasing company might increase because the products of the acquired company fill out its product line providing greater access to those customers who prefer a full-service vendor. Cost reductions can result from economies of scale. The combined firms may not need two full scale finance departments, HR departments, IT departments, and so on. These cost-reducing restructurings can, of course, be difficult for the individuals involved even when they make the combined organization more efficient. In addition to improving cash flow, acquisitions also have the potential to decrease the riskiness (volatility) in the cash flow of the combined firm. Having a diversified portfolio of products will reduce volatility by the greatest amount when the cash flow from different products are negatively correlated. For example, aggregate cash flow volatility is reduced if the firm has some products that do well when energy prices are high and other products that do well when energy prices are low.

The spreadsheet reproduced in Exhibit 9-8 illustrates that an acquisition's value is its stand-alone value plus the value of synergies achieved, minus the price paid and related deal costs. This summary spreadsheet utilizes stand-alone and synergy cash flow projections that were estimated through a process similar to that described in Exhibit 9-7. The synergy cash flow is negative in the first year because substantial one-time restructuring costs were anticipated. Unlike the example in Exhibit 9-7 where the transaction involved purchasing the stock of the acquired company, this example assumes the assets within one division of a corporation are being purchased. In an asset purchase, the purchasing firm does not assume responsibility for the liabilities of the division or company being acquired. This spreadsheet models a $4 billion purchase price plus $120 million in deal costs spread over 3 years. The net present value of the cash flow shown on Row 10 is calculated in cell B12. The approach is exactly the same as the one used in Exhibit 9-7. The formula in cell B12 is =NPV(C16,B10:H10)+(I10/(C16-C17)). If all these assumptions turned out to be correct, the acquisition would add $740 million in shareholder value.

	A	B	C	D	E	F	G	H	I
1	**NPV of a Strategic Acquisition**								
2	($ in Millions)	2013	2014	2015	2016	2017	2018	2019	2020
3									
4	Stand-Alone Cashflows	$ 113	$ 119	$ 125	$ 131	$ 138	$ 145	$ 152	$ 160
5									
6	Cash Flows from Synergies	$ (63)	$ 8	$ 8	$ 12	$ 16	$ 18	$ 20	$ 21
7									
8	Price Pay-Out + Deal Costs	$ 2,120	$ 1,000	$ 1,000					
9									
10	Stand Alone + Synergies - Price - Deal Costs	$ (2,070)	$ (873)	$ (867)	$ 143	$ 154	$ 163	$ 172	$ 181
11									
12	NPV of Acquisition	$740							
13									
14									
15	Assumptions:								
16	Weighted average cost of capital is	10%							
17	Beginning in 2020, annual growth in FCF will be	5%							
18	* Perpetual growth terminal value calculated as [FCF in 2020 / WACC - g]								

Exhibit 9-8 The pursuit of synergies can motivate M&A activity.

Weak Assumptions or Weak Execution?

Unfortunately, the empirical evidence suggests most acquisitions don't create much, if any, value for the acquiring company's shareholders. A study by the consulting firm McKinsey and Company looked at 1,415 acquisitions from 1997 through 2009. Its conclusion was that roughly one-third created value, one-third did not, and for the final third, the empirical results were inconclusive.[4] Why do so many acquisitions fail to achieve the benefits projected by models such as the ones previously illustrated? It's not because of flaws in the logic of these models. It's because either the assumptions plugged into these models were unrealistic or firms could not execute on the activities required to achieve these outcomes. Estimating a target company's current worth is always difficult, and projecting the synergies an acquisition will create is even more problematic. Cost reduction synergies may be relatively easy to quantify and deliver. Sales growth synergies are harder to project and attain. An acquisition that would not make economic sense without the projected synergies is a high-risk acquisition.

HR managers in their strategic partner role can greatly influence the likelihood that M&A activity leads to true value creation. HR's initial point of influence is in the design of a compensation system that rewards managers for pursuing value creating acquisitions without encouraging them to take excessive risks. This challenge is discussed in Chapter 12, "Creating Value and Rewarding Value Creation." HR plays a key role during the due diligence phase of the acquisition planning. Determining the value of the targeted company's workforce is an essential task that most investment bankers are unqualified to perform. Projecting the workforce restructuring costs and synergies is also an area in which substantial input from HR managers will be needed. Post-merger HR must, of course, play a central role in the merging of the workforces, systems, and cultures. This last step can be the primary determinant of whether an acquisition succeeds or fails. To function in these critical roles, HR managers must understand the firm's business strategy, the acquisition strategy, and the basics of the financial models used to evaluate the acquisition. This chapter has provided illustrations of the types of models you are likely to encounter. HR managers should not underestimate their ability to understand these models and to contribute to discussions of M&A plans or other strategic initiatives. Constructing these models will be done by the finance group. It has the easy job. The difficult task is determining the correct assumptions to plug in to these models. That's an area in which HR can make a huge contribution.

10

Equity-Based Compensation: Stock and Stock Options

During the 1980s, the pay packages of top executives were often unrelated to the success of the corporations they managed. How could that have occurred when their compensation consisted of salaries plus bonuses that were paid only if certain financial targets were achieved? In fact, CEOs received about 50% of their pay in the form of bonuses. The assumption was that the total compensation (salary plus bonus) received by these executives would be highly correlated with changes in company performance. The empirical data, however, failed to support that assumption. A frequently cited 1990 *Harvard Business Review* article by Michael C. Jensen and Kevin J. Murphy reported an extensive statistical analysis showing that annual changes in executive compensation did not reflect changes in corporate performance. Even though bonuses represented a large proportion of total compensation, Jensen and Murphy concluded that compensation for CEOs was "no more variable than compensation for hourly and salaried employees."[1] They and others argued for more aggressive pay-for-performance systems. Heeding this call, in the early 1990s corporate boards began to emphasize the creation of shareholder value. Equity compensation—that is, paying in stock and stock options—was seen as the most direct way to align shareholder interests and financial interests of managers. The use of equity compensation, particularly the granting of stock options, expanded dramatically during the 1990s. By 2003, 99% of large U.S. public corporations were granting stock options.[2]

How Do Stock Options Work?

Before looking at the specific characteristics of employee stock options, it may be helpful to review the use of exchange traded options. These are options publicly traded on a regulated exchange. These stock options are contracts that guarantee the option's owner the right to either buy or sell the underlying stock at a specified price during a specified time period. The key point is that the option owner has the right, but not the obligation, to make this transaction. A call option provides the right to purchase a share of stock, that is, to call it in. A put option provides the right to sell a share of stock, that is, to put it to the other person. Now look first at a real estate analogy to see why one person might sell an option and another might purchase an option. Suppose you want to buy my house but only if your company transfers you to central New Jersey. We could sign a contract giving you the right to buy my home for a specified price, say $500,000, anytime during the next 12 months. That contract would require me to sell you my home if you decide to go forward with the deal but would not require you to purchase it if you chose not to. Why would I agree to take my home off the market for 12 months waiting for you to make a decision? I would do that only if you paid me some negotiated amount, say $10,000, to purchase that call option on my house. If you decided not to go through with the deal, I would keep your $10,000 and put my house back on the market. Stock options are similar in that the option purchasers pay for the right to make a transaction at a future date if they decide it is in their interest to do so. The option sellers receive a fee for agreeing to those terms. The amount paid to purchase an option is usually referred to as the *premium*.

What Is the Intrinsic Value of an Option? What's the Time Value of an Option?

For a call option, the *intrinsic value* is the current stock price minus the exercise price. The *exercise price* is the price at which you have the right to exercise your option to purchase the stock. If a stock is currently selling for $45 and you have the right to buy it for $30, the intrinsic or minimum value of this option is $15. You could make a $15 profit by purchasing the stock at $30 and immediately reselling it at the current market price of $45. Why might the price of an option be greater than this minimum value? The possibility that the stock price could rise prior to the date the option expires makes its market value greater than its intrinsic value. If potential option buyers believe this stock's price will rise above $45 before the option expires, they will be willing to pay more than $15 for the option. In fact, an option with an intrinsic value of zero (for example, the right to buy any time during the next year for $80 a share a stock that is currently selling for $80 a share) could have a market value well above zero. The portion of an option's value attributable to the amount of time remaining before the option expires is referred to as the *time value* of that option.

Exchange Traded Options Are Sometimes Referred to as Listed Options

Exchange traded options are options traded on a regulated exchange that standardizes the contracts so that the underlying asset, quantity, expiration date, and strike price are known in advance. For example, Exhibit 10-1 shows the June 14, 2012, market price of call and put options on shares of Johnson & Johnson stock. On that date Johnson & Johnson stock was selling for $66.01 per share. The table shows the cost of purchasing call options with exercise prices (also called strike prices) ranging from $40 per share to $90 per share. For example, the market price of an option to purchase one share of J&J stock for $75.00 was $1.05. Why would anyone pay a $1.05 for the right to buy J&J stock at $75.00 when it was currently available for $66.01? You would buy that call option only if you believed that prior to the option's expiration on the third Friday of June 2013, the J&J stock price would exceed $76.05 (the $75.00 you would pay for the stock plus the $1.05 you have already paid for the option). Suppose, for example, prior to the option's expiration, the J&J stock price reaches $95.00. You could exercise your option to purchase the stock at $75.00 and then immediately resell it for $95.00. That $20.00 gain minus the $1.05 you paid for the option would leave you with a net profit of $18.95. If, on the other hand, on the day the option expired, the J&J stock price were below $75, you would let the option expire unexercised. There is an analogous case of buying a put option. You would pay $16 for the option to sell one share of J&J stock at $75 if you thought prior to the options expiration the J&J stock price would fall below $59 per share. If, for example, it fell to $40 per share, you could buy it at that price and then exercise your option to sell it at $75. Your profit would be $19 per share, the $35 per share gain minus the $16 you paid for the put option. You can profit from call options when the price of a stock goes up and from put options when the price of a stock goes down.

Price on June 14, 2012, of one share of Johnson & Johnson (JNJ) stock was $66.01.

Price on June 14, 2012, of calls & puts on JNJ stock expiring January 18, 2014.

STRIKE PRICE	Call	Put
$ 40.00	$ 26.00	$ 0.60
$ 45.00	$ 18.10	$ 0.80
$ 50.00	$ 15.75	$ 1.43
$ 55.00	$ 11.40	$ 2.26
$ 60.00	$ 7.35	$ 3.80
$ 65.00	$ 4.23	$ 6.30
$ 67.50	$ 3.05	$ 9.90
$ 70.00	$ 2.19	$ 11.90
$ 75.00	$ 1.05	$ 16.00
$ 80.00	$ 0.43	$ 21.00
$ 85.00	$ 0.42	$ 22.95
$ 90.00	$ 0.13	$ 28.15

Exhibit 10-1 Example of exchange traded options

Source: http://investing.money.msn.com/investments/equity-options?symbol=us%3ajnj.

Are Options High-Risk Investments?

Are options high-risk investments? The answer to that question (and the answer to most questions) is, "It depends." *Naked options* is the term used to describe trades in which the option purchaser does not also own shares of the underlying stock. Naked options can be extremely risky investments. Suppose the price of company X stock fell from $40 a share to $36 a share. If you had purchased $100,000 worth of stock when the price was at $40, you would have a 10% loss, but your investment would still be worth $90,000. What would your investment be worth if you had instead invested your $100,000 in options to buy company X stock at $40 per share? It would be worthless if on the day those options expired the stock price was $36. For the same movement in the stock price, the stock investment declined by 10% and the options investment declined by 100%. Covered options, on the other hand, can be a risk-reducing instrument. Covered options refer to trades in which the option buyer also owns shares of the underlying stock. Suppose you own 1,000 shares of Apple stock worth $700,000. You plan to retire in 1 year and are concerned that if the Apple stock price drops dramatically, your retirement will be much less comfortable. If you purchased for $8.00 each 1,000 put options giving you the option to sell 1,000 shares of Apple stock for $700 per share, you have limited your loss to $8,000. If the stock price fell to $350 per share but you have the right to sell your shares at $700, the $8,000 you paid for the put options prevented a $350,000 loss on the stock. You could think of that $8,000 as the cost of buying portfolio insurance. Of course, if the Apple stock price had risen by 10%, what would have been a $70,000 gain would be reduced by what you paid for the (unused) puts, and your net benefit would be only $62,000.

Options Trading Can Involve Many Different Strategies

Clever, but not always successful, traders have devised a large number of sometimes complex strategies for using options. These have colorful names such as Guts, Butterfly, Straddle, Strangle, Risk reversal, Bull put spreads, and on and on. You don't need to understand any of those to design and manage employee stock option programs. However, illustrating one simple one may provide some insight into how calls and puts can be pieced together. A strategy referred to as a *straddle* involves buying a put and a call on the same stock. Suppose Boeing and Airbus compete for a large jetliner contract. You don't have an opinion about which firm will win the contract, but you do believe that as soon as the winner is announced, the price of Boeing stock will soar if Boeing wins the contract or plummet if Boeing loses the contract. If Boeing stock price is currently selling for $75 per share, you could bet on that anticipated volatility by simultaneously buying calls giving you the right to purchase Boeing stock at $75 and puts giving you the right to sell Boeing stock at $75 a share. If the calls cost you, for example, $3 each and the puts $2 each, you have invested $5 per share to create this trade. If the stock moves up by more than $5, you exercise the call and make a profit. If the stock price falls by more than $5, you exercise the put and make a profit. Using straddles you can make money whether a stock price rises or falls, as long as the movement in one direction or the other is large enough.

How Do Employee Stock Options Differ from Exchange Traded Options?

Employee stock options cannot be bought or sold on public stock exchanges. Employers grant them, usually at no cost, to senior executives and sometimes also to non-executive employees. Employee stock options give the employee the right purchase shares of the employing company's stock at a specific price during a fixed time period. Suppose for example, the company's stock is currently selling for $50 a share and the employee is granted the right to purchase 1,000 shares at today's price any time in the next 10 years. If 6 years from now, the stock is selling for $80 a share and the employee exercises her option to buy 1,000 shares at $50 each, she will have an immediate gain of $30,000 ((80 – 50) x 1000). The hope is that the prospect of such gains will create an incentive for employees to behave in ways that will make the firm more successful and cause the stock price to rise faster. Employee stock options are by definition call options because they provide the right to purchase shares of stock. Employee stock options differ from exchange traded options in a number of important ways:

- They are granted or given to employees, so there is no purchase price.

- They are usually nontransferable; that is, they cannot be sold prior to exercise.

- They often have a vesting period, that is, the options are forfeited if the employee does not stay with that firm for a specified period of time.

- They tend to have longer exercise periods than exchange traded options. The average life of employee stock options is often 7 to 10 years. The exercise period for exchange traded options is typically months or at most a year or two.

As will be discussed next, these differences mean that the market price of exchange traded options is not usually a good proxy for the value of employee stock options.

Equity Compensation Can Be Options, Shares, or Both

The graph in Exhibit 10-2 is based on data reported by Frederic W. Cook and Company, Inc.,[3] a large consulting firm specializing in executive compensation. This firm conducts an annual survey of the executive compensation practices of the 250 largest U.S. companies in the Standard & Poor's 500 index. The trends shown in this graph are quite dramatic. In 2003, 99% of these large firms granted stock options to their senior executives. By 2011, the percentage granting options had declined to 70%. During the same period the proportion of firms offering their employees performance shares increased from 26% to 72%. Performance shares are shares of company stock given to managers only if certain companywide performance targets, such as an increase in revenues or earnings-per-share, are reached. The percentage of firms granting stock options may continue to decline, but for the foreseeable future, it is likely that options will continue to be used by the majority of large firms. Stock options are increasingly granted in combination with outright share grants or share grants contingent upon company performance. Possible explanations for the decreasing reliance on employee stock options are discussed in the following sections.

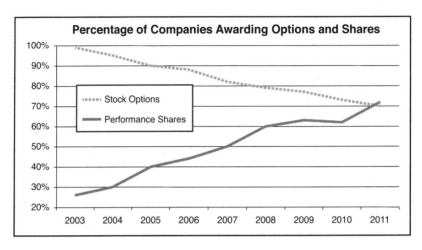

Exhibit 10-2 Trends in equity compensation

Source: Graph prepared with data extracted from the following reports released by Frederic W. Cook & Co., Inc.: *The 2004 Top 250*, September 2004, page 4. *The 2008 Top 250*, October 2008, page 5. *The 2011 Top 250*, October 2011, page 7.

Do Employees Prefer Options or Stock?

What are the key differences between paying in options and paying in shares of stock? If given the choice would employees prefer to receive options or shares? To explore these questions use the specific example described in Exhibit 10-3. The assumptions are that a company whose stock price is currently $40 per share is considering two alternatives. This firm will give employees either A) 1,000 shares of company stock or B) options to buy 8,000 shares of stock at today's $40 price any time during the next 10 years. These employee stock options are valued at $5 each. Is it more expensive to grant stock or options? As this example illustrates there need not be any cost difference. By adjusting either the number of shares or the number of options, it is straightforward to define two alternatives that would have the same cost to the company. If the cost is the same, how would you choose between these alternatives? That choice should not be left to the firm's finance department but should be based on the HR department's assessment of which alternative would have the most beneficial incentive effects. To begin that analysis look at the impact a $20 change in the stock price would have on stockholders and on option holders.

Assumptions: Current stock price is $40 per share. Company will offer employees either A or B.		**Cost to Employer**	
A. 1,000 shares @ $40 each		1,000 x $40 = $40,000	
B. 8,000 options valued at $5 each to buy shares @ $40		8,000 x $5 = $40,000	

Which would cost the company more, A or B?

Which would employees prefer?

Which would encourage more productivity?

	If stock price falls from $40 to $20	If stock price remains at $40	If stock price rises from $40 to $60
Value of 1,000 shares	$20,000	$40,000	$60,000
Value of option to buy 8,000 shares at $40	$0	$0	$160,000

Exhibit 10-3 Does a $40 change in stock have the same impact on stockholders and option holders?

Employees Granted Shares Benefit Even When the Stock Price Goes Down

This example reveals clearly that paying with options is a highly leveraged form of compensation. If the stock price is still $40 at the time the options expire, the value of the 8,000 options will be zero. Had employees received 1,000 shares instead of options and the stock price remained at $40, their equity compensation would be worth $40,000. That's a big difference. If the stock price doesn't change or falls, employees benefit substantially more from a grant of shares than from a grant of options. The situation reverses, however, if the stock price rises. If on the day the options expire the stock price is $60, the employee's 8,000 options will be worth $160,000 ([$60 – $40] × 8,000). The value of 1,000 shares on that date would be $60,000. That's $100,000 less than the value of 8,000 options.

Do All Employees Have the Same Risk Preferences?

Which alternative would employees prefer, and which alternative would create the stronger incentive effects?

The answer to those questions depends upon the personalities of the employees involved and their positions in your organization. Risk-averse employees would probably prefer to receive shares instead of options. For them it may be important to know that their equity compensation will be worth something even if share prices remain flat or decline. Regardless of personal risk preferences, employees at lower income levels may prefer shares because they would be less able to adjust their personal finances to accommodate large fluctuations in the value of their equity compensation. Less risk-averse employees and employees at higher income levels will probably prefer to receive a larger percentage of their compensation as options. These employees may be willing to accept some additional risk to have the possibility of a much larger payout. In the previous numerical illustration, at a stock price of $60 per share, the option holders received a payout of $160,000 compared to the $60,000 benefit they would've gotten from 1,000 shares. That's a $100,000 difference for the same movement in stock price. The difference gets even bigger as the share price continues to climb. At $85 per share 1,000 shares would be worth $85,000, whereas 8,000 options would be worth $360,000 ([$85 – $40] × 8000). At that the price level, the difference is $275,000!

The finance department can calculate the cost differences, but the HR department should be assessing which combinations of stock and options are more likely to motivate and retain key employees. The mix preferred by employees is not necessarily the mix corporations will prefer. HR managers must determine whether increasing the amount of at-risk pay is a desirable compensation strategy in each of the specific situations they encounter. Risk-averse employees might prefer cash over either stock or options, but that would not create the wanted incentive effects. Risk tolerant executives might prefer options over stock. Would a highly leveraged compensation package like that optimize executive incentives to increase performance, or would it encourage them to swing for the fences and expose the firm to unwarranted risk? These are not easy questions to answer, and the analysis of these behavioral issues should not be left to the finance department. For HR managers to participate in that discussion, they must understand the financial and accounting aspects of options so they can make judgments about how employees will respond. The data in Exhibit 10-2 shows a significant and consistent decline in the granting of stock options. What triggered this decline? Part of the explanation may be that firms concluded that the overuse of employee stock options was encouraging excessive risk-taking. That is, however, not the primary reason. The primary reason for this change in compensation practices was a change in accounting practices.

The Debate over the Expensing of Stock Options

The Financial Accounting Standards Board (FASB) in 2004 altered the existing generally accepted accounting principles to require for the first time that employee stock options had to be expensed in the year they are issued.[4] Prior to that time a company could choose to either include or not include the cost of employee stock options along with the other expenses shown on its income statement. If it chose not to recognize the cost of employee stock options on its income statement, it was required to show only in a footnote how large that expense would have been had it been included in its income statement. Sound like a strange rule? It was. Only a handful of major companies (for example, Coca-Cola, General Electric, Wachovia Bank, Bank One, and the Washington Post) chose to subtract the cost of employee stock options on their income statement.[5] Companies were reluctant to expense options because doing so would lower their reported net income and earnings per share. Of course, where on the page you chose to show that expense affects only the reported net income, not the actual business reality. The decision to expense or not expense options sometimes had a substantial effect on a firm's reported bottom line. One study by Merrill Lynch estimated that by not expensing options, companies in the Standard & Poor's 500 index overstated their earnings by 10%.[6]

The FASB decision followed years of debate during which much of corporate America argued that the expensing of options was not necessary because option grants were not a business expense but merely the transfer of an ownership interest from one group of individuals to another, that is, from current stockholders to employees.

If that argument had prevailed, it would have implied that paying in stock was also a nonexpense because it is also just a transfer of an ownership interest from current stockholders to employees. Direct stock grants have always been treated as a compensation expense, and there were no serious proposals to change that practice. The argument for expensing options is that if these equity instruments were not given to employees, they could be sold the public. The price the public would have paid for these options is the opportunity cost of giving them to a firm's employees. Berkshire Hathaway CEO Warren Buffett summarized the case for expensing option well when he asked, "If stock options aren't a form of compensation, what are they? If compensation isn't an expense, what is it? And, if expenses shouldn't go into the calculation of earnings, where in the world do they go?"[7]

Changes in the Accounting Treatment of Options Does Not Change Their True Cost

Now that the expensing of employee stock options is mandatory, firms are reducing the number of options granted. In 2003, 99% of large firms granted options to their top executives. The expensing of options became mandatory in 2004, and as was shown in Exhibit 10-2, the percentage of large firms granting options declined in that year and each subsequent year. By 2011, that percentage was down to 72%. Was this a rational response to the changing accounting rules? There are legitimate reasons to be concerned about the precision of the approaches used to estimate the cost of the employee stock options. Nevertheless, whatever the true cost of granting options is, the change in the accounting rules did not increase that true cost by one cent. If the accounting rules didn't increase the true cost of options, why are fewer firms using them? It seems that the extensive use of options prior to 2004 was not driven by judgments about the optimal compensation strategy but by the desire to maximize reported earnings. Speaking in 1998, Warren Buffet observed, "Accounting principles offer management a choice: Pay employees in one form and count the cost, or pay them in another form and ignore the cost. Small wonder then that the use of options has mushroomed."[8] This emphasis on reported, as opposed to true, earnings was obviously not in the best long-run interest of shareholders. Now that both option grants and stock grants must be expensed, the playing field has been leveled. Firms can now choose the mix of option and stock grants that they believe will create value for shareholders without having this decision distorted by the accounting rules.

Using Black-Scholes to Estimate the Cost of the Options Granted

Now that options expensing is mandatory, firms are paying greater attention to the methodologies used to calculate the dollar cost of option grants to their employees. The choice of methodology can have a direct effect on the firm's bottom line. The price of exchange traded options is set by the marketplace. It is determined by what buyers are willing to pay and what sellers are willing to accept. Because employee stock options usually differ from exchange traded options in a number of significant ways, the price of options traded in the marketplace is not a useful proxy for the value of options granted to employees. Most firms must rely on financial models to estimate the cost of their employee stock options. The most widely used of these is the Black-Scholes model,[9] named for Fisher Black and Myron Scholes, the two Nobel prize-winning economists who developed it. However, over the last few years, a significant number of firms have shifted to alternatives such as lattice models or Monte Carlo simulations. These alternatives are discussed next. Decisions about which model to use should not be left to the finance department. An understanding of employee behavior is required when choosing among alternative models, and the choice of model may influence future compensation strategy decisions. HR managers should be active contributors to these discussions.

The equations underlying the Black-Scholes model are complex, but HR managers without a mathematics background can still achieve a good intuitive understanding of what the model does and how they can use it to design and manage employee stock option programs. The Black-Scholes value of an option can be calculated by plugging a few numbers into a spreadsheet of the type described next. The Black-Scholes model estimates the present value of the expected payoff an employee will receive from an options grant. The logic and calculation of present values is discussed in Chapter 7, "Capital Budgeting and Discounted Cash Flow Analysis." The expected payoff is just the average payoff that an individual would receive if she purchased (or was granted) an option with these characteristics on many occasions. If you go to a casino and play a game where there is a 30% chance of winning $50 and a 70% chance of losing $25, the expected payoff is −$2.50 (.30 × $50 + .70 × −$25). If you played that game 1,000 times, your average outcome would be close to a loss of $2.50 per play. That expected payoff was calculated by multiplying each of the possible outcomes by the probability that outcome would occur and then summing those products. As you see next, the Black-Scholes model estimates all the possible payoffs from an option and the probability that each of those payoffs will occur. It then uses that information to calculate an expected payoff and expresses that expected payoff in present value terms.

The Black-Scholes model estimates the range of potential payoffs to an option by assuming that on average the price of the underlying stock will increase at the risk-free interest rate. The risk-free interest rate is the rate you could earn on a riskless investment such as U.S. government bonds. This assumption is illustrated in Exhibit 10-4. If the annual risk-free interest rate is 5%, the assumption is that stocks that trade at $38 a share at the beginning of the year will on average trade at $40 ($38 × 1.05) at year's end. Of course, that number is only an average. Roughly one-half the time, the price will be greater than $40 and roughly one-half the time less than $40. The distribution of possible stock prices around the expectation of $40 is represented by the curve in Exhibit 10-4. The specific shape of the curve assumed by the Black-Scholes is a lognormal distribution. This is just a variation on the normal or bell-shaped curve that you may be familiar with. Important characteristics of lognormal distributions are that they do not include values below zero and are skewed to the right. That makes sense because a stock's price can never fall below zero and has no fixed limit on the upside. The distribution is skewed to the right because a stock's price can drop only 100% but can rise by more than 100%. Because the distribution is skewed to the right, the mean of the distribution ($40) is slightly to the right of the dotted vertical line.

Stock prices slightly above or slightly below the mean are assumed to be more likely to occur than prices far above or far below the mean. In this example, stock prices between $40 a share and $50 a share are more likely to occur than prices between $50 and $60. Prices between $50 and $60 a share are more likely than prices between $60 and $70. Prices above $70 (or below $20) are possible but have an even lower likelihood of occurring. How rapidly the probability of occurrence drops off as the price deviates from the mean is determined by what statisticians call *the standard deviation of the distribution*. Roughly speaking the standard deviation is just the average deviation around the mean stock price. In this example, a low standard deviation would mean prices cluster tightly around the expected value of $40. A large standard deviation would mean prices are spread out over a much larger range. The simplest way to calculate the standard deviation in a stock's price is to use past history. Some analysts, however, prefer to use an estimate of what future price volatility will be. After you have an estimate of the mean stock price and standard deviation of the distribution, you can use the known properties of the lognormal distribution to calculate the probability of each possible stock price occurring. In Exhibit 10-4 that probability is shown graphically as the height of the curve at each stock price.

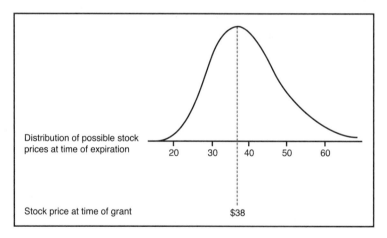

Exhibit 10-4 Log-normal curve to describe distribution of possible future stock prices

You can then convert your estimate of the distribution of possible stock prices at the time of exercise into an estimate of the distribution of possible option payoffs. For example, if the exercise price is $38 and the stock price at expiration is $50, the value of the option is $12

($50 – $38). And analogous calculation could be done for all possible stock prices. Of course, for all stock prices below the exercise price of $38, the value of the option will be zero. There is no value to having the right to buy something at $38 that is selling in the public market-place for less than that. Weighting each of these possible payoffs by the probability that it will occur, you can calculate the average payoff you would receive if you purchased an option like this many times. That average or expected payoff, when expressed in present value terms, is the value to the employee and the cost to the employer of this option grant. The cost per option would then be multiplied by the number of options granted to determine the total cost.

Understanding the Inputs to the Black-Scholes Model

The original Black-Scholes model did not take dividends into consideration. An extension of the original model proposed by Robert Merton in 1973[10] does incorporate the impact on option prices of dividend payments. It is this version that is most often used to price employee stock options. Fortunately, you do not need to master or even understand the Black-Scholes-Merton equations shown in Exhibit 10-5 to effectively use this model. Most corporations purchase commercial software to do these calculations on a large scale, but a quick Internet search would reveal numerous, free online calculators for determining the Black-Scholes value of a stock option. If you are willing to do a little typing, you can easily create your own Black-Scholes spreadsheet by following the model shown in Exhibit 10-6. The inputs describing the option are entered on Row 3. To calculate the Black-Scholes value based on these inputs, type in the following formulas:

in cell B6: =(LN(B3/C3)+(D3-G3+F3^2/2)*E3)/ (F3*SQRT(E3))

in cell C6: =B6-F3*SQRT(E3)

in cell D6: =NORMSDIST(B6)

in cell E6: =NORMSDIST(C6)

in cell D8: =D6*B3*EXP(-G3*E3)-E6*C3*EXP(-D3*E3)

$C = Se^{-qT}N(d_1) - (Xe^{-rT}N(d_2)$

where:

$d1 = [\ln(S/X) + (r - q + \sigma^2/2)T] / \sigma\sqrt{T}$
$d2 = d1 - \sigma\sqrt{T}$
$C =$ price of the call option
$S =$ price of the underlying stock
$N(d) =$ probability that a random draw from a standard normal distribution will be less than d
$q =$ dividend yield
$X =$ exercise price
$r =$ the continuously compounded risk-free rate
$\sigma =$ standard deviation of the natural log of stock prices
$T =$ time to exercise in years
$e =$ the mathematical constant (2.718282...) which is the base of the natural logarithm
$\ln =$ the natural logarithm of the indicated value

Exhibit 10-5 Black-Scholes-Merton option pricing formula

	A	B	C	D	E	F	G
1		Stock	Exercise	Risk-Free	Yrs to	Standard	Dividend
2		Price	Price	Rate	Maturity	Deviation	Yield
3	Inputs	$ 45.00	$ 45.00	4.5%	7	15.0%	2.5%
4							
5		d1	d2	N(d1)	N(d2)		
6	Outputs	0.55	0.15	0.71	0.56		
7							
8	Black Scholes value of call option is	$ 8.36					

Exhibit 10-6 Spreadsheet for calculating Black-Scholes value on an employee stock option

The six inputs to this model are

• Current stock price
• Price at which the option can be exercised
• Risk-free interest rate
• Years to maturity or expected life of the option
• Standard deviation in the price of the underlying stock
• Dividend yield on the underlying stock.

By adjusting each of these inputs up and down in the previous spreadsheet, you can quickly see the impact they have on the estimate of the options value. If you understand what makes an option valuable, you should not be surprised which changes increase the option's value and which lower it.

- **Stock price and exercise price:** The value of the option increases when the amount by which the current stock price exceeds the exercise price increases. The right to buy shares at $45 is more valuable when the current stock price is $65 than when the current stock price is $55. Employee stock options are typically granted with an exercise price equal to the current stock price. Their value depends upon how much the company's stock prices will rise in the future.

- **Risk-free interest rate:** The value of an option increases when the interest rate increases. One benefit of an option is that you get to hold onto your money until the option is exercised. If you buy 1,000 shares today at $45, you must immediately pay out $45,000. If you have the option to buy those same shares at the same price 7 years from now, you get to hold onto your $45,000 for an extra 7 years. The benefit from holding onto your $45,000 for 7 years depends on interest rates. The higher the interest rate, the more you can earn on your money during that 7-year period.

- **Years to maturity:** The value of an option increases when the years to maturity or the expected life of the option increases. Options have value for two reasons. They enable you to wait to see what happens to the stock price before making a decision about whether to purchase shares, and they enable you to hold onto your money until the option is exercised. Both of those benefits increase as the length of the option increases. With longer options, there is more time for the share prices to grow, and you get to retain your cash for a longer period.

- **Volatility of the stock price:** The value of an option increases when the volatility in the price of the underlying stock increases. Volatility is measured as the standard deviation in annual stock price changes expressed as percentage. A large standard deviation means there are large swings in the price of that stock. A lower standard deviation would mean the price fluctuations remain within a narrower range. For stock owners, higher price volatility means a greater chance of big gains and a greater chance of big losses. For option holders higher volatility means a greater chance of big gains, but not a greater chance of big losses. The value of an option increases as the stock price rises further above the exercise price. However, the value of an option does not change as the stock price falls further below the exercise price. The option value is zero whether on the date of expiration the stock price is $10 below the exercise price or $100 below the exercise price. Option holders benefit from greater volatility because it means a chance for bigger gains without exposure to the possibility of greater losses. The Black-Scholes value of an option is often more sensitive to changes in the volatility estimate than it is to changes in the other inputs to the model. In Exhibit 10-6, if you change only the volatility estimate from 15% to 25%, the value of the option rises from $8.36 to $11.81.

- **Dividend yield:** The value of an option decreases when the dividend yield on the underlying stock increases. The dividend yield is measured as the annual dividend paid divided by the average stock price in that year. What happens to the profits earned by the corporation during the period between the time the option is granted and the time it is exercised? Like all profits, they will either be distributed as dividends or retained in the corporation. If they are distributed as dividends, this value goes to current stockholders, not to the option holders. This will, other things equal, decrease the value of the shares the employee will in the future have the option to purchase. Simply put, option holders would prefer the company not distribute any dividends until they exercise their options and become shareholders.

- **Vesting periods and forfeiture rates:** The cost to the firm to grant employees stock options declines when the forfeiture rates increase. Employees who do not stay with the firm for the full vesting period often forfeit their right to these options. These factors are not inputs to the Black-Scholes model but can be used to adjust the results coming out of that model. For example, if the firm granting the options described in Exhibit 10-6 had a 2-year vesting period and a 5% employee exit rate, the value of the option would be $7.55 ($8.36 × .95 ×.95).

The Input Not Used by the Black-Scholes Model

It may seem counterintuitive, but expectations about whether the price of this stock will rise or fall are not an input to the Black-Scholes model or any other option costing model. Because options can be used to bet on a stock going up or down, the assumption is that the risk associated with any option could be exactly offset by creating a second portfolio whose value moved in the opposite direction. This ability to hedge away all risk allows options to be priced on a risk-neutral basis, that is, without any assumption about the direction of future movements in the stock price. It also allows options to be valued by assuming that the expected return on the underlying stock will equal the risk-free rate interest rate.

Firms Must Disclose the Methods and the Assumptions They Use to Cost Stock Options

The Financial Accounting Standards Board's Accounting Standards Codification 718 on Stock Compensation (ASC 718) requires that all equity compensation be expensed at "fair value." For awards such as restricted stock and performance shares, fair value is the current value of the stock. For stock options and stock appreciation rights, fair value is estimated using an option-pricing model such as Black-Scholes. For stock options that vest over time the compensation expense is recognized over that vesting period. ASC 718 also requires that in the footnotes to its financial statements a firm disclose information describing the nature and terms of its share-based payments, the method of estimating fair value, and the effect of these compensation costs on the income and cash flow statements. The list of specifics that must be disclosed is extensive. Exhibits 10-7 and 10-8 contain only excerpts from the stock option footnotes in the 2011 annual reports of Johnson & Johnson and Alcoa.

The fair value of each option award was estimated on the date of grant using the Black-Scholes option valuation model that uses the assumptions noted in the following table. Expected volatility represents a blended rate of 4-year daily historical average volatility rate and a 5-week average implied volatility rate based on at-the-money traded Johnson & Johnson options with a life of 2 years. Historical data is used to determine the expected life of the option. The risk-free rate was based on the U.S. Treasury yield curve in effect at the time of grant.

The average fair value of options granted was $7.47, $8.03, and $8.35, in 2011, 2010, and 2009, respectively. The fair value was estimated based on the weighted average assumptions of

	2011	2010	2009
Risk-Free Rate	2.41%	2.78%	2.71%
Expected Volatility	18.20%	17.40%	19.50%
Expected Life	6.0 yrs	6.0 yrs	6.0 yrs
Dividend Yield	3.60%	3.30%	3.30%

Exhibit 10-7 Excerpt from the 2011 stock option footnotes of Johnson & Johnson

Source: Johnson & Johnson 2011Annual Report, page 54.

J&J Used Black-Scholes to Price Employee Stock Options

The interpretation of the information in the Johnson & Johnson footnote is relatively straightforward. J&J's Black-Scholes model uses a risk-free interest rate of 2.41% based on U.S. Treasury bonds. J&J says that its historical experiences have been that employees exercise their options on average after about 6 years. In 2011, J&J stock paid dividends equal to 3.6% of the average stock price. The one assumption that may warrant some explanation is the expected volatility in the price of J&J stock. J&J reports that it was estimated using a combination of historical data and the implied volatility from exchange traded options on J&J stock. To find the volatility implied by the market price of J&J's exchange traded options, you can plug into the Black-Scholes formula the market price of those options and all the Black-Scholes variables other than volatility. Then solving algebraically for volatility, you can obtain an estimate of what the market on average was assuming about how much variability there will in the future prices of J&J stock. The disadvantage of using historical volatilities is that history may not repeat itself. The disadvantage of using implied volatilities is that they are only estimates of what may happen in the future. J&J chose to use a blend of the two.

The fair value of new options is estimated on the date of grant using a lattice-pricing model with the following assumptions:

	2011	**2010**	**2009**
Average risk-free interest rate	0.19–3.44%	0.14–3.62%	0.3–2.65%
Dividend yield	0.9%	1.1%	1.2%
Volatility	36–43%	47–51%	38–76%
Annual forfeiture rate	5%	4%	3%
Exercise behavior	45%	35%	43%
Life (years)	5.8	5.6	4.2

The exercise behavior assumption represents a weighted average exercise ratio (exercise patterns for grants issued over the number of years in the contractual option term) of an option's intrinsic value resulting from historical employee exercise behavior. The life of an option is an output of the lattice-pricing model based upon the other assumptions used in the determination of the fair value.

Exhibit 10-8 Excerpt from the 2011 stock option footnotes of Alcoa

Source: Alcoa 2011 Annual Report, page 126.

Alcoa Used a Lattice Model to Price Employee Stock Options

The footnote excerpted in Exhibit 10-8 shows that Alcoa used a lattice pricing model instead of Black-Scholes. Models such as the one illustrated in Exhibit 10-9 are often referred to as *lattice models* because of their lattice-like appearance. Before discussing why an increasing number of firms are shifting to lattice models, it is probably useful to review how these models work. Like the Black-Scholes models, lattice models estimate the present value of the expected payoff an employee will receive from an options grant. As in Black-Scholes, that expected payoff is calculated by multiplying each of the possible outcomes by the probability that outcome will occur and then summing those products. The difference is that in the Black-Scholes model the distribution of possible stock prices at the time of expiration is described by a continuous distribution, the lognormal curve discussed in the previous section. Under the lattice model, distribution of possible stock prices is represented by a range of discrete price points.

	A	B	C	D	E	F	G	H	I	J (Intrinsic Value)	K	L (Present Value)	M	N (Probability)	O	P (Present value x Probability)
1	Current stock price	$40								Intrinsic		Present				Present value
2	Exercise price of option	$40		Year 0	Year 1	Year 2	Year 3	Year 4		Value		Value		Probability		x Probability
3	Expected life of option	4														
4	Volatility of stock price is	25%						101.62		$61.62		$54.75		0.0625		$3.42
5	Risk-free interest rate	3%					$ 80.49									
6	Expected dividend yield	2%						$ 60.97		$20.97		$18.63		0.0625		$1.16
7						$63.76										
8	Fair value of option	$8.08						$ 60.97		$20.97		$18.63		0.0625		$1.16
9							$ 48.30									
10								$ 36.58		$0.00		$0.00		0.0625		$0.00
11					$50.50											
12								$ 60.97		$20.97		$18.63		0.0625		$1.16
13							$ 48.30									
14								$ 36.58		$0.00		$0.00		0.0625		$0.00
15						$38.25										
16								$ 36.58		$0.00		$0.00		0.0625		$0.00
17							$ 28.98									
18								$ 21.95		$0.00		$0.00		0.0625		$0.00
19																
20				$ 40.00												
21								$ 60.97		$20.97		$18.63		0.0625		$1.16
22							$ 48.30									
23								$ 36.58		$0.00		$0.00		0.0625		$0.00
24						$38.25										
25								$ 36.58		$0.00		$0.00		0.0625		$0.00
26							$ 28.98									
27								$ 21.95		$0.00		$0.00		0.0625		$0.00
28					$30.30											
29								$ 36.58		$0.00		$0.00		0.0625		$0.00
30							$ 28.98									
31								$ 21.95		$0.00		$0.00		0.0625		$0.00
32						$22.95										
33								$ 21.95		$0.00		$0.00		0.0625		$0.00
34							$ 17.39									
35								$ 13.17		$0.00		$0.00		0.0625		$0.00
36																
37														total		$8.08

Exhibit 10-9 Example of a simplified binomial options pricing model

Most lattice models assume that the price of the underlying stock will follow a binomial distribution, a type of probability distribution in which the underlying event has only one of two possible outcomes. These models break down the time to expiration into a series of discrete intervals, or steps. The assumption is that at each step the stock price will either increase by a specific amount or decrease by a specific amount. The simplified binomial model in Exhibit 10-9 assumes that the term of the option is 4 years and that each step equals 1 year. Therefore, at the end of year 1, there are only two possible stock prices. The year 2 stock price is dependent upon where the price ended year 1. As you can see in the diagram, this process means there are 4 possible prices at the end of year 2, 8 possible prices at the end of year 3, and 16 possible prices at the end of year 4. Had this model been extended out to the 10-year term of a typical employee stock option, the number of price possibilities at the end of the last year would be more than 1,000. Using this estimate of the distribution of possible stock prices at the time of expiration, you can calculate the expected payoff to the option holder.

If You Want to Know How the Spreadsheet Was Calculated

This simplified binomial model (see Exhibit 10-9) assumes the stock price in each period will grow at the risk-free interest rate minus the dividend rate. The price will then be that amount plus one standard deviation or that amount minus one standard deviation. The formula in cell E11 is =D20*(1+B5-B6)*(1+B4). The formula in cell E28 is =D20*(1+B5-B6)*(1-B4). Analogous formulas were entered into columns F, G, and H. The intrinsic value of the option, the amount of payoff that would be received at each price level, is shown in Column J. That amount is just the stock price minus the exercise price of $40 per share. Because those gains would be received 4 years from now, they need to be converted into present values. That calculation is done in Column L by dividing the intrinsic value from Column J by $(1+i)^t$. The formula in cell L4 is =+J4/(1+B5)^4. Column N shows the probability that each of those values will occur because there are 16 equally likely outcomes that probability is 1.0/16, which is .0625. The present values from Column L are multiplied by these probabilities, and the product is shown in Column P. The values in Column P are then summed in cell P37. The value in cell P37 is the weighted average of the possible outcomes that is the expected payoff from the option.

Why Do Some Firms Prefer Lattice Models over Black-Scholes?

The Black-Scholes model is easy to calculate. You enter the assumptions into a single equation and obtain an estimate of the option's value. However, the Black-Scholes model assumes the value of the input variables (volatility, interest-rate, and dividend yield) are fixed over the term of the option. That's not always the case. More important, it also assumes there is no early exercise, that is, that all employees will hold their options until the expiration date. That assumption is seldom, if ever, true. In practice, firms attempt to incorporate early exercise behavior into the Black-Scholes model by using the average number of years before exercise, rather than the maximum term of the option as the input assumption. Because the Black-Scholes assumptions are seldom perfectly satisfied, the results obtained with that model are at least open to question.

The lattice model is more cumbersome to calculate because you must specify perhaps hundreds of steps in a binomial tree. However, an advantage of the lattice model is that at each step, you can use different volatility, interest-rate, and dividend yield assumptions. The biggest advantage of the lattice model is that you can explicitly model early exercise behavior, and if you want you can model the exercise behavior differently for different groups of employees. The basics of modeling the early exercise are illustrated in Exhibit 10-10. In this example, you do not assume that all employees will hold their options until they expire at the end of 4 years. Instead, assume that employees will exercise their options if and when the current stock price reaches a level equal to or greater than 150% of the exercise price. In other words, the assumption is that when the reward from exercising gets large enough, employees will grab the bird-in-hand rather than continue to hold their options and expose themselves to the possibility that the stock price will fall. In Exhibit 10-10, one of the four possible stock prices at the end of year 2 satisfied this condition ($63.76 > (1.50 × $40). There is a 25% chance that the $63.76 price will be reached the end of year 2. If that happens the model assumes the option will be exercised at that point. The distribution of possible payoff values is adjusted and the expected payoff recalculated. In this example, explicitly modeling early exercise behavior reduced the option value to $7.93 from the $8.08 shown in Exhibit 10-9. The effect would have been larger if the example extended the binomial tree out to the 10-year term of a typical employee stock option. The effect would have also been larger if you assumed that less than a 50% increase in the stock price was required to trigger early exercise. The footnote shown in Exhibit 10-8 indicates that the Alcoa lattice model assumed early exercise would occur when the stock price grew by 45%.

	A	B	C	D	E	F	G	H	I	J	K	L	M	N	O	P
1	Current stock price	$40								Intrinsic		Present				Present value
2	Exercise price of option	$40		Year 0	Year 1	Year 2	Year 3	Year 4		Value		Value		Probability		x Probability
3	Expected life of option	?														
4	Volatility of stock price is	25%														
5	Risk-free interest rate	3%														
6	Expected dividend yield	2%														
7							$63.76			$ 23.76		$22.39		0.2500		$5.60
8	Fair value of option	$7.93														
9																
10																
11						$50.50										
12							$60.97			$20.97		$18.63		0.0625		$1.16
13							$ 48.30									
14							$36.58			$0.00		$0.00		0.0625		$0.00
15						$38.25										
16							$36.58			$0.00		$0.00		0.0625		$0.00
17							$ 28.98									
18							$21.95			$0.00		$0.00		0.0625		$0.00
19																
20				$ 40.00												
21							$60.97			$20.97		$18.63		0.0625		$1.16
22							$ 48.30									
23							$36.58			$0.00		$0.00		0.0625		$0.00
24						$38.25										
25							$36.58			$0.00		$0.00		0.0625		$0.00
26							$ 28.98									
27							$21.95			$0.00		$0.00		0.0625		$0.00
28					$ 30.30											
29							$36.58			$0.00		$0.00		0.0625		$0.00
30							$ 28.98									
31							$21.95			$0.00		$0.00		0.0625		$0.00
32						$22.95										
33							$21.95			$0.00		$0.00		0.0625		$0.00
34							$ 17.39									
35							$13.17			$0.00		$0.00		0.0625		$0.00
36																
37														total		$7.93

Exhibit 10-10 Assumes early exercise will occur when stock price reaches 150% of the exercise price

To summarize, lattice models enable the firm to build in assumptions about when early exercise will occur. If options are exercised prior to the expiration date, that changes the distribution of possible option payoffs. Changes in that distribution alter the average benefit employees receive from these options. That expected benefit is the value of the option used in the calculation of the firm's employee stock option expense. If the choice of the options pricing model affects the estimated value of the options, it also affects the expense shown on the income statement and the bottom-line net income that the company reports.

The lattice models in Exhibits 10-9 and 10-10 are simplifications created to illustrate the basic logic behind these approaches. In practice, the lattice model most often used to value employee stock options is the Hull-White model.[11] An example of the type of lattice models that can be designed following the Hull-White approach is shown in Exhibit 10-11. The simplified examples in Exhibits 10-9 and 10-10 were four-step binomial models. The example in Exhibit 10-11 is a 200-step trinomial model. A binomial model assumes there are two possible price outcomes at each step, an increase or a decrease. A trinomial model assumes there are three possible outcomes. The price will increase, stay the same, or decrease. A 200-step model is one that divides the time between the grant date and the expiration date into 200 periods.

Inputs

Grant date:	01-Jan-03
Exercise price:	95.70
Current stock price:	87.00
Maximum option life in years:	10
Volatility:	30%
Risk free rate:	4.50%
Dividend yield:	2.50%
Trinomial steps	200

ESO Grant Schedule

Results		**Vesting schedule**		
Vesting period (years):	1.5	2.0	2.5	3.0
Percent of grant vested:	40%	20%	20%	20%

Employee category	Options granted	Employee exit rate	Exercise multiple		Details by vesting period				Total Expense
Senior managers	56,000	3%	2.5	Option value	25.16	25.02	24.83	24.64	1,397,889
				Total expense	563,658	280,182	278,084	275,965	
				Expected option life	8.2	8.3	8.4	8.5	
Middle managers	41,000	5%	2.3	Option value	23.36	23.09	22.80	22.51	943,833
				Total expense	383,026	189,329	186,935	184,543	
				Expected option life	7.6	7.7	7.9	8.1	
Professional staff	45,500	8%	1.9	Option value	20.39	20.03	19.68	19.26	907,772
				Total expense	371,070	182,270	179,129	175,303	
				Expected option life	6.5	6.7	7.0	7.2	
Support staff	15,000	15%	1.5	Option value	14.84	14.43	13.94	13.40	214,366
				Total expense	89,050	43,281	41,829	40,205	
				Expected option life	4.8	5.2	5.6	6.0	
Total options granted:	157,500				Total option expense for 1-Jan-03 grant:				3,463,860

Exhibit 10-11 Worksheet from commercially available employee stock option software

Source: Hoadley Trading & Investment Tools website, http://www.hoadley.net/options/develtoolseso.htm, downloaded 8/24/2012.

The Black-Scholes model assumes a continuous distribution of possible stock prices. This distribution is illustrated by the curve in Exhibit 10-4. Lattice models assume a process that produces a distribution of discrete stock prices. This distribution is illustrated by the prices in Column H of the spreadsheet in Exhibit 10-9. However, as the number of steps in a lattice model increases, this distribution of discrete prices becomes a closer and closer approximation to the continuous distribution assumed by Black-Scholes. Using the same assumptions about the option terms and the underlying stock, Black-Scholes and 200-step lattice models such as the one shown in Exhibit 10-11 would yield almost exactly the same estimate of the option's value. Of course, the purpose of going to a lattice model is that it offers the flexibility to use different input assumptions. For each year, you could use a different estimate of the stock price volatility, the risk-free interest rate, and the dividend yield. The biggest difference is that with the lattice models, you can specifically model early exercise behavior and forfeitures due to employee exits. As illustrated in Exhibit 10-11, different assumptions can be specified for different employee groups. A firm's historical experience might indicate that, for example, less highly paid employees tend to exercise their options when the stock price exceeds 150% of the exercise price, but senior executives tend to not exercise early unless the stock price reaches 250% of the exercise price. Unlike the Black-Scholes model where expected time to exercise was one of the input variables, a lattice models such as the one in Exhibit 10-11 calculates the average life of the options based on the assumptions about the exercise multiples and the anticipated movements in the stock price. The Alcoa note in Exhibit 10-8 points out that this is the case.

Using Monte Carlo Simulation to Determine the Value of Employee Stock Options

Most firms still use a Black-Scholes model to estimate the cost of employee stock options. A growing number of firms use either a binomial or trinomial lattice model. A smaller percentage uses a Monte Carlo simulation. Each of these approaches uses a different method to estimate the distribution of possible stock prices at the time of expiration. The Black-Scholes model relies on a single equation that assumes that these prices can be described by a continuous lognormal distribution. Lattice models assume this distribution can be approximated by a series of discrete price points generated through a multistep binomial or trinomial tree. Monte Carlo simulations are the least rigid in their assumptions. These models perform a large number of random trials and observe the price distribution that results. A different application of Monte Carlo simulations was illustrated and discussed in Chapter 9, "Financial Analysis of a Corporation's Strategic Initiatives." When used to evaluate options, Monte Carlo models begin with an equation for predicting the future price of the underlying stock. That equation, which is the same one underlying in the Black-Scholes model, assumes that stock prices follow a random walk. Each period the stock price moves randomly either up or down. The magnitude of that movement is determined by the standard deviation of the changes in stock price. Monte Carlo simulations use random draws from a standard normal distribution to generate a sequence of random stock price movements and then calculate the stock price that would result. Each time that process is repeated, it generates one possible value of the stock price at expiration. That process is then repeated many thousands of times. The average of all these price possibilities is then used to calculate the expected payoff from the option. That expected payoff is then expressed in present value terms.

Dilution, Overhang, and Run Rates

Your CFO may have legitimate concerns about managing overhang. *Overhang* is the aggregate of the equity awards currently outstanding plus those authorized but not yet granted, divided by the fully diluted number of shares outstanding. In other words, a measure of how many shares have been or may in the future be issued through the firm's equity compensation programs. When the overhang is large, shareholders may become concerned the company's compensation practices will result in an excessive dilution of their ownership interests. Motivated by that same concern, companies carefully monitor their run rate, a measure of the rate at which they are issuing the shares under their shareholder-approved equity compensation plan. The higher the run rate, the sooner management needs to go back to the shareholders seeking an authorization for an increase in the share pool. Overhang and dilution are important constraints on the design of equity compensation programs. They should not, however, drive the design of these programs. Stock prices are a function of earnings-per-share. The denominator in the EPS ratio is the number of shares outstanding. Other things equal, if equity compensation programs increase that denominator, EPS and the stock prices will decline. That is the dilution effect that may be a concern to shareholders. However, if equity compensation programs are effective, other things will not be equal. Net income in the numerator will rise by more than enough to offset the larger denominator and EPS and the stock price will rise. Some forms of equity bases pay (for example, stock appreciation rights, restricted stock units, and performance share units) do not result in any dilution all. A brief description of these instruments is provided in Exhibit 10-12.

Stock options: A stock option is a right to purchase employer stock at a fixed price during a specified period of time. An expense is charged based on the option's fair value on the grant date. Fair value is estimated using a Black-Scholes, lattice, or Monte Carlo model.

Restricted stock: Restricted stock is employer stock granted to employees at no cost. It is subject to vesting requirements and transferability restrictions. An expense is charged equal to the number of shares granted multiplied by the grant date market value of the stock.

Restricted stock unit (RSU): Restricted stock units are not stock, but cash payments equal in value to one share of stock. Units do not represent any actual ownership interest and have no voting or dividend rights. The amount expensed is equal to the number of RSUs granted multiplied by the grant date fair market value of a share of company stock.

Stock appreciation rights (SAR): Stock appreciation rights provide the employee a payoff equal to the appreciation in a specified number of shares of employer stock. The SAR's fair value on the grant date is estimated using a Black-Scholes, lattice, or Monte Carlo model.

SARs provide a payoff to the employee only if the stock price appreciates. RSUs provide a payoff to the employee even if the stock price is flat or declines.

Performance shares: Performance shares are employer stock provided to employees if company performance reaches target levels. For Performance shares contingent upon financial performance (for example, EBIT, EPS, and ROE) at the end of the performance period, the expense is adjusted to equal the value of the shares that actually vest. Performance shares contingent upon stock market performance (for example, stock price change or TSR) are usually valued using a lattice model or Monte Carlo simulation. Black-Scholes models cannot easily incorporate the performance contingencies.

Performance share unit (PSU): Performance units are not stock, but cash payments equal in value to one share of stock that are made to employees if specified financial performance or stock performance targets are achieved. For PSUs contingent upon financial performance at the end of the performance period, the expense is adjusted to equal the value of the cash actually paid. PSUs contingent upon stock market performance are usually valued using either a lattice model or Monte Carlo simulation. Black-Scholes models cannot easily incorporate the performance contingencies.

Exhibit 10-12 Alternative forms of equity compensation

Equity Compensation Is One Tool for Aligning Executive and Shareholder Interests

HR managers need more than the ability to read and interpret the employee stock option footnotes in their firm's annual report. To effectively design and manage compensation programs, they must understand the financial characteristics of alternative forms of equity-based pay. In many companies employee stock options now represent a smaller percentage of total compensation. Options are still widely used but often combined with other forms of equity compensation. They are also often combined with cash bonuses tied to stock performance measures such as the total shareholder return. Stock-related measures are, however, only one tool for aligning executive and shareholder interests. The alternative is to replace or combine stock market-based measures with financial statement-based measures of the increase in shareholder value. A range of such measures is discussed in Chapter 12, "Creating Value and Rewarding Value Creation." Both approaches have their own strengths and weaknesses.

11

Financial Aspects of Pension and Retirement Programs

$6,080,800,000,000. That number is the value of the financial assets invested in U.S. private pension plans at the end of 2011.[1] Because it is sometimes difficult to grasp how large a number like $6 trillion is, it may be useful to provide a few comparison points. In fy 2011 total expenditures by the U.S. government, including the military, social security, Medicare and everything else, were $3.6 trillion. Total tax receipts were $2.3 trillion, and the federal budget deficit was $1.3 trillion.[2] It's hard to overstate the financial significance of pension plans in the U.S. economy. How this $6 trillion is invested has a substantial impact on both U.S. and global capital markets. At the corporate level, pension trusts are separate entities and not included in the assets shown on a firm's balance sheet. Nevertheless, pension finance can be among the most critical issues a firm faces. In some large firms the individuals managing their pension trusts are responsible for a portfolio of assets larger than the value of the firm. For example, at the end of 2011, the assets in Alcoa's pension trust were valued at $10.3 billion,[3] and the market value of Alcoa's outstanding stock was $9.2 billion. Lockheed Martin's pension trust at the end of that year was valued at $27.3 billion[4] while its market cap was $26.2 billion. At the individual level, there is no question about the importance of pensions and retirement savings in every family's financial planning. In the United States, there are basically three types of pension plans.

Defined Benefit (DB) Plans

Under *defined benefit (DB) plans* there is a formula established by management or negotiated with a union that defines the pension benefit employees will receive in the years after they retire. These benefits are typically tied to the employee's salary level and/or years of service. Firms pre-fund these plans by making contributions to a common pension trust. There are no individual employee accounts. If the investments in the trust do not perform well, the firm needs to make additional contributions to provide the promised benefits. The investment risk associated with DB plans therefore falls upon employers. DB plans are sometimes referred to as *traditional pension plans*.

Defined Contribution (DC) Plans

Under *defined contribution (DC) plans* employees are not guaranteed any specific level of retirement benefits. A formula determined by management or negotiated with the union defines the amount of the contributions a firm must make to each employee's account while they are employed. Separate investment accounts are established for each employee, and a contribution to this account is typically made each pay period. In some cases the employer contributions are supplemented by required or voluntary employee contributions. If the investments in an employee's DC account do not perform well, that individual will have less money to retire on. The investment risk associated with DC plans therefore falls upon employees. The most common form of DC plan in the United States is the 401(k). Section 401(k) of the U.S. Internal Revenue Code specifies the major tax advantages of these plans. Employers receive a tax deduction for their contribution to the employee's accounts, but those contributions and the earnings on those contributions are usually not taxable to the employee until they are distributed at retirement.

Hybrid Plans

Technically, *hybrid plans* are DB plans because there is a defined retirement benefit and all funds are invested in a common trust.

However, hybrid plans attempt to combine the most attractive features of DB and DC plans. The most common form of a hybrid plan is *a cash balance plan (CBP)*. Under a CBP employees accrue benefits under a fixed formula as they would in a traditional DB plan. Each period the firm allocates pay credits (not actual dollars) to an account in the employee's name. These credits are usually equal to a percentage of the individual's salary. The balances in these accounts are then increased each year by a plan-specified growth rate. At retirement employees receive a lump sum payment equal to the balance in their account or an annuity based on that balance. The investment risk to employees is less than in DC plans because the employer is obligated to pay the promised retirement benefit. The investment risk to the employer may be less than in traditional DB plans because the annual growth rate can be adjusted over time if actual investment returns fluctuate.

The Shift from DB Plans to DC Plans

Exhibit 11-1 shows that in 1975 there were twice as many participants in DB plans as in DC plans. That situation has reversed, and there are now twice as many participants in DC plans as in DB plans. In 1975, as shown in Exhibit 11-2, the dollar value of contributions to DB plans was greater than the dollar value of contributions to DC plans. Today, contributions to DC plans are almost 3 times contributions to DB plans. Most of that reversal is the result of the growth in DC plans, not a decline in the number of DB plan participants. The number of participants in DB plans is roughly the same today as 30 years ago (refer to Exhibit 11-1). Few new DB plans are created, but for years to come they will continue to have a significant impact on the U.S. economy and to be of critical importance to those firms with large DB plans. A number of explanations have been offered for the shift from DB to DC plans. DB plans are often back-loaded; that is, the largest increases in value occur as workers approach retirement. That feature is increasingly less attractive as workers become more mobile, changing jobs multiple times during their careers. DC plans are more portable and in most cases impose no penalty on workers who change jobs. From the employer's perspective DC plans have more predictable cash flow requirements, are not subject to invest risk, and are far easier to administer. Depending on the plan's features, DC plans may also be much less expensive to fund.

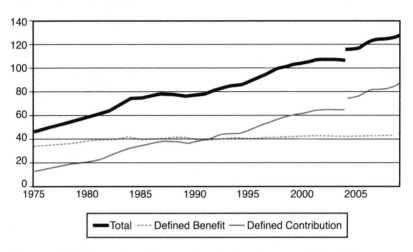

Exhibit 11-1 Millions of participants by pension plan type, 1975–2009

Source: U.S. Department of Labor Employee Benefits Security Administration, *Private Pension Plan Bulletin: Historical Tables and Graphs*, March 2012, page 6. The series breaks in 2005 are due to changes in the USDOL definition of plan participant.

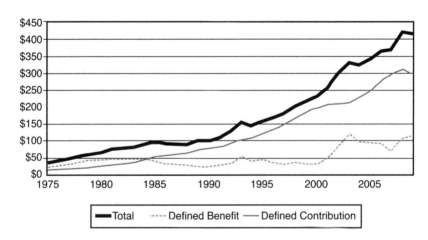

Exhibit 11-2 Pension plan contributions in billions by type of plan, 1975–2009

Source: U.S. Department of Labor Employee Benefits Security Administration, "Private Pension Plan Bulletin: Historical Tables and Graphs," March 2012, page 18.

Pension Accounting

Pension trusts and the firms that sponsor them are separate legal entities. The firm and the pension plan each have their own separate accounting records and financial statements. The following discussion is limited to the way pension costs and pension obligations are shown on the firm's financial statements. The accounting for DC plans is straightforward. The employer's annual pension expense is simply the amount that under the terms of its DC plan it is obligated to contribute to the pension trust. The employer reports a liability on its balance sheet only if it does not make that contribution in full. The employer records an asset only if it contributes more than the required amount. The accounting for DB plans is more complex. FASB Accounting Standards Codification Section 715 Compensation - Retirement Benefits: Defined Benefit Plans (formerly SFAS 87 and SFAS 106) spells out these requirements in considerable detail. Because this book is aimed at HR managers, not accountants, a discussion of these details is unnecessary. Instead, the key provisions of ASC 715 can be illustrated using excerpts from the pension footnotes in the 2008 annual report of Verizon Communications, Inc. Verizon is a global broadband and telecommunication company and a component of the Dow Jones industrial average.

Calculating Defined-Benefit Pension Obligations

Before looking at the Verizon case study, it is probably useful to review a few definitions and concepts. Defined benefit pension plans typically provide retirement benefits that are a function of years of service and final salary. For example, a firm might promise retirees an annual pension benefit equal to years of service × 2% × average salary in last 3 years of employment. Under that formula, an employee retiring with 30 years of service and an average final salary of $90,000 would receive an annual pension of $54,000 (30 × 2% × $90,000). Suppose this employee retires on his 65th birthday and the actuarial tables tell us his life expectancy is 85 years. How much does the firm need to have in its pension trust on the day he retires to have fully fund his retirement benefits? To have fully funded its pension obligation to this employee, the firm must have on hand the present value of $54,000 per year for 20 years. If you assume the annual investment return on the assets in the pension trust is 6%, that amount is $619,376. That amount was calculated in cell G11 of the spreadsheet in Exhibit 11-3 by entering the formula =NPV(0.06,C12:C31).

	A	B	C	D	E	F	G
1	Age	Pension Payments					
2	56		$0		PV at age 55		$345,856
3	57		$0				
4	58		$0				
5	59		$0				
6	60		$0				
7	61		$0				
8	62		$0				
9	63		$0				
10	64		$0				
11	65		$0		PV at age 65		$619,376
12	66		$54,000				
13	67		$54,000				
14	68		$54,000				
15	69		$54,000				
16	70		$54,000				
17	71		$54,000				
18	72		$54,000				
19	73		$54,000				
20	74		$54,000				
21	75		$54,000				
22	76		$54,000				
23	77		$54,000				
24	78		$54,000				
25	79		$54,000				
26	80		$54,000				
27	81		$54,000				
28	82		$54,000				
29	83		$54,000				
30	84		$54,000				
31	85		$54,000				

Exhibit 11-3 Calculating the present value of anticipated pension payments

Now suppose today is this employee's 55th birthday and he is still 10 years away from retirement. How much must the firm have on hand today to fully fund his retirement benefits that will not start for another 10 years? The answer is $345,856. That amount was calculated in cell G2 with the formula =NPV(6%,C2:C31). The amount needed today is less because it will grow for 10 years at a compounded annual rate of 6% before the firm begins drawing on it to make pension distributions. In the jargon of the pension accountants, that $345,856 number is the PBO, the projected benefit obligation to this employee. You can now calculate the PBO for the entire workforce by performing analogous calculations for each of the other plan participants and then summing those results.

You must understand the assumptions that were required to estimate the projected benefit obligation. Those assumptions include the fact the employee would not leave before he was vested in the pension plan, the age at which the employee would retire, years of service and final average salary on the retirement date, and the number of years the employee would live after retirement. An additional key assumption is the discount rate used to calculate the present value of the projected retirement benefits. Clearly it is possible, in fact probable, that a firm's actual experience will differ substantially from these assumptions. Nevertheless, the PBO is your best available estimate of the present value of what the firm has promised its employees under the terms of its defined-benefit plan. If you work with pensions, however, you see that firms utilize three different measures for their pension obligations. These are the projected benefit obligation (PBO), the accumulated benefit obligation (ABO), and the vested benefit obligation (VBO). Exhibit 11-4 shows the differences between these three measures.

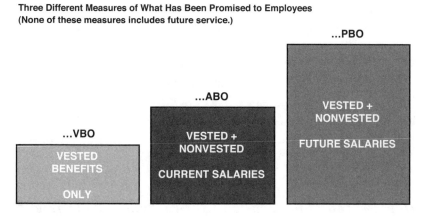

Three Different Measures of What Has Been Promised to Employees
(None of these measures includes future service.)

Exhibit 11-4 Vested benefit obligation, accumulated benefit obligation, and projected benefit obligation

Most DB plans require a specific number of years of service before an employee is vested in the plan. Employees who leave before becoming vested are not entitled to pension benefits. The vested benefit obligation, the VBO, is the present value of anticipated future payments to employees who are already vested. That is the most conservative, the smallest, of the three measures. It is the present value of the pension benefits that have already been earned. Stated another way, it is the present value of the benefits that must be paid if the firm went out of business today. The accumulated benefit obligation, the ABO, is the present value of anticipated future pension payments to both vested and nonvested employees based on their current salaries. The largest of the three measures is the PBO, the projected benefit obligation. It is based on projections of what employee salaries will be at the time they retire. In pension plans in which retirement benefits are not tied to salary level, the PBO equals the ABO.

Corporate financial reporting focuses primarily on the PBO, but the ABO must also be disclosed. The VBO is a measure used primarily by the Pension Benefit Guarantee Corporation (PBGC). The PBGC was created by the federal government through the Employee Retirement Income Security Act of 1974 (ERISA). The PBGC acts as an insurer that provides retirement benefits to participants in failed DB plans. The PBGC is not funded by tax revenues but by insurance premiums paid by the sponsors of defined benefit pension plans. The more underfunded a pension plan is, the larger the premiums it must pay. The PBGC measures the underfunding by comparing a plan's assets to its vested benefit obligation. When value of what's on hand (the plan assets) is less than the value of what has been promised (the VBO), the premium increases. The VBO is the smallest of the three benefit obligation measures, so this process results in smaller premium charges than if underfunding had been judged by comparisons to the ABO or the PBO.

How Do You Think Pension Expense Should Be Defined?

HR managers who do not understand how pension costs are calculated will find it difficult to effectively manage those costs. How do you think pension expense should be defined? Consider the following information describing Verizon's 2008 defined-benefit pension plans.

During that year

Verizon's pension investments lost	$10.7 billion
In benefits to retirees Verizon paid	$ 2.6 billion
	Total $13.3 billion

Some might argue based on that experience, Verizon should have subtracted $13.3 billion in pension expense on its 2008 income statement. Actually, Verizon subtracted no pension expense in 2008. Verizon added in $341 million of pension income! How did Verizon do that? They did it by complying with generally accepted accounting procedures. To understand how Verizon determined that it had pension income, not pension expense, you need to review the information contained in the footnotes to Verizon's financial statements.

Understanding the Pension Footnotes in a Firm's Annual Report

The data in Exhibit 11-5 is excerpted from the financial statement footnotes in Verizon's 2008 annual report. At the end of 2008, the projected benefit obligation (PBO) under Verizon's DB pension plans was $30.394 billion. The value of the assets in Verizon's pension trusts at the end of 2008 was $27.791 billion. These plans were underfunded by $2.6 billion ($30.395 billion in obligations minus $27.791 billion in assets). The difference between the PBO and the current fair value of plan assets is the funded status of the plan. That amount is shown on the bottom row of this table. Note that in 1 year, Verizon's pension plans went from being overfunded by approximately $10.2 billion to being underfunded by more than $2.6 billion—a swing of almost $13 billion in one year!

One of the most important changes brought about by ASC 715 was that in addition to disclosing the funded status of their DB plans in a footnote to their financial statements, firms must include the amount of any underfunding as a liability on their balance sheet. This makes it easier for financial statement users to assess the impact of DB plans upon a firm's financial condition. Verizon included a $10.2 billion pension related asset on its 2007 balance sheet. On its 2008 balance sheet, that became a pension related liability of $2.6 billion. Between 2007 and 2008, the value of Verizon's shareholders equity declined by almost $13 billion for reasons related to its pension plan and not to its business operations. ASC 715 requires that the liability shown on the balance sheet be the underfunding in the PBO. The ABO must however also be disclosed. In a paragraph that followed the table excerpted in Exhibit 11-5, Verizon reported that the accumulated benefit obligation under its DB pension plans was $29.405 billion and $31.343 billion on December 31, 2008, and December 31, 2007, respectively.

Obligations and Funded Status				(Dollars in Millions)
	Pension		**Healthcare and Life**	
At December 31	2008	2007	2008	2007
Change in Benefit Obligations				
Beginning of Year	$32,495	$34,159	$27,306	$27,330
Service Costs	382	442	306	354
Interest Cost	1,966	1,975	1,663	1,592
Plan Amendments	300	-	24	-
Actuarial (Gain) Loss, Net	(154)	123	(483)	(409)
Benefits Paid	(2,577)	(4,204)	(1,529)	(1,561)
Terminations, Curtailments, Settlements	(1,835)	-	(22)	-
Acquisitions and Divestitures, Net	(183)	-	(169)	-
End of Year	$30,394	$32,495	$27,096	$27,306
Change in Plan Assets				
Beginning of Year	$42,659	$41,509	$4,142	$4,303
Actual Return on Plan Assets	(10,680)	4,591	(1,285)	352
Company Contributions	487	737	1,227	1,048
Benefits Paid	(2,577)	(4,204)	(1,529)	(1,561)
Settlements	(1,867)	-	-	-
Acquisitions and Divestitures, Net	(231)	26	-	-
End of Year	$27,791	$42,659	$2,555	$4,142
Funded Status	($2,603)	$10,164	($24,541)	($23,164)

Exhibit 11-5 Excerpt from financial statement footnotes in Verizon 2008 Annual Report

Source: Verizon Communications 2008 Annual Report, page 61.

Other Post-Retirement Benefits

Verizon also provides medical and life insurance benefits to its retirees through its other post-retirement benefit plans. The obligations and assets associated with these nonpension plans are also shown in Exhibit 11-5. At the end of 2007 and 2008, these plans added approximately $24 billion more to Verizon's unfunded obligations. There is one significant difference between the accounting for pension plans and the accounting for other post-retirement benefits. For pension plans, ASC 715 requires that the funded status be measured as the difference between the fair value of plan assets and the *projected* benefit obligation. For other post-retirement benefits, ASC 715 requires that the funded status be measured as the difference between the fair value of plan assets and the *accumulated* benefit obligation. At the end of 2008, the total benefits-related liability shown on Verizon's balance sheet was more than $27 billion ($2.603 billion in pension liabilities + $24.541 billion in other post-retirement benefit programs). That's a number that will get the attention of any CFO.

Pension Expense Is One Component of the Operating Expenses Shown on the Income Statement

The previous discussion considered the pension-related assets or liabilities that show up on a firm's balance sheet. ASC 715 also specifies the process for calculating the pension expense that is recognized on a firm's income statement. As mentioned, in 2008, Verizon's pension investments lost $10.7 billion, and the company paid out $2.6 billion for retirement benefits. Still there was no pension expense shown on Verizon's income statement. Instead Verizon reported $341 million of pension income. How did it do that? It did it by following the requirements of ASC 715. The calculation Verizon used is shown in Exhibit 11-6. The general approach is to sum the components that increase a firm's PBO and then to subtract from that total the return on the assets in the pension trust. That makes sense. Your pension cost increases are offset to some degree by what you earn on funds that are already in the pension trust. The process is, however, a bit more complicated than that. At the beginning of each fiscal year, firms are required to project what they expect to earn on the assets in their pension trust. Financial statements are, of course, prepared after the fiscal year ends, and by that time, firms know both what they had expected to earn and what they actually did earn on the assets in the pension trust. Nevertheless, ASC 715 requires that when calculating pension expense, firms reduce their pension cost not by what the pension assets actually earned, but by what they had been expected to earn. That's done even in a year when the expectation is for large gains, and the actual performance turns out to be big losses. Why do that? Before exploring the logic behind this requirement, it is probably useful to clarify the definitions of the pension cost components, as shown in Exhibit 11-6.

Calculation of Net Periodic Cost (In Millions of Dollars)		
Year Ending December 31	2008	2007
Service Cost	$382	$442
Interest Cost	$1,966	$1,975
Amortization of Prior Service Cost	$62	$43
Actuarial Loss, Net	$40	$98
Expected Return on Plan Assets	($3,187)	($3,175)
Net Periodic Benefit (Income) Cost	($737)	($617)
Assumptions Used in Determining Net Periodic Cost		
Year Ending December 31	2008	2007
Discount Rate	6.50%	6.00%
Expected Return on Plan Assets	8.50%	8.50%
Rate of Compensation Increase	4.00%	4.00%

Exhibit 11-6 Calculation of pension expense recognized on Verizon's 2008 Income Statement

Source: Verizon Communications 2008 Annual Report, pages 62 and 63.

Service Cost

The *service cost* is the increase in the PBO that results from the fact that employees at the end of the year will have 1 more year of service than they did at the start of the year. The plan's benefit formula is, of course, key to determining the size of that increase.

Interest Cost

The *interest cost* is the increase in the PBO that results because at the end of the year employees will be 1 year closer to retirement than they were at the start of the year. For example, assuming as Verizon did a 6.5% discount rate, the present value of $100,000 needed 2 years from now is $88,166 ($88,166 × 1.065 × 1.065 = $100,000). The present value of $100,000 needed 1 year from now is $93,897 ($93,897 × 1.065 = $100,000). The difference between those two numbers ($5,731) is the interest cost of getting 1 year closer to retirement. The service cost reflects the increase in the amount of benefits the firm must pay. The interest cost results from the fact that there is now a shorter period before it must start paying them.

Amortization of Prior Service Cost

Prior service costs are incurred when a plan amendment increases the pension benefits attributable to service prior to the current period. These costs are not charged fully during the year in which the plan change occurs. They are amortized, that is, spread out over a number of years.

Actuarial Loss, Net

To estimate its future pension payments, a firm must make a large number of actuarial assumptions, for example, turnover rates, rate of future wage increases, retirement patterns, and life expectancies. These assumptions are continually reassessed, and when necessary pension cost estimates are adjusted to correct for actual experiences that are more or less costly than had been anticipated. In Exhibit 11-5 this adjustment was to recognize a net actuarial loss. The firm's pension expenses are $40 million more than implied by the earlier actuarial assumptions. Such adjustments can, of course, result in a net actuarial gain. That would occur when the firm's pension expenses are less than implied by the earlier actuarial assumptions.

Expected Return on Plan Assets

At the start of 2008, Verizon expected to earn an 8.5% return on the assets in its pension trust. This and the other assumptions that Verizon was required to make to estimate its pension expense are shown at the bottom of Exhibit 11-6. Multiplying the expected rate of return of 8.5% by the average value of the plan assets in 2008 yields the expected dollar return of $3.187 billion. The calculation in Exhibit 11-6 reduced Verizon's annual pension expense by the amount of this $3.187 billion expected return, rather than by the amount of the 2008 actual return (shown in Exhibit 11-5) which was a $10.680 billion loss. Now say that again. The pension expense was calculated assuming a $3.187 billion gain, whereas the reality was a $10.680 billion loss. The rationale for and the implications of this approach are discussed in the next section.

Why Base Costs on the Expected Rather Than the Actual Return on Plan Assets?

What would be the consequences if the net pension expense on a firm's income statement were calculated as current service and interest costs minus the actual earnings on the assets in the pension trust? Remember that many large firms have pension assets worth billions of dollars. In a year when the stock market rose by say 30%, the actual earnings on a firm's pension trust might be greater than the service and interest costs for its pension plan. In that year the firm would have net pension income rather than a net pension expense. That could produce a big jump in the net profit shown on the bottom line of the firm's income statement. Similarly, in a year when the stock market declined dramatically, the return on the pension assets could be a multibillion dollar loss, reducing the firm's pretax profit by an equal amount. Exhibit 11-5 shows Verizon's actual pension plan returns for 2007 and 2008. These assets grew in 2007 by almost $4.6 billion, but in 2008 they declined by almost $10.7 billion. That's a swing of almost $15.3 billion. Had Verizon's pension expense been calculated using these actual returns, its pension expense would have increased by almost $15.3 billion between 2007 and 2008. That would have produced a corresponding $15.3 billion drop in Verizon's corporate profits for reasons unrelated to the success of its telecommunications businesses. Smaller firms would experience smaller impacts, but those impacts could be just as significant relative to the size of their net profits. Some financial analysts argue that if pension expense were calculated using the actual earnings on the pension trust, the result-ing large swings in bottom-line net income would be misinterpreted by many individuals as fluctuations in the profitability of the firm's business operations. Others argue that calculating pension expense in this manner would lead to more accurate reporting. That's an ongoing debate.

At the moment, current accounting standards require firms to use the approach illustrated in Exhibit 11-6. Subtracting the expected return on plan assets rather than the actual return on plan assets is an attempt to smooth out the volatility in pension expense. The expected rate of return is the average rate of earnings expected over the long term given the mix of investments in the pension trust. If this assump-tion turns out to be correct, there will be just as many years when the actual return exceeds the expected return as there will be when the actual return falls short of the expected return. If over time the better-than-expected returns offset the less-than-expected returns, using this approach will produce no distortion in the firm's long-run pension expense. But what if this assumption is incorrect and the better-than-expected and the less-than-expected returns don't offset each other? To deal with this possibility, the accounting profession created a procedure known as the corridor method.

Corridor Method Used to Smooth Pension Expense

Under the *corridor method* prescribed by ASC 715, firms main-tain a record of the cumulative net amount by which the actual return on plan assets differs from the expected return. For example, if last year the assets of the pension trust earned $10 million more than expected and this year earned $12 million less than expected, the cumulative net balance would be –$2 million. This record is main-tained in an account called Other Comprehensive Income (OCI). If the firm has made a good estimate of the long-run rate of return, then over time the better-than-expected returns and the weaker-than-expected returns will be approximately the same magnitude, and the net balance in this OCI account will hover around zero. It is possible, however, that little or no offsetting will occur and that the balance in this account will grow to either a large positive or a large negative number.

Only when it becomes "too large" does the balance in this account affect the firm's income statement. ASC 715 defines too large as a positive or negative balance whose absolute value is greater than 10% of the size the pension plan. The size of the pension plan is measured as the PBO or the value of plan assets, whichever is the larger number. For example, suppose the PBO is the larger number and is $50 million. Ten percent of $50 million is $5 million. As long as the balance in this account ranges between –$5 million and +$5 million, the difference between the actual and expected earnings has no impact on the income statement. If the balance in this account were to fall to say –$7 million, an additional $2 million pension expense would be recognized on the firm's income statement. If the balance in this account rose to say +$6 million, $1 million in pension income would be recognized on the firm's income statement. The amount by which these balances are beyond the upper or lower limit of the corridor is not recognized fully on the current income statement but is amortized, that is, spread out, over a number of years. A graphical illustration of how the corridor width can change over time is shown in Exhibit 11-7.

Defined-Benefit Pension Plans Hit by the Perfect Storm

The perfect storm label is becoming a cliché, but it does seem appropriate when discussing the status of defined-benefit pension plans. These plans over the last decade have been hit with a perfect storm of economic forces. The demography of the workforce is changing. More individuals are in or are approaching retirement. These individuals are living longer. In manufacturing and other industries in which the workforce is declining, the ratio of retirees to active employees is rising. Since 2000, the investment returns earned on DB plan assets have been extremely volatile and often far less than expected. Interest rates are also at historic lows, which has caused the measures of DB plan obligations to surge. The combination of weaker investment returns and larger plan obligations have made underfunding a serious concern. As shown in Exhibit 11-8, pension plan underfunding in the largest U.S. corporations has grown to record levels. In aggregate these plans were fully funded in 2007 but now have a combined shortfall of almost $355 billion. Of the companies in the S&P 500 index, only 18 have fully funded DB plans. At the end of 2011, seven (General Electric, AT&T, Boeing, Exxon Mobil, Ford Motor, IBM, and Lockheed Martin) had DB plans underfunded by more than $10 billion. The company with the greatest underfunding was General Electric. GE's pension obligations exceeded its pension assets by $21.6 billion.[5]

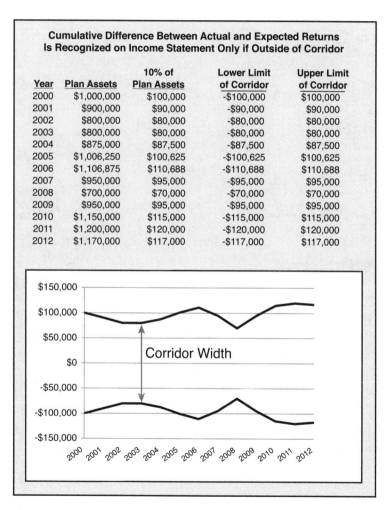

Cumulative Difference Between Actual and Expected Returns Is Recognized on Income Statement Only if Outside of Corridor

Year	Plan Assets	10% of Plan Assets	Lower Limit of Corridor	Upper Limit of Corridor
2000	$1,000,000	$100,000	-$100,000	$100,000
2001	$900,000	$90,000	-$90,000	$90,000
2002	$800,000	$80,000	-$80,000	$80,000
2003	$800,000	$80,000	-$80,000	$80,000
2004	$875,000	$87,500	-$87,500	$87,500
2005	$1,006,250	$100,625	-$100,625	$100,625
2006	$1,106,875	$110,688	-$110,688	$110,688
2007	$950,000	$95,000	-$95,000	$95,000
2008	$700,000	$70,000	-$70,000	$70,000
2009	$950,000	$95,000	-$95,000	$95,000
2010	$1,150,000	$115,000	-$115,000	$115,000
2011	$1,200,000	$120,000	-$120,000	$120,000
2012	$1,170,000	$117,000	-$117,000	$117,000

Corridor Width

Exhibit 11-7 Corridor method used to smooth pension expenses

Pension Plans of S&P 500 Companies			
Year	Funded Status (Billions of US$)	Discount Rate (%)	Expected Return (%)
1999	$280.0	7.44	9.13
2000	$226.0	7.43	9.17
2001	$2.9	7.13	9.15
2002	-$218.5	6.64	8.63
2003	-$164.8	6.09	8.38
2004	-$164.3	5.80	8.27
2005	-$140.4	5.11	8.13
2006	-$40.3	5.75	8.03
2007	$63.4	6.13	8.02
2008	-$308.4	6.29	7.95
2009	-$260.7	5.81	7.83
2010	-$245.0	5.31	7.73
2011	-$354.7	4.71	7.60

Exhibit 11-8   Pension underfunding at record levels

Source: *S&P 500 2011 Pension and Other Post Employment Benefits*, S&P Dow Jones, LLC., July 2012, Exhibit, page 5.

The Impact of Interest Rates on DB Plan Obligations

The Federal Reserve has forced interest rates to artificially low levels hoping that will stimulate the economic recovery. It is clear how weak economic conditions can lower the return on pension plan assets, but how do low interest rates affect pension plan obligations? The projected benefit obligation, the PBO, is the present value of the benefits a firm projects that it must provide under the terms of its DB pension plan. One of the requirements of ASC 715 is that a firm discloses the discount rate it uses to calculate this present value. The discount rate Verizon used in 2008 was 6.5%. The discount rate it used in 2011 was 5.0%. What's the impact of a discount rate reduction of that magnitude? You can easily create a simple spreadsheet to see the impact. The hypothetical described in Exhibit 11-9 is an employee who will retire in 10 years and receive a pension of $60,000 per year for the rest of her life. The formula in cell H7 is =NPV(6.5%,C2:C31) and the formula in cell H11 is =NPV(5%,C2:C31). The drop in the interest rate increases the present value of the pension obligations to this employee from $352,191 to $459,043. As discussed in Chapter 7, "Capital Budgeting and Discounted Cash Flow Analysis," the present value of any future amount rises as the interest rate declines. Suppose the firm's obligation to this employee had been fully funded when that obligation were calculated using a 6.5% discount rate. With no change in the amount of pension benefits the employee will receive and no change in the value of assets in the pension trust, a drop in the discount rate to 5% would mean the firm's pension obligation to this employee was suddenly underfunded by more than almost $100,000 ($413,139 – $316,972).

	A	B	C	D	E	F	G	H
1	**Age**		**Pension Payment**					
2	56		$0					
3	57		$0					
4	58		$0					
5	59		$0		**Present Value of Pension Obligation**			
6	60		$0					
7	61		$0			at 6.5 % is		$352,191
8	62		$0					
9	63		$0					
10	64		$0					
11	65		$0			at 5.00 % is		$459,043
12	66		$60,000					
13	67		$60,000					
14	68		$60,000					
15	69		$60,000					
16	70		$60,000					
17	71		$60,000					
18	72		$60,000					
19	73		$60,000					
20	74		$60,000					
21	75		$60,000					
22	76		$60,000					
23	77		$60,000					
24	78		$60,000					
25	79		$60,000					
26	80		$60,000					
27	81		$60,000					
28	82		$60,000					
29	83		$60,000					
30	84		$60,000					
31	85		$60,000					

Exhibit 11-9 Impact of interest rate on present value of pension benefits

How Do Firms Select the Appropriate Discount Rate?

ASC 715 requires that the discount rates firms use to determine their pension obligations be tied to the yield on high-quality corporate bonds. Because of the actions the Federal Reserve has taken in its efforts to stimulate the economy, interest rates in 2012 are at historically low levels. These low rates increase PBOs and reduce funded status, putting pressure on firms to make larger cash contributions to their DB plans. To ease this pressure, at least temporarily, Congress passed and President Obama signed into law on July 6, 2012, a provision that enables companies to calculate discount rates based on a 25-year average, instead of the 2-year average that had been previously mandated.[6] The average interest rate over the last 25 years is, of course, much higher than the average rate during the last 2 years. Using a higher rate reduces their calculated PBO, and a number of major firms have already begun to take advantage of this provision. For example, General Electric CEO Jeff Immelt has stated that because of the recent law change, GE's cash pension contributions in 2012 and 2013 will be $2.5 billion less than it had previously expected. Sears Holdings has also announced that because of this provision, it will cut its expected 2013 pension contribution by 40% to 50%.[7] Did this increase in the acceptable discount rates actually reduce pension costs? No, it reduced only the calculated PBO. This provision had no effect on the level of pension benefits firms must pay out in the future. It is certainly possible that the effect of reducing their short-term pension contributions will be that these firms must make larger contributions in the future.

Changes in Pension Assumptions Can Alter Corporate Profits

In 2008, Verizon projected that the long-run rate of return on the assets of its pension trust would be 8.5%. Exhibit 11-8 shows that Verizon's assumption was slightly above the 7.95% average for companies in the S&P 500 index. How does the expected return assumption affect a firm's financial statements? The expected investment return does not affect the funded status of a DB plan or the amount of pension liability shown on the firm's balance sheet. The level of underfunding or overfunding is determined at the end of each year by comparing the PBO to the value the assets in the pension trust (refer to Exhibit 11-5). The year-end value of those assets is a function of how much they actually gained or lost during the year. In 2007 (refer to Exhibit 11-5) the actual return on the assets in Verizon's pension plans was a gain was $4.6 billion, but in 2008, the actual return was a loss of $10.7 billion. It is the actual, not the expected, return on plan assets that determines funded status and the amount of the pension liability or pension asset shown on a firm's balance sheet.

The expected return does, however, impact a firm's bottom line profits, EPS, and possible its stock price. Under ASC 715, firms are required to estimate pension expense using the process shown in Exhibit 11-6. If everything else remained constant, making an aggressive (high) assumption about the expected return would reduce a firm's current pension expense. That in turn would increase the firm's bottom line profit. Of course, if the expected rate of return assumption is excessive, the firm will eventually accumulate a shortfall outside of the pension corridor and be forced to recognize an additional expense on its income statement. That recognition may, however, be many years into the future and may not serve as a deterrent to a management seeking a short-run earnings boost. Verizon lowered its expected investment return from 8.5% in 2008 to 8.0% in 2011. A change in that direction would, other things equal, increase pension expenses and decrease bottom-line profits.

De-Risking Defined Benefit Pension Plans

Many organizations are making changes designed to alter the risk associated with their DB pension plans. These changes are motivated at least in part by the recent increases in stock market volatility and the fact that a liability reflecting any pension underfunding pension must be included in a firm's balance sheet. Often referred to as *de-risking strategies*, these actions have as their goal either reducing pension risk or transferring that risk from the firm to another party. Risk reducing strategies are usually implemented through changes in the way the pension assets are invested. A number of firms have adopted a liability-driven investment strategy. These firms begin with estimates of the amount of cash that will be needed in each future year (the liabilities) and then select investments that provide cash in a pattern that corresponds with these needs. That typically means reducing the percentage of pension assets invested in stock and increasing the percentage invested in long-term bonds. The trade-off, of course, is that these more predictable investments provide lower returns. Some have argued that this may be a particularly inopportune time to shift to a strategy of this type because it would mean locking in interest rates that are at historically low levels. There are also variations on this strategy that use complex financial instruments designed to hedge interest rates and wage inflation. The expectation is that these instruments will rise in value if interest rates and wage inflation increase, thus offsetting, at least in part, the increases in pension costs that would be caused by higher interest rates and wage inflation.

Transferring DB Risk to Employees

As an alternative to, or sometimes in combination with risk-reducing strategies, a number of high-profile firms have adopted risk transfer strategies. These typically involve transferring pension risk from the firm to employees and/or insurance companies. For example, Ford and General Motors recently announced lump sum payout offers designed to transfer pension risk to participating former employees.[8] At the end of 2011, GM's pension obligation was $134 billion and Ford's was $74 billion. The offers were extended to more than 140,000 Ford and GM retirees. Retirees accepting the offer would in exchange for relinquishing their entitlement to pension benefits for life be given a one-time lump sum payment. When an individual accepts the offer, the costs to GM and Ford are fixed (the amount of the lump sum), and all investment risk is transferred to the retiree. Investing those lump sum payments, some close to $1 million in value, becomes the responsibility of the retiree. If the investments perform well, the former employees may enjoy retirement income greater than what they would have received under the terms of the pension plan. If the investments perform poorly, the reverse may be true. The attractiveness of the lump sum offer to individual employees depends upon their life expectancy and numerous other factors.

Transferring DB Risk to Insurance Companies

The GM plan also provides an example of transferring pension risk to an insurance company. For those employees who do not opt for the lump sum payment, GM will purchase annuity contracts from Prudential Insurance. These contracts require Prudential to provide the retirees with exactly the same income stream they would have received from GM's pension plan. This device fixes the cost to GM (the amount it pays Prudential for the annuity) and transfers all the investment risk. If Prudential's own investments perform poorly, they may find in the future that they underpriced those annuities. Of course, it's equally possible that Prudential's investments will perform better than they projected.

Freezing DB Pension Plans

Other firms (for example, IBM, HP, and Sears) have chosen to mitigate their pension risk by freezing their DB plans. Data gathered by Towers Watson, an HR consulting firm, shows that of the DB plan sponsors in the Fortune 1000, 56% have at least one plan that is either frozen or closed to new hires.[9] Some freezes enable current workers to continue in their existing DB plan but offer new workers only a DC plan. Other freezes end DB accruals entirely for all workers. Workers do not lose the defined benefits they have earned up to the date of the freeze, but these benefits no longer increase with future work or pay increases. In place of future DB accruals, employers typically offer a new DC plan. Typically, these replacement DC plans do not produce retirement benefit equal to what the workers would have received under the frozen DB plans. The net effect is that with these freezes employers generally have less risk and lower costs. Employees assume more investment risk, and unless they make additional contributions out of their personal funds will in most cases receive smaller retirement benefits.

DC plans Are Simpler for Employers, More Complex for Employees

Why do so many employees save so little for retirement? Part of the answer is simply that they have competing and more immediate needs that must be paid for from their current income. These competing needs place great pressure on many households, particularly those at lower-income levels. Nevertheless, studies in an emerging field called *behavioral finance* indicate that many individuals fail to allocate their financial resources in a manner that would be in their own best interest. One of the reasons for this is the tendency to avoid or at least delay complex decisions. DC plans require employees to make difficult decisions about whether to participate, how much to save, and how to invest. The tendency to put off or completely avoid complex decisions is a major factor affecting 401(k) enrollments. An increasing number of firms address this issue through provisions that automatically enroll employees in a 401(k) program unless they explicitly opt to not be included. Deciding how much to invest is a complex decision, which involves allocating limited resources across multiple goals (for example, providing a comfortable home for one's family, helping a child pay for college, and providing for one's own retirement). Some firms provide access to financial planning services as an employee benefit. Yet even with access to such services, you shouldn't underestimate the complexity of the planning tasks that DC plans impose on employees. Deciding how to invest is the task many employees find most intimidating. Many employees, including highly educated employees, have limited familiarity with alternative investment vehicles and are unfamiliar with the basic concepts of portfolio theory. Still, they will be required to make portfolio allocation decisions that could have a major impact on the quality of life during their retirement years.

Firms May Unintentionally Influence DC Plan Choices

The following is just one of many possible examples of how individual employees might manage their 401(k) assets differently than the way professionals manage DB plan assets. Assume that as shown in Scenario 1 in Exhibit 11-10 an employee's 401(k) plan offers a choice between only two investment vehicles: Investment B that is low risk and Investment C that is high risk. What investment mix should the employee choose? The answer, of course, depends on the individual's financial situation and his risk preferences. Suppose, however, that when faced with this choice, the employee reasons that he doesn't want to do anything extreme, so he puts 50% of his assets into Investment B and 50% into Investment C. To simplify this illustration, assume that the risk level associated with each of the investments in this example can be measured on a 1 to 4 scale. Investment B is a 2 and Investment C is a 3, so under scenario one, the average portfolio risk level would be 2.5.

Risk Measure	Investment A Very Low Risk 1	Investment B Low Risk 2	Investment C High Risk 3	Investment D Very High Risk 4	Average
Scenario 1		50%	50%		2.5
Scenario 2		0%	100%	0%	3.0
Scenario 3	0%	100%	0%		2.0

Exhibit 11-10 Allocation of 401(k) assets for a hypothetical employee

What would have happened if this employee had instead been faced with Scenario 2 (the option to choose among B, C, and D)? Under Scenario 2, would he have perceived Investment C to be the middle ground choice and given his strategy of avoiding extreme allocations, put 100% of his 401(k) assets into C (or equivalently divided his assets equally between B, C, and D)? If so, the risk level of the portfolio would have increased from 2.5 to 3.0, not because the employee's risk preferences increased, but because the range of alternatives offered colored the employees perception of investment C. An analogous hypothesis could be made that offering the alternatives in Scenario 3 would have led to a portfolio with an average risk level of 2.0. Of course, a professional investment manager believing that 2.5 was the optimal risk level could have easily achieved a portfolio matching that requirement under any of the three scenarios. One implication of this example is that firms may be unknowingly and unintentionally influencing the investment choices made by their employees. It is difficult to avoid unintentionally influencing employee investment decisions through the mix of choices offered and the way each of those choices are described. Academic studies using experiments and actual data from retirement plans have documented how the menu of funds has a strong effect on portfolio choices.[10]

Intentionally Influencing DC Plan Choices

One alternative to unintentionally influencing employee investment choices is to intentionally shape those choices. Critics might
argue that such strategies are inappropriately paternalistic, but a
number of firms are adopting plan design features intended to help
employees invest more wisely. The Pension Protection Act of 2006
expanded the ability of employers to implement such features without
fear of legal liability for market fluctuations or other adverse investment outcomes. This legislation sanctioned a new class of default
investments for DC plans, qualified default investment alternatives
(QDIAs). Life-cycle or target maturity funds, which qualify as QDIAs,
require employees to select a portfolio based only on an expected
year of retirement. The fund managers then make the initial portfolio
allocations and continue to rebalance the portfolio until the target or
maturity date. Although devices such as life-cycle funds may improve
investment outcomes for many individuals, there are downsides to
any one-size-fits-all approach. Such funds cannot take into consideration an employee's nonpension assets and financial obligations and
may therefore result in allocations different from those that would
come out of a more holistic financial planning process.

Improving Employee Ability to Make Their Own Choice

An alternative to providing employees with better default choices
is, of course, to increase the ability of employees to make good
choices. A January 2012 survey by the Society for Human Resource
Management found that 52% of U.S. employers offer financial education to their employees.[11] A study of financial education in the
workplace conducted by economists at the Federal Reserve Bank of
Kansas found strong evidence that such programs can improve personal financial outcomes and some evidence that such programs also
provide benefits to the employer.[12] Hopefully, there will be increases
in the frequency and effectiveness of such workplace programs combined with better financial education in high schools and colleges. In
the meantime, the low level of financial literacy among most employee
groups, including those with advanced degrees, is a serious concern
for a retirement system that relies heavily on DC retirement plans.

HR Implications Pension Plan Design

The goal of pension design is not to minimize risk or reduce costs. It is to design a cost-effective component of an overall compensation package that helps the firm attract, motivate, and retain the workforce it needs to successfully implement its business strategy. Doing this requires an understanding of the financial incentives created by different pension plans. Compared to DC plans, DB plans typically provide much stronger financial incentives for individuals to remain with their current employer. To see how these incentives are created, consider the example in Exhibit 11-11. Company A and Company B offer identical defined-benefit pension plans. In both cases individuals beginning at age 65 receive an annual pension benefit equal to their years of service times 2% times their final salary at that firm. If the pension plans are identical, why would an employee moving from Company A to Company B retire with less income? If the employee described in this example worked 40 years for Company A, her annual pension benefit starting at age 65 would be $96,021 (40 x 2% × $120,026). If she worked 20 years for Company A and then 20 years for Company B, her combined annual pension payment from the two firms would be $69,921. Her pension benefits would be $26,100 less per year for the rest of her life because of the midcareer job change. The detailed calculations are shown in Exhibit 11-11. Had the employee remained at Company A for her full career, her benefit would have been 80% of her salary at age 65. Changing jobs would mean that her combined retirement benefit would be 40% of her salary at age 65 at plus 40% of her salary at age 45. Because one-half of her benefit would be based on a lower salary, her retirement income would be substantially reduced.

DC plans such as 401(k)s are more portable and seldom penalize an employee for changing jobs. When firms shift from DB to DC plans, they often lose a powerful retention device. The pension savings that result from the shift to a DC plan may be offset, at least in part, by the cost of putting in place new programs to reduce employee turnover. This may, however, be a good opportunity to target the new retention incentives, for example, bonuses, promotions, or salary increases, for those employees who are most valuable to the firm. For retention, DB plans are blunt instruments creating incentives for both high performers and low performers to remain with their current employer.

Assumptions:

Company A and Company B have same defined-benefit formula:

Annual retirement benefit at age 65 = Years of service x 2%
x Final salary

Employee begins career at age 25 at an annual salary of $25,000.
Employee will retire at age 65 and has a life expectancy of 85.

Salary increases at rate of 4% per year, so salary at age 45 is ($25,000 x
1.04^20) = $ 54,778 and salary at age 65 is
($25,000 x 1.04^40) = $120,026.

* *

If employee works for 40 years at Company A, her retirement benefit will
be (40 yrs x 2% x $120,026) which = $96,021.

If at age 45 employee moves from Company A to Company B, her benefit
from A will be (20 yrs x 2% x $54,778),
which = $21,911.

Her benefit from B will be (20 yrs x 2% x $120,026)
which = $48,010.

Her combined benefit from A & B will be $69,921.

The penalty for changing jobs is $26,100 per year for 20 years!

Exhibit 11-11 DB pension plans discourage changing jobs.

DB Plans Encourage Retirement

For employees in their preretirement years, DB plans create incentives to stay put. However, after individuals reach retirement age, the situation reverses. DB plans are more likely than DC plans to encourage retirement. Consider again the employee described in Exhibit 11-11. If she worked an additional year beyond 65, the amount of her annual retirement benefit would increase to $102,358 (41 × 2% × $124,827). That's an increase of $6,337 per year, and using an 8% discount, the present value of $6,337 for 19 years is $60,862. Remember, however, that she gave up $96,021 in retirement benefits by retiring 1 year later. Postponing her retirement would actually cost her money. Under most DB plans the present value of the retirement benefits received decreases with additional years of service beyond the plan's normal retirement age. This creates a strong incentive for employees in DB plans to leave as soon as they reach this age. For individuals in DC plans, the situation is different. Delaying retirement increases their pension wealth by the amount of the additional contributions received and any increases in the market value of their DC plan assets. Unlike DB plan participants, they give up nothing by delaying the date on which they begin drawing retirement benefits. The funds they do not draw out at age 65 will still be in their account at age 66.

The Future?

It is likely that the shift from DB plans to DC plans will continue. However, for at least a decade or two, DB plans will remain a significant factor in the U.S. economy and a major issue for the CFOs and CHROs in many companies. The International Accounting Standards Board (IASB) has amended IAS 19 to eliminate many of the smoothing mechanisms in pension accounting. Beginning in 2013, non-U.S. companies that operate under the IASB guidelines will utilize the actual and not the expected earnings on pension assets to offset their annual pension expense. This may significantly increase the volatility of reported earnings of these companies. Given the ongoing attempts to achieve convergence between U.S. GAAP and International Financial Reporting Standards, many observers expect that FASB will also move in this direction.

A limited number of U.S. companies, for example, AT&T, Honeywell, and UPS, have already voluntarily changed their pension accounting procedures. These firms have not adopted a full mark-to-market approach, which would mean using actual rather than expected earnings to calculate annual pension expense. They have however given up some of the smoothing mechanisms available under ASC 715. Honeywell has, for example, adopted a modified mark-to-market approach under which it will still calculate annual pension using expected earnings, still maintain the nonrecognition corridor, and still defer losses inside the corridor. Honeywell will, however, in each year calculate the market value of its pension assets and then charge any losses outside of the corridor in the current year. Under current U.S. GAAP, the amount outside of the corridor can be amortized over a number of years. The maximum number of years is the average remaining service of active plan participants. Firms currently have the option to recognize gains and losses faster than required by ASC 715, and that is what Honeywell has decided to do. It's not clear yet how many other firms will choose to make similar voluntary changes in their pension accounting. It is certainly possible that most will wait to see whether FASB shifts U.S. GAAP to something closer to IAS 19.

The provisions of ASC 17 are often described as designed to smooth pension expense. It would be more accurate to say they are designed to smooth the reported pension expense. As the accounting moves away from smoothing the reporting of pension expense, there will certainly be more pressure to smooth actual pension expense. Smoothing actual pension expenses will require adopting DB funding strategies such as the liability-driven approach previously described and replacing traditional DB plans with DC or hybrid plans. These changes will create challenges and opportunities for HR managers. HR managers will need to understand the financing of and financial incentives created by alternative retirement benefit plans to select those that cost-effectively contribute to a firm's efforts to attract, motivate, and retain the talent it needs. Creative HR executives may propose plan features that would not have occurred to actuaries or pension plan managers. For example, J. Randall MacDonald, the senior vice-president for human resources at IBM, has speculated about melding retirement and health benefits into a performance-based 401(k) that rewards better performers with better benefits. He asks, "If everybody gets paid on performance, shouldn't there be benefits based on performance? That's what it means to be a performance-based culture."[13]

12

Creating Value and Rewarding Value Creation

At the time of the last economic census, there were 5,767,306 firms in the United States. Their business strategies differed, but they all had exactly the same goal, value creation. People invest in a business because they believe the value of their investment will increase enough to compensate them for the risk they took as well as for the time value of their money. Companies create value by investing capital at rates of return exceeding the cost of that capital. A company's capability to identify and implement such investments is determined by the quality of its management and workforce. These are the individuals who must develop and effectively execute the firm's business strategy. Selecting, motivating, and retaining these individuals is the responsibility of the firm's human resource management function. For this system to work properly HR managers must understand how value is created in their firm and then use that understanding to design a compensation system that encourages value creation. Enhancing the firm's capability to create shareholder value should also be the primary objective of all recruitment and selection and employee development activities.

Aligning Pay with Performance

Compensation arrangements should provide incentives for employees to execute the firm's business strategy in the best interests of the shareholders and other stakeholders. The Center on Executive Compensation has articulated this mandate more fully stating that

To pay for results, companies and their Compensation Committees must have a solid grasp of which measures will create value for the company and its shareholders. Typically, these measures are directly related to the company's business strategy and thus should be customized for each company. Value may be driven by profits, revenue, market share, new product development, or cash flow, just to name a few, or a combination of measures. The particular measures used may change over time as the company's business strategy and the global economic environment changes.[1]

Appendix A at the end of this chapter contains a list of several dozen financial performance measures currently in use. Selecting the financial performance measures that are most appropriate for a specific company at a specific point in time requires an understanding of the firm's business strategy, a few key financial concepts, and what can seem like an off-putting array of financial jargon. The goal of this chapter is to explain those concepts and decode at least some of that jargon. Hopefully, the following illustrations clarify the economic conditions under which value is created and the challenges involved in measuring value creation.

Isn't It All About Profit Maximization?

Why make this complicated? Why not just tie incentive pay to profitability? Doing that would, of course, require you to decide which definition of profit you are going to use.

Gross Profit

Gross profit (the difference between sales revenues and the cost of the merchandise sold) might be useful as one of multiple performance measures but is clearly not sufficient as a stand-alone measure. A firm can have positive gross profits, but if those gross profits are not large enough to cover operating expenses, interest, and taxes, the firm will have a bottom line net loss. Gross profit might be appropriate as one driver of short-term incentive pay when a firm's operating plans call for improvements in gross margins through increasing sales prices and/or reducing merchandise costs.

EBIT Versus Net Income

Earnings before interest and taxes are deducted are the profit generated by a firm's business operations. Bottom line net income is always the result of two things: the profitability of the firm's business operations and how that business was financed, that is, how much was borrowed at what interest rate. If the goal is to provide incentives for individuals such as divisional executives who can influence operating results but are not involved in how the business is financed, EBIT would be the more appropriate bonus driver. In most firms financing decisions (for example, whether to raise funds through the sale of stock or the sale of bonds) are made at the corporate level without the involvement of divisional managers.

EBIT Versus EBIT per Employee

EBIT per employee is a metric recommended by one of the world's largest consulting firms[2] and used by major corporations.[3] This measure may seem particularly appealing to HR managers because it highlights workforce productivity. It can, however, be misleading. Suppose an IT services firm could get the same output from two programmers paid $100,000 each or three programmers paid $60,000. Which is the better buy? The answer is obvious. There is no reason to pay $200,000 if you can get the same output for $180,000. Exhibit 12-1 shows what would happen if these two staffing strategies were compared on the basis of EBIT per employee. Scenario A would result in lower EBIT and lower net income, but higher EBIT per employee ($220 million divided by 2,000 employees = $110,000). The EBIT per employee under scenario B is less ($240 million divided by 3,000 employees = $80,000) even though this is obviously the better strategy. Consider a different hypothetical. Suppose an auto manufacturer has six welders earning $60,000 per year each. The firm has the option to replace three of those employees with a robotic welding machine leased for $200,000 per year. Automating the welding process would reduce profits but increase EBIT per employee. EBIT per employee is not just an imperfect measure of value creation; it can lead to rewarding strategies that destroy shareholder value. In the examples cited, EBIT would be a much better measure than EBIT per employee.

Suppose an IT services firm could get the same output from scenario A and scenario B.
Scenario A: 2,000 programmers with average salary of $100,000 per year
Scenario B: 3,000 programmers with average salary of $60,000 per year

Which staffing strategy should they adopt?

(Millions of $)	Scenario A (2,000 @ $100K)	Scenario B (3,000 @ $60K)
Revenues	$500	$500
- COGS	30	30
- Programmer Salaries	200	180
- Other Operating Expenses	50	50
EBIT	220	240
- Interest	10	10
Pretax Profit	210	230
- Tax @30%	63	69
NI	$147	$161
EBIT per Employee	$110,000	$80,000

Exhibit 12-1 EBIT per employee can be a misleading measure.

EBIT Versus EBITDA

As discussed in Chapter 2 ("The Income Statement: Do We Care About More Than the Bottom Line?"), EBIT is a measure of operating profit. EBITDA (earnings before interest taxes depreciation and amortization have been subtracted out) is a measure of cash flow from operations. Depreciation and amortization are accounting realloca-tions of expenses incurred in other periods but do not represent a cash outflow during the current period. EBITDA is a widely used performance metric, particularly in the telecommunications industry. If for the most recent quarter, EBITDA in a telecom company were positive, that indicates that during that quarter the subscriber fees charged to its customers were greater than the cost to provide tele-com services to these customers. The cost to provide those services did not, however, include depreciation. Depreciation is the charge that reflects the fiber and electronics costs of building the firm's net-work. After these networks are in place, the cost to provide monthly telecom services is relatively low. So if a telecom firm boasts that its EBITDA is positive, it may be saying nothing more than its current revenues are large enough to cover its expenses if you don't include its biggest expenses (fiber, electronics, and network construction). It is certainly possible for EBITDA to be positive while EBIT is negative; that is, the firm is losing money. If EBITDA were the sole basis for incentive pay, bonuses might well be distributed in years when the firm had large losses. EBITDA does however convey useful information. If EBITDA were negative, cash infusions would be required just to sustain the units operations. Because cash flow management is critical to all firms, EBITDA may be useful as one of several drivers of short-term incentive pay.

Profit per Dollar of Assets: ROA and ROIC

As a stand-alone, measure of performance EBIT, or operating profit, is almost meaningless. Is an operating profit of $300 million a good outcome, one warranting a large bonus payment? If you earn $300 in interest on your bank account, is that a good return? The answer to both questions obviously depends on how much was invested to earn that return. The simplest way to assess the level of performance indicated by a specific profit amount is to express that profit as a percentage of the assets invested to generate that profit. Return on assets (ROA) is usually defined as

ROA = net income / assets

However, as discussed net income is the result of both the success of a firm's business operations and the way it was financed. Net income, the bottom line of the income statement, is after interest expense has been subtracted out. If you want to compare the business operations of two firms before taking into consideration any differences in the way they were financed, a better measure would be the return on invested capital (ROIC). The return on invested capital (ROIC) is usually defined as

ROIC = after-tax operating profit / assets
= [EBIT × (1 – the tax rate)] / assets

The difference between ROA and ROIC is that the numerator of ROA is net income, whereas the numerator of ROIC is after-tax operating profit. Operating profit is, of course, before interest is subtracted out. If you want to know whether the business operations of United

Airlines were more successful than those of Delta Air Lines, before taking into consideration any differences in the way the two airlines were financed, comparing them on ROIC would be more informative than comparing them on ROA. If you want to establish bonus drivers for divisional managers, ROIC would probably be a more appropriate measure than ROA because divisional managers generally are not involved in the financing decisions that impact ROA.

ROIC Compared to the Firm's Weighted Average Cost of Capital (WACC)

What would your gain be if you borrowed money from your brother-in-law at 8% and put it into an investment earning 6%? You wouldn't have any gain. You can use exactly the same logic to determine what an acceptable ROIC level is for a firm. A firm's weighted average cost of capital (WACC) is what it costs the firm to raise the money it has invested in the business. If in a particular year, a firm's weighted average cost of capital were 8% and its ROIC were 6%, it would have created no economic value during that year. Actually, it would be losing economic value in every period during which that situation persisted. If you borrow money from your brother-in-law at 8%, you come ahead only when you can invest it at more than 8%. A firm generates economic value only when it's ROIC is greater than its WACC. ROIC is a widely used performance metric. Chapter 2 and Chapter 3 ("The Balance Sheet: If Your People Are Your Most Important Asset, Where Do They Show Up on the Balance Sheet?") reviewed the financial statements for Home Depot, Incorporated. Home Depot uses ROIC to assess its own financial performance. In a recent announcement the company indicated that it had been targeting achievement of the 15% ROIC by 2015 but now expects to reach 24% by that date.[4] Home Depot's WACC is probably not more than 10%, so an ROIC of that level would represent substantial value creation. How can you estimate the dollar amount of the value created?

Economic Value Added

Economic value added (EVA) is just a firm's after-tax operating profit minus the cost of financing the assets used to make that profit.

The cost of financing those assets is the dollar value of the capital employed times the firm's weighted average cost of capital. Suppose, for example, a large corporation has $200 million in assets invested in Division A. If that corporation's weighted average cost of capital is 10%, it costs them $20 million per year to provide those assets to Division A. That division will not generate any economic value for the corporation and its shareholders unless it produces an after-tax operating profit greater than $20 million per year. If its after-tax operating profit were $28 million, the economic value added by that division would be $8 million. If its after-tax operating profit had been $16 million, the divisional managers might have felt they were entitled to bonuses based on that profit, but that division would have reduced shareholder value by $4 million. When corporations tie bonuses to EVA, the message they are sending is that just making a profit is not good enough. To generate value (and justify management bonuses) a firm's business operations must produce a profit greater than the cost of financing the assets used to make that profit.

Exhibit 12-2 shows EVA can be calculated in either of two ways. You can subtract from after-tax operating profit, the cost of financing the assets used to make that profit, or you can multiply the amount by which ROIC exceeds WACC by the dollar value of the assets employed. Both methods produce the same result. Evaluating corporate performance in this manner is not a new idea. GM used a similar approach in the 1920s. However, much of the current interest in economic value added stems from the work during the 1980s by the Stern Stewart consulting firm. This firm refined the concept and trademarked the term EVA, which as trademarked by Stern Stewart differs from similar measures in that it is calculated using that company's proprietary procedures for making adjustments to the accounting data used to derive the estimates of after-tax operating profits and capital employed.[5] Closely related measures (under slightly different names) are used by many firms. Some use the more generic term economic profit (EP), and some have created their own labels. For example, Roche Pharmaceuticals determines performance bonuses based in part on a closely related measure it calls operating profit after capital charge (OPAC). The commonality in these approaches is that they are all based on after-tax operating profit minus the cost to finance the assets used to make that profit.

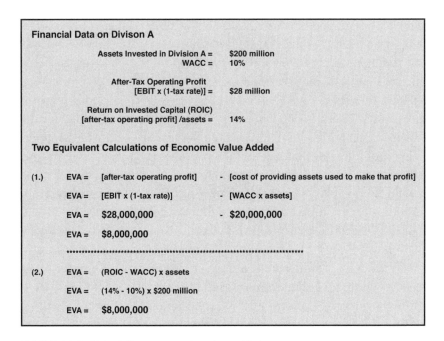

Financial Data on Divison A

Assets Invested in Division A =	$200 million
WACC =	10%
After-Tax Operating Profit [EBIT x (1-tax rate)] =	$28 million
Return on Invested Capital (ROIC) [after-tax operating profit] /assets =	14%

Two Equivalent Calculations of Economic Value Added

(1.) EVA = [after-tax operating profit] - [cost of providing assets used to make that profit]

EVA = [EBIT x (1-tax rate)] - [WACC x assets]

EVA = $28,000,000 - $20,000,000

EVA = $8,000,000

....

(2.) EVA = (ROIC - WACC) x assets

EVA = (14% - 10%) x $200 million

EVA = $8,000,000

Exhibit 12-2 Calculating economic value added

Why does EVA differ from accounting profits? Accounting profit, the net income figure on the bottom line of the income statement, is after subtracting out interest expense. Interest expense is the cost of debt, but an income statement does not include the cost of the equity capital used. EVA is after subtracting a capital charge based on WACC, which is the weighted average of the cost of debt and the cost of equity. It is therefore quite possible for accounting profits to grow while no value is created. Actually, as the hypothetical illustrated in Exhibit 12-3 demonstrates, it is possible for revenues, profits, and even ROE to grow while value is being destroyed. That statement has important implications for the use of revenue, profits, and ROE as bonus drivers.

The firm's revenues and net income grew each year and actually more than doubled between 2013 and 2020 (refer to Exhibit 12-3). The firm's ROE was also increasing and at seemingly respectable levels throughout this period. Millions of dollars in shareholder value were, however, destroyed in each year. Over the period, the total decline in shareholder value was more than 0.4 billion dollars.

That occurred because in each year the firm's ROIC was less than its weighted average cost of capital. In other words, in each year the firm made a profit, but in no year was that profit large enough to cover the cost of raising the funds needed to support the firm's business operations. Many, if not most firms, link incentive compensation to accounting measures such as revenue growth, profits (either EBIT or NI), and return on equity. These firms should understand that all those measures can increase even when no value is created.

(All $ Values in Millions) Year	2013	2014	2015	2016	2017	2018	2019	2020
Equity	2000	2200	2420	2662	2928	3221	3543	3897
Debt	2000	2200	2420	2662	2928	3221	3543	3897
Assets	4000	4400	4840	5324	5856	6442	7086	7795
WACC	10%	10%	10%	10%	10%	10%	10%	10%
Revenue	1500	1650	1815	2100	2310	2400	2775	3174
Cost of Goods Sold	600	660	726	868	954	956	1141	1337
Operating Expenses	400	440	484	532	586	644	709	779
EBIT	500	550	605	700	770	800	925	1058
Interest	100	110	121	133	146	161	177	195
Pretax Income	400	440	484	567	624	639	748	863
Tax	120	132	145	170	187	192	224	259
Net Income	280	308	339	397	437	447	523	604
EBIT x (1 - Tax Rate)	350	385	424	490	539	560	648	741
- Capital Charge	400	440	484	532	586	644	709	779
= EVA	-50	-55	-61	-42	-47	-84	-61	-39
ROE	14%	14%	14%	15%	15%	14%	15%	16%
ROIC	8.8%	8.8%	8.8%	9.2%	9.2%	8.7%	9.1%	9.5%

Exhibit 12-3 Revenues, profits, and ROE increased while value was destroyed.

Hoping to avoid situations such as the one just described, some firms have chosen to link incentive compensation to the dollar value of EVA, whereas others have chosen to link it to the amount by which ROIC exceeds WACC. For example, Kaiser Aluminum Corp. reports that its 2011 short-term incentive plan is designed to reward participants for economic value added above a specified dollar threshold.[6] On the other hand, Degussa Chemicals, now part of Evonik Industries, has explicitly targeted an ROIC at least 2 percentage points above its 9% cost of capital.[7] EVA and the amount by which ROIC exceeds WACC are closely related but not identical measures. EVA captures the value created by growth in addition to the value created by the ROIC-WACC difference. If growth means more assets (and ROIC and WACC remain unchanged), more shareholder value will be created. A firm that uses the ROIC-WACC difference as a performance metric will probably want to combine it with one or more measures of business growth.

Limitations in the EVA Measure

The concept behind EVA is relatively simple, but the calculation of EVA can become complex. Analysts have attempted to improve the precision of the EVA measure by making accounting adjustments to both the operating profit component and the capital employed component of EVA. For example, from an accounting standpoint R&D is an expense subtracted on the income statement. Some analysts would argue for purposes of calculating EVA, R&D should be treated as an investment. The accounting adjustments required to make that change would include adding back the R&D expense on the income statement, and then capitalizing R&D expenses and depreciating them over time as you would with investments in plant and equipment. Dozens of such accounting changes have been suggested. There are now EVA definitions that range from the basic one that uses unadjusted income statement and balance sheet data, to complex ones that make 150 or more adjustments to the data disclosed in a firm's financial statements.[8] With enough effort most of the concerns about the accounting data used to calculate EVA can be addressed. The trade-off is that these numerous adjustments make it harder for managers to understand what EVA is measuring and what actions they need to take to boost EVA. Another concern unrelated to the accounting data is that EVA does not correlate highly with stock prices. This may be because stock prices are driven by expectations about future performance, and EVA is a measure of past performance. Even if EVA is of limited usefulness as a stock-picking tool, that does not necessarily reduce its value as a planning tool and as a basis for allocating incentive compensation.

EVA is a much better measure of value creation than frequently used metrics such as revenue growth, operating profit, EPS, and return on equity (refer to Exhibit 12-3). Nevertheless EVA does share some limitations with these metrics. They can all create inappropriate incentives to maximize short-run performance at the expense of the long term. Some managers may overemphasize the short term believing that doing so will boost their incentive pay and/or the value of their stock and stock options. These individuals may reason that there is no guarantee that in the longer term they will even be employed at the same firm. Executives overly focused on short-term rewards might be tempted to take actions such as compromising product quality, reducing advertising expenditures, cutting back on new product development, limiting budgets for employee training and development, or offering less competitive pay packages. Even if they are not in the best long-run interest of the firm, any of these actions could increase current profit and EVA measures.

Cash Flow Return on Investment

Cash flow return on investment (CFROI), like EVA, is a metric designed to focus on value creation. Both EVA and CFROI emphasize that value is created only when rates of return exceed the firm's weighted average cost of capital. Operating profits are the key input to EVA calculations. Operating cash flows are the key input to CFROI models. CFROI is the internal rate of return on the inflation-adjusted cash flows produced with a firm's assets.[9] The calculation and interpretation of an internal rate of return (IRR) measure is discussed in Chapter 7, "Capital Budgeting and Discounted Cash Flow Analysis." A CFROI greater than the firm's cost of capital indicates that value is being created. Exhibit 12-4 shows the components used when calculating CFROI. Different firms use different computational approaches, but they all begin with an estimate of the amount a firm has invested in its existing assets. The book value of a firm's assets is, of course, the original purchase price of those assets minus accumulated depreciation. This process begins by adding back the accumulated depreciation to calculate the amount the firm originally paid. That amount is then converted to current dollars using estimates of the rate of inflation since those assets were purchased. In other words, estimate what it would cost to purchase all those assets today.

	A	B	C	D	E	F	G	H	I	J	K	L
1	**Four Inputs Needed to Calculate CFROI**											
2	1. Gross Investment (GI) = Net Assets + Cumulated Depreciation + Current Dollar Adjustment										-$3,517	million
3	2. Gross Cash Flow (GCF) = Adjusted EBIT (1-tax rate) + Current Year's Depreciation and Amortizat										$582	million
4	3. Expected Life of the Assets at the Time of the Original Investment										10	years
5	4. Salvage Value (SV) of Assets at End of Their Expected Life (in Today's Dollars)										$986	million
6												
7	**Year**	**GI**	**GCF**	**SV**	**FCF**							
8	0	-$3,517			-$3,517							
9	1		$582		$582							
10	2		$582		$582							
11	3		$582		$582							
12	4		$582		$582							
13	5		$582		$582							
14	6		$582		$582							
15	7		$582		$582							
16	8		$582		$582							
17	9		$582		$582							
18	10		$582	$986	$1,568							
19												
20				CFROI =	12.6%							

Exhibit 12-4 Calculating cash flow return on investment

The second input to this model is the annual cash flows those assets are currently producing. It is calculated by adding depreciation and amortization back to the usual measure of after-tax operating profit (EBIT × [1-tax rate]). As you know, depreciation and amortization do not represent cash outlays in the current period. The CFROI approach assumes the real (inflation-adjusted) cash flows on assets do not change over time. This may be a reasonable assumption for investments in mature firms. When this assumption is not correct, it is probably a conservative one. If investment returns do grow in real terms, this assumption causes the CFROI measure to underestimate the true value created.

The third input required for this calculation is an estimate of the average useful life the firm's assets. The estimate used is not the remaining life of these assets, but the total useful life of these assets from the date of the original investment. The final input required is an estimate of the salvage value, (that is, residual value) of these assets at the end of their expected useful life. This estimate is often the portion of the initial investment that was not depreciable. This amount is also adjusted to express it in today's dollars.

The spreadsheet (refer to Exhibit 12-4) shows the cash flow series based on these four inputs and calculates the IRR of that series in cell E20. The Excel formula in E20 is =IRR(E8:E18). The estimated

CFROI is 12.6%. That number should be compared to the firm's real, that is, inflation adjusted cost of capital. Value will be created only when the CFROI is greater than the real cost of capital. This is analogous to the standard capital budgeting use of IRR.[10]

As a basis for allocating incentive pay, CFROI has many of the same strengths and weaknesses as EVA. Their primary strength is that both measures focused directly on value creation. As discussed, measures like revenue, profit, and ROE can be positive and growing even when value is destroyed. On the downside EVA, and maybe more so CFROI, can be difficult to communicate to managers. If managers cannot see how changes in their behavior affect the measure, it will not produce the desired incentive effects. There is also always the danger these measures could be gamed by self-serving managers willing to boost near-term profits and cash flow in ways that would not be in the best long-run interest of the firm and its shareholders.

Economic Margin (EM)

Economic margin[11] is a performance metric that combines elements of both CFROI and EVA. EVA is operating profit minus a charge for the capital used to generate that profit. Economic margin is based on operating cash flow minus a charge for the capital used to generate that cash flow. That amount is then expressed as a percentage of total invested capital. The invested capital measure in the denominator of the economic margin ratio is similar to the one in the denominator of the CFROI ratio. The equation for economic margin can be written as

**Economic Margin = (operating cash flow –
capital charge) / total invested capital**

The capital charge is (debt plus equity) × WACC. As in the calculation of EVA and CFROI, a number of adjustment's are usually made to accounting measures of operating cash flow and total invested capital.[12] Proponents of the economic margin measure would argue that it is superior to EVA because it is based on cash flows and not on profits. Profits are influenced by accounting choices such as depreciation schedules. Cash flows are not.

Market Value Added (MVA)

ROIC, ROE, EVA, CFROI, and economic margin are performance measures based on financial statement data, not on stock
prices. Market value added (MVA) is a function of stock price and
usually defined as the market value of the company minus the book
value of the company's debt and equity capital. For example, if the
market cap of a company is $10 million and the book value of its
assets is $6 million, the market value added is $4 million. Management's objective should be to maximize the market value added, not
the market value of a firm, because the latter can be easily accomplished by investing ever-increasing amounts of capital. A company
that generates positive EVA should have a market value in excess of
its book value. In theory, the MVA should equal the present value of
the expected EVA stream. The economic value of any asset is just the
present value of the cash flows you could get out of owning. Looked at
this way EVA management can be thought of as a tool to maximize a
company's MVA. There is a sense in which MVA should be a particularly appealing measure to HR managers. MVA measures the value
of a company beyond the value of its physical assets. Why might two
companies with identical physical assets have different market values?
There are a number of possibilities (for example, brand value or first
mover advantage), but the most common reason is the differences in
the value of their workforces.

If a company's stock is not publicly traded, it is generally not possible to calculate MVA. MVA is a function of management's performance, external perceptions of that performance, and external market
conditions. Even if the amount contributed by management were
negative, the momentum from a soaring stock market might push a
firm's MVA into positive territory. In the year 2000, the average company in the S&P 500 had a market value five times its book. Over
the last decade it is more likely that market conditions would have
depressed a firm's MVA. As revealed in Exhibit 12-5, for companies
in the S&P 500, the ratio of market value to book value plummeted
during the economic crisis of 2008. Since that time the S&P 500 index
has regained most of its losses, but the ratio of market to value book
value remains below where it was in 2008 and is less than one-half of
what it was in 2000.

Exhibit 12-5 The top panel shows ratio of market value to book value among S&P 500 companies; the bottom panel shows value of S&P 500 index.

Source: Standard & Poor's, downloaded September 9, 2012 from http://www.vectorgrader.com/indicators/price-book

Total Shareholder Returns (TSR)

Total shareholder return (TSR) is just the change in the stock price plus dividends. It is often expressed as a percentage by dividing the change in the stock price plus dividends by the initial stock price. For example, if during 2012 a company's stock price increased from $40 per share to $46 per share and the company paid a dividend of $2 share, its 2011 TSR would be 20% (6 + 2 / 40). Compensation specialists have argued that incentive pay should be linked not just to company financials but also to TSR.[13] The implication of that statement is that managers should be rewarded not just based on estimates of how well the company performs but also on measures tied to the benefit received by the company's shareholders. TSR is viewed by some as the ideal measure for aligning executive compensation and shareholder interests.

How does TSR compare to MVA? TSR is a change measure; that is, the change in the stock price over the last year. MVA is a level measure; that is, the difference between market value and book value at a point in time. Suppose a company's market value increases from $40 million to $60 million, while its book value increases from $30 million to $50 million. If no dividends were paid, the TSR over that period would be 50% (60 – 40 / 40). The change in MVA over that period would be zero (40 – 30 = 60 – 50). If MVA had been measured as a ratio rather than as a difference, it would have declined by 13 percentage points (40 / 30 = 1.33 and 60 / 50 = 1.20). Even though they were each affected by stock price, TSR and the two measures of MVA would have resulted in different levels of incentive pay.

Relative TSR

Relative TSR is just a company's TSR relative to the average TSR among a reference group of other companies. Tying incentive pay to relative TSR instead of absolute TSR minimizes the impact of overall stock market fluctuations and industrywide changes in performance. Performance share plans (those that grant stock to employees based on company performance levels) are increasingly popular, and TSR is the most frequently used performance metric in these plans. For example, in February 2012, performance share units granted to GE CEO Jeff Immelt in 2007 were canceled because between 2007 and 2011 GE's TSR did not exceed that of the S&P 500.[14] Many companies feel relative TSR is the best measure they have to align executive compensation with shareholder interests. Still, a number of valid cautions about the use of TSR or relative TSR have been raised. One is that the composition of the reference group can dramatically change the impact of this measure. One high-tech company that measured its TSR relative to the S&P 500 later realized that market swings in the tech industry were much wider than cycles in the general economy. This meant the relative TSR measure it was using was capturing relative volatility, not relative performance.[15] Is the way to avoid that problem to compare a company's TSR with the average TSR in a small group of similar companies? Identifying a small group of highly similar companies is not always possible. Even when it is, unintended outcomes can occur. The average TSR among a small group of 4 to 6 firms could be greatly impacted by an unusual event, for example, an acquisition or a patent lawsuit at one of the firm's in the group. Such events could influence your firms incentive pay in ways unrelated to your firm's performance. An additional criticism has been that although TSR may do a good job to align executive pay and value creation, it does not do a good job signaling to executives how to create that value. Unlike TSR, internal financial and operating measures can be focused on the specific value drivers that have been targeted by the firm's business strategy.

Earnings per Share (EPS) and the Price/Earnings (P/E) Ratio

Earnings per share, which is just net income divided by the number of shares outstanding, gets a lot of attention. It is often the headline number first reported by the media when firms release their quarterly financial reports. The reason for this attention is that EPS is closely related to stock price. The price of any firm's stock can be expressed as it's EPS times its P/E ratio. If a company's P/E is 15, that is, its stock price is 15 times its EPS, and its EPS increases from $2 to $3, its stock price will increase from $30 to $45. Some executives have complained, however, that even though their EPS was rising (which they believed was a result of their performance), their stock prices fell because of lower P/E ratios (which they believed were unrelated to their performance).

The P/E ratio, the price per share divided by earnings per share, is the amount share purchasers are willing to pay for every $1 of earnings. Why do P/E ratios differ between companies? Why isn't $1 of earnings from Company A worth exactly the same thing as $1 of earnings from Company B? The answer is that P/E ratios are determined not by current earnings-per-share but by expected future earnings. Consider the example in Exhibit 12-6. Both companies are currently earning $2.00 per share, but the expectation in the market is that Company A's EPS will decline in the future, whereas company B's EPS will rise. Obviously, investors will pay more for Company B's stock even though both companies have the same current earnings-per-share. Investor expectations about future earnings-per-share are shaped by company-specific factors as well as by factors related to the overall market and the overall economy. During 2012, the median P/E for stocks in the S&P 500 was close to 16. High P/E stocks, (for example, those with a P/E above 25) tend to have higher growth rates or the expectation of a profit turnaround. Low P/E stocks (for example, those with a P/E below 10) tend to have slower growth or diminished prospects.

Companies A and B each have a current EPS of $2.00:

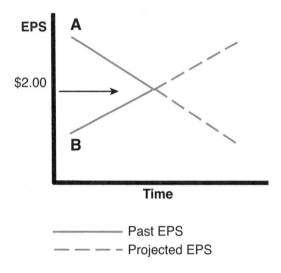

—————— Past EPS

— — — - Projected EPS

Exhibit 12-6 Stock price reflects expected not current EPS.

Managing EPS Expectations

It's not unusual to see a company's stock price fall immediately after it announces an increase in earnings-per-share. The explanation is typically that the company's EPS did not rise as much as financial analysts had expected. A company whose earnings had been expected to rise by 10% typically sees its stock price fall if it announces an earnings increase of 5%. A company whose earnings had been expected to rise by 2% typically sees its stock price jump if it announces an earnings increase of 5%. Managers concerned about their company's stock price worry about both EPS and the P/E ratio. The success of their current operations determines their EPS, and the guidance they give investors is one of the factors affecting the P/E ratio. When giving guidance about future earnings, companies have an incentive to not let expectations get too high. The higher the stock market's expectations for a company's performance, the better the company has to perform just to keep its stock price stable. Home Depot stock, for instance, lost one-half its value between 1999 and 2009 despite growing revenues at 11% per year and maintaining a value creating ROIC. A McKinsey and Co. analysis[16] suggested that a major reason for that drop was that the market was expecting an even higher and probably unobtainable level of performance. Justifying Home Depot's 1999 stock price would have required revenue growth of 26% per year for 15 years. That example highlights the importance of managing expectations as well as earnings.

The Impact of Financial Restructuring on EPS

Earnings-per-share is net income divided by the number of shares outstanding. The value of the ratio, of course, changes when there are changes in either the numerator or the denominator. If net income remains constant, the denominator decreases, and EPS rises when a company buys back shares. Managers sometimes mistakenly interpret increases in EPS due to financial restructuring as increases in business performance. When a company borrows to buy back shares, this increases EPS but does not change the cash flows from the firm's operations or add value to the firm. It changes only who has a claim to those cash flows, the shareholders or the debt holders. There would be no rationale for operating managers to receive EPS-based incentive pay in a situation such as this.

Acquisitions are a second area in which EPS changes are often misinterpreted. For example, when General Dynamics recently acquired the privately held munitions manufacturer Gayston, Corp., it did not disclose the terms of the deal but said it expected the transaction to be "accretive to earnings."[17] Many managers believe they should not undertake acquisitions unless those acquisitions are accretive, that is, they increase the acquirer's earnings-per-share. The example in Exhibit 12-7 demonstrates the fallacy in this reasoning. In this example, company A's weighted average cost of capital is 8%. Because the assets acquired in this transaction produce a return of only 7%, the economic value added, or in this case the economic value lost, is –$65 million (–1% x the $650 million acquisition price). Nevertheless, the deal is accretive in that the acquirer's EPS increases by 20%. The acquirer's EPS increases because the income from the new assets exceeds the after-tax interest expense on the new debt. It's important for managers to understand that that increase in EPS does not always mean an increase in economic value.

Company A's weighted average cost of capital is 8%.
Company A acquires company B for $650 million.
Company B's assets produce an after-tax return of 7%.
Therefore, the acquisition reduces shareholder value by $65 million (1% x $650 million).

Company A paid for the acquisition by borrowing $650 million at 6%.
Company A's after-tax interest cost is $650 million x 6% x (1- tax rate of 33%).

	Income in Millions	Shares Outstanding in Millions	EPS
Preacquisition Net Income of Company A	100.0	50	$2.00
Net Income from company B's Assets (7% x $650 million)	45.5		
Additional After-Tax Interest Expense (6% x $650 million) x .67	-25.4		
Post-Acquisition Net Income of Company A	120.2	50	$2.40

EPS rises by 20% even though shareholder value was reduced by $65 million!

Exhibit 12-7 Accretive acquisitions do not necessarily add value.

The Goldilocks Problem: Getting the Incentive Level Just Right

The Center on Executive Compensation advises that "incentive plans should be customized to the company to support the realization of its business strategy while limiting overly aggressive or overly conservative decision making."[18] Complying with that advice is not a simple task. In addition to selecting the most appropriate measures, a firm must ensure that the reward for increased performance is just right, not too little and not too much. During the 1980s, executive pay packages were often criticized because they were not tightly linked to corporate performance. One influential study concluded executive compensation did not reflect changes in corporate performance. Even though bonuses represented a large proportion of total compensation, CEO pay was "no more variable than compensation for hourly and salaried employees."[19] Corporations responded by increasing incentive pay and granting more stock options. Then in 2008, the financial crisis caused the pendulum to swing in the opposite direction. Many argued that the global economic crisis was due in part to executive compensation packages that encouraged excessive risk-taking. The allegation was that paying bonus payments tied to short-term profits, and granting options with a limited downside but an unlimited upside encouraged managers to take big risks in the pursuit of big rewards. During 2007 and 2008 many of these high-risk investments failed, causing shareholder value to plummet. Responding to these concerns, in December 2009, the Securities and Exchange Commission approved new rules requiring publicly traded companies to disclose information about how they have incorporated risk management into their compensation practices.[20]

Of course, businesses cannot operate without taking risks. The challenge is to avoid risks that are not justified by the potential rewards, and risks that, regardless of the size of the potential reward, might impose unacceptably severe costs on the firm or its stakeholders. Making decisions about which and how much risk a firm should accept is usually the responsibility of the CFO, perhaps with the CEO and others. It is HR's role to help design a compensation system that encourages individuals to adopt behaviors consistent with those decisions. To do that HR managers must understand the financial performance measures their firm uses and the behaviors that would be encouraged by linking incentive pay to these measures. They also need to understand that some forms of pay are inherently more risk-inducing than others. For example, suppose a firm's stock options vest after 3 years and are exercisable for 10 years. This creates a 7-year period during which executives could be exercising their options and then immediately selling those shares, benefiting from a short-term spike in the stock price. That could provide a substantial monetary incentive to undertake risky projects with short-term payoffs, even if they offer little prospect of long-term value creation. That inappropriate incentive could, of course, be negated or at least reduced if the firm required that shares be held for a period of time after the options were exercised.

Many firms are replacing options with performance share units (PSUs). PSUs represent the value of one share of the company's stock plus the dividends paid. The number of PSUs an employee receives typically depends upon some measure of the firm's financial performance. For example, an incentive formula might state that if the firm's EBITDA is below $50 million, the executive receives no PSUs. If EBITDA reaches $50 million the executive receives 1,000 PSUs plus an additional 20 PSUs for each $1 million of EBITDA more than $50 million. Formulas of that type can encourage either overly aggressive or overly conservative decision making. If the minimum threshold is difficult to achieve, executives may feel they must adopt risky strategies to earn any incentive pay. If the minimum threshold is a reasonable one, but the number of PSUs offered for amounts more than the threshold is too small, executives may have an incentive to be overly cautious seeking to avoid anything that might cause them to miss that minimum threshold. If the number of PSUs offered for amounts more than the threshold is large and uncapped, executives may be tempted to pursue high-risk strategies that offer the possibility of tremendous payoffs.

Risk Must Be Considered When Evaluating Financial Performance

You would not evaluate the financial performance of your personal investments without taking risk into consideration. You would not be happy with your stock mutual fund if it provided the same rate of return you could have earned on a government-guaranteed bank CD. The stock fund, to justify the extra risk you are taking, would need to provide a much higher return. That same principle should be applied when deciding how much incentive pay is warranted by a given level of corporate financial performance. Executives who achieve a strong level of financial performance without excessive risk-taking should be rewarded more highly than executives who achieve that same level of performance by exposing the company to great risk. Consider the following example from the home mortgage industry.

Employee A grants (with income checks) mortgages of $1 million that do not exceed 50% of the value of the underlying property. Employee B grants (without income checks) mortgages of $1 million that equal 90% of the value of the underlying property. A typical bonus program would be based only on the value of mortgages granted ($1 million in each case). The lack of integration between bonus and risk level encourages employees to maximize the dollar value mortgaged, limited only by the need to meet compliance and approval requirements. There is no incentive to grant less risky mortgages, and the consequence for granting risky mortgages is often not realized until a default many years after payment of the associated incentive amount.[21]

Some executive contracts contain *clawback provisions*. These provisions require the employee to repay bonus amounts that later turn out not to have been earned. However, these provisions are generally limited to situations in which a material misrepresentation results in a restatement of the company's earnings. They typically do not apply to situations where high-risk strategies turn out badly. A better way to have avoided the adverse incentives created by the compensation system in the preceding example would have been to reward loan officers for both the level of performance (the dollar value of mortgages granted) and the quality of that performance (the likelihood that the mortgages will be repaid in full). The probability that a mortgage would be repaid in full might be estimated based on factors such as borrower's credit score and the ratio of mortgage value to the home value. The average risk level of the mortgages approved by Employee A could then be calculated and used along with the dollar value of mortgages approved by Employee A to determine the size of her bonus.

Securities analysts when evaluating the performance of a portfolio of stocks, bonds, or other financial instruments use a variety of risk measures, for example, volatility, Sharpe ratio, Value at Risk (VAR), and risk adjusted return on capital (RAROC). In most industries these measures cannot be applied directly to assess the risk associated with firm performance or specific business proposals. In many cases, such as the previous mortgage example, firms can develop their own numerical risk indicators. However, even in firms where the level of risk cannot be easily quantified, managers and corporate boards must consider risk when evaluating and rewarding financial performance.

Putting It All Together

Both short-term and long-term financial measures should be designed to encourage long-term value creation. It will almost always be necessary to combine these financial measures with nonfinancial measures such as customer satisfaction, market share, product innovation, product quality, process efficiency, and the ability to attract and retain talented employees. Short-term metrics should be used to drive implementation of the firm's business strategy. These measures often include specific annual targets for items such as cash flow (EBITDA), revenue growth, operating margins (EBIT/ sales revenue), and return on invested capital (ROIC). Managers must not be allowed to game the system by maximizing one of these at the expense of the others. For example, revenue growth adds economic value only when ROIC is greater than the weighted average cost of capital (WACC). Rewarding revenue growth when ROIC is not greater than WACC would be a serious mistake. Firms should consider not rewarding improvements in any one measure unless each of the other measures is at or above a minimum threshold. Annual performance metrics should be specific to the firm's short-term operating strategy. That strategy might suggest that value creation can be maximized by setting an aggressive revenue growth targets while maintaining an acceptable ROIC level. On the other hand, a firm pursuing a strategy of targeting a narrow market niche that will pay a premium for a differentiated product might set an aggressive ROIC target while maintaining an acceptable pace of revenue growth.

Short-term performance metrics may also change over a product's life cycle. Exhibit 12-8 shows how this might occur. Following the introduction of a new product, firms invest to support growth. The expectation is that during this period sales will be growing rapidly and that the product will be profitable. At the same time cash flows may be low or even negative. The firm may be pouring large amounts of cash into the business to expand manufacturing, distribution, and sales facilities. This often results in a negative cash flow. However, because these large expenditures are not expensed on the current income statement but rather depreciated over many years, they do not prevent the firm from showing an accounting profit.

Investment Strategy Changes Over the Product Lifecycle

Strategy	Performance Expectation
Invest to Support Growth	Rapid Sales Growth Moderate ROIC Low or Negative Cash Flow
Reinvest to Maintain Market Share	Sales Growth Equal to Market High ROIC Large Positive Cash Flow
Invest Only to Optimize Cash Flow	Flat or Declining Sales Low or Negative ROIC Positive Cash Flow (Must Cover Variable Costs)

Exhibit 12-8 Linking performance measure to strategy

At some point the product reaches its peak where to maintain market share sales growth must equal that of the market. At this point the product should be generating large profits and large positive cash flows. Getting to this point was the reason the firm introduced the product in the first place. Eventually, the product will approach the end of its life cycle with sales that are flat or declining. To maintain sales in the face of competition from newer products, prices may need to be reduced substantially. This price reduction may lead to operating losses and a negative ROIC. Would a firm continue to produce this product if it shows a loss each quarter? It would as long as the cash flow from the product is positive and large enough to cover the variable costs. For example, suppose revenues are $100 million, variable costs are $50 million, and fixed costs are $30 million. The firm's profit is $20 million (+ 100 – 50 – 30). Variable costs are those that vary with the volume of output. Fixed costs do not vary on the number of units produced. Now supposed to compete with a competitor that has a newer model, this firm must reduce its price by 30%. If it continues to sell the same number of units, its accounting profit would be –$10 million (+ 70 – 50 – 30). Why not shut the plant down if it is losing $10 million a year? If the plant is closed, that eliminates the $50 million in variable costs but not the $30 million in fixed costs. If production continues for another year, the firm must put in another $50 million to cover the variable costs, but that amount will be more than offset by the $70 million in revenues generating by keeping the plant open. In other words, the cash inflows from keeping the plant open another year are greater than the cash outflows required to keep it open. As long as that is the case, there is a benefit to keep the plant open even if it shows an accounting loss.

Now step back and look at the implications of that last example. The performance metrics were the same in all three stages of this product's life cycle, but their interpretation shifted by 180 degrees. In the early stage no incentive bonus would be awarded unless sales were growing rapidly. In the latter stage the expectation is that sales would be flat or declining. In the early stage no incentive bonuses would be awarded unless profits and ROIC were positive. In the latter stage an acceptable performance might include losses and a negative ROIC. In the early stage an acceptable performance could include low or even negative cash flows. In the latter stage cash flows would have to be positive and large enough to cover all variable costs. What's the take away message in this example? Financial performance metrics cannot be interpreted independent of each other and without considering the business context.

Long-Term Measures of Value Creation

The short-term operating and financial measures a firm focuses on should be the drivers of long-term value creation. The metrics used to determine long-term incentive pay usually include a much heavier weighting on direct financial measures of value creation such as EVA, CFROI, and economic margin, and on stock market-based measures of value creation such as stock price, relative TSR, and market value added. These are usually combined with one or more forms of equity-based pay such as restricted stock, performance shares, stock appreciation rights, or stock options. In recent years there appears to be a trend toward using multiple forms of long-term incentives. Stock options now make up 50% or less expected of the value of long-term incentives. Among large firms, a measurement period of 3 years is often used to determine long-term incentive pay.[22] An argument could certainly be made that from the shareholder perspective 3 years should be considered an intermediate term, rather than a long-term performance. Almost all publicly traded large firms attempt to achieve an even longer term alignment between top executive and shareholder interests through the use of executive stock ownership guidelines. These guidelines often require that top executives hold company shares valued at 3 to 6 times their base salary. The assumption is that executives will be less likely to take excessive risk or over-emphasize short-term results if a significant portion of their personal wealth is tied up in company stock. Most stock ownership policies require compliance for as long as the executive remains employed at the firm. Some however extend into retirement. Exxon Mobil, for example, grants restricted stock with 50% vesting after 5 years and 50% vesting 10 years after retirement.[23]

Using Imperfect Metrics Well

All measures of business performance are imperfect. Each has its own weaknesses and limitations. The challenge is to combine them in ways so that in the aggregate they provide a useful basis to plan and evaluate business outcomes. Discounted cash flow measures such as net present value and internal rate of return are almost universally recognized as essential planning tools. They are just as applicable to investments within the HR function as they are to investments and other functional area. Even when formal DCF models are not prepared, all operating and strategic investments should be considered from this perspective. No expenditures should be made unless the anticipation is that the present value of future benefits will exceed the upfront costs. DCF techniques work well at the project level, even if the project is a huge one such as an acquisition. However, when assessing performance at the business unit or company level where many things are happening at once, additional measures are needed.

Accounting measures such as revenue growth, cash flow, and profit margins are easy to communicate and can be targeted at the specific changes required by a firm's business strategy. The weakness in these measures is more than just the assumptions the accountants must make to generate them. It is possible to grow revenues, cash flow, profits, and ROE while no shareholder value is created. Firms create value for their shareholders when, and only when, the return on invested capital is greater than the firms' weighted average cost of capital. That statement is simple and unquestionably true. The complexity and ambiguity arise when you try to measure the rate of return, the amount invested, and the weighted average cost of capital.

A number of direct measures of value creation have been proposed, for example, EVA, CFROI, and economic margin. The basic concept underlying these measures is easily understood. A firm does not generate value for its shareholders unless its after-tax operating profit is greater than the cost of financing the assets used to make that profit. Communicating that message to everyone within an organization is essential. Unfortunately, calculating these measures can require extensive reconfigurations of the underlying accounting data. These reconfigurations can obscure what is actually measured. Non-accountants may fail to see the forest for the trees and therefore miss the message about what it takes to create value. An important challenge facing HR managers is ensuring that all employees, whether or not their pay is tied to these measures, understand the economic conditions under which value is created and how their own activities impact value creation. Most employees do not need to understand the accounting detail. They do need to understand the determinants and consequences of changes in operating profits, the assets invested in their unit, and the cost of raising the money to purchase those assets.

Encouraging value creation through the use of equity-based pay (for example, restricted stock, stock options, and stock appreciation rights) or through bonuses tied to measures such as market value added avoids the reliance on accounting data. The trade-off is that market values that are highly volatile may be influenced by events, perhaps on the other side of the world, unrelated to firm performance. The value created when ROIC is greater than the cost of capital will over the long term be correlated with market value. Proponents would argue that in the short run, EVA and related measures are more useful than stock market-based measures because they are less impacted by factors beyond the control of the executive team. Most large firms use a combination of these measures. Selecting the mix that is most likely to attract, motivate, and retain talented employees can be a major determinant of a corporation's success. HR managers who do not understand the strengths and weaknesses of these alternative performance metrics cannot develop a compensation strategy that aligns executive incentives with the firm's business strategy.

HR's Role in Value Creation

The talent of its management and workforce is often the primary determinant of a corporation's success. HR professionals are the ones charged with responsibility to build that competitive advantage. There is no role more important than that. Successful HR strategies are those that align with and support the firm's business strategy. Successful business strategies are those that create shareholder value. Understanding the financial requirements for value creation is therefore critical to the strategy development process. This book was not intended to be a volume on business strategy or on HR strategy. It was intended to help HR managers increase their understanding of the financial tools they need to link HR strategy to business strategy. Line managers often see a lack of business acumen as the major factor limiting the success of their HR colleagues. Sometimes this is an accurate assessment. At other times, HR managers have the necessary business insights but cannot effectively communicate with line managers because they don't speak the language (finance) used to plan and evaluate business initiatives. In either case, the good news is that it does not take a degree in finance to overcome those limitations. When you get past the jargon, it is not difficult to obtain an intuitive understanding of the key finance principles that guide corporate operating and strategic decision making. These principles are no more complex than things HR managers deal with all the time. HR managers willing to make a reasonable effort to get up to speed in these areas should not underestimate their ability to contribute to discussions involving financial measures and financial models. If they do not do this, they are limiting what they can contribute to their companies and what they can achieve in their careers.

Appendix A: A Sample of Financial Measures Currently in Use

Caution: These measures are not defined by GAAP, and definitions may vary from company to company.

Measure	Definition
After-tax profit	See net income.
Bottom line growth	See net income.
Cash ROIC	[EBIT (1 – tax rate) + Depreciation and Amortization] / [Gross Fixed Assets + Noncash Working Capital]
Cash flow return on investment (CFROI)	Internal rate of return on existing investments based on real, as opposed to nominal, cash flows.
Earnings per share	Net income divided by number of shares outstanding.
EBIT	Earnings before interest and taxes are subtracted out.
EBIT per employee	EBIT divided by number of employees.
EBITA	Earnings before interest taxes and amortization are subtracted out.
EBITA multiple	Enterprise value divided by EBITA.
EBITDA	Earnings before interest, taxes, depreciation, and amortization are subtracted out.
Economic margin	(Operating cash flow – Capital charge) / Invested capital
Economic profit	[EBIT (1 – tax rate)] – [WACC x capital employed] which is same as [(ROIC – WACC)] x capital employed
Economic value added (EVA)	See economic profit.
Enterprise value	Market capitalization plus debt minus excess cash.
EPS	See earnings-per-share.
Free cash flow	EBITDA minus increase in working capital and increase in long-term assets
Gross margin	Gross profit / revenues.
Gross profit	Sales revenue minus costs of goods sold.
Market share	Company sales divided by industry sales.
Market value added (MVA)	Market capitalization minus book value of debt and equity.

Measure	Definition
Net earnings	Same as Net Income or Net Profit.
Net income	Bottom line of the income statement.
Net profit	See net income.
NOPAT	Net operating profit after tax = EBIT minus cash taxes.
Operating margin	EBIT divided by sales revenue.
Operating profit	See EBIT.
P/E ratio	Stock price per share divided by earnings per share.
Price to book (P/B) Ratio	Stock price/book value per share or market capitalization/total shareholders' equity.
Relative TSR	Total shareholder return for company divided by average total shareholder return in peer group.
Return on assets (ROA)	Net income divided by assets.
Return on equity (ROE)	Net income divided by equity.
Return on invested capital (ROIC)	[EBIT × (1 – tax rate)] / capital employed
Return on net assets (RONA)	See return on invested capital.
Revenue growth	Sales revenue in current period minus sales revenue in previous period.
Revenue per employee	Sales revenue divided by number of employees.
Risk Adjusted Return on Capital (RAROC)	Return minus expected loss divided / capital at risk.
Sales growth	See revenue growth.
Sales per employee	See revenue per employee.
Shareholder value	Enterprise value minus value of outstanding debt.
Stock price	Price per share.
Top line growth	See revenue growth.
Total shareholder return (TSR)	Change in stock price plus dividends divided by initial stock price.

Bibliography

Alcoa (2011). Annual report for the Year 2011. Accessed September 24, 2012, http://www.alcoa.com/global/en/investment/info_page/annual_report.asp.

Asaf, Samir (2004). *Executive Corporate Finance*, London: FT Prentice Hall.

Association for Financial Professionals (2011) "Current Trends in Estimating and Applying the Cost of Capital," Report of Survey Results Bethesda, Maryland: Association for Financial Professionals. Accessed September 24, 2012, www.AFPonline.org.

Baker, Stephen, and Keith L. Alexander (1993) "The Owners vs. the Boss at Weirton Steel," *Business Week*, November 15, 1993, p. 38.

Becker, Brian E., Mark A. Huselid and Richard W. Beatty (2009), *The Differentiated Workforce*, Boston, Massachusetts: Harvard Business Press.

Becker, Brian E., Mark A. Huselid and Dave Ulrich (2001) *The HR Scorecard*, Boston Massachusetts: Harvard Business Press.

Benartzi, S. and R.H. Thaler (2001). "Naïve Diversification Strategies in Retirement Saving Plans," *American Economic Review*, 91(1), 79–98.

Black, Fischer and Myron Scholes (1973). "The Pricing of Options and Corporate Liabilities," *Journal of Political Economy*, 81 (3): 637–654.

Bloomberg.com (2011). "Home Depot Sells $2 Billion of Debt." March 28, 2011. Accessed September 24, 2012, http://www.bloomberg.com/news/2011-03-28/home-depot-plans-2-billion-of-debt-to-replenish-cash-buy-stock.html.

Bragg, Steven M. (2011). GAAP 2012, Hoboken, NJ: John Wiley and Sons.

Bryan, Lowell (2005). "The new metrics of corporate performance: Profit per employee," *McKinsey Quarterly*, 2005, no 3, pp 26–35. Accessed September 24, 2012, http://download.mckinseyquarterly.com/bonus/mb_21stcentury.pdf.

Cascio, Wayne and John Boudreau (2011). *Investing in People*, Upper Saddle River, NJ: FT Prentice Hall.

Center on Executive Compensation (2012a). "Putting executive compensation principles into practice." Accessed September 24, 2012, http://www.executivecompensation.org/principles/principles_1.aspx.

Center on Executive Compensation (2012b). "Principled pay practices in detail." Accessed September 24, 2012, http://www.executivecompensation.org/principles/principles_short.aspx#customized.

Corporate Leadership Council (2008). "Building Next-generation HR Line Partnerships," Washington, DC: Corporate Executive Board.

Damodaran, Aswath (2011). *Applied Corporate Finance*, Hoboken, New Jersey: John Wiley & Sons, Inc.

Damodaran, Aswath (2012). *Investment valuation*, Hoboken New Jersey: John Wiley & Sons, Inc.

Degussa Corp. (2005). Annual Report for the Year, 2005. Accessed September 24, 2012, http://xingsha365.com/degussa/en/investors/fiscal_2005/annual_report_online_2005/.

Economist Magazine (1999). "Share and Share Alike" August 5, 1999. Accessed September 24, 2012, http://www.economist.com/node/230106.

Edmiston, Kelly D, Mary C. Gillett-Fisher, and Molly McGrath, (2009). "Weighing the effects of financial education and the workplace." Federal Reserve Bank of Kansas, October 2009, research working papers 09–01.

Ellig, Bruce R. (2007). "The complete guide to executive compensation," New York: McGraw-Hill.

Estrada, Javier (2011). *Understanding Finance*, New York: FT Prentice Hall.

Feldman, Amy (2009). "IBM Reinvents the 401(k)" *Bloomberg BusinessWeek*, July 02, 2009. Accessed September 24, 2012, http://www.businessweek.com/magazine/content/09_28/b4139058355275.htm.

Ferracone, Robin (2011). "Performance share plans the best of both worlds." Forbes.Com, March 3, 2011. Accessed September 24, 2012, http://www.forbes.com/sites/robinferracone/2011/03/03/performance-share-plans-the-best-of-both-worlds/.

Fitz-Enz, Jac (2010). *The New HR Analytics*, New York: Amacom, American Management Association.

Forbes.com (2001). "Warren Buffett: Value Man through and through." Accessed September 24, 2012, http://www.forbes.com/2001/04/26/buffett.html.

Frederic W. Cook & Co., Inc. (2004). "The 2004 Top 250," September 2004. Accessed September 24, 2012, http://www.fwcook.com/publications.html.

Frederic W. Cook & Co., Inc. (2008). "The 2008 Top 250," October 2008. Accessed September 24, 2012, http://www.fwcook.com/publications.html.

Frederic W. Cook & Co., Inc. (2011). "The 2011 Top 250," October 2011. Accessed September 24, 2012, http://www.fwcook.com/publications.html.

F. W. Cook & Co. (2010). "Executive Stock Ownership Policies," Sept 13, 2010, Accessed September 24, 2012, http://www.fwcook.com/alert_letters/09-13-10_Executive_Stock_Ownership_Policies_-_Trends_and_Developments.pdf.

General Electric (2012). Proxy Statement for Year 2011 submitted to US Securities Exchange Commission, Accessed September 24, 2012. http://www.ge.com/investors/financial_reporting/proxy_statements.html.

Harris, Milton and Artur Raviv (1991). "The Theory of Capital Structure," *Journal of Finance*, Vol. 46, No. 1, 297–355.

Hull, J. and A. White. (2004). "How to value employee stock options," Financial*Analysts Journal*, Vol. 60, No.1, January/February 2004, 114–119.

IBM (2011). Annual Report for Year 2011 Accessed September 24, 2012, http://www.ibm.com/annualreport/2011/bin/assets/2011_ibm_statements.pdf.

Jensen, Michael C. and Kevin J. Murphy (1990). "CEO Incentives: It's Not How Much You Pay, But How," Harvard University Press, 1998; *Harvard Business Review*, No. 3, May–June 1990.

Kaiser Aluminum Corp. (2011). Form 8K filed with the US securities exchange commission on March 7, 2011. Accessed September 24, 2012, http://investors.kaiseraluminum.com/sec.cfm.

Kieso, Donald E., Jerry J. Weygandt, and Terry D. Warfield (2012). *Intermediate Accounting*, 14th edition, Hoboken, NJ: John Wiley & Sons, Inc.

Koller, Tim, Richard Dobbs, and Bill Huyett (2011). *Value: The Four Cornerstones of Corporate Finance*, Hoboken, New Jersey: John Wiley & Sons, Inc.

Lockheed Martin Corporation (2012). Annual Report for the Year 2011. Accessed September 24, 2012, http://www.lockheedmartin.com/us/news/annual-reports.html.

McFarland, Brendan (2011). "Pension freezes among the Fortune 1000 in 2011," Towers Watson Insider, November 2011. Accessed September 24, 2012, http://www.towerswatson.com/assets/pdf/5858/Towers-Watson-Insider-Pension-Freeze-Nov2011.pdf.

Medland, Christina (2011). "Compensating to manage risk." Meridian client update issue 2011–1, March 30, 2011, Meridian Compensation Partners, LLC, Accessed September 24, 2012, http://www.meridiancp.com/images/uploads/client_update_040110r.pdf.

Mercer (2009) *Pay for Results*, Hoboken, NJ: John Wiley & Sons.

Mercer Human Resource Consulting (2007). "HR Transformation v2.0: it's all about the business," New York. Accessed September 24, 2012, http://www.imercer.com/products/2012/us-human-resources.aspx.

Merton, Robert C. (1973). "Theory of Rational Option Pricing." *Bell Journal of Economics and Management Science* (The RAND Corporation) 4 (1): 141–183.

Monga, Vipal (2012). "Companies rush to recalculate pension contributions." WSJ.com. July 9, 2012. Accessed September 24, 2012, http://mobile.blogs.wsj.com/cfo/2012/07/09/companies-rush-to-recalculate-pension-contributions/.

Morgan Stanley (2011). "Global IT Services: Per-employee Metrics are Key to Quality of Growth." Morgan Stanley research report, September 23, 2011. Accessed September 24, 2012, http://www.morganstanleychina.com/conferences/apsummit2011/research/30GlobalITServices.pdf.

Murphy, Maxwell (2012a). "Home Depot CFO says buybacks fueled new ROIC target." WSJ.com: June 6, 2012. Accessed September 24, 2012, http://blogs.wsj.com/cfo/2012/06/06/home-depot-cfo-says-buybacks-fuel-new-roic-target/.

Murphy, Maxwell (2012b). "GE Latest to Cut Pension Contribution on New Law," WSJ.com: July 20, 2012. Accessed September 24, 2012, http://blogs.wsj.com/cfo/2012/07/20/ge-latest-to-cut-pension-funding-on-new-law/.

Naughton, Keith (2012). "U.S. Automakers Cut Retirees Loose." *Bloomberg BusinessWeek*, June 27 2012, http://www.businessweek.com/articles/2012-06-27/u-dot-s-dot-automakers-cut-retirees-loose.

Norris, Floyd (2012). "Private pension plans, even at big companies, maybe underfunded." *The New York Times*, Business Day, July 20, 2012. Accessed September 24, 2012, http://www.nytimes.com/2012/07/21/business/pension-plans-increasingly-underfunded-at-largest-companies.html.

Pfizer, Inc. (2011). Annual Report for Year 2011. Accessed September 24, 2012, http://www.pfizer.com/files/annualreport/2011/financial/financial2011.pdf.

Rehm, Werner and Carsten Silvertsen, "A strong foundation for M&A in 2010," *McKinsey on Finance*, 34 (Winter 2010): 17 to 22.

Sammer, Joanne (2012). "Financial education", *HR Magazine*, June 2012, Vol. 57, No. 6, p. 72.

Schuler, Randall S. and Susan E. Jackson (2007). *Strategic Human Resource Management*, Second Edition, Malden, Ma: Blackwell Publishing.

Stern, J. M., G. B. Stewart, and D. A. Chew (1999). "The EVA Financial Management System," *Journal of Applied Corporate Finance* (Summer 1999).

Stires, David (2002). "A Little Honesty Goes a Long Way," *Fortune* (September 2, 2002), p. 186. Accessed September 24, 2012, http://money.cnn.com/magazines/fortune/fortune_archive/2002/09/02/327899/index.htm.

Tiffany & Co. (2012). Form 10K report submitted to U.S. Securities Exchange Commission for fiscal year ended January 31, 2012. Accessed September 24, 2012, http://investor.tiffany.com/sec.cfm?SortOrder=Type%20Ascending&DocType=&DocTypeExclude=&Year=.

Ulrich, Dave, et. al. (2012). *HR from the Outside In*, New York: McGraw-Hill.

UPI.com (2012). "General Dynamics buys Gayston." UPI.com. August 28, 2012. Accessed September 24, 2012, http://www.upi.com/Business_News/Security-Industry/2012/08/28/General-Dynmics-buys-Gayston-sector/UPI-16771346171509/.

U.S. Federal Reserve System (2012). Federal Reserve Statistical Release Z1, Flow of funds accounts of the United States, Private pension funds, March 8, 2012. Accessed September 24, 2012 http://www.federalreserve.gov/releases/z1/20120308/accessible/f118.htm.

U.S. Office of Management and Budget (2012). "Budget of the United States Government, fiscal year 2013." Office of Management and Budget: Washington, DC. Accessed September 24, 2012, http://www.whitehouse.gov/sites/default/files/omb/budget/fy2013/assets/budget.pdf.

U.S. Securities and Exchange Commission (2009). Release Nos. 33-9089; 34-61175: Washington, DC, Dec. 16, 2009. Accessed September 24, 2012, http://www.sec.gov/news/press/2009/2009-268.htm.

Endnotes

Chapter 1

1. Corporate Leadership Council (2008).
2. Mercer Human Resource Consulting (2007).
3. See for an example Schuler and Jackson (2007), Becker, Huselid, and Ulrich (2001), Becker, Huselid and Beatty (2009), and Mercer (2009).

Chapter 2

1. Pfizer, Inc. (2011), page 16.

Chapter 3

1. In addition if a company's operating cycle is longer than 1 year, an item is considered a current asset if it will be converted to cash or used up within one operating cycle. An operating cycle is the average time required to purchase or manufacture a product, sell it, and collect the cash from that sale, often between 60 and 180 days.
2. The concept and calculation of present value is discussed in detail in Chapter 7.
3. Baker and Alexander (1993).
4. Bloomberg.com (2011).
5. IBM (2011), page 72.

Chapter 5

1. Becker, Huselid, and Beatty (2009), page 51.
2. Tiffany & Co. (2012), page K3.

Chapter 6

1. Association for Financial Professionals (2011), page 5.
2. Ibid, page 6.
3. The Modigliani-Miller irrelevance proposition tells us that in theory the value the company should not depend on its capital structure. However, in practice not all of the assumptions of the Modigliani-Miller model are met, and empirical research suggests that increasing equity often decreases stock prices while increasing leverage often increases stock prices. See Harris and Raviv (1991).

Chapter 7

1. It is also possible that the cash flow patterns generated by certain projects will produce multiple or no solutions to the IRR equation. See Estrada (2011), pages 268–275.

Chapter 8

1. Cascio and Boudreau (2011), page 229–230. Becker, Huselid, and Ulrich (2001), page 90.
2. This software can be accessed at www.hrcosing.com.
3. Cascio and Boudreau (2011), page 104.

Chapter 9

1. Association for Financial Professionals (2011), page 4.
2. Ibid.

3. Ibid, page 6.
4. Rehm and Silvertsen (2010).

Chapter 10

1. Jensen and Murphy (1990).
2. Frederic W. Cook & Co. (2004), page 4.
3. Frederic W. Cook & Co. (2004), page 4. Frederic W. Cook & Co. (2008), page 5. Frederic W. Cook & Co. (2011), page 7.
4. FASB ASC 718 (formerly, FASB Statement 123R). See Bragg (2011), pages 994–1014.
5. Kieso, Weygandt, and Warfield (2012), p.919.
6. Stires (2002), page 186.
7. Forbes.com (2001).
8. *Economist Magazine* (1999).
9. Black and Scholes (1973).
10. Merton (1973).
11. Hull and White (2004).

Chapter 11

1. U.S. Federal Reserve System (2012).
2. U.S. Office of Management and Budget (2012).
3. Alcoa 2011 Annual report, page 137.
4. Lockheed Martin Corporation (2012).
5. Norris (2012).
6. Monga (2012).
7. Murphy, Maxwell (2012b).
8. Naughton (2012).
9. McFarland (2011).
10. Benartzi and Thaler (2001).
11. Sammer (2012).

12. Edmiston, Gillett-Fisher, and McGrath (2009).

13. Feldman, Amy (2009).

Chapter 12

1. Center on Executive Compensation (2012a).

2. Bryan (2005).

3. Morgan Stanley (2011).

4. Murphy (2012a).

5. Stern, Stewart, and Chew (1999).

6. Kaiser Aluminum Corp (2011).

7. Degussa (2005), page 43.

8. Asaf (2004), page 43.

9. Damodaran, (2011), page 311.

10. As discussed in Chapter 7, IRR measures make a reinvestment rate assumption that may not always be appropriate. A modification of the basic CFROI approach adopted by some firms involves adjusting the gross cash flow estimates downward by subtracting the amount that would have to be set aside replace these assets at the end of their projected life. That variation assumes that instead of being continually reinvested at the CFROI rate, at least a portion of the cash flows will be reinvested at the lower WACC rate. Calculations based on lower cash flows, of course, lead to lower estimates CFROI. See Damodaran (2012), page 885.

11. Asaf (2004), page 45.

12. Operating cash flow = net income + Depreciation and Amortization + after-tax interest expense + rental expense under operating leases + R&D expense + or – nonrecurring items. Invested capital = total assets + accumulated depreciation + asset inflation adjustment + Capitalized operating leases+ Capitalized R&D – nondebt current liabilities. Adding depreciation and amortization back to net income converts it from a profit measure to a cash flow measure. Removing nonrecurring, one-time expenditures is intended to produce a better estimate of

ongoing cash flows generated by these investments. The rental and R&D costs that were subtracted out when net income was calculated are added back because they are viewed as investments rather than as current expenses. The capitalized R&D and lease expenses are then added to the denominator.

13. Ellig (2007), page 598.

14. General Electric (2012), page 18.

15. Ferracone (2011).

16. Koller, Dobbs, and Huyett (2011) page 5.

17. UPI.com (2012).

18. Center on Executive Compensation (2012b).

19. Jensen and Murphy (1990).

20. U.S. Securities and Exchange Commission (2009).

21. Medland (2011).

22. Frederic W. Cook & Co. (2011) page 14.

23. F. W. Cook & Co. (2010), page 3.

Index

Numbers

401(k)s, 207-208
  influencing plan choices, 209-210
  pricing bonds, 90-91

A

ABO (accumulated benefit
  obligation), 192
accounting for pension plans, 189
  actuarial loss, net, 197
  amortization of prior service
    costs, 197
  DB (defined benefit) plan
    obligations, 189-192
  expected return on plan assets,
    197-198
  income statements, 195-196
  interest costs, 196-197
  pension footnotes, 193
  post-retirement benefits, 194-195
  service costs, 196
accounts receivable, 25
accounts receivable turnover ratio, 25
accumulated benefit obligation
  (ABO), 192
acquisition value, Monte Carlo
  simulations, 148-150
acquisitions
  DCFs (discounted cash flows),
    144-145
  EPS (earnings per share), 235
  Monte Carlo simulations, 150-151
actuarial loss, net, 197
Airbus, 157-158

Alcoa
  disclosure of methods and
    assumptions they use to cost stock
    options, 174-176
  pension trusts, 185
aligning pay with performance,
  217-218
alternative calculation of ROI, 41
amortization, 14-15
amortization of prior service costs,
  pension plans, 197
analysis, maximizing ROI (return on
  investment), 125-126
analyzing
  DCFs (discounted cash flows),
    mergers and acquisitions, 144-145
  expected NPV, 135-137
annual cash, 10
annual reports, pension footnotes, 193
Apple, 157
ASC 17, 214
ASC 715, 193
asset turnover, common size financial
  statements, 51-52
asset values, balance sheets, 35
AT&T, 214

B

balance sheets, 10, 23-25
  accounts receivable, 25
  accounts receivable turnover
    ratio, 25
  believing the numbers, 34-37
    asset values, equity value, 35
  book value versus market value of
    long-term assets, 35

X-Y-Z

THE APOSTLES
after ACTS

THE APOSTLES
after ACTS

A Sequel

THOMAS E. SCHMIDT

CASCADE *Books* · Eugene, Oregon

THE APOSTLES AFTER ACTS
A Sequel

Cascade Books
An Imprint of Wipf and Stock Publishers
199 W. 8th Ave., Suite 3
Eugene, OR 97401

www.wipfandstock.com

ISBN 13: 978-1-62032-617-6

Cataloguing-in-Publication data:

Schmidt, Thomas E.

    The apostles after Acts : a sequel / Thomas E. Schmidt.

    x + 216 pp. ; 23 cm. Includes bibliographical references and indexes.

    ISBN 13: 978-1-62032-617-6

    1. Church history—Primitive and early church, ca. 30–600. 2. Christianity—Origins. I. Title.

BR165 S347 2013

Manufactured in the U.S.A.

In memory of Lyle Hillegas 1934–2008

a witness of redemption

Contents

Contents

Maps

INTRODUCTION

A Hard Acts to Follow

QUESTIONS UNANSWERED

As a guide for faith and practice, the New Testament is a rich resource. As an account of Christian origins, however, it leaves much to be desired. The Gospels cover only portions of the last years of Jesus's life. The events in Acts cover almost three decades, but the book skips long periods; and the second half focuses on just one character, Paul, who is still awaiting trial at the end. We presume that he was killed, but what were the circumstances? This is only one of many questions that the New Testament leaves unanswered. What happened next, not only to Paul, but also to Peter and the rest of the apostles? Were they all martyred? How far did they travel to spread the gospel? What of other important characters, like Mary, and the Lord's brothers James and Jude? When and why did Roman emperors begin widespread persecutions? What became of the Jerusalem Christians when the Jews fought the Romans and the temple was destroyed? Why were the four Gospels written, and by whom?

From my earliest days as a believer, these kinds of questions intrigued me. I was soon to learn, however, that outside of the New Testament itself, it is difficult to find information about Christianity's first few decades. There are many reasons for this. To begin, non-Christian writers paid little or no attention to the movement until it grew to a significant size. Christian writers of the first hundred years focused on faith and practice, not events. When interest grew in the origins of the movement, writers were removed by a century or more from the events, and their sources were often tainted by pious imagination. We get little help from archaeology because the key locations were ravaged by wars, and the critical time period is so brief. New manuscripts and physical evidence occasionally come to light, but these discoveries add insight by inches rather than yards. Historical scholarship is slow to combine data into consensus, especially in matters of such complexity. These factors combine to throw a shroud of mist over early Christianity.

The picture, however, is not altogether bleak. Despite all of these obscuring layers, enough information is visible to allow some reconstruction of events, and there are reasonable techniques available to establish the probability—or at least plausibility—of many details and events.

METHOD OR MADNESS?

But how to present this information? The traditional "search for the apostles" traces the careers of key individuals within the New Testament and beyond. Other treatments work topically, analyzing ancient writings and artifacts to explore, for example, the role of women in leadership, the interaction of Christianity with pagan Roman and Jewish cultures, or the socio-economic status of early believers. While these approaches are useful, they tend to divide or classify rather than unify. That is, they supply data and explanation, but they do not offer the sweep of events, the sense of plot and movement that we get from reading the biblical Gospels and Acts. My intent, by contrast, is to bring together the work of many scholars to reconstruct this critical period *as a story*.

The result is a work of historical fiction—with a twist. It is not an attempt to create another book of the Bible, or even to suggest that this is what a sequel to the biblical Acts of the Apostles would look like if it had been written. Rather, it is an attempt to use a biblical format to convey what *may* have happened, relying on the data and techniques that scholarship makes available. Of course I am only one scholar, and my assumptions (stated below) influence my findings and presentation. Moreover, even if the general framework of my reconstruction is credible, there are infinite variations possible in terms of who went where, said what, and did this or that.

The "twist" is that the fictional element of this volume is not merely a work of imagination; it is a work of reconstruction. For that reason, the text is accompanied by a commentary which explains or quotes the sources behind stories, shows how the text harmonizes with data or themes in the New Testament, and offers other background information to help the reader understand the process of composition. Careful attention is given to the themes, content, and style of Acts, and even the vocabulary and cadence are an attempt to render the imagined Greek words and syntax into the English of the New Revised Standard Version. So to the extent that the text feels authentic to the reader, this is by design—but as a gesture of reverence, not as an attempt to mislead.

SORTING FACT FROM FICTION

A peach and an onion are similar in size, shape, weight, and even color. But peel away the peach skin and flesh, crack open the pit, and there is its essence, the seed or kernel. Peel away the onion skin, pry away layers beneath, and eventually you have nothing but smelly fingers. Applying the analogy to accounts of the apostles written a hundred or more years after their time, are we looking at peaches or onions?

"Form criticism" is a kind of educated guesswork in which scholars of ancient documents speculate backwards from the final "form" (what the text says) to the original events, or at least to the circumstances, that gave rise to the text. One of the principles they employ is "multiple attestation," which suggests that an event reported by a number of writers in different places at different times (and the earlier the better) is more likely to be a "peach"; that is, it may represent or at least approximate an historical event. So, for example, subtracting the sometimes contradictory or fantastic details in various tales of Peter's death, we are left with the "kernel" that he was martyred in Rome late in Nero's reign. Another principle is "dissimilarity," which suggests that an event that is either unique or not easily explained away by known circumstances is more likely to be a "peach." So, for example, Peter's crucifixion upside down is an unusual and, therefore, credible detail; but a story that pits him against the magician Simon (from Acts 8) in front of Nero looks suspiciously like other contemporary tales involving various apostles where Simon serves as a kind of super villain.

Time complicates questions of credibility in our sources. With the Gospels, we have a narrow window of no more than seventy years between events and writing. When asking what happened to the apostles after Acts, however, we have material written up to a thousand years later. Is any of it credible? Generally speaking, the earlier the source, the more reliable, although there can be exceptions for long-lost manuscripts or for traditions preserved in isolated areas. It is also important to note that literature is not our only source of information. Archaeology and other disciplines can sometimes confirm stories or give new information. For example, the discovery that a king named in the apocryphal *Acts of Thomas* was an historical figure, together with finds of early Roman coins on the Malabar coast, suddenly lent credibility to a heretofore "legendary" first-century Christian mission to India.

MAKING HISTORY

In my reconstruction of events here, I put words in the mouths of apostles, but I attempt only to paraphrase, clarify, or slightly extend New Testament teaching. Undoubtedly, considerable development of ideas occurred during the years covered by this volume, and we should expect different flavors of faith from apostles lesser known than Paul and Peter, who dominate Acts and the Epistles. But the purpose of this book is not to introduce new controversies, much less heresies, especially since it is designed to be consistent with the themes introduced in Luke-Acts. With that in view, I take a cautious approach regarding theology and ethics, and I am more speculative regarding events. At the end of the book I have included a chart that rates the probability of the proposed locations and deaths of each apostle.

The text describes several healings and prophecies, but I do fill the text with "signs and wonders" from apocryphal works, nor do I invent new ones. This is not because I doubt that miracles occurred in the ministries of the apostles, but because it is nearly impossible to discern fact from fiction in apocryphal miracle stories, and it seems presumptuous to invent new ones. Why? In the New Testament, healings or prophecy involve an obvious purpose, to get health or information by a direct act of God, whereas "signs and wonders" are tied to larger purposes and themes, some of which are beyond our understanding. Ignorance of this distinction is evident in early Christian apocryphal tales of the boy Jesus striking dead a playmate who foolishly knocks him down or of Peter causing the crash of a magician who flies through the air to impress Nero. While I could compose stories without such silliness, the invention of even a "plausible miracle" with a clear link to a larger theme would take my reconstruction beyond both peaches and onions, to blowing bubbles.

Is it possible to sort through the mess of dubious traditions to reconstruct a coherent, credible account of this critical period? The choice between peach and onion is an inexact science, and I am undoubtedly guilty at times of giving too much credit to legendary material or of overlooking an historical kernel. But the intent is to present a story both credible and readable. Where I must embellish in the interest of filling out the story, I attempt to do so in a manner consistent with the New Testament, particularly with the style and theology of Luke.

WHY NO MORE?

The reader may wonder why the events of this volume end about AD 75. Why not take the story to the end of the first century? Three reasons. One is the limitation of space. In the interest of authenticity, this sequel is the same length as Luke's Gospel and Acts (each about twenty-four thousand words), which is barely enough space to cover the known or likely events of the period AD 62–75. Of course, there could be yet another sequel, but a second limitation is Luke's life. It is unlikely that he was much younger than thirty when he became a travelling companion of Paul around AD 50, so his survival to the end of the century is unlikely. Finally, for the end of the first century and beginning of the second, we have a collection of a dozen works, some anonymous and others by Christian leaders, known together as the Apostolic Fathers. Although these writings contain little historical information, in many respects they pick up where this volumes leaves off, supplying a wealth of material about the early development of Christianity.

WHOSE HISTORY IS THIS?

Since I am writing as if this were a New Testament document, and because The New Testament assumes its own accuracy (as do early church writers), I will follow its claims of authorship. That supposition tips over other dominoes, including early dates of composition and traditional authors for the Gospels. Let me be clear, however, that my intention in this is not to dig in my heels for widely-disputed positions but to operate within the context of New Testament belief. The alternative would be to make complex judgments about New Testament documents in order to justify a revised history, and this would not be useful to most readers. I might, for example, reconstruct an early Christian history that stresses the leadership of women, social justice, harmony between ethnic groups, or "lost causes" like Gnosticism. But however interesting such versions of the period might be, they would owe more to a modern agenda than to the earliest documents and traditions, including those of the New Testament itself.

In general, therefore, this account operates from five assumptions that enable me to construct a coherent and I hope plausible sequence of events: 1) the canonical New Testament contains accurate information concerning the travels of the apostles that can be harmonized for the most part internally and with early church tradition; 2) the disputed letters 1–2 Timothy and Titus, or at least the travel details in them, are credible sources for Paul's later travels; 3) Mark, then Matthew and Luke, were written between AD 62–74 by the men whose names the early church attached to them; 4) accounts by second-to-fourth century writers, especially Clement, Irenaeus, Tertullian, and Eusebius, contain fairly accurate information that may help us reconstruct details of Christian origins; 5) the often imaginative or heretical writings and traditions of the first few centuries of the Christian era may be gleaned, with appropriate caution, for information about the first century.

One final note on method: In order to avoid cluttering the text with citations, I have cited scholars only when documenting technical information (e.g., details of Roman trial law) or supporting a position on a disputed matter (e.g., Paul's trip to Spain). Other information provided here is available in standard reference works such as encyclopedias, introductory textbooks, and major commentaries, including scholarly materials available online. At the end of the book is a list of works cited, which also serves as a partial bibliography for those who wish to pursue sources on their own.

JOURNEY OF WRITER AND READER

Writing this book was a renewal of faith. I was freshly struck by the truth that a tiny group of people, without force of arms and often in the face of violent opposition, persevered, wandered into distant lands, and drew converts to the bizarre idea that an executed Jewish convict was the savior of the world and the transformer of each individual. My hope, my prayer, is that readers will themselves find new cause to wonder at this story, at this Person who continues to produce sequels in the lives of many. As the anonymous first century *Epistle to Diognetus* puts it, "He it is who was from the beginning, who was born young and found to be old, and who is ever born new in the hearts of the saints."

The Apostles after Acts

CHAPTER 1

Prologue

1 In the second book, Theophilus, I wrote about all that the Holy Spirit accomplished from the beginning of the church in Jerusalem, [2]how the apostles preached the word of the Lord in many places, from Jerusalem to Rome, and how the number of believers multiplied. [3]Now, having seen myself, and also having learned from many eyewitnesses, how the Lord has continued to fulfill his promise to send the word to the ends of the earth, [4]I complete my account, trusting that by the truth of these things, the Spirit will make you bold to continue the work that he began through the apostles.

Paul Released to Travel

[5]In the seventh year of Nero, when Paul had been preaching unhindered in Rome for more than a year, Pudens, the son of a senator, heard the word of the Lord from Paul and believed, along with many of his household. [6]Pudens brought Paul into his own house, and he welcomed believers there from all over Rome. [7]And many more were added to the number of believers because of him.

[8]When Paul had been in Rome two years, and the Jews from Jerusalem had not yet appeared to accuse him before the emperor, the charges against him were dismissed. [9]Pudens also sent word to the emperor that he would commit to surety for Paul. [10]Because Paul had obeyed all the laws of Rome, and because Pudens promised houses and lands to ensure Paul's appearance at the will of the emperor, Paul was given over to Pudens. [11]Immediately Pudens determined to help Paul fulfill his desire to preach in Spain, providing for Paul and those who accompanied him out of his own possessions. [12]He sent with Paul as his steward his slave Quintipor, who was a believer. [13]Paul summoned Timothy from Ephesus and Titus from Corinth, and he also took with him Urbanus and Stachys from Rome.

Paul Preaches in Terraco

[14]When a moderate south wind began to blow, we set sail for Corsica, [15]and after waiting several days, we found favorable winds and sailed to Terraconensis, where we journeyed from the coast to the city of Terraco. [16]There was a synagogue of the Jews in the city, but Paul went instead to the marketplace, where he preached openly to those gathered there. [17]After some days, when several citizens had believed, certain leaders of the city asked Paul to speak to them.

[18]So Paul, standing on the steps of the palace of Augustus, said, [19]"Terraconians, you have achieved fame throughout the world, and great wealth for yourselves, by taking from the earth gold, silver, and other metals. [20]Even the scriptures of the Jews from ancient times speak of your greatness among the nations, and the kings of the earth who have traded with you. [21]But the prophets also speak of you together with one who is greater than any king, [22]one of whom the scriptures declare, 'the kings of Tarshish and of the isles render him tribute.' [23]Who is this greater one but the Messiah, whom the scriptures say must suffer, and whom the Jews rejected, but God raised him from the dead and seated him at his right hand? [24]Thus the scriptures say of God, 'You set a crown of fine gold on his head. He asked you for life; you gave it to him—length of days forever and ever. [25]His glory is great through your help; splendor and majesty you bestow on him.'

[26]Now why do the scriptures exalt him, and why do we call him Lord? [27]It is because in another place, Terraconians, when speaking of your city, God declares the foolishness of idols next to the worship of the true God: [28]'They are both stupid and foolish; the instruction given by idols is no better than wood! Beaten silver is brought from Tarshish, and gold from Uphaz. [29]They are the work of artisans, but the Lord is the true God; he is the living God and the everlasting King.' [30]Long ago, David, king of the Jews, declared to God that 'The law of your mouth is better to me than thousands of gold and silver pieces'; [31]and David's son Solomon, likewise, proclaimed that 'A good name is to be chosen rather than great riches, and favor is better than silver or gold.' [32]What is this better law but the law of the spirit of life which is in Christ Jesus? [33]And what is this good name but the name of Christ, who descended from these kings according to the flesh and whose name is now above all other names? [34]And what is this favor but the mercy of God poured out on those who call upon the name of the Lord? [35]And finally, what are gold and silver, lead and tin, next to the surpassing riches of knowing Christ as Savior?"

[36]With these and other proofs from scripture, Paul persuaded the people, and many believed, including several women and men of high standing. [37]Paul remained in Terraco for two months, preaching, healing, and strengthening the disciples.

Paul Expelled from Carthago Nuvo

[38]Then, leaving Stachys in the house of Abercius to continue building up the believers, we journeyed south by the Augustan Way to Carthago Nuvo, where Paul again preached in the marketplace to the leaders of the city. [39]And here many more believed; but the next day, the Jews of that city accused Paul before the officials, [40]saying, "This is the one about whom we have heard from our brothers in Jerusalem and Rome, that he teaches scorn for our law and our people, and also for the gods of Rome." [41]And the city officials, fearing further disturbance from the Jews or from the people, told Paul to leave the city.

Paul's Opponents Thwarted in Corduba

[42]We then traveled west to the province of Baetica, and the cities of Corduba and Gades. [43]In Corduba, Paul was welcomed into the house of Balbus, a silver merchant, who was the brother of Abercius. [44]When Paul entered the house, Balbus told him that his wife Claudia was lying ill in an inner chamber, and near to death with a fever that had afflicted her for eight days. [45]And Paul, entering the chamber, prayed for Claudia and raised her up. [46]Then Balbus and his entire household believed and were baptized

in the name of the Lord Jesus, and they received the Holy Spirit. [47]And word spread throughout the city, so that others brought sick people to Paul, and many were healed. [48]Now when the Jews of Carthago Nuvo sent messengers to accuse Paul, the city officials sent them away, [49]saying, "This man has done nothing but good since he came here, so whatever god he worships must be good, and the trouble that you warn about must be the trouble that you bring." [50]So the believers in Corduba rejoiced, and Paul remained with them four months, teaching and strengthening them in the Lord. [51]Then he told them, "The Lord has revealed to me that my time is short, but I have not yet reached the farthest point of my journey."

Paul Reaches the Western Sea

[52]So, leaving Urbanus in Corduba, we traveled south to Gades, which faces the great western sea, from which sailors journey to Gaul, Britain, and many strange lands. [53]When Paul saw the sea, he knelt down at the water's edge and said, "Here I have reached the limit of the west, and where the Lord sends me now, I must wait and pray to learn." [54]But we had been in Gades only three days when a ship arrived from Rome carrying a messenger from Pudens with a letter for Paul begging him to come to Ephesus, where the church was threatened by false teachers.

CHAPTER 2

Paul Preaches in Crete

1 Since it was now late in the year, Paul determined to leave Gades as soon as possible. [2]So we took passage on a ship carrying merchants, which put in at Carthage, Syracuse, and then Crete, where we disembarked to find passage to Ephesus. [3]There were good southwesterly winds at that time of year, and Paul was anxious to reach Ephesus, but the Lord told him to preach in Crete, so we traveled from the port of Chersonisos inland to Lyttos. [4]There Paul found among the Jews a household of believers who had been faithful to the Lord Jesus for many years, but they had made no converts either among the Jews or the Greeks. [5]So Paul preached day and night both in the synagogue and in the marketplace, and more were added to the number of believers, both from the Jews and the Greeks. [6]After a month, leaving Titus in Lyttos to strengthen the believers there and to preach in the other towns nearby, we sailed for Ephesus.

Paul Confronts Opponents in Ephesus

[7]Following a strong south wind, and touching at Naxos, we reached Ephesus on the third day. [8]When we arrived, the elders told Paul that the church there had divided into two factions, one that remained in the household of Onesiphorus, with Priscilla and Aquila and some others, while Hymenaeus and Alexander the silversmith drew many others away in opposition to Paul. [9]When Paul asked to meet with all the believers, including those who opposed him, only Alexander with a few others came to dispute with him. [10]Alexander said to those who had gathered, "Paul follows the Pharisees who hope for another life, because they are not content with the Lord in this life. [11]But many other Jews, and the wisdom

of the Greeks, and even your own eyes, tell you that there is no resurrection except in our new life in Christ. [12]Paul comes here again not to make you free in the Lord but to chain you to the body."

[12]And Paul replied, "Brothers and sisters, for two years I lived with you, and you saw by many miracles and healings that the Lord cared not only for your souls but also for your bodies. [13]Does the Lord no longer care, or have you now been led astray by the foolishness of these men that passes for wisdom? [14]For it was not I, but the Spirit through the scriptures who taught you that the Lord made the flesh of man and called it good. [15]Now we all know that the flesh is weak and prone to sin; but so also is the spirit of man fallen and prone to rebellion. [16]Nevertheless, both are saved by grace together, and both will be raised on the last day. [17]If it were not so, why would Christ Jesus be raised in the body? [18]And if he is not raised, but is only a spirit, why would God have sent him to you in the flesh, from the line of David? [19]For by the body you are made one with each other, and by the body you are part of all that God has done in the world from creation until now. [20]Without the body, therefore, there is no truth in what was accomplished through the prophets, or in the life and death of the Lord Jesus Christ, or even in you when you first came to faith. [21]Without the body, you are less than a leaf blown by every wind—first to false teachers, then to immorality, and finally to the ruin of your faith. [22]Furthermore, without the resurrection, the salvation that you know in Christ ends with your death. [23]And while you may thrive in the body for now, enjoying the pleasures of life, what of those who suffer by disease, or famine, or persecution? [24]For such is the lot of most men, and of many believers, especially in these last days. [25]Are you so short-sighted that you cling to this life only, but do not think of those for whom life is filled with trouble,

and resurrection their only hope? [26]And as for you, Alexander, if it is the body that you scorn, so from the body of Christ you shall be cut off until you repent and return to the word that you once received."

[27]When those who opposed Paul heard his words, some of them repented, but Alexander scoffed, and with Hymenaeus continued to teach against Paul. [28]Paul remained for three months and debated with them on several occasions; but wishing to reach Macedonia before the winter storms, he left Timothy there to strengthen the believers and journeyed to Miletus, where Paul wished to see the believers one last time.

Paul Teaches About Forgiveness in Corinth

[29]From Miletus we sailed along the coast to Troas, where Paul found Mark in the house of Carpus, and left with him his books and parchments. [30]From there we sailed to Neapolis, and traveled to Philippi and Thessalonica. [31]In all of these places, the believers rejoiced to see Paul, and many were encouraged in the faith.

[32]From Thessalonica, Paul journeyed to Corinth, where there were many believers, meeting in several households, but all were one in the Lord. [33]Apollos was in Corinth at this time, strengthening many. [34]And when Paul witnessed his great knowledge of scripture and ability to debate with both Jews and Greeks, he sent him with Zenas to help Titus in Crete and Timothy in Ephesus. [35]From there Apollos went to Rome and then to Alexandria, where he expounded the scriptures concerning Christ to the learned Jews, both in preaching and in writing.

[36]While Paul was in Corinth, the believers brought to him one of the elders and the wife of one of the deacons, who had been caught together in adultery. [37]Although they repented, the believers wanted to cast

them from the church, for they said to Paul, "You taught us to deliver such sinners to Satan." [38]But Paul said, "You do not understand the body of Christ. [39]For it is not the power to punish that binds you in the Lord, but the power to love. [40]If these two had not repented, you should exclude them until their desire for you would bring them back in sorrow and obedience. [41]But because they have repented, you must embrace them as though they had not sinned, although they should not have authority while they prove their obedience. [42]Anyone who would cast them out should himself be cast out, for that one denies Christ. [43]You did not receive the Spirit to build walls, but to pierce them." [44]And one of the elders said, "But they may sin again." [45]But Paul replied, "Which of you has not sinned two times, or three, or a thousand? At which number did the cup of the Lord's mercy become empty? [46]When you have emptied that cup for yourselves, you may show it empty to others whose trespasses offend you." [47]So by these and other words, Paul taught the believers to grow in Christ.

[48]But when Paul had been with the Corinthians for seven months, he received a letter from Pudens telling of a great fire in Rome and of certain Jews who whispered to Nero's wife Poppaea to blame the Christians, so that Paul, as one well known to them, was summoned to Rome to answer their accusations. [49]Despite the warning of Pudens to stay away, even if he would lose houses and lands, Paul immediately prepared to sail for Rome, [50]saying, "The lion roars, and I will go to him, trusting in the Lord for help. [51]For if I do not face the lion, what others might he devour while he seeks me?"

CHAPTER 3

The Great Fire in Rome

1 The next day, we found a ship sailing for Rome from the port of Lechaion. [2]Not yet knowing how great was the danger to others, Paul took with him Titus, Crescens, Tichycus, Eubulus, and Quintipor. [3]Setting sail with a fair south wind, after four days we put in at Rhegium, on the fifth day we reached Ostia.

[4]In Rome at this time, all was in an uproar over the fire. [5]For there are often fires in the city, because the streets are narrow and crowded with wooden buildings, but no fire had burned for so long or destroyed so great an area. [6]Beginning near the Circus Maximus, and blown by strong winds, flames spread quickly in every direction, burning for six days and six nights. [7]Soldiers roamed through the city stopping those who tried to put out the flames, either because they were under orders or because they hoped for spoil. [8]Many areas of the city were destroyed, including the Palatine Hill and many palaces, temples, and houses of leading citizens. [9]Most of the great buildings of the Forum, however, which were made of stone, were spared, as was most of the Campus Martius in the north, and the Esquiline Hill on the east.

[10]Most of the great men of Rome were away because of the heat of the summer, and Nero himself was at Antium. [11]When Nero rushed back to the city while the fire was still burning, he stood on a tower, played the lyre, and sang until the flames threatened even his palace. [12]After the fire, for the relief of the homeless, he built shelters in the Campus Martius, opened Agrippa's public buildings and his own Gardens there,

and had grain brought in to feed the people. [13]These acts, though popular, did not silence the rumor that Nero had given orders to start the fire because he wished to rebuild the city after his own plan, including a great new palace, which indeed he began while smoke still rose from the ruins.

Christians Blamed for the Fire

[14]At this time the Jews lived in several quarters across the river, and many of the believers lived among them, gathering in various households. [15]Most of the Jews lived at peace with them, but some of their leaders hated the believers, [16]especially Paul, for he had continually preached boldly in Rome and renounced the Jews for rejecting Christ Jesus. [17]Seeing an opportunity, a few of these Jews went to Nero's wife Poppaea, who was a friend to them, and told her that Nero might blame the believers for the fire. [18]For they said, "All Rome has heard these men say that the world will soon end by fire, nor can they dispute that they desire it. [19]Not only that, but they name Christ, and not Caesar, their Lord." [20]Poppaea reported all these things to Nero, who knew nothing of the Lord or of the believers. [21]But after listening to her, he gave orders for his soldiers to arrest every believer they could find.

[22]Now began a time of great suffering for the believers in Rome. [23]For whenever Nero's soldiers were able to find one who named Christ as Lord, they would torture that believer to confess the names of others, so that more were arrested, and all lived in fear. [24]The soldiers took those who confessed Christ Jesus, both men and women, to the Circus of Nero and chained them there in the place where wild beasts were kept. [25]Then, casting lots among them, the soldiers took some to be burned and others to be cast to the beasts. [26]Those who were to be burned were first covered with pitch, then crucified and placed along the roads or paths of the gardens. [27]They were left there to suffer during the day, and at night they were set on fire to light the gardens. [28]So many were killed in this way in the first days that the fire and smoke could be seen from across the river, so that many thought another part of the city was being destroyed.

[29]Others were thrown to the beasts, which were not given food for many days, and then released upon the believers, who were either tied to posts or made to run for the entertainment of those Romans who came to the circus. [30]But neither these believers nor those who were burned cried out, but instead sang songs of praise to the Lord, or prayed in silence until the beasts or flames consumed their bodies. [31]And so loud and joyful was their singing, or so strong were they in silence, that those who witnessed their suffering, both the soldiers and the crowds, knew their innocence and began to pity them and to despise Nero. [32]Moreover, many turned to the Lord because of their faith and boldness, so that for every one who suffered, two more were added to their number.

The Burning of Andronicus

[33]Among those arrested in the first days was Andronicus, whose household was among those where believers gathered. [34]Although he was beaten with rods, and then boiling water was poured on him, he did not reveal the names or whereabouts of any other believers. [35]Instead, filled with the Spirit, he cried out to the others who were arrested to be strong in the Lord. [36]And when he was crucified, until the fire was lit, he boldly sang the hymn taught to him by Paul:

> [37]Though in the form of God, our
>   Christ
> For gain of us knew pain and loss;
> [38]His emptiness alone sufficed
> To fill our cups, to lift his cross.

³⁹From servant to almighty Lord
Our God has now exalted him;
⁴⁰Each knee shall bow with one
    accord,
Each tongue confess and join our
    hymn.

⁴¹Andronicus continued to sing until a soldier came forward with a torch and touched it to the pitch covering him, yet he continued to sing until the flames covered him and he gave up his spirit to the Lord.

⁴²Other believers who witnessed the death of Andronicus were strengthened, both to proclaim Christ Jesus boldly and to refuse to tell the whereabouts of other believers, so that many were saved from arrest. ⁴³But for many weeks Nero continued to seek out the believers, and hundreds were killed, ⁴⁴some like Andronicus because the Jews accused them, and others because they came forward boldly and confessed Christ before the soldiers.

CHAPTER 4

Paul Arrives in Rome

1 When Paul reached Ostia, he stayed there that night in the house of Pudens. ²Pudens sent word to the believers who were in hiding, and some were bold to come to Paul, not fearing arrest; among those were Eubulus, Linus, and Claudia. ³Linus embraced Paul and told him of the great suffering that had occurred in Rome while they waited for Paul, of the multitude of believers who were thrown to beasts or burned, including Andronicus and many others beloved by Paul. ⁴All wept. ⁵Then Paul said, "Let us hope in the Lord, for surely those who died by fire will send up sparks to ignite the whole world. ⁶And do not fear on my behalf, for whether I live or die, Christ will be glorified." ⁷With these and many other words, the believers were comforted.

⁸The next day, wishing to show the Romans that all was done lawfully, Pudens chained Paul to the soldier Licinius, who was a believer, and went with them to Nero's palace. ⁹He also sent for leaders from the Jews who were not opposed to Paul, and certain believers who were Roman freedmen, to be witnesses on Paul's behalf, ¹⁰but out of fear of Nero, none came to Paul's defense. ¹¹Nero's prefect, who had commanded Pudens to summon Paul, now stated that without witnesses in Paul's defense, the charges against him could not be dismissed, and that he must also answer new charges concerning the fire. ¹²Then he commanded that Paul be held in the Praetorium until Nero might consider the matter.

¹³Paul was cast into a small hut where he suffered from the cold and many other indignities, but through the intercession of Pudens, visitors were permitted both to bring food and to help him prepare for his trial. ¹⁴Many believers, fearing arrest, would not come to him, but others were made bold in the Spirit and brought to Paul both food and comfort, and received comfort from him. ¹⁵Among these were Onesiphorus, and Pudens and his daughters Praxedes and Pudentiana, who also knew Nero's evil ways and counseled Paul concerning the best way to appeal to him. ¹⁶Learning that his trial would not occur before winter, Paul sent Titus to Dalmatia, Crescens to Galatia, and Tichycus to Ephesus with a letter to Timothy begging him to come. ¹⁷This Timothy did, bringing with him Aquila and Priscilla, Apollos, and also Mark, who brought Paul's

books and parchments, [18]but because winter was near, their journey was delayed by storms, and they did not arrive until many days after Paul was killed.

[19]After some time, the prefect called for Paul again, telling Pudens that Nero was ready to hear his defense. [20]So Paul, together with only Licinius, Pudens, and Quintipor, the slave of Pudens, went to the palace. [21]Soon after Paul entered, an attorney spoke for Nero, accusing Paul as before of causing sedition among the Jews, and adding the new charge that he was a leader of the sect of the Christians who were blamed for the fire. [21]And Nero, reclining on a dais, listened.

Paul Speaks to Nero

[22]When the prefect motioned to Paul, he stretched out his free hand and said, "I appeal to your benevolence, most excellent emperor, in dismissing these false charges, [23]trusting that you will confirm the judgment of your governors Gallio and Festus, that I have obeyed the law in all things, as have all those who follow Christ.

[24]"In the days before my birth, the Roman consul and hero Pompey traveled through the province of Cilicia and the city of Tarsus to make that province a part of Rome. [25]In that day the father of my father, a leather merchant, provided for Pompey to house all of his legions in tents and to cover them all with clothing. [26]In return for his service, he was made a Roman citizen, an honor given also to me, as the firstborn of his firstborn. [27]Now, many years later, I have come to Rome, not with an army, but on behalf of many brothers and sisters in Christ, [28]praying that as my earthly father once covered Caesar, Caesar will now cover me and my spiritual family. [29]I do not speak to Caesar of garments, but of spiritual things, knowing that he has power to cover those who believe in Christ Jesus with the mantle

of freedom to worship in peace. [30]So all who name Christ Jesus pray for Caesar and for all authorities, submitting to them in all humility and obedience, knowing that rulers are put in place by God.

[31]"Therefore the charges against me and those who follow Christ have no foundation but result only from certain misunderstandings among the Jews. [32]I have honored Caesar in all things from the days of my youth until now, whether free or in chains, following the vision once given to me of the risen Christ. [33]As a Jew, I have been bold to testify of those things told in our scriptures concerning this Christ, that he would suffer and rise from the dead, giving light and the hope of salvation to both Jew and gentile. [34]Through all of these trials, until this day, he has been my help. [35]Some of the Jews deny that he is the Messiah, and others deny the resurrection of the dead, and these have proclaimed themselves enemies both to me and to all who follow Christ. [36]But these are disputes among the Jews, and they cannot prove any other charge against me or my brothers and sisters regarding the laws of Rome. [37]Nor do they appear before you today—whether out of fear or shame I do not know—whereas I offer you not only my testimony but also the confirmation of the noble Gallio and Festus that I have done no wrong.

[38]"Thus I have waited in chains for these many years for the opportunity to answer these false accusations and to hear you, most benevolent emperor, proclaim to the world that those who follow Christ are lawful subjects of Caesar. [39]For to end the persecution of my brothers and sisters will redound to your honor both in Rome and throughout the world."

CHAPTER 5

Nero Debates Paul

1 When Paul had finished his defense, Nero spoke with several of his counselors who were standing near, among whom was Poppaea. [2]Then Nero said to Paul, "I have not yet heard why you who follow this Christ so hate Rome and Caesar that you would burn the city. [3]Do you not hope that your God will destroy all the earth with fire? Answer me this."

[4]Then Paul spoke again: "It is true, most excellent emperor, that God will destroy the earth in judgment on the day when Christ returns, [5]but his judgment and his triumph are not as men understand these things, nor is it given to men to bring these things about. [6]Our God does not dwell in a house made with hands, nor can any man build God's house by destroying the house of another. [7]On the contrary, we are commanded to live in peace with all men, and to honor earthly authority as sent by God. [8]These things all the Jews believe, and not only those who follow Christ."

[9]Now Nero, wishing to trap Paul into speaking against him, said, "You speak of 'authority.' [10]But is not Caesar their Lord and yours?"

[11]Paul answered, "Caesar is lord on earth, but Christ is Lord in heaven, and there is one God, the Father, who reigns over all. [12]Christ his Son dwelt on earth, and he will return in glory to fulfill the scriptures. [13]In that day all who dwell on earth, not only the Jews but also the Romans, and Caesar himself, will bow down before Christ the Lord."

[14]At these words, Nero cried out, "No more of this madness! [15]A Jew reigns in heaven with his father? [16]Is there no one left on earth to reign but Caesar? [17]Then let most excellent and benevolent Caesar judge. [18]This man shall not wait ten days to see his Lord, but shall die today by the sword. [19]And because he dishonors Rome, take him outside the city, along the road by which he came."

[20]When Pudens heard Nero's judgment, he came before him weeping and begged for mercy on account of Paul's age and infirmity. [21]And Nero embraced him and made a show before all that he sorrowed for the loss to Pudens, but that he must make an example of Paul. [22]Now Nero had already learned from Poppaea that Pudens was a believer, but he feared that to kill more leading citizens would stir up the nobles against him. [23]So Nero made a pretense of pity, but two days later he secretly gave orders to have Pudens murdered quietly in his own house. [24]Nevertheless, word spread that Nero and Poppaea were killing not only believers among the Jews but also many Romans who followed Christ, all of them blameless, and the people began to pity the believers and to hate Nero. [25]Hearing of this, Nero stopped the killing, but the people and especially the nobles still despised him and blamed him all the more for the fire. [26]Such was the tyrant Nero, who three years later in a rage killed Poppaea while she was pregnant; [27]and afterwards, when all Rome turned against him for his many crimes, ran from his own palace and begged his slave to kill him, for he did not have the courage. [28]So Nero's reign and his line ended, while the church in Rome and throughout the world continued to multiply.

The Beheading of Paul

[29]Immediately after his trial, Paul was taken from the palace by a centurion and a cohort

of soldiers outside the city along the Ostian Way. [30]Word spread quickly from Pudens and the slaves of his household, so that before they were outside the city, many believers had come, risking their lives, to follow with the crowd who wished to see an execution. [31]When the centurion had taken Paul some distance along the road, he grew anxious about the growing crowd, so [32]he gave the order to stop in an open field where a single fig tree stood. [33]Now the believers began to weep and to cry out against the soldiers, so Pudens asked the centurion to allow Paul to quiet them, and this was granted.

[34]Paul said, "My brothers and sisters, do not sorrow, for this is a day of victory that I have long awaited. [35]For many years I have endured hardships and faced death on account of the word, first at the hands of the Jews and now at the hands of the Romans, [36]but all is in the hands of the Lord, into which I will soon be delivered. [37]So do not grieve for me, the least of his servants, but give thanks in this as in all things. [38]For in Christ, when all is lost, all is found. [39]Therefore rejoice that I will soon gain the Lord, and have hope for yourselves. [40]For in Rome and throughout the world, the Lord will build his church upon the death of his saints. [41]If by fire, he will make of it a wind to scatter his seed, and if by the sword, he will make of it a plow to sow, [42]and so he will make such a harvest of faith and righteousness that Rome itself will be overshadowed, and the word of the Lord will go to the ends of the earth."

[43]With these words Paul knelt by the tree, lifted his eyes to heaven, and cried out, "Lord, receive my spirit." [44]Then the centurion, taking a long sword carried by a member of the cohort for that purpose, with one stroke struck Paul's head from his shoulders.

[45]And the soldiers were ready to throw Paul's body into a pit or cast it into the river, but when Pudens asked, they allowed him to take it. [46]Lucina, a believer who was one of those who witnessed Paul's death, had a house nearby with a burial place. [47]So Pudens, together with Quintipor and Licinius and many other believers who were there, took Paul's body there and buried it.

CHAPTER 6

The Crucifixion of Peter

1 Now all this time, following the fire, Peter had been in hiding, not out of fear, but at the urging of Linus and the others who wished to protect him. [2]Sometimes he was in the house of Priscilla, wife of Glabrio, and sometimes in other houses outside the city, where he comforted many whose family members had been killed by Nero. [3]And at this time he was in the house of Junia on the Triumphal Way, a mile from the city.

[4]Linus, after he had witnessed Paul's death and comforted the believers who mourned at the house of Lucina, came in the night with several of Paul's co-workers to tell Peter. [5]And Peter said, "I must go to Rome this night. [6]For today, as I walked in the road, the Lord appeared to me, walking the other way toward the city. [7]And I asked, 'Lord, where are you going?' [8]And he said, "To Rome, to be crucified again.' [9]And I cried out and said, 'No, it is I who must go.' [10]And immediately he was taken up from me into heaven."

[11]And Peter said, "Now that our brother Paul has entered into the Lord's presence, why should I wait another day or even until the morning? Let me go now." [12]Linus and the others pleaded with Peter to remain until daylight, but he would not. [13]And Elama, Peter's wife, begged to go with him, but he said no. [14]And she said, "How is it that I have walked this road so long with you, and you would deny me the last few steps? [15]For you are not the first to say, 'Where you go, I will go also.'"

[16]And so Peter, accompanied only by his wife, walked through the night until he reached the gardens of Nero, where so many of the saints had been killed, and where some were still hanging. [17]Because it was still night, and the cock had not yet crowed, there were only a few soldiers on watch. [18]And Peter was made bold in the Spirit, and proclaimed to them that Christ is Lord. [19]The soldiers, perceiving from his age and manner that he was mad, laughed at him and tried to send him away. [20]But he proclaimed Christ even louder. [21]Then a centurion came out from the barracks nearby and asked what the disturbance was. [22]One of the soldiers said, "This old man is among the mad followers of Christos who have burned the city." [23]The centurion bade soldiers to arrest Peter and to bring him forward. [24]And Elama ran to him and said that she would not be parted from him. [25]The centurion said to him, "Old man, answer this charge. For you know the decree of Nero that no one may live who names Christ as Lord." [26]And Peter answered in a great voice, "On the contrary, no one may live except those who name Christ as Lord." [27]So the centurion commanded the soldiers to crucify him and his wife. [28]Just then the cock crowed. [29]And as they took his wife away to the gardens to crucify her, Peter called out to her tenderly, "Elama, wherever you go, remember the Lord." [30]Then, turning to the soldiers, he said that he was not worthy to die in this manner. [31]And the soldiers mistook him, thinking that he wished to die some other way, so they told him that he must suffer as a traitor and a slave. [32]And Peter said, "I am indeed a slave, and I beg you to return me without delay to Christ my master. [33]I would not be spared the pain of the cross, but the honor of it, to die in the same manner as my Lord." [34]And he continued to preach boldly to them. [35]Then the soldiers mocked him, saying, "Because you are so eager to reach heaven, your feet shall go there first, and all shall see your journey." [36]So they took Peter to the center of the circus and crucified him with his feet uppermost, his arms stretched out, and his head down. [37]For a short time he called out praises to the Lord, but then he could not speak for pain, and in less than an hour he gave up his spirit. [38]All this was witnessed by Gavrus, one of the soldiers in the cohort, who became a believer because of the things he saw that day.

The Church in Rome

[39]When the other believers in Rome learned that Paul and Peter had been killed, one the day after the other, they were in great anguish of heart and debated whether to flee or hide. [40]But Linus and Eubulus were made strong in the Lord to encourage them. [41]Furthermore, believers among the nobles said that Nero's cruelty was soon spent, and that he had said of Paul that cutting off his head would cause the body, meaning the church, to bleed to death. [42]But through the winter, he continued to kill all the believers he found, including Priscilla and Aquila, who had come from Ephesus too late to find Paul alive, and were soon arrested in their house because of informers among the Jews. [43]Timothy and Mark, however, were delivered, and Timothy returned to Ephesus while Mark remained in Rome in the house

of Priscilla Glabria, whom Nero dared not harm, fearing the nobles. ⁴⁴After the winter, Nero gave orders to his soldiers to make no more arrests, and all rejoiced.

⁴⁵Thus through great suffering the word of the Lord continued to spread throughout the city, ⁴⁶including into the households of the great, who were baptized along with their households, and who gave shelter to many. ⁴⁷And many of the soldiers who had been commanded to arrest and kill believers marveled at their faith and endurance in suffering, and they too followed the Lord. ⁴⁸Even those in Rome who did not believe took pity on the believers, because all Rome hated Nero and did not believe his lies about the fire. ⁴⁹As for the tyrant himself, he turned his wrath from the believers to his own nobles; ⁵⁰and when he died, Rome was in turmoil until a new emperor arose, ⁵¹so that for a time the believers were left in peace. ⁵²So it is to this day, although some fear that a new Nero will arise.

CHAPTER 7

Simeon Calls the Apostles to Jerusalem

1 In the last days of Nero's persecutions, Aquila and Priscilla, together with Timothy, arrived in Ostia, where they learned that Paul had been killed. ²They proceeded to their house in Rome, but informants among the Jews brought soldiers to arrest them. ³Priscilla and Aquilla were crucified, and Timothy was in prison for many weeks, but the Lord delivered him. ⁴During this time, Mark and Apollos also arrived, but believers from the household of Pudens hid them in Ostia, where they remained for some time, writing and encouraging the believers. ⁵When Timothy was released, he went to Dalmatia to see Titus, and then, together with Mark and Apollos, they sailed to Alexandria to strengthen the church there.

⁶When word came to Jerusalem that Paul and Peter and many other believers were killed, Simeon and the apostles who were with him, John and Simon the Zealot, fasted and prayed to know the Lord's will and if this were the end that Christ Jesus had foretold. ⁷For certain leaders of the Jews were planning rebellion against Rome, and there were rumors of war. ⁸Moreover, many believers, including some of the apostles, had been called before councils and rulers to be killed for proclaiming Christ as Lord, ⁹while others in Judea and Galilee had been persecuted by the Jews because they refused to take up arms against Rome.

¹⁰Simeon now sent word to the apostles to meet in Jerusalem following Passover, in the eleventh year of Nero. ¹¹He summoned Andrew from Nicaea, Philip and Bartholomew from Hierapolis, Matthew from Damascus, and Judas son of James from Edessa. ¹²Knowing that Thomas was too far away to return, Simeon did not send for him. ¹³In addition to those of the twelve who still lived, Simeon sent for Jude the Lord's brother from Galilee, and Mark, Apollos, and Timothy from Alexandria.

Purpose of the Council

¹⁴When these were all gathered, along with other leaders of the church from Judea and nearby territories, Simeon addressed them, saying, ¹⁵"Brothers in Christ, it is now more years since the Lord was raised than it was from his birth to that day, and still we wait the promise of his coming. ¹⁶One sign he

gave us to look for may soon be upon us, if war comes to Jerusalem. ¹⁷Everywhere our fellow countrymen rise up in anger at Rome and tell us that we must resist Caesar as the enemy of God, at which time God will hasten to save us. ¹⁸Now if war comes, and we stand aside, will we be counted as those who oppose the Lord? ¹⁹No, for we have his command that we should not take up the sword, even in his defense. ²⁰Not only that, but we have for these many years awaited his coming while living at peace with all, despite persecution, sometimes at the hands of the Gentiles and other times at the hands of the Jews. ²¹We obey all laws, except when human authorities set laws against each other, in which case we obey the law of God. ²²In times past, God has used his enemies to punish his people for their hardness of heart. ²³So it was when our fathers were led into captivity in Babylon because, according to the Scriptures, 'All the leading priests and the people also were exceedingly unfaithful.' ²⁴But later, when the people turned to the Lord, he restored them. ²⁵So it may be again, that before the end the Lord may once again use the suffering of his people to fulfill his promise to gather them to himself.

²⁶Therefore, if we join the Jews in fighting Rome, we may keep them longer from following the Lord.

²⁷Now concerning the commission of the Lord to spread the word throughout the world, many have now fulfilled his commission and have entered into his presence rather than returning to ours. ²⁸They have been seeds planted in the ground of this earth, and by their deaths they have multiplied the harvest of heaven. ²⁹Of the twelve whom the Lord chose, only eight remain. ³⁰Now the Lord has instructed us that when he returns, we must be found doing, not waiting in idleness. ³¹Whether this is the end, no one knows, but such signs as we see increase our urgency. ³²So let us now send out those who remain to the places the Lord reveals to us. ³³Furthermore, because many eyewitnesses have now died, let a written account of the deeds and words of the Lord go with those who preach, to strengthen the churches in truth and righteousness. ³⁴To this end, let us examine the account of Mark and, if the Lord wills, let us also choose from among ourselves others who can write of these things."

CHAPTER 8

Commission to Write the Gospels

Now the writing of the life of the Lord in four different accounts happened in this way. ²When Peter was in Rome, the believers there, having heard his preaching, asked him to commit these things in writing. ³And Peter, not being a learned man, entrusted this task to John Mark. ⁴He wrote down what Peter had witnessed, how the Lord performed many miracles, and that his suffering and death were not a shame but a triumph greater than those celebrated by Caesar. ⁵Copies of this account were made for use by various households of believers, and the church in Rome was greatly strengthened by it. ⁶Furthermore, when the Gentiles heard it they were amazed and inquired about the truth of these things, so that many believed, seeing the Spirit at work in the lives of believers. ⁷For the more that Nero did to oppose the church, the more the Lord performed signs and wonders through the believers, and built them up in faith and righteousness.

[8]When the account written by Mark was read in Jerusalem to the apostles and others who were eyewitnesses, they heartily approved it. [9]But some said, "There are many other sayings and deeds of the Lord that we know are worthy to be written, and who will do this?" [10]Simeon and the other apostles, therefore, prayed and fasted for three days, asking the Lord for guidance.

[11]The Spirit indicated to the apostles that Matthew should write a fuller account for the Jews, [12]including proofs from the Scriptures that Jesus was the Messiah, as well as many of the Lord's teachings that have been collected in Hebrew, and others that Matthew remembered. [13]Matthew agreed, and he went to Alexandria, taking with him Apollos, who confounded the Jews there with his great learning and persuaded many to turn to the Lord. [14]Matthew remained in Alexandria for three years and wrote his account of the Lord, and then he traveled to Antioch, where he had many copies made of his account. [15]He had planned to send them to Jerusalem, but by this time all was in turmoil, so he gave them to the apostles to take on their journeys.

[16]Directed by the Spirit, Simeon also said to John that he should write an account of the deeds of the Lord. [17]At first John did not wish to do so, because he believed that he was unworthy, but the other apostles urged him, especially Andrew, to whom the Lord revealed that John should write an account. [18]And when John had prayed for many days, he said, "Mark writes of the last year in the ministry of the Lord, [19]but the Lord did many other miracles and deeds before he went up to Jerusalem to be killed, and he taught the disciples many other things that Mark has not written." [20]And so John agreed to write after the others, but not to repeat those things already told in their accounts.

[21]Finally, Simeon called me before the council and said, "Although you did not see the Lord, you have walked in the Way for many years, preaching the word with Paul and the other apostles. [22]You are beloved by many who saw the Lord, and you have been eyewitness yourself to much that the Spirit has done through the apostles in many places. [23]Furthermore, the Lord has given to you the beloved Theophilus as a patron who will enable you to travel or gather others to you in search of the truth concerning these things. [24]Therefore, we charge you to write for the Gentiles, and for the Jews who live among them, an account of all that has transpired from the birth of the Lord to the present day, including the acts of the apostles, according to the accounts of eyewitnesses from near and far."

[25]In this manner the Spirit began to provide four accounts of the life and teachings of Christ Jesus, of which copies would be made for the strengthening of the church and to aid in the spread of the word. [26]The apostles and all those gathered were of one accord regarding these four accounts, and all rejoiced.

Commission of Those Remaining of the Twelve

[27]On the next day, Simeon said, "Just as the Lord has provided that four will write in one Spirit, so he has created four winds to carry the word forth. [28]So the Spirit directs each of the twelve who remain to the four corners of the earth. [29]First, John, together with Timothy, will go north to Asia, bearing witness to the word of the Lord and strengthening the church in the region of Ephesus. [30]Philip and Bartholomew, likewise, will return to Hierapolis in Phrygia, and from there they will go as the Lord directs. [31]Andrew, together with Luke, will journey to the west, to Macedonia and Achaia. [32]Simon and Judas, likewise, will carry the word west to far lands, first through Cyrenaica and Mauretania, then if the Lord allows to Britain and Gaul. [33]Matthew will travel to the south,

first to Alexandria with Mark and Apollos, then to Ethiopia. ³⁴To the east Thomas has already gone, beyond Parthia and Persia, and as far as India. ³⁵When we learn about the progress of the word in these lands, the Lord may direct the apostles and others to go there, so that the mercy of God will reach farther than the sword of Rome, even farther than the dispersion of the Jews. ³⁶For when all the nations of the earth have heard the good news, the word of the Lord will be fulfilled, and the end will come."

CHAPTER 9

Leadership of Simeon

1 After Simeon had spoken, the apostles, together with all the believers gathered there, gave thanks for the direction that the Lord had given, and for the wisdom shown by Simeon. ²Now there were some among the believers in Jerusalem who opposed him, because they believed that the Lord would raise up prophets to lead the church, ³and that appointing men from the family of Jesus would give the appearance of rule by lineage, according to the traditions of men. ⁴But the apostles saw that Simeon, like James before him, was chosen by the Spirit not by reason of his nearness to the Lord by birth but by reason of his faith and righteousness.

Martyrdom of James, the Lord's Brother

⁵For James the brother of the Lord was beloved, not only by the household of faith but also by many of the Jews, even among those who did not believe in Christ Jesus. ⁶He was known from his youth as a righteous man, and he was in the habit of praying in the temple, ⁷begging forgiveness for the people, so that his knees became as hard as a camel's, and he was called by the people James the Just. ⁸Many believed in Christ Jesus because of his wise words and his good works. ⁹But during the Passover in the eighth year of Nero, when the city was crowded with strangers, the scribes and Pharisees saw an opportunity to accuse him. ¹⁰Taking him to the pinnacle of the temple, they demanded that he confess who Jesus was in sight and hearing of all the people. ¹¹And James, filled with the Spirit, shouted in a great voice, "Why do you ask me concerning Jesus, the Son of Man? ¹²He was crucified and raised from the dead, and he now sits in heaven at the right hand of the great Power, and is soon to come upon the clouds of heaven." ¹³Then the scribes and Pharisees, perceiving that the people were not angry but ready to hear more, cried out that he was a blasphemer and pushed him from the pinnacle of the temple. ¹⁴But James, who was not killed by the great fall, rose to his knees and prayed, "I beg you, Lord God our Father, forgive them." ¹⁵The crowd marveled at this, but the scribes and Pharisees came down from the pinnacle and began to stone James. ¹⁶One of the priests said, "Stop! Will you stone the one who prays for you?" ¹⁷And while they considered what to do, one of them came forward with a club and struck James on the head, and he gave up his spirit. ¹⁸When the crowd saw the evil that was done, and how James died praying for his accusers, even more believed; ¹⁹and others shouted out against the scribes and Pharisees, so that after this they did not persecute the believers openly, but only before their own councils.

Final Song and Death of Mary

[20]Now all this time Mary, the mother of the Lord, had lived in Bethlehem, where she was cared for by John. [21]Full of years and full of grace, she spent her days in care for the poor and earnest prayer for the saints. [22]When word came to her that James had been killed, she was filled with sorrow, and said,

[23]My heart faints within me;
Shuddering and sorrow seize my
flesh.
[24]I have come into deep waters, and
the flood sweeps over me.
[25]I am weary with weeping,
and my eyes grow dim with waiting
for my God.
[26]O Lord, do not cast me off in the
time of old age;
[27]Do not forsake me when my
strength is spent.
For I know that my Redeemer lives,
That when my flesh fails, I shall see
God,
[28]That when all is accomplished, he
will stand upon the earth.
[29]So even as my strength fades,
Let me proclaim your might to all
the generations to come;
[30]And even as my light grows weak,
Let your sun rise within me.
[31]You who have done great things,
O God, who is like you?
[32]You who have made me see many
troubles,
You will revive me again,
[33]You who have brought my flesh to
diminish,

Once again you will bring my soul to
magnify you.
[34]So fill my mouth with your praise,
and with your glory all of my days.

[35]Soon after this, Mary knew that she was near death, and John sent for her children. [36]Simon and Joses had died by this time, but Jude, together with his wife and sisters, and their husbands and children, gathered around Mary. [37]After blessing all of them, Mary raised her eyes to heaven and gave up her spirit; [38]and her family, together with the saints, mourned her for forty days.

Ministry of Jude

[39]After the death of Mary, Jude, who like James his brother became a believer after Christ was risen, returned to Galilee, testifying concerning the Lord and strengthening the believers there. [40]He was also known by both the Jews and Gentiles for his righteousness, and many believed because of him. [41]He would not remain in Jerusalem, because the Lord revealed to him that he should be a witness in the place where the Lord had lived, and among his people. [42]When the war came, his family suffered from the Jews, because he would not instruct his family to fight against Rome. [43]And after the war, the same Jews told the Romans that Jude and his family called themselves sons of David and desired to be kings when Jesus returned. [44]But when the Romans examined Jude and his sons, they saw that they were peaceful farmers and would fight for no earthly kingdom, so they let them go.

CHAPTER 10

Arrest of Matthias and James Son of Alphaeus

1 For two years following the death of James, all was quiet in Jerusalem, ²and the number of believers continued to grow, so that some of the Jews still plotted secretly against the church. ³Among these were some from the party of the Essenes, who lived near the Dead Sea and also in many towns and cities of Judea, studying the scriptures and practicing holiness. ⁴Many believers came from this party, including those who from the beginning had held their possessions in common and kept close to the law, with much fasting and prayer. ⁵Some of these lived in Jerusalem, including the apostle Matthias; and others lived in Bethany, including the apostle James son of Alphaeus. ⁶But when rumors of war began to be heard in all parts of the country, many from the party of the Essenes, who had been peaceful, decided to join with those who wished to rebel against Rome, ⁷for they believed that God would then destroy the Romans and make them reign over Jerusalem. ⁸They resented the believers because they would not fight, and also because they said that Jesus was the Messiah. ⁹And thinking that the believers would join with them if their leaders were taken from them, they accused Matthias and James of blasphemy, and they were brought before the chief priests and the entire council. ¹⁰At the council, the men who had tried to kill Paul and who had killed James accused them, ¹¹saying, "These two pretend to live quiet and righteous lives, but privately they turn their followers against the law. ¹²For they teach that God is not present in the temple, and that Jesus is the Messiah. ¹³Furthermore, they teach that he is exalted to the right hand of the Almighty, and so they blaspheme the Name." ¹⁴Then the chief priests demanded that Matthias and James give a defense.

Matthias Prophesies Before the Council

¹⁵And Matthias, filled with the Spirit, addressed the council with these words: ¹⁶"My brothers, we need not speak in our own defense, for all the people have observed us from the day of our Lord's resurrection until now, how we have lived among the poor of Jerusalem and in the villages nearby, ¹⁷following the way of life and renouncing the way of destruction, at peace with all men. ¹⁸We have devoted ourselves to fasting and prayer, taking part in the festivals of our people in strict observance of the law, and awaiting the appearance of our Lord and Savior.

¹⁹Now we are called before you by hypocrites who deliver us to the very ones they despise. ²⁰Know that the Lord could deliver us from them and from you, but he has brought us here to testify and to fulfill the scriptures. ²¹Therefore hear the word of the Lord concerning the chief priests, the Pharisees, and the other parties who have rejected Christ Jesus:

²²When David cried, 'My God, why hast thou forsaken me?' and his garments were divided, was it not a prophecy of destruction, not only of the wicked of at that time, but also of this generation? ²³For our Lord himself cried these words from the cross, while some of you looked on and mocked, and you did not fear God even when he rent the garment of the temple veil. ²⁴And after this, when he raised Jesus from the dead, and he appeared before many witnesses,

you still would not turn to him. [25]Since that time the Spirit has made us bold to bear witness in words and in deeds that he is the Christ, seated at the right hand of God, and that he will soon return in glory. [26]You bring judgment on yourselves, seeking to destroy his messengers as you once did the prophets, stoning some or giving them over to the Romans, mocking others or ignoring them.

[27]And because you have done nothing new, but only repeated your wickedness of old, the Lord does not send you a new word but repeats one of old. [28]For after David, speaking for the nation, says that he is forsaken, he continues, 'The poor shall eat and be satisfied, those who seek him shall praise the Lord.' [29]Now who comes to the table but the poor, whom you have despised and rejected? [30]So the same scripture proclaims, 'All the ends of the earth shall turn to the Lord; and all the families of the nations shall worship before him.' [31]Now who are these families but the Gentiles, whom you regard as unclean and unworthy? [32]And what of the dominion that you hope will come when God destroys these your enemies and makes you rule in their place? [33]'For dominion belongs to the Lord, and he rules over the nations.' [34]So it is not you, but the Lord who reigns, [35]as the scripture says: 'To him, indeed, shall all bow down. Posterity will serve him; future generations will be told about the Lord, and proclaim his deliverance to a people yet unborn, saying that he has done it.' [36]You doctors of the law, you guides of the people, your eyes are closed to these words of David your king, who after he sinned was blind until he was told by Nathan, 'Thou are the man.' [37]So David learned humility, and the son of David, the heir to his kingdom, likewise came as a servant, and in your pride you did not know him. [38]Now you have rejected the Lord and his prophets once more, so once more you will be forsaken, along with the temple and all that you have built with your hands, [39]while the nations will gather the blessings meant for you, until such time as you repent. [40]And may that be soon, before the day that Christ Jesus comes from the clouds in glory to gather his own."

Stoning of Matthias and James Son of Alphaeus

[41]The chief priests and Pharisees on the council, when they heard Matthias, agreed that he and James should die. [42]So they took them out to stone them. [43]And because Matthias, an unlearned man, had dared to quote scripture to them, they mocked him, [44]saying, "When will he die, and his name perish?" For in Hebrew, the word "when" is the same as the name Matthias. [45]But as Matthias and James were being stoned, they lifted up their eyes to heaven and begged the Lord to forgive their persecutors and to bring them to repentance. [46]When the believers who were together in Jerusalem and Bethany learned of their deaths and of their bold words before the council, they were strengthened in their faith, and not one followed the rebels. [47]But the scribes and Pharisees continued to look for an opportunity to accuse them, and as the war drew near, the hatred of the rebels grew.

CHAPTER 11

Jerusalem Church Moves to Pella

1 Now came a terrible time for all the Jews in Galilee and Judea, and a time of great suffering for the church. [2]For soon after the death of Matthias and James son of Alphaeus, word came to Jerusalem concerning the deaths of Paul and Peter, and then the council occurred. [3]By that time, rebels were already gathering in Galilee, and because the believers there would not join with them, many had to flee, leaving houses and lands, and later returned to nothing, their possessions having been destroyed.

[4]In Jerusalem, after the apostles were sent out, Simeon rose up and prophesied, [5]"Now, says the Lord, I have set my face against Jerusalem, and I send my servants to the nations to announce the good news of salvation. [6]Those who remain, looking to the teachers of the law and to false messiahs, will see only destruction. [7]Therefore, quickly, leave all that you own and come out from among them, and go to the place of refuge I have prepared for you in Perea across the Jordan." [8]So Simeon, and more than a thousand of the believers from Jerusalem and Judea, went to the vicinity of Pella in Perea. [9]The believers there welcomed as many as they could into their houses, and those who were able bought new houses and lands. [10]Even so, food was scarce, so that many suffered in the years of the war, and some moved away where they could find relatives or other places of safety. [11]So has the church of Jerusalem scattered, although many remain in Pella to this day, along with Simeon and other leaders.

Jews Rebel Against Rome

[12]Soon after the church moved from Jerusalem, the Lord brought a calamity upon the Jews such has never been seen, even in the days of the wicked kings of long ago. [13]For in the twelfth year of Nero, rebels among the Jews began to attack the Romans, and the high priest ceased prayers and sacrifices for the emperor. [14]In fear of the rebels, Agrippa fled Jerusalem, and the Jews defeated a legion of Roman troops in battle. [15]This raised the hopes of the rebels, and many joined them. [16]But Vespasian was sent to crush the rebellion, and he brought three legions, together with many auxiliaries, along with his son Titus, to destroy the Jews. [17]They began their conquest in Galilee, where some towns resisted them, and others gave up without a fight. [18]Then, after much tumult in Rome following the death of Nero, Vespasian became emperor and left Titus alone to crush the rebellion.

[19]The leading rebels, John of Giscala and Simon Bar Giora, fled to Jerusalem, and their followers killed all who wished to surrender to the Romans, together with their rivals among the Jews. [20]In the first year of Vespasian, the Romans surrounded Jerusalem with a great army, and they looked down upon the temple and the upper city from the Mount of Olives. [21]They began their siege during Passover, so that thousands were trapped inside the city. [22]When anyone tried to escape, the Romans captured them and crucified them within sight of those within, as many as five hundred in a single day. [23]Meanwhile, the soldiers destroyed the land around Jerusalem, cutting down all of the trees and burning the gardens and crops.

²⁴Inside the city, the followers of John and Simon hated each other more than they hated the Romans, and they continued to kill each other, even burning the food supply for the entire city. ²⁵As a result, there was terrible famine, and much disease, so that more Jews died from these causes than from fighting the Romans. ²⁶The rebels took by force what little food remained, leaving women and children to die of hunger.

Romans Destroy the Temple

²⁷In the second year of the siege, the Romans broke through the outer wall; and soldiers, killing all they could find and setting fires, destroyed much of the city. ²⁸But a group of rebels led by Eleazar ben Simon still held the temple area, while another group led by Simon held the upper city. ²⁹After two months, the Romans broke through to the temple, and after plundering the holy places and relics, the soldiers set fire to a building nearby, and soon the temple itself began to burn. ³⁰While these events took place, those who still held the upper city looked on in sorrow and fear, knowing that the temple was lost and that they would soon die. ³¹And many other Jews, including those already captured who awaited their fate and those outside who watched from afar, wailed and lamented when they saw the flames and smoke rising from the temple.

³²After the entire city was in the hands of Titus, and the fires had cooled, he gave orders for what was left of the temple to be torn down stone by stone, until nothing remained. ³³Thus the word of the Lord was fulfilled, and the temple, which had stood for a thousand years, was destroyed in a matter of days, ³⁴because of the hard hearts of the people, who turned to lawlessness against Rome rather than to salvation in Christ Jesus.

End of the Rebellion

³⁵In all, because so many Jews had been trapped in the city, more than a million died, either from crucifixion outside the walls, or battle and starvation within. ³⁶Of those who survived, many more were crucified, and a hundred thousand were made captive. ³⁷Some of these were sent to be killed in the arena by gladiators or by wild beasts, but most were made slaves to work in the mines or to labor until their deaths in lands far away. ³⁸A few of the rebels escaped, fleeing to the desert and to the fortresses of Herodium, Machaerus, and Masada, where Titus pursued them until all resistance was destroyed. ³⁹Of the parties of the Jews, one of the Pharisees, Johanan ben Zakai, opposed the rebellion and so obtained permission from Vespasian to move the council to Jamnia by the sea, to study the law there. ⁴⁰But as for Jerusalem, the city now lies desolate, awaiting the return of Christ Jesus its king.

CHAPTER 12

The Church in Pella

1 When word reached the church in Pella that the temple was destroyed, all mourned, especially for the suffering of their countrymen. [3]For there was not a family among the believers that had not lost members, either from the fighting or from famine and disease. [3]And many of those who lived were sold into slavery, while others were never heard from again. [4]In spite of their great sorrow, however, the saints were comforted by hearing the words of Christ Jesus concerning the last things, believing that what had occurred in Jerusalem was the sign of his return in glory. [5]Some no longer worked or even ate food, gathering instead in houses to pray and await the Lord's coming. [6]Therefore, Simeon and the elders began likewise to fast and pray, inquiring of the Lord whether this was the end, and what they should do. [7]And after three days, Simeon gathered all the saints and said to them,

The Delay of the Lord's Coming

[8]"Brothers and sisters, it has not been revealed to us that the Lord will return soon. [9]Now we all know the signs of his coming, and that the chief of these is the destruction of Jerusalem. [10]Nevertheless, the Lord did not say that this was the last war, but rather that it would be the beginning of the end, and that the time of the Gentiles must be fulfilled. [11]What could this mean but that more time must pass? [12]And who knows the number of days? [13]Moreover, Christ Jesus told us to look for other signs, and the chief of these is that the good news will be preached to the nations. [14]Has not

the Spirit sent out the apostles, some who still journey, and do they not continually tell us of new lands where Christ is not yet proclaimed? [15]Despite our sorrow, should we rejoice for the Lord's return before all the harvest is gathered in?

[16]Furthermore, the Lord said that no one knows the day, not even the Son, so who are we to claim such knowledge? [17]No, as the Lord taught, it is our duty to be watchful, and this does not mean to wait in idleness but to be found in faith and righteousness, doing his will. [18]And what is his will but to preach to the nations, to obey him in all things, to be one, and to endure with joy whatever suffering is before us? [19]So let us be on guard, as our Lord taught us, not as those who seek signs, but rather as those who seek righteousness. [20]In this manner, we will be found ready, whether we are guided by signs to look for his coming or are taken unawares. [21]May the Lord come soon!"

[22]The church heard Simeon's words with gratitude, and those who had been idle returned to their labors. [23]The believers in Pella continued to be strong in the Spirit and to grow in number, although many moved to other parts of the country. [24]At the same time, bands of rebels who had escaped from the Romans roamed throughout Galilee, Judea, and beyond the Jordan, robbing the poor of their crops and killing many who had not joined with them, including many believers. [25]So the judgment of the Lord fell not only upon Jerusalem and the temple, but also upon the entire land. [26]Yet still the hearts of the people were hardened, and the Spirit began to do greater works in other lands.

CHAPTER 13

Eight Remain of The Twelve

1 Now, dear Theophilus, I will return to the beginning, when the twelve and the other apostles first went out from the last council in Jerusalem, [2]to tell in order what the Spirit has accomplished through them, even in their deaths, to spread the good news of salvation throughout the world.

[3]The first of the twelve to be killed was James son of Zebedee, in the second year of Claudius, who was beheaded by Agrippa to please the Jews. [4]During that time the twelve came and went from Jerusalem, traveling alone or together to many lands, taking with them other apostles who are known to you from my second book. [5]Peter preached in the provinces of the north, and he traveled numerous times to Rome, where he spent many years building up the believers before he was killed. [6]The next to be killed, in the tenth year of Nero, were Matthias and James son of Alphaeus. [7]As a result, at the time of the council, John, Andrew, Philip, Bartholomew, Matthew, Judas son of James, Simon the Zealot, and Thomas all still lived, but some of these have died since, as this book will tell.

The Stoning of Barnabas

[8]There were many other apostles who are not numbered among the twelve, the chief of whom were James the brother of the Lord, and Paul. [9]I have written of the death of James, who gave guidance to the church in Jerusalem for many years and was beloved by all the people. [10]As for Paul, he journeyed throughout Asia, Macedonia, Greece, and even to Spain, establishing churches and often suffering persecution from both Jews and Greeks, until he was beheaded in Rome. [11]Many of those who traveled with Paul still live, but some of his coworkers have been killed. [12]The first of these was Barnabas, who was beloved by the twelve and all the saints for his faith and courage. [13]After he parted company with Paul in Antioch, he took John Mark with him to Cyprus, and through them the Spirit added many to the church. [14]After some years, John Mark left to join Peter in Rome, while Barnabas continued to preach, confounding his opponents in the synagogue and bearing witness to both Jews and Gentiles by his good works. [15]But the Jews of Salamis were jealous that Barnabas persuaded so many of their number to turn to Christ Jesus. [16]Therefore, one day they formed a mob and took Barnabas from a synagogue to a place outside the city, where they beat him; and when he refused to deny the Lord, they stoned him.

The Stoning of Silas

[17]Silas, who had served with both Paul and Peter for many years, came at last to Corinth, where he led the church until the tenth year of Nero. [18]When certain Greek merchants there heard about the evil that Nero did in Rome, they saw an opportunity to make an example of Silas. [19]So they accused him of blasphemy against the gods, and incited a mob to stone him, [20]thinking that the believers would scatter and the merchants would increase in riches from the sin and luxury of that city. [21]No one dared to oppose them at that time, because all feared the emperor, [22]but the persecution soon ended and many more turned to the Lord, because they knew that Silas was a good and law-abiding man.

The Church Thrives Through Suffering

²³Of the many apostles who were killed by Nero, together with hundreds of other believers there, it is not necessary to write further. ²⁴Likewise, many elders and believers from Judea and Galilee were killed, either put to the sword by the rebels, or stoned by Jews who say that those who follow Christ Jesus are blasphemers. ²⁵But the Spirit everywhere encouraged the saints, performing signs and wonders through the apostles, ²⁶refuting their opponents among both Jews and Greeks, and building up the church both in number and in faith, so that all were one and all hoped in Christ Jesus. ²⁷Even in Rome and Judea, where suffering at the hands of evil men was most severe and lasted the longest, the Spirit acted with the greatest power, ²⁸sowing the seed of so many witnesses into a harvest of yet more fruit.

CHAPTER 14

John and Timothy in Ephesus

1 When those of the twelve who remained were sent out by the Spirit from Jerusalem, John went with Timothy to Ephesus. ²John was gentle in spirit, having for many years devoted himself to prayer, provision for the poor, and care for Mary in her old age. ³And although he was almost sixty years old, he was a large man and strong in body, ⁴having in his youth been a fisherman who, together with James his brother, pulled great nets from the sea. ⁵Now, after many years in Jerusalem, he was eager to reap a harvest of men in distant lands, as had the other apostles.

John Raises a Woman

⁶When John and Timothy reached Ephesus, the saints rejoiced that Timothy was restored to them after escaping Nero and traveling for many months, ⁷and they were eager to honor John as one who had walked with the Lord. ⁸Soon after they arrived, a messenger came to John from Lycomedes, a magistrate and a man of great substance in Ephesus. ⁹At first the believers feared for John, but the messenger told them, "My master wishes you no harm. ¹⁰On the contrary, he hopes for help from you, and wishes for the man named John to come to him in haste." ¹¹John immediately went with him to Lycomedes, who fell on his face before him and said, "For seven days, my beloved wife Cleopatra has been ill with a palsy. ¹²First she shook in all her limbs, then her members became numb one by one, so that now I fear that she is near death. ¹³But three nights ago in a dream, one in shining garments appeared to me in a dream, ¹⁴saying to me, 'My servant, a man named John, will soon come to Ephesus; seek him among the Christians and ask from him whatever you wish.'"

¹⁵Lycomedes took John to his inner chamber, where Cleopatra lay. ¹⁶But when they entered the room, they saw that she was no longer breathing. Lycomedes, who loved her greatly, cried out that John was too late, and falling on the floor, said that he wished now to die as well. ¹⁷But John wept with him and comforted him. ¹⁸Then he knelt by the bed, laid his hands on Cleopatra, and prayed for an hour in silence, his tears falling on Cleopatra's hands. ¹⁹Meanwhile, the servants and some other citizens of Ephesus gathered in the outer rooms, and even in

the doorway. [20]Then John touched the face of Cleopatra and said, "In the name of the Lord Jesus, arise." [21]Immediately Cleopatra opened her eyes and sat upright, then began to move her arms and legs freely and to ask what had happened while she slept. [22]Lycomedes rose and leapt around the room for joy, embracing first Cleopatra, then John, and finally the servants and all those who had gathered in his house. [23]The next day he made a great feast, and all those of his household were baptized. [24]Word about Cleopatra spread quickly throughout the city, especially among the leading citizens who knew Lycomedes, so that many more believed in Christ Jesus.

The Death of Aelia

[25]Some days after this, the elders brought to John a young girl who had drowned in the river outside the city. [26]The name of the girl was Aelia, and although she was only ten years old, she loved the Lord and was known among the saints for singing hymns in a pure voice. [27]When they brought her before John, together with her mother and father, he wept with them, and he prayed in silence over the child as he had with Cleopatra, while all waited. [28]After an hour, he rose from the body of Aelia and said to her mother and father, "Beloved, this child will not return to you."

[29]Her mother and father bowed their heads and were silent, [30]but Menandros, one of the elders, said, "Why does the Lord raise the wife of Lycomedes, who was not a believer, but not this child, who loved the Lord? [31]Moreover, her parents have long followed Christ Jesus, in prayer and faithfulness, and they have no other child. [32]What is the Lord's purpose in taking one so young?" [33]And John said, "Beloved, the Lord's purpose is always the same, in suffering or in peace, and that is that is for us to believe and to love one another. [34]Nor does the Lord take children; he only gives them, this one for ten years, another for one hundred years, and it is not for us to know why each is given for a different number of days. [35]So do not look for purpose, but weep. [36]Did not the Lord weep for Lazarus, even when he knew that in the next moment he would raise him up? [37]How much more, therefore, does the Lord now weep, and we with him, for Aelia? [38]For now the storm waters rise up over the heads of all who loved her, but the day is coming when the troubled sea will pass away, and there will remain only a river of healing. [39]By that river, those who love Aelia will find her, although the road may be long for them and covered in shadow."

[40]But Menandros asked again, "How then shall we teach anyone concerning the Lord's will, if we cannot give a reason for the girl's death?" [41]And John answered him, "Beloved, do not contend with the Lord, or with one another, as do the Greeks, but only believe, and love. [42]Otherwise you may heap up 'therefore' and 'because' until you cannot see suffering behind your many words. [43]The Lord would not have us justify suffering, but endure it. [44]You must learn from him who, although more innocent than any child, went willingly to his death. [45]Some of the Greeks wish to stop suffering, thinking to compel their gods by casting spells. [46]Others put a mask over suffering, indulging in drunkenness or the pleasures of the flesh. [47]Still others seek to rise above suffering, denying that the body is real. [48]But not so with you, who must walk not against, or around, or above suffering, but through it, as did the Lord, finding in him your reward. [49]So, little children, endure a little while, loving one another, [50]and then you will see the Lord, who will turn your darkness to light, and your mourning to dancing."

[51]When Menandros and some others heard John's words, they turned away from John, because they said that everything

happens for a reason, and that John did not know the Lord's will. [52]But many were comforted by John's love, including the mother

and father of Aelia, who after their time of mourning began again to serve the Lord with hope and gladness.

CHAPTER 15

John Gathers the Poor Widows of Ephesus

1 On another day, John instructed his coworker Verus to find all the poor women in Ephesus who were more than sixty years old. [2]Verus returned and told John that there were nearly one hundred such women, but almost all were feeble or sick, and only four were sound in body. [3]John said, "Gather the sick ones into the great theater near the marketplace, and tell all the people of Ephesus to come and see the glory of God." [4]A great number came to the theater, and there Cleopatra and Lycomedes made all things ready for the care of the women.

John Preaches to the Ephesians

[5]Then John said to the crowd, "Here before you are the old and sick women of your city, whom the Lord has gathered to heal so that you will believe. [6]For if he cares for such weak vessels as these, how much more does he desire to accomplish works of love and goodness through you who are strong?

[7]But first let me sow in your ears the truth regarding your lives, so that you will not only marvel at the Lord's power but will also take care for your souls. [8]For the worst among you know that there is judgment after death, and because you fear God, you are ready to hear of his mercy. [9]But the best among you hide your troubled souls from others, and even from God, thinking that life is long and that today is one more spectacle

for your amusement. [10]Do not think that your time will be so long, for your life is but a moment; and the treasures of your household, like those of your great city, will fade. [11]You who are rich provide for yourselves things that make you unhappy, out of worry that you will lose them. [12]For a moment, while the sun shines, you delight in gold, in ivory and jewels, but when night falls, can you look at these things? [13]Behold, the night is coming, perhaps nearer for you than for these old women here before you. [14]Are you puffed up because your bodies, unlike theirs, are beautiful? [15]Yet every day you see your beauty fade, and your powders and potions can only delay the ruin that comes to all. [16]Where can you turn? [17]If you take pleasure in adultery, you find that both law and nature take vengeance upon you. [18]If you indulge in wrath and passion, you make of yourself a beast. [19]If you are a drunkard or a quarreler, you lose the control of your senses to a shameful desire. [20]Turn where you will, rich or poor, all roads lead to the same end. [21]But today your road brings you to life, abundant and eternal, if only you will believe in Christ Jesus."

John Heals the Ephesian Women

[22]And turning to the old women, who were sitting apart in the lowest circle of the theater, or in the case of the most sick, lying on pallets, John began to walk among them, laying hands on them and healing them of their diseases and weakness. [23]And those who watched from higher in the theater

pressed forward to see, and marveled that some whom they knew to be weak rose up and walked. ²⁴Many of the old women wept for joy, embracing one another. ²⁵And on that day almost a hundred of the widows and more than a thousand of those who looked on were added to the number of believers.

John's Ministry in Asia

²⁶After this, John was much sought after in Ephesus to heal, preach, and offer comfort, and through him the Lord saved many. ²⁷He also traveled in the region, as far north as Pergamum and inland to Laodicea. ²⁸In each city he preached boldly to the Greeks, healed both believers and unbelievers of sickness, and encouraged the saints to love one another. ²⁹In the winter months, when travel was difficult, he remained in Ephesus and began to write his account of the life of the Lord.

Mary Magdalene Visits John

³⁰After he had lived there for two years, Mary Magdalene came from Pella to minister to John and the other apostles in Asia. ³¹She followed Jesus from the beginning in Galilee, and together with Joanna and Susanna, gave of her possessions and remained with the Lord to the end, even when others deserted him. ³²Joanna set Mary over her possessions, and when she died, Mary continued to sell parcels of land and give the proceeds to the apostles, as the need arose. ³³When she became old, Mary traveled to Antioch, then to Ephesus and other cities, giving encouragement to the apostles and telling all of Christ Jesus and the events she had witnessed. ³⁴She knew John and Mary the mother of the Lord from the days when they walked with the Lord. ³⁵They rejoiced now in meeting, and the believers in Ephesus marveled to hear what they told concerning Christ Jesus. ³⁶Mary stayed in Ephesus with John for a year, ministering to the saints, ³⁷and then the Spirit told her to journey to Phrygia to see Philip and Bartholomew.

CHAPTER 16

Philip and Bartholomew in Hierapolis

1 When Simeon called the apostles to Jerusalem after the deaths of Paul and Peter, he summoned Philip and Bartholomew from Hierapolis in Phrygia. ²After the resurrection of the Lord, they had for many years preached together in Syria and further north in the regions of Galatia, Bithynia, Pontus, and Cappadocia. ³They returned to Hieropolis after the council to continue building up the church there. ⁴There were many Jews in the city, and many believers among them who met in the house of Epicrates.

Philip Arrested for the Healing of Nicanora

⁵At that time Vettius Niger, who was proconsul of Asia, lived in Hierapolis. ⁶His wife Nicanora had long suffered from various diseases, including a swelling of her eyes that made her nearly blind. ⁷When she heard that Philip healed the sick, she sent for him. And calling upon the name of

Christ Jesus, Philip released her from all her illnesses. [8]That same day Nicanora had her slaves carry her to the house of Epicrates to meet the other believers, [9]and there she was baptized together with her slaves.

[10]Niger was a tyrant, jealous of his wife and suspicious of all in the city but the other Romans. [11]When he learned that Nicanora had gone to the house of those who had healed her, he cried out, "By what trickery have these magicians pretended to cure her? Bring her to me." [12]And when Niconora heard of his anger, she returned to him [13]and said, "Do not be angry with me or my deliverer, for he reigns in heaven, and in his name I will be a better wife to you. [14]But my healing will not be complete until your soul is healed, when you turn from the idols we have worshiped and serve Christ Jesus the Lord." [15]When Niger heard these words, he was filled with anger. [16]Dragging Nicanora by the hair and kicking her, he cried, "If you do not deliver these deceivers who have bewitched and seduced you, I will cut off this hair, and then the head that has disgraced me." [17]But when he released her, Nicanora bowed before him and said, "My hair and my head are yours for as long as you grant me life; [18]and the sooner you take my life, the sooner my soul will fly to Christ Jesus my Lord." [19]Then Niger was torn between shame and wrath, because Nicanora humbled herself before him but would not deny Christ.

[20]When Niger forced Nicanora's slaves to reveal who had healed her, he sent soldiers to the house of Epicrates, and they brought Philip before him, while Bartholomew and Epicrates, together with some of the believers, followed. [21]Philip spoke to Niger without fear, telling him how he had laid hands on Nicanora and prayed for her in the name of the Lord Jesus to be healed, [22]and that now she was a disciple of Christ Jesus, having been baptized that day. [23]Once again Niger was enraged, and he commanded his soldiers to scourge Philip, together with Epicrates and Bartholomew, [23]and to drag Philip through the streets of the temple of Apollo, where he would be killed the next day in front of the people.

[24]The believers took Epicrates and Bartholomew and hid them, tending to their wounds, [25]and all prayed that the Spirit would deliver Philip or give him strength to face his tormentors. [26]The soldiers chained Philip to a column between the temples of Apollo and Pluto, and the next morning a great crowd of about seven thousand men gathered. [27]Even before Niger arrived, the priests of the temples were shouting against Philip, saying that he was one of the foreigners and magicians who seduced women and defied both the divine emperor and Apollo, the chief god of the city.

Philip's Speech

[28]But Philip, filled with the Spirit, said to the crowd, "Men of Hierapolis, it is fitting that you should hear the empty charges of these priests, for the true God has brought me here between the temples of their false gods, one of the sun and one of the underworld, [29]to proclaim to you that they are no gods at all, neither in the sky, nor under the earth, nor on the earth itself. [30]All of you know that these priests claim to descend to hell, but they only do tricks with poisonous vapors from a cave in the earth. [31]They also demand from you payments of gold and many sacrifices for healings, but they say that the same god brings plague. [32]They accuse those who are pure of seducing women, while their god fornicates with a thousand demons like himself. [33]In all of these things they are false, but they will learn the truth soon enough about hell and plague and demons.

[34]And what of the house of their god, this great temple? [35]Twice in this generation it has been destroyed by earthquakes,

and foolish men lavish years and fortunes to build it up again. [36]But when evil men destroyed the temple of Christ's body, God raised him up in three days and exalted him to heaven, from where he will soon come to reign over the earth. [37]Hear the truth, people of Hierapolis! [38]These so-called gods are nothing, but the priests would raise them up together with themselves. [39]Christ was great, but he became small for our sake, to raise us up together with him. [40]Do your hearts not tell you to come up out of hell and receive the true healing, a touch that will lift you beyond the sun to life everlasting?"

The Crucifixion of Philip

[41]Just then Niger came to the temple, and the priests ran to him, accusing Philip of defying the emperor and the temple. [42]Niger replied, "Why do you need to speak, when this man's own words and those of my wife are enough to condemn him? [43]She is still bewitched, speaking strange words and praying through the night to Jesus. [44]I will soon put an end to this man's enchantments." [45]And he ordered Philip to be hanged head downwards by iron hooks through his heels, opposite the temple from a certain tree. [46]Philip, although he was weak from the scourging and being chained through the night, did not cry out [47]but prayed in a loud voice for the Lord to save Niger, and for the people of Hierapolis to believe. [48]Soon, however, he could speak no more, and he gave up his spirit. [49]The priests of the temple rejoiced, but when the crowd saw the courage of Philip, and the cruelty of Niger, who killed the very man who had healed his wife, they mourned, and many believed in Christ Jesus. [50]The people of Hierapolis gave the body of Philip to Bartholomew, who buried him there.

CHAPTER 17

Bartholomew Journeys to Armenia

1 Soon after this, the tyrant Niger was sent back to Rome, and Bartholomew preached again openly in the city. [2]But he mourned greatly for Philip, because they had been like brothers and had traveled together since their youth. [3]So Bartholomew gathered the elders in the house of Epicrates and said to them, "The apostles in Jerusalem sent us back to you to finish our work here, and then to go where the Lord would send us. [4]Now the church in Hierapolis is strong, and the Lord calls me to go, but not again to the cities where I have preached with Philip, where I would hear the echo of his steps next to mine. [5]Instead, I will go to the cities of the East, beyond the reach of Rome, where the word of the Lord has not been heard. [6]Nevertheless, I will not go alone if the Lord will call any from among you to make this journey with me." [7]And the Spirit chose two men, Perseus and Nicator, to go with Bartholomew.

[8]In the spring, when they were able to travel through the passes, they journeyed along the king's road through the cities of Iconium, Caesarea, Comona, and Melitene. [9]In each place, they were welcomed by believers who begged them to preach and strengthen the church. [10]After Melitene, they crossed the Euphrates and journeyed south to Edessa, where Philip and Bartholomew had preached years before. [11]Here Bartholomew was greeted with joy by the church, and he remained through the winter. [12]Among the believers there were

some merchants who traveled on the trade routes, and they gave reports of Thomas in India and other apostles who had traveled to distant lands. ¹³They also told Bartholomew about the lands of Armenia, Albania, and Parthia in the north between the two great inland seas. ¹⁴When Bartholomew and the others heard that these people had not yet heard the word of the Lord, the Spirit stirred their hearts, and they determined to travel there as soon as they could cross the mountain passes.

¹⁵Taking with them Borus and Kalemos, who knew the languages of the region, Bartholomew, together with Perseus and Nicator, preached the word of the Lord throughout the towns of Armenia and Albania. ¹⁶Wherever they went, they healed the sick, cast out demons, and turned people from false idols to the worship of Christ Jesus. ¹⁷After a year, they made their way down the Araxes River to the coast, and from there went north to the city of Albanapolis.

Conversion of Polymius

¹⁸When they arrived in Albanapolis, Bartholomew sat apart by the shore for an hour and remembered Philip, because he said that the place was much like their home in Galilee, and that it was a good place to end his days. ¹⁹Soon after they entered the city, Bartholomew cast out a demon from a man who had long been shut up in his house out of fear that he would harm someone. ²⁰When word of this came to Polymius, the ruler of the city, he sent to Bartholomew on behalf of his daughter, who was also afflicted by a demon. ²¹He took Bartholomew to the chamber where she was kept and said, "See how she is kept in chains, because she bites anyone who comes near. ²²Our priests cannot help her, but if this new god you bring can free a wild man who has been tormented for years, perhaps he can help my child."

²³Bartholomew said to him, "Loose her, and let her go." ²⁴Polymius replied, "We have her in our power only when she is bound. Would you have us let her go?" ²⁵Again Bartholomew said, "Let her go, and when she has eaten and rested, early tomorrow bring her to me." ²⁶And after Bartholomew left, Polymius debated with himself for an hour, then decided to do as Bartholomew said. ²⁷And when he went in to his daughter, the demon was already gone, and his daughter was in her right mind.

²⁸Early the next day, Polymius loaded a cart with gold, pearls, and expensive garments and went to find Bartholomew at the inn. ²⁹When Bartholomew saw the treasure he said, "These things I fear more than the demons I cast out, for they bind with stronger chains. ³⁰Take them from me, and give them to the poor. ³¹But first stay and learn how your daughter was delivered." ³²And he taught Polymius from the scriptures about the hopes of the Jews and how they had all been fulfilled in Christ Jesus. ³³Polymius listened all day. ³⁴And in the evening, he took Bartholomew and those who were with him back to the palace, and there he was baptized together with his daughter and all his household. ³⁵Then he asked Bartholomew to remain in the palace and preach to the people.

Martyrdom of Bartholomew

³⁶Bartholomew preached in Albanopolis and the surrounding towns for several months, and many believed, ³⁷but the priests and some of the merchants hated Polymius and the believers for tearing down the temple of their idol. ³⁸So they sent to their king Astryages and reported to him that a stranger in Albanopolis was defying the gods and declaring that Jesus was the true king. ³⁹Astryages, who was the brother of Polymius, immediately sent soldiers

to arrest Bartholomew. [40]When he was brought before the king, Astryages asked him, "Are you the one who has turned my brother from the gods?" [41]Bartholomew answered, "Those were not gods from which he turned, but it is truly God to whom he has turned." [42]And the king asked, "Are you the one who caused our gods to be broken in pieces?" [43]Bartholomew answered, "Would you grieve over the empty houses of demons, when you should rejoice with your brother in the God who dwells in the heavens?" [44]Then Astryages said, "Your own mouth condemns you. [45]Because you have made my brother and the people reject our gods, now in front of them all I will make you reject your god and worship ours." [46]And he gave orders for Bartholomew to be beaten with rods, and then to have his skin torn from his body. [47]But when the apostle was silent and did not deny Christ, Astryages ordered for him to be beheaded. [48]Then, learning that Polymius took the remains of Bartholomew to be buried in the royal tomb, he ordered his body to be placed in a sack and thrown into the sea. [49]After Astryages and his soldiers left, Polymius and his household continued to worship the Lord, and Perseus and Borus remained there, [50]while Nicator and Kalemos returned to Edessa with a report of all that the Lord had done through Bartholomew.

CHAPTER 18

Andrew in Nicaea

1 The apostle Andrew was sent from the council to Macedonia and Achaia. [2]From there he hoped to continue west to Illyricum and to the northern regions of Italy, if the Lord would allow him. [3]But first, when we left Jerusalem, we journeyed to Caesarea to find a ship; and from there we followed fair winds to Tyre, Antioch, Myra, Miletus, and Troas, stopping in each city for a several weeks to encourage the believers. [4]For Andrew was a kindly man, and he did not hurry but spent many hours listening and talking to the to the saints one by one. [5]For he said, "The Lord heals and performs wonders in a moment, but the greatest of his works are those he does in the heart, with much patience. [6]For the greatest fish lie deepest in the sea, and it requires time and skill to draw them up to the light."

[7]Reaching Nicaea just before the storms, we remained there through the winter. [8]It was in Nicaea that Andrew had lived for a year before the council, and he was beloved by the saints. [9]Andrew and Peter his brother were the first to proclaim the word of the Lord in Nicaea, and they often returned there to wait for the Spirit to send them to new lands. [10]For Andrew and Peter had preached throughout Bithynia, Pontus, and Cappadocia; and when Peter went to Rome, Andrew sailed to the land of Scythia on the other side of the sea. [11]Whenever he returned from preaching the word of the Lord, the saints in Nicaea had made him welcome and provided for his further travels. [12]So now when the Spirit directed Andrew to depart, the Nicaeans were generous in sending him onward. [13]Providing all things necessary, they also sent with him Lamachos and Xenion, who preached and served with him to the end.

Andrew Journeys to Macedonia and Achaia

[14]Because it was still not safe to travel by sea, Andrew followed the road to Byzantium, where he had first preached and where Stachys now led the church. [15]After two months, he went to Heraclea, where he stayed three months. [16]From Heraclea he went to Philippi and then to Thessalonica, [17]remaining for a year in each city and building up the saints so that the seed once planted and nurtured by Paul became a strong tree bearing much fruit.

[18]After two years in Macedonia, Andrew traveled to Thebes, where you, most excellent Theophilus, welcomed him into your house and provided for him as you have for all the saints to this day, laying up treasure in heaven. [19]When Andrew was refreshed in spirit, he went to Corinth, where he lived for a year, strengthening the believers there. [20]Then the Lord sent him to Patras.

Andrew Crucified in Patras

[21]Now this was a time of great turmoil, for after the tyrant Nero died, four men sat on the throne in Rome until Vespasian was made emperor. [22]There were revolts in the provinces, and the greatest of these was in Judea, where Jerusalem was under siege. [23]So while all waited to learn the outcome of these events, the Jews feared that they would be persecuted, and those who hated them accused them of rebellion. [24]Moreover, Roman magistrates everywhere wished to assure the new emperor of their loyalty, so they were quick to punish any rumor of revolt.

[25]After Andrew had been in Patras for two months, a new proconsul, Lucius, arrived in the city. [26]The next day the merchant Demotoles gave a banquet for Lucius; and even before the food was served he began to accuse Andrew of sedition, [27]for he was angry that his son, having heard Andrew's preaching, had become a believer. [28]The the next day Lucius had Andrew arrested and brought before him in the theater. [30]Lucius said to him, "Is it true, as you are accused by a citizen of this city, that you are the leader the Christians?" [31]Andrew answered, "I am no leader but a servant of Christ who reigns in heaven, and of the emperor who reigns on earth." [32]Turning to the crowd that had gathered, Lucius said, "Having learned of this sect in Rome, I know they speak of loyalty to mask their crimes. [33]For they claim to teach virtue; but they refuse to worship Caesar or any of the gods, and they follow a god of the Jews who they claim will destroy the world. [34] Turning again to Andrew, he said, "Knowing that your life is in peril for such sedition, I ask you again, are you a Christian?" [35]Andrew said, "I am." [36]Then Lucius said, "In the ship that brought me here, there is a statue of Caesar ready to be set up in Corinth, where I will govern as proconsul. [37]Now, Christian, answer me this: If I were to place before you, on the one hand, this image of Caesar, for you to speak the words of invocation and offer wine together with incense; [38]and on the other hand, a cross to hang from, which would you choose?" [39]After waiting for a moment, Andrew spoke in a loud voice, "Proconsul, you honor me by asking three times so that I may consider carefully. [40]The choice I make is for life, but not as it is in your power to give; [41]for in offering me the cross, you let me suffer as did my Lord, before God raised him from the dead. [42]This is the life I choose, which is life everlasting." [43]Lucius waved his hand before the crowd and said, "You all see the evidence from his own mouth of his absurd and extravagant superstition. [44]This contagion has spread through many cities of the empire, affecting all ranks and ages, and it must be restrained before these fools lead more fools away from loyalty and order." [45]Then Lucius gave orders for Andrew

to be scourged and crucified along the road outside the city. [46]And in order to make his suffering last longer, he ordered the soldiers not to break Andrew's limbs but to hang him with thongs rather than nails on two crossed posts with his arms and feet apart. [47]In this manner he lived four days. [48]And some of the believers dared to visit Andrew while he lived, praying for him and begging the guards to give him water. [49]Meanwhile, he encouraged those who came, and he spoke of Christ Jesus to the guards. [50]Seeing the faith of Andrew and those who came to comfort him, Laenus, the chief of the cohort, believed and was baptized. [51]When Andrew had given up his spirit to Christ Jesus, the believers in Patras buried him there; [52]and immediately they began to ask the Lord which of them might preach the word of the Lord in Illyricum and Italy, as Andrew had intended.

CHAPTER 19

Simon and Jude Travel West

1 The apostles Simon the Zealot and Jude son of James were sent by the council to lands far in the west; first to Cyrenaica and Mauretania, then, if the Lord allowed, to Britain and Gaul. [2]In the years before the council, they had traveled together throughout Samaria and Galilee, and across the Jordan into Petraea and Arabia, showing great courage and endurance in preaching the word. [3]Wherever they traveled, Simon and Jude followed an ordered plan whereby they took three young disciples from each city and taught them as they journeyed concerning the word of God, preaching, and overseeing the church. [4]After they reached a new city, when a month or two had passed, they sent one of the new disciples home, appointed one to remain in the new city for a time, and took the third with them to the next city. [5]In this manner, although Simon and Jude were quick to move on, they built a kinship in the Lord between believers in nearby cities and trained many young men to preach the word. [6]Furthermore, those they left behind trained others in the same manner to preach in the neighboring villages, and in this manner many came to Christ in a short time.

Instructions to Disciples

[7]When Simon and Jude found new disciples, they taught them how to give their lives to the Lord, [8]saying, "To follow Christ Jesus, there are three things you must give up, and a fourth. [9]First, you must give up your possessions. [10]For if you trust the Lord completely, you will hold nothing back for your own security; [11]and you cannot give in your heart only, for only what you do with your treasure proves the devotion of your heart. [12]Second, you must give up your family. [13]For if you cling to father or mother, or if you take on a wife, you will go no further than your duty to them will allow. [14]Find instead a new family in Christ Jesus, which will provide for you a full table of fellowship and many beloved children in those who are saved. [15]Third, you must give up your life. [16]For any day you may be killed for the Lord's sake; and if even once you say to yourself, 'I must live one more day, until tomorrow,' you will put tomorrow before the word of the Lord, and then another day, [17]until the word is further away from

you than it was before you first heard it; and your condemnation will be worse than if you had never known the truth."

¹⁸"These three things the Lord taught while he was in the flesh; but in the Spirit he has taught us a fourth thing: that you must give up judgment. ¹⁹For you will be accused of blasphemy or hypocrisy or evil, and you will suffer from hunger and thirst and various perils on the road or at sea. ²⁰You will be threatened by rulers of synagogues, magistrates of Rome, or authorities of other lands; ²¹and crowds will gather to mock you and amuse themselves at the spectacle of your death. ²²But if you become bitter that you are treated so, or if you hate your despisers, your bitterness will become a poison to the saints and to the word of the Lord; ²³your heart will be lost, your mind will abandon the word of God, and your mouth will deny Christ before your persecutors. ²⁴Moreover, your body will turn in secret to the false comfort of women, or strong drink, or luxuries. ²⁵All of this begins in the moment that you judge what you deserve rather than trusting God to judge. ²⁶But remember always that he who chose you deserved the greatest honor but received the worst shame; ²⁶and that even now he sees all, even your heart; ²⁷and he knows all, even what you can endure; ²⁸and he forgives all, even your darkest thought. ²⁹Keep these things before your heart, beloved, and you will grow to be like him. ³⁰Remember also that those who persecute you are only blind until the love of Christ opens their eyes, and then you will be merciful toward them and severe toward the devil."

Simon and Jude Cross North Africa

³¹Gathering and teaching disciples in this manner, Simon and Jude preached for two years along the entire coast, from Alexandria to Gades in Spain. ³²First they went to Cyrene, where they found that there were many believers among the Jews because of the work of the Spirit through Alexander and Rufus. ³³The church there welcomed Simon and Andrew; and the Jews in that place were ready to listen to them when they saw that they followed the law in all things and also taught the mercy of God in Christ Jesus. ³⁴After they preached for a month in Cyrene, the saints there sent them, together with three young disciples, to the cities of Ptolemais, Berenike, and Boreum, where once again they preached and found new disciples. ³⁵From Cyrenaica they sailed to the province of Africa, first to the city of Oea and then to Carthage. ³⁶For six months Simon and Jude preached in Carthage, Utica, and Hippo, and many believed in Christ Jesus. ³⁷Then the Spirit directed them to sail to the province of Mauretenia and the cities of Caesarea and Tingis. ³⁸In all of these places Simon and Jude followed their custom of raising up disciples who accompanied them part of the way; ³⁹and after the apostles continued west, they returned to preach and teach in the region of their homes. ⁴⁰In this manner, the number of believers multiplied quickly throughout Cyrenaica, Africa, and Mauretenia.

⁴¹Crossing over the straits to Spain, Simon and Jude remained for several months in Baetica, where they were made welcome by the elders of the church in Gades, which had been established by Urbanus. ⁴²It was now winter, so they remained in Gades, preaching and building up the church until spring, when they could find a good ship and fair winds to sail to Britain.

CHAPTER 20

Simon and Jude Preach in Britain

1 Because there were no large cities along the coasts of Spain and Gaul, the ship that carried Simon and Jude north made its way slowly, putting in at small ports along the way. [2]After two months, they made landfall in Britain at the port city of Noviomagus; and from there they traveled on the Roman roads to Corinium, Eburacum, Lindum, and Londinium. [3]The people of Britain, who were recently conquered by the Romans, followed strange gods and were slow to hear the word of the Lord; but Simon and Jude preached to many of the Jews and Romans in the cities who believed and were baptized.

Simon and Jude are Sent East from Gaul

[4]Wishing to move to warmer lands before winter came, the apostles crossed over to the port of Gesoriacum in Gaul and traveled along the Roman road to Lugdunum. [5]There they remained for the winter, preaching in that city; and they planned to travel throughout Gaul in the spring. [6]But one night, while Simon was in the synagogue in Lugdunum studying the scriptures, the Spirit directed him to the place in the prophet Isaiah where it is written, "I will bring your offspring from the east, and from the west I will gather you." [7]Simon wondered what this might mean; [8]and immediately the Spirit showed him where David wrote, "As far as the east is from the west, so far he removes our transgressions from us." [9]Simon's heart burned within him all night. [10]In the morning he told Jude, who said, "So it is with me. [11]For in a dream last night, a man appeared to me in rich robes of the East, with the sun rising behind him and carrying a sword covered in blood. [12]He spoke no word, but with his other hand he beckoned for me to come." [13]Therefore Simon and Jude agreed that the Lord was directing them to the other side of the world to die; [14]and when spring came, they traveled to the port of Masilia and looked for a ship to take them east.

Simon and Jude Preach in the Lands of the East

[15]After sailing for two months, they put in at Antioch, where the saints rejoiced to see them and to hear of all those whom the Lord had saved through their preaching in far lands. [16]When they had received encouragement from the church there, they went inland to Edessa. [17]There they learned that Bartholomew had been killed; and Jude said, "It is as my dream foretold. [18]For the blood on the sword was not my own, yet the hand that beckoned was for me. [19]So let us go immediately, for I would see as many as possible saved before I see the Lord."

[20]Following their custom of taking with them disciples from each city where they preached, Simon and Jude went immediately to Babylon, where there were many Jews, and preached in the synagogues there. [21]After some weeks, they traveled to Susa, and then to Persepolis in Persia. [22]There, too, they found many Jews, and many were saved. [23]After returning some distance along the same road, they went north into Parthia and Assyria, to the cities of Ectabana and Ninevah.

Simon and Jude are Killed in Armenia

²⁴Thus Simon and Jude traveled throughout the kingdoms of the East for two years, rejoicing that they were allowed to live long enough to see so many saved. ²⁵When they came at last to Armenia, they were arrested in Ardaze below Mount Ararat by Gisak, the ruler of that region. ²⁶Gisak had heard from his priests that Simon and Jude stirred up many in the cities and towns of his land to defy the gods that he served. ²⁷He took the apostles to the hillside above the city and ordered his soldiers to beat them and pierce them with swords, hoping they would deny Christ and shame themselves before the people who had gathered. ²⁸But Simon, just before he died, said, "Do you think my brother and I would turn away from the prize now, after we have journeyed twice across the world to reach it?" ²⁹So Gisak ordered Simon to be cut into pieces, and Jude to be pierced with a spear. ³⁰And Aggaeus, a disciple who accompanied Simon and Jude, went back to Edessa to tell of their deaths before returning to preach to his countrymen in Persia.

CHAPTER 21

Mark Preaches to Worshipers of Serapis

1 For many years before the council, John Mark traveled with Paul, Barnabas, Peter, and Matthew. ²It was Mark who wrote, on Peter's behalf, the first account of the life of the Lord. ³He was also among the first to preach in Alexandria, and he was beloved by the church there. ⁴After the council, he went to Alexandria with Matthew and Apollos. ⁵Leaving them in the Jewish quarter, he went to the Greek quarter to the house of Eustathis and rejoiced that the believers had multiplied in that part of the city. ⁶There he remained for two years, building up the saints and preaching to the Greeks. ⁷But in the fourteenth year of Nero, it happened that the day of the Lord's resurrection occurred on the same day as the festival of Serapis. ⁸Hearing that the Christians were worshiping, a mob came from the Serapeum nearby and surrounded the house of Eustathis, demanding that the believers come out and pay homage to the idol. ⁹Immediately Mark came out and spoke boldly to the crowd: ¹⁰"Men and women of Alexandria, do not be angry that we worship our God on the day of your festival. ¹¹For the day was not chosen by men to insult you, but by God to enlighten you. ¹²Moreover, it is not the day that matters, but the truth regarding the one we worship. ¹³For all know that Serapis was made from the gods of Egypt and the Greeks; and this is no shame, for the true God has sent stories to all men to show himself in part until the whole is revealed. ¹⁴So it is told that a bull rises when it is killed to give life to all; that a three-headed dog guards the gates of hell; that a snake heals diseases. ¹⁵All these are pictures of the truth, but their fulfillment is in Christ Jesus. ¹⁶For he came not in a story but in the flesh; ¹⁷and when his own people turned against him, God raised him from the dead and gave him glory and all authority over heaven and hell and over all diseases and demons. ¹⁸He shines brighter than any sun and gives life to all who call upon him."

Mark Killed in Alexandria

[19]At these words, some in the crowd were moved and wished to hear more about the Lord; [20]but those who believed that he insulted Serapis shouted so loudly that he could no longer be heard. [21]Then the mob seized him, and tying him with ropes, they dragged him through the streets. [22]When they saw that he was still alive, they imprisoned him in the Serapeum overnight; and the next morning they dragged him through the streets again until he gave up his spirit. [23]They intended to burn his body, but just then a great rain began to fall; and with no crowd to watch their cruelty, they left Mark's body in the street for the dogs and returned to their homes. [24]While the rain fell and the wind blew, some of the saints carried off his body in secret and buried it in the house of Eustathis.

Matthew Travels to Antioch, Egypt, and Axum

[25]At this time Matthew and Apollos were in the Jewish quarter, where Matthew finished writing his account of the life of the Lord while Apollos preached to the Jews and built up the believers among them. [26]Soon after the death of Mark, Matthew and Apollos went to Antioch, where Matthew had copies made of his writings for use by the church there and by any apostles who traveled through the city to preach in faraway lands. [27]When he had stayed in Antioch for three months, he left Apollos there and returned to Alexandria. [28]At this time Vespasian was in the city, while his armies fought to make him emperor and to defeat the Jews. [29]Therefore, fearing trouble either from the Romans or the followers of Serapis, the believers in Alexandria equipped Matthew with all he would need to journey south, sending with him Leontis and Propylus.

[30]Matthew traveled first by boat to the cities of upper Egypt, then by roads into Axum. [31]When he found synagogues of the Jews, he showed them by many proofs from the scriptures that Jesus is the Christ. [32]But as he journeyed further south, he came eventually to cities where there were no Jews, and he found many who had never heard the word of God. [33]Whenever he came to such a place, he gathered the leaders or any who would listen and spoke to them in this manner:

Matthew Preaches to New Hearers

[34]"Although I am a stranger, I bring a story that you will know in part, for it begins in every heart. [35]Among my people, a promise from long ago was fulfilled when one came to save us from bondage. [36]But he came as a humble child, not as the king the people desired; and he preached peace and forgiveness, not war and conquest. [37]So despite the truth of his words and the miracles and healings he performed, his own people rejected him and delivered him to the authorities to be killed. [38]For their hatred these people have suffered greatly, most of all in their hearts. [39]For who among us does not long for mercy from God, and how much more those who have long waited for a promised deliverer? [40]Now as for this deliverer, Christ Jesus by name, God raised him from the dead and took him up to heaven, as I and many others witnessed. [41]But before God took him up, Christ Jesus promised to return and reward those who believe in him, not only among the Jews but also among the nations. [42]So I come to you, to increase the harvest of salvation before he returns.

[43]And who am I to ask you to believe these things? [44]I was not always as you see me now, an old man with few possessions. [45]When I was young I learned to read and speak in different tongues and to reckon

numbers, but up to the time of my calling by Christ Jesus I used my learning only to make wealth for one man—myself. [46]Now I am able to count many who are made rich in spirit by hearing the word of God, and I am able to tell of his greatness in many tongues. [47]Furthermore, although I am an old man, I have many spiritual children among whom my heart moves like a young father. [48]And while I carry no gold or silver, I am free from the burden of their care; [49]moreover, I have no fear for tomorrow, and I have treasure laid up in the kingdom of heaven, toward which I am bound with every step. [50]Who would not count mine a profitable exchange, to give up that which I could never keep in order to gain what I cannot lose? [51]And now I ask you to consider, as I once did, the ties that bind you, the worries of this life, and the fear of death and what lies beyond. [52]Does your heart not cry within you for a god greater than those you have known? [53]And do you not hear the call of Christ Jesus in your spirit as I heard him call to me in the flesh many years ago? [54]Listen! For it is not only my voice that you hear but the power of his Spirit calling you to salvation."

[55]And wherever Matthew went, whether to the Jews or to those in the furthest parts of Axum who heard the word of God for the first time, the Spirit bore fruit through him in those who were saved.

CHAPTER 22

The Lord Sends Thomas to the East

1 Eight years after the Lord was taken up into heaven, Thomas was in Jerusalem when the Spirit directed him to travel east and preach in the regions of Persia, Parthia, and India. [2]From his journeys during these many years, Thomas sent word to Jerusalem by messenger or letter concerning the progress of the gospel, which the church rejoiced to hear. [3]Therefore, when Simeon called a council to send out the apostles, he did not send for Thomas, knowing that he was far away preaching as the Lord had instructed him.

[4]Soon after his calling, Thomas traveled to Edessa, and from there he preached the word of the Lord throughout the regions of Osrohoene, Assyria, and Media. [5]In cities along the trade routes where he found Jewish settlements, he remained for a time preaching in the synagogues, and many believed. [6]Thomas did not take silver or gold from any; [7]but as need arose, he worked with his own hands building houses, as he had done from his youth in Tiberius.

Thomas Reaches India

[8]When the Lord told Thomas that he should journey further east into lands far beyond the reach of Rome, he met a merchant from India named Abbanes who was sent by his king to find carpenters who could build palaces after the fashion of the Romans. [9]Abbanes agreed to take Thomas with him and to begin to teach him the language of India. [10]After many months along the trade routes through Persia and Parthia, they arrived in Taxila, the chief city of king Gundaphorus in India.

Thomas Builds a Palace for King Gundaphorus

[11]Abbanes took Thomas to the king, who instructed Thomas to build a palace for him in Pindi, a city nearby. [12]He gave Thomas gold for this purpose, and he sent with him a slave who could speak both Greek and the Indian tongue.

[13]When Thomas came to the city where Gundaphorus desired a palace, he saw how poor the people were and how many were afflicted with disease. [14]Moved with pity, he gave to the poor all of the king's gold, and took up his residence among them. [15]He healed many and preached to them as well as he could, for he did not yet know their language well; and the king's slave had run away in fear. [16]After two months passed, the king sent a steward to see the progress of the palace, and he found nothing. [17]Hearing this report, Gundaphorus sent soldiers to search for Thomas. [18]They found him living openly with the poor, who followed him as one of their holy men.

[19]The soldiers brought Thomas before the king, who demanded what had become of the palace and the gold he had given to him. [20]Thomas said to him, "Your palace is finished." [21]Gundaphorus replied, "Who will tell me the truth? For my steward says that nothing has been done. When can I see this palace?" [22]Thomas said, "Your steward tells you the truth that he sees, but the truth that he does not see is that the palace is in heaven, which you purchased with your gold; and you will see it when you die." [23]Gundaphorus was enraged; and throwing Thomas into prison, he asked his counselors how best to torture him before killing him.

[24]Now that very night in a palace nearby, Gad, the brother of the king, was struck with a fever and seemed to die. [25]But in the morning, while his wife and household were preparing to mourn him, he returned to health and hurried to the king to tell him of the strange dream he had. [26]He said to Gundaphorus, "In my dream I went to paradise, and a man came to me whose face shone so brightly that I could not see his features. [27]He took me by the hand and led me to a marvelous palace; [28]and he said to me, 'This is the mansion that your brother built, and it waits for him. [29]But return to your brother immediately, and he will know how to build another such palace for you.'"

[30]When Gundaphorus heard his brother's words, he covered his face with his hands and wept. [31]Then he sent his soldiers to bring Thomas from the prison, and he told his brother Gad the story of the gold that Thomas had given to the poor. [32]When Thomas was brought to them, the king and his brother knelt before him and asked who his God was and how they could worship him. [33]Then Thomas explained to them all things concerning Christ Jesus; and that same day they were baptized, together with their wives and many members of their household. [34]And Thomas remained with them for a year, living at times with the king and at other times with the poor. [35]He began to preach in the language of the people, and many believed in both Taxali and Pindi. [36]Gundaphorus gave Thomas much more gold to give to the poor, [37]for he said, "The palace in heaven for my brother must be as great as mine."

[38]But after two years, the kingdom of Gundaphorus was invaded by armies from the north. [39]And when word came to the king that his army was defeated, he sent Thomas away by ship, [40]saying to him, "My brother and I may soon see our new palaces, but you have other houses to build."

CHAPTER 23

Thomas Establishes Churches in Malabar

1 Thomas traveled down the Indus River to the port of Patala. [2]From there he sailed along the coast to the region of Malabar, where he found settlements of Jews who traded with Rome by ship. [3]When Thomas embarked at the port of Muziris, he preached in the synagogue there. [4]One of the first who believed among the Jews was Samuel, who became a brother in the Lord to Thomas; [5]and after many years with the apostle he returned to Antioch to tell of all that the Lord has done in India.

[6]Thomas remained in Muziris for two years, where he learned the language of that region and began to preach among the people. [7]Many believed because they saw the signs that Thomas did, healing many of their diseases and casting out demons. [8]Moreover, they saw that Thomas lived as one of their poor, wearing a simple garment and eating only bread and water. [9]He remained in the region of Malabar for twenty years, and there he established churches in the seven cities of Muziris, Palayoor, Paravur, Kokkamangalam, Niranam, Kollam, and Chayal. [10]In each place he remained for three years, building up the church; [11]then he journeyed futher south and east, leaving behind many believers trained in righteousness and the word of God.

[12]When Thomas prepared to leave Chayal on the far side of India, the believers there warned him not to go further up the coast because they feared the zealous priests of that country. [13]By this time Thomas was an old man, weakened by much fasting; [14]but he said, "The Lord calls to me continually from the rising sun, and that way I must go until I find the end of the world or the end of my life; either end will be a joy to me."

Thomas Preaches in India

[15]Taking with him only Samuel, Thomas reached the city of Mylapore in the region of Soras, where he began to preach as he had in Malabar, in this manner:

[16]"I see that the custom of this land is to wash in a river, or to chant the names of the gods, or to perform tasks for them in order to gain salvation. [17]But I say to you that these are the doctrines of priests, who are the same in every land, including my own. [18]They lay burdens on men, causing them to live in fear that their good deeds will not be enough to please God, nor are they ever pleased except when they are ruling others. [19]They take the last coins of the poor to build their temples, not knowing that the true God lives not in a building but in our hearts; [20]and the house of a poor man is sufficient to gather for the worship of the Lord.

[21]"Moreover, I see that the custom of this land is to honor those with light skin and make outcasts of those with dark skin. [22]But I say to you that all men shed blood that is red, [23]and red was the blood of Christ Jesus, shed for all men. [24]So do not despair if the traditions of men appoint a low place for you, for in Christ Jesus you are promised a place in the heavens, [25]where all are one in him and all are white as snow, for they reflect his glory.

[26]"Again, I learn that your philosophers say that all things are God, or that there is no god but the one within them. [27]But I say to you that this seems good only when the crops ripen at the right time or when a mother suckles her child. [28]It does not seem so, however, when one suffers from the cruelty of other men or when sickness takes an infant. [29]Moreover, if man is a god to himself, then it is not you only but your neighbor who is a god. [30]And how fortunate

if the god that is your neighbor is a merciful god, but how unfortunate if he takes your goat or your wife. [31]Look at the sinfulness of man—lying, unjust, hurtful; always at war with nature, others, and himself—and see what gods these men are and how the world is to be pitied, ruled by such gods. [32]No, God must be other than us, or we are doomed to die in misery and confusion. [33]And God must be one, or we serve lesser gods who are not gods at all."

Thomas Arrested in Mylapore

[34]Thomas had preached in this manner for two months, and many believed, especially among the poor. [35]But when the priests of Mylapore learned that a man was preaching the word of the Lord in opposition to their gods, they went to Misdaeus, the king of that place, and had Thomas arrested.

[35]The king asked Thomas to answer the reports he had heard about his preaching. [36]And when the apostle spoke boldly to him concerning the ways of the priests and the nature of God, Misdaeus saw that Thomas spoke with wisdom and authority, and he wished to hear more, but he feared the priests. [37]Then the priests said to him, "Make this man show you a sign; for we hear that he is a healer, and he and his god should be put to the test."

[38]Thomas refused, saying, "My God does not perform wonders out of obedience to men but out of his mercy, which is not ours to command. [39]Now if you come with me to the houses of the poor, surely you will see such signs. [40]But a moment later you will doubt them and ask for more. [41]They will become like wine to you, always sweet and never enough, until you stagger and fall. [42]I once demanded proofs and learned that I was a fool when I saw that my mind made a wall before my heart. [43]And although I cried to escape, my mind placed more stones to raise the wall higher, until my mind built

a fortress to imprison my heart. [44]But then my Lord came to me through the wall—and this was not in a dream or as a ghost but in his body before my eyes—and I was ashamed of the wall I had built. [45]Such is each of you until the Lord makes a door in your wall. [46]Therefore, Misdaeus, bid him enter, and you will know the truth. [47]For he sees all things about you, he demands all things from you, and yet he has mercy in all things concerning you. [48]Seek not the stones of proof but the waters of grace, and the wall of doubt that imprisons you will soften and melt away."

Thomas Speared by Soldiers

[49]Again Misdaeus perceived that Thomas was a good man, and he would have released him; [50]but the priests continued to demand that he be killed. [51]And while the king feared the priests, he also feared the people; [52]for many already believed, and even those who did not considered Thomas a holy man. [53]Therefore, at the king's command, four of his soldiers took Thomas outside the city, pretending to protect him on the road. [54]But when they were out of sight of the crowd that had followed for some way, they took Thomas up a mountain and there killed him, piercing him with spears. [55]Samuel and a few of the believers from Mylapore still followed, [56]and when they saw the soldiers come down from the mountain without Thomas, they went up and found his body and took it to the city where they buried him. [57]Nevertheless, even in the short time he was with them, many believed because of Thomas. [58]And Samuel, promising to send others to encourage the new believers in Mylapore, went back through the seven churches in Malabar telling of the apostle's death before he sailed for Antioch.

CHAPTER 24

Luke Summarizes the Three Volumes

[1]When the believers in Antioch learned of the death of Thomas, they sent word to the churches in Pella, Alexandria, Rome, Corinth, and Ephesus. [2]In every place, the saints mourned because of his death but rejoiced because of what the Lord did through him. [3]For Thomas was the first of the twelve to carry the good news of Christ Jesus beyond the areas ruled by Rome, and through him the Lord began to show the way to a harvest of salvation in the farthest of lands. [4]So now, most excellent Theophilus, having written in order how the Spirit has taken the word of the Lord to the four corners of the world, I come to the end of these three volumes. [5]And what is there to say regarding the end of this account, or regarding the earthly end of the apostles, that is not also a beginning?

[6]For we have seen that all but two of the twelve have died—some by the sword, some by stoning, and some by the cross. [7]Some were falsely accused of blasphemy by the Jews, while others were blamed when people turned from false gods. [8]Some were hated by merchants who lost wealth gotten by wickedness and wrong belief or rulers who lost the loyalty of their family or subjects. [9]Yet all of these, the twelve and the others whose suffering is recorded here, were righteous and faithful to the end, and their deaths led many more to believe. [10]This is the testimony of every witness, and the evidence in every place where the church grows upon ground watered by the blood of the saints.

[11]For though many have suffered, through them the Lord has laid a foundation of obedience and hope throughout the world. [12]Consider the perfect wisdom of God. [13]When a farmer allows a tree to reach the time for dropping seeds, new trees may grow, but only nearby. [14]However, when he takes ripe seeds from the tree and plants them in new places that he has prepared, they grow faster and stronger, and the harvest is great. So it is with God.

[15]And so it is, beloved Theophilus, that the end of this account is but the beginning of what the Lord will do. [16]For in the first volume, we saw that the Father has given us his Son, through whom we have salvation. [17]In the second volume, we witnessed that the Son gave us his Spirit, through whom we have the church. [18]Now in this third volume, we have seen the Spirit give boldness to the apostles to preach the word, even to the point of death. [19]And through the death of the saints, the Lord has built up his church in every place to hasten the harvest of salvation. [20]All of our labor is to that end, which is the beginning of everlasting glory.

1

Paul's Mission to Spain

1 In the second book, Theophilus, I wrote about all that the Holy Spirit accomplished from the beginning of the church in Jerusalem, ²how the apostles preached the word of the Lord in many places, from Jerusalem to Rome, and how the number of believers multiplied. ³Now, having seen myself, and also having learned from many eyewitnesses, how the Lord has continued to fulfill his promise to send the word to the ends of the earth, ⁴I complete my account, trusting that by the truth of these things, the Spirit will make you bold to continue the work that he began through the apostles.

[1–4] Comparison to the prologues in Luke's Gospel and Acts will reveal similar wording but also some progression. The first two verses summarize the familiar themes of Spirit-guided evangelism, geographic progress, and growth of the church. But now Luke, who is present for many of the key events in this narrative—indeed, perhaps from the beginning of the "we" passages in Acts 16[1]—acknowledges himself as an eyewitness. Furthermore, he cites "many eyewitnesses" to anticipate questions about his reporting on such far-flung events. It is also significant that this prologue ends with a charge to continue the work of the apostles, as if they are past tense—because by AD 75, as we will see, most of them were martyred.

Theophilus, whose name appears in the New Testament only in Luke's prologues, has not been identified with certainty. He may be a patron who is otherwise unknown, or a pseudonym for someone of influence whose identity Luke wished to protect. Some have suggested the mid-first century high priest Theophilus ben Ananus, who is mentioned by the first-century Jewish historian Josephus (*Jewish Antiquities* 18.5.3), an identification which may account for some particulars of content, especially the interest in the temple in the early chapters of the Gospel. Other scholars believe that Luke creates a fictional name for his dedication, in which case Theophilus ("lover of God") is a kind of "everyman" designation meant to apply to any Gentile reader. For the purposes of this narrative, Theophilus is a real character who sponsors Luke's writing (see chapter 8 below).

---

1. Porter, "'We' Passages," 545–74; Bock, *Acts* 14.

⁵In the seventh year of Nero, when Paul had been preaching the word of the Lord unhindered in Rome for more than a year, Pudens, the son of a senator, heard the word of the Lord from Paul and believed, along with many of his household. ⁶Pudens brought Paul into his own house, and he welcomed believers there from all over Rome. ⁷And many more were added to the number of believers because of him.

⁸When Paul had been in Rome two years, and the Jews from Jerusalem had not yet appeared to accuse him before the emperor, the charges against him were dismissed.

---

[5] The seventh year of Nero is AD 61, midway through the period most scholars assign to Paul's Roman imprisonment. Literally the last word in Acts is "unhindered," a term that occurs only once in the New Testament and makes a strong statement that Paul was completely free to preach. The point is not only to show that Paul's activity is legal but also that Rome, up to this point, is showing tolerance for Christian missionary activity.

The large role for Pudens in Paul's last days is plausible for several reasons. He is a biblical character, mentioned among the Romans in Paul's last letter (2 Tim 4:21). Historically, he is identified as the son of Quintus Cornelius Pudens, a Roman senator. Tradition states that the wife of the elder Pudens, Priscilla, was converted by Peter and provided shelter for him and others. Her family and many Christians were buried in the northeastern part of the ancient city in the catacombs beneath her house, which are preserved today. As chapter 4 will recount, the daughters of Pudens may have continued to aid believers during persecutions. The evidence is strong, therefore, that the family of Pudens was influential in the early Roman church, and it is reasonable to suppose that Pudens himself was able to offer protection to Paul, and to survive himself at least until Nero's persecution, when tradition states that he was martyred.

Reference to Pudens in 2 Timothy 4:21 introduces the issue of Paul's authorship of 1–2 Timothy and Titus, the Pastoral Epistles. In chapters 1–5 of this reconstruction, an attempt is made to harmonize Paul's movements as recorded in Acts with information garnered from these letters, especially the personal details at the end of 2 Timothy. This follows from the assumption stated in the introduction that Paul wrote these letters, or at least the parts of them containing travel details, and that he did so after the events recorded in Acts.[2] Those who regard the Pastoral Epistles as forgeries from the late first century will need to put the next few chapters in "square brackets" and either move up the date of Paul's death or account some other way for the last several years of his life.

[6–7] This is the first of many references in this account to a "house church," already familiar from Acts (e.g., 2:44–46, 16:11–15, 17:1–9), which usually involved a well-to-do convert providing space for worship, instruction, and sometimes safety.[3] The "church" as a separate building was not common until the fourth century.

[8] Roman law required that accusers appear at a trial, and there may have been a two-year statute of limitations for Paul's opponents to appear in Rome.[4] Paul's release, however, did not constitute his innocence, and he was subject to re-arrest. The supposition here, that Pudens guarantees his return, is a more formal or controlled version of these circumstances.

2. See, e.g., Knight, *Pastoral Epistles*, 4–52; Klinker-deClerck, "Pastoral Epistles," 101–8.

3. Blue, "House Church," 119–222.

4. Tajra, *Trial*, 194–96.

⁹Pudens also sent word to the emperor that he would commit to surety for Paul. ¹⁰Because Paul had obeyed all the laws of Rome, and because Pudens promised houses and lands to ensure Paul's appearance at the will of the emperor, Paul was given over to Pudens. ¹¹Immediately Pudens determined to help Paul fulfill his desire to preach in Spain, providing for Paul and those who accompanied him out of his own possessions. ¹²He sent with Paul as his steward his slave Quintipor, who was a believer. ¹³Paul summoned Timothy from Ephesus and Titus from Corinth, and he also took with him Urbanus and Stachys from Rome.

[9–10] "Entrustment to surety"⁵ was a form of confinement in which a prisoner, usually of high rank or importance, was released to the care of a private citizen, who had to produce him on demand or forfeit house and lands.

[11] Paul's intention to visit Spain is clear from Romans 15:23–24, 28: "I desire, as I have for many years, to come to you when I go to Spain. . . . I will set out by way of you to Spain."⁶ Of course, this intention was expressed long before the lengthy series of trials and imprisonments which culminated in his death. Paul's journey to Spain, however, is supported by an early and strong tradition (*See* primary sources below), including the compelling reference in Clement of Rome written just thirty years later, within the living memory of the writer (*1 Clement* 5:5–7). Assuming that Paul was released in AD 62, this leaves at least two years for further travel before his martyrdom late in Nero's reign. As chapters 2–5 suggest, this period also allows for further travel to the east and a final, more severe imprisonment in line with the Pastoral Epistles.

[12–13] Six companions may seem a large number to readers who think Paul traveled alone or with one coworker, but this is because Luke usually mentions only the main actors; in Acts 20:4–5, however, he lists no less than eight members of Paul's retinue on his third missionary journey.

While no traditional sources name traveling companions for Paul's last journeys, those proposed here are chosen because, with one exception, they are associated with his later ministry. Only Quintipor is a fictitious character. The supposition is that Pudens would entrust a Christian slave to accompany Paul on his journeys while representing Pudens, perhaps even in a financial capacity. Pudens' proenomen (second of three names) was Quintius, and a slave's name was often formed by adding to it the suffix *-por* ("child").

Timothy and Titus are plausible companions because they figure importantly in Paul's last movements and writings. We do not know their whereabouts during the four years supposed here between Paul's third missionary journey and his letters to them. Ephesus is the most likely place for Timothy, since he is associated with that city in both the New Testament and early church tradition. As for Titus, he is stationed for a time in Crete (Tit 1:5), then he accompanies Paul to Rome before he moves on to Dalmatia (2 Tim 4:9). We have no information about his location before Crete or after Dalmatia; however, because 2 Corinthians makes it clear that Titus had an important conciliatory role in Corinth, this narrative places him there.

---

5. Rapske, *Roman Custody*, 32–35.

6. All Scripture quotations are from the *New Revised Standard Version*.

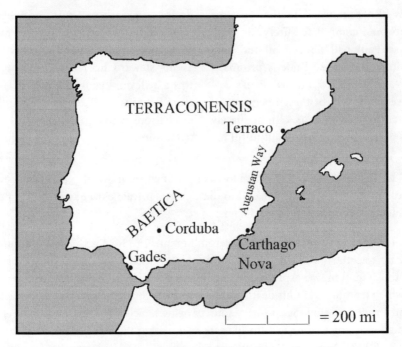

Map 1: Spain

[Note: Maps are provided near the first reference in the commentary to the
area described; only places mentioned in the text of *The Apostles after Acts* are
included on the maps.]

---

[14]When a moderate south wind began to blow, we set sail for Corsica, [15]and after waiting several days, we found favorable winds and sailed to Terraconensis, where we journeyed from the coast to the city of Terraco.

Urbanus and Stachys are chosen from the long list to whom Paul sends greetings when he writes to the Romans; in 16:9, Paul refers to the former as "our coworker in Christ" and to the latter as "my beloved." Since Urbanus is a Roman name and Stachys is a Greek name, they are suitable for a mission to the large, Romanized cities of Spain. Stachys appears later in this narrative in the position that later tradition assigned to him, bishop of Byzantium (18:14).

Luke, a loyal companion of Paul to the end (2 Tim 4:11), does not name himself, but he is traditionally regarded as the source of the "we" passages in Acts, which are typically mission trips that begin with the words "we sailed" (16:10–17; 20:5–15; 21:1–18; 27:1—28:18).

[14] Luke shows considerable interest in winds, using similar wording elsewhere for the beginning of journeys (e.g., Acts 27:13). Multi-directional, rapidly-shifting winds made westerly sailing particularly difficult in ancient times.

[15] Hugging the coast from Rome and following currents and south winds, this would be the likely first stop in Spain. Strong evidence of an early Christian community in Terraco supports the idea that Paul evangelized the city.[7]

7. Tajra, *Martyrdom,* 104.

¹⁶There was a synagogue of the Jews in the city, but Paul went instead to the marketplace, where he preached openly to those gathered there. ¹⁷After some days, when several citizens had believed, certain leaders of the city asked Paul to speak to them.

¹⁸So Paul, standing on the steps of the palace of Augustus, said, ¹⁹"Terraconians, you have achieved fame throughout the world, and great wealth for yourselves, by taking from the earth gold, silver, and other metals.

[16–17] The later chapters of Acts indicate a transition from Paul's earlier missionary approach, which was to go first to the synagogue and preach to the Jews. In Corinth he declares, "From now on I will go to the Gentiles" (Acts 18:6); in Ephesus he moves from the synagogue to a lecture hall (Acts 19:9); in Rome he meets in his rented house with Jewish leaders, and after they reject his message he pronounces judgment: "Let it be known to you that this salvation of God has been sent to the Gentiles; they will listen" (Acts 28:28). Coming at the very end of Acts, this passage clearly signals movement to a predominant, if not exclusive, mission to Gentiles. Paul's choice here to preach in the marketplace finds precedent in his mission to Athens (Acts 17:17–34).

[18–19] Paul's sermon at the Areopagus in Athens (Acts 17:22–31) serves as a pattern in that a local source of civic pride—there a monument, here the precious metals industry—serves as a vehicle to introduce the gospel.[8] In this fictional account, as in Acts, Paul wants to show both the futility of pagan idolatry and the superiority of the gospel, especially in light of its fulfillment of scripture.[9] The fact that Tarshish, which is identified by most scholars with Tarracona, is mentioned no less than twenty-eight times in the Old Testament—most often in prophetic denunciations of its trading partner Tyre—gives Paul a specific point of reference. The repeated biblical references to gold and silver reflect the main source of the region's wealth. While grain, olives, and other metals such as tin and lead flowed from the province of Hispania to Rome, gold from the north (Tarraco) and silver from the south (Corduba and Gades) made the region indispensable to Rome.

8. Schnabel, "Paul in Athens," 172–90.
9. Jipp, "Areopagus Speech," 567–88.

---

²⁰Even the scriptures of the Jews from ancient times speak of your greatness among the nations, and the kings of the earth who have traded with you. ²¹But the prophets also speak of you together with one who is greater than any king, ²²one of whom the scriptures declare, 'the kings of Tarshish and of the isles render him tribute.' ²³Who is this greater one but the Messiah, whom the scriptures say must suffer, and whom the Jews rejected, but God raised him from the dead and seated him at his right hand? ²⁴Thus the scriptures say of God, 'You set a crown of fine gold on his head. He asked you for life; you gave it to him—length of days forever and ever. ²⁵His glory is great through your help; splendor and majesty you bestow on him.'

²⁶Now why do the scriptures exalt him, and why do we call him Lord? ²⁷It is because in another place, Terraconians, when speaking of your city, God declares the foolishness of idols next to the worship of the true God: ²⁸"They are both stupid and foolish; the instruction given by idols is no better than wood! Beaten silver is brought from Tarshish, and gold from Uphaz. ²⁹They are the work of artisans, but the

Lord is the true God; he is the living God and the everlasting King.' ³⁰Long ago, David, king of the Jews, declared to God that 'The law of your mouth is better to me than thousands of gold and silver pieces'; ³¹and David's son Solomon, likewise, proclaimed that 'A good name is to be chosen rather than great riches, and favor is better than silver or gold.' ³²What is this better law but the law of the spirit of life which is in Christ Jesus? ³³And what is this good name but the name of Christ, who descended from these kings according to the flesh and whose name is now above all other names? ³⁴And what is this favor but the mercy of God poured out on those who call upon the name of the Lord? ³⁵And finally, what are gold and silver, lead and tin, next to the surpassing riches of knowing Christ as Savior?"

³⁶With these and other proofs from scripture, Paul persuaded the people, and many believed, including several women and men of high standing. ³⁷Paul remained in Terraco for two months, preaching, healing, and strengthening the disciples. ³⁸Then, leaving Stachys in the house of Abercius to continue building up the believers, we journeyed south by the Augustan Way to Carthago Nuvo, where Paul again preached in the marketplace to the leaders of the city. ³⁹And here many more believed; but the next day, the Jews of that city accused Paul before the officials, ⁴⁰saying, "This is the one about whom we have heard from our brothers in Jerusalem and Rome, that he teaches scorn for our law and our people, and also for the gods of Rome." ⁴¹And the city officials, fearing further disturbance from the Jews or from the people, told Paul to leave the city.

[20–32] Although Paul usually uses the word "law" in contrast to the gospel, in Rom 8:2 he uses precisely these words to indicate the gospel itself. This is entirely appropriate in such a context, where the contrast is not to Jewish legalism but to pagan immorality.

[23–32] The Old Testament texts in Pauls sermon are as follows: V. 22 = Psalm 72:10; v. 24 = Psalm 21:3–4; v.29 = Jeremiah 10:8–9; v.30 = Psalm 119:72; v.31 = Proverbs 22:1.

[33–36] The same description of high-status converts is used following Paul's preaching in Beroea (Acts 17:10).

[37–38] Paul's overland route is determined by the newly-constructed Via Augusta, which ran along the east coast from the Pyranees through Tarraco (modern Terragona), which was the capitol of the territory of Terraconensis and center of the gold trade; south to the silver center, coastal Cathargo Nova (modern Cartagena); west into the heavily Romanized territory of Baetica, with its capital Corduba (Cordoba); finally, to the Atlantic port and Roman naval center Gades (Cadiz), which contained the highest concentration of upper class citizens after Rome and Padua. An analogous modern mission might involve traveling from New York (= Rome) to San Francisco, then down the California coast to Malibu, inland to Beverly Hills, and south to Coronado—Paul was definitely on the five-star tour.

[39–41] Opposition from Jewish leaders in response to Paul's preaching is a familiar theme in Paul's ministry (e.g., Acts 13:45; 14:2, 5, 19), and after thirty years of missionary activity, including two in Rome, he was undoubtedly well known. Furthermore, his appeal to Caesar against the jurisdiction of Jewish authorities (Acts 25:11–12) would have been perceived as a kind of renunciation of citizenship, a symbolic break with Judaism.[10] In this instance, there is certainly enough truth to the accusation to warrant expulsion on the part of city officials. Paul would be the first to recognize that Christianity must at some point receive official sanction as a religion distinct from Judaism, because the Jews were not content to shelter under their umbrella a group that so differed in fundamental respects; and Romans would regard the Lordship of Christ a direct affront to the gods and to emperor worship.

10. Tajra, *Trial*, 198.

---

[42]We then traveled west to the province of Baetica, and the cities of Corduba and Gades. [43]In Corduba, Paul was welcomed into the house of Balbus, a silver merchant, who was the brother of Abercius. [44]When Paul entered the house, Balbus told him that his wife Claudia was lying ill in an inner chamber, and near to death with a fever that had afflicted her for eight days.[45]And Paul, entering the chamber, prayed for Claudia and raised her up. [46]Then Balbus and his entire household believed and were baptized in the name of the Lord Jesus, and they received the Holy Spirit. [47]And word spread throughout the city, so that others brought sick people to Paul, and many were healed. [48]Now when the Jews of Carthago Nuvo sent messengers to accuse Paul, the city officials sent them away, [49]saying, "This man has done nothing but good since he came here, so whatever god he worships must be good, and the trouble that you warn about must be the trouble that you bring." [50]So the believers in Corduba rejoiced, and Paul remained with them four months, teaching and strengthening them in the Lord. [51]Then he told them, "The Lord has revealed to me that my time is short, but I have not yet reached the farthest point of my journey." [52]So, leaving Urbanus in Corduba, we traveled south to Gades, which faces the great western sea, from which sailors journey to Gaul, Britain, and many strange lands. [53]When Paul saw the sea, he knelt down at the water's edge and said, "Here I have reached the limit of the west, and where the Lord sends me now, I must wait and pray to learn." [54]But we had been in Gades only three days when a ship arrived from Rome carrying a messenger from Pudens with a letter for Paul begging him to come to Ephesus, where the church was threatened by false teachers.

---

[42] Baetica, which was the most Romanized part of Spain. Corduba, like Terracona, contained a strong Christian community from a very early date.[11]

[43] Both Abercius and Balbus are fictitious characters, their names taken from a list of Roman cognomens (the third of three Roman names, and the one commonly used in informal designations). Any person of high standing in a first-century Spanish city was almost certain to be a Roman citizen.

[44] This incident follows the pattern of Acts 28:7–10.

[45–46] On the baptism of entire households, see Acts 10:24, 44–48; 11:14; 16:15, 31–34.

[47] Acts 28:9 records a similar response to an individual healing.

11. Mullen, *Expansion*, 251–54.

[48–50] There is no indication in Acts or Paul's letters what length of time was required to establish a church before he moved on. In some locations (e.g., Athens) it appears that no one was converted; in other places (e.g., Philippi, Corinth, Ephesus) Paul leaves suddenly, but his letters indicate that a church had been established. The supposition here, that Paul spends several months following up on a successful preaching mission, also allows his Spanish mission to begin and end between winters, when sea passage would be unlikely.

PRIMARY SOURCES

Luke's Prologues

Luke 1:1–4: Since many have undertaken to set down an orderly account of the events that have been fulfilled among us, just as they were handed on to us by those who from the beginning were eyewitnesses and servants of the word, I too decided, after investigating everything carefully from the very first, to write an orderly account for you, most excellent Theophilus, so that you may know the truth concerning the things about which you have been instructed.

Acts 1:1–8: In the first book, Theophilus, I wrote about all that Jesus did and taught from the beginning until the day when he was taken up to heaven, after giving instructions through the Holy Spirit to the apostles whom he had chosen. After his suffering he presented himself alive to them by many convincing proofs, appearing to them during forty days and speaking about the kingdom of God. While staying with them, he ordered them not to leave Jerusalem, but to wait there for the promise of the Father. "This," he said, "is what you have heard from me; for John baptized with water, but you will be baptized with the Holy Spirit not many days from now." So when they had come together, they asked him, "Lord, is this the time when you will restore the kingdom to Israel?" He replied, "It is not for you to know the times or periods that the Father has set by his own authority. But you will receive power when the Holy Spirit has come upon you; and you will be my witnesses in Jerusalem, in all Judea and Samaria, and to the ends of the earth."

Paul in Spain

Clement of Rome (AD 96) 1 *Clement* 5:5–7: Through jealousy and strife Paul showed the way to the prize of endurance; seven times he was a herald both in the East and in the West, he gained the noble fame of his faith, he taught righteousness to all the world, and when he had reached the limits of the West he gave his testimony before the rulers, and thus passed from the world and was taken up into the Holy Place—the greatest example of endurance.[12] ["The limits of the West" clearly means Spain, according to multiple contemporary references.[13]]

---

12. Clement is quoted from *The Apostolic Fathers.*
13. E.g., Tajra, *Martyrdom,* 110–11.

Muratorian Canon (AD 170) 2: [Luke] shows . . . that the principle on which he wrote was, to give only what fell under his own notice, by the omission of the passion of Peter, and also of the journey of Paul, when he went from the city Rome to Spain.[14]

Irenaeus (AD 180) *Against Heresies* 1.10.2: For the Churches which have been planted in Germany do not believe or hand down anything different, nor do those in Spain, nor those in Gaul, nor those in the East, nor those in Egypt, nor those in Libya, nor those which have been established in the central regions of the world. [Irenaeus does not name Paul, but the reference to an established church in Spain by the mid-second century suggests early missionary activity there.]

Tertullian (AD 200) *An Answer to the Jews* 7: For whom have the nations believed. . . . the Moors, all the limits of Spain, and the diverse nations of the Gauls, and the haunts of the Britons— inaccessible to the Romans, but subjugated to Christ. [Again, there is no reference here to Paul but to an early established church in Spain.]

Cyril of Jerusalem (AD 375) *Catechetical Lectures* 17.26: [Paul] fully preached the Gospel, and instructed even imperial Rome, and carried the earnestness of his preaching as far as Spain, undergoing conflicts innumerable, and performing signs and wonders.

John Chysostom (AD 390) *Homily* 10 *on* 2 *Timothy* 4:20: For after he had been in Rome, he returned to Spain, but whether he came thence again into these parts, we know not.

---

14. *The Muratorian Canon* and all apocryphal and early church writings before AD 325 are quoted from Roberts, Donaldson, and Coxe, *The Ante-Nicene Fathers,* unless otherwise noted.

2

Paul Returns to Greece and Asia Minor

1 Since it was now late in the year, Paul determined to leave Gades as soon as possible. ²So we took passage on a ship carrying merchants, which put in at Carthage, Syracuse, and then Crete, where we disembarked to find passage to Ephesus. ³There were good southwesterly winds at that time of year, and Paul was anxious to reach Ephesus, but the Lord told him to preach in Crete, so we traveled from the port of Chersonisos inland to Lyttos. ⁴There Paul found among the Jews a household of believers who had been faithful to the Lord Jesus for many years, but they had made no converts either among the Jews or the Greeks. ⁵So Paul preached day and night both in the synagogue and in the marketplace, and more were added to the number of believers, both from the Jews and the Greeks. ⁶After a month, leaving Titus in Lyttos to strengthen the believers there and to preach in the other towns nearby, we sailed for Ephesus.

[1–3] Paul's movements in this chapter are based in part on references in the Pastoral Epistles, which imply travel after his initial Roman imprisonment. Further travel is also indicated in the apocryphal *Acts of Paul*, written about AD 160.[1] This book, only about one quarter of which survives, may have been based on word-of-mouth records of Paul's final activities, and its very creation may in fact indicate early dissatisfaction with the incompleteness of Acts.[2] Tertullian (*Concerning Baptism* 17:5) reports that the author was an elder in Asia Minor whose progressive views on the role of women (i.e., Paul's coworker Thecla in the story) led to his demotion and suppression of the document. Because the beginning of the document is missing, there is no way to tell if the original described a trip to Spain. While most of the action in the surviving fragments takes place in Pisidian Antioch and Myra, The *Acts of Paul* also has Paul visiting Iconium, Lystra, Sidon, Tyre, Philippi, Corinth, Crete, and Ephesus.

Assuming a final journey to the eastern Mediterranean, a number of proposals have been made for an itinerary. The sequence here combines plausible sailing routes with places and circumstances described in the Pastoral Epistles to create a simple circle moving counterclockwise around the Aegean Sea from Crete to Corinth, with an elapsed time of about one year, from early fall 63 to late summer 64.

1. For a thorough introduction, see Klauck, *Apocryphal Acts*, 47–79.
2. Bauckam, "Acts of Paul," 105–52.

[4] The fact that Cretans, along with representatives of many other lands, are present at Pentecost (Acts 2:11) suggests to many scholars that these first converts from far-flung regions were also the first evangelists to those regions, and were perhaps discovered later through the travels of others (as were some of John's disciples in Ephesus twenty years after his death, Acts 19:1–7).

[5–6] Titus 1:5: "I left you behind in Crete for this reason, so that you should put in order what remained to be done, and should appoint elders in every town, as I directed you."

---

[7]Following a strong south wind, and touching at Naxos, we reached Ephesus on the third day. [8]When we arrived, the elders told Paul that the church there had divided into two factions, one that remained in the household of Onesiphorus, with Priscilla and Aquila and some others, while Hymenaeus and Alexander the silversmith drew many others away in opposition to Paul. [9]When Paul asked to meet with all the believers, including those who opposed him, only Alexander with a few others came to dispute with him. [10]Alexander said to those who had gathered, "Paul follows the Pharisees who hope for another life, because they are not content with the Lord in this life. [11]But many other Jews, and the wisdom of the Greeks, and even your own eyes, tell you that there is no resurrection except in our new life in Christ. [12]Paul comes here again not to make you free in the Lord but to chain you to the body."

[7–8] Paul greets Onesiphorus, Priscilla, and Aquila in 2 Timothy 4:19, suggesting that they are leaders who have remained loyal. 1 Timothy 1:20 records that Hymenaeus and Alexander "have suffered shipwreck in the faith" and have been "turned over to Satan" (see also 1 Cor 5:3–5) "so that they may learn not to blaspheme." In 2 Timothy 2:17, a specific charge is laid against Hymenaeus, and another named Philetus, "who have swerved from the truth by claiming that the resurrection has already taken place." In 2 Timothy 4:14–15, Paul warns once more against Alexander the silversmith as one who damaged Paul and "strongly opposed our message." There are two or more people named Alexander associated with Ephesus.[3] Alexander "the silversmith" is specified by vocation here and in 2 Timothy 4:14 to distinguish him from a Jewish leader by the same name who opposed Paul to the civil authorities (Acts 19:33–41).

[9–12] The key phrase to illuminate this schism is "the resurrection has already taken place" (2 Tim 2:17). The strength of Alexander's argument is that many Jews, the Greek philosophers, and the lack of observable evidence for an afterlife combine against Paul's teaching. In this speech, Alexander's ideas approximate those of the Gnostics, whose rejection of the body would lead to rejection of the Old Testament, the humanity of Jesus, and much of the New Testament. The Gnostics countered these with numerous apocryphal Gospels and Acts that expressed their ideas, some of which have only recently been discovered (e.g., *The Gospel of Judas*). These works, written a century or more after the events they describe, have no scholarly advocates as alternative histories of the New Testament period, but they help us to understand how the Gnostics became serious rivals to orthodox Christianity for the next two centuries.

---

3. Knight, *Pastoral Epistles*, 110–11.

Map 2: Greece and Asia Minor

[12]And Paul replied, "Brothers and sisters, for two years I lived with you, and you saw by many miracles and healings that the Lord cared not only for your souls but also for your bodies. [13]Does the Lord no longer care, or have you now been led astray by the foolishness of these men that passes for wisdom? [14]For it was not I, but the Spirit through the scriptures who taught you that the Lord made the flesh of man and called it good. [15]Now we all know that the flesh is weak, and prone to sin; but so also is the spirit of man fallen and prone to rebellion. [16]Nevertheless, both are saved by grace together, and both will be raised on the last day. [17]If it were not so, why would Christ Jesus be raised in the body? [18]And if he is not raised, but is only a spirit, why would God have sent him to you in the flesh, from the line of David? [19]For by the body you are made one with each other, and by the body you are part of all that God has done in the world from creation until now. [20]Without the body, therefore, there is no truth in what was accomplished through the prophets, or in the life and death of the Lord Jesus Christ, or even in you when you first came to faith. [21]Without the body, you are less than a leaf blown by every wind—first to false teachers, then to immorality, and finally to the ruin of your faith. [22]Furthermore, without the resurrection, the salvation that you know in Christ ends with your death. [23]And while you may thrive in the body for now, enjoying the pleasures of life, what of those who suffer by disease, or famine, or persecution? [24]For such is the lot of most men, and of many believers, especially in these last days. [25]Are you so short-sighted that you cling to this life only, but do not think of those for whom life is filled with trouble, and resurrection their only hope? [26]And as for you, Alexander, if it is the body that you scorn, so from the body of Christ you shall be cut off until you repent and return to the word that you once received."

[12–26] Paul's response here (with some reference to 1 Cor 15) summarizes the arguments of orthodox Christianity from ancient times to modern, from the Gnostics to the Existentialists, against Greek philosophy (and much Eastern religion), which has influenced many to regard the soul as transcendent or superior to the body. As the words given to Paul imply, this notion can lead not only to moral decline ("What difference does it make what the [mere] body does?") but also to dismissal of Christ's resurrection ("What need had he of a [lowly] body?") and ultimately rejection of the afterlife ("Our [spiritual] encounter with God in this life is sufficient"). Furthermore, such mind-body dualism tends to disengage humanity from history, i.e., from God's intervention on behalf of Israel or in the Incarnation. Finally—but not addressed by Paul in this account—disparagement of the body opens the door to treatment of people as abstractions who then become grouped and expendable in a cause, or as enemies. By contrast, to preserve the view of each person as a unity of flesh and spirit, as an embodied soul, encourages the treatment of each individual with dignity. It also connects each person to the physical, historical world, and in that sense it makes history matter.

---

[27]When those who opposed Paul heard his words, some of them repented, but Alexander scoffed, and with Hymenaeus continued to teach against Paul. [28]Paul remained for three months and debated with them on several occasions; but wishing to reach Macedonia before the winter storms, he left Timothy there to strengthen the believers and journeyed to Miletus, where Paul wished to see the believers one last time. [29]From Miletus we sailed along the coast to Troas, where Paul found Mark in the house of Carpus, and left with him his books and parchments. [30]From there we sailed to Neapolis, and traveled to Philippi and Thessalonica. [31]In all of these places, the believers rejoiced to see Paul, and many were encouraged in the faith.

[32]From Thessalonica, Paul journeyed to Corinth, where there were many believers, meeting in several households, but all were one in the Lord. [33]Apollos was in Corinth at this time, strengthening many. [34]And when Paul witnessed his great knowledge of scripture and ability to debate with both Jews and Greeks, he sent him with Zenas to help Titus in Crete and Timothy in Ephesus.

[27–28] Since Timothy is in Ephesus when Paul writes his two letters to him, this narrative leaves him here now. Since Paul "left Trophimus ill in Miletus" (2 Tim 4:20), this somewhat indirect route to Troas accomplishes several things in terms of the overall harmony of itinerary details. It gets Paul to Miletus after parting with Timothy; it gets Paul from Crete to Ephesus without delay; and it replaces a land journey from Ephesus to Troas with a sea journey from Miletus to Troas.

[29] Paul later instructs Timothy to "get" Mark (2 Tim 4:11), so Mark is presumably not in Ephesus, but close enough to retrieve. In the next sentence (2 Tim 4:12), Paul asks Timothy to bring his cloak, books, and parchments, all of which were left in Troas. While the wording does not link the books and parchments directly to Mark, it is reasonable to imagine Paul leaving his manuscripts with author Mark, who was perhaps writing his Gospel during a stay in Troas, and thinking that he would return for them (and his cloak) the following winter—until news from Rome changed his plans.

[30–34] Luke elsewhere offers high praise for the abilities of Apollos (Acts 18:24–28). This highly-educated Alexandrian Jew had ministered in Corinth previously during at least two periods (1 Cor 1:12; 3:4–6; 16:12); and according to Jerome, he became the first bishop of Corinth. His obvious importance to this church, and the detail that he and Zenas carry the letter to Titus (Tit 3:13), together suggest that he was in Corinth during Paul's final visit. His later movements are unknown.

Scholars have long noted that the contents of 1 Timothy and Titus are very similar, and they are likely to have been written at the same time. They could have been sent either from Macedonia or Achaia (Corinth). Paul mentions to Titus his intention to winter in Nicopolis (Tit 3:12), a city on the west coast of Greece that Paul had not yet visited; but in this reconstruction he remains instead in Corinth, presumably due to the needs of the church. It was not uncommon for Paul's travel plans to change on short notice due to changing circumstances (e.g., Acts 16:6–10).

---

[35]From there Apollos went to Rome and then to Alexandria, where he expounded the scriptures concerning Christ to the learned Jews, both in preaching and in writing.

[36]While Paul was in Corinth, the believers brought to him one of the elders and the wife of one of the deacons, who had been caught together in adultery. [37]Although they repented, the believers wanted to cast them from the church, for they said to Paul, "You taught us to deliver such sinners to Satan." [38]But Paul said, "You do not understand the body of Christ. [39]For it is not the power to punish that binds you in the Lord, but the power to love. [40]If these two had not repented, you should exclude them until their desire for you would bring them back in sorrow and obedience. [41]But because they have repented, you must embrace them as though they had not sinned, although they should not have authority while they prove their obedience. [42]Anyone who would cast them out should himself be cast out, for that one denies Christ. [43]You did not receive the Spirit to build walls, but to pierce them." [44]And one of the elders said, "But they may sin again." [45]But Paul replied, "Which of you has not sinned two times, or three, or a thousand? At which number did the cup of the Lord's mercy become empty? [46]When you have emptied that cup for yourselves, you may show it empty to others whose trespasses offend you." [47]So by these and other words, Paul taught the believers to grow in Christ.

---

[35] Apollos is one of several candidates for authorship of the anonymous Epistle to the Hebrews. Differences in style and content from Paul's other works make it unlikely that Paul wrote the letter. While no early church tradition attributes the work to Apollos, his known credentials match its content. The writer has a high level of education, a sophisticated knowledge of the scriptures, and an assumption of authority that could only belong to an apostle or one of his associates. See commentary on 7:5 below for more detail concerning the movements of Apollos and Timothy in relation to Hebrews.

[36–47] Acts does not show Paul dealing with the ethical or theological difficulties of particular churches, but their dominance in his correspondence, the moral issues of the Corinthian church, the growing challenge of church discipline in the post-apostolic period, and the just-referenced "delivery to Satan" of the Ephesian false teachers all make such a passage plausible. "Delivery to Satan," that is, exclusion from the church, was to be the sentence of the combined church, not individuals, for unrepentant defiance.[4] Moreover, it was remedial ("that they may learn," 1 Tim 1:20; "so that his spirit may be saved," 1 Cor 5:5), not a sentence of damnation. Thus the Pharisees' practice of "banning" as a punitive measure to ensure doctrinal or moral compliance stands in stark contrast with Paul's community-centered, draw-to-repentance approach, which is extended here from other passages in his epistles (Rom 14:10–12; 15:1–6; 2 Cor 2:5–8; Gal 6:1–5; Col 3:12–15; 1 Thess 5:14; 2 Tim 2:24–25) and, of course, Luke's Gospel (6:27–38; 7:36–50; 15:11–32; 17:1–4).

4. Knight, *Pastoral Epistles*, 111.

---

[48]But when Paul had been with the Corinthians for seven months, he received a letter from Pudens telling of a great fire in Rome and of certain Jews who whispered to Nero's wife Poppaea to blame the Christians, so that Paul, as one well known to them, was summoned to Rome to answer their accusations. [49]Despite the warning of Pudens to stay away, even if he would lose houses and lands, Paul immediately prepared to sail for Rome, [50]saying, "The lion roars, and I will go to him, trusting in the Lord for help. [51]For if I do not face the lion, what others might he devour while he seeks me?"

[48–51] Paul could have been arrested while on his travels, or he could have been recalled. In this account, he is warned of the likelihood of death but chooses to return to Rome. From the time of his first appeal to Rome (Acts 25:11), it is apparent that Paul recognizes his unique position to represent Christianity as a legitimate faith to be protected either under the umbrella that sheltered Judaism or independently. At this point, the narrative suggests that Pudens wrote in haste and that Paul has incomplete knowledge of Nero's designs. His return may be motivated in part by a desire to protect Pudens, or by a hope that the new accusations may allow him to revive his original purpose in gaining legitimacy for Christianity. Nevertheless, his reference to Nero as "lion" echoes 2 Timothy 4:17, and the metaphor suggests that he has little real hope of escape, let alone legal victory.

PRIMARY SOURCES

Coworkers and Opponents Following Paul's Roman Imprisonment

Titus 1:3: I left you behind in Crete for this reason, so that you should put in order what remained to be done, and should appoint elders in every town, as I directed you.

Titus 3:12–13: When I send Artemas to you, or Tychicus, do your best to come to me at Nicopolis, for I have decided to spend the winter there. Make every effort to send Zenas the lawyer and Apollos on their way, and see that they lack nothing.

1 Timothy 1:3: I urge you, as I did when I was on my way to Macedonia, to remain in Ephesus so that you may instruct certain people not to teach any different doctrine.

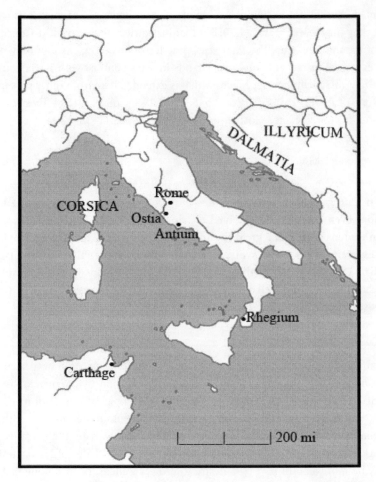

Map 3: Italy

2 Timothy 1:15–18: You are aware that all who are in Asia have turned away from me, including Phygelus and Hermogenes. May the Lord grant mercy to the household of One-siphorus, because he often refreshed me and was not ashamed of my chain; when he arrived in Rome, he eagerly searched for me and found me—may the Lord grant that he will find mercy from the Lord on that day! And you know very well how much service he rendered in Ephesus.

2 Timothy 2:16–18 Avoid profane chatter, for it will lead people into more and more impi-ety, and their talk will spread like gangrene. Among them are Hymenaeus and Philetus, who have swerved from the truth by claiming that the resurrection has already taken place. They are upsetting the faith of some.

2 Timothy 4:9–21: Do your best to come to me soon, for Demas, in love with this present world, has deserted me and gone to Thessalonica; Crescens has gone to Galatia, Titus to Dalmatia. Only Luke is with me. Get Mark and bring him with you, for he is useful in my ministry. I have sent Tychicus to Ephesus. When you come, bring the cloak that I left with Carpus at Troas, also the books, and above all the parchments. Alexander the coppersmith

did me great harm; the Lord will pay him back for his deeds. You also must beware of him, for he strongly opposed our message. At my first defence no one came to my support, but all deserted me. May it not be counted against them! But the Lord stood by me and gave me strength, so that through me the message might be fully proclaimed and all the Gentiles might hear it. So I was rescued from the lion's mouth. The Lord will rescue me from every evil attack and save me for his heavenly kingdom. To him be the glory for ever and ever. Amen. Greet Priscilla and Aquila, and the household of Onesiphorus. Erastus remained in Corinth; Trophimus I left ill in Miletus. Do your best to come before winter. Eubulus sends greetings to you, as do Pudens and Linus and Claudia and all the brothers and sisters.

3

Nero's Persecution

1 The next day, we found a ship sailing for Rome from the port of Lechaion. ²Not yet knowing how great was the danger to others, Paul took with him Titus, Crescens, Tichycus, Eubulus, and Quintipor. ³Setting sail with a fair south wind, after four days we put in at Rhegium, on the fifth day we reached Ostia.

⁴In Rome at this time, all was in an uproar over the fire. ⁵For there are often fires in the city, because the streets are narrow and crowded with wooden buildings, but no fire had burned for so long or destroyed so great an area. ⁶Beginning near the Circus Maximus, and blown by strong winds, flames spread quickly in every direction, burning for six days and six nights. ⁷Soldiers roamed through the city stopping those who tried to put out the flames, either because they were under orders or because they hoped for spoil. ⁸Many areas of the city were destroyed, including the Palatine Hill and many palaces, temples, and houses of leading citizens. ⁹Most of the great buildings of the Forum, however, which were made of stone, were spared, as was most of the Campus Martius in the north, and the Esquiline Hill on the east.

---

[1] The port of Lechaion, about three miles west on the Gulf of Corinth, allowed transport west toward Rome; Cenchrae, on the east side of the Isthmus of Corinth, was the doorway east to the Aegean Sea. This double-port status of Corinth, which allowed ships to avoid dangerous waters south of Achaia, was the main source of the city's wealth.

[2–3] The list of Paul's companions is determined by references in 1 Timothy 4, the assumption that Luke is indicated by the first person plural, and the supposition that Quintipor would return to Pudens. Another recurrent companion mentioned in 1 Timothy 4:10 (also Phm 24, Col 4:14) is Demas, who left for Thessalonica before Paul's return to Rome as one "having loved this present world." This suggests that he was either wary of the danger or was drawn away by an interest that Paul disapproved.[1]

[4–9] Modern scholars explain that ignorance of fire prevention and urban squalor made fire a constant menace to ancient Rome.[2] The description here of the great fire of AD 64 is paraphrased from the accounts of three ancient historians, most notably Tacitus, which are included below.

1. Knight, *Pastoral Epistles*, 464.
2. Canter, "Conflagrations," 276.

¹⁰Most of the great men of Rome were away because of the heat of the summer, and Nero himself was at Antium. ¹¹When Nero rushed back to the city while the fire was still burning, he stood on a tower, played the lyre, and sang until the flames threatened even his palace. ¹²After the fire, for the relief of the homeless, he built shelters in the Campus Martius, opened Agrippa's public buildings and his own Gardens there, and had grain brought in to feed the people. ¹³These acts, though popular, did not silence the rumor that Nero had given orders to start the fire because he wished to rebuild the city after his own plan, including a great new palace, which indeed he began while smoke still rose from the ruins.

¹⁴At this time the Jews lived in several quarters across the river, and many of the believers lived among them, gathering in various households. ¹⁵Most of the Jews lived at peace with them, but some of their leaders hated the believers, ¹⁶especially Paul, for he had continually preached boldly in Rome and renounced the Jews for rejecting Christ Jesus. ¹⁷Seeing an opportunity, a few of these Jews went to Nero's wife Poppaea, who was a friend to them, and told her that Nero might blame the believers for the fire. ¹⁸For they said, "All Rome has heard these men say that the world will soon end by fire, nor can they dispute that they desire it. ¹⁹Not only that, but they name Christ, and not Caesar, their Lord." ²⁰Poppaea reported all these things to Nero, who knew nothing of the Lord or of the believers. ²¹But after listening to her, he gave orders for his soldiers to arrest every believer they could find.

[10–13] The ancient historians wrote from the standpoint of the aristocrats, who hated and eventually ousted Nero, so their criticisms may be exaggerated. Despite his antics, such as the tower-top concert that generated the phrase "fiddling while Rome burns" (it was actually a lyre), it is debatable that Nero would order the fire; and of course he would have little control over it once it started. He may have been overly eager to rebuild Rome, and to finance the reconstruction out of the pockets of the upper classes, but to his credit Nero moved quickly to provide relief to victims. Not to excuse him, but it must be remembered that he had little preparation for ruling the world: Nero was seventeen years old when he became emperor, twenty-seven when Rome burned, and thirty-one when he died.

[14] Historians estimate that as many as fifty thousand Jews lived on the outskirts of the city center, with the greatest concentrations on the northwest and west across the Tiber.³ For the most part, these Jews were free, working poor, but there were some more wealthy and influential individuals among them.

[15–21] Of the three Roman historians who described the fire, only Tacitus details the persecution of Christians. In fact, the account of Tacitus, written in AD 105, is the oldest undisputed reference to Christianity by a non-Christian author. The roles of the Jews as accusers and of Nero's consort Poppaea as their abettor are conjectural. Poppaea is described by Josephus as a friend to high-ranking Jews in Rome, including those with ties to Judea (Josephus *Antiquities* 20.11.8; *Life* 3, 16). It is reasonable to suppose that she would exert influence on their behalf against Paul. If not, we might wonder how Nero would know of them. According to Suetonius (*Claudius* 25.4; see also Acts 18:2), Nero's predecessor temporarily expelled Jews from Rome in AD 49 for rioting over "Chrestus," which most scholars

3. Clarke, "Rome and Italy," 466; Levinskaya, *Diaspora*, 182–85.

believe indicates a disturbance involving Jews and Christians.[4] But it is unlikely that Nero knew of this incident—or for that matter, of Christianity. Even if a generous ten percent of Roman Jews had converted, plus a similar number of Gentiles, this would amount to no more than one percent of the city's population. We should not expect the emperor to understand the issues pertaining to this tiny group any more than we should expect a modern U.S. president to be aware of a spinoff church in the suburbs of Washington D.C.

Once Nero was made aware of the Christian sect, his concern is not likely to have gone beyond an interest in their loyalty to the empire and to his person. Rome's highest value was order, symbolically expressed by participation in the official religion, which included the emperor cult. Thus, simply naming Christ rather than Caesar as Lord was perceived as a threat to the entire structure of society, a "mischievous superstition" meriting death (Tacitus *Annals* 15.44). In the second century and beyond, official opposition to Christianity became more specific. Accusers suspected the Christians' habit of secret meetings, which in other new religions often involved drunkenness or sexual aberration; and they misunderstood the eucharist, which led to accusations of cannibalism.[5]

4. Frend, *Martyrdom*, 121–22.

5. Benko, *Pagan Rome*, 1–24, 54–74; Frend, *Martyrdom*, 77–93, 123–32.

---

[22]Now began a time of great suffering for the believers in Rome. [23]For whenever Nero's soldiers were able to find one who named Christ as Lord, they would torture that believer to confess the names of others, so that more were arrested, and all lived in fear. [24]The soldiers took those who confessed Christ Jesus, both men and women, to the Circus of Nero and chained them there in the place where wild beasts were kept. [25]Then, casting lots among them, the soldiers took some to be burned and others to be cast to the beasts. [26]Those who were to be burned were first covered with pitch, then crucified and placed along the roads or paths of the gardens. [27]They were left there to suffer during the day, and at night they were set on fire to light the gardens. [28]So many were killed in this way in the first days that the fire and smoke could be seen from across the river, so that many thought another part of the city was being destroyed. [29]Others were thrown to the beasts, which were not given food for many days, and then released upon the believers, who were either tied to posts or made to run for the entertainment of those Romans who came to the circus. [30]But neither these believers nor those who were burned cried out, but instead sang songs of praise to the Lord, or prayed in silence until the beasts or flames consumed their bodies. [31]And so loud and joyful was their singing, or so strong were they in silence, that those who witnessed their suffering, both the soldiers and the crowds, knew their innocence and began to pity them and to despise Nero. [32]Moreover, many turned to the Lord because of their faith and boldness, so that for every one who suffered, two more were added to their number.

[22–23] The second-century jurist Gaius explains that prisoners were often kept alive before execution to torture them into implicating others.[6]

[24–28] Tacitus records these gruesome public punishments of "multitudes" of Christians and Nero's enjoyment of the spectacle. But while Nero's sadistic tendencies were objectionable even at that time, these particular punishments were not unusual. On the contrary, as the Roman laws quoted below make clear, arson was such a serious crime in Rome that the required penalty was for perpetrators to be burned or thrown to wild beasts. From the Roman public's point of view, therefore, the objection was not so much that the punishment did not fit the crime but that the punished did not commit the crime.

[29–32] There is no record from Christian sources of the martyrdoms under Nero; only Tacitus describes in general the forms of punishment and the public's disgust with Nero over his sadistic revels. Increasingly from the second century on, however, similar punishments were administered to believers as thousands died simply for naming Christ as Lord. Dying for an idea, especially one as preposterous to Roman ears as the one Christians proclaimed, was unusual—if not unprecedented—in the ancient world. Undoubtedly some believers denied their faith, some implicated others under torture, and some died screaming in terror. But others exhibited great courage, often before large crowds prepared to mock them, and such deaths had a powerful impact.[7] Indeed, in one of the great ironies of history, the violent death of Christian martyrs facilitated the nonviolent conquest of the very empire their deaths were designed to preserve.

6. Rapske, *Roman Custody*, 12.
7. Frend, *Martyrdom*, 1–21.

---

[33]Among those arrested in the first days was Andronicus, whose household was among those where believers gathered. [34]Although he was beaten with rods and then boiling water was poured on him, he did not reveal the names or whereabouts of any other believers. [35]Instead, filled with the Spirit, he cried out to the others who were arrested to be strong in the Lord.

[36]And when he was crucified, until the fire was lit, he boldly sang the hymn taught to him by Paul:

> [37]Though in the form of God, our Christ
>   For gain of us knew pain and loss;
> [38]His emptiness alone sufficed
>   To fill our cups, to lift his cross.
> [39]From servant to almighty Lord
>   Our God has now exalted him;
> [40]Each knee shall bow with one accord,
>   Each tongue confess and join our hymn.

[33–35] Andronicus and his wife Julia, who maintained a church in their house, were "prominent among the apostles" in Rome, and they may have been witnesses of Jesus's life or resurrection, since Paul mentions that "they were in Christ before me" (Rom 16:7). They are among the first to whom Paul sends greetings in his letter to the Romans, but we know nothing else about them. Scholars debate about whether Paul's words indicate that they are considered important apostles or important to the apostles, and of course the term applied to both of them bears on the subject of women's leadership in the early church. For the purposes of this narrative, the name of Andronicus is useful as a plausible candidate for martyrdom by Nero; Junia appears again in chapter 5.

[36–40] This is a poetic rendering of the profound "kenosis" (emptying) hymn of Philippians 2:6–11, which Paul probably quotes rather than composes, and which scholars regard as one of the earliest and most sophisticated statements of Christian theology. It proclaims the paradox of Christ's sacrifice of divine attributes for our sake, with the result that he attains an even higher place and higher praise.

---

⁴¹Andronicus continued to sing until a soldier came forward with a torch and touched it to the pitch covering him, yet he continued to sing until the flames covered him and he gave up his spirit to the Lord. ⁴²Other believers who witnessed the death of Andronicus were strengthened, both to proclaim Christ Jesus boldly and to refuse to tell the whereabouts of other believers, so that many were saved from arrest. ⁴³But for many weeks Nero continued to seek out the believers, and hundreds were killed, ⁴⁴some like Andronicus because the Jews accused them, and others because they came forward boldly and confessed Christ before the soldiers.

[41–44] Consistent with themes introduced in Acts, the narrative takes every opportunity to stress the innocence of believers before the law, their willingness to proclaim Christ boldly in public, and the fact that persecution was fuel for growth rather than a detriment to the Christian movement.

PRIMARY SOURCES

The Fire in Rome, AD 64

Tacitus (AD 105) *Annals* 15.38–41: A disaster followed, whether accidental or treacherously contrived by the emperor, is uncertain. . . . It had its beginning in that part of the circus which adjoins the Palatine and Caelian hills, where, amid the shops containing inflammable wares, the conflagration both broke out and instantly became so fierce and so rapid from the wind that it seized in its grasp the entire length of the circus. . . . The blaze in its fury ran first through the level portions of the city, then rising to the hills, while it again devastated every place below them, it outstripped all preventive measures; so rapid was the mischief and so completely at its mercy the city, with those narrow winding passages and irregular streets, which characterised old Rome. . . . And no one dared to stop the mischief, because of incessant menaces from a number of persons who forbade the extinguishing of the flames, because again others openly hurled brands, and kept shouting that there was one who gave them authority, either seeking to plunder more freely, or obeying orders. Nero at this time was at Antium, and did not return to Rome until the fire approached his house, which he had built to connect the palace with the gardens of Maecenas. It could not, however, be stopped from devouring the palace, the house, and everything around it. However, to relieve the people, driven out homeless as they were, he threw open to them the Campus Martius and the public buildings of Agrippa, and even his own gardens, and raised temporary structures to receive the destitute multitude. Supplies of food were brought up from Ostia and the neighbouring towns, and the price of corn was reduced to three sesterces a peck. These acts, though popular, produced no effect, since a rumour had gone forth everywhere that, at the very time when the city was in flames, the emperor appeared on a private stage and sang of the destruction of Troy, comparing present misfortunes with the calamities of antiquity. At last, after five days, an end was put to the conflagration at the foot of the Esquiline hill, by the destruction of all buildings on a vast space, so that the violence of the fire was met by clear ground and an open sky. But before people had laid aside their fears, the flames returned, with no less fury this second time, and especially in the spacious districts of the city . . . Rome, indeed, is divided into fourteen districts, four of which remained uninjured, three were levelled to the ground, while in the other seven were left only a few shattered, half-burnt relics of houses.[8]

Suetonius (AD 120) *Nero* 38: But he showed no greater mercy to the people or the walls of his capital. When someone in a general conversation said: "When I am dead, be earth consumed by fire," he rejoined, "Nay, rather while I live," and his action was wholly in accord. For under cover of displeasure at the ugliness of the old buildings and the narrow, crooked streets, he set fire to the city so openly that several ex-consuls did not venture to lay hands on his chamberlains although they caught them on their estates with tow and fire-brands, while some granaries near the Golden House, whose room he particularly desired, were demolished by engines of war and then set on fire, because their walls were of stone. For six days and seven nights destruction raged, while the people were driven for shelter to monuments and tombs. At that time, besides an immense number of dwellings, the houses of leaders of old were burned, still adorned with trophies of victory, and the temples of the gods vowed and dedicated by the kings and later in the Punic and Gallic wars, and whatever else interesting and noteworthy had survived from antiquity. Viewing the conflagration from the tower of Maecenas and exulting, as he said, in "the beauty of the flames," he sang the whole of the "Sack of Ilium," in his regular stage costume. Furthermore, to gain from this calamity too all the spoil and booty possible, while promising the removal of the debris and dead bodies free of cost he allowed no one to approach the ruins of his own property; and from the contributions which he not only received, but even demanded, he nearly bankrupted the provinces and exhausted the resources of individuals.[9]

Dio Cassius (AD 225) *Roman History* 62.16–18: After this Nero set his heart on accomplishing what had doubtless always been his desire, namely to make an end of the whole city and realm during his lifetime. . . . Accordingly he secretly sent out men who pretended to be drunk or engaged in other kinds of mischief, and caused them at first to set fire to one or two or even several buildings in different parts of the city, so that people were at their wits' end, not being able to find any beginning of the trouble nor to put an end to it, though they constantly were aware of many strange sights and sounds. . . . Now this did not all take place on a single day, but it lasted for several days and nights alike. Many houses were destroyed for want of anyone to help save them, and many others were set on fire by the same men who came to lend assistance; for the soldiers, including the night watch, having an eye to plunder, instead of putting out fires, kindled new ones. While such scenes were occurring at various points, a wind caught up the flames and carried them indiscriminately against all the buildings that were left. . . . While the whole population was in this state of mind and

---

8. Tacitus is quoted from the translation by Church and Brodribb.
9. Suetonius is quoted from the translation by Rolfe.

many, crazed by the disaster, were leaping into the very flames, Nero ascended to the roof of the palace, from which there was the best general view of the greater part of the conflagration, and assuming the lyre-player's garb, he sang the "Capture of Troy," as he styled the song himself, though to the enemies of the spectators it was the Capture of Rome. The calamity which the city then experienced has no parallel before or since, except in the Gallic invasion. The whole Palatine hill, the theatre of Taurus, and nearly two-thirds of the remainder of the city were burned, and countless persons perished. There was no curse that the populace did not invoke upon Nero, though they did not mention his name, but simply cursed in general terms those who had set the city on fire. . . .He now began to collect vast sums from private citizens as well as from whole communities, sometimes using compulsion, taking the conflagration as his pretext, and sometimes obtaining it by voluntary contributions, as they were made to appear.[10]

Persecution of Christians Following the Fire

Tacitus (AD 105) *Annals* 15.44: But all human efforts, all the lavish gifts of the emperor, and the propitiations of the gods, did not banish the sinister belief that the conflagration was the result of an order. Consequently, to get rid of the report, Nero fastened the guilt and inflicted the most exquisite tortures on a class hated for their abominations, called Christians by the populace. Christus, from whom the name had its origin, suffered the extreme penalty during the reign of Tiberius at the hands of one of our procurators, Pontius Pilatus, and a most mischievous superstition, thus checked for the moment, again broke out not only in Judaea, the first source of the evil, but even in Rome, where all things hideous and shameful from every part of the world find their centre and become popular. Accordingly, an arrest was first made of all who pleaded guilty; then, upon their information, an immense multitude was convicted, not so much of the crime of firing the city, as of hatred against mankind. Mockery of every sort was added to their deaths. Covered with the skins of beasts, they were torn by dogs and perished, or were nailed to crosses, or were doomed to the flames and burnt, to serve as a nightly illumination, when daylight had expired. Nero offered his gardens for the spectacle, and was exhibiting a show in the circus, while he mingled with the people in the dress of a charioteer or stood aloft on a car. Hence, even for criminals who deserved extreme and exemplary punishment, there arose a feeling of compassion; for it was not, as it seemed, for the public good, but to glut one man's cruelty, that they were being destroyed.

Penalty for Arson in Roman Law

Laws of the Twelve Tables (450 BC) 8.10: Any person who destroys by burning any building or heap of corn deposited alongside a house shall be bound, scourged, and put to death by burning at the stake provided that he has committed the said misdeed with malice aforethought; but if he shall have committed it by accident, that is, by negligence, it is ordained that he repair the damage or, if he be too poor to be competent for such punishment, he shall receive a lighter punishment.[11]

10. Dio Cassius is quoted from the translation by Cary.
11. Quoted from Theron, *Evidence of Tradtion*.

Caius (AD 150) *On the Law of the 12 Tables Book 4*: Anyone who sets fire to a house, or a pile of grain near a house shall be chained, scourged, and put to death by fire, provided he committed the act knowingly and deliberately.[12]

Ulpian (AD 200) *On the Duties of Proconsuls Book 8*: Persons of low rank who designedly cause a fire in a town shall be thrown to wild beasts and those of superior station shall suffer death, or else be banished to some island.[13]

12. Quoted from Benko, *Pagan Rome*, 27.
13. Quoted from Benko, *Pagan Rome*, 27.

4

Paul before Nero

1 When Paul reached Ostia, he stayed there that night in the house of Pudens. ²Pudens sent word to the believers who were in hiding, and some were bold to come to Paul, not fearing arrest; among those were Eubulus, Linus, and Claudia. ³Linus embraced Paul and told him of the great suffering that had occurred in Rome while they waited for Paul, of the multitude of believers who were thrown to beasts or burned, including Andronicus and many others beloved by Paul. ⁴All wept. ⁵Then Paul said, "Let us hope in the Lord, for surely those who died by fire will send up sparks to ignite the whole world. ⁶And do not fear on my behalf, for whether I live or die, Christ will be glorified." ⁷With these and many other words, the believers were comforted.

⁸The next day, wishing to show the Romans that all was done lawfully, Pudens chained Paul to the soldier Licinius, who was a believer, and went with them to Nero's palace.

---

[1] See the note on Pudens in 1:5. Pudens had a house near that of his mother Priscilla in central Rome and at least one other, recently discovered in Ostia.

[2] Of these three, from whom Paul sends greetings in 2 Timothy 4:21, we can identify only Linus, who was appointed to lead the church in Rome by Peter and lived to AD 79. Clement, the fourth bishop (AD 92–101, following Anacletus) was probably a young man at this time and may have known Peter and Paul.

[3] Paul sends greetings in Romans 16 to no less than twenty-eight people even before he has visited the city, contradicting the caricature of Paul as a controversial rather than relational figure. He must have known hundreds more believers after ministering for two years in Rome. It is impossible to overstate the shock of learning that a large percentage of these had probably been tortured and killed in a matter of days or weeks.

[4–7] Paul's words here are dependent on Romans 14:8, and his role as comforter is familiar from Acts 20:36–38 and in his letter to these very believers (Rom 5:1–5; 8:18–39).

[8] The name of Licinius is fictitious, but the situation is plausible; one of the dominant themes of Luke's writing is to show the law-abiding nature of Christians. Chains, might attach to one or all four limbs, and sometimes the neck as well, could weigh up to 30 lbs.,

and would constitute severe hardship to a prisoner, compounded by attachment to a resentful soldier.[1] Here Pudens, anticipating the need to show Paul in chains, presumably made inquiries to find a soldier who could be trusted to treat Paul as well as the circumstances would allow, and he employs the relatively mild form of chaining, arm-to-arm. We do not know where Nero took up temporary housing after the fire destroyed most of the palaces in central Rome, but because Tacitus tells us that he watched the fire from the tower of the palace of Macaenas, on the hill overlooking the city from the northeast, this serves as a plausible location for the events that follow.

1. Rapske, *Roman Custody*, 25–32, 206–9.

---

⁹He also sent for leaders from the Jews who were not opposed to Paul, and certain believers who were Roman freedmen, to be witnesses on Paul's behalf, ¹⁰but out of fear of Nero, none came to Paul's defense. ¹¹Nero's prefect, who had commanded Pudens to summon Paul, now stated that without witnesses in Paul's defense, the charges against him could not be dismissed, and that he must also answer new charges concerning the fire. ¹²Then he commanded that Paul be held in the Praetorium until Nero might consider the matter. ¹³Paul was cast into a small hut where he suffered from the cold and many other indignities, but through the intercession of Pudens, visitors were permitted both to bring food and to help him prepare for his trial.

[9–10] 2 Timothy 4:16: "In my first defense no one came to my support, but all deserted me. May it not be counted against them!" The "first defense" probably refers to a preliminary hearing.[2] Acts 17:29 tells of two meetings with Roman Jewish leaders who seem at least neutral at first, but do not convert and are denounced by Paul with a quotation of Isaiah 6:9–10. With up to 40,000 Jews in the city, there was undoubtedly a range of response to Paul and the Christian movement, but Luke's interest in the spread of the gospel to the gentiles typically leads him to focus on those Jews who reject the gospel. The wording here stresses Nero's evil rather than the Christians' cowardice, but in the midst of such an intense persecution, whatever surviving believers of influence who might support Paul would be reluctant to appear at a judicial proceeding, fearing a trap. Paul's exclamation "May it not be held against them" (2 Tim 4:16) implies that their action is forgivable under the circumstances.[3]

[11] As in Acts 28:16, the official is not named. Given the weakness of the case that brought Paul's appeal to court, it seems likely that it might remain on the books as a pretense, while the real agenda would be to eliminate an influential leader of the Christians.

[12–13] Paul reports a harsh final imprisonment that he anticipates will end with his death (2 Tim 2:9, 4:6–8), but not before an opportunity to proclaim the gospel so that "all the Gentiles might hear it" (2 Tim 4:17). Imprisonment in the Praetorian camp was one of several possibilities for a prisoner awaiting trial, and not as bad as one of the prisons but harsh enough.[4] The location proposed here is close to the palace of Macaenas on the east side Rome, from which Tacitus tells us that Nero watched Rome burn and which is, therefore,

2. Knight, *Pastoral Epistles*, 468–70.
3. Knight, *Pastoral Epistles*, 470.
4. Rapske, *Roman Custody*, 176–225.

a plausible location for Nero's residence following the fire. The famous Mamertine prison, associated in later tradition with both Paul and Peter, is highly unlikely to have housed either.[5]

5. Tajra, *Martyrdom*, 99–101.

---

[14]**Many believers, fearing arrest, would not come to him, but others were made bold in the Spirit and brought to Paul both food and comfort, and received comfort from him.** [15]**Among these were Onesiphorus, and Pudens and his daughters Praxedes and Pudentiana, who also knew Nero's evil ways and counseled Paul concerning the best way to appeal to him.**

[16]**Learning that his trial would not occur** **before winter, Paul sent Titus to Dalmatia, Crescens to Galatia, and Tichycus to Ephesus with a letter to Timothy begging him to come.** [17]**This Timothy did, bringing with him Aquila and Priscilla, Apollos, and also Mark, who brought Paul's books and parchments,** [18]**but because winter was near, their journey was delayed by storms, and they did not arrive until many days after Paul was killed.**

[14–15] In 1 Timothy 1:16–17, Paul commends Onesiphorus for seeking out Paul during his final imprisonment. Luke is there as well ("Luke alone is with me" 1 Tim 4:11), but he would not mention himself in the text. Tradition states that Pudens was martyred by Nero, but at least two of his children, daughters Praxedes and Pudentiana, who were believers and possibly martyrs later, boldly ministered to others during the persecutions.[6] While the evidence for them may be thin, their inclusion here is fitting. Luke makes reference in his Gospel to women who ministered to Jesus (8:1–3), and young, female visitors from a powerful family might be the safest source of aid in the midst of Nero's persecution.

[16] These are Paul's directions according to 2 Timothy 4:10–12, 21. Paul mentions several others, and he states that "only Luke is with me" (2 Tim 4:11); but of course Luke does not mention himself in the narrative. Since Timothy is in Ephesus, Tichycus is presumably the bearer of the letter (as he is elsewhere: Eph 6:21; Col 4:7; Tit 3:12). I leave open the possibility suggested by some scholars that the differences in style and content in the rest of 2 Timothy may reflect a writing secretary during this final imprisonment, or that other parts of the letter were composed later. Certainly the personal details in the last chapter have a strong claim to authenticity.

[17–18] Paul sends greetings to Aquila and Priscilla (2 Tim 4:19), and we know that they had a house in Rome which was presumably a meeting place for believers (Rom 16:4). For Apollos, see notes on 2:33–35 and 7:1–5. Paul asks Mark to bring "the books, and above all the parchments" (2 Tim 4:13), which may have included scriptures and Paul's writings in progress, or copies of his previous letters. Indeed, it is intriguing to suppose that Paul traveled with copies of his own writings, which might help to explain why they were studied widely at an early date (2 Pet 3:16). This might also help to explain why the Pastoral Epistles were not always included in early lists of New Testament books: they were sent east just as Paul's other letters, i.e., those later collected, were being sent west.

6. Edmundson, *The Church in Rome*, 245; McBirnie, *The Twelve*, 221.

If, as this narrative suggests, Paul was soon after writing 2 Timothy, in the fall when conditions would warrant the request for Timothy to bring his cloak (2 Tim 4:13), the sea passage would be dangerous and unlikely to get Paul's friends there in time. Traditions differ as to whether Aquila and Priscilla were killed by Nero or, after this last visit to Rome, by pagan rioters in Ephesus. Tradition suggests that Mark went to Rome once more before his martyrdom in Alexandria in AD 68.[7] According to Hebrews 13:23, Timothy was arrested in Rome and later released, which might correspond to the end of Nero's persecution.

7. Atiya, *Eastern Christianity*, 27.

---

[19] After some time, the prefect called for Paul again, telling Pudens that Nero was ready to hear his defense. [20] So Paul, together with only Licinius, Pudens, and Quintipor, the slave of Pudens, went to the palace. [21] Soon after Paul entered, an attorney spoke for Nero, accusing Paul as before of causing sedition among the Jews, and adding the new charge that he was a leader of the sect of the Christians who were blamed for the fire. [21] And Nero, reclining on a dais, listened.

[**19–21**] Roman law dictated that accusers appear;[8] the supposition here is that Nero himself is the accuser, and the earlier charges against Paul from the Jews have become secondary.

It is worthwhile here to set the stage visually for this historic confrontation. Historians do not describe actual trials before emperors, and most of us are influenced by notoriously inaccurate movie depictions of ancient Rome and its emperors. If Nero would hear such a case himself,[9] the trial would have taken place in central Rome, either in a public building or, as depicted here, in a palace. Neither description nor remains of the palace of Macaenas survive, but based on other buildings, we should picture a large room of several hundred square feet with high ceilings, walls painted with frescos, crowds of litigants and attendants, and Nero himself reclining on a raised dais at one end of the room. We do not know if the emperor would address the litigant directly or merely hear the exchange between litigants and pass judgment through an attendant. In this case, the importance of the case might bring Nero: Paul had status as a leader of the movement, he had well-placed friends like Pudens, and Nero needed to make at least a show of justice for the fire.

Movies portray Nero as old and fat, but in fact he was only twenty-seven years old in AD 64. The Roman historian Suetonius, who despised Nero, describes him as having long, curly, blond hair, blue eyes, a thick neck, prominent stomach, skinny legs, bad skin, and nasty body odor. This may be code for "effeminate and profligate."

According to the second century apocryphal *Acts of Paul*, the apostle was "little of stature, thin-haired upon the head, crooked in the legs, of good state of body, with eyebrows joining, and nose somewhat hooked." By our standards, this is as unflattering as the portrait of Nero; however, according to the ancients, small stature indicated intelligence; bowed legs and unibrows were attractive; and a hooked nose signified magnanimity.[10] Baldness is the only feature here that ancients would perceive negatively, so it is more likely than the other details to reflect historical rather than idealized description. In any case, Paul could not have

8. Tajra, *Trial*, 193–94.

9. *See* Tajra, *Martyrdom*, 14–17, 169.

10. Omerzu, "Portrayal," 252–79; Bauckam, "Acts of Paul," 138–49.

been an imposing figure at this time: at least sixty years old, scarred and worn by past and recent beatings, filthy from confinement, and at least one arm weighed down with an iron chain.

---

²²When the prefect motioned to Paul, he stretched out his free hand and said, "I appeal to your benevolence, most excellent emperor, in dismissing these false charges, ²³trusting that you will confirm the judgment of your governors Gallio and Festus, that I have obeyed the law in all things, as have all those who follow Christ.

²⁴"In the days before my birth, the Roman consul and hero Pompey traveled through the province of Cilicia and the city of Tarsus to make that province a part of Rome. ²⁵In that day the father of my father, a leather merchant, provided for Pompey to house all of his legions in tents and to cover them all with clothing. ²⁶In return for his service, he was made a Roman citizen, an honor given also to me, as the firstborn of his firstborn.

[22–23] Paul's speech follows a formal pattern prescribed by ancient judicial proceedings, which is well documented.[11] The court scenes in Acts 24 and 26 follow this pattern, which is required in such cases and may be taken from official documents in Luke's possession.[12] Over two hundred such documents survive, and the rules and stylistic strategies for presentation of a legal case are laid out by first century rhetorician Quintillian. Luke's audience would recognize the pattern, and its careful conveyance is consistent with his priority to present Christianity as legitimate from a legal standpoint. We do not have a record of an actual trial before Nero, but Tacitus (*Annals* 14) records a formal exchange between the emperor and the disgraced Seneca that includes relevant elements and style. These and other surviving documents help us to understand the constituents of a typical trial speech.

A legal presentation opens with an *exordium* or formal appeal for help, including a respectful form of address called the *captivatio benevolentiae* (literally, "capturer of good will"). How would Paul address Nero to gain his good will without calling him "divine" or "Lord," as many solicitors would? The wording here is borrowed from two ancient documents. "Most excellent emperor" is one of the forms of address used by Pliny the Younger in his correspondence with Trajan, and Tacitus (*Annals* 14) records that Seneca predicts honor for Nero from granting his request. Paul uses a similar formal opening in Acts 26:2–3.

Paul's strongest defense against the charges brought by the Jews would be the dismissal of the case by Roman governors Gallio (Acts 18:12–17) and Festus (Acts 24–26), who probably sent formal documents attesting to Paul's innocence. The original appeal to Rome, therefore, may have been motivated not by a desire on Paul's part to preserve his own life but by a hope to attain legal protection for Christians as distinct from the Jews. This would have been a delicate distinction from a Roman perspective and a risky venture, since the Jews had enjoyed extraordinary protection by the Romans for a century; on the other hand, as Paul may have foreseen, they were on the brink of open revolt against Roman rule in Palestine.

[24] Following the opening of the defense is the *narratio*, also familiar from Acts 26:4–18.

---

11. Satterthwaite, "Classical Rhetoric," 337–79.
12. Winter, "Forensic Speeches," 305–36.

[**25–26**] This is conjecture based on a combination of known factors. Roman citizenship "from birth" (Acts 22:28) was usually conferred as an honor to an individual for service,[13] which means that Paul's father or grandfather, citizens of the wealthy city of Tarsus, may have received perpetual citizenship in return for some favor, presumably of a commercial nature. Tents were not made from linen but from hides of cattle or goats, and it is conceivable that Pompey, traveling through with his legions about 65 B.C., found himself in need of what only a local leather merchant could provide quickly, in quantity. Paul calls himself a tentmaker by trade (Acts 18:3), but it is possible that this was a skill acquired in a successful family enterprise, along the lines of a building contractor's son who must learn the business "from the ground up." As a promising scholar, however, he could not have lingered long in the trade before making his way to Jerusalem for his religious education (Acts 22:3). His fellow tent-makers, Priscilla and Aquila, are wealthy enough to travel widely (e.g., Acts 18:18) and sponsor house churches in Ephesus (1 Cor 16:19; 2 Tim 4:19) and Rome (Rom 16:3); furthermore, they are sophisticated enough to instruct the erudite Apollos (Acts 18:26). Paul himself often travels and houses himself—most notably while imprisoned for two years in Rome "at his own expense" (Acts 28:30) without any stated means of support. Indeed, nowhere in Acts or in his own writings does Paul plead personal poverty, except once in a metaphorical sense (2 Cor 6:10). These factors combine to suggest that while Paul may have traveled with a sewing kit, he was a person of considerable means with affluent professional contacts. At the very least, he was born into such circumstances, and that would be enough to substantiate an appeal such as that depicted here.

13. Rapske, *Roman Custody*, 86; Tajra, *Trial*, 82.

---

[27]Now, many years later, I have come to Rome, not with an army, but on behalf of many brothers and sisters in Christ, [28]praying that as my earthly father once covered Caesar, Caesar will now cover me and my spiritual family. [29]I do not speak to Caesar of garments, but of spiritual things, knowing that he has power to cover those who believe in Christ Jesus with the mantle of freedom to worship in peace. [30]So all who name Christ Jesus pray for Caesar and for all authorities, submitting to them in all humility and obedience, knowing that rulers are put in place by God.

[**27–28**] We know from Paul's letters that he is fond of garment metaphors (2 Cor 5:1–4; Rom 13:14; Gal 3:37) and this kind of application of a mundane theme to spiritual realities (e.g., building in 1 Cor 10:15; athletics in 1 Cor 9:24–27; armor in Eph 6:13–17). While such word play may appear not to suit the gravity of the occasion, to the contrary, just such rhetorical flourishes are recommended in trial speeches by the first century Roman Quintilian.[14] A clever speaker shows confidence and may win over the judge by his wit.

[**29–30**] This is familiar Pauline language. On the distinction from the material realm to "spiritual things," see Romans 2:29; 1 Corinthians 15:44. On freedom to worship, see Acts 24:11, 14; 27:23. On prayer for and obedience to authorities see Romans 13:1–7; 1 Timothy 2:1–2.

14. Winter, "Forensic Speeches," 319.

³¹"Therefore the charges against me and those who follow Christ have no foundation but result only from certain misunderstandings among the Jews. ³²I have honored Caesar in all things from the days of my youth until now, whether free or in chains, following the vision once given to me of the risen Christ. ³³As a Jew, I have been bold to testify of those things told in our scriptures concerning this Christ, that he would suffer and rise from the dead, giving light and the hope of salvation to both Jew and gentile. ³⁴Through all of these trials, until this day, he has been my help. ³⁵Some of the Jews deny that he is the Messiah, and others deny the resurrection of the dead, and these have proclaimed themselves enemies both to me and to all who follow Christ. ³⁶But these are disputes among the Jews, and they cannot prove any other charge against me or my brothers and sisters regarding the laws of Rome. ³⁷Nor do they appear before you today—whether out of fear or shame I do not know—whereas I offer you not only my testimony but also the confirmation of the noble Gallio and Festus that I have done no wrong.

³⁸"Thus I have waited in chains for these many years for the opportunity to answer these false accusations and to hear you, most benevolent emperor, proclaim to the world that those who follow Christ are lawful subjects of Caesar.³⁹For to end the persecution of my brothers and sisters will redound to your honor both in Rome and throughout the world."

---

[31] The third section of a formal defense is the *probatio,* in which the defendant asserts the lack of proof against him. We have a model of this formal aspect in Paul's defense before Felix, Acts 24:12–13.

[32–33] This is the fourth formal element in Paul's defense, the *refutatio*, in which he defends himself against his absent accusers among the Jews. The wording here is familiar from Paul's previous defenses, especially Acts 24:14–18 and 26:18, 22–23.

[34] The fifth and final element of a formal appeal is the *peroratio*, a summary signaled by the word "help." In Acts 26:22, Paul does not use the traditional appeal for help from the judge but claims that "to this day I have had help from God." So it is here, and we might suppose that this variation on the expected wording would raise Nero's blond eyebrow. For Paul and for Luke as recorder, it is the key phrase that lifts the situation out of the judicial and into the spiritual. For ultimately, this trial is not about Nero's judgment and deliverance but God's.

[35–36] Note that in his summary, Paul moves subtly from his own defense to that of his fellow believers. Rather than speaking of the fire directly, he stresses the moral, law-abiding nature of believers.

[37] Paul's "ace-in-the-hole" is the dismissal of his charges by other high officials, who may well have passed on in writing their judgment that Paul's troubles reflected a religious dispute and would have resulted in his release if he had not appealed to Caesar (Acts 26:32).

[38] This is an explicit appeal to have Christianity declared *religio licita,* an approved religion under the protection of imperial Rome distinct from Judaism. This would end official persecution, including that instigated by hostile Jews, and it would also protect Christians

from being lumped together with Jews when the latter were persecuted. Paul may have been aware of the rising unrest in Judea and Galilee, which would result in open rebellion only two years later.

[39] The phrase "redound to your honor" was used by Seneca in his defense before Nero (Tacitus *Annals* 14). "Throughout the world" is a further appeal to Nero's vanity, with an ironic allusion to the theme of Luke's work.

PRIMARY SOURCES

Paul before Nero

The Acts of Paul (AD 150–200) 10.3: And among the many Paul also was brought bound; to him all his fellow-prisoners gave heed, so that Caesar observed that he was the man in command. And he said to him: "Man of the great king, but (now) my prisoner, why did it seem good to thee to come secretly into the empire of the Romans and enlist soldiers from my province?" But Paul, filled with the Holy Spirit, said before them all: "Caesar, not only from thy province do we enlist soldiers, but from the whole world. For this charge has been laid upon us, that no man be excluded who wishes to serve my king. If thou also think it good, do him service! For neither riches nor the splendor of this present life will save thee, but if thou submit and entreat him, then shalt thou be saved. For in one day he will destroy the world with fire." When Caesar heard this, he commanded all the prisoners to be burned with fire, but Paul to be beheaded according to the law of the Romans.[15]

---

15. *The Acts of Paul* is quoted from the translation by M. R. James.

5

Martyrdom of Paul

1 When Paul had finished his defense, Nero spoke with several of his counselors who were standing near, among whom was Poppaea. [2]Then Nero said to Paul, "I have not yet heard why you who follow this Christ so hate Rome and Caesar that you would burn the city. [3]Do you not hope that your God will destroy all the earth with fire? Answer me this." [4]Then Paul spoke again: "It is true, most excellent emperor, that God will destroy the earth in judgment on the day when Christ returns, [5]but his judgment and his triumph are not as men understand these things, nor is it given to men to bring these things about. [6]Our God does not dwell in a house made with hands, nor can any man build God's house by destroying the house of another. [7]On the contrary, we are commanded to live in peace with all men, and to honor earthly authority as sent by God. [8]These things all the Jews believe, and not only those who follow Christ."

[9]Now Nero, wishing to trap Paul into speaking against him, said, "You speak of 'authority.' [10]But is not Caesar their Lord and yours?"

---

[1] As noted above (3:17), Nero's consort Poppaea was a friend to high-ranking Jews in Rome, including those with ties to Judea; she could have exerted influence on their behalf against Paul.

[2–3] Paul's neglect to this point of direct reference to the fire is a strategic maneuver to lift the issues out of the immediate circumstances and to avoid antagonizing Nero. Roman historians of the period provide ample evidence, however, that Nero was quick to provoke a crisis in order to serve his purposes.

[4–8] Paul again appeals to the law-abiding nature of Christian practice, avoids reference to fire even in consigning judgment to God, and draws the blanket of (legal) Judaism over these beliefs.

[9–10] What historians call "the imperial cult" required official allegiance and sacrifice to the emperor, including use of titles like "Lord," "Savior," and even "God." The highest titles—and divine status—were normally reserved for emperors after their death,[1] but we know

1. Rankin, *Clement to Origen*, 24.

that Nero flirted with the claim of deity in his lifetime (Tacitus *Annals* 15.74) and had coins minted calling him "Savior of the world." The imperial cult was loosely enforced, and Jews were exempt entirely; but it could be engaged at any time to test loyalty, as we know from Pliny the Younger's correspondence with Trajan (Letter 97).

---

[11]Paul answered, "Caesar is lord on earth, but Christ is Lord in heaven, and there is one God, the Father, who reigns over all. [12]Christ his Son dwelt on earth, and he will return in glory to fulfill the scriptures. [13]In that day all who dwell on earth, not only the Jews but also the Romans, and Caesar himself, will bow down before Christ the Lord." [14]At these words, Nero cried out, "No more of this madness! [15]A Jew reigns in heaven with his father? [16]Is there no one left on earth to reign but Caesar? [17]Then let most excellent and benevolent Caesar judge. [18]This man shall not wait ten days to see his Lord, but shall die today by the sword. [19]And because he dishonors Rome, take him outside the city, along the road by which he came."

[20]When Pudens heard Nero's judgment, he came before him weeping and begged for mercy on account of Paul's age and infirmity. [21]And Nero embraced him and made a show before all that he sorrowed for the loss to Pudens, but that he must make an example of Paul. [22]Now Nero had already learned from Poppaea that Pudens was a believer, but he feared that to kill more leading citizens would stir up the nobles against him. [23]So Nero made a pretense of pity, but two days later he secretly gave orders to have Pudens murdered quietly in his own house. [24]Nevertheless, word spread that Nero and Poppaea were killing not only believers among the Jews but also many Romans who followed Christ, all of them blameless, and the people began to pity the believers and to hate Nero. [25]Hearing of this, Nero stopped the killing, but the people and especially the nobles still despised him and blamed him all the more for the fire.

[11–13] It is apparent from Paul's previous judicial proceedings that he recognized when the cause was lost, and he used these occasions for a clear declaration suited to the audience (e.g., Acts 28:24–28).

[14–19] The oldest traditions concerning Paul's death agree that he died by beheading, which was considered a method appropriate to his status as a Roman citizen. Other forms of execution used for treasonable offenses included crushing the victim beneath large rocks, throwing him down from a great height, and, of course, crucifixion. This narrative suggests a reason for Paul's being taken so far outside the city, which traditional accounts do not explain; they may be reconstructing the event from the location of his burial place.

[20–23] Nero used the ruse of public sympathy in Seneca's trial, ordering him killed a short time later (Tacitus *Annals* 14). Normally, half or more of the victim's possessions were forfeit to the state. Because traditional accounts suggest that the children of Pudens survived and provided further aid to the church, Nero may have been content with the death of Pudens, or at least dared not take out his wrath further on this powerful family. For Poppaea, see notes on 3:17 above.

[24–25] The account of Nero's persecution in Tacitus appears to indicate an episode rather than an extended campaign.[2] It is unlikely that Nero would go on killing for an extended period, even if he could find enough victims. We know that he was preoccupied with major building projects and would probably not want to keep drawing attention to the fire, which was being blamed on him despite his Christian scapegoats. Finally, there is no evidence of an empire-wide, official, or permanent ban on Christianity, which we would expect from an extended persecution. On the contrary, it is reasonable to suppose that the terror was intense but brief and that Christians were once again tolerated, albeit grudgingly, even in the later years of Nero's reign. After AD 64, we do not learn of further official persecution until late in the reign of Domitian, about AD 95, then again under Trajan about AD 110.

2. Frend, *Martyrdom*, 127.

---

[26]Such was the tyrant Nero, who three years later in a rage killed Poppaea while she was pregnant; [27]and afterwards, when all Rome turned against him for his many crimes, ran from his own palace and begged his slave to kill him, for he did not have the courage. [28]So Nero's reign and his line ended, while the church in Rome and throughout the world continued to multiply.

[29]Immediately after his trial, Paul was taken from the palace by a centurion and a cohort of soldiers, outside the city along the Ostian Way. [30]Word spread quickly from Pudens and the slaves of his household, so that before they were outside the city many believers had come, risking their lives, to follow with the crowd who wished to see an execution. [31]When the centurion had taken Paul some distance along the road, he grew anxious about the growing crowd, [32]so he gave the order to stop in an open field where a single fig tree stood.

[26–28] Tacitus, Suetonius, and Dio Cassius agree that Nero murdered the pregnant Poppaea by kicking or jumping on her; the latter two historians describe Nero's ignominious death following a coup initiated by the nobles. Nero was the last of the Julio-Claudian emperors.

[29] The following portion of the narrative is entirely conjectural. Traditional accounts agree that Paul was taken along the Ostian Way, but the stories diverge at that point and include fantastic accounts of Paul's severed head either spouting milk or bouncing three times and creating permanent water fountains.

[30–32] The Ostian Way location of Paul's execution was later shifted about a mile east to the Aquae Salviae, a tradition with no historical basis.[3] The fourth-century *Acts of Peter and Paul* contains the interesting detail that there was a lone pine tree at the site. The change here to a fig tree adds a poetic or prophetic touch in allusion to Luke 13:6–7; 21:29. Of course, if this were actually scripture, scholars would exhaust themselves arguing about whether or not the tree bore figs.

3. Tajra, *Martyrdom*, 152–54.

³³Now the believers began to weep and to cry out against the soldiers, so Pudens asked the centurion to allow Paul to quiet them, and this was granted. ³⁴Paul said, "My brothers and sisters, do not sorrow, for this is a day of victory that I have long awaited. ³⁵For many years I have endured hardships and faced death on account of the word of the Lord, first at the hands of the Jews and now at the hands of the Romans, ³⁶but all is in the hands of the Lord, into which I will soon be delivered. ³⁷So do not grieve for me, the least of his servants, but give thanks in this as in all things. ³⁸For in Christ, when all is lost, all is found. ³⁹Therefore, rejoice that I will soon gain the Lord, and have hope for yourselves. ⁴⁰For in Rome and throughout the world, the Lord will build his church upon the death of his saints. ⁴¹If by fire, he will make of it a wind to scatter his seed, and if by the sword, he will make of it a plow to sow, ⁴²and so he will make such a harvest of faith and righteousness that Rome itself will be overshadowed, and the word will go to the ends of the earth."

⁴³With these words Paul knelt by the tree, lifted his eyes to heaven, and cried out, "Lord, receive my spirit." ⁴⁴Then the centurion, taking a long sword carried by a member of the cohort for that purpose, with one stroke struck Paul's head from his shoulders. ⁴⁵And the soldiers were ready to throw Paul's body into a pit or cast it into the river, but when Pudens asked, they allowed him to take it. ⁴⁶Lucina, a believer who was one of those who witnessed Paul's death, had a house nearby with a burial place. ⁴⁷So Pudens, together with Quintipor and Licinius and many other believers who were there, took Paul's body there and buried it.

[33–36] Paul's words borrow from his farewell to the Ephesian elders in Acts 20:18–35 and his last written words to Timothy (2 Tim 4:6–7).

[37] This wording derives from 1 Corinthians 15:9; Ephesians 3:8; and 1 Thessalonians 5:18.

[38] This line finds no parallel in Paul; it is borrowed from *Godric* by Frederick Buechner, an historical novel about the eleventh-century hermit and saint.

[39] In Philippians 1:21, Paul asserts that "for me, living is Christ and dying is gain," and in 2 Timothy 4:8 he states that "from now on there is reserved for me the crown of righteousness" which the Lord will give "also to all who have longed for his appearing."

[40–42] See 1 Corinthians 3:6–9 for a similar use by Paul of an agricultural metaphor. The references to wind and "ends of the earth" connect the narrative to the important themes of Spirit-empowered evangelism introduced in Acts 2:2 and 1:8, respectively.

[43–44] While apocryphal accounts indulge in long farewell speeches for apostles just at the point of execcution, often followed by wonders or miraculous healings of bystanders, the account here follows the simple death described for Stephen (Acts 7:60).

[45–47] With no knowledge of sanitation, Romans typically cast their many victims in pits or into the Tiber,⁴ but it is reasonable to suppose that in this situation they might be open to an alternative, especially for a bribe. It is also possible that friends of Paul appealed to his right as a Roman citizen to proper burial.⁵ We know nothing of Lucina except that the name

4. Rapske, *Roman Custody*, 14.
5. Tajra, *Martyrdom*, 24–25.

appears in traditions about the burial of martyrs, including Paul, on her property along the Ostian Way, not far from the location of Paul's execution.[6] Another tradition is that Pudens had an estate on the Ostian Way and that Paul was buried there.[7]

PRIMARY SOURCES

The Death of Paul

The Acts of Paul (AD 150–200) 10.5: Then Paul stood with his face to the east, and lifting up his hands to heaven prayed at length; and after communing in prayer in Hebrew with the fathers he stretched out his neck without speaking further. But when the executioner struck off his head, milk spurted upon the soldier's clothing. And when they saw it, the soldier and all who stood by were amazed, and glorified God who had given Paul such glory.

Tertullian (AD 200) *Prescription Against Heretics* 36: [in Rome] Paul was crowned with John's death.

Tertullian (AD 213) *Scorpiace* 15: That Peter is struck, that Stephen is overwhelmed *by stones*, that James is slain as is a victim at the altar, that Paul is beheaded has been written in their own blood. And if a heretic wishes his confidence to rest upon a public record, the archives of the empire will speak, as would the stones of Jerusalem. We read the lives of the Cæsars: At Rome Nero was the first who stained with blood the rising faith. Then is Peter girt by another, when he is made fast to the cross. Then does Paul obtain a birth suited to Roman citizenship, when in Rome he springs to life again ennobled by martyrdom.

Peter of Alexandria (306 AD) *De Poenitentia: Epistola Canonica* 9: The renowned Paul, having been oftentimes delivered up and brought in peril of death, having endured many evils, and making his boast in his numerous persecutions and afflictions, in the same city [Rome] was also himself beheaded; who, in the things in which he gloried, in these also ended his life.

Eusebius (AD 325) *Ecclesiastical History* 2.25.5: Thus [Nero] publicly announcing himself as the first among God's chief enemies, he was led on to the slaughter of the apostles. It is, therefore, recorded that Paul was beheaded in Rome itself, and that Peter likewise was crucified under Nero. This account of Peter and Paul is substantiated by the fact that their names are preserved in the cemeteries of that place even to the present day.[8]

Acts of Peter and Paul (AD 350): And they beheaded him at the place called Aquae Salviae, near the pine tree.

---

6. Tajra, *Martyrdom*, 160–62.
7. McBirnie, *The Twelve*, 221.
8. Eusebius is quoted from the translation by Lake.

6

Martyrdom of Peter

1 Now all this time, following the fire, Peter had been in hiding, not out of fear, but at the urging of Linus and the others who wished to protect him. ²Sometimes he was in the house of Priscilla, wife of Glabrio, and sometimes in other houses outside the city, where he comforted many whose family members had been killed by Nero.

---

[1] We know little of Peter's movements from the AD 44 Jerusalem Council (Acts 15) to his martyrdom, traditionally in Rome. His two epistles show that he spent considerable time in Asia Minor, but he wrote one from Rome (1 Pet 5:13). We know from Galatians 2:11 that he ministered in Antioch, and tradition claims that he was bishop there for seven years. Early and strong tradition has him in Rome before AD 50, then periodically until his death. The fact that Luke says nothing of his presence during Paul's first imprisonment (AD 60–62) suggests that he may have been back in Asia Minor at that time.

Interest in Peter's travels, death, and likely burial site (where the Vatican now stands) has generated many volumes of research from Roman Catholic scholars;[1] and his life inspired more interest than any other apostle among apocryphal writers. This narrative chooses a few details that seem at least plausible, if not historically demonstrable, in order to construct a coherent narrative. Having accepted the likely location of Rome as Peter's place of martyrdom, the next challenge is to choose a date. Early church historians offer dates in Nero's reign from AD 64–67, either before or after the death of Paul, and Eusebius (AD 325) makes the intriguing statement that Peter and Paul died "at the same time" (*Ecclesiastical History* 2.25.8). In Greek as in English this phrase can indicate anything from the same day to the same year, but the timing of Nero's persecution probably limits the range to a few months at most. This narrative offers the conjecture that Peter's death was in part a consequence of Paul's. The situation envisioned here is that the ever-impulsive Peter cannot bear to remain in hiding after Paul's public proclamation of faith before Nero.

[2] Priscilla, mother of Pudens, had a large house of her own along the Salarian Way in the northeast part of Rome, not far from the palace of Macaenas. The reference here to her husband distinguishes her from another prominent Priscilla, the wife of Aquila. This Priscilla

---

1. E.g., O'Connor, *Peter in Rome*, 50–59.

and her husband, Roman consul Manius Acilius Glabrio, were believers who, according to tradition, were martyred by Domitian (AD 81–96). In Glabrio's case, the martyrdom is confirmed by the account of contemporary Roman historians, making him the highest-ranking convert that we know in the first century. Excavations confirm that their property became an early center of Christian worship, and their catacombs are preserved today. The house is claimed by tradition as Peter's headquarters during his visits to Rome. Luke would probably not name Priscilla and Glabria unless he perceived that they were safe at the time of writing.

---

³And at this time he was in the house of Junia on the Triumphal Way, two miles from the city. ⁴Linus, after he had witnessed Paul's death and comforted the believers who mourned at the house of Lucina, came in the night with several of Paul's co-workers to tell Peter. ⁵And Peter said, "I must go to Rome this night. ⁶For today, as I walked in the road, the Lord appeared to me, walking the other way toward the city. ⁷And I asked, 'Lord, where are you, going?' ⁸And he said, 'To Rome, to be crucified again.' ⁹And I cried out and said, 'No, it is I who must go.' ¹⁰And immediately he was taken up from me into heaven."

¹¹And Peter said, "Now that our brother Paul has entered into the Lord's presence, why should I wait another day or even until the morning? Let me go now." ¹²Linus and the others pleaded with Peter to remain until daylight, but he would not.

---

[3] Almost any of the twenty-eight people to whom Paul sends greetings in Romans 16 would be a candidate for a "safe house" in or near the city. Junia (Rom 16:7) is chosen here due to her importance in that list. She and husband Andronicus are called "prominent among the apostles," and they were early converts in Judea, suggesting a possible connection to Peter as well as Paul. The location of her house is entirely conjectural, and the reference to her without Andronicus is meant to imply that he has been martyred. The distance of her house from the city might provide some measure of protection.

[4] Note that Linus, who according to tradition was Peter's successor in leadership of the Roman church, is taking an increasing leadership role. The term "bishop" is not used here or elsewhere in this book to designate early church leaders. Although the term came into common use in some areas in the early second century, it is more in keeping with Luke's usage and understanding to employ the term "leader" here.²

[5–10] This is an adaptation of the "Quo Vadis" legend, first recorded in the apocryphal second-century *Acts of Peter*.³ Although we cannot know if the story is historical, its drama and consistency with what we know of Peter's character merit its inclusion here. The famous phrase is Latin for "where are you going?" In the Latin translation of the Bible, these words are used in the Peter's exchange with Jesus about following "where I am going" (John 13:36–37).

[11–12] Peter's impulsive nature is indicated in passages like Mark 8:31–33; Matthew 14:28–31; and John 18:10–11. The most well-known, of course, is his promise to follow Jesus just before denying him (Mark 14:66–72 and parallels). It is the last incident that serves as the backdrop here, where Peter is intent to get to Rome and proclaim Christ before dawn.

---

2. *See* Weiss, *Earliest Christianity*, 766–68.

3. For a thorough introduction, see Klauck, *Apocryphal Acts*, 81–112.

¹³And Elama, Peter's wife, begged to go with him, but he said no. ¹⁴And she said, "How is it that I have walked this road so long with you, and you would deny me the last few steps? ¹⁵For you are not the first to say, 'Where you go, I will go also.'"

¹⁶And so Peter, accompanied only by his wife, walked through the night until he reached the gardens of Nero, where so many of the saints had been killed, and where some were still hanging. ¹⁷Because it was still night, and the cock had not yet crowed, there were only a few soldiers on watch. ¹⁸And Peter was made bold in the Spirit, and proclaimed to them that Christ is Lord. ¹⁹The soldiers, perceiving from his age and manner that he was mad, laughed at him and tried to send him away. ²⁰But he proclaimed Christ even louder. ²¹Then a centurion came out from the barracks nearby and asked what the disturbance was. ²²One of the soldiers said, "This old man is among the mad followers of Christos who have burned the city." ²³The centurion bade soldiers to arrest Peter and to bring him forward. ²⁴And Elama ran to him and said that she would not be parted from him. ²⁵The centurion said to him, "Old man, answer this charge. For you know the decree of Nero that no one may live who names Christ as Lord." ²⁶And Peter answered in a great voice, "On the contrary, no one may live except those who name Christ as Lord." ²⁷So the centurion commanded the soldiers to crucify him and his wife. ²⁸Just then the cock crowed. ²⁹And as they took his wife away to the gardens to crucify her, Peter called out to her tenderly, "Elama, wherever you go, remember the Lord." ³⁰Then, turning to the soldiers, he said that he was not worthy to die in this manner.

[13–15] We know that Peter was married (Mark 1:30) and that his wife accompanied him (1 Cor 9:5), but there are no early, reliable accounts of her. Later traditions call her Perpetua ("everlasting"), a Latin name that is highly unlikely, so it is changed here to its Hebrew equivalent. Clement of Alexandria (AD 180–200) does not name her but reports that she was martyred with Peter (*Stromata* 7.11). The phrase *quo vadis* occurs in the Latin Bible not only at John 13:36–37 but also at Ruth 1:16, alluded to here. Of course it is unlikely that Peter and his wife would be speaking Latin, but the common phrase "where you are going" could produce the same associations in any language.

[16–18] The theme of boldness, especially in the face of impending arrest or persecution, is a dominant theme of Acts (e.g., 9:27–28; 13:46; 18:26).

[19–28] The narrative here deliberately parallels Peter's denial of Christ in Mark 14:66–72.

[29] The account here follows Clement of Alexandria, who reports that "the blessed Peter, on seeing his wife led to death, rejoiced on account of her call and conveyance home, and called very encouragingly and comfortingly, addressing her by name, 'Remember the Lord'" (*Stromata* 7.11). The addition here of "wherever you go" is an allusion to *quo vadis*.

[30] The early traditions, while differing in detail, agree that Peter requested an inverted crucifixion because he felt unworthy to die as Christ had. Many interpeters take the words of Jesus to Peter in John 21:18b–19 as a veiled reference to his crucifixion: "When you grow old, you will stretch out your hands, and someone else will fasten a belt around you and take you where you do not wish to go." Here, to highlight the cruelty of the soldiers, the form of crucifixion is their idea.

³¹And the soldiers mistook him, thinking that he wished to die some other way, so they told him that he must suffer as a traitor and a slave. ³²And Peter said, "I am indeed a slave, and I beg you to return me without delay to Christ my master. ³³I would not be spared the pain of the cross, but the honor of it, to die in the same manner as my Lord." ³⁴And he continued to preach boldly to them. ³⁵Then the soldiers mocked him, saying, "Because you are so eager to reach heaven, your feet shall go there first, and all shall see your journey." ³⁶So they took Peter to the center of the circus and crucified him with his feet uppermost, his arms stretched out, and his head down. ³⁷For a short time he called out praises to the Lord, but then he could not speak for pain, and in less than an hour he gave up his spirit. ³⁸All this was witnessed by Gavrus, one of the soldiers in the cohort, who became a believer because of the things he saw that day.

³⁹When the other believers in Rome learned that Paul and Peter had been killed, one the day after the other, they were in great anguish of heart and debated whether to flee or hide. ⁴⁰But Linus and Eubulus were made strong in the Lord to encourage them.

[31–37] Tradition describes Peter's crucifixion in the exact center of Nero's circus (arena), an area now within the Vatican. Peter's quick expiration is likely, given his age and the form of crucifixion. No reference is made here to the circumstances or site of his burial, which are the subject of much subsequent study. Crucifixion normally involved leaving the body on the cross for some time; and as noted above, disposal was usually in a pit or the river. This is the most likely scenario if Peter was killed during Nero's persecution. It is possible, however, that actual events transpired in a way similar to those described here for Paul, with a more public execution and influential friends granted permission to dispose of the body. Modern scholars, combining literary and historical sources with archaeological evidence, confirm that the area of the present Vatican, just across the Tiber northwest of the old city center, is the most likely site of Peter's death and burial.

[38] The name of Gavrus is fictional. While Luke does not explicitly reveal his sources, he states that the events he records "were handed on to us by those who from the beginning were eyewitnesses and servants of the word" (Luke 1:2). In this narrative, Licinius and Quintipor are the implied sources for Paul's trial and death. To show that Peter's less public and more humiliating death also glorified God, a soldier who was converted by the events would be the ideal witness. It may be for similar reasons that in Acts 27, the centurion Julius is named and then referenced repeatedly in the account of Paul's journey to Rome.

[39–40] Other than the name of Eubulus, and the knowledge that Linus led the Roman church following Peter's death, we have no historical information about the period during and after Nero's persecution. Believers undoubtedly experienced grief, fear, and expectation of the end of all things. These were not only Christians but also residents of the greatest city in the world, the most grand sections of which were reduced to charred rubble. Hundreds of their family members were dying horrible deaths, and now the two most famous founders of their faith had been murdered. Undoubtedly, as in any tragedy, some despaired, some looked for miraculous intervention, and others put one foot in front of the other, trusting that somehow God would show the way.

[41]Furthermore, believers among the nobles said that Nero's cruelty was soon spent, and that he had said of Paul that cutting off his head would cause the body, meaning the church, to bleed to death. [42]But through the winter, he continued to kill all the believers he found, including Priscilla and Aquila, who had come from Ephesus too late to find Paul alive, and were soon arrested in their house because of informers among the Jews. [43]Timothy and Mark, however, were delivered, and Timothy returned to Ephesus while Mark remained in Rome in the house of Priscilla Glabria, whom Nero dared not harm, fearing the nobles. [44]After the winter, Nero gave orders to his soldiers to make no more arrests, and all rejoiced.

[45]Thus through great suffering the word of the Lord continued to spread throughout the city, [46]including into the households of the great, who were baptized along with their households, and who gave shelter to many. [47]And many of the soldiers who had been commanded to arrest and kill believers marveled at their faith and endurance in suffering, and they too followed the Lord. [48]Even those in Rome who did not believe took pity on the believers, because all Rome hated Nero and did not believe his lies about the fire. [49]As for the tyrant himself, he turned his wrath from the believers to his own nobles. [50]And when he died, Rome was in turmoil until a new emperor arose, [51]so that for a time the believers were left in peace. [52]So it is to this day, although some fear that a new Nero will arise.

---

[41] The supposition that Nero calculated ending the movement by rounding up the leaders was certainly typical of his manner of operation, which was undoubtedly well known to highly-situated members of the church.

[42] As noted above, we do not know when Nero's persecution ended, but he probably soon turned his attention from destruction of people to construction of buildings. Tradition suggests that Priscilla and Aquila were among the Neronic martyrs. Since they are in Ephesus when 2 Timothy is written (4:19), this narrative brings them to Rome either with those whom Paul summons or soon after in response to news of Paul's death. As owners of a house where believers met (Rom 16:5), they would be easy for informants to identify.

[43] As noted above, the house of Priscilla is a plausible place of refuge, especially for one like Mark who had been a companion of Peter. Tradition has Timothy return to Ephesus, where he served as bishop until his martyrdom at the hands of pagans in AD 80. We are told by Eusebius that Mark, whose movements will be described in later chapters, left Rome not long after Peter's death for Alexandria (*Ecclesiastical History* 2.16.1).

[47] The wording here summarizes the last three chapters, which is typical of Luke when ending subsections of his longer works (e.g., 2:43–47; 4:32–37; 6:7; 14:21–28; 28:30–31). In this case the key themes are rejoicing, giving shelter, suffering, the conversion of many, and the spread of the gospel.

[48] According to Roman historian Tacitus, "there arose a feeling of compassion; for it was not, as it seemed, for the public good, but to glut one man's cruelty, that they were being destroyed" (*Annals* 15.44).

[**49–51**] As noted above, we know of no more general persecutions until late in the the reign of Domitian (AD 81–96). This does not exclude the occasional exposure and persecution of believers, especially among the nobility, who were more likely to experience the notice and resentment of Roman rulers.

[**52**] This possibility, which is an important aspect of the biblical book of Revelation, did not begin with Christians. Roman historians Tacitus (*Histories* 1.78, 2.8) and Suetonius (*Nero* 57) relate the origin of the so-called "Nero *redivivus*" myth, which started with the rumor that the tyrant did not die but escaped east to Parthia, from whence he would return to destroy Rome. Given Nero's young age in AD 68, this fear could remain viable well into the second century. There is also evidence that early Christians considered a later emperor who acted like Nero to be Nero, perhaps in the same sense that some thought John the Baptist or Jesus to be Elijah (Tertullian, *Apology* 5.4; Eusebius, *Ecclesiastical History* 3.17). Here Luke takes a more conservative approach, directing such fear toward a figurative, "new" Nero.

PRIMARY SOURCES

The Quo Vadis Legend

The Acts of Peter (AD 150–200) 35: The rest of the brethren together with Marcellus entreated him to withdraw, but Peter said to them, "Shall we act like deserters, brethren?" But they said to him, "No, it is so that you can go on serving the Lord." So he assented to the brethren and withdrew by himself, saying, "Let none of you retire with me, but I shall retire by myself in disguise." And as he went out of the gate he saw the Lord entering Rome; and when he saw him he said, "Lord, whither goest thou here?" [*Domine, quo vadis?*] And the Lord said to him, "I am coming to Rome to be crucified." And Peter said to him, "Lord, art thou being crucified again?" He said to him, "Yes, Peter, I am being crucified again." And Peter came to himself; and he saw the Lord ascending into heaven; then he returned to Rome rejoicing and giving praise to the Lord, because he said, "I am being crucified"; since this was to happen to Peter.

The Death of Peter

Ascension of Isaiah (AD 80–200) 4:2–3: After it is consummated, Beliar the great ruler, the king of this world, will descend, who hath ruled it since it came into being; yea, he will descent from his firmament in the likeness of a man, a lawless king, the slayer of his mother: who himself (even) this king. Will persecute the plant which the Twelve Apostles of the Beloved have planted. Of the Twelve one will be delivered into his hands.[4]

Acts of Peter (AD 150–200) 37: And having approached and standing by the cross he began to say: O name of the cross, thou hidden mystery! O grace ineffable that is pronounced in the name of the cross! O nature of man, that cannot be separated from God! O love (friendship) unspeakable and inseparable, that cannot be shown forth by unclean lips! I

---

4. *The Ascension of Isaiah* is quoted from the translation by Charlesworth.

seize thee now, I that am at the end of my delivery hence (or, of my coming hither). . . . But now it is time for thee, Peter, to deliver up thy body unto them that take it. Receive it then, ye unto whom it belongeth. I beseech you the executioners, crucify me thus, with the head downward and not otherwise: and the reason wherefore, I will tell unto them that hear. [The account continues for an entire page with Peter, upside-down, explaining the symbolism of his position, then dying.]⁵

Tertullian (AD 200) *Prescription Against Heretics* 36: What a happy Church is that [Rome] on which the Apostles poured out their doctrine with their blood; where Peter had like passion with the Lord.

Tertullian (AD 213) *Scorpiace* 15: Then is Peter girt by another, when he is made fast to the cross.

Origen (AD 250) *Commentary on Genesis* 3: Peter was crucified at Rome with his head downwards, as he himself had desired to suffer.

Lactantius (AD 315) *De mortibus persecutorum* 2.6: And while Nero reigned, the Apostle Peter came to Rome, and, through the power of God committed unto him, wrought certain miracles, and, by turning many to the true religion, built up a faithful and steadfast temple unto the Lord. When Nero heard of those things, and observed that not only in Rome, but in every other place, a great multitude revolted daily from the worship of idols, and, condemning their old ways, went over to the new religion, he, an execrable and pernicious tyrant, sprung forward to raze the heavenly temple and destroy the true faith. He it was who first persecuted the servants of God; he crucified Peter, and slew Paul.

Eusebius (AD 325) *Ecclesiastical History* 3.1.2: Peter seems to have preached to the Jews in Pontus and Galatia and Bithynia, Cappadocia, and Asia, and at the end he came to Rome and was crucified head downwards, for so he had demanded to suffer.

Jerome (AD 400) *De viris illustribus* 1: Simon Peter the son of John, from the village of Bethsaida in the province of Galilee, brother of Andrew the apostle, and himself chief of the apostles, after having been bishop of the church of Antioch and having preached to the Dispersion—the believers in circumcision, in Pontus, Galatia, Cappadocia, Asia and Bithynia— pushed on to Rome in the second year of Claudius to overthrow Simon Magus, and held the sacerdotal chair there for twenty-five years until the last, that is the fourteenth, year of Nero. At his hands he received the crown of martyrdom being nailed to the cross with his head towards the ground and his feet raised on high, asserting that he was unworthy to be crucified in the same manner as his Lord.⁶

The Deaths of Paul and Peter "At the Same Time"

Eusebius (AD 325) *Ecclesiastical History* 2.25.8: And that they both suffered martyrdom at the same time is stated by Dionysius, bishop of Corinth, in his epistle to the Romans, in the

5. *The Acts of Peter* is quoted from the translation by M. R. James.
6. Jerome and other early church writers after AD 325 are quoted from Schaff and Wace, *Nicene and Post-Nicene Fathers.*

following words: You have thus by such an admonition bound together the planting of Peter and of Paul at Rome and Corinth. For both of them planted and likewise taught us in our Corinth. And they taught together in like manner in Italy, and suffered martyrdom at the same time (Greek: *kata ton auton kairon*).

Jerome (AD 392) *Liber de Viris illustribus* 5: Accordingly in the 14th year of Nero's reign, on the same day as Peter, in Rome, he was beheaded for Christ, and was buried at the via Ostiense, in that the 37th year after Our Lord's Passion.

Jerome (AD 392) *Tractate on Psalm 96* lines 176–183: How then were Peter and Paul condemned to death on one day by the impious Nero, if the Lord preserves the souls of his saints? Consider carefully what is being said. The Lord preserves the souls of his saints, their souls, not their bodies.

The Death of Peter's Wife

Clement of Alexandria (AD 180–200) *Stromata* 7.11: And blessed Peter saw his wife being led to her death. They say, accordingly, that the blessed Peter, on seeing his wife led to death, rejoiced on account of her call and conveyance home, and called very encouragingly and comfortingly, addressing her by name, "Remember the Lord."

7

Simeon Calls the Apostles to Jerusalem

1 In the last days of Nero's persecutions, Aquila and Priscilla, together with Timothy, arrived in Ostia, where they learned that Paul had been killed. ²They proceeded to their house in Rome, but informants among the Jews brought soldiers to arrest them. ³Priscilla and Aquilla were crucified, and Timothy was in prison for many weeks, but the Lord delivered him. ⁴During this time, Mark and Apollos also arrived, but believers from the household of Pudens hid them in Ostia, where they remained for some time, writing and encouraging the believers. ⁵When Timothy was released, he went to Dalmatia to see Titus, and then, together with Mark and Apollos, they sailed to Alexandria to strengthen the church there.

---

[1] For the movements of these individuals, see above, 4:16–18, and 2 Timothy 4:9. Aquila and Priscilla are in Ephesus with Timothy when Paul writes (2 Tim 4:19). We do not know that they went to Rome at that time, but we know that they had a house there and that they had once before "risked their lives" on Paul's behalf (Rom 16:3–4). According to much later tradition, they were martyred either in Asia Minor or Rome. The supposition here is that they, together with others to whom Paul wrote in 2 Timothy, were drawn back to the emergency too late to help Paul and found themselves in mortal danger.

[2–3] The writer of Hebrews (13:23), suggested here as Apollos (see commentary above on 2:32–35), does not explain the circumstances of Timothy's temporary incarceration. If, as it appears, this was during Nero's persecution, it is remarkable—perhaps miraculous—that he escaped death.

[4] Mark presumably came as requested in 2 Timothy 4:11, and he may have picked up Apollos from Corinth on the way, arriving separately. It is reasonable to put the two together near Rome at this time, given Mark's writing and their later travel together to Alexandria (according to tradition).

[5] At the end of Hebrews, the writer expressed the hope that Timothy "if he comes in time . . . will be with me when I see you" (13:23). Since Titus was probably still in Dalmatia (2 Tim 4:10), and he and Timothy were old travel companions, it is reasonable to imagine Apollos waiting for Timothy's return from visiting Titus before sailing with him to the destination of the letter, Alexandria.

Hebrews closes, "those from Italy greet you" (13:24), so it is most likely written from Rome (less likely *to* Rome). Since the epistle's reference to an earlier persecution (10:32–34) does not match the severity of Nero's persecution, and since it does not mention the temple's destruction, it was probably written before AD 70 to a prominent community of Jewish believers such as Antioch, Jerusalem, or Alexandria. Here it is connected to Timothy's release, presumably in the winter of AD 65, with the supposition that Timothy accompanied Apollos and Mark from Rome to Alexandria soon after the epistle was sent. In this scenario, the persecution referred to in Hebrews is at the hands of hostile Jewish leaders.

---

⁶When word came to Jerusalem that Paul and Peter and many other believers were killed, Simeon and the apostles who were with him, John and Simon the Zealot, fasted and prayed to know the Lord's will, and if this were the end that Christ Jesus had foretold. ⁷For certain leaders of the Jews were planning rebellion against Rome, and there were rumors of war. ⁸Moreover, many believers, including some of the apostles, had been called before councils and rulers to be killed for proclaiming Christ as Lord, ⁹while others in Judea and Galilee had been persecuted by the Jews because they refused to take up arms against Rome.

¹⁰Simeon now sent word to the apostles to meet in Jerusalem following Passover, in the eleventh year of Nero.

---

[6] According to Eusebius (*Ecclesiastical History* 3.11), the surviving apostles gathered after the martyrdom of James the Lord's brother in AD 62 to choose Simeon as his successor to lead the Jerusalem church. Simeon was the son of Clopas, who was Joseph's brother, making him a cousin of Jesus. Eusebius reports that Simeon led the church to Pella (chapter 10 below) and that he was crucified in the early second century at the remarkable age of 120. Beyond these details, we know nothing of his life and very little of the Jerusalem church during this period.

[7–9] As previous chapters have shown, the breach between Christianity and Judaism was a growing problem for both groups, and there was no middle ground: Jesus was either the Messiah or he was not. The stakes were understandably higher in Jerusalem than in the far-flung regions of the empire, where Jews were less insulated and less equipped to enforce orthodoxy. Still, even in Palestine, there was not constant persecution. For rank and file Christians and Jews, daily life was dominated by work and domestic concerns, and theological differences had little practical effect. Even in terms of personal piety and community worship, the groups could operate on parallel tracks in synagogue and house church, while sharing festivals and the temple. But for some leaders of the Sadducees and Pharisees, who saw themselves as the protectors of Judaism, compromise and coexistence were impossible. From time to time they resorted to force to make examples of Christian leaders—usually through judicial proceedings, but on occasion by inciting mobs. Another form of pressure on Christians appears to have increased, however, as war approached. Militant groups like the Zealots and followers of the rebellion's leaders demanded the allegiance and aid of their fellow countrymen. As the uprising grew more desperate in the face of overwhelming Roman force, the need for help increased; and so did reprisals against those who refused to join the cause.

[10] Although there is no direct evidence of such a council, there are good reasons to suppose that a meeting occurred to commission both the Gospels and the surviving apostles before the war, which began in AD 66. We know from Acts that the apostles' pattern in the face of a crisis was to call a meeting in Jerusalem and to respond as a group. Eusebius records the meeting to choose Simeon in AD 62, and he also reports that around the time of the war, the apostles divided evangelistic regions by lot (*Ecclesiastical History* 3.1). Any one of several critical developments at this time could have precipitated such a meeting, and in combination the significance of these events was enormous: the deaths of the primary apostles Paul and Peter, the deaths of other apostles and leaders in the immediately preceding years, the end of the natural lives of eyewitnesses of Jesus, and the clear signs of impending war with Rome. The timeline proposed here allows only six to eight months between Peter's death and the council, but such a meeting could have occurred a year later and still preceded the war, which did not in fact reach Jerusalem for several years.

---

[11]He summoned Andrew from Nicaea, Philip and Bartholomew from Hierapolis, Matthew from Damascus, and Judas son of James from Edessa. [12]Knowing that Thomas was too far away to return, Simeon did not send for him. [13]In addition to those of the twelve who still lived, Simeon sent for Jude the Lord's brother from Galilee, and Mark, Apollos, and Timothy from Alexandria.

[14]When these were all gathered, along with other leaders of the church from Judea and nearby territories, Simeon addressed them, saying, [15]"Brothers in Christ, it is now more years since the Lord was raised than it was from his birth to that day, and still we wait the promise of his coming. [16]One sign he gave us to look for may soon be upon us, if war comes to Jerusalem. [17]Everywhere our fellow countrymen rise up in anger at Rome and tell us that we must resist Caesar as the enemy of God, at which time God will hasten to save us.

[11–13] Subsequent chapters will detail the movements and circumstances of these and other key figures. In summary at this point, it is likely that five of the original twelve had died by AD 66: Judas Iscariot, James son of Zebedee, Matthias, James son of Alphaeus, and Peter. Other key leaders who had been martyred by this time include James the Lord's brother, Paul, Barnabas, and Silas. Andrew, Bartholomew, Simon, and Judas were likely martyred by AD 69, and Thomas by AD 72, leaving only John, Philip, and Matthew alive at the time that this theoretical narrative was written.

Luke refers to the original group of apostles as "the twelve" only once in Acts (6:2), preferring "the apostles" (e.g., 1:2; 2:43; 8:14). The designation is used here and later to distinguish the group, especially in light of its diminishment by martyrdom during this period.

[14–16] "When you hear of wars and insurrections, do not be terrified; for these things must take place first, but the end will not follow immediately" (Luke 21:9); "When you see Jerusalem surrounded by armies, then know that its destruction has come near" (Luke 21:20).

[17] It was typical of false messiahs and zealous patriots, including those who would soon instigate the rebellion against Rome, to maintain that the great battle once begun by the faithful would end with God's intervention on their behalf.

[18]Now if war comes, and we stand aside, will we be counted as those who oppose the Lord? [19]No, for we have his command that we should not take up the sword, even in his defense. [20]Not only that, but we have for these many years awaited his coming while living at peace with all, despite persecution, sometimes at the hands of the Gentiles and other times at the hands of the Jews. [21]We obey all laws, except when human authorities set laws against each other, in which case we obey the law of God. [22]In times past, God has used his enemies to punish his people for their hardness of heart. [23]So it was when our fathers were led into captivity in Babylon because, according to the Scriptures, 'All the leading priests and the people also were exceedingly unfaithful.' [24]But later, when the people turned to the Lord, he restored them. [25]So it may be again, that before the end the Lord may once again use the suffering of his people to fulfill his promise to gather them to himself. [26]Therefore, if we join the Jews in fighting Rome, we may keep them longer from following the Lord.

[27]Now concerning the commission of the Lord to spread the word throughout the world, many have now fulfilled his commission and have entered into his presence rather than returning to ours. [28]They have been seeds planted in the ground of this earth, and by their deaths they have multiplied the harvest of heaven. [29]Of the twelve whom the Lord chose, only eight remain. [30]Now the Lord has instructed us that when he returns, we must be found doing, not waiting in idleness. [31]Whether this is the end, no one knows, but such signs as we see increase our urgency. [32]So let us now send out those who remain to the places the Lord reveals to us. [33]Furthermore, because many eyewitnesses have now died, let a written account of the deeds and words of the Lord go with those who preach, to strengthen the churches in truth and righteousness. [34]To this end, let us examine the account of Mark and, if the Lord wills, let us also choose from among ourselves others who can write of these things."

[18–19] Luke 22:51; 6:27; and Matthew 26:52 teach the renunciation of violence. The early church was consistently pacifist for several centuries, even at times refusing to baptize soldiers if they did not first give up their vocations.

[20–21] Once again (see, e.g., 1:10, 48–49; 4:8 above), Luke takes every opportunity to stress the law-abiding nature of Christians, in this case even under pressure from their fellow countrymen.

[22–24] This is the consistent message of the prophets: God will restore his people to prosperity when they return to obedience (see, e.g., Jer 29:14; Ezek 39:25; Hos 6:11). V. 23 = 2 Chronicles 36:14.

[25–26] This argument turns on its head that of the militants, suggesting that avoidance of conflict, not participation in it, will hasten the end of salvation.

[27–30] The Gospel and Acts include several passages that stress active watchfulness: Luke 12:35–48; 21:34–36; Acts 20:28–31.

[31–34] At this point in the narrative, Mark's Gospel is not yet approved, nor has a link been established between Gospel composition and the current crisis. There are no indications in the Gospels themselves that their production was motivated by persecution and the death of the first generation of believers, but this is reasonable to suppose. Peter's death in Rome may have precipitated, or perhaps accelerated, not only the writing of the Gospel but also its particular emphasis on Christ's passion as an ironic triumph.

PRIMARY SOURCES

Possible Pre-War Meeting to Commission Apostles

Acts of Thomas (AD 225) 1: AT that time we the apostles were all in Jerusalem—Simon called Peter, and Andrew his brother; James the son of Zebedee, and John his brother; Philip and Bartholomew; Thomas, and Matthew the tax-gatherer; James of Alphæus and Simon the Cananæan; and Judas of James;—and we portioned out the regions of the world, in order that each one of us might go into the region that fell to him, and to the nation to which the Lord sent him.

Eusebius (AD 325) *Ecclesiastical History* 3.1: Such was the condition of things among the Jews [when it happened that the war blazed up in the twelfth year of the reign of Nero], but the holy Apostles and disciples of our Saviour were scattered throughout the whole world. Thomas, as tradition relates, obtained by lot Parthia, Andrew Scythia, John Asia (and he stayed there and died in Ephesus), but Peter seems to have preached to the Jews of the Dispersion . . . and at the end he came to Rome and was crucified head downwards, for so he had demanded to suffer.

8

The Gospels are Commissioned and Apostles Sent Out

1 Now the writing of the life of the Lord in four different accounts happened in this way. ²When Peter was in Rome, the believers there, having heard his preaching, asked him to commit these things in writing. ³And Peter, not being a learned man, entrusted this task to John Mark. ⁴He wrote down what Peter had witnessed, how the Lord performed many miracles, and that his suffering and death were not a shame but a triumph greater than those celebrated by Caesar.

---

[1] With minor alterations to accommodate the narrative to the circumstances of a theoretical council convened in AD 65, this account follows the traditions of the early church regarding the composition of the four Gospels, which are provided in the primary source material below.

[2–4] The sequence here reflects the consensus of scholars that Mark wrote first, and that Matthew and Luke then used Mark plus a common source, designated Q (German for *quelle* = source) and additional sources of their own. The primary evidence for this is that 95% of Mark's content appears in either Matthew or Luke, sometimes word-for-word and sometimes in shortened versions of particular passages. The sequence of events and agreements of detail also support Mark's priority. Scholars debate whether the Q source was written, and if so, whether it was in one form or in one language. This shared material, largely sayings of Jesus, comprises about 25% of Matthew and Luke; and each contains an additional 20% of unique material, most of it in the birth narratives.

The early church did not describe the purpose of Mark's Gospel in these terms, but a thorough examination reveals in every passage its message of victory, culminating in the triumph of the cross.[1] In the Greco-Roman world, honor and shame were constant themes. The greatest humiliation imaginable was crucifixion, reserved for traitors and slaves; conversely, the greatest symbolic honor was the *triumph*, a parade through Rome to proclaim the emperor's achievements, even his divinity. No Roman who heard Mark's account would fail to miss the dozen or more details in the passage describing the Lord's death that precisely parallel those

---

1. Gundry, *Mark*.

of a typical Roman triumph.[2] Far from downplaying the suffering of Christ, Mark devotes half his Gospel to the Lord's last few days, and his account of the crucifixion is a masterpiece of irony, exalting Christ precisely as it subverts Nero.

2. Schmidt, "Crucifixion," 1–18.

---

[5]Copies of this account were made for use by various households of believers, and the church in Rome was greatly strengthened by it. [6]Furthermore, when the Gentiles heard it they were amazed and inquired about the truth of these things, so that many believed, seeing the Spirit at work in the lives of believers. [7]For the more that Nero did to oppose the church, the more the Lord performed signs and wonders through the believers, and built them up in faith and righteousness.

[8]When the account written by Mark was read in Jerusalem to the apostles and others who were eyewitnesses, they heartily approved it. [9]But some said, "There are many other sayings and deeds of the Lord that we know are worthy to be written, and who will do this?" [10]Simeon and the other apostles, therefore, prayed and fasted for three days, asking the Lord for guidance. [11]The Spirit indicated to the apostles that Matthew should write a fuller account for the Jews, [12]including proofs from the Scriptures that Jesus was the Messiah, as well as many of the Lord's teachings that have been collected in Hebrew, and others that Matthew remembered.

[5–7] Affirming the effect of Mark's Gospel both confirms its legitimacy despite its creation as an indirect reminiscence and suggests that it was useful for edification and evangelism—provided that the lives of believers represented the Gospel. It is difficult, but instructive, to imagine a time when this challenge was fresh, when Mark's Gospel was not an ancient and revered document but a revolutionary call to "follow me" (1:14; 2:15), because "truly this man was God's Son" (15:39).

[8–12] As a tax collector (Mark 2:14; Matt 9:9), Matthew was affluent and educated, conversant in several languages, and therefore the most obvious candidate among the original twelve to record the ministry of Jesus. His Gospel is notable for its many quotations of Scripture to show Jesus as the fulfillment of Scriptural expectations concerning the Messiah. He also shows great interest in the birth and lineage of Jesus. Furthermore, the arrangement of the Lord's teaching in five great sermons, corresponding to the first five books of the Bible, portray Jesus as the new Moses. These factors combine to convince scholars that Matthew's Gospel was written primarily for Jewish believers.

The persistent ancient tradition that Matthew wrote in the Hebrew language is contradicted by the obvious dependence of his Gospel on Mark and the identical form of some sayings also in Luke, both of which were written in Greek. The fourth-century scholar Origen recognized this problem and maintained that a Hebrew document written by Matthew was re-written soon after as the Gospel we know, but by an unknown author. If indeed Matthew went to Alexandria around this time, Apollos or some other educated believer could have performed this task. It is also possible that the sayings source Q or some other document circulated in Hebrew and was associated with Matthew. Rather than enter into speculation about the details of composition, the account here simply follows the early tradition that attributes the Gospel in general terms to Matthew.

¹³Matthew agreed, and he went to Alexandria, taking with him Apollos, who confounded the Jews there with his great learning and persuaded many to turn to the Lord. ¹⁴Matthew remained in Alexandria for three years and wrote his account of the Lord, and then he traveled to Antioch, where he had many copies made of his account. ¹⁵He had planned to send them to Jerusalem, but by this time all was in turmoil, so he gave them to the apostles to take on their journeys.

¹⁶Directed by the Spirit, Simeon also said to John that he should write an account of the deeds of the Lord. ¹⁷At first John did not wish to do so, because he believed that he was unworthy, but the other apostles urged him, especially Andrew, to whom the Lord revealed that John should write an account. ¹⁸And when John had prayed for many days, he said, "Mark writes of the last year in the ministry of the Lord, ¹⁹but the Lord did many other miracles and deeds before he went up to Jerusalem to be killed, and he taught the disciples many other things that Mark has not written." ²⁰And so John agreed to write after the others, but not to repeat those things already told in their accounts.

²¹Finally, Simeon called me before the council and said, "Although you did not see the Lord, you have walked in the Way for many years, preaching the word with Paul and the other apostles. ²²You are beloved by many who saw the Lord, and you have been eyewitness yourself to much that the Spirit has done through the apostles in many places. ²³Furthermore, the Lord has given to you the beloved Theophilus as a patron who will enable you to travel or gather others to you in search of the truth concerning these things. ²⁴Therefore, we charge you to write for the Gentiles, and for the Jews who live among them, an account of all that has transpired from the birth of the Lord to the present day, including the acts of the apostles, according to the accounts of eyewitnesses from near and far."

[13–15] Matthew's ministry and the composition of his Gospel are often associated not only with Alexandria but also with Antioch, which contained a large Jewish community. The city would also provide a convenient travel hub for distribution of a Gospel, and it would be much safer than Jerusalem during the tumult of the later first century. The availability of Matthew's Gospel may help to explain its early prominence; from the beginning it was listed first.

[16–20] It was obvious to the first readers that John's Gospel differed greatly from the other three, and the account here conveys the earliest explanation. The oldest source is the second-century *Muratorian Fragment*, and further details are added by Eusebius and Jerome. In the late second century Clement of Alexandria distinguishes John as the "spiritual" Gospel, since it includes much teaching about belief and love.

Eusebius reports that John read the other three Gospels before he wrote his own. This account places his commission early, with the others; but it leaves open the exact time of his composition, which could allow for him to read the Gospels of Matthew and Luke later, especially since he was easily accessible in Ephesus (or on Patmos, from AD 82–96).

[21–24] Luke consistently refrains from naming himself, but use of the pronoun "me" is consistent with the "we" passages in Acts and in the earlier chapters here. The content of Simeon's commission extends the claims of Luke's own prologues to suggest that he was in a unique position to record the beginnings of Christianity. He had proven himself faithful over time and through adversity, he was himself an eyewitness to much of Paul's ministry, and he is now in a position to act as historian under the generous patronage of Theophilus. Such help should not be underestimated, for the composition of documents the size and scope of the Gospel and Acts would require substantial time, food, lodging, and safety. Even before the writing could begin, there would be costs for research: hand-copied written resources like the Old Testament and the other Gospels, travel to visit witnesses or to bring witnesses to Luke, and messengers to communicate with others. Then copies would have to be made for distribution. All in all, the production of Luke's Gospel and Acts—much less a sequel to them—had to have been a complex and expensive project.

---

²⁵In this manner the Spirit began to provide four accounts of the life and teachings of Christ Jesus, of which copies would be made for the strengthening of the church and to aid in the spread of the word of the Lord. ²⁶The apostles and all those gathered were of one accord regarding these four accounts, and all rejoiced.

²⁷On the next day, Simeon said, "Just as the Lord has provided that four will write in one Spirit, so he has created four winds to carry the word forth. ²⁸So the Spirit directs each of the twelve who remain to the four corners of the earth.

²⁹First, John, together with Timothy, will go north to Asia, bearing witness to the word of the Lord and strengthening the church in the region of Ephesus.

[25–26] Here and in 8:5 above, reference is made to copies of the Gospels, but the descriptions of the Gospels' origins do not include accounts of their reproduction. We may infer the existence of copies or collections from one New Testament reference to "all his [Paul's] letters" and "other scriptures" (2 Pet 3:16). Also noteworthy is the discovery of a papyrus fragment of John's Gospel from the early second century found in Egypt, far from the Gospel's place of composition. This suggests that the Gospels were copied and distributed widely from an early date. Undoubtedly, documents carried by missionaries or held by church leaders were destroyed during persecutions, and some were reproduced on fragile materials that did not last. Complete manuscripts on expensive, long-lasting materials like parchment do not appear until the fourth century.

[27–28] The coincidence of "four Gospels" and "four winds," plus the fact that "spirit" and "wind" are the same word in Hebrew, provides a fitting image for the commissioning of the surviving apostles. The sequence of directions is not arbitrary, but follows a pattern shown in Acts, which in turn derives from Old Testament passages like 1 Chronicles 1 and Ezekiel 5, where "tables of kings" proceed outward in a spiral emanating counterclockwise from Jerusalem—first north, then west, south, and east.[3] This pattern provides the sequence for the journeys of the apostles here, the detailed accounts of which begin in chapter 14.

[29] As the record of Acts and the letters of Paul show, the apostles tended to travel in pairs, or with at least one associate. The directions and pairings here are based on tradition and conjecture regarding the movements of the apostles, which are detailed in later chapters.

---

3. Scott, "Geographical Horizon," 526–27.

³⁰Philip and Bartholomew, likewise, will return to Hierapolis in Phrygia, and from there they will go as the Lord directs. ³¹Andrew, together with Luke, will journey to the west, to Macedonia and Achaia. ³²Simon and Judas, likewise, will carry the word west to far lands, first through Cyrenaica and Mauretania, then if the Lord allows to Britain and Gaul. ³³Matthew will travel to the south, first to Alexandria with Mark and Apollos, then to Ethiopia. ³⁴To the east Thomas has already gone, beyond Parthia and Persia, and as far as India. ³⁵When we learn about the progress of the word in these lands, the Lord may direct the apostles and others to go there, so that the mercy of God will reach farther than the sword of Rome, even farther than the dispersion of the Jews. ³⁶For when all the nations of the earth have heard the good news, the word of the Lord will be fulfilled, and the end will come."

[30–36] As is the case in Acts, and as subsequent chapters will show, the initial directions of missionaries often changed for any number of reasons. Travel beyond the boundaries of the empire involved risky journeys into the unknown yet signified the reach of the gospel not to the known world but beyond, to the ends of human habitation. While Acts 1:8 charges the disciples to take the gospel "to the ends of the earth" before Christ's return, Matthew 24:14 links evangelism directly to the end: "And the good news of the kingdom will be proclaimed throughout the world, as a testimony to all the nations, and then the end will come."

PRIMARY SOURCES

Papias (AD 110–140) quoted in Eusebius, *Ecclesiastical History* 3.39.15–16: This also the presbyter said: Mark, having become the interpreter of Peter, wrote down accurately, though not in order, whatsoever he remembered of the things said or done by Christ. For he neither heard the Lord nor followed him, but afterward, as I said, he followed Peter, who adapted his teaching to the needs of his hearers, but with no intention of giving a connected account of the Lord's discourses, so that Mark committed no error while he thus wrote some things as he remembered them. For he was careful of one thing, not to omit any of the things which he had heard, and not to state any of them falsely. These things are related by Papias concerning Mark. But concerning Matthew he writes as follows: So then Matthew wrote the oracles in the Hebrew language, and every one interpreted them as he was able.

Muratorian Fragment (AD 170–200): Those things at which he was present he placed thus. The third book of the Gospel, that according to Luke, the well-known physician Luke wrote in his own name in order after the ascension of Christ, and when Paul had associated him with himself as one studious of right. Nor did he himself see the Lord in the flesh; and he, according as he was able to accomplish it, began his narrative with the nativity of John. The fourth Gospel is that of John, one of the disciples. When his fellow-disciples and bishops entreated him, he said, "Fast ye now with me for the space of three days, and let us recount to each other whatever may be revealed to each of us." On the same night it was revealed to Andrew, one of the apostles, that John should narrate all things in his own name as they called them to mind. And hence, although different points are taught us in the several books of the Gospels, there is no difference as regards the faith of believers, inasmuch as in all of them all things are related under one imperial Spirit, which concern the *Lord's* nativity, His passion, His resurrection, His conversation with His disciples, and His twofold advent, the first in the humiliation of rejection, which is now past, and the second in the glory of royal power, which is yet in the future.

Irenaeus (AD 180) *Against Heresies* 3.1.1: Matthew also issued a written Gospel among the Hebrews in their own dialect, while Peter and Paul were preaching at Rome, and laying the foundations of the Church. After their departure, Mark, the disciple and interpreter of Peter, did also hand down to us in writing what had been preached by Peter. Luke also, the companion of Paul, recorded in a book the Gospel preached by him. Afterwards, John, the disciple of the Lord, who also had leaned upon His breast, did himself publish a Gospel during his residence at Ephesus in Asia.

Clement of Alexandria (AD 200) quoted in Eusebius, *Ecclesiastical History* 6.14.5–7: Again, in the same books, Clement gives the tradition of the earliest presbyters, as to the order of the Gospels, in the following manner: The Gospels containing the genealogies, he says, were written first. The Gospel according to Mark had this occasion. As Peter had preached the Word publicly at Rome, and declared the Gospel by the Spirit, many who were present requested that Mark, who had followed him for a long time and remembered his sayings, should write them out. And having composed the Gospel he gave it to those who had requested it. When Peter learned of this, he neither directly forbade nor encouraged it. But, last of all, John, perceiving that the external facts had been made plain in the Gospel, being urged by his friends, and inspired by the Spirit, composed a spiritual Gospel. This is the account of Clement.

Origen (AD 220) quoted in Eusebius, *Ecclesiastical History* 6.24.4–7: Among the four Gospels, which are the only indisputable ones in the Church of God under heaven, I have learned by tradition that the first was written by Matthew, who was once a publican, but afterwards an apostle of Jesus Christ, and it was prepared for the converts from Judaism, and published in the Hebrew language. The second is by Mark, who composed it according to the instructions of Peter, who in his Catholic epistle acknowledges him as a son, saying, 'The church that is at Babylon elected together with you, salutes you, and so does Marcus, my son.' And the third by Luke, the Gospel commended by Paul, and composed for Gentile converts. Last of all that by John.

Eusebius (AD 325) *Ecclesiastical History* 3.24.5–15: Of all the disciples of the Lord, only Matthew and John have left us written memorials, and they, tradition says, were led to write only under the pressure of necessity. For Matthew, who had at first preached to the Hebrews, when he was about to go to other peoples, committed his Gospel to writing in his native tongue, and thus compensated those whom he was obliged to leave for the loss of his presence. And when Mark and Luke had already published their Gospels, they say that John, who had employed all his time in proclaiming the Gospel orally, finally proceeded to write for the following reason. The three Gospels already mentioned having come into the hands of all and into his own too, they say that he accepted them and bore witness to their truthfulness; but that there was lacking in them an account of the deeds done by Christ at the beginning of his ministry. And this indeed is true. For it is evident that the three evangelists recorded only the deeds done by the Saviour for one year after the imprisonment of

John the Baptist, and indicated this in the beginning of their account. . . . They say, therefore, that the apostle John, being asked to do it for this reason, gave in his Gospel an account of the period which had been omitted by the earlier evangelists, and of the deeds done by the Saviour during that period; that is, of those which were done before the imprisonment of the Baptist. . . . One who understands this can no longer think that the Gospels are at variance with one another, inasmuch as the Gospel according to John contains the first acts of Christ, while the others give an account of the latter part of his life. . . . But as for Luke, in the beginning of his Gospel, he states himself the reasons which led him to write it. He states that since many others had more rashly undertaken to compose a narrative of the events of which he had acquired perfect knowledge, he himself, feeling the necessity of freeing us from their uncertain opinions, delivered in his own Gospel an accurate account of those events in regard to which he had learned the full truth, being aided by his intimacy and his stay with Paul and by his acquaintance with the rest of the apostles.

Jerome (AD 392) *Illustrious Men* 3, 7–9: Matthew, also called Levi, apostle and aforetimes publican, composed a gospel of Christ at first published in Judea in Hebrew for the sake of those of the circumcision who believed, but this was afterwards translated into Greek, though by what author is uncertain. The Hebrew itself has been preserved until the present day in the library at Cæsarea which Pamphilus so diligently gathered. I have also had the opportunity of having the volume described to me by the Nazarenes of Berœa, a city of Syria, who use it. . . .

Luke a physician of Antioch, as his writings indicate, was not unskilled in the Greek language. An adherent of the apostle Paul, and companion of all his journeying, he wrote a Gospel. . . . He also wrote another excellent volume to which he prefixed the title *Acts of the Apostles*, a history which extends to the second year of Paul's sojourn at Rome, that is to the fourth year of Nero.

Mark the disciple and interpreter of Peter wrote a short gospel at the request of the brethren at Rome embodying what he had heard Peter tell. When Peter had heard this, he approved it and published it to the churches to be read by his authority. . . . So, taking the gospel which he himself composed, he went to Egypt and first preaching Christ at Alexandria, he formed a church so admirable in doctrine and continence of living that he constrained all followers of Christ to his example. . . . He died in the eighth year of Nero and was buried at Alexandria, Annianus succeeding him.

John, the apostle whom Jesus most loved, the son of Zebedee and brother of James, the apostle whom Herod, after our Lord's passion, beheaded, most recently of all the evangelists wrote a Gospel, at the request of the bishops of Asia, against Cerinthus and other heretics and especially against the then growing dogma of the Ebionites, who assert that Christ did not exist before Mary. On this account he was compelled to maintain His divine nativity. But there is said to be yet another reason for this work, in that when he had read Matthew, Mark, and Luke, he approved indeed the substance of the history and declared that the things they said were true, but that they had given the history of only one year, the one, that is, which follows the imprisonment of John and in which he was put to death. So passing by this year the events of which had been set forth by these, he related the events of the earlier period before John was shut up in prison, so that it might be manifest to those who should diligently read the volumes of the four Evangelists. This also takes away the discrepancy which there seems to be between John and the others.

9

The Family of Jesus

1 After Simeon had spoken, the apostles, together with all the believers gathered there, gave thanks for the direction that the Lord had given, and for the wisdom shown by Simeon. ²Now there were some among the believers in Jerusalem who opposed him, because they believed that the Lord would raise up prophets to lead the church, ³and that appointing men from the family of Jesus would give the appearance of rule by lineage, according to the traditions of men. ⁴But the apostles saw that Simeon, like James before him, was chosen by the Spirit not by reason of his nearness to the Lord by birth but by reason of his faith and righteousness.

---

[1] The account of Eusebius confirms that Simeon's blood relation to Jesus contributed to his selection, which brings up the interesting question of church leadership and a "family dynasty." Concerning leadership, it is clear throughout the New Testament that leaders were appointed by other leaders, acting either individually (Mark 3:14; Tit 1:5), by groups of leaders (Acts 14:23), or even by lot from among worthy candidates (Acts 1:20–26). Judging from the concerns about evaluating those who claimed to be prophets (e.g., Matt 7:15; 1 Cor 14), however, there were probably some difficulties discerning leadership roles. The *Didache*, or *Teaching of the Twelve*, an anonymous first-century document produced in Palestine, goes into some detail about this problem.

While the notion of a literal family dynasty comprising physical descendants of Jesus is a modern myth, there is no doubt that his relatives played an important role in the early Palestinian church, adding lineage to the criteria of leadership attributes, at least for the Jerusalem church. There is no record of a controversy, but the hint of one here reflects the known differences in views of leadership in the early days of the church.

How important were the relatives of Jesus? We know that James and Simeon, successively, led the Jerusalem church into the second century; and Jude was influential enough to write the epistle bearing his name from a position of authority. We know a little of James from the New Testament, including his epistle, and we have the source described below for his martyrdom; but beyond this, we know little about the family of Jesus. Eusebius (*Ecclesiastical History* 1.17) referred to the family as the *desposynoi* ("those of the master"), which suggests that they must have been of some interest. But apart from the information that they lived around Nazareth and preserved family records to substantiate the claim that they were descended from David, he offers no details.

---

⁵For James the brother of the Lord was beloved, not only by the household of faith but also by many of the Jews, even among those who did not believe in Christ Jesus.

⁶He was known from his youth as a righteous man, and he was in the habit of praying in the temple, ⁷begging forgiveness for the people, so that his knees became as hard as a camel's, and he was called by the people James the Just. ⁸Many believed in Christ Jesus because of his wise words and his good works. ⁹But during the Passover in the eighth year of Nero, when the city was crowded with strangers, the scribes and Pharisees saw an opportunity to accuse him. ¹⁰Taking him to the pinnacle of the temple, they demanded that he confess who Jesus was in sight and hearing of all the people. ¹¹And James, filled with the Spirit, shouted in a great voice, "Why do you ask me concerning Jesus, the Son of Man? ¹²He was crucified and raised from the dead, and he now sits in heaven at the right hand of the great Power, and is soon to come upon the clouds of heaven." ¹³Then the scribes and Pharisees, perceiving that the people were not angry but ready to hear more, cried out that he was a blasphemer and pushed him from the pinnacle of the temple. ¹⁴But James, who was not killed by the great fall, rose to his knees and prayed, "I beg you, Lord God our Father, forgive them." ¹⁵The crowd marveled at this, but the scribes and Pharisees came down from the pinnacle and began to stone James. ¹⁶One of the priests said, "Stop! Will you stone the one who prays for you?" ¹⁷And while they considered what to do, one of them came forward with a club and struck James on the head, and he gave up his spirit. ¹⁸When the crowd saw the evil that was done, and how James died praying for his accusers, even more believed; ¹⁹and others shouted out against the scribes and Pharisees, so that after this they did not persecute the believers openly, but only before their own councils.

²⁰Now all this time Mary, the mother of the Lord, had lived in Bethlehem, where she was cared for by John.

---

[5] Roman Catholic tradition later asserted that Mary remained a virgin, and that, therefore, the siblings must have come from a previous marriage of Joseph. While this is technically possible, it appears to be a clear case of invention after the fact, and this narrative assumes the most natural meaning of the Gospel texts, that they are full blood relations.

The wording here follows closely the account of Hegesippus, a second-century source quoted by Eusebius (*See* primary sources below). The specific and plausible details suggest that the story is historically reliable. The pinnacle of the temple, the southwest corner of the gigantic platform on which the temple stood, was about one hundred feet from the valley below.

[6–19] The last two sentences here differ from the Hegesippus narrative, which adds the editorial suggestion that the temple was destroyed in direct response by God to the martyrdom of James.

[20] The notion that John cared for Mary is based partly on the Gospel, which reports that John took Mary into his home following the ministry of Jesus (John 19:25–27). This of course implies that Joseph, who is not mentioned in the Gospels after the birth narratives,

was by this time dead. Traditions differ regarding John's movements before the war, and the time and place of Mary's death, but it is likely that John remained in or close to Jerusalem until her death.[1] Bethlehem, about five miles south of Jerusalem, is chosen here for its associations with the birth of Jesus. To survive this late, Mary would have been at least eighty, so this chapter admittedly stretches credibility in order to link the events of the narrative with the lives of Jesus's family members.

1. Ruffin, *The Twelve*, 93–95.

---

[21]Full of years and full of grace, she spent her days in care for the poor and earnest prayer for the saints.

[22]When word came to her that James had been killed, she was filled with sorrow, and said,

[23]My heart faints within me; Shuddering and sorrow seize my flesh. [24]I have come into deep waters, and the flood sweeps over me. [25]I am weary with weeping, and my eyes grow dim with waiting for my God. [26]O Lord, do not cast me off in the time of old age; [27]Do not forsake me when my strength is spent. For I know that my Redeemer lives, That when my flesh fails, I shall see God, [28]That when all is accomplished, he will stand upon the earth. [29]So even as my strength fades, Let me proclaim your might to all the generations to come; [30]And even as my light grows weak, Let your sun rise within me. [31]You who have done great things, O God, who is like you? [32]You who have made me see many troubles, You will revive me again, [33]You who have brought my flesh to diminish, Once again you will bring my soul to magnify you. [34]So fill my mouth with your praise, and with your glory all of my days.

---

[21] "Full of grace" is a nod to Roman Catholic readers, who may find it difficult to forgive the designation of James and Jude as full brothers of Jesus. Stephen is similarly described as "full of grace and power" in Acts 6:8. The activity of Mary in her later years is unknown, but devotion to the poor echoes the Magnificat (Luke 1:52–53); and prayer was the vocation of the elderly Anna, who prophesied that the infant Jesus would be the Messiah (Luke 2:36–38). Luke does not often refer to the believers as "saints" (Acts 9:13, 32, 41; 26:10), but it fits this context.

[22] The composition of Mary's "*Nunc dimittis*" (*See* Luke 2:29–33) is intended to complement the Magnificat, her hymn of praise in response to the news that she will give birth to the Messiah (Luke 1:46–55). That song melds a primary biblical passage (1 Sam 2:1–10) with several others, adds original material, and stresses paradoxes that defy human expectations. Likewise here, the primary passage is Psalm 71, and the movement of thought is from a realistic lament over loss to increasingly strong expressions of hope.

[23–30] These paradoxes are closest to Psalm 71:18. More specifically, the Old Testament derivations here are as follows: v. 23a = Psalm 19:7; v. 23b = Psalm 21:6; v. 24 = Psalm 69:3; vv. 26–27a = Psalm 71:9; vv. 27b–28 = Job 19:25–26; v. 31 = Psalm 71:18; v. 32 = Psalm 71:20.

[31–33] This flesh/soul, diminish/magnify paradox brings the song back full circle to Luke 1:46, "My soul magnifies the Lord."

[34] Psalm 71:6–8. The point of the Magnificat, the point of this song, and indeed the point of Mary, is to direct glory not to herself but to the Lord.

³⁵Soon after this, Mary knew that she was near death, and John sent for her children. ³⁶Simon and Joses had died by this time, but Jude, together with his wife and sisters and their husbands and children, gathered around Mary.

³⁷After blessing all of them, Mary raised her eyes to heaven and gave up her spirit; ³⁸and her family, together with the saints, mourned her for forty days. ³⁹After the death of Mary, Jude, who like James his brother became a believer after Christ was risen, returned to Galilee, testifying concerning the Lord and strengthening the believers there. ⁴⁰He was also known by both the Jews and Gentiles for his righteousness, and many believed because of him. ⁴¹He would not remain in Jerusalem, because the Lord revealed to him that he should be a witness in the place where the Lord had lived, and among his people. ⁴²When the war came, his family suffered from the Jews, because he would not instruct his family to fight against Rome. ⁴³And after the war, the same Jews told the Romans that Jude and his family called themselves sons of David and desired to be kings when Jesus returned. ⁴⁴But when the Romans examined Jude and his sons, they saw that they were peaceful farmers and would fight for no earthly kingdom, so they let them go.

[35–36] The death of Mary provides a convenient entry for the rest of the family. Mark 6:3 names the brothers of Jesus: James, Jude, Simon, and Joses. It also mentions sisters, but they are not named either by the New Testament or church tradition. Likewise, we have no more information about Simon and Joses. Acts 1:14 reports that just after the resurrection of Jesus, the apostles were together with Mary and "the brothers" of Jesus, but this may be only James and Jude, who became leaders in the church. 1 Corinthians 9:5 affirms that wives accompanied "the other apostles and the brothers of the Lord and Cephas"; but again, the reference is most likely to the well-known James and Jude. 1 Corinthians 15:7 reports that the resurrected Christ appeared to James, but makes no reference to other family members, nor does the New Testament tell how family members who were skeptics (Mark 3:21; John 7:5) became believers, even leaders in the early church.

By the time the Gospels were written, the siblings of Jesus would have been old by first-century standards, and it is reasonable to suppose that some would have died of natural causes. If they had died as martyrs, some tradition is likely to have survived. It is intriguing to wonder who these brothers and sisters were, and what stories they could tell, but they are lost to history.

[37–41] In the brief epistle of Jude, the author designates himself humbly as "a servant of Jesus Christ and brother of James" (v. 1). The letter opposes an early form of false teaching that involved immoral behavior, but neither its theology nor practices are described in detail. There is little doubt that the epistle is authentic, because Jude was too obscure a figure to attract forgeries in his name. We can infer from the letter, from what we know of James, and from general knowledge of first-century Palestinian Christianity, that Jude had a strong interest in personal righteousness as the expression of faith in Christ.

[42–44] Persecution of Jude and the family of Jesus by the Jews in Galilee is speculative but certainly possible, given the circumstances. We know that the Jewish rebellion began in Galilee, and that it was clearly a lost cause as soon as Rome committed a substantial force to quell the uprising. Locals who refused to fight, as the early Christians did, would face wrath and reprisal from their fellow countrymen. The story of Roman interrogation is generally accurate; nevertheless, it happened not to Jude but to his grandsons in the early second century, as Eusebius reports (see below). Evidently the Romans were rounding up anyone who could be suspected of Messianic pretensions, and the family members of Jesus would be prime candidates.

PRIMARY SOURCES

Simeon Chosen to Lead Church

Eusebius (AD 325) *Ecclesiastical History* 3.11.1–2: After the martyrdom of James and the capture of Jerusalem which immediately followed, the story goes that those of the Apostles and of the disciples of the Lord who were still alive came together from every place with those who were, humanly speaking, of the family of the Lord, for many of them were then still alive, and they all took counsel together as to whom they ought to adjudge worthy to succeed James, and all unanimously decided that Simeon the son of Clopas, whom the scripture of the Gospel also mentions, was worthy of the throne of the diocese there. He was, so it is said, a cousin of the Saviour, for Hegesippus relates that Clopas was the brother of Joseph.

Eusebius (AD 325) *Ecclesiastical History* 4.22.4: The same author also describes the beginnings of the heresies which arose in his time, in the following words: And after James the Just had suffered martyrdom, as the Lord had also on the same account, Symeon, the son of the Lord's uncle, Clopas, was appointed the next bishop. All proposed him as second bishop because he was a cousin of the Lord.

The Death of James

Hegesippus (AD 170) quoted in Eusebius, *Ecclesiastical History* 2.23.3–19
The charge of the Church passed to James the brother of the Lord, together with the Apostles. He was called the "Just" by all men from the Lord's time to ours, since many are called James, but he was holy from his mother's womb. He drank no wine or strong drink, nor did he eat flesh; no razor went upon his head; he did not anoint himself with oil, and he did not go to the baths. He alone was allowed to enter into the sanctuary, for he did not wear wool but linen, and he used to enter alone into the temple and be found kneeling and praying for forgiveness for the people, so that his knees grew hard like a camel's because of his constant worship of God, kneeling and asking forgiveness for the people. So from his excessive righteousness he was call the Just and Oblias, that is in Greek, "Rampart of the people and righteousness," as the prophets declare concerning him. Thus some of the seven sects among the people . . . inquired of him what was the "gate of Jesus," and he said that he was the Saviour. Owing to this some believed that Jesus was the Christ. The sects . . . did not believe either in the resurrection or in the one who shall come to reward each according to his deeds, but as many as believed did so because of James. Now, since many even of the rulers believed, there was a tumult of the Jews and the Scribes and Pharisees saying that the whole

111

people was in danger of looking for Jesus as the Christ. So they assembled and said to James, "We beseech you to restrain the people since they are straying after Jesus as though he were the Messiah. We beseech you to persuade concerning Jesus all who come for the day of the Passover, for all obey you. For we and the whole people testify to you that you are righteous and do not respect persons. So do you persuade the crowd not to err concerning Jesus, for the whole people and we all obey you. Therefore stand on the battlement of the temple that you may be clearly visible on high, and that your words may be audible to all the people, for because of the Passover all the tribes, with the Gentiles also, have come together." So the Scribes and Pharisees mentioned before made James stand on the battlement of the temple, and they cried out to him and said, "Oh, just one, to whom we all owe obedience, since the people are straying after Jesus who was crucified, tell us what is the gate of Jesus?" And he answered with a loud voice, "Why do you ask me concerning the Son of Man? He is sitting in heaven on the right hand of the great power, and he will come on the clouds of heaven." And many were convinced and confessed at the testimony of James and said, "Hosanna to the Son of David." Then again the same Scribes and Pharisees said to one another, "We did wrong to provide Jesus with such testimony, but let us go up and throw him down that they may be afraid and not believe him." And they cried out saying, "Oh, oh, even the just one erred." And they fulfilled the Scripture written in Isaiah, "Let us take the just many for he is unprofitable to us. Yet they shall eat the fruit of their works." So they went up and threw down the Just, and they said to one another, "Let us stone James the Just," and they began to stone him since the fall had not killed him, but he turned and knelt saying, "I beseech thee, O Lord, God and Father, forgive them, for they know not what they do." And while they were thus stoning him one of the priests of the sons of Rechab, the son of Rechabim, to whom Jeremiah the prophet bore witness, cried out saying, "Stop! What are you doing? The Just is praying for you." And a certain man among them, one of the laundrymen, took the club with which he used to beat out the clothes, and hit the Just on the head, and so he suffered martyrdom. And they buried him on the spot by the temple, and his gravestone still remains by the temple. He became a true witness both to the Jews and to Greeks that Jesus is the Christ, and at once Vespasian began to besiege them. This account is given at length by Hegesippus, but in agreement with Clement. Thus it seems that James was indeed a remarkable man and famous among all for righteousness, so that the wise even of the Jews thought that this was the cause of the siege of Jerusalem immediately after his martyrdom, and that it happened for no other reason than the crime which they had committed against him.

Jude the Brother of Jesus

Eusebius (AD 325) *Ecclesiastical History* 3.20.1–5: Now there still survived of the family of the Lord grandsons of Judas, who was said to have been his brother according to the flesh, and they were delated as being of the family of David. These the officer brought to Domitian Caesar, for, like Herod, he was afraid of the coming of the Christ. He asked them if they were of the house of David and they admitted it. Then he asked them how much property they had, or how much money they controlled, and they said that all they possessed was nine thousand denarii between them, the half belonging to each, and they stated that they did not possess this in money but that it was the valuation of only thirty-nine plethra [20 acres] of ground on which they paid taxes and lived on it by their own work. They were asked concerning the Christ and his kingdom, its nature, origin, and time of appearance, and explained that it was neither of the world nor earthly, but heavenly and angelic, and it would be at the end of the world, when he would come in glory to judge the living and the dead and to reward every man according to his deeds. At this Domitian did not condemn them at all, but despised them as simple folk, released them, and decreed and end to the persecution against the church.

10

Martyrdom of Matthias
and James Son of Alphaeus

1 For two years following the death of James, all was quiet in Jerusalem; ²and the number of believers continued to grow, so that some of the Jews still plotted secretly against the church. ³Among these were some from the party of the Essenes, who lived near the Dead Sea and also in many towns and cities of Judea, studying the scriptures and practicing holiness. ⁴Many believers came from this party, including those who from the beginning had held their possessions in common and kept close to the law, with much fasting and prayer. ⁵Some of these lived in Jerusalem, including the apostle Matthias; and others lived in Bethany, including the apostle James son of Alphaeus.

[1–2] This chapter is highly speculative, because sources reveal little about the Jerusalem church in the years immediately preceding the war of AD 66–74, and we know almost nothing about the apostles Matthias and James son of Alphaeus. Piecing together hints and possibilities from numerous sources, the most that can be claimed is that these are the kind of events that could have occurred.

[3–4] The consensus of scholars is that the Essenes were the group that produced the Dead Sea Scrolls. According to first-century Jewish historian Josephus, they had communities in towns around Judea (*Wars of the Jews* 2.124). Bethany (v. 5 below) was about a mile and a half south of Jerusalem. Scholars believe that there was an Essene community in Jerusalem, probably in the part of the city where the church began. They had many beliefs in common with the early Christians, including high standards of holiness, common property, ritual washings, and communal meals. Some have linked the Essenes to the early believers who practiced community of possessions (Acts 2:43–47; 4:32–35). Others believe that this more radical form of Christianity was practiced by an offshoot group like those responsible for the *Didache*, which offers instructions about righteous living and about how to evaluate those who claim to be prophets.

[5] These are the two least-known apostles. Matthias was chosen to replace Judas (Acts 1:21–26), but the New Testament does not mention him again. James son of Alphaeus is the brother of Matthew, as distinguished from the apostle James, son of Zebedee and brother

of John. A third James, the Lord's brother, featured in chapter 9 above, was not an apostle, but he led the Jerusalem church and figures prominently in the New Testament. To make matters more confusing, there is one other reference to "James the less" (Mark 16:2; a reference to his physical size, not his importance), who is probably the son of Alphaeus. Apart from his name on lists of apostles (e.g., Luke 6:15; Acts 1:13), the activities of James son of Alphaeus are not described in the New Testament.

In the fourth century, without naming his source, Eusebius reported that "Matthias also taught in the same manner that we ought to fight against and abuse the flesh, and not give way to it for the sake of pleasure, but strengthen the soul by faith and knowledge" (*Ecclesiastical History* 3.29.4). A few late traditions associate him with missions to Armenia and Ethiopia; but the evidence is thin, and some confusion may be caused by the similarity of his name to that of Matthew. With such a common name, James son of Alphaeus may be the victim of even more confusion. Some maintain that the occurrence of his name next to that of Simon the Zealot in lists of apostles suggest a more radical form of discipleship like that portrayed here.[1]

The fact that both apostles disappear from view so quickly and do not reappear until centuries later in unreliable or contradictory traditions means that they probably died early, either in Jerusalem or nearby.[2] This is more likely to have occurred in a period of turmoil like that just before the war. So although the facts regarding these two are few, in combination they support the circumstances described here.

1. McBirnie, *The Twelve*, 146.
2. Ruffin, *The Twelve*, 79.

---

[6]But when rumors of war began to be heard in all parts of the country, many from the party of the Essenes, who had been peaceful, decided to join with those who wished to rebel against Rome, [7]for they believed that God would then destroy the Romans and make them reign over Jerusalem. [8]They resented the believers because they would not fight, and also because they said that Jesus was the Messiah. [9]And thinking that the believers would join with them if their leaders were taken from them, they accused Matthias and James of blasphemy, and they were brought before the chief priests and the entire council.

[6–7] If scholars are correct that the Essenes produced the Dead Sea Scrolls, we know from their writings that they expected that God would soon break in to history on their behalf. We also know from excavations of their settlement at Qumran that this was a tragic and final error; the community was destroyed by the Romans, and the sect disappeared from history. The war also wiped out the Zealots, and without the temple, the high priestly party of the Sadducees disappeared. Only the Pharisees survived, reconstituting Judaism around the study of the law.

[8–9] The Essenes held themselves aloof from temple activities, believing that the temple administration was spiritually corrupt. Nevertheless, apart from vigilante activity, the only way to punish a rival or breakaway group—if that was how the Essenes perceived the Christians—would be to bring an accusation of blasphemy to the Sandhedrin, the ruling council, consisting of both Sadducees ("the chief priests" in the Gospels) and Pharisees.

¹⁰At the council, the men who had tried to kill Paul and who had killed James accused them, ¹¹saying, "These two pretend to live quiet and righteous lives, but privately they turn their followers against the law. ¹²For they teach that God is not present in the temple, and that Jesus is the Messiah. ¹³Furthermore, they teach that he is exalted to the right hand of the Almighty, and so they blaspheme the Name." ¹⁴Then the chief priests demanded that Matthias and James give a defense.

¹⁵And Matthias, filled with the Spirit, addressed the council with these words: ¹⁶"My brothers, we need not speak in our own defense, for all the people have observed us from the day of our Lord's resurrection until now, how we have lived among the poor of Jerusalem and in the villages nearby, ¹⁷following the way of life and renouncing the way of destruction, at peace with all men. ¹⁸We have devoted ourselves to fasting and prayer, taking part in the festivals of our people in strict observance of the law, and awaiting the appearance of our Lord and Savior. ¹⁹Now we are called before you by hypocrites who deliver us to the very ones they despise.

²⁰Know that the Lord could deliver us from them and from you, but he has brought us here to testify and to fulfill the scriptures. ²¹Therefore hear the word of the Lord concerning the chief priests, the Pharisees, and the other parties who have rejected Christ Jesus:

²²When David cried, 'My God, why hast thou forsaken me?' and his garments were divided, was it not a prophecy of destruction, not only of the wicked of at that time, but also of this generation? ²³For our Lord himself cried these words from the cross, while some of you looked on and mocked, and you did not fear God even when he rent the garment of the temple veil.

[10–14] The reference to Paul alludes to previous actions of the Sanhedrin (Acts 23), and the death of James at the hands of scribes and Pharisees is detailed in the previous chapter here. The content of the charge is similar to that brought against Paul (Acts 21:28). Although Sadducees and Pharisees disagreed about many fundamental issues, they were united in their passionate defense of the name of God, which represented God's character. To exalt any other god, much less any human (as they believed Jesus to be) to "the right hand of the Almighty" was to claim equality with God, and such blasphemy was punishable by death. The minor charge here of dishonoring the temple was still near to blasphemy given the belief in God's presence there. Christians taught that God's presence should be understood in terms of Holy Spirit in the heart of the believer.

[15] The following speech of Matthias is an explication of Psalm 22. The psalm begins with David's expression of dereliction, including the famous quote delivered by Jesus from the cross, and ends with the promise of salvation to the nations. The confrontational style of Matthias here is even more bold than other speeches recorded in Acts; this is intended to reflect the more radical, prophet-driven approach of a radical community of believers like that proposed here for Matthias and James.

[16–18] These details summarize the *Didache,* which includes much of the teaching of Jesus from the Sermon on the Mount (Matt 5–7) and extends it in other specific and strict ways. The document begins with a contrast between the "way of life" and the "way of death."

[**19**] As noted above, the Essenes considered the temple administration corrupt, so a denunciation to the Sanhedrin would in their minds have to involve a compromise of principle in the interest of justice.

[**20–23**] It is an intriguing possibility that the cry of Jesus from the cross was not a cry of despair—at least not *only* a cry of despair—but a cry of judgment. Jesus understood himself to be a representative of the nation, and his quotation of David in Psalm 22 can be applied to both the king and the nation. Moreover, just after Jesus quoted the Psalm, the Spirit of God symbolically left the temple when the curtain was torn. Whether or not modern scholars are correct in interpreting the Gospel text this way,[3] such associations between biblical texts and events were possible, even typical, among rabbis of the time. Matthias, in other words, is speaking authentically in this context.

3. Schmidt, "Cry," 145–53.

---

[24] And after this, when he raised Jesus from the dead, and he appeared before many witnesses, you still would not turn to him. [25] Since that time the Spirit has made us bold to bear witness in words and in deeds that he is the Christ, seated at the right hand of God, and that he will soon return in glory. [26] You bring judgment on yourselves, seeking to destroy his messengers as you did once the prophets, stoning some or giving them over to the Romans, mocking others or ignoring them.

[27] And because you have done nothing new, but only repeated your wickedness of old, the Lord does not send you a new word but repeats one of old. [28] For after David, speaking for the nation, says that he is forsaken, he continues, 'The poor shall eat and be satisfied, those who seek him shall praise the Lord.' [29] Now who comes to the table but the poor, whom you have despised and rejected? [30] So the same scripture proclaims, 'All the ends of the earth shall turn to the Lord; and all the families of the nations shall worship before him.' [31] Now who are these families but the Gentiles, whom you regard as unclean and unworthy? [32] And what of the dominion that you hope will come when God destroys these your enemies and makes you rule in their place? [33] 'For dominion belongs to the Lord, and he rules over the nations.' [34] So it is not you, but the Lord who reigns, [35] as the scripture says: 'To him, indeed, shall all bow down. Posterity will serve him; future generations will be told about the Lord, and proclaim his deliverance to a people yet unborn, saying that he has done it.' [36] You doctors of the law, you guides of the people, your eyes are closed to these words of David your king, who after he sinned was blind until he was told by Nathan, 'Thou are the man.'

[24–29] The poor, especially in Luke-Acts, are understood not only as the economically disadvantaged but largely, due to their circumstances, as those who depend utterly on God. The renunciation of possessions to form a community (Acts 2, 4) is a dramatic expression of this dependence. Matthias now applies it to all who likewise acknowledge their need for God's salvation, namely, the nations who are henceforth included in the proclamation of the gospel.

[30–36] The reference to his audience as "doctors" and "guides" is of course ironic, and it is followed by a sharply-pointed reference to David's blindness before the prophet exposes the king's adultery (2 Sam 12:7).

---

³⁷So David learned humility, and the son of David, the heir to his kingdom, likewise came as a servant, and in your pride you did not know him. ³⁸Now you have rejected the Lord and his prophets once more, so once more you will be forsaken, along with the temple and all that you have built with your hands, ³⁹while the nations will gather the blessings meant for you, until such time as you repent. ⁴⁰And may that be soon, before the day that Christ Jesus comes from the clouds in glory to gather his own."

⁴¹The chief priests and Pharisees on the council, when they heard Matthias, agreed that he and James should die. ⁴²So they took them out to stone them. ⁴³And because Matthias, an unlearned man, had dared to quote scripture to them, they mocked him, ⁴⁴saying, "When will he die, and his name perish?" For in Hebrew, the word "when" is the same as the name Matthias.

⁴⁵But as Matthias and James were being stoned, they lifted up their eyes to heaven and begged the Lord to forgive their persecutors and to bring them to repentance. ⁴⁶When the believers who were together in Jerusalem and Bethany learned of their deaths and of their bold words before the council, they were strengthened in their faith, and not one followed the rebels. ⁴⁷But the scribes and Pharisees continued to look for an opportunity to accuse them, and as the war drew near, the hatred of the rebels grew.

[37–40] The *Didache* ends, "Then shall the world behold the Lord coming on the clouds of heaven" (16:8). As in many passages in Luke-Acts, the condemnation of the Jewish religious authorities is sharp, and grows ever sharper as the Spirit moves from them to the Gentiles—but never without hope held out that the Jews will turn to Christ. This perpetual tension is a dominant theme in Luke's writing,[4] and so it continues here.

[41–44] An intriguing passage in the Babylonian Talmud (*See* primary sources below) reports the first-century execution for blasphemy of a "Mattai" who was a "student" of "Yeshu" with this mockery of his name. The individual could be Matthias, but probably not Matthew, because the execution would have to take place before the war of AD 66–74, leaving inadequate time for the composition of the Gospel. Yeshu was a common enough name and could be a teacher other than Jesus. But once again, the pieces can be fitted together in a plausible whole that fits this context.

[45–47] As in Acts, martyrs are shown to be innocent, while their persecutors are ineffective. In most persecutions throughout history, killing the leaders tends to strengthen and multiply the followers—suggesting that the real motive is not remedial, but punitive.

---

4. Marguerat, *First Christian Historian*, 229; Tannehill, *Narrative Unity*, 344–57.

PRIMARY SOURCES

Babylonian Talmud (AD 500) *Sanhedrin* 43a: Our Rabbis taught: Yeshu had five disciples, Matthai, Nakai, Nezer, Buni and Todah. When Matthai was brought [before the court] he said to them [the judges], Shall Matthai be executed? Is it not written, *Matthai* [when] *shall I come and appear before God?* (Ps 42.2b). Thereupon they retorted; Yes, Matthai shall be executed, since it is written, *When Matthai* [when] *shall* [he] *die and his name perish.* (Ps 41.5b).[5]

---

5. *The Babylonian Talmud* is quoted from the translation by Schachter.

11

Jerusalem and the Temple are Destroyed

1 Now came a terrible time for all the Jews in Galilee and Judea, and a time of great suffering for the church. ²For soon after the death of Matthias and James son of Alphaeus, word came to Jerusalem concerning the deaths of Paul and Peter, and then the council occurred. ³By that time, rebels were already gathering in Galilee, and because the believers there would not join with them, many had to flee, leaving houses and lands, and later returned to nothing, their possessions having been destroyed.

⁴In Jerusalem, after the apostles were sent out, Simeon rose up and prophesied, ⁵"Now, says the Lord, I have set my face against Jerusalem, and I send my servants to the nations to announce the good news of salvation. ⁶Those who remain, looking to the teachers of the law and to false messiahs, will see only destruction. ⁷Therefore, quickly, leave all that you own and come out from among them, and go to the place of refuge I have prepared for you in Perea across the Jordan." ⁸So Simeon, and more than a thousand of the believers from Jerusalem and Judea, went to the vicinity of Pella in Perea. ⁹The believers there welcomed as many as they could into their houses, and those who were able bought new houses and lands. ¹⁰Even so, food was scarce, so that many suffered in the years of the war, and some moved away where they could find relatives or other places of safety. ¹¹So has the church of Jerusalem scattered, although many remain in Pella to this day, along with Simeon and other leaders.

[1–3] Interestingly, the rebellion of the Jews was limited to their homeland, and there is no record of reprisals against Jews in Rome or elsewhere. Evidently the Romans believed that the war was attributable to local rebel leaders. Nor is there any evidence that Jews of the Diaspora (those outside Palestine) lent military or financial aid. Within the country, however, the rebels were strong, and quick to punish those who did not support them.

[4–7] Eusebius reports that believers were directed from Jerusalem to Pella by a prophecy, but he offers further details. Here the prophecy is put in the mouth of Simeon, and its content is a logical extension of the speech of Matthias in chapter 10. The wording "set his face" is an allusion to Luke 9:51–52, in which Jesus "set his face to go to Jerusalem. And he sent messengers ahead of him." Just as this signals the fulcrum of geographical movement in the Gospel, so Simeon's words here, coupled with the council's commission of the apostles as messengers, signal movement now "to the ends of the earth."

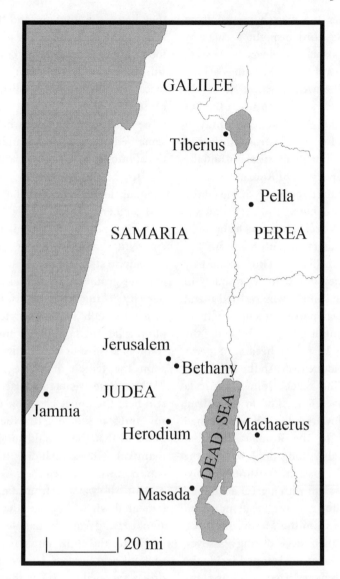

GALILEE

Tiberius

Pella

SAMARIA   PEREA

Jerusalem
Bethany

JUDEA

Jamnia

Herodium

DEAD SEA

Machaerus

Masada

|_____| 20 mi

Map 4: Palestine

[8–11] While we have no historical record of the transfer of the Jerusalem church moved to Pella and it is difficult to estimate numbers, the descent of hundreds or even scores on any town would present a long term hardship to all those involved. Presumably some came with the means to reduce the burden on local believers, and the wording here echoes that of Acts 2:45; 4:34–37, where the more affluent sold property to provide for the group. Even so, it is likely that the protraction of the war and of the Lord's return eventually required further scattering. As tensions continued into the second century between Rome and militant Jewish factions, Christians for the most part steered clear of trouble spots like Jerusalem.

[12]Soon after the church moved from Jerusalem, the Lord brought a calamity upon the Jews such has never been seen, even in the days of the wicked kings of long ago. [13]For in the twelfth year of Nero, rebels among the Jews began to attack the Romans, and the high priest ceased prayers and sacrifices for the emperor. [14]In fear of the rebels, Agrippa fled Jerusalem, and the Jews defeated a legion of Roman troops in battle. [15]This raised the hopes of the rebels, and many joined them. [16]But Vespasian was sent to crush the rebellion, and he brought three legions, together with many auxiliaries, along with his son Titus, to destroy the Jews. [17]They began their conquest in Galilee, where some towns resisted them, and others gave up without a fight. [18]Then, after much tumult in Rome following the death of Nero, Vespasian became emperor and left Titus alone to crush the rebellion.

[19]The leading rebels, John of Giscala and Simon Bar Giora, fled to Jerusalem; and their followers killed all who wished to surrender to the Romans, together with their rivals among the Jews. [20]In the first year of Vespasian, the Romans surrounded Jerusalem with a great army, and they looked down upon the temple and the upper city from the Mount of Olives. [21]They began their siege during Passover, so that thousands were trapped inside the city. [22]When anyone tried to escape, the Romans captured them and crucified them within sight of those within, as many as five hundred in a single day. [23]Meanwhile, the soldiers destroyed the land around Jerusalem, cutting down all of the trees and burning the gardens and crops.

[24]Inside the city, the followers of John and Simon hated each other more than they hated the Romans, and they continued to kill each other, even burning the food supply for the entire city. [25]As a result, there was terrible famine and much disease, so that more Jews died from these causes than from fighting the Romans. [26]The rebels took by force what little food remained, leaving women and children to die of hunger.

[27]In the second year of the siege, the Romans broke through the outer wall; and soldiers, killing all they could find and setting fires, destroyed much of the city. [28]But a group of rebels led by Eleazar ben Simon still held the temple area, while another group led by Simon held the upper city. [29]After two months, the Romans broke through to the temple, and after plundering the holy places and relics, the soldiers set fire to a building nearby, and soon the temple itself began to burn. [30]While these events took place, those who still held the upper city looked on in sorrow and fear, knowing that the temple was lost and that they would soon die. [31]And many other Jews, including those already captured who awaited their fate and those outside who watched from afar, wailed and lamented when they saw the flames and smoke rising from the temple.

[32]After the entire city was in the hands of Titus and the fires had cooled, he gave orders for what was left of the temple to be torn down stone by stone, until nothing remained. [33]Thus the word of the Lord was fulfilled, and the temple, which had stood for a thousand years, was destroyed in a matter of days, [34]because of the hard hearts of the people, who turned to lawlessness against Rome rather than to salvation in Christ Jesus.

---

[12] The narrative here is a summary of the lengthy account of Flavius Josephus (*The Wars of the Jews* 2–7). Josephus, a Jew who initially took part in the rebellion in the north and then served as a negotiator for the Romans, offers a pro-Roman perspective, consistently blaming rebel leaders for the slaughter. He even goes so far as to attribute the burning of the

temple to out-of-control soldiers rather than to Titus himself, who almost certainly ordered the destruction. The more brief account by Roman historian Dio Cassius helps to balance the picture.

[13–18] Following the death of Nero, Rome was thrown into turmoil. After the "year of four emperors," Vespasian took control in AD 69. This distraction undoubtedly fed the hopes of the Jewish rebels. Still, apart from a few early victories against fairly small and unprepared forces, the Jewish War was not a seesaw battle but a methodical slaughter, as an overwhelming Roman force moved from the north toward the inevitable siege of Jerusalem.

[19–34] The narrative here contrasts rebellion with lawlessness, but it also comes close to attributing the destruction of Jerusalem and its temple to the Jews' rejection of Christ. The early church began to make this transition in the second century, as we have seen, by blaming the carnage on the martyrdom of James. While the predictions of Jesus recorded in the Gospels urge repentance, they do not link Jerusalem's demise directly to his, and he certainly never encouraged anything stronger than verbal persuasion in the face of opposition. Luke elsewhere includes pronouncements of judgment on the people, but it puts the verdict and penalty entirely in God's hands (Acts 18:8; 19:41–44; 21:13, 22, 28). It is perhaps the greatest shame in the history of Christianity that Jewish rejection of Jesus became an excuse to persecute the Jews as a people. How did this happen? As Jews gradually became the minority group, they became subjects of the same suspicion or resentment once directed toward Christians, or toward "the other" in any culture, and for the same reasons: isolation, mysterious practices, and economic success. Then at some point, after Christians acquired secular power and abandoned their early pacifism, the belief that God had punished the Jews for rejecting Christ gave way to a belief that Christians could themselves be instruments of God's punishment. The late fourth century saw the beginning of an appalling history, first with destruction of synagogues and expulsion from countries, then with massacres during the Crusades, and finally with the complicity of many Christians during the Holocaust. In the New Testament period, the notion of Christians as instruments of God's judgment was unimaginable, not because believers lacked power but because they renounced it. The "upside down kingdom," according to its Founder, would prevail not by force but by the Spirit acting through witnesses whose lives would embody mercy, kindness, and service.

---

³⁵In all, because so many Jews had been trapped in the city, more than a million died, either from crucifixion outside the walls, or battle and starvation within. ³⁶Of those who survived, many more were crucified, and a hundred thousand were made captive. ³⁷Some of these were sent to be killed in the arena by gladiators or by wild beasts, but most were made slaves to work in the mines or to labor until their deaths in lands far away. ³⁸A few of the rebels escaped, fleeing to the desert and to the fortresses of Herodium, Machaerus, and Masada, where Titus pursued them until all resistance was destroyed.

[35–38] The last stronghold of the rebellion, the desert fortress of Masada overlooking the Dead Sea, held out until AD 73, when the Romans forced Jewish captives to build a gigantic siege ramp to its walls. When they broke through, they found the corpses of 960 Jews who chose suicide over Roman conquest. Despite the decisive Roman victory, unrest continued;

and the Jews revolted once again in AD 132 under another false messiah, Simon bar Co-chba. When they were defeated in 135, the emperor Hadrian expelled Jews from Jerusalem and built a pagan temple on the site of the Jewish temple. The Jews did not achieve political independence in the land until 1948.

---

³⁹Of the parties of the Jews, one of the Pharisees, Johanan ben Zakai, opposed the rebellion and so obtained permission from Vespasian to move the council to Jamnia by the sea to study the law there. ⁴⁰But as for Jerusalem, the city now lies desolate, awaiting the return of Christ Jesus its king.

---

[39] Within twenty years of the destruction of the temple, the Jews under Johanan's leadership had ratified the canon of scripture (for Christians, the Old Testament) and reconstituted Judaism around the study of the law. Ben Zakai was an important contributor to the Mishnah, which was taking shape during this time. By the fifth century, the Talmud was completed in Babylon, which had become a center of Jewish study. There were many other important Jewish writings produced during this era, but the three key components of Scripture, Mishnah, and Talmud may be seen as concentric circles, with Scripture at the center and the other texts as layers of interpretive commentary by the great rabbis.

[40] It is not clear how complete was the devastation of Jerusalem, or how quickly the city was rebuilt before the revolt in AD 132. The time frame supposed here would place Luke's writing very close to the end of the rebellion, so it is likely that the city and the surrounding countryside were in complete ruins and sparsely inhabited.

PRIMARY SOURCES

The Church Migrates to Pella

Eusebius (AD 325) *Ecclesiastical History* 3.5.3: The people of the church of Jerusalem were commanded by an oracle given by revelation before the war to those in the city who were worthy of it to depart and dwell in one of the cities of Perea which they called Pella. To it those who believed on Christ migrated from Jerusalem, that when holy men had altogether deserted the royal capital of the Jews and the whole land of Judea, the judgment of God might at last overtake them for all their crimes against the Christ and his Apostles, and all that generation of the wicked be utterly blotted out from among men.

The Destruction of the Temple

Josephus (AD 95) *Wars of the Jews* 6.249–266: So Titus retired into the tower of Antonia, and resolved to storm the temple the next day, early in the morning, with his whole army, and to encamp round about the holy house. But as for that house, God had, for certain, long ago doomed it to the fire; and now that fatal day was come . . . one of the soldiers, without staying for any orders, and without any concern or dread upon him at so great an undertaking, and being hurried on by a certain divine fury, snatched somewhat out of the materials that were on fire, and being lifted up by another soldier, he set fire to a golden window, through which there was a passage to the rooms that were round about the holy house, on the north side of it. As the flames went upward, the Jews made a great clamor, such as so mighty an affliction required, and ran together to prevent it; and now they spared not their lives any longer, nor suffered anything to restrain their force, since that holy house was perishing, for whose sake it was that they kept such a guard about it. . . . Then did Caesar, both by calling to the soldiers that were fighting, with a loud voice, and by giving a signal to them with his right hand, order them to quench the fire. But they did not hear what he said . . . as still some of them were distracted with fighting, and others with passion. But as for the legions that came running thither, neither any persuasions nor any threatenings could restrain their violence . . . and when they were come near the holy house, they made as if they did not so much as hear Caesar's orders to the contrary; but they encouraged those that were before them to set it on fire. As for the seditious, they were in too great distress already to afford their assistance [towards quenching the fire]; they were everywhere slain, and everywhere beaten; and as for a great part of the people, they were weak and without arms, and had their throats cut wherever they were caught. Now round about the altar lay dead bodies heaped one upon another, as at the steps going up to it ran a great quantity of their blood, whither also the dead bodies that were slain above [on the altar] fell down. And now, since Caesar was no way able to restrain the enthusiastic fury of the soldiers, and the fire proceeded on more and more, he went into the holy place of the temple, with his commanders, and saw it, with what was in it. . . . But as the flame had not as yet reached to its inward parts, but was still consuming the rooms that were about the holy house, and Titus supposing what the fact was, that the house itself might yet he saved, he came in haste and endeavored to persuade the soldiers to quench the fire . . . yet were their passions too hard . . . as was their hatred of the Jews, and a certain vehement inclination to fight them, too hard for them also. Moreover, the hope of plunder induced many to go on, as having this opinion, that all the places within were full of money, and as seeing that all round about it was made of gold. And besides, one of those that went into the place prevented Caesar, when he ran so hastily out to restrain the soldiers, and threw the fire upon the hinges of the gate, in the dark; whereby the flame burst out from within the holy house itself immediately, when the commanders retired, and Caesar with them, and when nobody any longer forbade those that were without to set fire to it. And thus was the holy house burnt down, without Caesar's approbation.[1]

The Destruction of Jerusalem

Josephus (AD 95) *Wars of the Jews* 7.1.1: Now as soon as the army had no more people to slay or to plunder, because there remained none to be the objects of their fury, (for they would not have spared any, had there remained any other work to be done,) Caesar gave orders that they should now demolish the entire city and temple, but should leave as many of the towers standing as were of the greatest eminency; that is, Phasaelus, and Hippicus, and Mariamne; and so much of the wall as enclosed the city on the west side. This wall was spared, in order to afford a camp for such as were to lie in garrison, as were the towers also

1. Josephus is quoted from the translation by Whiston.

spared, in order to demonstrate to posterity what kind of city it was, and how well fortified, which the Roman valor had subdued; but for all the rest of the wall, it was so thoroughly laid even with the ground by those that dug it up to the foundation, that there was left nothing to make those that came thither believe it had ever been inhabited. This was the end which Jerusalem came to by the madness of those that were for innovations; a city otherwise of great magnificence, and of mighty fame among all mankind.

Josephus (AD 95) *Wars of the Jews* 6.1.1: And truly the very view itself of the country was a melancholy thing; for those places which were before adorned with trees and pleasant gardens were now become a desolate country every way, and its trees were all cut down: nor could any foreigner that had formerly seen Judea and the most beautiful suburbs of the city, and now saw it as a desert, but lament and mourn sadly at so great a change: for the war had laid all the signs of beauty quite waste: nor if any one that had known the place before, had come on a sudden to it now, would he have known it again; but though he were at the city itself, yet would he have inquired for it notwithstanding.

12

Simeon Addresses the Delay of Christ's Coming

1 When word reached the church in Pella that the temple was destroyed, all mourned, especially for the suffering of their countrymen. ³For there was not a family among the believers that had not lost members, either from the fighting or from famine and disease. ³And many of those who lived were sold into slavery, while others were never heard from again. ⁴In spite of their great sorrow, however, the saints were comforted by hearing the words of Christ Jesus concerning the last things, believing that what had occurred in Jerusalem was the sign of his return in glory. ⁵Some no longer worked or even ate food, gathering instead in houses to pray and await the Lord's coming. ⁶Therefore, Simeon and the elders began likewise to fast and pray, inquiring of the Lord whether this was the end, and what they should do. ⁷And after three days, Simeon gathered all the saints and said to them,

---

[1] There is no historical record of the church in Pella. Undoubtedly such a group of refugees from Jerusalem suffered greatly at the loss of the temple, but perhaps more severely at the loss of friends, neighbors, and relatives left behind.

[3–5] Paul apparently faced a similar problem with believers in Thessalonica who misunderstood his teaching about the end (2 Thess 2:1–3; 3:6–13).

[6–7] Simeon's exhortation makes reference to several signs of the end recorded in the Gospels, and he stresses the responsibility of believers not to predict the end but to be found doing God's will.

Most modern believers are familiar with attempts to account for the delay of Christ's second coming by an "already/not yet" scenario. In this understanding, some of the biblical predictions were fulfilled during the lives of the first generation of believers, while other predictions await fulfillment at some future date, just before the end. Such explanations introduce as many questions as they answer, and Christians since the first century have continued to propose new solutions. One of these is *preterism*, which maintains that the Gospel predictions were fulfilled in part (except the resurrection of the dead and the Second Coming) or in full (symbolically) in the events of AD 70. Some argue that this view was present in the early church, but the evidence is weak. The early works excerpted below illustrate a belief that the end was near but that certain conditions, such as further evangelism or greater purity in the church, needed to be met. Others believed that reference to the "day" of his coming might (based on Psalm 90:4) be interpreted as a thousand years, and that therefore the end might be delayed by millennia.

There are many interpretive schemes possible, and the point here is not to take sides in a modern debate but to let Simeon's speech suggest one possible avenue of early speculation. In order to remain true to the intent of Scripture, however, any explanation of the end must stress faithful obedience, not predictive accuracy, as the responsibility of the waiting Church.

---

[8]"Brothers and sisters, it has not been revealed to us that the Lord will return soon. [9]Now we all know the signs of his coming, and that the chief of these is the destruction of Jerusalem. [10]Nevertheless, the Lord did not say that this was the last war, but rather that it would be the beginning of the end, and that the time of the Gentiles must be fulfilled. [11]What could this mean but that more time must pass? [12]And who knows the number of days? [13]Moreover, Christ Jesus told us to look for other signs, and the chief of these is that the good news will be preached to the nations. [14]Has not the Spirit sent out the apostles, some who still journey, and do they not continually tell us of new lands where Christ is not yet proclaimed? [15]Despite our sorrow, should we rejoice for the Lord's return before all the harvest is gathered in?

[16]Furthermore, the Lord said that no one knows the day, not even the Son, so who are we to claim such knowledge? [17]No, as the Lord taught, it is our duty to be watchful, and this does not mean to wait in idleness but to be found in faith and righteousness, doing his will. [18]And what is his will but to preach to the nations, to obey him in all things, to be one, and to endure with joy whatever suffering is before us? [19]So let us be on guard, as our Lord taught us, not as those who seek signs, but rather as those who seek righteousness. [20]In this manner, we will be found ready, whether we are guided by signs to look for his coming or are taken unawares. [21]May the Lord come soon!"

[8–14] The intent here is to anticipate the coming chapters, which chronicle the missions of the apostles. Simeon's words are derived largely from the Gospels: V. 9 = Mark 13:2; v. 10a = Mark 13:8; v. 10b = Luke 21:24; v. 13 = Mark 13:9; v. 16 = Mark 13:32; v. 17 = Luke 21:34; v. 18 = Luke 21:19; v. 19 = Matthew 6:33.

[15] As the early church texts excerpted below suggest, the need for an unknown number of people to be saved was the most common, and presumably most persuasive, explanation for the delay.

[16–17] The same theme is common in other early church documents, e.g., *1 Clement* 28:1; *Didache* 16:1–2; *Epistle of Barnabas* 4:9–14; 21:2–6; Ignatius, *Epistle to the Ephesians* 11:1.

[18–21] This expression (Aramaic *Maranatha* = our Lord, come!), which appears in several early documents (1 Cor 16:22; *Didache* 10:6; probably behind Rev 22:20), clearly represents the common hope of believers in the middle decades of the first century, when Aramaic was the dominant language of the church.

²²The church heard Simeon's words with gratitude, and those who had been idle returned to their labors. ²³The believers in Pella continued to be strong in the Spirit and to grow in number, although many moved to other parts of the country. ²⁴At the same time, bands of rebels who had escaped from the Romans roamed throughout Galilee, Judea, and beyond the Jordan, robbing the poor of their crops and killing many who had not joined with them, including many believers. ²⁵So the judgment of the Lord fell not only upon Jerusalem and the temple, but also upon the entire land. ²⁶Yet still the hearts of the people were hardened, and the Spirit began to do greater works in other lands.

[22–26] In the circumstances proposed for this document, Luke is writing just as the major fighting of the war has ended, not long after the fall of Masada. Mop-up operations undoubtedly continued, along with brigandage and reprisals against rebels' perceived enemies among the Jewish people. The fact that information about the activities of Christians in Palestine is scarce from this period suggests that believers may have been barely holding their own. Even apart from persecution, the entire country was devastated, its population reduced, and farming interrupted. It is unlikely that the arid region of Pella could sustain for long the large influx of believers from Jerusalem. These factors combine to help explain the decline, or at least silence, of the late first-century church in its place of origin. From this point, therefore, the focus of this document returns to the apostles sent out in chapter 8 to take the gospel to "the ends of the earth."

PRIMARY SOURCES

Delay of the Parousia (Second Coming)

2 Peter 3:4, 3:8–9: Where is the promise of his coming? For ever since our ancestors died, all things continue as they were from the beginning of creation! . . . But do not ignore this one fact, beloved, that with the Lord one day is like a thousand years, and a thousand years are like one day. The Lord is not slow about his promise, as some think of slowness, but is patient with you, not wanting any to perish, but all to come to repentance.

Revelation 6:9–11: When he opened the fifth seal, I saw under the altar the souls of those who had been slaughtered for the word of God and for the testimony they had given/ they cried out with a loud voice, "Sovereign Lord, holy and true, how long will it be before you judge and avenge our blood on the inhabitants of the earth?" They were each given a white robe and told to rest a little longer, until the number would be complete both of their fellow servants and of their brothers and sisters, who were soon to be killed as they themselves had been killed.

Clement of Rome (AD 96) *1 Clement* 23:3–5: Let this Scripture be far from us in which he says "Wretched are the double-minded, who doubt in their soul and say 'We have heard these things even in the days of our fathers, and behold we have grown old, and none of these things has happened to us.' Oh, foolish men, compare yourselves to a tree: take a vine, first it sheds its leaves, then there comes a bud, then a leaf, then a flower, and after this the unripe grape, then the full bunch." See how in a little time the fruit of the tree comes to ripeness. Truly his will shall be quickly and suddenly accomplished, as the Scripture also bears witness that "he shall come quickly and shall not tarry; and the Lord shall suddenly come to his temple, and the Holy One for whom ye look."

Clement of Rome (AD 130–160) *2 Clement* 12:1, 5–6: Let us then wait for the kingdom of God, from hour to hour, in love and righteousness, seeing that we know not the day of the appearing of God. . . . When a brother sees a sister he should have no thought of her as female, nor she of him as male. When you do this, he says, the kingdom of my Father will come.

Shepherd of Hermas (AD 150) *Similitudes* 9.5.1–2: And on that day the building was finished, but the tower was not completed, for it was going to be built on to, and there was a pause in the building. . . . I said to the shepherd: "Why, Sir," said I, "was the building of the tower not completed?" "The tower," said he, "cannot yet be completed unless its lord come and test this building, in order that if some stones prove to be rotten, he may change them, for the tower is being built according to his will."

Shepherd of Hermas, Similitudes 9.31.2: But this world and the vanities of their riches must be cut away from them, and then they will be meet for the kingdom of God.

Shepherd of Hermas, Similitudes 5.2.5; 5.5.2: After a time the master of the servant and the field came, and entered into the vineyard, and seeing the vineyard beautifully fenced, and moreover dug, and all the weeds pulled up and vines fertile, he was greatly pleased at the acts of the servant. . . . The absence of the Master is the time which remains before his coming.

Shepherd of Hermas, Similitudes 9.14.2; 10.4.4: For this cause also there was a pause in the building, in order that, if they repent, they may go away into the building of the tower. But if they do not repent then others will enter and they will finally be rejected. . . . Therefore do good deeds, all you have learnt of the Lord, lest the building of the tower be finished while you delay to do them. For the work of the building has been broken off for your sake. Unless therefore you hasten to do right the tower will be finished and you will be shut out.

Shepherd of Hermas, Visions 3.8.9: And I began to ask her about the times, if the end were yet. But she cried out with a loud voice saying, "Foolish man, do you not see the tower still being built? Whenever therefore the building of the tower has been finished, the end comes. But it will quickly be built up; ask me nothing more. This reminder and the renewal of your spirits is sufficient for you and for the saints.

Irenaeus (AD 180) *Against Heresies* 5:28:3: For in as many days as this world was made, in so many thousand years shall it be concluded. And for this reason the Scripture says: Thus the heaven and the earth were finished, and all their adornment. And God brought to a conclusion upon the sixth day the works that He had made; and God rested upon the seventh day from all His works. This is an account of the things formerly created, as also it is a prophecy of what is to come. For the day of the Lord is as a thousand years; and in six days created things were completed: it is evident, therefore, that they will come to an end at the sixth thousand year.

13

Apostles Martyred prior to the Council

1 Now, dear Theophilus, I will return to the beginning, when the twelve and the other apostles first went out from the last council in Jerusalem, ²to tell in order what the Spirit has accomplished through them, even in their deaths, to spread the good news of salvation throughout the world.

³The first of the twelve to be killed was James son of Zebedee, in the second year of Claudius, who was beheaded by Agrippa to please the Jews. ⁴During that time the twelve came and went from Jerusalem, traveling alone or together to many lands, taking with them other apostles who are known to you from my second book. ⁵Peter preached in the provinces of the north, and he traveled numerous times to Rome, where he spent many years building up the believers before he was killed. ⁶The next to be killed, in the tenth year of Nero, were Matthias and James son of Alphaeus. ⁷As

a result, at the time of the council, John, Andrew, Philip, Bartholomew, Matthew, Judas son of James, Simon the Zealot, and Thomas all still lived, but some of these have died since, as this book will tell.

⁸There were many other apostles who are not numbered among the twelve, the chief of whom were James the brother of the Lord, and Paul. ⁹I have written of the death of James, who gave guidance to the church in Jerusalem for many years and was beloved by all the people. ¹⁰As for Paul, he journeyed throughout Asia, Macedonia, Greece, and even to Spain, establishing churches and often suffering persecution from both Jews and Greeks, until he was beheaded in Rome. ¹¹Many of those who traveled with Paul still live, but some of his coworkers have been killed. ¹²The first of these was Barnabas, who was beloved by the twelve and all the saints for his faith and courage.

[1–2] This chapter includes some review, serving as a transition to the missionary activities of the apostles and resuming the chronology which begins with the council in midyear AD 65. The renewal of direct address to Theophilus reinforces the notion of accurate, ordered accounting. The text also reiterates familiar themes: Spirit guidance, boldness, unity, and church growth through suffering, especially of the martyrs.

[3–5] Chapter 6 did not recount Peter's missionary activity except to establish his recurrent presence in Rome. While in Rome he wrote to believers from his previous missionary journey to "Pontus, Galatia, Cappadocia, Asia, and Bithynia" (1 Pet 1:1), provinces which span the northern half of Asia Minor.

[6–12] Barnabas is a key figure in the New Testament. He first appears as the one who heroically risked introducing the new convert Saul (later named Paul) to the Jerusalem church when many feared that Saul was a spy (Acts 9:26–30). Barnabas traveled extensively with Paul, helping to establish the important church in Antioch; but he is not mentioned after splitting with Paul in order join his cousin John Mark on his home island of Cyprus (Acts 15:36–40). The fact that Paul later makes reference to Mark without Barnabas (Col 4:10) suggests that by this time (probably late in Paul's first Roman imprisonment, AD 60–62), Barnabas had died.

The *Epistle of Barnabas,* in the collection known as the Apostolic Fathers, was long attributed to him, but scholars now consider it a late first-century composition from someone in Alexandria, writing in his name. The *Acts of Barnabas* is a fifth-century document, and the *Gospel of Barnabas*, although it may contain older material, is largely medieval. While these documents are too late to give us historic details about Barnabas, their existence confirms the importance of his name in the early church.

---

¹³After he parted company with Paul in Antioch, he took John Mark with him to Cyprus, and through them the Spirit added many to the church. ¹⁴After some years, John Mark left to join Peter in Rome, while Barnabas continued to preach, confounding his opponents in the synagogue and bearing witness to both Jews and Gentiles by his good works. ¹⁵But the Jews of Salamis were jealous that Barnabas persuaded so many of their number to turn to Christ Jesus. ¹⁶Therefore, one day they formed a mob and took Barnabas from the synagogue to a place outside the city, where they beat him; and when he refused to deny the Lord, they stoned him.

¹⁷Silas, who had served with both Paul and Peter for many years, came at last to Corinth, where he led the church until the tenth year of Nero.

[13–16] This account of the martyrdom of Barnabas is based on one of several late traditions, none of which are certain. It is, however, typical of the kind of opposition faced earlier by Paul and Barnabas in Cyprus and elsewhere (Acts 13–14). In Salamis, Cyprus, the reputed tomb of Barnabas is contained in a monastery built in the fifth century.

[17] Silas is another companion of Paul (Acts 15–18) whose later activities are unknown. He is identified with Sylvanus, who is a co-writer of Paul's Thessalonian correspondence (1 Thess 1:1, 2 Thess 1:1), a coworker of Paul in Corinth (2 Cor 1:19), and Peter's ghost writer (1 Pet 5:12). His work with Peter suggests that he was in Rome in the early 60s. Tradition places him in Corinth as its first bishop, which there is no reason to doubt, but this account supposes that he is with Peter when Paul visits Corinth (chapter 2 above) and returns to give leadership to the church until his death.

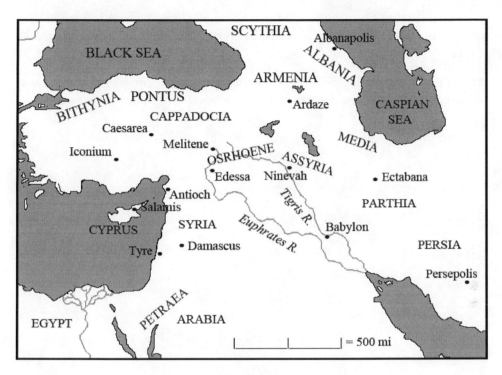

Map 5: Asia

[18]When certain Greek merchants there heard about the evil that Nero did in Rome, they saw an opportunity to make an example of Silas. [19]So they accused him of blasphemy against the gods, and incited a mob to stone him, [20]thinking that the believers would scatter and the merchants would increase in riches from the sin and luxury of that city. [21]No one dared to oppose them at that time, because all feared the emperor, [22]but the persecution soon ended and many more turned to the Lord, because they knew that Silas was a good and law-abiding man.

[23]Of the many apostles who were killed by Nero, together with hundreds of other believers there, it is not necessary to write further. [24]Likewise, many elders and believers from Judea and Galilee were killed, either put to the sword by the rebels, or stoned by Jews who say that those who follow Christ Jesus are blasphemers. [25]But the Spirit everywhere encouraged the saints, performing signs and wonders through the apostles, [26]refuting their opponents among both Jews and Greeks, and building up the church both in number and in faith, so that all were one and all hoped in Christ Jesus. [27]Even in Rome and Judea, where suffering at the hands of evil men was most severe and lasted the longest, the Spirit acted with the greatest power, [28]sowing the seed of so many witnesses into a harvest of yet more fruit.

[**18–22**] Other than a late tradition that he was martyred in Macedonia in the mid-60s, nothing is known of the circumstances of the death of Silas. The account here owes something to the merchant riot in Ephesus (Acts 19) that nearly resulted in Paul's death, and the knowledge that Corinth, as a wealthy port city with a reputation for decadence, would naturally contain many high-powered enemies of the church. Although there was no official empire-wide ban on Christianity until the third century, periodic local persecution was common; and word of Nero's violence could have supplied the pretense for the martyrdom of Silas.

[23–28] The wording here echoes that of previous passages, summarizing the themes that will now advance with the various trajectories of the apostles sent out from Jerusalem.

14

North to Ephesus with John

1 When those of the twelve who remained were sent out by the Spirit from Jerusalem, John went with Timothy to Ephesus. [2]John was gentle in spirit, having for many years devoted himself to prayer, provision for the poor, and care for Mary in her old age. [3]And although he was almost sixty years old, he was a large man and strong in body, [4]having in his youth been a fisherman who, together with James his brother, pulled great nets from the sea. [5]Now, after many years in Jerusalem, he was eager to reap a harvest of men in distant lands, as had the other apostles. [6]When John and Timothy reached Ephesus, the saints rejoiced that Timothy was restored to them after escaping Nero and traveling for many months, [7]and they were eager to honor John as one who had walked with the Lord. [8]Soon after they arrived, a messenger came to John from Lycomedes, a magistrate and a man of great substance in Ephesus.

---

[1] Chapter 8:29 above. The date of John's move to Ephesus is unknown, but it is unlikely that he moved there before the mid-60s, since he is not mentioned in Paul's later correspondence.

[2–5] Although there are no physical or character descriptions of John in scripture or tradition, the description here is not arbitrary. Given the emphasis on belief and love in John's Gospel and epistles, it is likely that his life embodied these priorities. The fact that Jesus commissioned him to care for his mother (John 19:26–27, chapter 9 above) also suggests that he was compassionate. Credible sources from the early church report that he lived into his nineties, suggesting a robust physical nature. Finally, it is reasonable to suppose that after years of caring for Mary while the other apostles traveled, he would be eager to take part in missionary activity.

[6–8] *The Acts of John*, which includes the story of Lycomedes and Cleopatra (chapters 17–26), was written in the mid-second century.[1] It is attributed to Leucius Charinus, a one-time companion of John whose writings were later condemned and their heretical portions removed. (Charinus was a Gnostic or Docetic, denying the humanity of Christ.) The two stories recounted here and in chapter 16 may be legendary; on the other hand, Leucius wrote within the living memory of eyewitnesses, and he names several individuals pre-

1. For a thorough introduction, see Klauck, *Apocryphal Acts*, 15–46.

sumably be known to the church in Ephesus who could verify or deny the accounts. The story of the raising of Cleopatra (a common name in the Hellenistic world after the famous Egyptian queen) is streamlined and modified here to preserve a plausible core from *The Acts of John*; details preserved include Lycomedes' prominence, his vision to summon John, the illness and death of Cleopatra, John's touching of her face, and the response of salvation for the household and many witnesses.

---

[9]At first the believers feared for John, but the messenger told them, "My master wishes you no harm. [10]On the contrary, he hopes for help from you, and wishes for the man named John to come to him in haste." [11]John immediately went with him to Lycomedes, who fell on his face before him and said, "For seven days, my beloved wife Cleopatra has been ill with a palsy. [12]First she shook in all her limbs, then her members became numb one by one, so that now I fear that she is near death. [13]But three nights ago in a dream, one in shining garments appeared to me in a dream, [14]saying to me, 'My servant, a man named John, will soon come to Ephesus; seek him among the Christians and ask from him whatever you wish.'" [15]Lycomedes took John to his inner chamber, where Cleopatra lay. [16]But when they entered the room, they saw that she was no longer breathing. Lycomedes, who loved her greatly, cried out that John was too late, and falling on the floor, said that he wished now to die as well. [17]But John wept with him and comforted him. [18]Then he knelt by the bed, laid his hands on Cleopatra, and prayed for an hour in silence, his tears falling on Cleopatra's hands. [19]Meanwhile, the servants and some other citizens of Ephesus gathered in the outer rooms, and even in the doorway. [20]Then John touched the face of Cleopatra and said, "In the name of the Lord Jesus, arise." [21]Immediately Cleopatra opened her eyes and sat upright, then began to move her arms and legs freely and to ask what had happened while she slept. [22]Lycomedes rose and leapt around the room for joy, embracing first Cleopatra, then John, and finally the servants and all those who had gathered in his house. [23]The next day he made a great feast, and all those of his household were baptized. [24]Word about Cleopatra spread quickly throughout the city, especially among the leading citizens who knew Lycomedes, so that many more believed in Christ Jesus.

[25]Some days after this, the elders brought to John a young girl who had drowned in the river outside the city. [26]The name of the girl was Aelia, and although she was only ten years old, she loved the Lord and was known among the saints for singing hymns in a pure voice.

[9–25] This story does not appear in any traditional account of John's ministry, but some readers will recognize Aelia and the other characters. The inclusion of such a story here reflects Luke's pattern of pairing characters in successive stories, often to show a contrast between responses: Zacchaeus follows the rich young ruler (Luke 18–19), Ananias follows Barnabas (Acts 4–5), the Ethiopian eunuch follows Simon the magician (Acts 8), etc. In this case, good things happen to bad people, then bad things happen to good people, then Christians make matters worse by attempting to explain God's reasons. The account here of John's response applies the style and pattern of his writings to the issue, stressing empathy over explanation.

[26] A similar description is offered in Acts 9:36–43 for a woman named Dorcas, who is raised by Peter.

²⁷When they brought her before John, together with her mother and father, he wept with them, and he prayed in silence over the child as he had with Cleopatra, while all waited. ²⁸After an hour, he rose from the body of Aelia and said to her mother and father, "Beloved, this child will not return to you."

²⁹Her mother and father bowed their heads and were silent, ³⁰but Menandros, one of the elders, said, "Why does the Lord raise the wife of Lycomedes, who was not a believer, but not this child, who loved the Lord? ³¹Moreover, her parents have long followed Christ Jesus, in prayer and faithfulness, and they have no other child. ³²What is the Lord's purpose in taking one so young?" ³³And John said, "Beloved, the Lord's purpose is always the same, in suffering or in peace, and that is for us to believe and to love one another. ³⁴Nor does the Lord take children; he only gives them, this one for ten years, another for one hundred years, and it is not for us to know why each is given for a different number of days. ³⁵So do not look for purpose, but weep. ³⁶Did not the Lord weep for Lazarus, even when he knew that in the next moment he would raise him up? ³⁷How much more, therefore, does the Lord now weep, and we with him, for Aelia? ³⁸For now the storm waters rise up over the heads of all who loved her, but the day is coming when the troubled sea will pass away, and there will remain only a river of healing. ³⁹By that river, those who love Aelia will find her, although the road may be long for them and covered in shadow."

⁴⁰But Menandros asked again, "How then shall we teach anyone concerning the Lord's will, if we cannot give a reason for the girl's death?" ⁴¹And John answered him, "Beloved, do not contend with the Lord, or with one another, as do the Greeks, but only believe, and love. ⁴²Otherwise you may heap up 'therefore' and 'because' until you cannot see suffering behind your many words. ⁴³The Lord would not have us justify suffering, but endure it. ⁴⁴You must learn from him who, although more innocent than any child, went willingly to his death. ⁴⁵Some of the Greeks wish to stop suffering, thinking to compel their gods by casting spells. ⁴⁶Others put a mask over suffering, indulging in drunkenness or the pleasures of the flesh. ⁴⁷Still others seek to rise above suffering, denying that the body is real. ⁴⁸But not so with you, who must walk not against, or around, or above suffering, but through it, as did the Lord, finding in him your reward. ⁴⁹So, little children, endure a little while, loving one another, ⁵⁰and then you will see the Lord, who will turn your darkness to light, and your mourning to dancing." ⁵¹When Menandros and some others heard John's words, they turned away from John, because they said that everything happens for a reason, and that John did not know the Lord's will. ⁵²But many were comforted by John's love, including the mother and father of Aelia, who after their time of mourning began again to serve the Lord with hope and gladness.

[27–32] Menandros is a fictional character; an earlier Greek dramatist by that name is famous for moral maxims, including, "Whom the gods love die young." There are several similar Christian platitudes, all of which are offensive to both heart and mind. As one pastor advised, "The next time someone says, 'God wanted your loved one to be with him,' tell them, 'I hope God wants *you* next.'" John's response here makes the same point, but more gently, that compassion is the only appropriate response to an untimely death.

[33] The author of 1 John often refers to his readers as either "beloved" or "little children"; in this context, the latter would cause confusion. The dominant themes of John's Gospel and his epistles are belief and mutual love.

[34–39] The wording here echoes Mary's song (9:24 above, from Ps 69:2) as well as Revelation 21:1; 22:1–2. It is fitting that a fisherman like John would use water imagery. The sea was a symbol of chaos in the ancient world, and storm or flood imagery is common in the Psalms for human confusion and despair. Rivers and streams, on the other hand, are commonly symbols of life, and the culminating vision in Revelation describes the river of healing, the place of reunion and endless light.

[36] John 11:35.

[40–50] The catalogue of human responses to the problem of pain is recognizable in both the ancient and modern world, especially in the forms of stopping or masking pain. In the case of transcending pain, there were several ancient philosophies that attempted such rationalization, including the Stoic argument that human experience was merely the out-working of the cosmic Mind, and the Gnostic notion that the spirit could rise above the body. There are of course modern equivalents, especially in Asian religion and New Age spirituality. The orthodox Christian belief has always been that suffering is both real and redemptive.

[51–52] A similar turning away from Jesus occurred after his teaching concerning the nature of his own suffering (John 6:52–66). The contrast of "words" and "love" between the two groups reflects the distinction made by John.

15

John and Mary Magdalene

1 On another day, John instructed his coworker Verus to find all the poor women in Ephesus who were more than sixty years old. [2]Verus returned and told John that there were nearly one hundred such women, but almost all were feeble or sick, and only four were sound in body. [3]John said, "Gather the sick ones into the great theater near the marketplace, and tell all the people of Ephesus to come and see the glory of God." [4]A great number came to the theater, and there Cleopatra and Lycomedes made all things ready for the care of the women. [5]Then John said to the crowd, "Here before you are the old and sick women of your city, whom the Lord has gathered to heal so that you will believe. [6]For if he cares for such weak vessels as these, how much more does he desire to accomplish works of love and goodness through you who are strong?

---

[1] The story of the healing of the widows in the Ephesian theater is contained in *The Acts of John* 30–37, including a series of paradoxes in his evangelistic sermon, some of which are paraphrased here. Other specific details conveyed here from the story include Verus's counting four ambulatory old women, the arrangement of the women—some on beds—in the theater, and their provision by Cleopatra and Lycomedes.

[2–4] Ephesus was the third largest city in the empire, containing about a quarter of a million people,[1] so it would not be difficult to find a hundred old women and a thousand people eager to witness either a spectacular success or an embarrassing failure.

[5–6] It may strike modern readers that a staged public healing is a strange and risky approach to evangelism, but there are numerous similar accounts in the early sources, leading scholars to conclude that healings and other miracles were the primary method of verifying the faith to new hearers.[2] Were people converted by hearsay, or did miracles occur? It is difficult to account otherwise for the growth of a movement to 10% of the empire (six million souls) in two hundred years. This is half a million new converts per generation—all without an organized plan, in the face of local opposition from proponents of established belief systems, and despite long periods of official persecution.

1. Treblico, "Asia," 307.
2. MacMullen, *Christianizing*, 17–24.

⁷But first let me sow in your ears the truth regarding your lives, so that you will not only marvel at the Lord's power but will also take care for your souls. ⁸For the worst among you know that there is judgment after death, and because you fear God, you are ready to hear of his mercy. ⁹But the best among you hide your troubled souls from others, and even from God, thinking that life is long and that to-day is one more spectacle for your amusement. ¹⁰Do not think that your time will be so long, for your life is but a moment; and the treasures of your household, like those of your great city, will fade. ¹¹You who are rich provide for yourselves things that make you unhappy, out of worry that you will lose them. ¹²For a moment, while the sun shines, you delight in gold, in ivory and jewels, but when night falls, can you look at these things? ¹³Behold, the night is coming, perhaps nearer for you than for these old women here before you. ¹⁴Are you puffed up because your bodies, unlike theirs, are beautiful? ¹⁵Yet every day you see your beauty fade, and your powders and potions can only delay the ruin that comes to all. ¹⁶Where can you turn? ¹⁷If you take pleasure in adultery, you find that both law and nature take vengeance upon you. ¹⁸If you indulge in wrath and passion, you make of yourself a beast. ¹⁹If you are a drunkard or a quarreler, you lose the control of your senses to a shameful desire. ²⁰Turn where you will, rich or poor, all roads lead to the same end. ²¹But today your road brings you to life, abundant and eternal, if only you will believe in Christ Jesus."

²²And turning to the old women, who were sitting apart in the lowest circle of the theater, or in the case of the most sick, lying on pallets, John began to walk among them, laying hands on them and healing them of their diseases and weakness. ²³And those who watched from higher in the theater pressed forward to see, and marveled that some whom they knew to be weak rose up and walked. ²⁴Many of the old women wept for joy, embracing one another. ²⁵And on that day almost a hundred of the widows and more than a thousand of those who looked on were added to the number of believers.

²⁶After this, John was much sought after in Ephesus to heal, preach, and offer comfort, and through him the Lord saved many. ²⁷He also traveled in the region, as far north as Pergamum and inland to Laodicea.

[7] Most of the challenges to the audience are adapted from *The Acts of John* 34–36. Such an Ephesian theater audience would include all classes, including affluent citizens, especially after the raising of the magistrate's wife and their public appearance with John. Pagan hearers would believe in an afterlife, but they would be unfamiliar with judgment and resistant to the notion of bodily resurrection. Contrary to modern assumptions, they would be only vaguely polytheistic, because under the influence of the Greek philosophers, most people simply promoted a favorite deity (usually Artemis in Ephesus) to create a virtual monotheistic understanding. In the popular view, the primary purpose of religion was to attain success in this life, particularly health. And under the influence of the philosophers, virtue and right living were important concerns. For all these reasons, John's sermon as recorded in *The Acts of John* is a plausible rendition of the kind of message that early Christian evangelists would direct toward a Greek audience.

[8–27] These are among two cities in the area around Ephesus that are listed in Revelation 2–3 in a circle beginning with the major city of Ephesus, suggesting that the author was a kind of "circuit preacher," or at least that the book would circulate in this well-laid geographical sequence.

---

²⁸In each city he preached boldly to the Greeks, healed both believers and unbelievers of sickness, and encouraged the saints to love one another. ²⁹In the winter months, when travel was difficult, he remained in Ephesus and began to write his account of the life of the Lord.

³⁰After he had lived there for two years, Mary Magdalene came from Pella to minister to John and the other apostles in Asia.

[28–29] It is significant that John's authorship of the Gospel in Ephesus is reported by Irenaeus (*Against Heresies* 3.1.1), because he was mentored by Polycarp of (nearby) Smyrna, who in turn was trained by John, providing a direct, two-generation link to the apostle. Unfortunately, the writing of Revelation is not so clear, because the early church makes reference to an "elder John" who may or may not be identified as the apostle. In the chronology proposed here, all of the writings attributed to John are completed after AD 75, but the discussion of authorship is readily available in commentaries and New Testament introductory texts.

As for John's later career, early church writers report that he was exiled to Patmos in AD 82 and was released to return to Ephesus in AD 96. He was the last of the apostles to die, and the only one known to have died of old age—in his ninety-fourth year, about AD 100 (Irenaeus *Against Heresies* 3.3.4; Jerome *Illustrious Men* 9). Either before or after his exile (traditions disagree), John was reportedly sent to Rome and tortured with boiling oil (Tertullian, *Prescription Against Heretics* 36). A beautiful story is told by Jerome (*Commentary on Galatians* 6.10), that when John was too old to preach, he was carried every week into the assembly of believers, where he whispered repeatedly, "My dear children, love one another." When asked why he repeated this, he replied, "Because it is the Lord's commandment, and if you do only this, you do enough."³

[30] It is difficult to overstate the importance of Mary Magdalene as a witness of the resurrection of Jesus. She is mentioned first in the list of female witnesses to the resurrection (Luke 23:55—24:10) and she is listed before Mary the mother of Jesus in Matthew 28:9. In Mark 16:9 and John 20:16, she is only witness to the resurrection. She is sometimes mistakenly identified with the unnamed female "sinner" in Luke 7:35–50, and a sixth-century pope was the first to refer to her as a recovered prostitute. The unfounded tradition of Mary's questionable morality persists into the modern age in films like *Jesus Christ Superstar* and novels like *The DaVinci Code*. Although Mary does not appear in Acts, another passage mentions her as a benefactress of Jesus and the disciples: Along with Joanna and Susanna, Mary "ministered to them out of their possessions" (Luke 8:3). Susanna is never mentioned again; Joanna is mentioned again only once, as among the first witnesses to the resurrection (Luke 24:10). Mary is not mentioned in Acts. Joanna, as the wife of Herod's steward, must not have lived long after the ministry of Jesus, and it is supposed here that Mary continued to dispose of her resources for the early church as did other unnamed individuals (Acts 2:45; 4:34–37).

3. Quoted in Cain, *Jerome*, 121.

[31]She followed Jesus from the beginning in Galilee, and together with Joanna and Susanna, gave of her possessions and remained with the Lord to the end, even when others deserted him. [32]Joanna set Mary over her possessions, and when she died, Mary continued to sell parcels of land and give the proceeds to the apostles, as the need arose. [33]When she became old, Mary traveled to Antioch, then to Ephesus and other cities, giving encouragement to the apostles and telling all of Christ Jesus and the events she had witnessed. [34]She knew John and Mary the mother of the Lord from the days when they walked with the Lord. [35]They rejoiced now in meeting, and the believers in Ephesus marveled to hear what they told concerning Christ Jesus. [36]Mary stayed in Ephesus with John for a year, ministering to the saints, [37]and then the Spirit told her to journey to Phrygia to see Philip and Bartholomew.

[31–32] It would be unusual in the patriarchal culture of first-century Palestine, but technically possible, for a woman of means like Joanna to have such power over her possessions.[4]

[33] Was Mary a figure of authority in the early church? Several traditions suggest that she survived long enough to travel among the early churches, and undoubtedly her stature would carry significant weight. In the tenth century, writers first gave Mary Magdalene the title *apostola apostolorum,* "apostle of (or to) the apostles," which meant not that she had authority over them but that she was sent by God on their behalf. On this basis, it is anachronistic to ascribe to her equal status with the twelve. Gnostic writings like the second-century *Gospel of Mary* put her in a place of prominence as the one who truly understood the (Gnostic!) ideas of Jesus, with Peter as her rival.[5] The notion that Mary was a major figure whose power was curtailed by the patriarchal male apostles[6] appeals to some today, but there is little to commend it historically. On the other hand, whether or not Mary traveled, it is highly unlikely that she simply announced the resurrection of Jesus and then went back to the kitchen. This chapter takes a middle position, suggesting that Mary was revered as a primary witness, a benefactress, and a loyal follower of Jesus from the earliest days of his ministry—but stopping short of giving her the title or authority of an apostle. This is certainly appropriate in adapting the style of Luke, whose writings are notable for showing the importance of women in early Christianity[7] but do not go beyond his sources to promote women's leadership.[8] Mary is brought into this account in relation to John because his Gospel gives her the greatest prominence.[9]

[34] There can be no doubt that Mary the mother of Jesus, Mary Magdalene, and John had a long history together that extended at least into the middle decades of the first century. Traditions differ about the times of death of the two women, and whether they lived together for a length of time in Jerusalem or Ephesus.

[35–37] Since Bartholomew was killed in AD 68 (chapter 16), Mary in this chronology must visit him just before his martyrdom.

4. Ricci, *Mary Magdalene,* 159–60.

5. See treatment of Gnostic texts in Thimme, "Memory and Revision," 205–17.

6. E.g., Brock, *Mary Magdalene,* 161–75.

7. Arlandson, *Women,* 186–93.

8. Ricci, *Mary Magdalene,* 64–72.

9. Thimme, "Memory and Revision," 200–201.

16

North to Phrygia with Phillip and Bartholomew

1 When Simeon called the apostles to Jerusalem after the deaths of Paul and Peter, he summoned Philip and Bartholomew from Hierapolis in Phrygia. [2]After the resurrection of the Lord, they had for many years preached together in Syria and further north in the regions of Galatia, Bithynia, Pontus, and Cappadocia.

---

[1] The apostle Philip figures in several passages in the Gospel of John, but elsewhere only in lists of the twelve; there is no reference to his activities in Acts. There is a second Philip, referred to as a deacon and evangelist (Acts 6:5; 8:4–40; 21:8–9), who is not to be identified with the apostle. The name was common, and the apostle Philip would not also have been a deacon. Moreover, Luke is careful to distinguish the second Philip as "the evangelist, one of the seven" (Acts 21:8–9). That passage also adds the unusual detail that the deacon "had four unmarried daughters who had the gift of prophecy"; several later sources that associate prophetess daughters with the apostle are almost certainly a result of confusing the two Philips.

Traditions regarding the movements of the apostles Philip and Bartholomew are unreliable and contradictory. Some locations are more likely than others, but the order of events is less certain, and reliable details are scarce. There is good authority for placing Philip's later ministry in Hierapolis. Eusebius quotes the early second-century writer Papias, who was bishop of Hierapolis just fifty years later; and the late second-century writer Polycrates, who both report that Philip worked and died in Hierapolis with his daughters. The reference to the daughters may indicate either early confusion with Philip the deacon/evangelist or later confusion by Eusebius; it could also mean that it was the deacon/evangelist and not the apostle who worked in Hierapolis.

[2] Traditions often pair Philip with Bartholomew (a.k.a. Nathanael) in later ministry, perhaps because New Testament lists often pair them and because Philip introduced Bartholomew to Jesus (John 1:45–51). The fourth-century apocryphal work *Acts of Philip*[1] reports that they worked together in Syria, Greece, and Phrygia. The supposition here that they also worked in northern and eastern Asia Minor provides for evangelization of this early-Christianized area (Peter may have been the first apostle there, according to 1 Pet 1:1), and it offers a transition to Bartholomew's later movement due east from the region.

---

1. For an introduction, see Klauck, *Apocryphal Acts*, 232–43.

³They returned to Hieropolis after the council to continue building up the church there. ⁴There were many Jews in the city, and many believers among them who met in the house of Epicrates.

⁵At that time Vettius Niger, who was proconsul of Asia, lived in Hierapolis. ⁶His wife Nicanora had long suffered from various diseases, including a swelling of her eyes that made her nearly blind. ⁷When she heard that Philip healed the sick, she sent for him. And calling upon the name of Christ Jesus, Philip released her from all her illnesses. ⁸That same day Nicanora had her slaves carry her to the house of Epicrates to meet the other believers, ⁹and there she was baptized together with her slaves.

¹⁰Niger was a tyrant, jealous of his wife and suspicious of all in the city but the other Romans. ¹¹When he learned that Nicanora had gone to the house of those who had healed her, he cried out, "By what trickery have these magicians pretended to cure her? Bring her to me."

[3–4] Research on first-century tombs in Hierapolis suggests that the population by the second century was about 100,000, almost half of them Jews. This would explain the focus here of early missionary activity. The city was first evangelized by Paul's coworker Epaphras, along with nearby Laodicea and Colossae (Col 4:13).

[5] Phrygia was a region of the province of Asia, and M. Vettius Niger was its proconsul during the latter years of Nero's reign. Traditions usually place Philip's martyrdom and Bartholomew's near martyrdom between AD 80–90, but this is probably too late to include the extensive later travels ascribed to Bartholomew. One way to harmonize the traditions is to separate the two apostles; the alternative, chosen here, is to move the date of Philip's death up to about AD 66. The story below is adapted from the ending of the fourth-century *Acts of Philip*, which names Nicanora, but not the proconsul. The account is too late to be reliable, but parts are plausible and may represent a core of fact. Details from the story employed here include Nicanora's healing and conversion, the proconsul's strange rage, Nicanora's attempts to convert her husband, and Philip's public crucifixion. The apocryphal story places the church in the house of Stachys, adds a sister of Philip, and reports the doubtful detail that Bartholomew was removed from the cross and released by a sympathetic crowd.

[6–11] The ancients drew a distinction between magic and religion, outlawing practitioners of magic and viewing them as modern people view cult leaders. Traveling charlatans were common, and they were severely punished. A high Roman official who learned of a family member's involvement would, like Niger, fear the worst.

---

¹²And when Niconora heard of his anger, she returned to him ¹³and said, "Do not be angry with me or my deliverer, for he reigns in heaven, and in his name I will be a better wife to you. ¹⁴But my healing will not be complete until your soul is healed, when you turn from the idols we have worshiped and serve Christ Jesus the Lord." ¹⁵When Niger heard these words, he was filled with anger. ¹⁶Dragging Nicanora by the hair and kicking her, he cried, "If you do not deliver these deceivers who have bewitched and seduced you, I will cut off this hair, and then the head that has disgraced me." ¹⁷But when he released her, Nicanora bowed before him and said, "My hair and my head are yours for as long as you grant me life; ¹⁸and the sooner you

take my life, the sooner my soul will fly to Christ Jesus my Lord." [19]Then Niger was torn between shame and wrath, because Nicanora humbled herself before him but would not deny Christ.

[20]When Niger forced Nicanora's slaves to reveal who had healed her, he sent soldiers to the house of Epicrates, and they brought Philip before him, while Bartholomew and Epicrates, together with some of the believers, followed. [21]Philip spoke to Niger without fear, telling him how he had laid hands on Nicanora and prayed for her in the name of the Lord Jesus to be healed, [22]and that now she was a disciple of Christ Jesus, having been baptized that day. [23]Once again Niger was enraged, and he commanded his soldiers to scourge Philip, together with Epicrates and Bartholomew, [23]and to drag Philip through the streets of the temple of Apollo, where he would be killed the next day in front of the people.

[24]The believers took Epicrates and Bartholomew and hid them, tending to their wounds, [25]and all prayed that the Spirit would deliver Philip or give him strength to face his tormentors. [26]The soldiers chained Philip to a column between the temples of Apollo and Pluto, and the next morning a great crowd of about seven thousand men gathered. [27]Even before Niger arrived, the priests of the temples were shouting against Philip, saying that he was one of the foreigners and magicians who seduced women and defied both the divine emperor and Apollo, the chief god of the city. [28]But Philip, filled with the Spirit, said to the crowd, "Men of Hierapolis, it is fitting that you should hear the empty charges of these priests, for the true God has brought me here between the temples of their false gods, one of the sun and one of the underworld, [29]to proclaim to you that they are no gods at all, neither in the sky, nor under the earth, nor on the earth itself. [30]All of you know that these priests claim to descend to hell, but they only do tricks with poisonous vapors from a cave in the earth. [31]They also demand from you payments of gold and many sacrifices for healings, but they say that the same god brings plague. [32]They accuse those who are pure of seducing women, while their god fornicates with a thousand demons like himself.

[**12–27**] Up to this point, the narrative here largely follows the *Acts of Philip*. The speech of Philip prior to his martyrdom, which is original, is intended to reflect religious beliefs and practices that prevailed in Hierapolis at this time.

[**28–30**] The Plutonium was a shrine to Pluto, god of the underworld. It was a small cave from which naturally emanated carbon dioxide gas, and priests learned to feign immunity to the poisons (and favor from Pluto) by holding their breath while carrying in animals, which died from the fumes. Several contemporary historians exposed this clever ruse, which was probably well known by the mid-first century.

[**31–32**] In Hierapolis, the temple of Apollo, next to the Plutonium, was the focus of this belief. Among other roles, Apollo was the god of the sun, light, truth, healing, and plague—all of which figure in Philip's speech. Apollo's list of sexual liaisons was long; the immorality of the gods, especially in an age when virtue was increasingly sought, was a common theme of Christian apologists.

³³In all of these things they are false, but they will learn the truth soon enough about hell and plague and demons.

³⁴And what of the house of their god, this great temple? ³⁵Twice in this generation it has been destroyed by earthquakes, and foolish men lavish years and fortunes to build it up again. ³⁶But when evil men destroyed the temple of Christ's body, God raised him up in three days and exalted him to heaven, from where he will soon come to reign over the earth. ³⁷Hear the truth, people of Hierapolis! ³⁸These so-called gods are nothing, but the priests would raise them up together with themselves. ³⁹Christ was great, but he became small for our sake, to raise us up together with him. ⁴⁰Do your hearts not tell you to come up out of hell and receive the true healing, a touch that will lift you beyond the sun to life everlasting?"

⁴¹Just then Niger came to the temple, and the priests ran to him, accusing Philip of defying the emperor and the temple.

⁴²Niger replied, "Why do you need to speak, when this man's own words and those of my wife are enough to condemn him? ⁴³She is still bewitched, speaking strange words and praying through the night to Jesus. ⁴⁴I will soon put an end to this man's enchantments." ⁴⁵And he ordered Philip to be hanged head downwards by iron hooks through his heels, opposite the temple from a certain tree. ⁴⁶Philip, although he was weak from the scourging and being chained through the night, did not cry out ⁴⁷but prayed in a loud voice for the Lord to save Niger, and for the people of Hierapolis to believe. ⁴⁸Soon, however, he could speak no more, and he gave up his spirit. ⁴⁹The priests of the temple rejoiced, but when the crowd saw the courage of Philip, and the cruelty of Niger, who killed the very man who had healed his wife, they mourned, and many believed in Christ Jesus. ⁵⁰The people of Hierapolis gave the body of Philip to Bartholomew, who buried him there.

[33–35] Hierapolis was damaged by an earthquake in AD 17 and completely destroyed by another in AD 60. Immediately afterwards, the city was rebuilt with the financial support of Nero. The emperor probably had a loyal following there, including worship of his image as a god, which was more common in the provinces than in Rome.

[36–37] In direct challenge to the cult of Apollo, god of truth, Philip repeatedly makes reference to the truth of the gospel and the falsehood of the pagan priests.

[38–40] The most direct challenge to the local deity is Philip's closing reference to "touch." The word is *paeon* in Greek—one of the most important epithets for Apollo, and the word for the formal song which was sung before battle, when launching a fleet, or after a victory was won. The phrase "beyond the sun," likewise, declares Christ's superiority to Apollo the sun god.

[41] The narrative here resumes dependence on the *Acts of Philip*, which include the proconsul's dramatic speech regarding his wife's intercession, the cruel mode of death, and Bartholomew's burial of his fellow apostle.

[42–50] This last detail may have been confirmed by the discovery in 2011 of a *martyrium* (place of pilgrimage) in which artifacts were discovered indicating that it was the tomb of Philip. It was destroyed by an earthquake in the seventh century, and the city of Hierapolis, sparsely populated for centuries, was finally abandoned after in the fourteenth century.

PRIMARY SOURCES

Papias (AD 110–140) quoted in Eusebius, *Ecclesiastical History* 3.39.8–9: But it is fitting to subjoin to the words of Papias which have been quoted, other passages from his works in which he relates some other wonderful events which he claims to have received from tradition. That Philip the apostle dwelt at Hierapolis with his daughters has been already stated. But it must be noted here that Papias, their contemporary, says that he heard a wonderful tale from the daughters of Philip. For he relates that in his time one rose from the dead. And he tells another wonderful story of Justus, surnamed Barsabbas: that he drank a deadly poison, and yet, by the grace of the Lord, suffered no harm.

Polycrates (AD 190) quoted in Eusebius, *Ecclesiastical History* 5.24.2: For in Asia also great lights have fallen asleep, which shall rise again on the day of the Lord's coming, when he shall come with glory from heaven, and shall seek out all the saints. Among these are Philip, one of the twelve apostles, who fell asleep in Hierapolis; and his two aged virgin daughters, and another daughter, who lived in the Holy Spirit and now rests at Ephesus.

17

Bartholomew Martyred in Armenia

1 Soon after this, the tyrant Niger was sent back to Rome, and Bartholomew preached again openly in the city. ²But he mourned greatly for Philip, because they had been like brothers and had traveled together since their youth. ³So Bartholomew gathered the elders in the house of Epicrates and said to them, "The apostles in Jerusalem sent us back to you to finish our work here, and then to go where the Lord would send us. Chapter 8:30 above. ⁴Now the church in Hierapolis is strong, and the Lord calls me to go, but not again to the cities where I have preached with Philip, where I would hear the echo of his steps next to mine. ⁵Instead, I will go to the cities of the East, beyond the reach of Rome, where the word of the Lord has not been heard. ⁶Nevertheless, I will not go alone if the Lord will call any from among you to make this journey with me." ⁷And the Spirit chose two men, Perseus and Nicator, to go with Bartholomew.

⁸In the spring, when they were able to travel through the passes, they journeyed along the king's road through the cities of Iconium, Caesarea, Comona, and Melitene. ⁹In each place, they were welcomed by believers who begged them to preach and strengthen the church. ¹⁰After Melitene, they crossed the Euphrates and journeyed south to Edessa, where Philip and Bartholomew had preached years before.

[1–2] The New Testament only rarely reports the emotional response of characters to events, but an occasional hint shows that, while these men may have been heroic, they were also human. It is not hard to imagine Bartholomew's pain in parting after more than thirty years of traveling with Philip.

[3–8] These are the main cities, about four hundred miles apart, along the major east-west trade route that eventually reached India. Only the wealthy were carried by animals along these rugged paths, often at high elevation; missionaries traveled by foot.

[9] Whether or not these cities were directly evangelized, their placement along a main road—and the likely presence of a Jewish population in each—made it likely that there were at least a few believers present by the middle decades of the first century.

[10] Edessa became an important early center of Christianity. Situated at the top edge of the Fertile Crescent, between the Tigris and Euphrates, it is now in southeastern Turkey; but at the time it was the northwestern capital of the kingdom of Osroene. Unreliable traditions claim that it was evangelized by several different apostles; what is indisputable is that by the mid-second century, Edessa had a large Christian population.

---

[11]Here Bartholomew was greeted with joy by the church, and he remained through the winter. [12]Among the believers there were some merchants who traveled on the trade routes, and they gave reports of Thomas in India and other apostles who had traveled to distant lands. [13]They also told Bartholomew about the lands of Armenia, Albania, and Parthia in the north between the two great inland seas. [14]When Bartholomew and the others heard that these people had not yet heard the word of the Lord, the Spirit stirred their hearts, and they determined to travel there as soon as they could cross the mountain passes.

[15]Taking with them Borus and Kalemos, who knew the languages of the region, Bartholomew, together with Perseus and Nicator, preached the word of the Lord throughout the towns of Armenia and Albania. [16]Wherever they went, they healed the sick, cast out demons, and turned people from false idols to the worship of Christ Jesus. [17]After a year, they made their way down the Araxes River to the coast, and from there went north to the city of Albanapolis.

[11–12] The narrative has already established that Thomas is in India (chapter above). Other apostles, most notably Simon and Jude (chapters 19–20 below), have already passed through but are not named in order to preserve the geographic sequence of the account.

[13] Ancient Armenia, which encompassed the area from Asia Minor to the Caspian Sea, was the first country to declare Christianity its official religion, in AD 301. The area to the north, between the Black and Caspian Seas, was mountainous and remote, and little is known of its history during this period. Albania, the ancient name of the west coast of the Caspian Sea, is not to be confused with the modern country on the Adriatic coast. Parthia's borders changed constantly, and the term was applied to almost every area east of Roman control. Just north of this region is Scythia, which according to a few late traditions was also evangelized by apostles.

[14–15] These are all Greek names typical of those found in Hellenistic cities, but the individuals and their activities are fictional.

[16–17] Modern Derbend on the Caspian Sea is the location of Bartholomew's martyrdom according to one tradition,[1] and most traditions place his death in the general area. One modern writer, however, believes that the evidence points to Bartholomew's martyrdom in India.[2]

---

1. Atiya, *Eastern Christianity*, 316.
2. Ruffin, *The Twelve*, 116–19.

18When they arrived in Albanapolis, Bartholomew sat apart by the shore for an hour and remembered Philip, because he said that the place was much like their home in Galilee, and that it was a good place to end his days. 19Soon after they entered the city, Bartholomew cast out a demon from a man who had long been shut up in his house out of fear that he would harm someone. 20When word of this came to Polymius, the ruler of the city, he sent to Bartholomew on behalf of his daughter, who was also afflicted by a demon. 21He took Bartholomew to the chamber where she was kept and said, "See how she is kept in chains, because she bites anyone who comes near. 22Our priests cannot help her, but if this new god you bring can free a wild man who has been tormented for years, perhaps he can help my child." 23Bartholomew said to him, "Loose her, and let her go." 24Polymius replied, "We have her in our power only when she is bound. Would you have us let her go?" 25Again Bartholomew said, "Let her go, and when she has eaten and rested, early tomorrow bring her to me." 26And after Bartholomew left, Polymius debated with himself for an hour, then decided to do as Bartholomew said. 27And when he went in to his daughter, the demon was already gone, and his daughter was in her right mind.

28Early the next day, Polymius loaded a cart with gold, pearls, and expensive garments and went to find Bartholomew at the inn. 29When Bartholomew saw the treasure he said, "These things I fear more than the demons I cast out, for they bind with stronger chains. 30Take them from me, and give them to the poor. 31But first stay and learn how your daughter was delivered." 32And he taught Polymius from the scriptures about the hopes of the Jews and how they had all been fulfilled in Christ Jesus. 33Polymius listened all day. 34And in the evening, he took Bartholomew and those who were with him back to the palace, and there he was baptized together with his daughter and all his household. 35Then he asked Bartholomew to remain in the palace and preach to the people.

36Bartholomew preached in Albanopolis and the surrounding towns for several months, and many believed, 37but the priests and some of the merchants hated Polymius and the believers for tearing down the temple of their idol. 38So they sent to their king Astryages and reported to him that a stranger in Albanopolis was defying the gods and declaring that Jesus was the true king. 39Astryages, who was the brother of Polymius, immediately sent soldiers to arrest Bartholomew.

[18–19] Allowing for travel and a stay in Edessa, it is now sometime in AD 68. The basic plot of the following narrative is adapted from the *Acts of Andrew and Bartholomew*, the latter section of which is also known as the *Martyrdom of Bartholomew*. The work is a fifth-century composition that, like other apocryphal works already described, may combine fabrication with a core of historical material. Certainly the pattern—healing, successful preaching (often involving an influential individual), then local reprisals—is familiar from the early chapters of Acts, and it formed a model for the spread of Christianity for almost a thousand years.

[20–28] This detail from the *Martyrdom of Bartholomew* seems quite plausible: the grateful ruler assumes that the wandering healer expects to be paid.

[29–39] The brother-kings Polymius and Astryages are not known from sources other than the *Martyrdom of Bartholomew*. The story could be entirely fictional, but the unusual relationship, coupled with the survival of Polymius to lead the Albanopolis church, may suggest an historical basis.

---

[40]When he was brought before the king, Astryages asked him, "Are you the one who has turned my brother from the gods?" [41]Bartholomew answered, "Those were not gods from which he turned, but it is truly God to whom he has turned." [42]And the king asked, "Are you the one who caused our gods to be broken in pieces?" [43]Bartholomew answered, "Would you grieve over the empty houses of demons, when you should rejoice with your brother in the God who dwells in the heavens?" [44]Then Astryages said, "Your own mouth condemns you. [45]Because you have made my brother and the people reject our gods, now in front of them all I will make you reject your god and worship ours." [46]And he gave orders for Bartholomew to be beaten with rods, and then to have his skin torn from his body. [47]But when the apostle was silent and did not deny Christ, Astryages ordered for him to be beheaded. [48]Then, learning that Polymius took the remains of Bartholomew to be buried in the royal tomb, he ordered his body to be placed in a sack and thrown into the sea. [49]After Astryages and his soldiers left, Polymius and his household continued to worship the Lord, and Perseus and Borus remained there, [50]while Nicator and Kalemos returned to Edessa with a report of all that the Lord had done through Bartholomew.

[40–46] Flaying a prisoner was a punishment typical in the ancient East, but not in the Roman empire.

[47–48] The poetic irony of this detail, with which the *Martyrdom of Bartholomew* closes, was probably not intended by the original writer: Bartholomew the fisherman and, later, fisher of men, finally joins the fishes.

PRIMARY SOURCES

Eusebius (AD 320) *Ecclesiastical History* 5.10.3: Pantænus was one of these, and is said to have gone to India. It is reported that among persons there who knew of Christ, he found the Gospel, according to Matthew, which had anticipated his own arrival. For Bartholomew, one of the apostles, had preached to them, and left with them the writing of Matthew in the Hebrew language, which they had preserved till that time. ["India" at the time included anything east of the Roman empire.]

Moses of Chorene (AD 480) *History of Armenia* 9: There came then into Armenia the Apostle Bartholomew, who suffered martyrdom among us in the town of Arepan. [Some scholars believe that this document was composed as late as the seventh century.]

18

West to Macedonia and Achaia with Andrew

1 The apostle Andrew was sent from the council to Macedonia and Achaia. ²From there he hoped to continue west to Illyricum and to the northern regions of Italy, if the Lord would allow him. ³But first, when we left Jerusalem, we journeyed to Caesarea to find a ship; and from there we followed fair winds to Tyre, Antioch, Myra, Miletus, and Troas, stopping in each city for a several weeks to encourage the believers. ⁴For Andrew was a kindly man, and he did not hurry but spent many hours listening and talking to the to the saints one by one. ⁵For he said, "The Lord heals and performs wonders in a moment, but the greatest of his works are those he does in the heart, with much patience. ⁶For the greatest fish lie deepest in the sea, and it requires time and skill to draw them up to the light."

[1–2] Andrew's later goal is not mentioned in 8:31 because it was realized by others, as this chapter anticipates. The area proposed here for his missionary activity, from Scythia to northern Italy, lies along a west-east plane about 1,500 miles long, and most of it is easily accessible by either land or sea. In this chapter, Andrew covers less than one-fifth of that area.

[3] The movements and manner attributed here to Andrew are largely speculative. Tradition supplies a few plausible locations for his later ministry and death, but further details lack credibility. Andrew is a common subject of later apocryphal works. The earliest of these is the *Acts of Andrew*, probably written in the mid-second century, perhaps by the same Leucius Charinus who was responsible for the *Acts of John* and *Acts of Peter*.[1] It may be based on earlier traditions, and its general itinerary for Andrew's later ministry is followed here—but little of the content, which is for the most part a series of preposterous miracle stories. It may in fact be a Christian re-telling of *The Odyssey*. Eusebius dismissed it as heretical and absurd (*Ecclesiastical History* 3.25.7). An even more fantastic *Acts of Andrew and Matthias,* probably also written by Leucius, takes the two apostles to an unknown land for an adventure among cannibals. The tale may, however, support the tradition that Andrew journeyed to Scythia; strange cultures on the fringes of the empire were often associated with such barbaric practices.

---

1. For a thorough introduction, see Klauck, *Apocryphal Acts*, 113–40.

[4–6] The biblical material does not offer enough detail to reconstruct a personality for Andrew. He was a fisherman, of course, and brother to the famously impulsive Peter. The glimpse into his manner here reflects this background and sets up a foil to the fast-paced approach of Simon and Jude in the next chapter.

---

⁷Reaching Nicaea just before the storms, we remained there through the winter. ⁸It was in Nicaea that Andrew had lived for a year before the council, and he was beloved by the saints [see primary sources below]. ⁹Andrew and Peter his brother were the first to proclaim the word of the Lord in Nicaea, and they often returned there to wait for the Spirit to send them to new lands. ¹⁰For Andrew and Peter had preached throughout Bithynia, Pontus, and Cappadocia; and when Peter went to Rome, Andrew sailed to the land of Scythia on the other side of the sea. ¹¹Whenever he returned from preaching the word of the Lord, the saints in Nicaea had made him welcome and provided for his further travels. ¹²So now when the Spirit directed Andrew to depart, the Nicaeans were generous in sending him onward.

¹³Providing all things necessary, they also sent with him Lamachos and Xenion, who preached and served with him to the end. ¹⁴Because it was still not safe to travel by sea, Andrew followed the road to Byzantium, where he had first preached and where Stachys now led the church. ¹⁵After two months, he went to Heraclea, where he stayed three months. ¹⁶From Heraclea he went to Philippi and then to Thessalonica, ¹⁷remaining for a year in each city and building up the saints so that the seed once planted and nurtured by Paul became a strong tree bearing much fruit.

¹⁸After two years in Macedonia, Andrew traveled to Thebes, where you, most excellent Theophilus, welcomed him into your house and provided for him as you have for all the saints to this day, laying up treasure in heaven.

---

[7] The "we" section for this chapter ends with v. 7, implying that Andrew left Luke in Nicaea and that Luke does not have details of Andrew's subsequent ministry. The supposition here is that Andrew went west with other co-workers while Luke went to Theophilus in Thebes to begin writing the Gospel and Acts; and the two met again in Thebes before Andrew went to Corinth and Patras near the end of his life (*See* notes on v. 18 below).

[8–10] Peter's missionary activity was centered in this area (1 Pet 1:1), and given the fact that the apostles went out in pairs, it is reasonable to suppose that he was accompanied by his brother. Peter spent time in Rome, but there is no record of Andrew there. There are, however, reports from Eusebius (*Ecclesiastical History* 3.1.1) and other early church writers that Andrew went east from Asia Minor to Scythia,[2] which is now southern Russia. The "sea" here is the Black Sea.

[11–14] Early tradition affirms Andrew as the founder and first bishop of Byzantium; he is the patron saint of Constantinople. In this reconstruction, Stachys, who is a traveling co-worker of Paul (16:9), traveled earlier with Paul from Rome to Spain (1:13), then remained behind to help establish the church in Terraco (1:38).

---

2. Peterson, *Andrew*, 25; Brownrigg, *Twelve*, 47; Budge, *Contendings*, 214–21.

[15–18] Luke 12:32–34 promises this reward to those who by generosity show their devotion to the kingdom. The location of Theophilus is unknown, but it is reasonable to suppose that Luke worked nearby or in his house. There is no reason to doubt the early tradition that Luke wrote in Achaia and Boeotia; the latter includes Thebes, just north of Corinth. This location was central in the empire and near ports, facilitating the collection of data for Luke's writing. Theophilus was presumably well placed, perhaps a Roman official, and therefore capable of giving both protection and provision to Luke while he wrote his Gospel and Acts. Different traditions have Luke dying naturally or as a martyr, and in Achaia or Bithynia (*See* note on 24:1 below).

---

[19]When Andrew was refreshed in spirit, he went to Corinth, where he lived for a year, strengthening the believers there. [20]Then the Lord sent him to Patras.

[21]Now this was a time of great turmoil, for after the tyrant Nero died, four men sat on the throne in Rome until Vespasian was made emperor. [22]There were revolts in the provinces, and the greatest of these was in Judea, where Jerusalem was under siege. [23]So while all waited to learn the outcome of these events, the Jews feared that they would be persecuted, and those who hated them accused them of rebellion. [24]Moreover, Roman magistrates everywhere wished to assure the new emperor of their loyalty, so they were quick to punish any rumor of revolt.

[25]After Andrew had been in Patras for two months, a new proconsul, Lucius, arrived in the city. [26]The next day the merchant Demotoles gave a banquet for Lucius; and even before the food was served he began to accuse Andrew of sedition, [27]for he was angry that his son, having heard Andrew's preaching, had become a believer.

[19–24] These details locate this part of the story in early AD 70. Following Nero's death in AD 68, a brief civil war in Rome was followed by the short reigns of Galba, Otho, and Vitellius; Vespasian prevailed in December AD 69 and ruled for ten years. The siege and destruction of Jerusalem followed on the heels of his succession, March-September AD 70. Since Vespasian had begun the crushing of the Jewish revolt before leaving his son Titus in charge, Jews throughout the empire would have been watched for signs of sedition. Christians, who proclaimed a Jewish messiah, could easily have been subject to charges of disloyalty during this period of high tension.

[25] After the departure in AD 53 of Gallio (who figures in Acts 18), there is no record of subsequent Achaian proconsuls. Lucius, however, was a common name among proconsuls and serves the need for a name here.

[26–27] From this point the chapter follows the remarkable correspondence (included below) of AD 112 between another proconsul, Pliny the Younger, and the emperor Trajan concerning the growing "Christian problem." Although that exchange occurred forty years after Andrew's death, it offers insight into the rationale and method of Roman attempts to suppress Christianity.[3] From the perspective of the empire, order was foremost, and the very life of a proconsul depended on his ensuring it. As Pliny discovered, Christians defied Roman order by refusing the symbolic act of worshiping Caesar. After being asked

3. Frend, *Martyrdom*, 155–72.

twice, if Christians refused to recant, he had them tortured and killed. Trajan approved this approach, suggesting only that the proconsul wait for Christians to be brought to him and not "go out of your way to look for them."

---

[28]The the next day Lucius had Andrew arrested and brought before him in the theater. [30]Lucius said to him, "Is it true, as you are accused by a citizen of this city, that you are the leader the Christians?" [31]Andrew answered, "I am no leader but a servant of Christ who reigns in heaven, and of the emperor who reigns on earth." [32]Turning to the crowd that had gathered, Lucius said, "Having learned of this sect in Rome, I know they speak of loyalty to mask their crimes. [33]For they claim to teach virtue; but they refuse to worship Caesar or any of the gods, and they follow a god of the Jews who they claim will destroy the world." [34]Turning again to Andrew, he said, "Knowing that your life is in peril for such sedition, I ask you again, are you a Christian?" [35]Andrew said, "I am." [36]Then Lucius said, "In the ship that brought me here, there is a statue of Caesar ready to be set up in Corinth, where I will govern as proconsul. [37]Now, Christian, answer me this: If I were to place before you, on the one hand, this image of Caesar, for you to speak the words of invocation and offer wine together with incense; [38]and on the other hand, a cross to hang from, which would you choose?" [39]After waiting for a moment, Andrew spoke in a loud voice, "Proconsul, you honor me by asking three times so that I may consider carefully. [40]The choice I make is for life, but not as it is in your power to give; [41]for

in offering me the cross, you let me suffer as did my Lord, before God raised him from the dead. [42]This is the life I choose, which is life everlasting." [43]Lucius waved his hand before the crowd and said, "You all see the evidence from his own mouth of his absurd and extravagant superstition. [44]This contagion has spread through many cities of the empire, affecting all ranks and ages, and it must be restrained before these fools lead more fools away from loyalty and order." [45]Then Lucius gave orders for Andrew to be scourged and crucified along the road outside the city. [46]And in order to make his suffering last longer, he ordered the soldiers not to break Andrew's limbs but to hang him with thongs rather than nails on two crossed posts with his arms and feet apart. [47]In this manner he lived four days.

[48]And some of the believers dared to visit Andrew while he lived, praying for him and begging the guards to give him water. [49]Meanwhile, he encouraged those who came, and he spoke of Christ Jesus to the guards. [50]Seeing the faith of Andrew and those who came to comfort him, Laenus, the chief of the cohort, believed and was baptized. [51]When Andrew had given up his spirit to Christ Jesus, the believers in Patras buried him there; [52]and immediately they began to ask the Lord which of them might preach the word in Illyricum and Italy, as Andrew had intended.

[28–47] According to the *Acts of Andrew*, Andrew was tied rather than nailed to the cross and lived four days. The earliest accounts do not, however, report that he was suspended from a cross in the shape of an X, which became known as the St. Andrew's cross or "Saltire." This detail was added centuries later. Late traditions also borrowed the detail from accounts of Peter's death that Andrew expressed unworthiness to be crucified like Jesus and was instead hung upside down.

[48–50] The conversion of the soldier is not taken from the *Acts of Andrew*, but it reflects a theme of soldiers' responding to the suffering of believers. This began with the centurion at the foot of the cross (Luke 23:47) and another centurion as the first Gentile convert (Acts 10). The tradition of soldiers converting and sometimes immediately suffering martyrdom, extends several centuries into the Christian era and includes such notables as Sebastian, Alban, and Victor (see also 3:31–32; 6:32, 47).

[51–52] The last verse is directed in part to the reader, implying an ongoing missionary charge to continue and complete the work begun by the apostles.

PRIMARY SOURCES

Andrew in Nicaea

The Teaching of the Apostles (AD 180–200): Nicæa, and Nicomedia, and all the country of Bithynia, and of Inner Galatia, and of the regions round about it, received the apostles' ordination to the priesthood from Andrew, the brother of Simon Cephas, who was himself Guide and Ruler in the church which he had built there, and was priest and ministered there.

Luke (and Theophilus) in Achaia

Anti-Marcionite Lucan Prologue (AD 200): The holy Luke is an Antiochene, Syrian by race, physician by trade. As his writings indicate, of the Greek speech he was not ignorant. He was a disciple of the apostles, and afterward followed Paul until his confession, serving the Lord undistractedly, for he neither had any wife nor procreated sons. [A man] of eighty-four years, he slept in Thebes, the metropolis of Boeotia, full of the holy spirit. He, when the gospels were already written down, that according to Matthew in Judea, but that according to Mark in Italy, instigated by the holy spirit, in parts of Achaea wrote down this gospel.[4]

Monarchian Lucan Prologue (AD 200–300) Luke: Luke, Syrian by nationality, an Antiochene, physician by art, disciple of the apostles, later followed Paul up until his confession, serving God without fault. For, never having either a wife or sons, he died in Bithynia at seventy-four years of age, full of the holy spirit. When the Gospels of Matthew in Judea, and Mark in Italy, had already been written, he wrote this gospel at the instigation of the holy spirit in the regions of Achaea, he himself also signifying in the beginning that others had been written beforehand.

Jerome (AD 398) *Preface to Commentary on Matthew*: The third is Luke, the physician, by birth a native of Antioch, in Syria, whose praise is in the Gospel. He was himself a disciple of the Apostle Paul, and composed his book in Achaia and Bœotia. He thoroughly investigates certain particulars and, as he himself confesses in the preface, describes what he had heard rather than what he had seen.

---

4. The *Latin Prologues* are quoted from the translation by Ben C. Smith.

Pliny and Trajan Conspire to Suppress Christianity

Pliny the Younger (AD 112) *Epistles* 10.96: To the Emperor Trajan: It is my invariable rule, Sir, to refer to you in all matters where I feel doubtful; for who is more capable of removing my scruples, or informing my ignorance? Having never been present at any trials concerning those who profess Christianity, I am unacquainted not only with the nature of their crimes, or the measure of their punishment, but how far it is proper to enter into an examination concerning them. Whether, therefore, any difference is usually made with respect to ages, or no distinction is to be observed between the young and the adult; whether repentance entitles them to a pardon; or if a man has been once a Christian, it avails nothing to desist from his error; whether the very profession of Christianity, unattended with any criminal act, or only the crimes themselves inherent in the profession are punishable; on all these points I am in great doubt. In the meanwhile, the method I have observed towards those who have been brought before me as Christians is this: I asked them whether they were Christians; if they admitted it, I repeated the question twice, and threatened them with punishment; if they persisted, I ordered them to be at once punished: for I was persuaded, whatever the nature of their opinions might be, a contumacious and inflexible obstinacy certainly deserved correction. There were others also brought before me possessed with the same infatuation, but being Roman citizens, I directed them to be sent to Rome. But this crime spreading (as is usually the case) while it was actually under prosecution, several instances of the same nature occurred. An anonymous information was laid before me containing a charge against several persons, who upon examination denied they were Christians, or had ever been so. They repeated after me an invocation to the gods, and offered religious rites with wine and incense before your statue (which for that purpose I had ordered to be brought, together with those of the gods), and even reviled the name of Christ: whereas there is no forcing, it is said, those who are really Christians into any of these compliances: I thought it proper, therefore, to discharge them. Some among those who were accused by a witness in person at first confessed themselves Christians, but immediately after denied it; the rest owned indeed that they had been of that number formerly, but had now (some above three, others more, and a few above twenty years ago) renounced that error. They all worshipped your statue and the images of the gods, uttering imprecations at the same time against the name of Christ. They affirmed the whole of their guilt, or their error, was, that they met on a stated day before it was light, and addressed a form of prayer to Christ, as to a divinity, binding themselves by a solemn oath, not for the purposes of any wicked design, but never to commit any fraud, theft, or adultery, never to falsify their word, nor deny a trust when they should be called upon to deliver it up; after which it was their custom to separate, and then reassemble, to eat in common a harmless meal. From this custom, however, they desisted after the publication of my edict, by which, according to your commands, I forbade the meeting of any assemblies. After receiving this account, I judged it so much the more necessary to endeavor to extort the real truth, by putting two female slaves to the torture, who were said to officiate' in their religious rites: but all I could discover was evidence of an absurd and extravagant superstition. I deemed it expedient, therefore, to adjourn all further proceedings, in order to consult you. For it appears to be a matter highly deserving your consideration, more especially as great numbers must be involved in the danger of these prosecutions, which have already extended, and are still likely to extend, to persons of all ranks and ages, and even of both sexes. In fact, this contagious superstition is not confined to the cities only, but has spread its infection among the neighbouring villages and country. Nevertheless, it still seems possible to restrain its progress. The temples, at least, which were once almost deserted, begin now to be frequented; and the sacred rites, after a long intermission, are again revived; while there is a general demand for the victims, which till lately found very few purchasers. From all this it is easy to conjecture what numbers might be reclaimed if a general pardon were granted to those who shall repent of their error.

Epistles 10.97: Trajan to Pliny: You have adopted the right course, my dearest Secundus, in investigating the charges against the Christians who were brought before you. It is not possible to lay down any general rule for all such cases. Do not go out of your way to look for them. If indeed they should be brought before you, and the crime is proved, they must be punished; with the restriction, however, that where the party denies he is a Christian, and shall make it evident that he is not, by invoking our gods, let him (notwithstanding any former suspicion) be pardoned upon his repentance. Anonymous informations ought not to he received in any sort of prosecution. It is introducing a very dangerous precedent, and is quite foreign to the spirit of our age.[5]

---

5. Pliny is quoted from the translation by Melmoth, revised by Bosanquet.

19

West across Africa with Simon the Zealot and Jude Son of James

1 The apostles Simon the Zealot and Jude son of James were sent by the council to lands far in the west; first to Cyrenaica and Mauretania, then, if the Lord allowed, to Britain and Gaul.

²In the years before the council, they had traveled together throughout Samaria and Galilee, and across the Jordan into Petraea and Arabia, showing great courage and endurance in preaching the word of the Lord. ³Wherever they traveled, Simon and Jude followed an ordered plan whereby they took three young disciples from each city and taught them as they journeyed concerning the word of God,

preaching, and overseeing the church. ⁴After they reached a new city, when a month or two had passed, they sent one of the new disciples home, appointed one to remain in the new city for a time, and took the third with them to the next city. ⁵In this manner, although Simon and Jude were quick to move on, they built a kinship in the Lord between believers in nearby cities and trained many young men to preach the word of the Lord. ⁶Furthermore, those they left behind trained others in the same manner to preach in the neighboring villages, and in this manner many came to Christ in a short time.

---

[1] These two apostles are listed together in the Gospels and Acts and almost always joined in traditions about their later ministries and deaths. To distinguish him from Simon Peter, Simon is called either the Canaanite (Matt 10:4; Mark 3:18) or the Zealot (Luke 6:15; Acts 1:13) by the evangelists. "Canaanite" is not a place name but a transliteration of the Hebrew *qana*, "the zealous one." Whether this appellation refers to Simon's temperament or to his membership in the first-century sect of that name, it is reasonable to suppose that he was energetic in his approach and strict in his adherence to the Jewish law. Luke refers to the apostle Judas (English: Jude) as "[son] of James" to distinguish him from Judas Iscariot. It is not known if this "James" is one of the Twelve or another. Judas is identified with Thaddeus (Matt 10:3; Mark 3:18), which may be another name used to distinguish him from Judas Iscariot. He is not to be confused with Jude the Lord's brother and author of the New Testament epistle. For ease of reference, this chapter will refer to the two apostles simply as Simon and Jude.

[2–6] There is no historical basis for the pattern of ministry supposed here for Simon and Jude. It is evident from Acts that Paul traveled with a group, focused on cities, and left co-workers behind, a pattern followed in chapters 1–2 above. An approach as methodical as the one described here for Simon and Jude is certainly possible, and it would help to explain the rapid expansion of Christianity around the empire and from urban to rural areas.

[7]When Simon and Jude found new disciples, they taught them how to give their lives to the Lord, [8]saying, "To follow Christ Jesus, there are three things you must give up, and a fourth. [9]First, you must give up your possessions. [10]For if you trust the Lord completely, you will hold nothing back for your own security; [11]and you cannot give in your heart only, for only what you do with your treasure proves the devotion of your heart. [12]Second, you must give up your family. [13]For if you cling to father or mother, or if you take on a wife, you will go no further than your duty to them will allow. [14]Find instead a new family in Christ Jesus, which will provide for you a full table of fellowship and many beloved children in those who are saved. [15]Third, you must give up your life. [16]For any day you may be killed for the Lord's sake; and if even once you say to yourself, 'I must live one more day, until tomorrow,' you will put tomorrow before the word of the Lord, and then another day, [17]until the word is further away from you than it was before you first heard it; and your condemnation will be worse than if you had never known the truth."

[18]"These three things the Lord taught while he was in the flesh; but in the Spirit he has taught us a fourth thing: that you must give up judgment. [19]For you will be accused of blasphemy or hypocrisy or evil, and you will suffer from hunger and thirst and various perils on the road or at sea. [20]You will be threatened by rulers of synagogues, magistrates of Rome, or authorities of other lands; [21]and crowds will gather to mock you and amuse themselves at the spectacle of your death. [22]But if you become bitter that you are treated so, or if you hate your despisers, your bitterness will become a poison to the saints and to the word of the Lord; [23]your heart will be lost, your mind will abandon the word of God, and your mouth will deny Christ before your persecutors. [24]Moreover, your body will turn in secret to the false comfort of women, or strong drink, or luxuries. [25]All of this begins in the moment that you judge what you deserve rather than trusting God to judge. [26]But remember always that he who chose you deserved the greatest honor but received the worst shame; [26]and that even now he sees all, even your heart; [27]and he knows all, even what you can endure; [28]and he forgives all, even your darkest thought. [29]Keep these things before your heart, beloved, and you will grow to be like him. [30]Remember also that those who persecute you are only blind until the love of Christ opens their eyes, and then you will be merciful toward them and severe toward the devil."

[31]Gathering and teaching disciples in this manner, Simon and Jude preached for two years along the entire coast, from Alexandria to Gades in Spain.

[7] The first three exhortations echo various passages from Luke's Gospel on the cost of discipleship, including the command to give up possessions (12:21, 33–34; 14:33; 16:10–14; 18:22–25), to leave behind family (5:11, 28; 8:21; 9:57–62; 14:26), and to sacrifice life itself (9:25; 14:27; 17:33). Jesus also warned disciples not to be "choked by the cares and riches and pleasures of life."

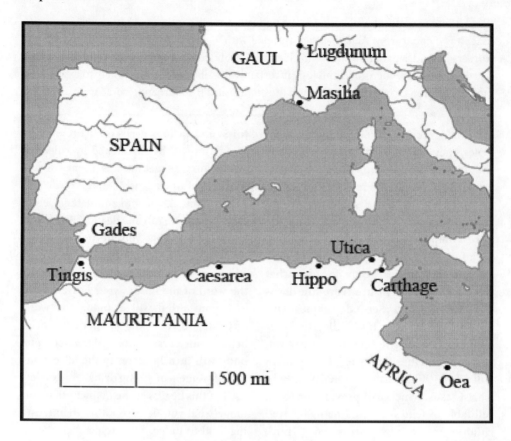

Map 6: Western North Africa

[8–18] The pattern of "three things . . . and a fourth" is a Jewish pattern of instruction familiar from the Old Testament (Prov 30; Amos 1–2); the number four is symbolic of completeness. The catalogue of hardships is familiar from passages like Luke 6:22; 21:12–19. The word "judgment" here introduces the problem of evaluating one's circumstances in terms of justice or fairness. In the first century or the twenty-first, one who has sacrificed ego and worldly comforts in the service of Christ is tempted at some point to resent getting a raw deal, or to fall prey to temptations that go with isolation or "life on a pedestal."

[19–31] It is important at this point to consider both the direction and the distance attributed her to Simon and Jude. Their traditional areas of missionary activity are literally all over the map, which may indicate either that they traveled extensively or that ignorance of their movements made them convenient subjects for invention. At least a few late traditions, curiously, assign them to both Mauretenia (modern Morocco) and Britain.[1] Others place them in Egypt, Arabia, Syria, and as far east as Babylonia, and Persia. Most of the stories of their martyrdom are set in the east. This narrative includes all of the above, and it moves them through Gaul, as well.

1. McBirnie, *The Twelve*, 162–64.

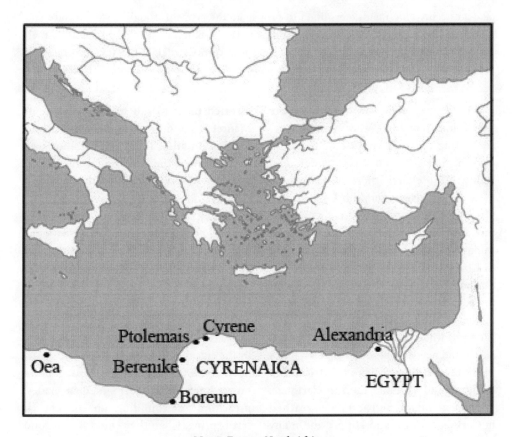

Map 7: Eastern North Africa

The next chapter will discuss the eastern travels of Simon and Jude; consider for now the possibility of Africa and Britain. From Alexandria to Tingis (Morocco) is 2,300 miles as the crow flies, and somewhat farther as the apostle walks or sails. A person in good shape can walk thirty miles per day, and ancient people on good roads probably covered distances greater than thirty miles on foot. Walking at this rate for six days per week, it would take about twelve weeks to hike the north coast of Africa. Ancient ships covered about 150 miles per day with fair winds; therefore, sailing at least half the distance, as proposed here, would cut the time required by more than half. Allowing for stops of one month per city for the ten cities listed would easily allow for the two-year time frame proposed here.

What of Britain and Gaul? To a modern reader, they may seem so far from Judea that the notion of travel there, especially by apostles in the first century, can only be the stuff of legend. And granted, there are some outlandish traditions, such as that of Joseph of Arimethea taking the boy Jesus to Glastonbury, England—conveniently enough, also the resting place of King Arthur. But is an apostolic missionary venture to the northern fringes of the empire out of the question? First century Roman roads were excellent, and it was a time of relative peace. By land, it is about 2,600 miles from Jerusalem to London. At the pace described above, the journey could be made on foot in four months—or six months with fewer miles per day or longer stops. By sea, the journey is quicker, but perhaps more hazardous. Now, take a dozen young men determined to propagate the gospel throughout the empire and give them about fifty years to accomplish it (say AD 35–85), for a total of six hundred man years. Is it unreasonable to think of just one of those years devoted to Britain, and one more to Gaul?

---

[32]First they went to Cyrene, where they found that there were many believers among the Jews because of the work of the Spirit through Alexander and Rufus. [33]The church there welcomed Simon and Andrew; and the Jews in that place were ready to listen to them when they saw that they followed the law in all things and also taught the mercy of God in Christ Jesus. [34]After they preached for a month in Cyrene, the saints there sent them, together with three young disciples, to the cities of Ptolemais, Berenike, and Boreum, where once again they preached and found new disciples. [35]From Cyrenaica they sailed to the province of Africa, first to the city of Oea and then to Carthage. [36]For six months Simon and Jude preached in Carthage, Utica, and Hippo, and many believed in Christ Jesus. [37]Then the Spirit directed them to sail to the province of Mauretenia and the cities of Caesarea and Tingis. [38]In all of these places Simon and Jude followed their custom of raising up disciples who accompanied them part of the way; [39]and after the apostles continued west, they returned to preach and teach in the region of their homes. [40]In this manner, the number of believers multiplied quickly throughout Cyrenaica, Africa, and Mauretenia.

[41]Crossing over the straits to Spain, Simon and Jude remained for several months in Baetica, where they were made welcome by the elders of the church in Gades, which had been established by Urbanus. [42]It was now winter, so they remained in Gades, preaching and building up the church until spring, when they could find a good ship and fair winds to sail to Britain.

---

[32] The province of Cyrenaica (modern Libya) was a Roman province, and Cyrenian Jews had their own synagogue in Jerusalem (Acts 6:9). Scholars believe that the reference to Simon of Cyrene, who carried Jesus's cross, as the father of Alexander and Rufus (Mark 15:21) suggests that these men were known to readers of the Gospel; this may be the same Rufus to whom Paul sends greetings in Romans 16:13. An early Christian presence in Cyrene is also implied by reference to believers from the city in Acts 11:19 and 13:1.

[33–35] The heavily-populated Roman province of Africa, especially the area in the vicinity of Carthage, was a center of Christianity from the second century,[2] making it likely that it was evangelized in the first century, possibly by apostles.

[36–41] Urbanus was left in nearby Corduba around 63 (1:52), so it has been five or six years—presumably enough time for him to continue the evangelistic ministry of Paul, who left Gades within days of his arrival (1:54—2:2 above).

---

2. Rankin, *Clement to Origen*, 55; Mullin, *Expansion of Christianity*, 301–8.

PRIMARY SOURCES

Christianity in Britain, Gaul, and Beyond the Empire

Irenaeus (AD 180) *Against Heresies* 1.10.2: As I have already observed, the <u>Church</u>, having received this preaching and this faith, although scattered throughout the whole world, yet, as if occupying but one house, carefully preserves it. . . . For the Churches which have been planted in Germany do not believe or hand down anything different, nor do those in Spain, nor those in Gaul, nor those in the East, nor those in Egypt, nor those in Libya, nor those which have been established in the central regions of the world.

Tertullian (AD 200) *An Answer to the Jews* 7.4: For upon whom else have the universal nations believed, but upon the Christ who is already come? For whom have the nations believed—Parthians, Medes, Elamites, and they who inhabit Mesopotamia, Armenia, Phrygia, Cappadocia, and they who dwell in Pontus, and Asia, and Pamphylia, tarriers in Egypt, and inhabiters of the region of Africa which is beyond Cyrene, . . . the varied races of the Gætulians, and manifold confines of the Moors, all the limits of Spain, and the diverse nations of the Gauls, and the haunts of the Britons—inaccessible to the Romans, but subjugated to Christ, and of the Sarmatians, and Dacians, and Germans, and Scythians, and of many remote nations, and of provinces and islands many, to us unknown, and which we can scarce enumerate?

20

Simon and Jude in Britain, Gaul, and Persia

1 Because there were no large cities along the coasts of Spain and Gaul, the ship that carried Simon and Jude north made its way slowly, putting in at small ports along the way. ²After two months, they made landfall in Britain at the port city of Noviomagus; and from there they traveled on the Roman roads to Corinium, Eburacum, Lindum, and Londinium. ³The people of Britain, who were recently conquered by the Romans, followed strange gods and were slow to hear the word of the Lord; but Simon and Jude preached to many of the Jews and Romans in the cities who believed and were baptized.

[1–2] Noviomagus is modern Chichester on the south coast of England. The modern versions of the other cities listed on this circular route are Cirencester, York, Lincoln, and London. These were all Roman administrative centers on major roads.

[3] As the primary sources below affirm, Christianity took hold in Britain as early as the second century, but scholars think it probably first spread to Roman soldiers and urban dwellers and was slow to penetrate the countryside. This is consistent with the picture throughout Acts and this account of evangelism focusing on cities—and often featuring prominent converts—followed by later infiltration of rural areas.[1] In fact, the word "heathen" literally refers to those outside cities who dwelt "among the heath."

SIMON AND JUDE ARE SENT EAST FROM GAUL

⁴Wishing to move to warmer lands before winter came, the apostles crossed over to the port of Gesoriacum in Gaul and traveled along the Roman road to Lugdunum. ⁵There they remained for the winter, preaching in that city; and they planned to travel throughout Gaul in the spring.

---

[4] Gesoriacum is Boulogne in northern France; Lugdunum is Lyon in central France.

---

1. Gill, "Urban Elites," 105–18.

Map 8: Britain

[5] The following account of the interruption of the apostles' brief time in Gaul is speculative. It is curious that multiple traditions place Simon and Jude in Africa and Britain, while multiple others locate one or both of them in Persia. If indeed they traveled to the far end of the known world, then back even further in the opposite direction, their dramatic direction change must have been motivated by a force greater than expedience or logic.

⁶But one night, while Simon was in the synagogue in Lugdunum studying the scriptures, the Spirit directed him to the place in the prophet Isaiah where it is written, "I will bring your offspring from the east, and from the west I will gather you." ⁷Simon wondered what this might mean; ⁸and immediately the Spirit showed him where David wrote, "As far as the east is from the west, so far he removes our transgressions from us." ⁹Simon's heart burned within him all night. ¹⁰In the morning he told Jude, who said, "So it is with me. ¹¹For in a dream last night, a man appeared to me in rich robes of the East, with the sun rising behind him and carrying a sword covered in blood. ¹²He spoke no word, but with his other hand he beckoned for me to come." ¹³Therefore Simon and Jude agreed that the Lord was directing them to the other side of the world to die; ¹⁴and when spring came, they traveled to the port of

Masilia and looked for a ship to take them east.

¹⁵After sailing for two months, they put in at Antioch, where the saints rejoiced to see them and to hear of all those whom the Lord had saved through their preaching in far lands. ¹⁶When they had received encouragement from the church there, they went inland to Edessa. ¹⁷There they learned that Bartholomew had been killed; and Jude said, "It is as my dream foretold. ¹⁸For the blood on the sword was not my own, yet the hand that beckoned was for me. ¹⁹So let us go immediately, for I would see as many as possible saved before I see the Lord."

²⁰Following their custom of taking with them disciples from each city where they preached, Simon and Jude went immediately to Babylon, where there were many Jews, and preached in the synagogues there. ²¹After some weeks, they traveled to Susa, and then to Persepolis in Persia. ²²There, too, they found many Jews, and many were saved. ²³After returning some distance along the same road, they went north into Parthia and Assyria, to the cities of Ectabana and Ninevah.

²⁴Thus Simon and Jude traveled throughout the kingdoms of the East for two years, rejoicing that they were allowed to live long enough to see so many saved. ²⁵When they came at last to Armenia, they were arrested in Ardaze below Mount Ararat by Gisak, the ruler of that region. ²⁶Gisak had heard from his priests that Simon and Jude stirred up many in the cities and towns of his land to defy the gods that he served. ²⁷He took the apostles to the hillside above the city and ordered his soldiers to beat them and pierce them with swords, hoping they would deny Christ and shame themselves before the people who had gathered. ²⁸But Simon, just before he died, said, "Do you think my brother and I would turn away from the prize now, after we have journeyed twice across the world to reach it?" ²⁹So Gisak ordered Simon to be cut into pieces, and Jude to be pierced with a spear. ³⁰And Aggaeus, a disciple who accompanied Simon and Jude, went back to Edessa to tell of their deaths before returning to preach to his countrymen in Persia.

[6–9] This may look like the modern pious practice of opening the Bible at random to find guidance, but Simon is not seeking direction; rather, he discovers the juxtaposition of the two passages, then considers its application to his ministry. Such free association, both between verses and between verses and their application, was common and acceptable in ancient Judaism. The verses that Simon quotes are Psalm 103:12 (v. 6) and Isaiah 43:5 (v. 8).

[10–12] Direction from visions and dreams is familiar to Luke's readers (Acts 2:17; 9:10; 10:3; 11:5; 18:9), including the critical appearance of a Macedonian man beckoning Paul to come evangelize his country (16:9).

[13–14] Masilia is modern Marseille on the south coast of France.

[15–20] After the Babylonia exile in the sixth century BC, most Jews remained in the area. The city became a center for study, in the fifth century AD producing the Talmud, which is the central text in Judaism to this day.

[21–23] The furthest point of this journey is between Edessa and Persepolis, a journey along a major trade route of about one thousand miles. From Persepolis north to Ninevah (modern Mosul, Iraq) is about seven hundred miles. This account allows Simon and Jude two years to cover this route, including stays of a month or two in each major city. Their deaths occur, therefore, about AD 71, which is within the wide range of AD 50–80 given by most traditions. This date allows ample time for Luke to learn of the events before writing this account in the mid-70s.

[24–25] Gisak and other Armenian names are fictional. The tradition that Simon and Jude were killed in this place—Simon by sword—is late and may be an attempt by an Armenian writer to claim the apostles for the area. On the other hand, Armenia was the first kingdom to make Christianity its official religion (AD 301), and the choice of a small town like Ardaze (modern Makou) seems an unusual one as compared to other cities claimed as sites for the apostles' martyrdom. A fourth-century apocryphal work, the *Passion of Simon and Jude* (followed by the later martyrologies of Jerome, Bede, etc.) reports that the apostles were killed in the unidentified Persian city of Suanir by priests.[2]

[26–30] The late second-century Syrian *Teaching of the Apostles* (*See* primary sources below) mentions Aggaeus as a disciple of Jude who, following the apostle's death, continued preaching in Persia to the borders of India. His inclusion here is in keeping with the pattern throughout this narrative of accounting for Luke's sources and of implying that the work of evangelism did, and should, continue.

PRIMARY SOURCES

Simon and Jude in the East

The Teaching of the Apostles (AD 180–200): Edessa, and all the countries round about it which were on all sides of it, and Zoba, and Arabia, and all the north, and the regions round about it, and the south, and all the regions on the borders of Mesopotamia, received the apostles' ordination to the priesthood from Addæus [Jude] the apostle. . . . The whole of Persia, of the Assyrians, and of the Armenians, and of the Medians, and of the countries round about Babylon, the Huzites and the Gelæ, as far as the borders of the Indians, and as far as the land of Gog and Magog, and moreover all the countries on all sides, received the apostles' ordination to the priesthood from Aggæus, a maker of silks, the disciple of Addæus the apostle.

Acts of Thaddeus (AD 300): And Thaddæus [Jude] along with Abgarus destroyed idol-temples and built churches; ordained as bishop one of his disciples, and presbyters, and deacons, and gave them the rule of the psalmody and the holy liturgy. And having left them, he went to the city of Amis, great metropolis of the Mesechaldeans and Syrians, that is, of Mesopotamia-Syria, beside the river Tigris. . . . Having therefore remained with them for five years, he built a church; and having appointed as bishop one of his disciples, and presbyters, and deacons, and prayed for them, he went away, going round the cities of Syria, and teaching, and healing all the sick; whence he brought many cities and countries to Christ through His teaching. Teaching, therefore, and evangelizing along with the disciples, and healing the sick, he went to Berytus, a city of Phœnicia by the sea; and there, having taught and enlightened many, he fell asleep on the twenty-first of the month of August.

2. Schneemelcher, *Apocrypha*, 481–82.

Eusebius (AD 325) *Ecclesiastical History* 1.13.10: After the ascension of Jesus, Judas, who was also called Thomas, sent to him Thaddeus, an apostle, one of the Seventy. When he had come [to Edessa] he lodged with Tobias, the son of Tobias.

Moses of Chorene (AD 480) *History of Armenia* 9: There came then into Armenia the Apostle Bartholomew, who suffered martyrdom among us in the town of Arepan. As to Simon, who was sent unto Persia, I cannot relate with certainty what he did, nor where he suffered martyrdom. It is said that one Simon, an apostle, was martyred at Veriospore. Is this true, or why did the saint come to this place? I do not know; I have only mentioned this circumstance that you may know I spare no pains to tell you all that is necessary.

21

South to Alexandria and Axum with Matthew

1 For many years before the council, John Mark traveled with Paul, Barnabas, Peter, and Matthew. ²It was Mark who wrote, on Peter's behalf, the first account of the life of the Lord. ³He was also among the first to preach in Alexandria, and he was beloved by the church there. ⁴After the council, he went to Alexandria with Matthew and Apollos. ⁵Leaving them in the Jewish quarter, he went to the Greek quarter to the house of Eustathis and rejoiced that the believers had multiplied in that part of the city. ⁶There he remained for two years, building up the saints and preaching to the Greeks. ⁷But in the fourteenth year of Nero, it happened that the day of the Lord's resurrection occurred on the same day as the festival of Serapis. ⁸Hearing that the Christians were worshiping, a mob came from the Serapeum nearby and surrounded the house of Eustathis, demanding that the believers come out and pay homage to the idol.

---

[1] For Mark's travels, see Acts 12:12, 25; 15:37, 39; Col 4:10; 1Thess 3:17; 1 Tim 6:21; 2 Tim 4:11; Phm 24; 1 Pet 5:13; and in this account 1:29; 2:17, 44; 3:4; 7:4–5, 13, 34; 8:3–8, 18–19, 34; 13:13–14.

[2–3] A strong and early tradition associates Mark with Alexandria and names him as its first bishop; but understandably, given his itinerant career, the dates and lengths of his visits are uncertain (Eusebius *Ecclesiastical History* 2.16, 24; Jerome *On Virtue* 7; Epiphanius *Heresies* 51.6).

[4–6] The timing here is conjectural, and the name Eustathis is fictional.

[7] The account of Mark's martyrdom below is adapted from a Coptic/Egyptian tradition reported by,[1] which also gives the date at AD 68. In the account presented here, only Mark's speech is new material.

[8] The facts support the Coptic tradition concerning Mark's death. Serapis, the official chief god of Hellenistic Egypt, was a composite god introduced by Ptolemy I (305–285 BC), whose intent was to unite native Egyptians and Greek colonists. Serapis combined the

---

1. Atiya, *Eastern Christianity*, 27–28.

features of various gods and beliefs from both cultures. His highly popular cult focused on healing and fertility, and followers were promised eternal life. The Serapeum was a huge complex of buildings on the west side of Alexandria, near the location of the Christian catacombs.

---

[9]Immediately Mark came out and spoke boldly to the crowd: [10]"Men and women of Alexandria, do not be angry that we worship our God on the day of your festival. [11]For the day was not chosen by men to insult you, but by God to enlighten you. [12]Moreover, it is not the day that matters, but the truth regarding the one we worship. [13]For all know that Serapis was made from the gods of Egypt and the Greeks; and this is no shame, for the true God has sent stories to all men to show himself in part until the whole is revealed. [14]So it is told that a bull rises when it is killed to give life to all; that a three-headed dog guards the gates of hell; that a snake heals diseases. [15]All these are pictures of the truth, but their fulfillment is in Christ Jesus. [16]For he came not in a story but in the flesh; [17]and when his own people turned against him, God raised him from the dead and gave him glory and all authority over heaven and hell and over all diseases and demons. [18]He shines brighter than any sun and gives life to all who call upon him." [19]At these words, some in the crowd were moved and wished to hear more about the Lord; [20]but those who believed that he insulted Serapis shouted so loudly that he could no longer be heard. [21]Then the mob seized him, and tying him with ropes, they dragged him through the streets. [22]When they saw that he was still alive, they imprisoned him in the Serapeum overnight; and the next morning they dragged him through the streets again until he gave up his spirit. [23]They intended to burn his body, but just then a great rain began to fall; and with no crowd to watch their cruelty, they left Mark's body in the street for the dogs and returned to their homes. [24]While the rain fell and the wind blew, some of the saints carried off his body in secret and buried it in the house of Eustathis.

[25]At this time Matthew and Apollos were in the Jewish quarter, where Matthew finished writing his account of the life of the Lord while Apollos preached to the Jews and built up the believers among them.

[9–13] The notion of paganism as preparation rather than competition for the gospel was popularized in the last century by J. R. R. Tolkien and C. S. Lewis, but there is no reason that it could not have been advanced in the first century. Indeed, Mark's close attention to parallels between the crucifixion of Jesus and the Roman triumphal procession (*See* comments on 8:4 above) shows that he was ready to make use of pagan imagery to advance the gospel. His speech here is simply an extension of that principle.

[14] Serapis is usually depicted as a human (occasionally with a bull's head), accompanied by a three-headed dog and a snake.

[15–18] The logic of paganism as preparation suggests that stories set in other worlds (Olympus, Valhalla, etc.) made people ready to hear the same principles conveyed in the Christian story, with the superior difference that the Christian story happened in this world. The last line here is the most risky for Mark: Serapis was a sun god, adapted in part from the Egyptian deity Ra and often depicted with a seven-pointed star on his brow. To claim that

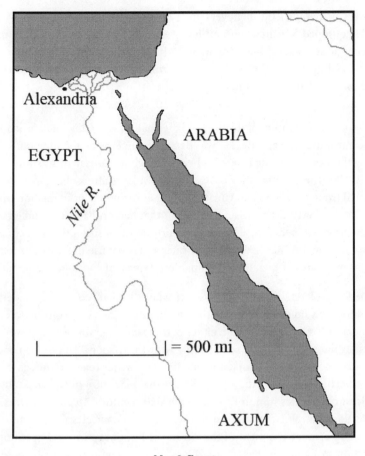

Map 9: Egypt

Jesus is "brighter than any sun" would be construed as either profound or provocative, as the diverse reaction of Mark's audience shows. The details of ropes, an overnight imprisonment, and the intended cremation stopped by a storm are all from the Coptic account.

[19–24] There is no evidence to place Matthew and Apollos in Alexandria at this time; but with no competing claims for their presence, they serve the narrative here. Alexandria was a major city in the first century, with about 400,000 inhabitants and a sizeable Jewish quarter in the northeast part of the city. It is plausible, therefore, that two prominent Christian leaders (Matthew and Apollos) could labor on one end of the city independently of a third (Mark). Nevertheless, the martyrdom of one would put the others in danger, making this an opportune moment to visit Antioch.

[26]Soon after the death of Mark, Matthew and Apollos went to Antioch, where Matthew had copies made of his writings for use by the church there and by any apostles who traveled through the city to preach in faraway lands. [27]When he had stayed in Antioch for three months, he left Apollos there and returned to Alexandria. [28]At this time Vespasian was in the city, while his armies fought to make him emperor and to defeat the Jews. [29]Therefore, fearing trouble either from the Romans or

the followers of Serapis, the believers in Alexandria equipped Matthew with all he would need to journey south, sending with him Leontis and Propylus.

³⁰Matthew traveled first by boat to the cities of upper Egypt, then by roads into Axum. ³¹When he found synagogues of the Jews, he showed them by many proofs from the scriptures that Jesus is the Christ.

[26–29] Vespasian was in Egypt during the latter half of AD 69, while his armies consolidated his control over the empire. He was declared emperor by the Egyptians in the summer and by the Roman Senate in December. Meanwhile, Jerusalem was under siege until March of AD 70. These factors may have created a volatile atmosphere in Alexandria or at least potential trouble for Jews and Christians, either separately or in relation to each other. Moreover, Mark's martyrdom was a recent event that had probably not cooled the ardor of diehard Serapis worshipers. These factors support the supposition that someone as notable among the Christians as Matthew would be safer and more useful far from Alexandria. Leontis and Propylus are fictional travel companions typical of apostolic missionary journeys.

[30] "Upper" Egypt refers to upriver Egypt, where Roman control extended along the Nile for a thousand miles. Further south was the important kingdom of Axum (roughly equivalent to modern Ethiopia). From either of these areas, Arabia was accessible by several large ports on the Red Sea. Why send Matthew to this region? Traditions concerning his travels are so sketchy, contradictory, and late that one writer refers to him as the "phantom apostle."[1] Nevertheless, among the late traditions that place him in Persia, Arabia, and elsewhere, at least one locates him in Ethiopia (the sixth-century *Apostolic History of Abdias*). The supposition that he traveled even farther south is conjectural. But the discovery of an early-second century fragment of the Gospel of John in southern Egypt, together with the production in Egypt of several early Gnostic texts, confirms that the Nile valley was evangelized in the first century, which opens the possibility of an apostolic mission. The Nile was a convenient highway, there were land and sea routes into Arabia, and there were Jewish settlements throughout the region. Apostles could have traveled south beyond the borders of the empire just as they (more certainly) traveled to other compass points. The story of the Ethiopian eunuch (Acts 8:27–39) supports at least an awareness of the region and, perhaps, a connection to it through this early convert. Together, these factors support at least the possibility of an apostolic journey far up the Nile. Since Matthew is the only one of the Twelve with any traditional connection to the area; and since he is not strongly connected anywhere else, this account designates him the southernmost apostolic missionary.

[31] Given the dominance in his Gospel of scriptural fulfillment texts concerning the ministry of Jesus, it would be natural to recount Matthew's ministry to the Egyptian Jews. But because the movement of the narrative is away from the Jewish mission and toward "the ends of the earth," it is appropriate to imagine what it was like to preach the gospel in places where even Judaism was unknown. The evangelistic sermon that follows is an attempt to convey, in terms appropriate to the first century and to a particular apostle, the challenge of such a mission.

---

1. Ruffin, *The Twelve*, 140.

³²But as he journeyed further south, he came eventually to cities where there were no Jews, and he found many who had never heard the word of God. ³³Whenever he came to such a place, he gathered the leaders or any who would listen and spoke to them in this manner:

³⁴"Although I am a stranger, I bring a story that you will know in part, for it begins in every heart. ³⁵Among my people, a promise from long ago was fulfilled when one came to save us from bondage. ³⁶But he came as a humble child, not as the king the people desired; and he preached peace and forgiveness, not war and conquest. ³⁷So despite the truth of his words and the miracles and healings he performed, his own people rejected him and delivered him to the authorities to be killed. ³⁸For their hatred these people have suffered greatly, most of all in their hearts. ³⁹For who among us does not long for mercy from God, and how much more those who have long waited for a promised deliverer? ⁴⁰Now as for this deliverer, Christ Jesus by name, God raised him from the dead and took him up to heaven, as I and many others witnessed. ⁴¹But before God took him up, Christ Jesus promised to return and reward those who believe in him, not only among the Jews but also among the nations. ⁴²So I come to you, to increase the harvest of salvation before he returns.

⁴³And who am I to ask you to believe these things? ⁴⁴I was not always as you see me now, an old man with few possessions. ⁴⁵When I was young I learned to read and speak in different tongues and to reckon numbers, but up to the time of my calling by Christ Jesus I used my learning only to make wealth for one man—myself. ⁴⁶Now I am able to count many who are made rich in spirit by hearing the word of God, and I am able to tell of his greatness in many tongues. ⁴⁷Furthermore, although I am an old man, I have many spiritual children among whom my heart moves like a young father. ⁴⁸And while I carry no gold or silver, I am free from the burden of their care; ⁴⁹moreover, I have no fear for tomorrow, and I have treasure laid up in the kingdom of heaven, toward which I am bound with every step.

[32–36] Of the four Gospel writers, Matthew devotes the most attention to the birth of Jesus, his fulfillment of scripture, and the disconnect between Jewish hopes and the mission of Jesus.

[37–38] This is, of course, a veiled reference to the destruction of Jerusalem, which had recently occurred when this sermon was delivered. But to offer details would distract hearers from the point of the sermon, which is to connect the story that Matthew brings to the spiritual longings of his audience.

[39–45] Of the Twelve, only Matthew is clearly an educated man at the time of his calling by Jesus (Matt 9:9). A Galilean tax collector would have to be literate and conversant in three or four languages. The work involved a contract with the Romans to provide, under their protection, certain revenues; to these the collector would add "what the market could bear" to pay himself. This imprecise system understandably alienated many and led to the lumping together of "tax collectors and sinners" (e.g., Matt 9:11; 11:19).

[46] The phrase "rich in spirit" is a deliberate play on the expression "poor in spirit," which occurs only in Matthew (5:3).

[**47–49**] The Gospels of Matthew and Luke contain numerous teachings of Jesus about giving up worldly possessions to gain heavenly treasure (e.g., Matt 6:19–20; Luke 12:33–34).

---

⁵⁰Who would not count mine a profitable exchange, to give up that which I could never keep in order to gain what I cannot lose? ⁵¹And now I ask you to consider, as I once did, the ties that bind you, the worries of this life, and the fear of death and what lies beyond. ⁵²Does your heart not cry within you for a god greater than those you have known? ⁵³And do you not hear the call of Christ Jesus in your spirit as I heard him call to me in the flesh many years ago? ⁵⁴Listen! For it is not only my voice that you hear but the power of his Spirit calling you to salvation."

⁵⁵And wherever Matthew went, whether to the Jews or to those in the furthest parts of Axum who heard the word of God for the first time, the Spirit bore fruit through him in those who were saved.

[**50**] The last part of this question adapts a quote attributed to mid-century missionary martyr Jim Elliot, who wrote in his journal in 1949: "He is no fool who gives what he cannot keep to gain that which he cannot lose." His source was the seventeenth-century preacher Philip Henry who wrote, a bit less elegantly, "He is no fool who parts with that which he cannot keep, when he is sure to be recompensed with that which he cannot lose." Both quotes ultimately derive from the words of Jesus about the futility of gaining the world while losing one's soul (Matt 16:26; Luke 9:25).

[**51–55**] As in previous chapters and throughout Acts, a summary is provided to affirm the success and progress of the gospel. In this case, however, the narrative leaves Matthew still preaching rather than telling of his martyrdom. The earliest tradition available, from the late second century (Clement of Alexandria *Stromata* 4.9), reports that Matthew died a natural death. Stories of Matthew's martyrdom emerge much later and are unreliable. Indeed, the very existence of a tradition of apostolic death by natural causes in an historical context where violent death was almost expected makes it highly likely that Matthew was not a martyr.

22

East to India with Thomas

1 Eight years after the Lord was taken up into heaven, Thomas was in Jerusalem when the Spirit directed him to travel east and preach in the regions of Persia, Parthia, and India. [2]From his journeys during these many years, Thomas sent word to Jerusalem by messenger or letter concerning the progress of the gospel, which the church rejoiced to hear.

[3]Therefore, when Simeon called a council to send out the apostles, he did not send for Thomas, knowing that he was far away preaching as the Lord had instructed him.

[4]Soon after his calling, Thomas traveled to Edessa, and from there he preached the word of the Lord throughout the regions of Osrohoene, Assyria, and Media.

---

[1] The supposition that Thomas traveled as far as India seems at first glance legendary, but the evidence is actually stronger than that for other apostles reaching Britain or Gaul. Early tradition consistently places Thomas in India, including accounts in Eusebius, Jerome, Gregory of Nazianzus, Ephrem, and Ambrose. In the sixteenth century, European explorers found a Christian population on the southwest coast (Malabar) that claimed spiritual descent from Thomas. They claimed to have memorialized his ministry in the *Rabban Pattu* song, which offers detail of the churches he founded and miracles he performed. The "Thomas Churches" and the Christian presence in Malabar remains strong to this day.

Some of the most interesting evidence comes from the early third-century *Acts of Thomas*.[1] This work is Gnostic in character and contains much obviously legendary material, but it also appears to preserve some historically credible traditions.[2] Scholars dismissed it as unreliable until historical and literary investigations revealed some remarkably accurate features. Chief among these is the discovery by modern archaeologists that a king mentioned in the text, Gundaphorus, was an actual historical character[3]—knowledge available only to someone who had traveled to the region at that time. There is some debate about which Gundaphorus this is of several who went by that name in the general period, with the fourth reigning over what is now northeast Pakistan in the mid-first century. Evidence has also come to light that both land and sea routes were used by first-century traders to visit

1. For a thorough introduction, see Klauck, *Apocryphal Acts*, 141–80.
2. McGrath, "Acts of Thomas," 297–311.
3. Neill, *India*, 27–28; Chinnappan, "Thomas," 207–22.

the southwest coast of India, called Malabar, which contained Jewish settlements.[4] Several other details in the *Acts of Thomas* may reflect knowledge of ancient India; but most of the names and other aspects of the story appear to be of later, Syrian origin.

[2–4] These are regions of modern Iraq and Iran that follow the ancient trade routes southeast toward Afghanistan and India.

> 4. Neill, *India*, 31–32; Menachery, "St. Thomas," 25–30.

---

[5]In cities along the trade routes where he found Jewish settlements, he remained for a time preaching in the synagogues, and many believed. [6]Thomas did not take silver or gold from any; [7]but as need arose, he worked with his own hands building houses, as he had done from his youth in Tiberius.

[8]When the Lord told Thomas that he should journey further east into lands far beyond the reach of Rome, he met a merchant from India named Abbanes who was sent by his king to find carpenters who could build palaces after the fashion of the Romans. [9]Abbanes agreed to take Thomas with him and to begin to teach him the language of India. [10]After many months along the trade routes through Persia and Parthia, they arrived in Taxila, the chief city of king Gundaphorus in India.

[11]Abbanes took Thomas to the king, who instructed Thomas to build a palace for him in Pindi, a city nearby. [12]He gave Thomas gold for this purpose, and he sent with him a slave who could speak both Greek and the Indian tongue.

[5–8] Although the figure of Abbanes in the *Acts of Thomas* is probably fictional, archaeologists have discovered that Gundaphorus was an avid builder who commissioned many structures in the Greek style. This confirms active communication between his kingdom and the West and strengthens the credibility of this aspect of the *Acts of Thomas*.

[9–10] The borders of the king's domain extended into modern Afghanistan on the west, parts of modern India on the east, and much of modern Pakistan in the center. Since borders were indistinct in the ancient world, it may not be contradictory for ancient writers (see primary sources below) to place Thomas in Parthia rather than India.

The story that follows is adapted from the *Acts of Thomas* 17–29: the apostle is commissioned to build a palace but gives the money to the poor; when confronted, he tells the king that the palace is already built, but in heaven; the enraged king considers how to kill him; his brother Gad has a near-death experience in which angels show him the king's heavenly palace; Gad tells the king, and the two are converted by Thomas; the apostle enjoys their patronage in establishing the church. Such drama and plot twisting make this arguably the best story in all of the apocryphal acts—but is it true? The writer's knowledge of an historical Gundaphorus lends some credibility to the account. Beyond that, the reader may judge the apostle's outrageous behavior and his deliverance by a timely dream as either the products of an extraordinary imagination or events so remarkable that they were passed on through several generations until the composition of the *Acts of Thomas*. In either case, the account deserves inclusion here on its merits as an effective and edifying story.

[11] Taxila would be in northeast Pakistan today, near Islamabad. Rawalpindi is about twenty miles southeast.

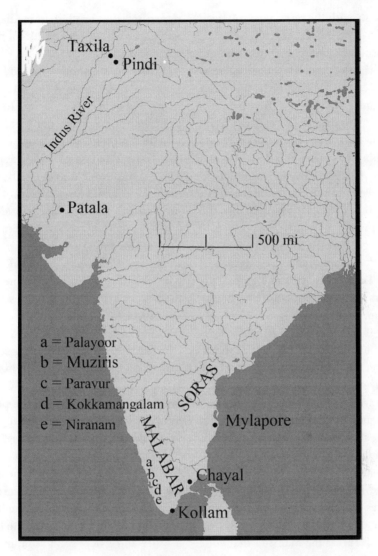

Map 10: India

[12] The slave-interpreter, who is not in the *Acts of Thomas*, is added here for realism. Thomas would need an interpreter and help to hire workmen. Once Thomas gave away the money for construction, the king's representative would either have reported the apostle's actions or (as below) run away in dread of the royal wrath, leaving someone else to discover later that there was no building.

[13]When Thomas came to the city where Gundaphorus desired a palace, he saw how poor the people were and how many were afflicted with disease. [14]Moved with pity, he gave to the poor all of the king's gold, and took up his residence among them. [15]He healed many and preached to them as well as he could, for he did not yet know their language well; and the king's slave had run away in fear. [16]After two months passed, the king sent a steward to see the progress of the palace, and he found nothing. [17]Hearing this report, Gundaphorus sent soldiers to search for Thomas. [18]They found him

living openly with the poor, who followed him as one of their holy men.

[19]The soldiers brought Thomas before the king, who demanded what had become of the palace and the gold he had given to him. [20]Thomas said to him, "Your palace is finished." [20]Gundaphorus replied, "Who will tell me the truth? For my steward says that nothing has been done. When can I see this palace?" [22]Thomas said, "Your steward tells you the truth that he sees, but the truth that he does not see is that the palace is in heaven, which you purchased with your gold; and you will see it when you die." [23]Gundaphorus was enraged; and throwing Thomas into prison, he asked his counselors how best to torture him before killing him.

[24]Now that very night in a palace nearby, Gad, the brother of the king, was struck with a fever and seemed to die. [25]But in the morning, while his wife and household were preparing to mourn him, he returned to health and hurried to the king to tell him of the strange dream he had. [26]He said to Gundaphorus, "In my dream I went to paradise, and a man came to me whose face shone so brightly that I could not see his features. [27]He took me by the hand and led me to a marvelous palace; [28]and he said to me, 'This is the mansion that your brother built, and it waits for him. [29]But return to your brother immediately, and he will know how to build another such palace for you.'"

[30]When Gundaphorus heard his brother's words, he covered his face with his hands and wept. [31]Then he sent his soldiers to bring Thomas from the prison, and he told his brother Gad the story of the gold that Thomas had given to the poor. [32]When Thomas was brought to them, the king and his brother knelt before him and asked who his God was and how they could worship him. [33]Then Thomas explained to them all things concerning Christ Jesus; and that same day they were baptized, together with their wives and many members of their household. [34]And Thomas remained with them for a year, living at times with the king and at other times with the poor. [35]He began to preach in the language of the people, and many believed in both Taxali and Pindi. [36]Gundaphorus gave Thomas much more gold to give to the poor, [37]for he said, "The palace in heaven for my brother must be as great as mine."

[38]But after two years, the kingdom of Gundaphorus was invaded by armies from the north. [39]And when word came to the king that his army was defeated, he sent Thomas away by ship, [40]saying to him, "My brother and I may soon see our new palaces, but you have other houses to build."

[13–19] How ironic that Thomas is, in Catholic tradition, the patron saint of builders. Perhaps modern contractors derive inspiration from this story for similarly imaginative reports of their progress.

[20–26] In the *Acts of Thomas* 22–23, angels rather than this Christ figure show the palace to Gad, and Gad returns with the intent of buying the palace from the king; his report confirms the claim of Thomas and leads to the conversion of the brothers.

[27–39] This invasion and the end of the reign of Gundaphorus in AD 52 is known by historians, but it is not recorded in the *Acts of Thomas* as the reason for the apostle's departure; nor does the book record a parting scene like the one depicted here. The Indus River was navigable only closer to the ocean and in the dry season, so Thomas would have traveled by road to a port city on the Indian Ocean in order to make his way further south.

PRIMARY SOURCES

Thomas Sent to India

The Teaching of the Apostles (AD 180–200): India, and all the countries belonging to it and round about it, even to the farthest sea, received the apostles' ordination to the priesthood from Judas Thomas, who was guide and ruler in the church which he had built there, in which he also ministered there.

Acts of Thomas (AD 225) 1: At that season all we the apostles were at Jerusalem . . . we portioned out the regions of the world, in order that each one of us might go into the region that fell to him, and to the nation to which the Lord sent him. By lot, then, India fell to Judas Thomas, also called Didymus. And he did not wish to go, saying that he was not able to go on account of the weakness of the flesh; and how can I, being an Hebrew man, go among the Indians to proclaim the truth? And while he was thus reasoning and speaking, the Saviour appeared to him through the night, and said to him: Fear not, Thomas; go away to India, and proclaim the word; for my grace shall be with you.

Eusebius (AD 325) *Ecclesiastical History* 3.1.1: The holy apostles and disciples of our Saviour were scattered throughout the whole world. Thomas, as tradition relates, obtained by lot Parthia.

23

Martyrdom of Thomas

1 Thomas traveled down the Indus River to the port of Patala. [2]From there he sailed along the coast to the region of Malabar, where he found settlements of Jews who traded with Rome by ship. [3]When Thomas embarked at the port of Muziris, he preached in the synagogue there. [4]One of the first who believed among the Jews was Samuel, who became a brother in the Lord to Thomas; [5]and after many years with the apostle he returned to Antioch to tell of all that the Lord has done in India.

[6]Thomas remained in Muziris for two years, where he learned the language of that region and began to preach among the people. [7]Many believed because they saw the signs that Thomas did, healing many of their diseases and casting out demons. [8]Moreover, they saw that Thomas lived as one of their poor, wearing a simple garment and eating only bread and water. [9]He remained in the region of Malabar for twenty years, and there he established churches in the seven cities of Muziris, Palayoor, Paravur, Kokkamangalam, Niranam, Kollam, and Chayal.

[1–2] Patala was both the end of the ancient land route from the west and the port at the mouth of the Indus. Its modern location is disputed, but some identify it with the city of Thatta in Pakistan.

[3] The Malabar coast stretches about 250 miles along the southwest tip of India. First-century Roman geographer Pliny the Elder (*Natural History* 6.101) describes extensive trade with India, and the discovery of Roman coins in Malabar confirm that it was a major trade center, connecting India to Red Sea ports, Alexandria, and the rest of the empire.[1] There is also evidence of extensive Jewish settlement.[2] These factors add credibility to confirm the Indian oral tradition regarding early evangelism of the area, which they attribute to the apostle Thomas.

[4–5] Samuel is a fictional character here, added to account for information regarding Thomas to reach Luke in the time frame allotted to this volume.

---

1. Mullen, *Expansion of Christianity*, 71–72.
2. McGrath, "Acts of Thomas," 304.

[6–9] The general outline of this chapter is adapted from Indian tradition concerning Thomas, which may contain an historical kernel around which more legendary elements grew.[3] The cities listed here are the so-called Thomas Churches of Indian tradition that survive to this day. The lengthy *Rabban Pattu* song (see note on 22:1 above) gives details of the ministry of Thomas, including healings, exorcisms, notable conversions. It is also from Indian tradition that this account derives dates for Thomas's move to Malabar in AD 52 and his death in AD 72.

3. Atiya, *Eastern Christianity*, 359–88.

---

[10]In each place he remained for three years, building up the church; [11]then he journeyed futher south and east, leaving behind many believers trained in righteousness and the word of God.

[12]When Thomas prepared to leave Chayal on the far side of India, the believers there warned him not to go further up the coast because they feared the zealous priests of that country. [13]By this time Thomas was an old man, weakened by much fasting; [14]but he said, "The Lord calls to me continually from the rising sun, and that way I must go until I find the end of the world or the end of my life; either end will be a joy to me."

[15]Taking with him only Samuel, Thomas reached the city of Mylapore in the region of Soras, where he began to preach as he had in Malabar, in this manner:

[16]"I see that the custom of this land is to wash in a river, or to chant the names of the gods, or to perform tasks for them in order to gain salvation. [17]But I say to you that these are the doctrines of priests, who are the same in every land, including my own. [18]They lay burdens on men, causing them to live in fear that their good deeds will not be enough to please God, nor are they ever pleased except when they are ruling others. [19]They take the last coins of the poor to build their temples, not knowing that the true God lives not in a building but in our hearts; [20]and the house of a poor man is sufficient to gather for the worship of the Lord.

[21]"Moreover, I see that the custom of this land is to honor those with light skin and make outcasts of those with dark skin. [22]But I say to you that all men shed blood that is red, [23]and red was the blood of Christ Jesus, shed for all men. [24]So do not despair if the traditions of men appoint a low place for you, for in Christ Jesus you are promised a place in the heavens, [25]where all are one in him and all are white as snow, for they reflect his glory.

[26]"Again, I learn that your philosophers say that all things are God, or that there is no god but the one within them. [27]But I say to you that this seems good only when the crops ripen at the right time or when a mother suckles her child. [28]It does not seem so, however, when one suffers from the cruelty of other men or when sickness takes an infant. [29]Moreover, if man is a god to himself, then it is not you only but your neighbor who is a god. [30]And how fortunate if the god that is your neighbor is a merciful god, but how unfortunate if he takes your goat or your wife. [31]Look at the sinfulness of man—lying, unjust, hurtful; always at war with nature, others, and himself—and see what gods these men are and how the world is to be pitied, ruled by such gods. [32]No, God must be other than us, or we are doomed to die in misery and confusion. [33]And God must be one, or we serve lesser gods who are not gods at all."

[34]Thomas had preached in this manner for two months, and many believed, especially among the poor. [35]But when the

priests of Mylapore learned that a man was preaching the word of the Lord in opposition to their gods, they went to Misdaeus, the king of that place, and had Thomas arrested.

³⁵The king asked Thomas to answer the reports he had heard about his preaching. ³⁶And when the apostle spoke boldly to him concerning the ways of the priests and the nature of God, Misdaeus saw that Thomas spoke with wisdom and authority, and he wished to hear more, but he feared the priests.³⁷Then the priests said to him, "Make this man show you a sign; for we hear that he is a healer, and he and his god should be put to the test."

³⁸Thomas refused, saying, "My God does not perform wonders out of obedience to men but out of his mercy, which is not ours to command.

[10–11] Indian tradition actually has Thomas travelling further east for a missionary trip into Maylasia before returning to establish the Indian churches. Further travel is certainly possible given the evidence of extensive trade from the port of Mylapore, which is the traditional location of the martyrdom and burial of the apostle. The city is now the southern part of Tamil Nadu.

[12–15] The accounts of Thomas's preaching in the *Acts of Thomas* are largely Gnostic in content and have nothing to do with India. The sermon here is an attempt to address key differences between Hinduism and Christianity in the style of a first-century evangelist. The three paragraphs, offered in the "it is said . . . but I say" style of the Sermon on the Mount (Matt 5), adapt New Testament teaching about salvation by works or appearances, division due to ethnic or status differences, and the nature of God.

[16–35] Misdaeus is the name of the king in the brief martyrdom account of the *Acts of Thomas* (below). If the account is based on actual events, the name Misdaeus may be an attempt to render in Greek the name of an unknown Indian monarch.

[35–36] In the Indian oral tradition, it is not the king and his soldiers who kill Thomas. Instead, a group of Brahmin priests who resent the conversion of many locals from Hinduism confront Thomas, who destroys their temple, and they kill him in reprisal. This version of the story exacerbates modern tensions between Indian Christians and Hindus. The account presented here combines the responsibility of the king and the priests in a pattern by now familiar, from both Acts and this volume, in which religious leaders enlist the aid of secular authorities to protect their interests.

[37–38] The response of Thomas extends the lessons presumably learned from the "doubting Thomas" episode in the Gospel of John (20:24–29). The wall imagery reflects the traditional understanding that Thomas was a builder by trade.

---

³⁹Now if you come with me to the houses of the poor, surely you will see such signs. ⁴⁰But a moment later you will doubt them and ask for more. ⁴¹They will become like wine to you, always sweet and never enough, until you stagger and fall. ⁴²I once demanded proofs and learned that I was a fool when I saw that my mind made a wall before my heart. ⁴³And although I cried to escape, my mind placed more stones to raise the wall higher, until my mind built a fortress to imprison my heart. ⁴⁴But then my Lord came to me through the wall— and this was not in a dream or as a ghost

but in his body before my eyes—and I was ashamed of the wall I had built. ⁴⁵Such is each of you until the Lord makes a door in your wall. ⁴⁶Therefore, Misdaeus, bid him enter, and you will not know the truth. ⁴⁷For he sees all things about you, he demands all things from you, and yet he has mercy in all things concerning you. ⁴⁸Seek not the stones of proof but the waters of grace, and the wall of doubt that imprisons you will soften and melt away."

⁴⁹Again Misdaeus perceived that Thomas was a good man, and he would have released him; ⁵⁰but the priests continued to demand that he be killed. ⁵¹And while the king feared the priests, he also feared the people; ⁵²for many already believed, and even those who did not considered Thomas a holy man. ⁵³Therefore, at the king's command, four of his soldiers took Thomas outside the city, pretending to protect him on the road. ⁵⁴But when they were out of sight of the crowd that had followed for some way, they took Thomas up a mountain and there killed him, piercing him with spears. ⁵⁵Samuel and a few of the believers from Mylapore still followed, ⁵⁶and when they saw the soldiers come down from the mountain without Thomas, they went up and found his body and took it to the city where they buried him. ⁵⁷Nevertheless, even in the short time he was with them, many believed because of Thomas. ⁵⁸And Samuel, promising to send others to encourage the new believers in Mylapore, went back through the seven churches in Malabar telling of the apostle's death before he sailed for Antioch.

PRIMARY SOURCES

Death of Thomas

Acts of Thomas (AD 225) 164, 168: When the apostle had said these things, Misdaeus considered how he should put him to death; for he was afraid because of the much people that were subject unto him, for many also of the nobles and of them that were in authority believed on him. He took him therefore and went forth out of the city; and armed soldiers also went with him. And the people supposed that the king desired to learn somewhat of him, and they stood still and gave heed. And when they had walked one mile, he delivered him unto four soldiers and an officer, and commanded them to take him into the mountain and there pierce him with spears and put an end to him, and return again to the city. And saying thus unto the soldiers, he himself also returned unto the city. . . . And when [Thomas] had . . . prayed he said unto the soldiers: Come hither and accomplish the commandments of him that sent you. And the four came and pierced him with their spears, and he fell down and died. And all the brethren wept; and they brought beautiful robes and much and fair linen, and buried him in a royal sepulchre wherein the former (first) kings were laid.[4]

4. *The Acts of Thomas* is quoted from the translation by M. R. James.

24

Luke Concludes His Work

1 When the believers in Antioch learned of the death of Thomas, they sent word to the churches in Pella, Alexandria, Rome, Corinth, and Ephesus. ²In every place, the saints mourned because of his death but rejoiced because of what the Lord did through him. ³For Thomas was the first of the twelve to carry the good news of Christ Jesus beyond the areas ruled by Rome, and through him the Lord began to show the way to a harvest of salvation in the farthest of lands. ⁴So now, most excellent Theophilus, having written in order how the Spirit has taken the word of the Lord to the four corners of the world, I come to the end of these three volumes. ⁵And what is there to say regarding the end of this account, or regarding the earthly end of the apostles, that is not also a beginning?

⁶For we have seen that all but two of the twelve have died—some by the sword, some by stoning, and some by the cross.

---

[1] These cities would be the logical communication hubs in AD 73–74, when the news of the death of Thomas might have arrived from India. The exiled Jerusalem church was headquartered in Pella while the war between Rome and the Jews was winding down. The other four cities probably contained the largest Christian populations at this time, and the two surviving apostles were in Alexandria (Matthew) and Ephesus (John). This narrative left Luke near Corinth in Thebes (see notes on 18:7, 18 above). Luke's later ministry and martyrdom—or natural death, depending on the source—may have taken place in Nicaea (*The Teachings of the Apostles* 8) or Byzantium/Constantinople (Jerome *Illustrious Men* 7).

[2–4] The "four corners of the earth" allusion is to 8:28 above.

[5] The obvious problem for Luke—and for the early church—was to find the value in persecution. This entire volume is symptomatic of the challenge, because the details of travel, church establishment, and preaching make less of an impression than the repeated accounts of violent death. Of course, even if the apostles all died from natural causes, any history of this period would record at least twelve important deaths. But the likelihood that most of them were killed, coupled with increasing Roman persecution as Christianity grew, requires that any history of this period address the Christian response to violence. For many in the early church, martyrdom became "an idealized form of Christian attitude toward death."[1]

---

1. Middleton, *Radical Martyrdom*, 172; *see also* Frend, *Martyrdom*; Boyarin, *Martyrdom*.

If a first-century writer had chronicled the deaths of the apostles, he would have had to address the question of the purpose of all this violence. So in this proposed summary of Luke's three-part work, he reiterates several of the themes developed throughout Acts and this volume (boldness, Spirit direction, ever-distant evangelism) but devotes the greatest stress to the meaning of martyrdom.

[6] To be more specific, according to the accounts presented here based on traditions of various strength, five of the twelve were killed by blades (Bartholomew, James son of Zebedee, Judas son of James, Simon the Zealot, and Thomas), two were stoned (James son of Alphaeus and Matthias), and two were crucified (Andrew, Peter, and Phillip). Other martyrdoms recorded here were by blade (Paul), stoning (Barnabas, James the Just, and Silas), and beating (Mark).

---

⁷Some were falsely accused of blasphemy by the Jews, while others were blamed when people turned from false gods. ⁸Some were hated by merchants who lost wealth gotten by wickedness and wrong belief or rulers who lost the loyalty of their family or subjects. ⁹Yet all of these, the twelve and the others whose suffering is recorded here, were righteous and faithful to the end, and their deaths led many more to believe.¹⁰This is the testimony of every witness, and the evidence in every place where the church grows upon ground watered by the blood of the saints.

¹¹For though many have suffered, through them the Lord has laid a foundation of obedience and hope throughout the world. ¹²Consider the perfect wisdom of God. ¹³When a farmer allows a tree to reach the time for dropping seeds, new trees may grow, but only nearby. ¹⁴However, when he takes ripe seeds from the tree and plants them in new places that he has prepared, they grow faster and stronger, and the harvest is great. So it is with God.

¹⁵And so it is, beloved Theophilus, that the end of this account is but the beginning of what the Lord will do. ¹⁶For in the first volume, we saw that the Father has given us his Son, through whom we have salvation. ¹⁷In the second volume, we witnessed that the Son gave us his Spirit, through whom we have the church. ¹⁸Now in this third volume, we have seen the Spirit give boldness to the apostles to preach the word, even to the point of death. ¹⁹And through the death of the saints, the Lord has built up his church in every place to hasten the harvest of salvation. ²⁰All of our labor is to that end, which is the beginning of everlasting glory.

[7–15] The summary of the three volumes is expressed in terms of the Trinity, a term that does not appear in the New Testament but which later theologians coined to designate what they called the three persons of the Godhead: Father, Son, and Holy Spirit. The three names appear in close proximity throughout Luke's writing (e.g., 1:8–17; 3:22; 12:8–12; Acts 2:38–39), perhaps the best example of which is the prayer of Jesus in Luke 10:21–22.

[16–20] The notion of identifying the three volumes with both the Trinity and the main topic of each volume gives a theological flavor to the structure of the whole collection. The progression of this summary also reflects the geographical movement within each volume (to Jerusalem, to Rome, to the ends of the earth) and the movement of the whole toward eternal reward. The explanation of this fictional conclusion, however, is not intended to advance the proposal that Luke wrote or intended a third volume. Rather, it is intended to show how a theoretical third volume might be included with Luke and Acts. If, having read these pages, the reader wishes it were "real," then perhaps the same Spirit is still at work penetrating the sludge of doubtful sources, many centuries, and the flaws of this writer.

Appendix

Why Does Acts End with Paul Awaiting Trial?

AT THE VERY END of Acts, Paul is living under house arrest in Rome, and his trial has not yet taken place: "He lived there two whole years at his own expense and welcomed all who came to him, proclaiming the kingdom of God and teaching about the Lord Jesus Christ with all boldness and without hindrance" (28:30–31). The typical reader is struck with the inconclusive nature of this ending. We have followed Paul's career from his conversion in chapter 9 through danger-fraught missionary journeys, and the last quarter of the book details the dramatic legal process that sends him to Rome. We are told that he has appealed to Caesar and that he expects to die. And now—no trial, no death.

There are three possible explanations for this. One is that Luke published his work while Paul was awaiting trial in Rome, about AD 62. The second possibility is that Luke wrote or planned another volume following Acts which was lost or never written. The third option is that Luke wrote several years after Paul's execution but found that the book's purpose was fulfilled, and its ending complete, with the gospel being preached in Rome. I will consider each of these theories in turn, beginning with the last.

THE MAJORITY VIEW: ACTS IS COMPLETE AS IS

Most nonspecialist readers are surprised to learn that the majority position among scholars is that Acts was written ten to twenty years after the events it records and that Luke chooses not to report Paul's death.[1] In this view, the final trial and execution of Paul would leave the reader with an individual tragedy and with the implication that Christianity is illegal. Instead, by ending with Paul preaching freely in Rome, Luke leaves the focus on his major themes of progress and fulfillment. The gospel has symbolically reached "the ends of the earth" (Acts 1:8), and the reader is obliged to continue Paul's work of preaching "with all boldness and without hindrance."

To the extent that this explanation stresses Luke's theological purposes, it is persuasive. But on closer inspection, it runs up against some major objections. For one, it is incongruous for Luke to devote the last quarter of Acts to the process leading up to Paul's appeal

---

1. Tannehill, *Narrative Unity*, 356; Trompf, "Death of Paul," 232–35; Conzelmann, *Acts*, 228; Fitzmyer, *Acts*, 791, 797; Marguerat, *First Christian Historian*, 205–30; Pervo, *Acts*, 688–90; Puskas, *Conclusion*, 131–40; Johnson, *Acts*, 474–76; Witherington, *Acts*, 808–12; Peterson, *Acts*, 724, 726.

before Caesar, only to decide that the culmination of that story is beside the point. As for the themes of fulfillment and promise, Luke has already shown, with the story of Stephen's martyrdom in Acts 7, that he can incorporate these themes into a story of martyrdom. Moreover, it is questionable—perhaps even anachronistic—to count Paul's arrival in Rome as fulfillment of the commission to take the gospel to "the ends of the earth": Rome is Paul's goal only after Acts 25, and the city does not figure importantly elsewhere in Acts.

Further objections to the "know, don't tell" theory focus on timing issues. If Acts is written ten to twenty years after the events it reports, as most commentators suggest, why does it contain no indication of the destruction of the temple, which would greatly strengthen the response to Jewish opponents? Neither does Acts offer a hint of Nero's persecution in AD 64, a critical event that effectively erased Luke's lengthy efforts to establish the legal viability of Christianity through Paul's various judicial proceedings. Furthermore, Acts shows no awareness of Paul's letters, which were well known and in circulation by the later dates proposed for composition.

THE CRITICAL ISSUE: PROPHECIES BY JESUS

The response to most of these objections is indirect, and it centers not on Acts but on Luke's Gospel, which was clearly written first. According to many modern scholars, the Gospel had to have been written after AD 70 because it contains predictions by Jesus of the destruction of Jerusalem and its temple. The assumption of these scholars is that Jesus couldn't possibly know such things forty years in advance; therefore, his predictions must be put in his mouth to make him appear to have prophetic powers. There are other minor arguments in support of a late date for Acts that I will consider below, but this is the main one.

Are the predictions in the Gospel of the destruction of Jerusalem a compelling reason to assign a post-70 date to Acts? I will argue that they are not, and then I will consider again the alternate explanations for the ending of Acts.

Of course discussion of this question ends before it begins if we assume that Jesus is the Son of God and capable, in his prophetic function, of predicting the future. But let us suppose, for the sake of argument, that Jesus had no supernatural foresight. Are his recorded predictions of the future after-the-fact fabrications?

ARE THE PROPHECIES IN MARK'S GOSPEL PROPHETIC?

The response to this question actually begins with Mark's Gospel, which Luke clearly used in composing his own account. In places he copied Mark word for word; sometimes he shortened passages; at other times he added material, often based on additional sources he had at his disposal. Such decisions in the composition process reflect Luke's themes, which emerge clearly from detailed study, especially from a comparative consideration of the four Gospels.

In the case of Jesus's predictions of the coming destruction, Mark's Gospel records the declaration of Jesus, "Do you see all these great buildings? Not one stone will be left here upon another; all will be thrown down" (13:2). Later he says there will be "wars and rumors of wars" (Mark 13:7), persecutions of his followers, various signs in the heavens, and then his return in glory.

In Luke's account, the prediction of the temple's destruction is exactly the same (21:6), as are the general predictions of wars, persecution, and the end; but there are a few additional details as well. In Luke 13:35, Jesus declares to the Jews, "Your house is abandoned." In 19:41, Jesus predicts that "your enemies will set up ramparts around you and surround you, and hem you in on every side." In 21:20, he says, "When you see Jerusalem surrounded by armies, then know that its desolation is at hand." Finally, in 21:24 he predicts that "they will fall by the edge of the sword and be taken away as captives among all nations; and Jerusalem will be trampled on by the Gentiles, until the times of the Gentiles are fulfilled." These predictions, which appear to be more specific than those in Mark, have led many scholars to the conclusion that Luke put these details in Jesus's mouth to make his "predictions" conform to known details of Jerusalem's destruction.[2]

We will return attention to these additional details in Luke's account a bit later. For now, consider the predictions of Jesus in Mark that within the lifetime of his hearers there will be a military conflict, that the temple will be completely dismantled, and that his followers will be persecuted. Would it require a prophet to predict these things in the hotbed of rebellion and messianic expectation that was first-century Judea? If there had been internet polls then, one can imagine a survey like this: "The most likely outcome of our resentment of Roman occupation will be (a) God will destroy Rome (b) the Romans will destroy Jerusalem (c) we will all learn to get along." Wouldn't a certain percentage of reasonable respondents choose "b" without being called prophets? And if someone committed their prediction to writing, would those who discovered this later be right to insist that it was written after AD 70? Again, I am not suggesting that Jesus lacked prophetic powers, only that his predictions were not surprising.

But vagueness or predictability are not the only problems with the supposition that the prophecies of Jesus were created after-the-fact. We might also question their accuracy. The Gospel prophecies do not mention the Romans, mass starvation during the siege, the burning of the temple, or the fact that the Jewish rebels killed almost as many of their own as did the Romans—all notable details that would lend credibility to Jesus as prophet. In terms of accuracy, we might also question the extent of the destruction. Josephus reports the burning and dismantling of the temple itself, many of the surrounding structures, and parts of the city's defensive walls. But some of the city must have been spared, because the Jews returned and rebuilt much of it. Just sixty years later, following the Bar Cochba revolt of AD 132–135, Roman historian Dio Cassius reports that the temple complex and city were completely destroyed (*Roman History* 69). In that rebellion, a larger number of people were killed than in the first revolt; and afterward, the surviving Jews were deported en masse and prohibited from entering Jerusalem. The destruction of the temple in AD 70, therefore, may not have fulfilled the predictions of the Gospels. In fact, one specific prediction does not appear to have been fulfilled until AD 135 when the emperor Hadrian installed statues of himself and of Jupiter on the site of the temple. Here is "the desolating sacrilege set up where it ought not to be" predicted in Mark 13:14. Yet this occurred far too late for an after-the-fact fabrication. Should scholars allow Jesus one lucky guess, or should they argue on the basis of Mark 13:14 that the Gospels were written in the mid-second century?

2. E.g., Fitzmyer, *Acts*, 54; Witherington, Acts, 61.

Appendix

A further consideration in terms of accuracy is that the return of Jesus and the destruction of the temple appear in the Gospels to be nearly simultaneous events. If the Gospels were written after the destruction of the temple, shouldn't we expect clarification in this regard? The events of AD 70 undoubtedly caused a furor of expectation that the end was imminent; yet the Gospels perpetuate confusion about the timing of the Lord's return. If the writers were carefully crafting predictions to make Jesus look prophetic, why did they not take the next step and resolve the key issue by distancing his return from the destruction of the temple? It is quite reasonable to suppose that at the time they wrote there was no issue because there was still a temple.

DO ADDITIONAL DETAILS IN LUKE REQUIRE A LATE DATE?

Now we return to the additional details in Luke's Gospel, which are regarded by many scholars as evidence that Luke wrote after AD 70. I disagree. The passages are typical of apocalyptic literature (or preaching), which involved predictions and vivid imagery concerning the end times, much of it taken from Old Testament passages. Its point was not to showcase the predictive powers of the speaker but to elicit a response of repentance and obedience to the speaker's message. And here is the key point: It had all happened before. That is, the images and the message—"Repent, for judgment is coming"—had been familiar to the Jews for centuries, from the time of the Old Testament prophets.

The fact that similar events had happened before is the key to understanding not only the predictions of Jesus in Mark's Gospel but also to the additional details in Luke.[3] For while the new specifics appear at first to reflect precise events in the war, they are still vague, and in fact they are all mentioned in Old Testament passages. Prophecies of Jerusalem being surrounded or besieged by enemy armies are common (Amos 3:11; Ps 118:10–12; Zech 12:2; Mic 5:1), and some even specify the use of siege ramps (Jer 6:6; 32:24; Ezek 21:22). Other passages mention the Jews' house being abandoned (Jer 22:5–6), falling by the edge of the sword (Jer 21:7), captivity (Ezek 32:9), and being trampled by the Gentiles (Dan 8:13). In other words, all of the "extra" material in Luke as compared to Mark can be attributed to Old Testament prophetic language just as easily as to contemporary events. The events of AD 70 should not be understood as contemporary so much as cyclical. The pattern of disobedience, followed by conquest, followed by restoration was familiar to Jesus's audience and to the biblically literate in Luke's audience. At the time Jesus delivered these predictions, the point was not for his audience to wait for the fulfillment of these things in order to establish that Jesus had been a prophet. Too late then! Rather, the point was to elicit repentance at that moment.

A final point concerning the notion of after-the-fact prophecies: If Luke's intent was to add details about the destruction of the temple to make Jesus look more accurate, we have to ask why he did not do the same in Acts. Surely it would add punch to the encounters of Stephen and Paul with the Jewish leaders if they could hint that Jerusalem and the temple were soon to be judged. The fact that Luke does not do this strengthens the argument that the prophetic additions in his Gospel are either Old Testament allusions, authentic statements by Jesus from Luke's additional sources, or both.

3. Munck, *Acts*, xlvii.

THE EARLY DATE THEORY

Once we remove the argument that the Gospels must be written after AD 70 because Jesus could not have predicted the destruction of the temple, we can look at other possibilities for the date of composition of the Gospels, and then for Acts.

The first possibility mentioned above for the abrupt ending of Acts is that Luke wrote up to the point that events had occurred; i.e., Paul was still awaiting trial at the time of writing. A thorough study by New Testament scholar Colin Hemer makes a persuasive case for this position against the climate of contemporary scholarship,[4] and an early date is supported by a number of other modern scholars.[5]

An oft-mentioned objection to this view is that Paul makes a long goodbye speech to the elders at Miletus, including the statement that "none of you . . . will ever see my face again (Acts 20:25).[6] For many reasons, this is a weak basis upon which to conclude that Paul is already dead at the time of writing.[7] Like the predictions of Jesus, this one by Paul is hardly surprising to anyone who knows his history. Moreover, he makes reference in the context to his coming danger in Jerusalem, not to his death in Rome. If Luke wants to hint about what happens next, why do so only once—eight chapters before the end? Indeed, if Luke is in the habit from his Gospel of adding more convincing details to the predictions of Jesus, why not here or elsewhere make reference to the circumstances of Paul's death? The most obvious grist for that mill, of course, would be the destruction of the temple, which in the mouth of Stephen (Acts 7) or Paul (Acts 28) would clinch the argument that these deaths were not tragic but transitional in the progress of the gospel from the Jews to the nations.

All of the objections to the late date of Acts constitute additional support for the view that the book is written in AD 62 with Paul awaiting trial.[8] First among these is the continuing ministry to the Jews without even a hint in Acts of the temple's destruction. Likewise, Acts offers no hint of Nero's persecution in AD 64 and the obvious implications of that official repression for the legality of Christianity—a theme developed as early as Acts 18 and dominating the later chapters. A third argument for an early date is that Acts shows no awareness of Paul's letters, which is understandable in AD 62 but less and less likely as the date of Acts is pushed back five, ten, or more years. Last but not least, the view that Acts is published while Paul awaits trial has in its favor the obvious and simple observation that this is where the narrative ends.

Modern scholars have established a principle that the simplest explanation, the one that best accounts for the others, is likely the right one—and yet, in this case, many set that principle aside. Scholar after scholar acknowledges the internal indications of an early date—then they brush them aside in favor of a purely "theological" ending that flies in the face of common sense. Luke could easily incorporate an account of Paul's death into his affirmation that the gospel is now being preached to the nations. To cling to a post-70 date because of a misunderstanding of the nature of Jesus's predictions is unacceptable. For all these sound reasons, the completion of Acts in AD 62 must remain a strong option.

4. Hemer, *Acts,* 383–410.

5. Munck, *Acts*, 260; Kistemaker, *Acts*, 22–24; Carson, Moo, and Morris, *Introductrion*, 190–94; Longenecker, *Acts*, 28–31; Bock, *Acts*, 25–27, 758–60. See also Eusebius, *Ecclesiastical History*, 2.22.6.

6. E.g., Conzelmann, *Acts*, 228.

7. Hemer, *Acts*, 407.

8. These objections are summarized in Munck, *Acts*, xlviii–liv; Fitzmyer, *Acts*, 52.

What this option does not explain, of course, is why Luke chose to publish before Paul's trial. It does not appear that he was in a hurry or cut off in the midst of writing: Acts maintains consistent style and themes to the end, and it is the same length as Luke's Gospel. Indeed, the very survival of the book suggests that it was written at a time of relative safety for its author. These factors can, of course, be marshaled to support the "theological" explanation for the ending of Acts, with or without a late date.

THE MISSING SEQUEL THEORY

The challenges to Luke's ending of Acts before Paul's trial leave open a third alternative, that Luke wrote or intended a third volume. The reader may expect me to champion this view, since it would help to justify this book. Alas, the arguments for it are mostly arguments from silence or combinations of objections to the other alternatives. It seems likely that if Luke had produced even part of another volume, there would be some record to that effect in the early church. One scholar suggests that the second-century apocryphal *Acts of Paul* amounts to a recognition that Luke's second volume required a sequel.[9] Be that as it may, most scholars dismiss the option summarily on the ground that the two volumes appear complete. Before closing the door, however, I will suggest one argument in its favor that I have not seen in the scholarly literature.[10]

A comparison of the ending of Luke's Gospel with the ending of Acts reveals several common elements:

> And see, I am sending upon you what my Father promised; so stay here in the city until you have been clothed with power from on high." Then he led them out as far as Bethany, and, lifting up his hands, he blessed them. While he was blessing them, he withdrew from them and was carried up into heaven. And they worshiped him, and returned to Jerusalem with great joy; and they were continually in the temple blessing God. (Luke 24:49–53)

> Let it be known to you then that this salvation of God has been sent to the Gentiles; they will listen." He lived there two whole years at his own expense and welcomed all who came to him, proclaiming the kingdom of God and teaching about the Lord Jesus Christ with all boldness and without hindrance. (Acts 28:28–31)

In both passages, there is a promise that God is about to do something else: bestow the Spirit, preach to the Gentiles. In both passages, the faithful do not simply wait but engage in appropriate behavior: "continually . . . blessing God," "proclaiming . . . with all boldness." In both passages, a location is specified that the audience knows is temporary: the disciples "returned to . . . the temple," Paul "lived there two whole years."

Keeping these parallels in mind, it is notable that Acts begins not with the apostles in the temple but back in Galilee for a final appearance of the resurrected Jesus. Then the apostles return to Jerusalem, receive the Spirit, and the story of the Church begins. In other words, there is not a precise break between the volumes but a bit of overlap. In the second volume,

---

9. Bauckam, "Acts of Paul," 105–52.

10. Puskas, *Conclusion*, 16 and others he cites acknowledge the parallels between Luke 24 and Acts 28 but do not discuss them in relation to a third volume.

this serves to remind the reader of what has gone before. But for purposes of comparison to the end of Acts, it is intriguing that the end of Luke's Gospel leaves out a few critical details that are supplied at the beginning of the second volume.

This leads to the question, Why not the same pattern for a third volume? In keeping with the parallels between the ends of the first two volumes, a third volume could begin as Acts does, backing up a bit to announce Paul's trial before Nero, then perhaps recording a speech by Paul (parallel to that of Jesus at the beginning of Acts) that promises the spread of the gospel to the Gentiles following his death. This would provide a smooth transition between Acts and the third volume, and the narrative could proceed in any number of directions, from a detailed account of Paul's trial to a catalogue of further activities among the Gentiles.

The parallels between the endings of Luke and Acts present a viable precedent for resumption of the story in a third volume. The supposition of such a volume supplies an answer to the question of why Paul is left waiting trial, but it also honors the observation of many scholars that Acts can be understood as complete—just as the Gospel can: but *more* complete with the overlapping subsequent volume.

The possibility that Luke intended a sequel to Acts is not an argument that it would look like the reconstructed account offered in this book. If Luke had indeed written or planned a third volume, naturally it would begin with Paul—but beyond that, who knows? If we had to predict the content of Acts based only on Luke's Gospel, we might be surprised to find that Acts focuses on Peter, James the Lord's brother, and the previously unknown Paul, while the rest of the apostles are scarcely mentioned. Therefore, my account of the careers of the Twelve in a "biblical" format is not a proposal for the content of Luke's theoretical third volume. Rather, it is an attempt to render the challenges of technical scholarship into a creative format. My hope is that the account will engage the imagination, transporting the reader to a time when these events were new and alive, the truths life-transforming. To the extent that such engagement occurs, this book itself may serve as a transition to yet another work—one yet to be written in the reader's own life.

Appendix

LOCATIONS AFTER ACTS AND DEATHS OF THE TWELVE

Apostle	Area/City of Activity	P*	Date & Place of Death	P
Andrew	Macedonia, Achaia, Parthia, Scythia	B	69 *Patras* Crucifixion	B
Bartholomew a.ka. Nathanael	Asia Minor, Armenia	B	68 *Albanopolis* flayed and beheaded	C
James "Greater," son of Zebedee	*Jerusalem*	A	42 *Jerusalem* beheaded	A
James "Lesser" son of Alphaeus	Judaea	C	62 *Jerusalem* stoning	C
John	Asia Minor, *Ephesus*	A	100 *Ephesus* natural death	A
Judas Iscariot	*Jerusalem*	A	33 suicide	A
Judas son of James a.k.a. Thaddaeus	Samaria, Galilee, Africa, Britain, Gaul, Persia	C	71 Persia speared	C
Matthew a.k.a. Levi	Egypt, Ethiopia	D	90 Ethiopia natural death	D
Matthias	Judaea	C	62 *Jerusalem* stoning	D
Peter	*Antioch*, Asia Minor, *Rome*	A	64 *Rome* crucifixion	A
Philip	Asia Minor, *Hierapolis*	B	66 *Hierapolis* crucifixion	C
Simon the Zealot	Samaria, Galilee, Africa, Britain, Gaul, Persia	C	71 Persia hacked with swords	C
Thomas	Persia, India	B	72 India speared	C

*Probability is indicated by letter to indicate the degree of certainty:

A: Nearly certain. Early, credible, or multiple sources.

B: Probable. Sources are few, debated, or late, but plausible.

C: Possible. Sources differ or are weak, but there may be truth behind the tradition.

D: Unlikely. Late, contradictory, or weak sources, so any conclusion is largely conjecture.

LOCATIONS AFTER ACTS AND DEATHS OF OTHER KEY FIGURES

Figure	Area/City of Activity	P*	Date & Place of Death	P
Paul	Asia Minor, Greece, *Rome*, Spain	A	64 *Rome* beheaded	A
Apollos	Greece, Asia Minor, Egypt	B	*Corinth* natural death	D
Barnabas	Greece, Asia Minor, Cyprus	B	61 *Salamis*, Cyprus stoned	C
James brother of Jesus aka "the Just"	*Jerusalem*	A	62 *Jerusalem* stoned	A
Jude brother of Jesus	Galilee	B	natural death	B
Luke	Greece, Asia Minor, *Rome*, Spain	B	80 Greece natural death	C
Mark	Greece, Asia Minor, Egypt	B	67 *Alexandria* beaten to death	B
Mary mother of Jesus	Judaea	B	60 *Jerusalem* natural death	B
Mary Magdalene	Syria, Asia Minor, *Ephesus*	C	*Ephesus* natural death	C
Silas	Greece, Asia Minor	D	54 *Corinth* stoned	D
Timothy	Greece, Asia Minor, *Ephesus*	B	80 *Ephesus*	B
Titus	Greece, Asia Minor, Crete	B	107 Crete natural death	B

Questions for Discussion

1:18–35: If Paul were placed in today's culture and a specific location, what images might he use as a springboard for an evangelistic sermon?

2:7–26: How does Paul's notion of the body affirm resurrection and the truth of the gospel?

2:36–47: How would the judgment and discipline issues be affected if the offenders had been guilty of theft or assault instead of adultery? Are sexual sins worse?

3:22–44: Other than persecution—which rarely works—what would be the most effective way to stop the spread of a new religion?

4:22–39: If you had to advise Paul regarding his defense, what would you add or subtract from this speech?

5:1–19: What case could be made to either a Roman official or a Christian that Caesar and Christ could coexist as Lord in their respective realms?

6:1–15: If Peter had not received a vision, what would the arguments be for and against having him—or other Christian leaders—remain in hiding for a while?

6:39–52: While there were many willing martyrs during the periods of persecution, the church struggled with its stance toward those who recanted and then returned to the church. How would you approach this issue?

8:1–26: Apart from these traditional explanations for the writing of the Gospels, what advantages and disadvantages do you see in having four accounts of the ministry of Jesus?

8:27–36: What organizational approach, other than the "four winds" geographical distribution proposed here, might have been used to spread the gospel?

9:1–44: What issues do these chapters introduce regarding spiritual merit in relation to family connections, and do you see parallels in modern church leadership?

9:20–34: How does this account suggest that Mary has changed or remained the same through her experiences since the birth of Jesus?

10:15–40: How does the speech of Matthias help to account for the movement of Christianity from Palestine and the Jews toward the Gentiles?

11:1–40: Many in the early church believed that the destruction of Jerusalem was judgment for the stoning of James, the crucifixion of Jesus, or the Jews' rejection of the gospel. Do you agree that God acted—or still acts—in this manner with nations?

12:8–21: Does Simeon's speech account for the delay of Jesus's return, or is there a better explanation? How might his speech differ after two thousand years?

14:25–50: How do John's words contrast with common Christian explanations of loss—and do you agree?

15:1–25: How and why does John's public group healing differ from what would be appropriate for ordinary believers then and now?

15:30–36: What were the possibilities and limitations of leadership in the first century for Mary Magdalene? Does her role then have implications for women in leadership today?

16:1–4: What were the advantages and disadvantages for the apostles' traveling in pairs over long periods of time?

17:15–35: The conversion of Polymius is one of several in Acts and this account involving prominent converts. What are the advantages and limitations of evangelizing influential people?

18:25–52: In light of this account of Andrew's martyrdom and the letter of Pliny to Hadrian (commentary), how do misconceptions of Christianity in the first century differ from misconceptions of Christianity today?

19:1–6: How would you assess the approach described here for the establishment of churches on the part of Simon and Jude?

19:7–30: What would you add to, or subtract from, Simon's instruction to potential disciples?

20:4–14: What is the appropriate place of dream interpretation in discerning God's will?

21:10–18: What is the best way to address differences in belief with a hostile audience?

21:34–54: How do you assess Matthew's sermon to an audience of new hearers? Does he strike the right balance of information and invitation?

22:11–37: Is Thomas's action irresponsible or daringly obedient to God? To what extent does the story suggest that the reader should emulate the apostle?

23:16–33: How do you assess Thomas's response to Hinduism and to pantheism ("all things are God")? How does his series of contrasts compare to the approach of Jesus in the Sermon on the Mount (Matthew 5–7)?

23:38–48: How does Thomas's speech address the tension between reason and faith?

24:6–14: If martyrdom serves to "increase the harvest," how do you assess those who have walked into danger seeming to seek martyrdom? Are periods of tolerance for Christianity due to watered-down discipleship?

What new insights have you gained from this book about the early church in the period after Acts?

What questions does the account leave unanswered about this period?

What affect might these insights and questions have on your life?

Bibliography

*The Apostolic Fathers, Volume I: I Clement. II Clement. Ignatius. Polycarp. Didache. Barnabas.*Translated by Kirsopp Lake. Loeb Classical Library. Harvard: University Press, 1912.

The Apostolic Fathers, Volume II: The Shepherd of Hermas. The Martyrdom of Polycarp. The Epistle to Diognetus. Translated by Kirsopp Lake. Loeb Classical Library. Harvard: University Press, 1913.

Arlandson, James M. *Women, Class, and Society in Early Christianity: Models from Luke-Acts.* Peabody, MA: Hendrickson, 1997.

Atiya, Aziz S. *A History of Eastern Christianity.* London: Methuen & Co., 1968.*Babylonian Talmud, The.* Edited by I. Epstein. Tractate Sanhedrin translated by Jacob Schechter. Talmudic Books at Halakhah. com. On line: http://halakhah.com/

Bauckam, Richard. "*The Acts of Paul* as a Sequel to Acts." In *The Book of Acts in Its Ancient Literary Setting,* edited by Bruce W. Winter and Andrew D. Clarke. The Book of Acts in Its First Century Setting 1, 105-152. Grand Rapids: Eerdmans, 1993.

Benko, Stephen. *Pagan Rome and the Early Christians.* Indiana: University Press, 1986.

Blue, Bradley. "Acts and the House Church." In *The Book of Acts in Its Graeco-Roman Setting,* edited by David W. J. Gill and Conrad Gempf, 119–222. The Book of Acts in Its First Century Setting 2. Grand Rapids: Eerdmans, 1994.

Bock, Darrell. *Acts.* Grand Rapids: Baker Academic, 2007.

Boyarin, Daniel. *Dying for God: Martyrdom and the Making of Christianity and Judaism.* Stanford: University Press, 1999.

Brock, Ann Graham. *Mary Magdalene, the First Apostle: The Struggle for Authority.* Harvard: University Press, 2003.

Budge, E. A. *The Contendings of the Apostles.* 3rd ed. London: The British Museum, 1935.

Butler, Alban. *The Lives of the Fathers, Martyrs and Other Principal Saints.* Dublin: James Duffy, 1866. Reprint New York: Bartleby.com, 2010. On-line: http://www.bartleby.com/210/

Cain, Andrew. *St. Jerome: Commentary on Galatians.* Fathers of the Church 121. Washington, DC: Catholic University of American Press, 2010.

Canter, H. V. "Conflagrations in Ancient Rome." *The Classical Journal* 27.4 (January 1932) 270–88. On-line: http://penelope.uchicago.edu/Thayer/E/Journals /CJ/27/4/ Conflagrations*.html

Carson, Donald A., Douglas J. Moo, and Leon Morris. *An Introduction to the New Testament.* Grand Rapids: Zondervan, 1992.

Charlesworth, James H. *The Apocrypha and Pseudepigrapha of the Old Testament.* 2 vols. New York: Doubleday, 1983.

Chinnapan, S. "St. Thomas and the North Indian King Gundaphorus." In *Early Christianity in India,* edited by G. John Samuel, 207–22. Chennai, India: Institute of Asian Studies, 2008.

Clarke, Andrew D. "Rome and Italy." In *The Book of Acts in Its Graeco-Roman Setting,* edited by David W. J. Gill and Conrad Gempf. The Book of Acts in Its First Century Setting 2, 455–82. Grand Rapids: Eerdmans, 1994.

Conzelmann, Hans. *Acts of the Apostles.* Philadelphia: Fortress, 1988.

Dio Cassius. *Roman History.* Translated by Ernest Cary. Loeb Classical Library. Harvard: University Press, 1914–1927. On-line: http://penelope.uchicago.edu/thayer/e/roman /texts/cassius_dio/home.html

Eusebius. *Ecclesiastical History, Books I–V.* Translated by Kirsopp Lake. Loeb Classical Library, Harvard: University Press, 1926.

Fitzmyer, Joseph. *The Acts of the Apostles.* New Haven, CT: Yale University Press, 1998.

Frend, W. H. C. *Martyrdom and Persecution in the Early Church: A Study of a Conflict from the Maccabees to Donatus.* New York: New York University Press, 1967.

Gill, David W. J. "Acts and the Urban Elites." In *The Book of Acts in Its Graeco-Roman Setting,* edited by David W. J. Gill and Conrad Gempf, 105–18. The Book of Acts in Its First Century Setting 2. Grand Rapids: Eerdmans, 1994.

Goodspeed, Edgar J. Goodspeed. *The Twelve.* New York: Collier, 1957.

Gundry, Robert H. *Mark: A Commentary on His Apology for the Cross.* Grand Rapids: Eerdmans, 1993.

Bibliography

Hemer, Colin J. *The Book of Acts in the Setting of Hellenistic History*. Edited by Conrad J. Gempf. Winona Lake, IN: Eisenbrauns, 1990.

James, M. R. *The Apocryphal New Testament*. Oxford: Clarendon, 1924.

Jipp, Joshua W. "Paul's Areopagus Speech of Acts 17:16–34 as Both Critique and Propaganda." *Journal of Biblical Literature* 131 (Fall, 2012) 567–88.

Johnson, Luke Timothy. *The Acts of the Apostles*. Collegeville, MN: Liturgical, 1992.

Josephus, Flavius. *The Works of Flavius Josephus*. Translated by William Whiston. Auburn and Buffalo: John E. Beardsley, 1895. http://www.ccel.org/j/josephus/works/josephus.htm

Kistemaker, Simon J. *Acts. New Testament Commentary*. Grand Rapids: Baker Academic, 1991.

Klauck, Hans Josef. *The Apocryphal Acts of the Apostles: An Introduction*. Waco, TX: Baylor University Press, 2008.

Klinker-De Klerck, Myriam. "The Pastoral Epistles: authentic Pauline writings." *European Journal of Theology* 17.2 (October 2008) 101–8.

Knight, George W., III. *The Pastoral Epistles: A Commentary on the Greek Text*. Grand Rapids, Eerdmans, 1992.

Latin Prologues: The Anti-Marcionite and Monarchian Prologues to the Canonical Gospels. Translated by Ben C. Smith. August 23, 2007. http://www.textexcavation.com/latinprologues.html

Levinskiya, Irina. *The Book of Acts in Its Diaspora Setting*. The Book of Acts in Its First Century Setting 5. Grand Rapids: Eerdmans, 1996.

Longenecker, Richard. *Acts*. Grand Rapids: Zondervan, 1995.

Marguerat, Daniel. *The First Christian Historian: Writing the 'Acts of the Apostles.'* Cambridge: Cambridge University Press, 2004.

McBirnie, William S. *The Search for the Twelve Apostles*. Carol Stream, IL: Tyndale House, 1973.

McGrath, James F. "History and Fiction in the Acts of Thomas: The State of the Question," *Journal for the Study of the Pseudepigrapha* 17 (2008) 297–311.

MacMullen, Ramsay. *Christianizing the Roman Empire (A.D. 100–400)*. New Haven, CT: Yale University Press, 1984.

Menachery, George. "Early Christianity in Kerala." In *First International Conference on the History of Early Christianity in India*, edited by G. John Samuel, 7–50. Chennai, India: Institute for Asian Studies, 2005.

Middleton, Paul. *Radical Martyrdom and Cosmic Conflict in Early Christianity*. New York: Routledge, 2002.

Mullen, R. L. *The Expansion of Christianity: A Gazetteer of its First Three Centuries*. Leiden: Brill, 2004.

Munck, Johannes. *The Acts of the Apostles*. Translated by W. F. Albright and C. S. Mann. Garden City, NY: Doubleday, 1967.

Neill, Stephen. *A History of Christianity in India: The Beginnings to 1707*. Cambridge: University Press, 1984.

New Revised Standard Version Bible. National Council of Churches of Christ, 1989.

O'Connor, Daniel W. *Peter in Rome: The Literary, Liturgical, and Archeological Evidence*. New York: Columbia, 1969.

Omerzu, Heike. "The Portrayal of Paul's Outer Appearance in the Acts of Paul and Thecla. Re-Considering the Correspondence between Body and Personality in Ancient Literature." *Religion & Theology* 15 (2008) 252–79.

Pervo, Richard I. *Acts: A Commentary*. Minneapolis, MN: Fortress, 2009.

Peterson, David G. *The Acts of the Apostles*. Grand Rapids: Eerdmans, 2009.

Peterson, Peter M. *Andrew, Brother of Simon Peter*. Leiden: Brill, 1963.

Pherigo, Lindsay P. "Paul's Life after the Close of Acts," *Journal of Biblical Literature* 70 (1951) 277–84.

Pliny the Elder. *Correspondence with Trajan*. Translated by William Melmoth. Revised by F. C. T. Bosanquet. http://ancienthistory.about.com/library/bl/bl_text_plinyltrstrajan.htm

Porter, Stanley E. "The 'We' Passages." *The Book of Acts in Its Graeco-Roman Setting*, edited by David W. J. Gill and Conrad Gempf. The Book of Acts in Its First Century Setting 2, 545–74. Grand Rapids: Eerdmans, 1994.

Puskas, Charles B., Jr., *The Conclusion of Luke-Acts: The Function and Significance of Acts 28:16–31*. Eugene, OR: Wipf & Stock, 2008.

Rankin, David Ivan. *From Clement to Origen: The Social and Historical Context of the Church Fathers.* Burlington, VT: Ashgate, 2006.

Rapske, Brian. *The Book of Acts and Paul in Roman Custody.* The Book of Acts in Its First Century Setting 3. Grand Rapids: Eerdmans, 2004.

Ricci, Carla. *Mary Magdalene and Many Others: Women who Followed Jesus.* Minneapolis, MN: Fortress, 1994.

Roberts, Alexander, James Donaldson, and A. Cleveland Coxe, editors. *Ante-Nicene Fathers.* Buffalo, NY: Christian Literature, 1885. Reprint, Grand Rapids: Eerdmans, 1951.

Ruffin, C. Bernard. *The Twelve: The Lives of the Apostles After Calvary.* Huntington, IN: Our Sunday Visitor, 1998.

Satterthwaite, Philip E. "Acts Against the Background of Classical Rhetoric." In *The Book of Acts in Its Ancient Literary Setting,* edited by Bruce W. Winter and Andrew D. Clarke, 337–79. The Book of Acts in Its First Century Setting 1. Grand Rapids: Eerdmans, 1993.

Schaff, Philip, and Henry Wace, editors. *Nicene and Post-Nicene Fathers.* Edited by. 2nd series. Buffalo, NY: Christian Literature, 1892. Reprint, Grand Rapids: Eerdmans, 1956.

Schmidt, Thomas E. "Cry of Dereliction or Cry of Judgment: Mark 15:34 in Context." *Bulletin for Biblical Research* 4 (1994) 145–53.

———. "Mark 15:16–32: The Crucifixion Narrative and the Roman Triumphal Procession." *New Testament Studies* 41:1 (January 1995) 1–18.

Schnabel, Eckhard J. "Contextualising Paul In Athens: The Proclamation Of The Gospel Before Pagan Audiences In The Graeco-Roman World." *Religion & Theology* 12.2 (2005) 172–90.

Schneemelcher, Wilhelm, editor. *New Testament Apocrypha* 2. Translated by H. R. McLaren Wilson. Revised edition, Louisville, KY: Westminster John Knox, 1992.

Scott, James M. "Luke's Geographical Horizon." In *The Book of Acts in Its Graeco-Roman Setting,* edited by David W. J. Gill and Conrad Gempf. The Book of Acts in Its First Century Setting 2, 483–544. Grand Rapids: Eerdmans, 1994.

Suetonius. *The Lives of the Twelve Caesars.* Translated by J. C. Rolfe. Loeb Classical Library, Harvard: University Press, 1914. http://penelope.uchicago.edu/Thayer/E/ Roman/Texts/Suetonius/12Caesars/home.html

Tacitus. *Annals.* Translated by Alfred J. Church and William J. Brodribb. The Internet Classics Archive. http://classics.mit.edu/Tacitus/annals.html

Tajra, Harry W. *The Martyrdom of St. Paul.* Tübingen: J. C. B. Mohr, 1994.

———. *The Trial of St. Paul: A Juridical Exegesis of the Second Half of the Acts of the Apostles.* Tübingen: J. C. B. Mohr, 1989.

Tannehill, Robert C. *The Narrative Unity of Luke-Acts: A Literary Interpretation.* Volume 2: *The Acts of the Apostles.* Minneapolis: Fortress, 1990.

Theron, Daniel J. *Evidence of Tradition: Selected Source Material for the Study of the History of the Early Church, the New Testament Books, the New Testament Canon.* Grand Rapids: Baker, 1958.

Thimmes, Pamela. "Memory and Re-vision: Mary Magdalene Research since 1975." *Currents In Research: Biblical Studies* 6 (October 1998) 193–222.

Trebilco, Paul. "Asia." In *The Book of Acts in Its Graeco-Roman Setting,* edited by David W. J. Gill and Conrad Gempf. The Book of Acts in Its First Century Setting 2, 291–362. Grand Rapids: Eerdmans, 1994.

Trompf, G. W. "On Why Luke Declined to Recount the Death of Paul: Acts 27–28 and Beyond." In *Luke-Acts,* edited by Charles A. Talbert, 225–39. New York: Crossroads, 1984.

Weiss, Johannes. *Earliest Christianity: A History of the Period A.D. 30–150.* Vol. 2. Translated by F. C. Grant and Sherman E. Johnson. New York: Harper & Row, 1959.

Winter, Bruce W. "Official Proceedings and the Forensic Speeches in Acts 24–26." In *The Book of Acts in Its Ancient Literary Setting,* edited by Bruce W. Winter and Andrew D. Clarke, 305–36. The Book of Acts in Its First Century Setting 1. Grand Rapids: Eerdmans, 1993.

Witherington III, Ben. *The Acts of the Apostles: A Socio-Rhetorical Commentary.* Grand Rapids: Eerdmans, 1997.

Ancient Document Index

~

NEW TESTAMENT

~

RABBINIC WRITINGS

~

GRECO-ROMAN WRITINGS

~

~

EARLY CHRISTIAN WRITINGS

Subject Index

Notes: Page numbers in **bold** indicate subjects mentioned in the text of *The Apostles after Acts* (therefore entered here twice); page numbers in regular font indicate subjects treated in the commentary. All persons and places mentioned both in the Bible and in *The Apostles after Acts* are listed in the index. Places visited by apostles only in *The Apostles after Acts* are indexed by region rather than individual city. Fictional names are not indexed, nor are the terms *apostle, Christ, God, Jesus, Lord*, and *Spirit*, which appear on nearly every page.